# Lecture Notes in Artificial Intelligence 1208

Subseries of Lecture Notes in Computer Science
Edited by J. G. Carbonell and J. Siekmann

## Lecture Notes in Computer Science

Edited by G. Goos, J. Hartmanis and J. van Leeuwen

**Springer**
*Berlin*
*Heidelberg*
*New York*
*Barcelona*
*Budapest*
*Hong Kong*
*London*
*Milan*
*Paris*
*Santa Clara*
*Singapore*
*Tokyo*

Shai Ben-David  (Ed.)

# Computational Learning Theory

Third European Conference, EuroCOLT '97
Jerusalem, Israel, March 17-19, 1997
Proceedings

 Springer

Series Editors
Jaime G. Carbonell, Carnegie Mellon University, Pittsburgh, PA, USA
Jörg Siekmann, University of Saarland, Saarbrücken, Germany


Volume Editor

Shai Ben-David
Technion - Israel Institute of Technology
Computer Science Department
Haifa 32000, Israel
E-mail: shai@cs.technion.ac.il


Cataloging-in-Publication Data applied for


Die Deutsche Bibliothek - CIP-Einheitsaufnahme

**Computational learning theory** : third European conference ;
proceedings / EuroCOLT '97, Jerusalem, Israel, March 17 - 19,
1997. Shai Ben-David (ed.). - Berlin ; Heidelberg ; New York ;
Barcelona ; Budapest ; Hong Kong ; London ; Milan ; Paris ;
Santa Clara ; Singapore ; Tokyo : Springer, 1997
  (Lecture notes in computer science ; 1208 : Lecture notes in artificial
  intelligence)
  ISBN 3-540-62685-9
NE: Ben-David, Shai [Hrsg.]; EuroCOLT <3, 1997, Yerûšãlayim>; GT


CR Subject Classification (1991): I.2.6, I.2.3, F.4.1, F.1.1, F.2

ISBN 3-540-62685-9 Springer-Verlag Berlin Heidelberg New York

© Springer-Verlag Berlin Heidelberg 1997
Printed in Germany

Typesetting: Camera ready by author
SPIN 10550390      06/3142 – 5 4 3 2 1 0     Printed on acid-free paper

# Foreword

This volume contains the papers presented at the Third European Conference on Computational Learning Theory (EuroCOLT'97), held during March 17-19, 1997, in Kibbutz Ma'ale-Hachamisha, Jerusalem, Israel.

This conference is the third in a series of bi-annual conferences established in 1993. The topics discussed in these meetings range over all areas related to Computational Learning Theory with an emphasis on mathematical models of machine learning. The conferences bring together researchers from a wide variety of related fields, including machine learning, neural networks, statistics, inductive inference, computational complexity, information theory, and theoretical physics. We hope that these conferences stimulate an interdisciplinary scientific interaction that will be fruitful in all represented fields.

Thirty-six papers were submitted to the program committee for consideration, 25 of these were accepted for presentation at the conference and publication in these proceedings. In addition, invited talks were presented by A. Ya Chervonenkis, Tali Tishby and Manfred K. Warmuth.

This year the IFIP WG 1.4 Scholarship is awarded to Mr Juris Smotrovs of the Institute of Mathematics and Computer Science, Latvia, for submitting the best paper to Eurocolt '97 written by a student.

We would like to thank all individuals and organizations that contributed to the success of this meeting. We are especially grateful to our program committee for their thorough evaluation of all submitted papers:

Peter Auer (TU Graz, Austria)
Peter Bartlett (ANU, Canberra, Australia)
Shai Ben-David (Technion, Haifa, Israel)
Francesco Bergadano (Torino Univ., Italy)
Pascal Koiran (LIP, Lyon, France)
Eyal Kushilevitz (Technion, Haifa, Israel)
Rob Schapire (AT&T, NJ, USA)
John Shawe-Taylor (Royal Holloway, London, England)
Hans Ulrich Simon (Univ. Dortmund, Germany)
Frank Stephan (Karlsruhe Univ., Germany)
Naftali Tishby (Hebrew Univ., Jerusalem, Israel)
Thomas Zeugmann (Kyushu Univ., Fukuoka, Japan)

We also owe thanks to Yvonne Sagi for acting as the conference secretary and to the conference Local Arrangement Chair, Hava Siegelmann.

March 1997                                                    Shai Ben-David

# Table of Contents

# Sample Compression, Learnability, and the Vapnik-Chervonenkis Dimension[*]

Manfred Warmuth
Department of Computer Science
University of California

## Abstract

Within the framework of pac-learning, we explore the learnability of concepts from samples using the paradigm of sample compression. We first show that any *Occam algorithm* that when given samples of size $m$ chooses a consistent hypotheses from a hypotheses class of size $2^{m-1/p(m)}$ is a weak learning algorithm and can thus be "boosted" to a strong learning algorithm. Thus the Occam algorithm compresses the sample of size $m$ to $m$ minus $1/p(m)$ many bits, where $p(.)$ is is any polynomial. Curiously enough compression of samples of size $m$ to $m + 1$ bits does not suffice to produce a weak learner. So the open problem is what is the maximum number of bits that still produces a weak learner.

Secondly we discuss compression of the sample to a small unlabeled subsample. The classical example is the following compression scheme for orthogonal rectangles in two-dimensional Euclidean space. Any labeled sample of an orthogonal rectangle can be compressed to up to four unlabeled points from the sample such that these points define the boundaries of a rectangle that is consistent with the whole original sample. Note that the VC dimension of orthogonal rectangles is four as well.

More generally a *sample compression scheme* of size $k$ for a concept class $C \subseteq 2^X$ consists of a compression function and a reconstruction function. The compression function receives a finite sample set labeled with some concept in $C$ and chooses a subset of at most $k$ unlabeled examples from the sample as the compression set. The reconstruction function forms a hypothesis on $X$ from a compression set of $k$ examples. For any sample set of a concept in $C$ the compression set produced by the compression function must lead to a hypothesis consistent with the whole original sample set when it is fed to the reconstruction function.

We give a one-page proof that the existence of a sample compression scheme of fixed-size for a class $C$ is sufficient to ensure that the class $C$ is pac-learnable. Previous work has shown that a class is pac-learnable if and only if the Vapnik-Chervonenkis (VC) dimension of the class is finite. The sample size bound for compression schemes are similar to the bounds that use the VC dimension (In the sample size bounds the size of the compression set takes the place of the VC dimension).

Finally we explore the intriguing relationship between sample compression schemes and the VC dimension. A concept class $C \subseteq 2^X$ of VC dimension $d$ is

---

[*] This reports on joint work with N. Littlestone, S. Floyd and D. P. Helmbold.

*maximum* if for every set of $m$ points of $X$ the maximum number of concepts is induced, i.e. $\sum_{i=0}^{d} \binom{m}{i}$ many. For every maximum class of VC dimension $d$, there is a sample compression scheme of size $d$, and for sufficiently large maximum classes there is no sample compression scheme of size less than $d$. For the above upper bound we let the compression set consist of a *labeled* subsample of the original sample.

One of the most beautiful an open problems is whether every class of VC dimension $d$ has a sample compression scheme of size $d$. The best general bound on the size of compressions schemes are based on the boosting algorithms of weak learning algorithms by Freund and Schapire. One can show essentially that there always are compression schemes of size $O(d \log m)$, where $d$ is again the VC dimension and $m$ is the size of the sample.

# Learning Boxes in High Dimension

Amos Beimel[1,*] and Eyal Kushilevitz[2,**]

[1] DIMACS Center, Rutgers University, P.O. Box 1179, Piscataway, NJ 08855.
[2] Department of Computer Science, Technion, Haifa 32000, Israel.

**Abstract.** We present exact learning algorithms that learn several classes of (discrete) boxes in $\{0, \ldots, \ell - 1\}^n$. In particular we learn: (1) The class of unions of $O(\log n)$ boxes in time poly$(n, \log \ell)$ (solving an open problem of [15, 11]). (2) The class of unions of disjoint boxes in time poly$(n, t, \log \ell)$, where $t$ is the number of boxes. (Previously this was known only in the case where all boxes are disjoint in one of the dimensions). In particular our algorithm learns the class of decision trees (over $n$ variables that take values in $\{0, \ldots, \ell - 1\}$) with comparison nodes in time poly$(n, t, \log \ell)$, where $t$ is the number of leaves (this was an open problem in [8] which was shown in [3] to be learnable in time poly$(n, t, \ell)$). (3) The class of unions of $O(1)$-degenerate boxes (that is, boxes that depend only on $O(1)$ variables) in time poly$(n, t, \log \ell)$ (generalizing the learnability of $O(1)$-DNF and of boxes in $O(1)$ dimensions). The algorithm for this class uses only equivalence queries and it can also be used to learn the class of unions of $O(1)$ boxes (from equivalence queries only).

## 1 Introduction

The learnability (under various learning models) of geometric concept classes was studied in many papers (e.g., [7, 10, 12, 4]). A particular attention was given to the case of discretized domains of points (i.e., $\{0, \ldots, \ell - 1\}^n$) and concept classes which are defined as union of boxes in this domain (e.g., [21, 22, 14, 2, 15, 16, 23]).

One of the reasons that unions of boxes seem to be interesting concepts is that they naturally extend DNF formulae (in other words, in the case $\ell = 2$ any union of $t$ boxes is equivalent to a DNF formula with $t$-terms). That is, a box can be viewed as a conjunction of non-boolean properties of the form "the attribute $x_i$ is in the range between $a_i$ and $b_i$". Similar to the special case of DNF functions, the learnability of unions of boxes in time poly$(n, t, \log \ell)$ (where $t$ is the number of boxes in the union) is an open problem in all models of learning.[3] Research on the problem of learning the class of unions of boxes (again, with

---

\* E-mail: beimel@dimacs.rutgers.edu. http://dimacs.rutgers.edu/~beimel. Part of this research was done while the author was a Ph.D. student at the Technion.

\*\* E-mail: eyalk@cs.technion.ac.il. http://www.cs.technion.ac.il/~eyalk. This research was supported by Technion V.P.R. Fund 120-872 and by Japan Technion Society Research Fund

[3] Note that to represent such a function $\Theta(t \cdot n \cdot \log \ell)$ bits are required. Hence efficiency is defined as polynomial in $t, n$ and $\log \ell$.

similarity to the case of DNF formulae) attempts to learn sub-classes of this class. There are two main directions: (1) Sub-classes in which the number of dimensions, $n$, is limited to $O(1)$. In this case unions of boxes (and more general geometric concept classes) are known to be learnable in the PAC model [12] and even in the weaker on-line model [4]. (2) Sub-classes in which the number of boxes in the union is limited to $O(1)$ (but the number of dimensions in not restricted). Again, this sub-class is learnable in the PAC model [20] and in the on-line model [23].

In this work we generalize some of the state-of-the-art results in *exact learning*[4] of DNF formulae [5, 3], hence strengthening several results in direction (2) above. In particular we show:

1. The class of all unions of $O(\log n)$ boxes can be learned in time $\text{poly}(n, \log \ell)$ (solving an open problem of [15, 11]). This generalizes a similar result for the class of DNF [6, 8, 9, 18, 3].
2. The class of all unions of disjoint boxes (and, more generally, unions of boxes in which each point belongs to at most $O(1)$ boxes) can be learned in time $\text{poly}(n, t, \log \ell)$, where $t$ is the number of boxes. This generalizes similar results for learning disjoint DNF and satisfy-$O(1)$ DNF [5, 3]. (Previously this was known only in the case where all boxes are disjoint in one of the dimensions [10, 13]; in this case in fact equivalence queries are sufficient.) In particular our algorithm learns the class of decision trees with comparison nodes in time $\text{poly}(n, t, \log \ell)$, where $t$ is the number of leaves (the learnability of this class was an open problem in [8]; in [3] it was shown that this class is learnable in time $\text{poly}(n, t, \ell)$).
3. The class of all unions of $O(1)$-degenerate boxes, that is boxes that depend only on $O(1)$ variables, can be learned in time $\text{poly}(n, t, \log \ell)$, where $t$ is the number of boxes. In this case we use only equivalence queries, i.e. we learn this class in the on-line model [19]. This result generalizes the learnability of $O(1)$-DNF and of boxes in $O(1)$ dimensions. The class of $k$-degenerate boxes was previously considered in [16, 17, 23]. Our algorithm for this class also learns the class of unions of $O(1)$ boxes from equivalence queries only.

The first two results are obtained in two steps: First, in Section 3, we show how to learn these classes but with complexity which is polynomial in $\ell$ (and the other parameters of the problem). This is done by a quite straightforward generalization of results in [3]. Then, in Section 4, we prove the main result of this paper: we show how to (adaptively) select a "small" subset of the domain $\{0, 1, \ldots, \ell - 1\}$ which is sufficient for the learning. Hence, we give a reduction that converts any algorithm for learning unions of boxes whose complexity is

---

[4] In the exact learning model [1], the algorithm is equipped with two types of queries: membership queries (MQs) in which the algorithm can ask for the value of the target function $f$ on points $x$ of its choice; and equivalence queries (EQs) in which the algorithm can suggest an hypothesis $h$ and gets as an answer either "YES" (i.e., $h \equiv f$) or "NO" together with a counterexample $y$ (i.e., a point such that $h(y) \neq f(y)$).

polynomial in $\ell$ to an algorithm with complexity which is polynomial only in $\log \ell$ (and the other parameters of the problem). Finally, in Section 5 we show how to convert a simple $\text{poly}(n, t, \ell)$ algorithm that learns unions of $O(1)$-degenerate boxes into a $\text{poly}(n, t, \log \ell)$ algorithm. In this case, the $\text{poly}(n, t, \ell)$ algorithm that we start with does not use membership queries. We use a refined conversion which does not use memberships queries as well; hence we get an algorithm with equivalence queries only. This conversion uses specific properties of the $\text{poly}(n, t, \ell)$ algorithm.

## 2  Preliminaries

In this section we define the classes of boxes we use in this paper. We consider unions of $n$-dimensional boxes in $[\ell]^n$ (where $[\ell]$ denotes the set $\{0, 1, \ldots, \ell-1\}$). Formally, a box in $[\ell]^n$ is defined by two corners $(a_1, \ldots, a_n)$ and $(b_1, \ldots, b_n)$ (in $[\ell]^n$) as follows:

$$B_{a_1,\ldots,a_n,b_1,\ldots,b_n} = \{(x_1, \ldots, x_n) \ : \ \forall i, \ a_i \leq x_i \leq b_i \ \}.$$

We view such a box as a boolean function that gives 1 for every point in $[\ell]^n$ which is inside the box and 0 to each point outside the box. Denote by $\text{BOX}_t$ the set of all functions that correspond to unions of $t$ boxes and by $\text{DISJ-BOX}_t$ the set of all functions that correspond to unions of $t$ *disjoint* boxes. A $k$-degenerate box is a box that depends only on $k$ variables, where a box *depends* on the $i$th variable if either $a_i \neq 0$ or $b_i \neq \ell - 1$. Denote by $k - \text{DBOX}_t$ the set of all functions that correspond to unions of $t$ $k$-degenerate boxes. Note that for the case $\ell = 2$ the class $\text{BOX}_t$ corresponds to the class of $t$-term DNF, the class $\text{DISJ-BOX}_t$ corresponds to the class ($t$-term) disjoint DNF and the class $k-\text{DBOX}_t$ corresponds to the class ($t$-term) $k$-DNF. Note that the number of terms, $t$, for a function in $k - \text{DBOX}_t$ can be at most $\binom{n}{k} \cdot \ell^{2k}$. This is $\text{poly}(n, \ell)$, for $k = O(1)$, but may be much larger than $\log \ell$.

*Notation:* We end this section with some useful notation. Given a set $L \subseteq [\ell]$ and a letter $a \in [\ell]$ we denote by $\lfloor a \rfloor$ the largest value in $L$ which is at most $a$, that is, $\lfloor a \rfloor \triangleq \max\{\sigma \in L : \sigma \leq a\}$. Similarly, we denote $\lceil a \rceil \triangleq \min\{\sigma \in L : \sigma > a\}$. (Whenever we use this notation the ground set $L$ will be clear from the context.)

## 3  Learning Boxes Using Hankel Matrices

We consider the learnability, in the exact-learning model, of the classes $\text{DISJ-BOX}_t$ and $\text{BOX}_{O(\log n)}$. We construct our algorithm in two stages. In this section we show an algorithm whose complexity is polynomial in $\ell$ (and in the other parameters of the problem). Then, in the next section, we show how to reduce the complexity to be polynomial in $\log \ell$. For the first stage, we use a recent result of [3]. Let $\mathcal{K}$ be a field, $\Sigma$ be an alphabet, and $f : \Sigma^n \to \mathcal{K}$ be a function. The *Hankel matrix* corresponding to $f$, denoted $F$, is defined as follows: each row of $F$ is indexed by a string $x \in \Sigma^{\leq n}$; each column of $F$ is indexed by a string $y \in \Sigma^{\leq n}$; the $(x, y)$ entry of $F$ contains the value of $f(x \circ y)$ if $x \circ y$ is of length (exactly) $n$ and 0 otherwise.

**Theorem 1 (BBBKV96).** *Let $\mathcal{K}$ be a field. There exists an algorithm that learns every function $f : \Sigma^n \to \mathcal{K}$ in time (and query) complexity which is $poly(n, rank(F), |\Sigma|)$, where rank is defined with respect to the field $\mathcal{K}$.*

By the above theorem, to prove the learnability of a concept class it is sufficient to give an upper bound on $rank(F)$ for the matrices corresponding to functions in the class. For convenience (and efficiency), we fix $\mathcal{K}$ to be GF(2) (although the next lemma holds for any field).

**Lemma 2.** *Let $B_1, \ldots, B_t$ be $t$ boxes in $[\ell]^n$ such that there is no point $x \in [\ell]^n$ which belongs to more than $s$ boxes and let $f$ be the function corresponding to the union of these boxes (e.g., for $s = 1$ we get the functions in DISJ-BOX$_t$). Then, $rank(F) \leq (n + 1) \cdot \sum_{i=1}^{s} \binom{t}{i}$.*

*Proof.* Let $F^d$ denote the submatrix of $F$ whose rows are indexed by strings $x \in \Sigma^d$ and whose columns are indexed by strings $y \in \Sigma^{n-d}$ (see Fig. 1). Note that by the definition of $F$ all entries which are not in one of the sub-matrices $F^d$ are zeroes. Hence, by linear algebra, $rank(F) = \sum_{d=0}^{n} rank(F^d)$. Therefore, it is sufficient to prove, for every $d$, that $rank(F^d) \leq \sum_{i=1}^{s} \binom{t}{i}$.

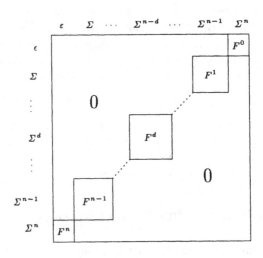

**Fig. 1.** The Hankel matrix $F$

Let $B$ be any box and denote the two corners of $B$ by $(a_1, \ldots, a_n)$ and $(b_1, \ldots, b_n)$. Define functions (of a single variable) $p_j(z_j) : [\ell] \to \{0, 1\}$ to be 1 if $a_j \leq z_j \leq b_j$ $(1 \leq j \leq n)$. Let $g : [\ell]^n \rightarrow \{0,1\}$ be defined by $\prod_{j=1}^n p_j(z_j)$ (i.e., $g(z_1,\ldots,z_n)$ is 1 if and only if $(z_1,\ldots,z_n)$ belongs to the box $B$). Let $G$ be the Hankel matrix corresponds to $g$ and $G^d$ its corresponding submatrix. Every row of $G^d$ is indexed by $x \in \Sigma^d$, and it can be written as $G_x^d(y) = g(x \circ y) = (\prod_{j=1}^d p_j(x_j))(\prod_{j=d+1}^n p_j(y_{j-d}))$. Now, for every $x$, the term $\prod_{j=1}^d p_j(x_j)$ is just a constant $\alpha_x \in \{0,1\}$. This means, that every row $G_x^d(y)$ is just a constant times the vector whose $y$-th coordinate is $\prod_{j=d+1}^n p_j(y_{j-d})$. This implies that $\text{rank}(G^d) \leq 1$. Finally, note that if $g_i$ is the function corresponding to the box $B_i$ then $f$ can be expressed as:

$$f = 1 - \prod_{i=1}^t (1 - g_i) = \sum_i g_i - \sum_{i,j}(g_i \wedge g_j) + \ldots + (-1)^{t+1} \sum_{|S|=t} \bigwedge_{i \in S} g_i$$
$$= \sum_i g_i - \sum_{i,j}(g_i \wedge g_j) + \ldots + (-1)^{s+1} \sum_{|S|=s} \bigwedge_{i \in S} g_i,$$

where the last equality is by the assumption that no point belongs to more than $s$ boxes. Also note that each term of the form $h = \bigwedge_{i \in S} g_i$ is an intersection of boxes which is a box by itself. Hence, by the above, the rank of the matrix $H^d$ corresponding to each of these terms is at most 1. Since we wrote $f$ as a linear combination of $\sum_{i=1}^s \binom{t}{i}$ such terms we get, by linear algebra, that $\text{rank}(F^d) \leq \sum_{i=1}^s \binom{t}{i}$. $\qquad\square$

Combining the above lemma with Theorem 1 we get:

**Corollary 3.** *The class* BOX$_{O(\log n)}$ *can be learned in time* poly$(n, \ell)$.

**Corollary 4.** *The class* DISJ-BOX *can be learned in time* poly$(n, t, \ell)$ *(where $t$ is the number of boxes in the target functions).*

## 4  Reducing the Dependency on $\ell$

In this section we reduce the dependency of our algorithm on $\ell$. For this, we define the notion of *sensitive* letters:

**Definition 5.** A letter $\sigma \in [\ell]$ is called *i-sensitive* with respect to $f$ if there exist letters $c_1,\ldots,c_{i-1},c_{i+1},\ldots,c_n \in [\ell]$ such that

$$f(c_1,\ldots,c_{i-1},\sigma - 1,c_{i+1},\ldots,c_n) \neq f(c_1,\ldots,c_{i-1},\sigma,c_{i+1},\ldots,c_n).$$

A letter $\sigma$ is called *sensitive* with respect to $f$ if $\sigma$ is *i*-sensitive for some $i$.

**Lemma 6.** *Let $f$ be a function in* BOX$_t$. *Then, there are at most $2nt$ sensitive letters with respect to $f$.*

*Proof.* If $f(c_1 \ldots c_{i-1}, \sigma - 1, c_{i+1} \ldots c_n) = 0$ and $f(c_1 \ldots c_{i-1}, \sigma, c_{i+1} \ldots c_n) = 1$ then for some box $B_j$ the letter $\sigma$ is the $i$th coordinate of the lower corner. If $f(c_1, \ldots, c_{i-1}, \sigma - 1, c_{i+1}, \ldots, c_n) = 1$ and $f(c_1, \ldots, c_{i-1}, \sigma, c_{i+1}, \ldots, c_n) = 0$ then for some box $B_j$ the letter $\sigma - 1$ is the $i$th coordinate of the upper corner. Since there are $t$ boxes, in $n$ dimensions, and each is defined by its two corners, the lemma follows. $\square$

The idea of our algorithm is as follows. As part of learning the function $f \in \text{BOX}_t$ we will learn the set of sensitive letters. At each stage, with the set of current letters, denoted $L$, we will try to learn the function using the algorithm of [3]. Either we will succeed, or we will find another sensitive letter and start again. Denote by $f_L$ the function $f$ restricted to the range $L^n$. Note that this function is by itself a union of at most $t$ boxes. Formally, our algorithm works as follows:

1. $L \leftarrow \{0\}$
2. Learn the function $f_L$ using the algorithm of [3].
   To answer membership queries about $f_L$ simply use the oracle for $f$, since for every $x \in L^n$ we have $f_L(x) = f(x)$.
   To simulate an equivalence query $EQ(h)$ to $f_L$, using the corresponding oracle for $f$, do the following:
   (a) Define $h' : [\ell]^n \rightarrow \{0, 1\}$ as

   $$h'(x_1, \ldots, x_n) = h(\lfloor x_1 \rfloor, \ldots, \lfloor x_n \rfloor) \ .$$

   Ask whether $h' \equiv f$.
   If the answer is "YES" halt with output $h'$.
   Otherwise, we have a counterexample $(y_1, \ldots, y_n) \in [\ell]^n$.
   (b) If $f(y_1, \ldots, y_n) = f(\lfloor y_1 \rfloor, \ldots, \lfloor y_n \rfloor)$ (this is checked using a membership query) then $(\lfloor y_1 \rfloor, \ldots, \lfloor y_n \rfloor)$ is a counterexample to $h$ – pass this counterexample to the algorithm for learning $f_L$ and continue its execution.
   Otherwise, proceed to Step (3).
3. If $f(y_1, \ldots, y_n) \neq f(\lfloor y_1 \rfloor, \ldots, \lfloor y_n \rfloor)$ then find an index $i$ s.t.

   $$f(\lfloor y_1 \rfloor \ldots \lfloor y_{i-1} \rfloor, y_i \ldots y_n) \neq f(\lfloor y_1 \rfloor \ldots \lfloor y_{i-1} \rfloor, \lfloor y_i \rfloor, y_{i+1} \ldots y_n)$$

   (this is found with $O(\log n)$ MQs using a binary search).
   Then, find a letter $\sigma$ such that $\lfloor y_i \rfloor + 1 \leq \sigma \leq y_i$ and

   $$f(\lfloor y_1 \rfloor \ldots \lfloor y_{i-1} \rfloor, \sigma - 1, y_{i+1} \ldots y_n) \neq f(\lfloor y_1 \rfloor \ldots \lfloor y_{i-1} \rfloor, \sigma, y_{i+1} \ldots y_n)$$

   (this is found with $O(\log \ell)$ MQs using a binary search).
   Set $L \leftarrow L \cup \{\sigma\}$ and start Step (2) again.

Using this algorithm we show the following results:

**Theorem 7.** *The class* $\text{BOX}_{O(\log n)}$ *can be learned in time* $poly(n, \log \ell)$.

*Proof.* We use the above algorithm to learn the class $\text{BOX}_{O(\log n)}$. As remarked, for every $L$ the function $f_L$ is also a union of $O(\log n)$ boxes. By Corollary 3, learning the function $f_L$ (Step (2)) ends within time $\text{poly}(n, |L|)$. So either we identify the target function $f$, or we add a new sensitive letter to $L$ (Step (3)). In addition, once $L$ contains all sensitive letters then for every point $(y_1, \ldots, y_n) \in [\ell]^n$,

$$f(y_1, \ldots, y_n) = f(\lfloor y_1 \rfloor, \ldots, \lfloor y_n \rfloor) \ . \tag{1}$$

At this point, since there are no more sensitive letters, the algorithm for $f_L$ will find a hypothesis $h \equiv f_L$ which by Equation (1) implies $h' \equiv f$. By Lemma 6 the size of $L$, and hence the number of times Step (3) is executed, is $O(n \log n)$. At each time that a new letter is inserted to $L$ we spend $\text{poly}(n, \log \ell)$ time in searching for a sensitive letter. All together, our algorithm learns the class $\text{BOX}_{O(\log n)}$ in time $\text{poly}(n, \log \ell)$. □

The above theorem solves an open problem of [15, 11]. The following theorem shows the learnability of disjoint boxes in time $\text{poly}(n, t, \log \ell)$. This significantly improves over [10, 13] where a similar result was shown for the case where there exists a dimension in which all the boxes are disjoint.

**Theorem 8.** *The class* DISJ-BOX *can be learned in time* $\text{poly}(n, t, \log \ell)$ *(where $t$ is the number of boxes in the target function).*

*Proof.* Again, we use the above algorithm to learn this class. By Lemma 6 the size of $L$, and hence the number of times Step (3) is executed, is $O(nt)$. At each time that a new letter is inserted to $L$ we spend $\text{poly}(n, \log \ell)$ time in searching for a sensitive letter. By Corollary 4 learning the function $f_L$ (Step (2)) takes time $\text{poly}(n, t, |L|)$ (observe that the function $f_L$ always consists of a union of at most $t$ disjoint boxes). All together, our algorithm learns any function in DISJ-BOX$_t$ in time $\text{poly}(n, t, \log \ell)$. □

A special case of disjoint boxes are functions which are represented by decision trees where each node contains a query of the form "Is $x_i \geq \theta$?" (and where the variables $x_i$ and the constants $\theta$ take values in $[\ell]$). The learnability of this class was an open problem in [8]. In [3] it was shown that this class is learnable in time $\text{poly}(n, t, \ell)$ (where $t$ here denotes the number of leaves in the tree corresponding to $f$). Our algorithm shows that this class can in fact be learned in time $\text{poly}(n, t, \log \ell)$.

**Remark 9.** Obviously, Corollary 4 and Theorem 8 can be easily extended to the case where no point $x$ is contained in more than $s$ boxes, for $s = O(1)$ (note that Lemma 2 is already formulated in a way that allows this extension). Also, Theorem 7 can be extended to show the learnability of *any* function of $O(\log n)$ boxes (and not only *unions* on boxes).

**Remark 10.** An improved complexity can be obtained if instead of collecting the sensitive letters (i.e., the set $L$) we would maintain a separate set $L_i$ for the $i$-sensitive letters.

**Remark 11.** A box is just the product of $n$ intervals one in each dimension. We can consider more general boxes which are products of $m$ intervals in each dimension. Such a general box can be viewed as the union of $m^n$ "regular" boxes. Nevertheless, it can be easily seen that our algorithms can be extended to this case as well with a small increase in the complexity. For example, the union of $t$ disjoint, general boxes can be learned in time which is $\mathrm{poly}(n, t, \log \ell, m)$. This is because Lemma 2 still holds, and since the number of sensitive letters is now bounded by $2mnt$.

## 5  Learning $O(1)$-Degenerate Boxes

In this section we show how to learn the class $k - \mathrm{DBOX}_t$, for $k = O(1)$, using only EQs (or equivalently, in Littlestone's on-line model [19]). This generalizes the learnability of unions of boxes in $O(1)$ dimensions and, as will be shown, can be used to learn unions of $O(1)$ boxes in $[\ell]^n$. Again, we start with an algorithm which is polynomial in $\ell$ and convert it into an algorithm which is polynomial in $\log \ell$. We use a refined transformation which does not use MQs. However, this transformation is not general and uses specific properties of the algorithm that we start with.

We start by defining *width one boxes* which is a certain class of boxes that we use in our algorithm.

**Definition 12.** A *width one box* is a box in which for every dimension either the width is 1 (i.e., $a_i = b_i$) or the box does not depend on the $i$th variable (i.e., $a_i = 0$ and $b_i = \ell - 1$).

It is a simple observation that every $k$-degenerate box can be written as the union of at most $\ell^k$ width one $k$-degenerate boxes, and hence every function in $k-$ DBOX$_t$ can be written as the union of at most $t \cdot \ell^k$ width one $k$-degenerate boxes. The following simple algorithm, which is a variant of the standard elimination algorithm for learning $k$-DNF [24], learns the class $k - \mathrm{DBOX}_t$ with complexity which is polynomial in $\ell$, for $k = O(1)$.

---

1. Make a list $Q$ of all width one $k$-degenerate boxes.
2. Define a hypothesis $h$ as the union of all boxes in the list $Q$.
3. Ask EQ($h$).
   If the answer is "YES" halt with output $h$.
4. Otherwise, the answer is "NO" and $y$ is a counterexample.
   Remove all the boxes in $Q$ that contain $y$.
   Goto 2.

---

We start with a simple observation about the algorithm.

*Claim 13. Let $f$ be a function in $k - \mathrm{DBOX}_t$. In every step of the algorithm $f \leq h$.*

*Proof.* As remarked, $f$ can be represented as a union of width one $k$-degenerate boxes. Let $Q^*$ be the set of these boxes. For proving the claim, it suffices to prove that at any time $Q^\star \subseteq Q$. This is obviously true at the beginning, since $Q$ contains *all* width one $k$-degenerate boxes. Whenever a counterexample $y$ is received, since $Q^\star \subseteq Q$ it must be that $h(y) = 1$ and $f(y) = 0$; hence, when we remove from $Q$ all the boxes to which $y$ belongs, none of them is in $Q^\star$. Therefore, after $Q$ is modified in Step (4) still $Q^\star \subseteq Q$. □

We next prove that the algorithm is correct.

**Lemma 14.** *The above algorithm learns the class* $k - \text{DBOX}_t$, *for* $k = O(1)$, *in time (and query) complexity* $\text{poly}(\ell, n)$. *Moreover, it uses only EQs (i.e., no MQs).*

*Proof.* If the algorithm halts then its hypothesis is equivalent to $f$. We have to prove that the algorithm must halt within $\text{poly}(\ell, n)$ time. By Claim 13, for every counterexample, $h(y) = 1$ while $f(y) = 0$. Thus, every EQ removes at least one width one $k$-degenerate box from $Q$. The size of $Q$ when the algorithm starts is the number of width one $k$-degenerate boxes which is less than $\ell^k n^k$. Thus, the algorithm uses at most $\ell^k n^k$ EQs, and runs in time $\text{poly}(\ell^k, n^k)$. □

Using the transformation of Section 4 we can learn the class $k - \text{DBOX}_t$ in time $\text{poly}(n, t, \log \ell)$ with EQs and MQs. However, our goal is an algorithm that does not use MQs and still has complexity which is polynomial in $\log \ell$. The idea is again to adaptively learn the sensitive letters. There are two problems in learning the sensitive letters without MQs. The first problem is that when the algorithm of Section 4 gets a counterexample $(y_1, \ldots, y_n)$ it checks whether it can return $(\lfloor y_1 \rfloor, \ldots, \lfloor y_n \rfloor)$ as a counterexample to the algorithm that learns the restricted function $f_L$ (Step (2b)). Since we know that every counterexample in the previous algorithm is a negative counterexample (that is, $f(y) = 0$ while $h(y) = 1$), we will pass only negative counterexamples to the algorithm for $f_L$, and every positive counterexample will be used to look for a sensitive letter (we prove below that this strategy works). The second problem that we face is how to search for a sensitive letter without using membership queries. We use an idea of [10, 11]: if there is a sensitive letter in a set $\{a, a + 1, \ldots, b\}$ where $a$ and $b$ are in $L$ then add $\lfloor (a + b)/2 \rfloor$ to $L$. In this case the set $L$ of letters that is used by the algorithm will be a super-set of the sensitive letters. However, the size of $L$ will still be relatively small. We next describe our algorithm.

1. $L \leftarrow \{0, \ell - 1\}$.
2. Make a list $Q$ of all width one $k$-degenerate boxes over the current set $L$.
3. Define a hypothesis $h : L^n \to \{0, 1\}$ as the union of all boxes in $Q$. Extend the hypothesis to $[\ell]^n$ by:
$$h'(x_1, ..., x_n) \triangleq h(\lfloor x_1 \rfloor, ..., \lfloor x_n \rfloor).$$
4. Ask EQ($h'$).
   If the answer is "YES" halt with output $h'$.
   Otherwise, the answer is "NO" and $y$ is a counterexample.
5. If $h'(y) = 1$ and $f(y) = 0$ then remove all boxes that contain $(\lfloor y_1 \rfloor, ..., \lfloor y_n \rfloor)$ from $Q$.
   Goto (3).
6. ($h'(y) = 0$ and $f(y) = 1$.)
   For every $i$ add $\lfloor (\lceil y_i \rceil + \lfloor y_i \rfloor)/2 \rfloor$ to $L$.
   Goto (2).

Every time that the algorithm reaches Step (6) it adds at least one new letter to $L$. Furthermore, if $L$ contains all the sensitive letters than the algorithm finds a hypothesis that is equivalent to $f$. Thus, since $L \subseteq [\ell]$, the algorithm will eventually halt with the right answer. As in Lemma 14, if $L$ is the set of letters when the algorithm halts then the complexity of the algorithm is poly$(|L|^k, t^k, n^k)$. Thus, it remains to prove that when the algorithm halts $L$ is small. This is based on the next claim.

**Claim 15.** *Every time the algorithm reaches Step (6) there exists an index $i$ and a sensitive letter $\sigma$ in $\{\lfloor y_i \rfloor + 1, ..., \lceil y_i \rceil - 1\}$.*

*Proof.* If the algorithm reaches Step (6) then $f(y) = 1$, i.e. there exists some $k$-degenerate box $B = B_{a_1, ..., a_n, b_1, ..., b_n}$ in $f$ that contains the counterexample $y$. Consider the box $B' = B_{a'_1, ..., a'_n, b'_1, ..., b'_n}$ where if $a_i = 0$ and $b_i = \ell - 1$ then $a'_i = 0$ and $b'_i = \ell - 1$, otherwise $a'_i = b'_i = \lfloor y_i \rfloor$. This is a width one $k$-degenerate box over $L$ that contains $(\lfloor y_1 \rfloor, ..., \lfloor y_n \rfloor)$. Since $h(\lfloor y_1 \rfloor, ..., \lfloor y_n \rfloor) = 0$, this box $B'$ is not in $Q$. Let $z$ be the counterexample that removed $B'$ from $Q$ (in some execution of Step (5)). For $1 \le i \le n$ define $w_i = y_i$ if $B$ depends on the $i$th variable and $w_i = z_i$ otherwise. By definition, $f(w_1, ..., w_n) = 1$ while $f(z_1, ..., z_n) = 0$. Thus, there exists an index $i$ such that $f(w_1, ..., w_{i-1}, w_i, z_{i+1}, ..., z_n) = 1$ while $f(w_1, ..., w_{i-1}, z_i, z_{i+1}, ..., z_n) = 0$. This implies that there exists a sensitive letter $\sigma$ such that either $z_i < \sigma \le y_i$ or $y_i < \sigma \le z_i$. Furthermore, $z_i \ne w_i$ and $B$ depends on the $i$th variable. Therefore, $\lfloor z_i \rfloor = \lfloor y_i \rfloor$ (since $z \in B'$) which implies $\lfloor y_i \rfloor \le z_i < \lceil y_i \rceil$. To conclude, if $z_i < \sigma \le y_i$ then $\lfloor y_i \rfloor \le z_i < \sigma \le y_i < \lceil y_i \rceil$. Thus, the sensitive letter $\sigma$ is in the interval $\{\lfloor y_i \rfloor + 1, ..., \lceil y_i \rceil - 1\}$. The case $y_i < \sigma \le z_i$ is similar. □

The next theorem completes the analysis of the above algorithm.

**Theorem 16.** *The class $k - \text{DBOX}_t$, for $k = O(1)$, can be learned in time (and query) complexity poly$(n, t, \log \ell)$ using equivalence queries only.*

*Proof.* We use the above algorithm to learn the class $k-\text{DBOX}_t$, for $k = O(1)$. If $L$ contains all sensitive letters then, by Claim 15, we can get only counterexamples $y$ such that $h'(y) = 1$ and after at most $|Q|$ such counterexamples the algorithm finds an hypothesis equal to $f$. Therefore, again by Claim 15, the algorithm reaches Step (6) at most $\log \ell$ times per each sensitive letter. By Claim 6, there are $O(nt)$ sensitive letters; hence, the algorithm reaches Step (6) only $O(nt \log \ell)$ times, and each time it adds at most $n$ new letters to $L$. That is, $|L| = O(n^2 t \log \ell)$ and the number of boxes in $Q$ (each time the algorithm reaches Step (2)) is $O(|L|^k n^k) = \text{poly}(n^k, t^k, \log^k \ell)$. Each time the algorithm asks an equivalence query and does not reach Step (6) it holds that $h(y) = 1$. I.e., there is a box in $Q$ that contains $(\lfloor y_1 \rfloor, \ldots, \lfloor y_n \rfloor)$ and the algorithm removes this box from $Q$. In other words, after at most $|Q| = \text{poly}(n^k, t^k, \log^k \ell)$ EQs the algorithm reaches Step (6). That is, the running time is $\text{poly}(n^k, t^k, \log^k \ell)$ which is $\text{poly}(n, t, \log \ell)$ for $k = O(1)$. □

**Remark 17.** The above algorithm can be used to learn the class of all unions of $O(1)$ boxes with only equivalence queries. (This was an open problem in [14] that was later solved in [23].) The idea is that if we have a function that can be represented as a union of $O(1)$ boxes, then its negation can be represented as a union of $O(1)$-degenerate boxes. Let $f$ be a union of $k$ boxes, that is (using the notation of the proof of Lemma 2) there exists functions $p_{m,j} : [\ell] \to \{0, 1\}$ for $1 \le m \le k$ and $1 \le j \le n$ such that $f = \vee_{m=1}^k \prod_{j=1}^n p_{m,j}(x_j)$, and $p_{m,j}(x_j) = 1$ if $x_j$ is in some interval. Therefore,

$$\overline{f} = \bigvee_{i_1,\ldots,i_k \in \{1,\ldots,n\}} \prod_{j=1}^k \overline{p_{j,i_j}(x_{i_j})} .$$

In words, a point $x$ is not in the union of $k$ boxes if for every box $B_j$ there exists a coordinate $i_j$ such that $x_{i_j}$ is not in the $i_j$-interval of the box (i.e., $p_{j,i_j}(x_{i_j}) = 0$). Note that $\overline{p_{j,i_j}(x_{i_j})}$ is a union of (at most) two intervals. Thus, $\overline{f}$ can be represented as a union of at most $n^k$ generalized boxes as defined in Remark 11. Each such generalized box can be represented as a union of at most $2^k$ (simple) $k$-degenerate boxes. Thus, $\overline{f}$ can be represented as a union of $O(kn^k)$ $k$-degenerate boxes, and our algorithm, as it is, learns the class of union of $O(1)$ boxes in time $\text{poly}(n, \log \ell)$.

# References

1. D. Angluin. Queries and concept learning. *Machine Learning*, 2(4):319–342, 1988.
2. P. Auer. On-line learning of rectangles in noisy environments. In *Proc. of 6th Annu. ACM Workshop on Comput. Learning Theory*, pages 253–261, 1993.
3. A. Beimel, F. Bergadano, N. H. Bshouty, E. Kushilevitz, and S. Varricchio. On the applications of multiplicity automata in learning. In *Proc. of 37th Annu. IEEE Symp. on Foundations of Computer Science*, pages 349–358, 1996.

4. S. Ben-David, N. H. Bshouty, and E. Kushilevitz. A composition theorem for learning algorithms with applications to geometric concept classes. manuscript, 1996.

5. F. Bergadano, D. Catalano, and S. Varricchio. Learning sat-$k$-DNF formulas from membership queries. In *Proc. of 28th Annu. ACM Symp. on the Theory of Computing*, pages 126–130, 1996.

6. A. Blum and S. Rudich. Fast learning of $k$-term DNF formulas with queries. In *Proc. of 24th ACM Symp. on Theory of Computing*, pages 382–389, 1992.

7. A. Blumer, A. Ehrenfeucht, D. Haussler, and M. K. Warmuth. Learnability and the Vapnik-Chervonenkis dimension. *Journal of the ACM*, 36:929–965, 1989.

8. N. H. Bshouty. Exact learning via the monotone theory. In *Proc. of 34th Annu. IEEE Symp. on Foundations of Computer Science*, pages 302–311, 1993. Journal version: *Information and Computation*, 123(1):146–153, 1995.

9. N. H. Bshouty. Simple learning algorithms using divide and conquer. In *Proc. of 8th Annu. ACM Workshop on Comput. Learning Theory*, pages 447–453, 1995.

10. N. H. Bshouty, Z. Chen, and S. Homer. On learning discretized geometric concepts. In *Proc. of 35th Annu. Symp. on Foundations of Computer Science*, pages 54–63, 1994.

11. N. H. Bshouty, P. W. Goldberg, S. A. Goldman, and H. D. Mathias. Exact learning of discretized geometric concepts. Technical Report WUCS-94-19, Washington University, 1994.

12. N. H. Bshouty, S. A. Goldman, H. D. Mathias, S. Suri, and H. Tamaki. Noise-tolerant distribution-free learning of general geometric concepts. In *Proc. of 28th Annu. ACM Symp. on Theory of Computing*, pages 151–160, 1996.

13. Z. Chen and S. Homer. The bounded injury priority method and the learnability of unions of rectangles. *Annals of Pure and Applied Logic*, 77(2):143–168, 1996.

14. Z. Chen and W. Maass. On-line learning of rectangles. In *Proc. of 5th Annu. ACM Workshop on Comput. Learning Theory*, 1992.

15. P. W. Goldberg, S. A. Goldman, and H. D. Mathias. Learning unions of boxes with membership and equivalence queries. In *Proc. of 7th Annu. ACM Workshop on Comput. Learning Theory*, 1994.

16. J. C. Jackson. An efficient membership-query algorithm for learning DNF with respect to the uniform distribution. In *35th Annu. Symp. on Foundations of Computer Science*, pages 42–53, 1994.

17. J. C. Jackson. *The Harmonic Sieve: A Novel Application of Fourier Analysis to Machine Learning Theory and Practice*. PhD thesis, Technical Report CMU-CS-95-184, School of Computer Science, Carnegie Mellon University, 1995.

18. E. Kushilevitz. A simple algorithm for learning $O(\log n)$-term DNF. In *Proc. of 9th Annu. ACM Workshop on Comput. Learning Theory*, pages 266–269, 1996.

19. N. Littlestone. Learning when irrelevant attributes abound: A new linear-threshold algorithm. *Machine Learning*, 2:285–318, 1988.

20. P. M. Long and M. K. Warmuth. Composite geometric concepts and polynomial predictability. In *Proc. of 3rd Annu. ACM Workshop on Comput. Learning Theory*, pages 273–287, 1990.

21. W. Maass and G. Turan. On the complexity of learning from counterexamples. In *Proc. of 30th Annu. Symp. on Foundations of Computer Science*, pages 262–273, 1989.

22. W. Maass and G. Turan. Algorithms and lower bounds for on-line learning of geometrical concepts. *Machine Learning*, 14:251 – 269, 1994.

23. W. Maass and M. K. Warmuth. Efficient learning with virtual threshold gates. In *Proc. 12th International Conference on Machine Learning*, pages 378–386. Morgan Kaufmann, 1995.
24. L. G. Valiant. A theory of the learnable. *Communications of the ACM*, 27(11):1134–1142, 1984.

# Learning Monotone Term Decision Lists

David Guijarro[1*], Víctor Lavín[1**] and Vijay Raghavan[2***]

[1] Department LSI, Universitat Politècnica de Catalunya,
Pau Gargallo 5, Barcelona 08028, Spain,
{david, vlavin}@goliat.upc.es
[2] Box 1679-B, Computer Science Department,
Vanderbilt University, Nashville, TN 37235,
raghavan@vuse.vanderbilt.edu

**Abstract.** We study the learnability of monotone term decision lists in the exact model of equivalence and membership queries. We show that, for any constant $k \geq 0$, $k$-term monotone decision lists are exactly and properly learnable with $n^{O(k)}$ membership queries in $O(n^{k^3})$ time. We also show $n^{\Omega(k)}$ membership queries are necessary for exact learning. In contrast, both $k$-term monotone decision lists ($k \geq 2$) and general monotone decision lists are not learnable with equivalence queries alone.

## 1 Introduction

Decision lists were introduced by Rivest [Riv87], who showed that the class of $k$-decision lists is properly PAC-learnable in polynomial time, for constant $k \geq 0$. Here the constant $k$ refers to the maximum number of literals in a term of the decision list. Related results on learning decision lists can be found in [Sim94].

It is not easy to generalize Rivest's results to allow arbitrary number of literals in a term. Such a generalization would include all boolean functions—moreover, the smallest decision list representation of a boolean function is no bigger than the DNF representation. Therefore, predictability of general decision lists would imply the predictability of DNF formulas, a hard open problem.

In this paper, we take a different approach to studying the learnability of decision lists with terms of arbitrary length—we restrict the terms to be monotone. This is not as big a restriction as may seem initially: we show that all boolean functions can still be represented with decision lists with monotone terms only. An advantage of this restriction is that monotone term decision lists are amenable to basic operations on representations. For example, we show that it is polynomial-time decidable if a given monotone term decision list is irredundant (i.e., if it contains no irrelevant variables in a term and no irrelevant term) and make it irredundant if it is not. We also show that there is a polynomial-time equivalence test for monotone term decision lists. In contrast, for general

* Supported by the Esprit EC program under project 7141 (ALCOM-II), the Working Group 8556 (NeuroColt), and the Spanish DGICYT (project PB92-0709)
** Supported by grant FP93 13717942 from the Spanish Government
*** This work was supported by NSF grant CCR-9510392.

decision lists, these operations cannot be done in polynomial time unless $P = NP$.

Our main results in the learnability of monotone term decision lists are as follows. First, we show that $k$-term decision lists are representable as $k$-decision lists. Consequently, for any constant $k$, $k$-term decision lists are PAC-learnable as $k$-decision lists using Rivest's algorithm [Riv87]. Proper learnability of $k$-term monotone decision lists is a more difficult question. We do not know if this class is properly PAC-learnable. However, we do show that this class is properly and exactly learnable with $n^{O(k)}$ membership queries alone in $n^{O(k^3)}$ time by a *non-adaptive* learning algorithm (i.e., the algorithm always makes membership queries on a fixed set of assignments). From this it follows that $k$-term monotone decision lists are "simple-PAC" learnable in the sense of Li and Vitányi [LV91].

Let us note that learnability of the class of functions representable by $k$-term monotone decision lists can be derived from [B95], but this derivation leads to a an improper algorithm. Kushilevitz's result in [K96] is also related to our wotk, it implies learnability of $O(\log n)$-term monotone decision lists improperly with equivalence and membership queries, and again proper learning of subclasses of monotone decision lists seems to be a difficult quetion.

We also show that $n^{\Omega(k)}$ membership queries are necessary for exact learning of this class and that equivalence queries will not suffice for exact learning when $k \geq 2$. Finally, we use Angluin's approximate fingerprint technique [Ang90] to show that equivalence queries do not suffice for exact learning of monotone term decision lists of arbitrary number of terms. An open problem, not resolved in this paper, is whether general monotone term decision lists are exactly learnable with equivalence and membership queries.

The rest of the paper is organized as follows. Section 2 presents definitions used in the rest of the paper. (For definitions of exact/PAC, and improper/proper learnability, the reader is referred to [Ang88, Ang90, AB92, HPRW96, Val84].) Section 3 contains some essential properties of monotone decision lists. Sections 4 and 5, respectively, contain our results for $k$-term monotone decision lists and general monotone decision lists.

## 2 Definitions

A *decision list* is an ordered list of pairs of boolean functions. Each pair $\langle t, o \rangle$ in a decision list is called a *node* of the decision list, the function $t$ being the *test* function and the function $o$ the *output* function. The last node in a decision list is called the *default* node and has a constant test function that evaluates to 1 (true). The evaluation of a decision list $\langle \langle t_1, o_1 \rangle, \langle t_2, o_2 \rangle, ... \rangle$ on an assignment $\alpha$ is obtained by first finding the least $i$ such that $t_i(\alpha) = 1$ and then outputting $o_i(\alpha)$. In the following sections, we say that assignment $\alpha$ *reaches* the node $\langle t_i, o_i \rangle$, if $i$ is the least integer such that $t_i(\alpha) = 1$.

A $k$-decision list [Riv87] is a decision list in which all the test functions are monomials with at most $k$ literals and the output functions are the constants 0 and 1. A *monotone decision list* is a decision list in which all the test functions (or *terms*) are monotone monomials and the output functions are the constants 0 and 1. If the output function associated with a term is 0, we say that the term is *negative*; otherwise it is *positive*. In this paper, we focus on monotone decision lists in general and $k$-term monotone decision lists in particular, where $k > 0$ is some fixed integer constant. (A $k$-term monotone decision list has at most $k$ nodes, not counting the default.)

A monotone decision list is *minimal* (or *irredundant*) if no node or variable within a term can be deleted without changing the boolean function represented by the decision list. Without loss of generality, we will suppose that all decision lists considered in this paper are minimal.

We denote the set of assignments with at most $l$ zeroes by $A_l$. The set of variables that are set to 1 in an assignment $\alpha$ is denoted by $ones(\alpha)$, and respectively, the set of variables that are set to 0 by $zeroes(\alpha)$. The natural partial order $\succ$ over assignments, given by $\alpha \succ \beta$ if and only if $ones(\alpha) \supset ones(\beta)$, defines a lattice called the *boolean lattice*. The set of variables of a term $t$ is denoted by $vars(t)$. Finally, for any assignment $\alpha$, the assignment $\alpha_{v \leftarrow b}$ is the assignment obtained by setting the variable $v$ to $b$ and all the other variables as in $\alpha$.

## 3 Some Properties of Monotone Decision Lists

We prove some essential properties of monotone decision lists, which will be used in the next section to develop a learning algorithm. We begin by showing that the general class of monotone decision lists has the power to represent all boolean functions.

**Property 1** *Every boolean function can be represented as a monotone decision list.*

*Proof.* Let $f$ be any boolean function. To represent $f$ using a monotone decision list, walk through the boolean lattice of assignments in topological order (i.e., starting at the assignment of all 1's and ending at the assignment of all 0's.) For each assignment $\alpha$, create a node $\langle t_\alpha, f(\alpha) \rangle$, where $t_\alpha$ is a monotone monomial containing precisely the variables in $ones(\alpha)$. (Note that the evaluation of $f$ on the all 0's assignment will form the output of the default node.) The decision list thus constructed represents $f$ since each assignment $\alpha$ in the boolean hypercube reaches the corresponding node $\langle t_\alpha, f(\alpha) \rangle$. $\square$

We now show that the class of $k$-term decision lists is contained in the class of $k$-decision lists considered by Rivest. From this it follows that $k$-term decision lists are PAC-learnable as $k$-decision lists, using Rivest's algorithm [Riv87].

**Property 2** *Every $k$-term decision list can be represented by a $k$-decision list.*

*Proof.* Let $L$ be a $k$-term decision list. We transform $L$ to an equivalent $k$-decision list $L'$ as follows: Initially $L'$ is the empty list. We begin by adding to

$L'$ a set of nodes that classify correctly the assignments that reach the default in $L$, i.e., we add to $L'$ nodes $\langle t, b \rangle$, where $b$ is the classification of the default of $L$, and each $k$-DNF term $t$ is obtained by picking one literal from each (non-default) term of $L$ and complementing the at most $k$ literals. Next, for each node from the last node of $L$ down to the second node of $L$, we use a similar procedure to classify all assignments that reach the node. That is, if $\langle t_i, b \rangle$ is the $i$-th node of $L$, we add to $L'$ one node $\langle t, b \rangle$ for every term $t$ obtained by picking one literal from each of the $i - 1$ terms of $L$ prior to $\langle t_i, b \rangle$ and complementing the at most $i - 1$ literals. Finally, we set the default of $L'$ to be the classification of the first node of $L$. □

The remaining properties in this section have to do with $k$-term monotone decision lists. We begin by showing that the set $A_{2k}$ is a specification set [GK91] for $k$-term monotone decision lists.

**Property 3** *Let $L_1$ and $L_2$ be $k$-term monotone decision lists. $L_1 \equiv L_2$ if and only if for all assignments $\alpha \in A_{2k}$, $L_1(\alpha) = L_2(\alpha)$.*

*Proof.* The "only if" part is trivial. For the "if" part, suppose that $\alpha$ is an assignment such that $L_1(\alpha) \neq L_2(\alpha)$. In particular, let $\langle t_1, b \rangle$ and $\langle t_2, \bar{b} \rangle$ be the respective nodes of $L_1$ and $L_2$ reached by $\alpha$. Let $T$ be the set of terms that precede $t_1$ in $L_1$ or $t_2$ in $L_2$. Note that $ones(\alpha) \supseteq vars(t_1) \cup vars(t_2)$, and $zeroes(\alpha)$ must contain at least one variable from each term in $T$. This implies that an assignment $\alpha'$ in which $zeroes(\alpha')$ is a minimal subset of $zeroes(\alpha)$ which contains at least one variable from each term in $T$ will also satisfy $L_1(\alpha') \neq L_2(\alpha')$. Such an assignment $\alpha'$ must be in $A_{2k}$ since $|T| \leq 2k$. □

Property 3 implies that $k$-term monotone decision lists are polynomial-query learnable with $|A_{2k}| = n^{O(k)}$ membership queries alone. In the next section, we show that we can infer the target $k$-term monotone decision list from membership queries on $A_{2k}$ in $n^{O(k^3)}$ time. The following property shows that it suffices to know the evaluation of a $k$-term monotone decision list $L$ on $A_{2k}$ in order to infer, in polynomial time, the evaluation of $L$ on any assignment.

**Property 4** *Let $f$ be a boolean function representable as a $k$-term monotone decision list, $\alpha$ be any assignment, and $b \in \{0, 1\}$. Then $f(\alpha) = b$ if and only if there exists some set $S \subseteq zeroes(\alpha)$ of at most $k$ variables, such that for all assignments $\beta \in A_{2k}$ that satisfy $zeroes(\beta) \supseteq S$ and $ones(\beta) \supseteq ones(\alpha)$, $f(\beta) = b$.*

*Proof.* Assume that $\alpha$ reaches the $i$-th node $\langle t_i, b \rangle$ of some $k$-term monotone decision list representation $L$ of $f$. For any pairwise disjoint sets $Y$ and $Z$ of variables, let $p(Y, Z)$ denote the partial assignment that sets to 0 all the variables in $Y$ and to 1 the variables in $Z$.

To prove the "only if" part, let $S \subseteq zeroes(\alpha)$ be a set of at most $i - 1$ variables whose negation falsify the first $i-1$ terms of $L$. Now consider the partial assignment $p(S, ones(\alpha))$. Clearly, all extensions of $p(S, ones(\alpha))$—in particular those that contain at most $2k$ 0's—reach $\langle t_i, b \rangle$, and are therefore classified as $b$.

Conversely, for any assignment $\alpha$ suppose there exists a set $S$ as in the property. Suppose, for contradiction, that $\alpha$ reaches the node $\langle t_i, \bar{b} \rangle$ in some $k$-term monotone decision list representation $L$ of $f$. Now consider the assignment $\beta$ that sets to 0 the variables in $S$, sets to 0 one variable in $vars(t) - (vars(t_i) \cup ones(\alpha))$ for each term $t$ in $L$ before $t_i$ that does not contain any variable of $S$, and sets to 1 the remaining variables. Clearly, $\beta$ is in $A_{2k}$ and is an extension of $p(S, ones(\alpha))$; however, $\beta$ reaches $\langle t_i, \bar{b} \rangle$, which contradicts the supposition that every extension of $p(S, ones(\alpha))$ evaluates to $b$. □

The following corollary is immediate.

**Corollary 5** *Let $f$ be a boolean function representable as a $k$-term monotone decision list. Given $f(\beta)$ for each assignment $\beta \in A_{2k}$, we can determine $f(\alpha)$ for any assignment $\alpha$ in $n^{O(k)}$ time.*

**Property 6** *Let $L$ be a minimal $k$-term monotone decision list and let $\langle t, b \rangle$ be a node of $L$. Then there exists a set $S \subseteq A_k$ such that*

*(i)* $|S| \leq k$,
*(ii)* *For each $\alpha \in S$, $L(\alpha) = b$, and*
*(iii)* *For each variable $v$, $v \in vars(t)$ if and only if $L(\alpha_{v \leftarrow 0}) = \bar{b}$, for some $\alpha$ in $S$.*

*Proof.* The minimality of $L$ guarantees that for any variable $v$ in $vars(t)$ there exists an assignment $\alpha$ that justifies the necessity of $v$ in $t$, i.e. $\alpha$ reaches $\langle t, b \rangle$ but $\alpha_{v \leftarrow 0}$ reaches some node $\langle t', \bar{b} \rangle$ after $\langle t, b \rangle$. (We say that $t'$ validates $v$ in $t$.)

We now prove that if a term $t'$ validates each variable in $V = \{v_1, v_2, ..., v_l\} \subseteq vars(t)$, then there exists a single assignment $\alpha \in A_k$ that justifies all the variables in $V$. To do this, we claim that every term of nodes prior to $\langle t', \bar{b} \rangle$ in $L$ either (a) contains a superset of $V$ or (b) contains some variable not in $vars(t) \cup vars(t')$. To prove the claim, suppose, to the contrary, that there is some term $r$ of a node prior to $\langle t', \bar{b} \rangle$ such that $r$ does not contain some variable $v$ of $V$ and $vars(r) \subset vars(t) \cup vars(t')$. Let $\alpha$ be a justifying assignment for $v$ in $t$, such that $\beta = \alpha_{v \leftarrow 0}$ reaches $\langle t', \bar{b} \rangle$. Since $ones(\beta) \supseteq vars(r)$, $\beta$ cannot reach any node beyond the one that contains $r$, a contradiction. It follows from the claim that the assignment $\alpha$ that sets to 0 one variable not in $vars(t) \cup vars(t')$ for each term that satisfies case (b), and sets to 1 the remaining variables is a justifying assignment for all variables in $V$, and has at most $k$ 0's.

All the variables in $vars(t)$ must be validated by at most $k$ terms. To finish the proof of the property, let $S$ be a set of assignments which contains, for each node $\langle t', \bar{b} \rangle$ that follows $\langle t, b \rangle$ in $L$, one assignment $\alpha \in A_k$ that reaches $\langle t, b \rangle$ and that justifies all the variables in $vars(t)$ validated by $t'$. The set $S$ then contains assignments that validate all the variables in $vars(t)$. Moreover, no variable not in $vars(t)$ will be justified by assignments in $S$ since all the assignments in $S$ reach $\langle t, b \rangle$. □

Property 6 motivates the following definition. We say that $\langle t, b \rangle$ is a *candidate node* (in a $k$-term monotone decision list representation) of a boolean function

$f$ if there exists a set $S \subseteq A_k$ with at most $k$ assignments, such that for each $\alpha \in S$, $f(\alpha) = b$ and such that $vars(t)$ is precisely the set of variables justified by assignments in $S$. Note that all candidate nodes of $f$ can be found in $n^{O(k^2)}$ time. Moreover, the set of candidate nodes of a boolean function is a superset of all possible nodes $\langle t, b \rangle$ which can appear in a minimal $k$-term monotone decision list representation of $f$.

## 4 Learning $k$-term Monotone Decision Lists

We begin by showing that $k$-term monotone decision lists are properly learnable in $n^{O(k^3)}$ time, using $n^{O(k)}$ membership queries. Next, we show that any proper membership-query learning algorithm for this class must use $n^{\Omega(k)}$ queries, proving that our algorithm is reasonably tight. An easy consequence of our learning algorithm is that $k$-term monotone decision lists are "simple-PAC" learnable. Finally, we show that this class is not learnable with equivalence queries alone.

The algorithm below follows directly from Properties 3 and 6 and Corollary 5 of the previous section.

### Algorithm Learn_$k$-term_monotone_decision_lists

1. Make membership queries on all assignments in $A_{2k}$.
2. Find the classification of the default.
3. Find all candidate nodes of the target function.
4. Construct all possible $k$-term monotone decision lists using candidate nodes and the default classification.
5. From the $k$-term monotone decision lists constructed in step (4), output the first one which agrees with the target function on the classification of the assignmnents in $A_{2k}$.

**Correctness:** In Step 1, we ask membership queries with all the assignments in $A_{2k}$. By using Corollary 5 to establish the evaluation of the target function on the all-zeroes assignment (or with a direct membership query), we decide the classification of the default node in the target function (Step 2).

Next, in Step 3, we use Property 6 to produce a set of $n^{O(k^2)}$ candidate nodes that are guaranteed to contain all the nodes of the target function represented as a $k$-term monotone decision list. Using all possible permutations of at most $k$ nodes from the set of candidate nodes, we end up with a set of candidate $k$-term monotone decision lists (Step 4). Property 6 ensures that at least one of these decision lists will be equivalent to the target. By Property 3, testing the candidate decision lists for consistency with the target function over $A_{2k}$ is enough to determine one which is equivalent to the target (Step 5).

**Query Complexity:** Only membership queries are used and then only in the first step. The number of queries is $|A_{2k}|$, which is at most $2kn^{2k} = n^{O(k)}$.

**Time Complexity:** The steps that take the most time are 4 and 5. Since Step 3 produces $n^{O(k^2)}$ candidate nodes, the number of candidate decision lists created in Step 5 is $n^{O(k^3)}$. This bound dominates the overall time, which remains $n^{O(k^3)}$.

The comments on correctness and complexity have effectively proved the following theorem.

**Theorem 7** *The class of k-term monotone decision lists can be properly learned with $n^{O(k)}$ membership queries in $n^{O(k^3)}$ time.*

Note that the learning algorithm is non-adaptive, i.e., it uses membership queries only on the fixed set $A_{2k}$, independent of the target $k$-term monotone decision list. Therefore, it follows that $k$-term monotone decision lists are learnable in the "simple-PAC" model of Li and Vitányi [LV91].

**Theorem 8** *Any membership-query learning algorithm for k-term monotone decision lists must use at least $\sum_{i=1}^{k-1} \binom{n}{i}$ queries.*

*Proof.* Let $\alpha$ be any assignment with at most $k-1$ zeroes. The singleton boolean function which is true precisely on the assignment $\alpha$ can be represented as a $k$-term monotone decision list. To construct such a representation, first create nodes $\langle v, 0 \rangle$ for each variable $v$ in $zeroes(\alpha)$, thus using at most $k-1$ nodes. Next, create a node $\langle t, 1 \rangle$, where $vars(t) = ones(\alpha)$, and finally set the default to 0.

From the above, it follows that the number of $k$-term monotone decision lists that can represent singletons is at least $\sum_{i=0}^{k-1} \binom{n}{i}$. Using a standard adversary argument with singletons, we get the result. $\qquad\square$

It is an easy exercise to show that 1-term monotone decision lists are learnable with equivalence queries alone. We now show that the class of $k$-term monotone decision lists has approximate fingerprints for $k \geq 2$, and therefore cannot be learned with equivalence queries alone. (For a definition of approximate fingerprints, and a proof that they are sufficient for non-learnability with equivalence queries alone, see [Ang90].) We start with a lemma.

**Lemma 9** *Let L be a k-term monotone decision list, $k \geq 2$. Then there exists an assignment $\alpha = \alpha(L)$ such that either*

*(a) $\alpha$ has at most $k-1$ zeroes, and $L(\alpha) = 0$, or*
*(b) $\alpha$ has at most $n/k$ ones, and $L(\alpha) = 1$.*

*Proof.* If $L$ is the constant function 1 then (b) holds. Otherwise, if $L$ is not a monotone boolean function, or $L$ has fewer than $k$ terms, or if two terms in $L$ share a variable, it is easy to construct an assignment that satisfies (a). Otherwise, all the $k$ terms in $L$ have distinct set of variables and $L$ is a monotone Boolean function. Therefore, there must be a positive term in $L$ with at most $n/k$ variables. An assignment with ones exactly in the positions of the variables in such a term satisfies (b). $\qquad\square$

**Theorem 10** *The class of $k$-term monotone decision lists, $k \geq 2$, has approximate fingerprints.*

*Proof.* Let $T_{n,k}$ be the target class of $k$-term monotone decision lists in which all the terms are positive, the default is negative, and each term has exactly $n/k$ variables that do not occur in any other term. To avoid floors and ceilings, assume that $n$ is a multiple of $k$.

In order to prove the approximate fingerprint property, it suffices to show that the number of functions in $T_{n,k}$ that either classify an assignment of at most $k-1$ 0's as 0 or classify an assignment with at most $n/k$ 1's as 1, is a superpolynomially small fraction of $|T_{n,k}|$.

Note that $|T_{n,k}| = \frac{n!}{[(n/k)!]^k k!}$. No function in $T_{n,k}$ classifies an assignment with at most $k-1$ zeroes as 0. Moreover, the fraction of the functions in $T_{n,k}$ that classify an assignment with at most $n/k$ ones as 1 is at most

$$\frac{|T_{n-n/k,k-1}|}{|T_{n,k}|} = \frac{(n-n/k)!(n/k)!k}{n!} = \frac{k}{\binom{n}{n/k}}$$

which, after a routine use of Stirling's approximation, can be seen to be superpolynomially small in $n$ for $k \geq 2$. $\square$

**Corollary 11** *The class of $k$-term monotone decision lists, $k \geq 2$, is not learnable with equivalence queries alone.*

*Proof.* Follows from Theorem 10 and Angluin's theorem [Ang90] on the approximate fingerprint property. $\square$

## 5   General Monotone Decision Lists

General monotone decision lists are monotone term decision lists with no *a priori* bound on the number of nodes. As shown in section 2, this class can represent all boolean functions. Here we show that there is a polynomial time algorithm for testing the equivalence of two general decision lists. Our results on the learnability of this representation class are sparse and, unfortunately, all negative. First of all, it follows from Theorem 8 that general decision lists are not learnable with membership queries alone. We show below that equivalence queries alone also do not suffice for learnability.

**Theorem 12** *There is an $O(n(p+q)pq)$ time algorithm that tests equivalence of two monotone decision lists on $n$ variables, $L_1$ and $L_2$, with $p$ and $q$ nodes respectively. The algorithm also supplies an assignment that witnesses the inequivalence, if $L_1 \not\equiv L_2$.*

*Proof.* For any pair of terms $t_1$ and $t_2$ from $L_1$ and $L_2$ respectively, define the assignment $\beta(t_1, t_2)$ by $ones(\beta(t_1, t_2)) \coloneqq vars(t_1) \cup vars(t_2)$. Clearly, if there exists a term $t_1$ in $L_1$ and a term $t_2$ in $L_2$ such that $L_1(\beta(t_1, t_2)) \neq L_2(\beta(t_1, t_2))$, then $L_1 \not\equiv L_2$. Conversely, if $L_1 \not\equiv L_2$, then there exists some assignment $\alpha$ such that $L_1(\alpha) \neq L_2(\alpha)$. Assume that $\alpha$ reaches nodes $\langle t_1, b \rangle$ in $L_1$ and $\langle t_2, \bar{b} \rangle$ in $L_2$. Consider the assignment $\beta = \beta(t_1, t_2)$. Now $\beta$ reaches both $\langle t_1, b \rangle$ and $\langle t_2, \bar{b} \rangle$, and $L_1(\alpha) = L_1(\beta) \neq L_2(\beta) = L_2(\alpha)$.

From the above, it follows that testing $L_1$ and $L_2$ for equivalence is tantamount to checking if $L_1(\beta(t_1, t_2)) = L_2(\beta(t_1, t_2))$ for all pairs $t_1$ in $L_1$ and $t_2$ in $L_2$. There are $O(pq)$ pairs of terms to consider, and each evaluation takes $O(n(p+q))$ time. $\qquad\square$

Note that the algorithm for testing equivalence can be used to test if a general monotone decision list is minimal—all one needs to do to decide if a particular variable in a term (or a particular node) is redundant is to delete the variable from the term (or the entire node) and test the resultant decision list for equivalence with the original.

We now show that monotone decision lists have approximate fingerprints. Note that this result does not follow immediately from the earlier proof of approximate fingerprints. We begin with a lemma.

**Lemma 13** *Let $L$ be a $p$-term monotone decision list on $n$ variables. There is an assignment $\alpha = \alpha(L)$ such that either*

*(a) $L(\alpha) = 0$ and $\alpha$ contains at most $\sqrt{n \ln p}$ 0's, or*
*(b) $L(\alpha) = 1$ and $\alpha$ contains at most $\sqrt{n \ln p}$ 1's.*

*Proof.* Let $m = \sqrt{n \ln p}$. If the first term in $L$ is negative, then clearly the all 1's assignment satisfies (a). If the default is positive, then the all 0's assignment satisfies (b). Otherwise, let $p' \leq p$ be the number of positive terms in $L$. If any such positive term, say $t$, has at most $m$ variables, then the assignment $\alpha$ such that $ones(\alpha) = vars(t)$ satisfies (b). Finally, if all the positive terms of $L$ have more than $m$ variables, then we show the existence of an assignment $\alpha$ that satisfies (a) as follows.

Pick $r = m$ variables at random and set them to 0, setting the remaining variables to 1. The probability that such an assignment is accepted by some positive term of $L$ is at most

$$(1 - m/n)^r p' \leq \left(1 - \sqrt{\frac{\ln p}{n}}\right)^r p < e^{-r\sqrt{\frac{\ln p}{n}}} p$$

For our choice of $r$, the last quantity in the above expression is 1. Therefore, there exists some set $X$ of at most $r$ variables such that the assignment $\alpha$ formed by setting all the variables in $X$ to 0 and the remaining variables to 1 is not accepted by any positive term of $L$. Such an assignment satisfies (a). $\qquad\square$

**Theorem 14** *The class of general monotone decision lists has approximate fingerprints.*

*Proof.* Let $T_n$ be the class of $q = \sqrt{n}$-term monotone decision lists in which all the terms are positive, the default is negative, and each term has exactly $q$ variables which do not occur in any other term. (Assume that $q$ is an integer in order to avoid floors and ceilings.) Note that this is the same target class as the one used in [AHK93] to show that read-once formulas cannot be identified with equivalence queries alone. The number of logically distinct Boolean functions in $T_n$ is $\frac{n!}{(q!)^{q+1}}$.

Let $p = n^c$ for some fixed constant $c > 0$ and let $L$ be any monotone decision list of $p$ terms. Let $\alpha = \alpha(L)$ be the assignment whose existence is guaranteed by Lemma 13. To show the approximate fingerprint property, it suffices to show that the fraction of concepts in $T_n$ that classify $\alpha$ as $L$ does is superpolynomially small. As in Lemma 13, let $m = \sqrt{n \ln p}$. If $L(\alpha)$ is 1, the number of concepts in $T_n$ that classify $\alpha$ as $L$ does is at most $\binom{m}{q} \frac{(n-q)!}{(q!)^{q-1}(q-1)!}$. If $L(\alpha)$ is 0, the number of concepts in $T_n$ that classify $\alpha$ as $L$ does is at most $\binom{m}{q} \frac{(n-q)!}{[(q-1)!]^q q!})$. In either case, the fraction of concepts in $T_n$ that classify $\alpha$ as $L$ does is at most $\binom{m}{q} \frac{(n-q)! q^q}{n!}$, which (after plugging in the values of $m$ and $q$) is less than $\frac{(\sqrt{nc \ln n})^{\sqrt{n}}}{(\sqrt{(n)})!} \cdot \frac{(\sqrt{n})^{\sqrt{n}}}{(n-\sqrt{n})^{\sqrt{n}}}$. This quantity can be seen to be superpolynomially small in $n$. $\square$

**Corollary 15** *The class of general monotone decision lists is not learnable with equivalence queries alone.*

*Proof.* Follows from Theorem 14 and Angluin's theorem [Ang90] on the approximate fingerprint property. $\square$

# 6 Acknowledgments

The authors wish to thank Professors José L. Balcázar, Ricard Gavaldà and Jorge Castro for suggesting the problem and participating in the discussion. We also thank some anonymous referees who pointed us to related results and contributed to the readability of some proofs.

# References

[Ang88] D. Angluin. "Queries and Concept Learning." Machine Learning 2, 319–342, 1988.

[Ang90] D. Angluin. "Negative Results for Equivalence Queries." Machine Learning, vol. 5, 121–150, 1990.

[AB92] M. Anthony and N. Biggs. "Computational Learning Theory: An Introduction." Cambridge University Press, 1992.

[AHK93] D. Angluin, L. Hellerstein, and M. Karpinski. "Learning Read-Once Formulas with Queries." Journal of the ACM, vol. 40, number 1, 185–210, 1993.

[B95] N. Bshouty. "Simple Learning Algorithms Using Divide and Conquer." Proceedings of the Eighth Annual Workshop on Computational Learning Theory, 447-453, 1995.

[GK91] S. Goldman and M. Kearns. "On the Complexity of Teaching." Proceedings of the Fourth Annual Workshop on Computational Learning Theory, 303–314, 1991.

[HPRW96] L. Hellerstein, K. Pillaipakkamnatt, V. Raghavan, D. Wilkins. "How Many Queries are Needed to Learn?" Journal of the ACM, Vol. 43, No. 5, September 1996, pp. 840-862.

[K96] E. Kushilevitz. "A Simple Algorithm for Learning $O(\log n)$-Term DNF." Proceedings of the Ninth Annual Workshop on Computational Learning Theory, 266-269, 1996.

[LV91] M. Li and P. Vitányi. "Learning Simple Concepts under Simple Distributions." SIAM Journal of Computing 20, 911–935, 1991.

[Riv87] R. Rivest. "Learning Decision Lists." Machine Learning 2, 229–246, 1987.

[Sim94] H. U. Simon. "Learning Decision Lists and Trees with Equivalence Queries." Proceeding of the 2nd European Conference EUROCOLT, pp 322-336, 1995.

[Val84] L. Valiant. "A Theory of the Learnable." Communications of the ACM 27:11, 1134–1142, 1984.

# Learning Matrix Functions over Rings

## (Extended Abstract)

Nader H. Bshouty[1] and Christino Tamon[*2] and David K. Wilson[1]

[1] Dept. Computer Science, University of Calgary, 2500 University Drive NW,
Calgary, AB, T2N 1N4 Canada
[2] Dept. Mathematics and Computer Science, Clarkson University, P.O. Box 5815,
Potsdam, NY 13699-5815, U.S.A.

**Abstract.** Let $R$ be a commutative Artinian ring with identity and let $X$ be a finite subset of $R$. We present an exact learning algorithm with a polynomial query complexity for the class of functions representable as

$$f(x) = \prod_{i=1}^{n} A_i(x_i)$$

where for each $1 \leq i \leq n$, $A_i$ is a matrix-valued mapping $A_i : X \to R^{m_i \times m_{i+1}}$ and $m_1 = m_{n+1} = 1$. These functions are referred to as *matrix functions*. Our algorithm uses a decision tree based hypothesis class called *decision programs* that takes advantage of linear dependencies. We also show that the class of matrix functions is equivalent to the class of decision programs.

Our learning algorithm implies the following results.

1. Multivariate polynomials over a finite commutative ring with identity are learnable using equivalence and substitution queries.
2. Bounded degree multivariate polynomials over $Z_n$ can be interpolated using substitution queries.

This paper generalizes the learning algorithm for automata over fields given in [4].

## 1 Introduction

The learnability of multiplicity automata over the field of rationals using equivalence and substitution queries was shown to be possible by Bergadano and Varricchio [7]. Their algorithm was a direct generalization of Angluin's algorithm for learning deterministic finite automata [1]. Using algebraic techniques, Beimel et al. [4] found a simpler algorithm for the above class which lead to the discovery of additional learnable concept classes. These new classes include multivariate polynomials over finite fields, bounded degree multivariate polynomials over infinite fields and the $XOR$ of terms. This new algorithm also provided

---

* Work done partly while the author was a student at the Dept. Computer Science, University of Calgary.

better query complexity for some other classes already known to be learnable such as decision trees and polynomials over GF(2).

We present a learning algorithm that generalizes the learning in [4] to functions over rings that contain a finite bound on any sequence of ideals. Our algorithm uses a target class of matrix functions defined as follows. Let $R$ be a commutative Artinian ring with identity and let $X$ be a finite subset of $R$. A function $f : X^n \to R$ is called a *matrix function* if it can be written as

$$f(x) = \prod_{i=1}^{n} A_i(x_i)$$

for some set of mappings $A_i : X \to R^{m_i \times m_{i+1}}$ with $m_1 = m_{n+1} = 1$. An assignment $x = (x_1, \ldots, x_n) \in X^n$ determines which matrices, $A_i(x_i)$, should be multiplied together to give a value for $f(x)$. The size of a matrix function $f$ is the maximum dimension of any matrix in any equivalent form of $f$ that minimizes $\Sigma_{i=2}^{n} m_i$. This representation is similar to that used in [3].

We introduce a target representation called *decision programs* which we show is equivalent to the class of matrix functions. These programs are a special type of decision tree that compute functions from $X^n$ to $R$ where $X$ is a finite subset of $R$. The root of the program is on level 1 and there are $n+1$ levels in total. Level $n+1$ consists of sinks or leaves that are labeled with values from $R$. Only nodes on level $n+1$ are referred to as leaves. The remaining nodes found on levels 1 through $n$ are classified as either independent or dependent. Independent nodes have outdegree $|X|$ with each exiting edge, labeled by a distinct member of $X$, entering a node on the next level. Dependent nodes have outdegree 0 and are labeled by a linear combination of some other independent nodes from the same level. Specifically, if $v_j$ is a dependent node then $v_j = \Sigma_{t \in I} \lambda_t v_t$ where $I$ holds the subscripts of the independent nodes on that level and $\lambda_t \in R$. All nodes have indegree exactly one except for the source. The *size* of a decision program is equal to the total number of nodes (independent, dependent, and sinks).

Given an assignment $x = (x_1, \ldots, x_n)$, a decision program evaluates $x$ in the following recursive manner. The computation to evaluate $x$ starts at the root. If during the computation we reach a node $v$ at level $j$ then we do the following based on whether $v$ is independent or dependent. If $v$ is independent then we follow the edge labeled $x_j$ to the next level. If $v$ is dependent then the value of the computation is the same linear combination of the computation values on the independent nodes using the same assignment. If $v$ is a sink then we return the label of $v$.

Our learning algorithm takes advantage of the linear dependencies that exist in the decision program representation and we show our algorithm implies the following results.

1. Multivariate polynomials over a finite commutative ring with identity are learnable using equivalence and substitution queries.
2. Bounded degree multivariate polynomials over $Z_n$ can be interpolated using substitution queries.

The former follows after we show how to represent multivariate polynomials as matrix functions. The latter follows using a generalization of Schwartz's Lemma [9] after a bound on the number of possible zeros of any target has been established.

The remainder of the paper is organized as follows. Section 2 contains some relevant definitions required for an understanding of our learning algorithm. Section 3 contains a description of our algorithm along with its analysis of correctness and complexity. Section 4 contains descriptions of how our learning algorithm can be used to learn multivariate polynomials over finite rings and to interpolate multivariate polynomials over $Z_n$. Section five presents one additional result that can also be solved using the algorithm of [4].

## 2 Preliminaries

This section gives the relevant preliminary definitions necessary for the presentation of our learning algorithm. We begin with a brief review of the learning model that we use. Following this we provide some relevant definitions from algebra including ideals and modules. We also state and prove two lemmas that are concerned with the length of any sequence of ideals within a ring. The final subsection is devoted to showing the equivalence of the classes of matrix functions and decision programs.

### 2.1 Learning Model

Our learning algorithm is set in the exact learning model which means it has access to two types of queries which answer questions about an unknown target formula $f$. The first type of question is a substitution query, $SuQ(x)$, which takes as input a member of the target domain, some $x \in X^n$, and outputs $f(x)$. The second type of question is an equivalence query, $EQ(h)$, which takes as input some hypothesis $h$ from a hypothesis representation class $H$ and answers YES if $h$ and $f$ are equivalent, otherwise, a counterexample, $c \in X^n$, is returned such that $f(c) \neq h(c)$. More information about this model can be found in [2]. We note that substitution queries are a generalization of membership queries.

### 2.2 Algebraic Definitions

We will assume familiarity with some basic algebraic structures such as Abelian groups, rings and fields. Let $R$ be a commutative ring with identity. An *ideal I* of $R$ is a subset of $R$ that forms an additive subgroup and is closed under scalar multiplication by elements of $R$. The notation $Ra$, for $a \in R$, will stand for the set $\{ra | r \in R\}$ and the notation $Ra_1 + \ldots + Ra_m$, for $a_i \in R$, will stand for the set $\{\sum_{i=1}^m r_i a_i | r_i \in R\}$. The former is known as the principal ideal generated by $a$ and the latter is known as the ideal generated by $a_1, \ldots, a_m$. We let $\{0\}$ represent the trivial ideal generated when $a = 0$.

An $R$-*module* $M$ is an Abelian group equipped with a multiplication from $R \times M$ to $M$ such that the following is satisfied for all $r, s \in R$ and $a, b \in M$:

$$r(a + b) = ra + rb, \quad (r + s)a = ra + sa, \quad (rs)a = r(sa), \quad 1a = a.$$

Note that if $R$ was a field then $M$ would be a vector space over $R$. We call $N$ an *submodule* of $M$ if $N$ is a subgroup of $M$ and $N$ is an $R$-module. An example of an $R$-module is $R^n$.

A ring is called *Artinian* if for any descending chain of ideals $I_0 \supset I_1 \supset I_2 \cdots$ there is an $r$ such that $I_r = I_{r+1} = I_{r+2} = \cdots$. A ring is called *Noetherian* if for any ascending chain of ideals $I_0 \subset I_1 \subset \cdots$ there is an $r$ such that $I_r = I_{r+1} = \cdots$. It is known that an Artinian ring is also Noetherian (see Theorem 3.2, page 16, [8]). Note that any finite ring is trivially Artinian. In addition to $R$ being a commutative ring with identity we will also assume that it Artinian. We now formally define the rank of an ordered set of elements from an $R$-module.

**Definition 1.** Let $M$ be an $R$-module and $v_1, \ldots, v_m \in M$. We define $rank(v_1, \ldots, v_m)$ to be the number of distinct sets in the sequence $Rv_1, Rv_1 + Rv_2, \cdots, Rv_1 + \ldots + Rv_m$. We say that the sequence $v_1, v_2, \ldots, v_m$ is independent if $rank(v_1, \ldots, v_m) = m$.

We will use $l(M)$ to denote the longest ascending chain of submodules in $M$. This is a measure of the number of changes in the sequence. The following two lemmas provide important relationships concerning the rank of members of $R^n$ and the longest ascending chain in $R^n$. If $v \in R^n$ we let $v = \mathbf{0}$ represent the all zero vector, that is, all $n$ coordinates of $v$ are equal to zero.

**Lemma 2.** *If* $v_1, v_2, \ldots, v_m \in R^n$ *and* $v_1 \neq \mathbf{0}$ *then* $rank(v_1, \ldots, v_m) \leq n \cdot l(R)$.

**Lemma 3.** *The length of the longest chain of submodules in* $R^n$ *is* $n$ *times the length of the longest chain of ideals in* $R$, *that is,*

$$l(R^n) = n \cdot l(R).$$

## 2.3 Equivalence of Matrix Functions and Decision Programs

In this subsection we state two theorems that imply that a function is a matrix function if and only if it is computable by a decision program. Both proofs can be found in the appendix.

**Theorem 4.** *If a function* $f$ *is computable by some decision program then* $f$ *is a matrix function.*

**Theorem 5.** *Any matrix function* $f(x) = \prod_{i=1}^{n} A_i(x_i)$ *over* $R$, *where* $A_i : X \to R^{m_i \times m_{i+1}}$, $X$ *is a finite subset of* $R$, *and* $m_1 = m_{n+1} = 1$, *is computable by some decision program of size at most*

$$(|X| + 1) + |X| l(R) \sum_{i=2}^{n} m_i.$$

# 3 Learning Matrix Functions

This section contains a description of our algorithm for learning matrix functions followed by an analysis which establishes both its correctness and its complexity. Before these are given we introduce a construct that plays an important part in our learning process. This initial discussion also includes a description of the event that implies our learning algorithm is making progress.

## 3.1 Dependency Tables

The algorithm uses decision programs as its hypothesis class along with a set of related tables that are used to determine the dependencies of nodes on the same level. The algorithm will maintain one table each level from 2 to $n$ with rows labeled by prefixes of vectors from $X^n$ and columns labeled by suffixes of vectors from $X^n$. Specifically, a table at level $j$ will have each row labeled with a vector from $X^{j-1}$ and each column labeled with a vector from $X^{n-j+1}$. For any level $j$ the content of the table at the row labeled $(x_1, \ldots, x_{j-1})$ and the column labeled $(x_j, \ldots, x_n)$ is $f(x_1, \ldots, x_n)$. The entries for all tables are provided by substitution queries. The size of a table is the number of rows times the number of columns.

We now describe the relationship between a table and the nodes that exist on the same level in the hypothesis decision program. Each node on level $j$ will be associated with a vector composed of the following. Let $w_0$ be the vector of length $j - 1$ that leads from the root of the hypothesis to the node $v_j^i$. If the labels of the columns of the table on level $j$ are $w_1, w_2, \ldots, w_k$ then the vector associated with $v_j^i$ is

$$(f(w_0 w_1), f(w_0 w_2), \ldots, f(w_0 w_k)).$$

This associated vector only appears as a row in the table on level $j$ if it cannot be represented as a linear combination of the associated vectors for nodes that are above it in the table. The index of this row would be $w_0$. If the associated vector can be expressed as a linear combination of the rows in the table then this node is labeled with this equation. We can designate which rows appear in this equation using the names of the nodes associated with these rows. These associated vectors determine the classification of each node in the existing hypothesis decision program given the current state of information known about the target.

We will show that an increase in the size of any table during the running of our algorithm indicates that progress is being made towards finding an equivalent representation of the target. A row is added to the bottom of a table any time an independent node is added to the hypothesis or an existing dependent node is found to be independent. When a column is added to the table it indicates that the dependecy of an existing node is going to change, i.e., the label of a dependent node will change or a dependent node will become independent.

We now address some related notation that will be useful during the description of our learning algorithm. We let $T_j$ denote the dependency table on level

$j$. As learning progresses our algorithm will be adding nodes to the hypothesis decision program. We will let $v_j^i$ denote the $i$th node added to the hypothesis on level $j$. We can view each node on level $j$ as computing a function over $X^{n-j+1}$. We will use $h_j^i(x)$ for $x \in X^n$ to denote the output value of the hypothesis decision program when the computation begins at node $v_j^i$. Notice this computation is independent of the first $j-1$ components of $x$. We will let $f_j^i(x)$ denote the output value of the target with an input composed of the prefix that leads from the root of the hypothesis to $v_j^i$ concatenated with the last $n-j+1$ components of $x$. Again, this computation is independent of the first $j-1$ components of $x$. Finally, if $v_j^i$ is an independent node we will use $v_j^i(x)$ to denote the node on level $j+1$ that is reached following the edge labeled $x_j$ that exits $v_j^i$. Now we give the description of the algorithm.

## 3.2   The Learning Algorithm

Our algorithm consists of three main steps. The first step initializes the hypothesis. The second step consists of asking an equivalence query using the current hypothesis as the input. The third step processes any counterexample returned by the equivalence query by updating the hypothesis accordingly. Steps two and three are repeated until the equivalence query replies YES.

For purposes of simplicity, we define an artificial representation for the constant zero function. This will consist of a root with $|X|$ uniquely labeled edges leading to a seperate dependent node on the next level. Each dependent node will be labeled with $0 \cdot v_I$ where $v_I$ is an imaginary vector. Also, during the running of the algorithm, if a table has no rows yet and an associated vector with a particular node is all zero, then it can be labeled with $0 \cdot v_I$. The algorithm starts by setting $h \equiv 0$.

The second step consists of asking an equivalence query using the current hypothesis $h$. If the query returns an answer of YES then the algorithm outputs $h$ and halts. If a counterexample $c$ is returned then the algorithm proceeds to step three which uses $c$ to modify the hypothesis. If $c$ is the counterexample returned due to a query with $h \equiv 0$, the algorithm will add an initial column to each table $T_j$, $3 \le j \le n$, labeled $c_j, \ldots, c_n$. The third step employs a recursive procedure called *Process* which traces through the current hypothesis looking for an appropriate place of modification. The counterexample $c$ and a test point $v_j^i$ are the two arguments of this procedure. The processing of any returned counterexample $c$ starts with a call of *Process* $(c, v_1^1)$ and proceeds according to two cases based on whether the input node is independent or dependent.

*Case 1:* Node $v_j^i$ is independent.

This node will not be modified further so the algorithm proceeds to the next level of the hypothesis by calling *Process* $(c, v_j^i(c))$.

*Case 2:* Node $v_j^i$ is dependent.

This means $v_j^i$ is labeled by some linear combination of independent nodes from that level, i.e., $v_j^i = \Sigma_{t \in I_j} \lambda_t v_j^t$ where $I_j$ contains the superscripts of the independent nodes on that level. First the algorithm checks the value of each $h_j^t(c)$, according to the order that the $v_j^t$'s were placed in the table, and compares it with $f_j^t(c)$. The first found disagreement, i.e., $h_j^t(c) \neq f_j^t(c)$, results in a call to $Process$ $(c, v_j^t(c))$. If no disagreements are found then a column is added to the table on level $j$ labeled with the suffix $(c_j, \ldots, c_n)$. The algorithm now revaluates all labels of dependent nodes in the order in which they were placed in the decision program. Each time a dependent node is found to be independent, a row is added to the bottom of the table on this level corresponding to this node. This is done before checking the label of the next dependent node. If any dependent nodes become independent during this pass through the dependent nodes then the process of checking labels is done again. This is repeated until a pass through the dependent nodes does not result in any dependent node changing to an independent one. If none of the nodes change to independent ones during the above then the processing is considered complete. If there are new independent nodes the algorithm must complete the hypothesis decision program through the addition of appropriate nodes and edges. The algorithm uses another recursive procedure called $CleanUp$ to complete the decision program. For each new independent node, $v_j^i$, the algorithm calls $CleanUp$ $(v_j^i)$ which proceeds according to the value of $j$.

*Case 1: $j = n$.*

The algorithm will add $|X|$ leaves to the last level. Each new leaf will have one incoming edge from $v_j^i$ labeled with a distinct element from $X$. If $(a_1, \ldots, a_{n-1})$ is the prefix that leads to $v_j^i$ then each new leaf is labeled by $f(a_1, \ldots, a_{n-1}, x)$ if its incoming edge is labeled by $x \in X$.

*Case 2: $j < n$.*

The algorithm adds $|X|$ new nodes to level $j + 1$ in an arbitrary order each with an incoming edge from $v_j^i$ labeled with a distinct element of $X$. Each new node is checked, in order, to see if it can be labeled by a linear equation of independent nodes on that level. If it cannot then a new row is added to the bottom of the table for this node. This is done before moving on to check the dependency of the next new node. As above, if any new nodes are found to be independent then passes are made through the dependent nodes, in the order they were added, until no nodes change from dependent to independent. If no nodes are found to be independent then the processing is complete. For any node $v_{j+1}^k$ found to be independent, call $CleanUp$ $(v_{j+1}^k)$.

## 3.3  Analysis of the Algorithm

We begin by stating several useful claims. Each claim holds for any time during the execution of the algorithm.

**Claim 1** *Every table contains rows of independent vectors at any time during the execution of the algorithm.*

**Claim 2** *For $2 \le j \le n$, $T_j$ contains at most $l(R)m_j$ rows.*

**Claim 3** *For $2 \le j \le n+1$, the number of nodes on level $j$ is at most $l(R)m_{j-1}|X|$.*

**Claim 4** *For any fixed set of $r$ rows in any table $T_j$, the number of times the linear combination of any dependent node on level $j$ changes with respect to the $r$ rows is at most $l(R)(r+1)$. Note that although the number of rows is fixed we still allow the addition of columns to the table.*

**Claim 5** *For $2 \le j \le n$, the number of columns in $T_j$ is at most*

$$|X|l(R)m_{j-1} \times l(R)\Sigma_{i=1}^{l(R)m_j}(i+1).$$

For each leaf $l$ of $h$, there is a unique path $P_l = (v_1, v_2, \ldots, v_{n+1})$, where $v_1$ is the root, $v_{n+1} = l$, and $v_2, \ldots, v_n$ are independent nodes. With each such unique path $P_l$, we can associate an assignment $b_l \in D^n$ where $b_j$ is the edge label of $(v_j, v_{j+1})$, for $j = 1, 2, \ldots, n$.

**Claim 6** *Suppose $h$ is a hypothesis decision program of the algorithm. For any leaf $l$ in $h$, $f(b_l) = h(b_l)$.*

**Correctness of the Algorithm** We know that if the algorithm halts it will output an equivalent form of the target because the algorithm halts when the equivalence query returns an answer of YES. We must now argue that the algorithm makes progress towards finding an equivalent hypothesis to the target. We do this with the following lemma.

**Lemma 6.** *Let $c$ denote the counterexample returned by an equivalence query using the current hypothesis $h$. A call of Process $(c, v_1^1)$ will result in an increase in the number of columns of at least one dependency table associated with $h$.*

**Proof** We know that $f(c) \ne h(c)$ and we now show that this disagreement is due to an incorrect labeling of a dependent node somewhere on a level between 2 and $n$. The disagreement will not be due to any independent node by Claim 1 nor will it be due to a labeling of a leaf by Claim 6. These two observations imply that the current contents of levels 1 or $n+1$ are not the cause of error. Now note that each label of a node on level $j$ reflects the information contained in $T_j$ because the processing of a level is not complete until all nodes that could have been classified independent have been. This is done by repeated checks of the labels until no dependent nodes turn independent, i.e., $T_j$ remains the same while checking the labels of all of the dependent nodes. The above implies that *Process* will eventually find a dependent node that has an incorrect label. At this point *Process* adds a new column to the table at this level so that the hypothesis may gain some of the information given by $c$. □

**Complexity** The number of equivalence queries asked in the algorithm is directly related to the number of columns of the dependency tables. The number of substitution queries associated with level $j$ of the hypothesis is related to the number of columns appearing in $T_j$ and the number of nodes on the same level. From the above claims it is easy to establish that the number of both types of queries is polynomial in $|X|$, $l(R)$, $m$, and $n$, where $m$ is the size of the target matrix function.

We note that the time complexity of the learning algorithm is dependent upon whether linear dependencies can be solved in polynomial time for the underlying ring.

## 4 Some Applications

### 4.1 Polynomials over Finite Commutative Rings with Identity

In this section we show that the class of multivariate polynomials over finite commutative rings with identity admits a representation as a matrix function over the same ring.

**Lemma 7.** *Let $R$ be a finite commutative ring with an identity. Let $f(x_1, \ldots, x_n)$ be a multivariate polynomial over $R$. Then there is a matrix function $A(x_1, \ldots, x_n) = \prod_{j=1}^{n} A_j(x_j)$ over $R$ that computes $f$.*

A corollary of Lemma 7 is that the class of multivariate polynomials over a finite commutative ring with identity is exactly learnable from equivalence and substitution queries. The learning complexity will depend on the number of variables, the cardinality of $R$, and the maximum degree of each variable in the target polynomial.

### 4.2 Randomized Interpolation of Polynomials over $Z_n$

The result from the previous subsection implies that multivariate polynomials over $Z_n$ are exactly learnable from equivalence and substitution queries. In this section we will show a randomized interpolation algorithm for multivariate polynomials over $Z_n$. First we will prove a generalization of Schwartz's Lemma [9] to the ring $Z_n$.

For a polynomial $p(x)$, we let $z(p)$ be the set of all zeroes of $p$, i.e., $z(p) = \{a : p(a) = 0\}$. Note that $|z(p)|$ is the number of zeroes of the polynomial $p$. For a natural number $n$, let $\delta(n)$ denote the minimal constant $d$ so that there is a polynomial of degree $d$ over $Z_n$ with nonzero coefficients and that is equivalent to the zero polynomial. For a natural number $n$, let $\rho(n)$ denote the smallest prime that divides $n$. We mention without proof the fact that $\delta(n) = \rho(n)$, for any $n$.

**Lemma 8.** *Let $n$ be a natural number. If $p(x)$ is a univariate polynomial of degree $d < \delta(n)$ over $Z_n$, then*

$$|z(p)| \leq \frac{dn}{\rho(n)}.$$

*Moreover there is a univariate polynomial of degree $d$ over $Z_n$ that has $\frac{dn}{\rho(n)}$ zeroes.*

The above lemma can be restated in the following more general form.

**Corollary 9.** *Let $n$ be a natural number and let $D \subseteq Z_n$. Let $p(x)$ be a univariate polynomial of degree $d < \delta(n)$ over $Z_n$. Then*

$$\Pr_{x \in_U D}[p(x) = 0] \leq \frac{dn}{|D|\rho(n)}.$$

Let $p(x_1, \ldots, x_k)$ be a multivariate polynomial over $Z_n$ with $k$ variables. We say that $p$ has degree $d$ if each variable $x_i$ has degree at most $d$ in the terms of $p$. The following lemma is based on the result due to Schwartz [9]

**Lemma 10.** *Let $n$ be a natural number and let $D \subseteq Z_n$. For any multivariate polynomial $p$ of degree $d < \delta(n)$ over $Z_n$ with $k$ variables,*

$$\Pr_{x \in D^k}[p(x) = 0] \leq \frac{dkn}{|D|\rho(n)}.$$

We are now ready to state the randomized interpolation algorithm for polynomials over $Z_n$.

**Theorem 11.** *Let $n$ be a natural number and let $kd < \frac{1}{2}\rho(n)$. Then any multivariate polynomial of degree $d$ over $Z_n$ can be interpolated in randomized polynomial time.*

In fact $d \leq \rho(n)(1 - 1/poly(\log n, d))$ is sufficient for above theorem to hold. Note that the above result relied on the assumption that $\rho(n)$ is rather large. We show next that if $\rho(n)$ is small then interpolation is hard even for the univariate case. We illustrate this for $\rho(n) = 2$.

**Lemma 12.** *Let $n$ be a natural number such that $\rho(n) = 2$. Then there is no polynomial time interpolation algorithm for the following class of polynomials over $Z_n$,*

$$\left\{ \frac{n}{2} \prod_{i=1}^{m}(x_i + \alpha_i) \mid \alpha_i \in \{0,1\}, \ 1 \leq i \leq m \right\}.$$

## 4.3 Constant-depth circuits with restricted MOD gates

We mention one more application which can also be solved using the algorithm from [4].

**Lemma 13.** *Let $p$ be a fixed prime. The class of constant depth circuits that contain MOD gates, where the modulus are prime powers of $p$, is exactly learnable from equivalence and membership queries.*

The proof of this lemma requires the following fact due to Beigel and Tarui.

**Fact 4.1** *[6] Let $p$ be a prime and let $e \geq 1$. Then there is a polynomial $r(x_1, \ldots, x_n)$ of degree $p^e - 1$ such that for each $x \in \{0, 1\}^n$, $mod_{p^e}(x_1, \ldots, x_n) \equiv r(x_1, \ldots, x_n) \pmod{p}$.*

# References

1. Angluin, D.: Learning Regular Sets from Queries and Counterexamples. Information and Computation, **75** (1987) 87–106.
2. Angluin, D.: Queries and Concept Learning. Machine Learning, **2** (1988) 319–342.
3. Bergadano, F., Bshouty, N.H., Varricchio, S.: Learning Multivariate Polynomials from Substitution and Equivalence Queries. Manuscript (1996).
4. Beimel, A., Bergadano, F., Bshouty, N.H., Kushilevitz, E., Varricchio, S.: On the Applications of Multiplicity Automata in Learning. Proc. 37th IEEE Ann. Symp. on Foundations of Computer Science, (1996) 349–358.
5. Bergadano, F., Catalano, D., Varricchio, S.: Learning Sat-$k$ DNF Formulas from Membership Queries. Proc. 28th ACM Ann. Symp. on Theory of Computing, (1996) 126–130.
6. Beigel, R., Tarui, J.: On ACC. Computational Complexity, **4** (1994) 350–366.
7. Bergadano, F., Varricchio, S.: Learning Behaviors of Automata from Multiplicity and Equivalence Queries. Proc. 2nd Italian Conference on Algorithms and Complexity, vol. 778 LNCS (1994) 54–62.
8. Matsumura, H.: Commutative Ring Theory. Cambridge University Press (1986).
9. Schwartz, J.T.: Probabilistic Algorithms for Verification of Polynomial Identities. Journal of the Assoc. for Comp. Mach, **27** (1980) 701–717.

# Learning from Incomplete Boundary Queries Using Split Graphs and Hypergraphs (Extended Abstract)

Robert H. Sloan[1]* and György Turán[2]**

[1] Dept. of EE & Computer Science, University of Illinois at Chicago
851 S. Morgan St. Rm 1120, Chicago, IL 60607-7053, USA
[2] Dept. of Mathematics, Stat., & Computer Science, University of Illinois at Chicago,
Research Group on Artificial Intelligence, Hungarian Academy of Sciences

**Abstract.** We consider learnability with membership queries in the presence of incomplete information. In the incomplete boundary query model introduced by Blum et al. [7], it is assumed that membership queries on instances near the boundary of the target concept may receive a "don't know" answer.

We show that zero–one threshold functions are efficiently learnable in this model. The learning algorithm uses split graphs when the boundary region has radius 1, and their generalization to split hypergraphs (for which we give a split-finding algorithm) when the boundary region has constant radius greater than 1. We use a notion of indistinguishability of concepts that is appropriate for this model.

## 1   Introduction

Learning in the presence of noise is one of the major issues that must be dealt with in order to design practical learning algorithms. Finding noise models that are both tractable and realistic is a nontrivial question in itself. For *PAC* learning, some of the the models considered are random noise affecting only the labels of examples, arbitrary noise affecting labels, arbitrary malicious noise, and, for instance space $\{0,1\}^n$, various models involving random noise affecting the instance bits [4, 11, 21, 23].

There are several recent approaches dealing with noise in query-based models of learning, in particular, for learning with membership and equivalence queries. Sakakibara [20] proposed a model where membership queries receive the wrong answer at random, but the noise is not persistent for any one instance, so repeated queries can overcome that noise. Angluin and Slonim [5] introduced a model where a random subset of the membership queries asked persistently receive the answer, "(I) don't know." Queries that may receive that response are referred to as *incomplete*. We previously studied the case where an adversary

---

* Partially supported by NSF grant CCR-9314258. Email: sloan@eecs.uic.edu.
** Partially supported by NSF grant CCR-9208170, OTKA grant T-14228, and Phare TDQM grant 9305-02/1022 (ILP2/HUN). Email: U11557@uicvm.uic.edu.

picks the subset of queries that receive a "don't know" response, and Angluin and Kriķis studied a model where an adversary picks a subset of queries that receive the wrong response [2, 3, 22].

A practical motivation for studying noisy membership queries comes from the experiments of Lang and Baum [15], which confirm the intuition that erroneous answers to membership queries are more frequent close to the boundary of the target concept. Blum et al. [7] formulated interesting models that try to capture this phenomenon by assuming that the answers to the membership queries are all correct *except in a neighborhood of a fixed radius* of the boundary of the target concept. (A point is close to the boundary of the target concept if its classification can change if a few of its components are flipped.) In the neighborhood of the boundary the answers to the membership queries are assumed to be either correct or "don't know" (the *incomplete boundary query* (IBQ) model), or they are assumed to be either correct or incorrect (the *unreliable boundary query* (UBQ) model). These models are extended to allow equivalence queries by requiring that the counterexamples be chosen from outside the boundary region. Efficient learning algorithms are required to be polynomial in the usual learning parameters. Thus, although the boundary of the target concept may be exponentially large, and so there may be exponentially many instances that receive a "don't know" answer, a learning algorithm is still required to identify the target concept after only polynomially many queries.

One of the main tasks in the area of learning from noisy data is to develop further learning algorithms for basic concept classes that may lead to general techniques for noise-tolerant learning. In this paper, we provide a step in this direction. We consider the incomplete boundary query model, which is the milder of the two models proposed in [7], and we discuss learning from membership queries alone (thus, we do not use equivalence queries).

Blum et al. [7] gave a learning algorithm for the intersection of two halfspaces in Euclidean space in the UBQ model. For the Boolean case, they considered learning subclasses of monotone DNF in a modified version of the UBQ model with only one-sided error. Notice that every learning algorithm in the UBQ model or the one-sided UBQ model can run in the IBQ model by changing every "don't know" answer it receives to 1. Thus some subclasses of monotone DNF are efficiently learnable in the IBQ model.

In this paper, we look at the learnability of *zero–one threshold functions* in the IBQ model. These are functions of the form $Th_k(\mathbf{y})$, where $\mathbf{y} = (y_1, \ldots, y_m)$ is a subset of the variable set $\{x_1, \ldots, x_n\}$. The variables in $(y_1, \ldots, y_m)$ are the *relevant variables* and $k$ is the *threshold*. An instance $v \in \{0, 1\}^n$ belongs to the concept $Th_k(\mathbf{y})$ if at least $k$ of the variables $(y_1, \ldots, y_m)$ have value 1 in $v$.

Zero–one threshold functions are a well-studied class [13, 14, 16, 19]. In particular, Hegedüs showed that this class can be learned with $O(n)$ membership queries [14]. In fact, one can even learn the larger class of *read-once compositions* of zero–one threshold functions (i.e., zero–one threshold formulas) with polynomially many membership queries [8]. On the other hand, *weighted monotone threshold functions*, that is, monotone halfspaces in $\{0, 1\}^n$, *cannot* be learned with polynomially many membership queries [6].

The (noise-free) membership query algorithm for learning zero–one threshold functions [14] is as follows. Starting with the all-ones vector $1^n$, turn components to 0 as long as this still gives a positive example of the target concept. The variables that are set to 1 in the final vector are all relevant, and their number is equal to the threshold of the target concept. Turning one more 1 to 0 we get a negative example. The remaining relevant variables are those 0 components of this negative example, which, when turned to 1, give a positive example.

This algorithm fails if answers to boundary queries may be incomplete. In fact, all the essential information obtained is in the boundary region of the target concept.

In this paper we show that zero–one threshold functions are *learnable with polynomially many incomplete boundary queries*. We give a detailed proof for the case when the radius of the boundary region is 1, and we outline the proof for the general case of radius $r$.

The learning algorithm for zero–one threshold functions is based on the observation that, given a positive example near the boundary of the target concept, switching a sufficient number of relevant variables from 1 to 0 will "break on through to the other side," and thus a query to this modified instance will receive a negative (i.e., 0) answer from the oracle. On the other hand, switching a set of irrelevant variables from 1 to 0 will lead to a positive example. Hence the oracle must give a positive (i.e., 1) or "don't know" answer to these queries. This gives a dichotomy that can be used to identify a set of candidates for the minimal point found in the first stage of the noise-free algorithm. A similar idea can be used to simulate the second stage of the algorithm.

The dichotomy can be formulated conveniently in terms of *split graphs* for the case of radius 1, and in terms of *split hypergraphs* in the general case. Split graphs were defined by Földes and Hammer [9] (see also [12, 17].). Split graphs have nice characterizations and efficient algorithms. The general case of split hypergraphs does not appear to have been studied before. We give an algorithm to determine whether an $r$-uniform hypergraph is a split hypergraph, and if so, to output a split, in polynomial time. This is used in showing that our learning algorithms require only a polynomial amount of computation.

Another component of our learning algorithm is a characterization of a notion of *indistinguishability* of two concepts, which is used to filter out those candidate hypotheses that are not acceptable as outputs of the learning algorithm.

It is hoped that the method used in the learning algorithm will be useful for learning other classes with incomplete boundary queries. In the last section of this paper, we mention some of the numerous open problems suggested by this work.

## 2  Definitions

We follow the standard model of learning from membership queries. The goal of the learner is to infer an unknown *target concept* from some given *concept class*

$C$ over a given *instance space* or *domain*. We will view concepts interchangeably as subsets of the instance space and as 0–1 functions on the instance space.

For the standard noise-free model, *proper exact identification* is required. This means that the learner must output precisely the correct target concept, and that the output must be in a specified syntactic form.

Fix a target concept $C$. An ordinary or *complete membership query* on instance $v$, denoted $MQ(v)$, returns $C(v)$. In this paper we study the *incomplete boundary membership oracle*, proposed by Blum et al. [7]. For the instance space $\{0,1\}^n$, the *distance to the boundary* of instance $v$ is the Hamming distance to the nearest instance $w$ such that $C(w) \neq C(v)$. The *boundary region of radius $r$ of $C$* is the set of all instances whose distance to the boundary is at most $r$. The incomplete boundary oracle returns either the correct classification of the instance, $C(v)$, or "don't know," which we will denote by $*$. The response $*$ can be given only for instances in the boundary region of radius $r$. The radius is a fixed, known constant.

Queries to this oracle about instance $v$ will be denoted $IBQ(v)$. In what follows, we often use expressions such as "$v$ has IBQ 1" for $IBQ(v) = 1$. A *positive instance* means any instance $v$ in the target concept regardless of whether $IBQ(v) = 1$ or $IBQ(v) = *$, and similarly for negative instances.

The requirement for successful learning in this noise model is that we must output a hypothesis that agrees with the target concept on all instances that are not in the boundary region of the target concept [7]. Moreover, the learner is allowed only a number of queries bounded by a polynomial in $n$, regardless of the frequency of $*$ responses. In general, there will be exponentially many instances in the boundary region even for constant $r$.

Let us briefly compare this model to the *limited membership query model* [3, 22]. On the one hand, in the limited membership query model, the oracle is allowed to respond $*$ on any instance it chooses, not only on boundary instances. On the other hand, in that model the learner is allowed a number of queries polynomial in both $n$ *and the number of $*$ responses received*. In particular, our algorithm for learning monotone DNF from limited membership plus equivalence queries could receive an exponential number of $*$ responses (in the "Up" phase of that algorithm [3, 22]) even if the $*$ responses are restricted to a boundary region of radius 1. Thus the two models appear to be incomparable.

## 2.1 Terminology for $\{0,1\}^n$

As do others (e.g., [5, 10]), we will view $\{0,1\}^n$ as a partially ordered set. The top element is the vector $1^n$ and the bottom element is $0^n$. The *descendants* of an instance $v$ are all instances $w$ such that $w \leq v$, where $x \leq y$ if each bit of $x$ is less than or equal to the corresponding bit of $y$. The *ancestors* of an element $v$ are all elements $w$ such that $w \geq v$. The *children* of $v$ are all descendants of $v$ with Hamming distance 1 from $v$; the *parents* of $v$ are all ancestors of $v$ with Hamming distance 1 from $v$. The norm $|v|$ of $v$ is the number of $v$'s components set to 1.

A *minterm* of a function $f$ is a set $S$ of variables such that for any assignment $v$ that sets all the variables in $S$ to 1, it holds that $f(v) = 1$, but this is not true for any subset of $S$. We will sloppily refer to both $S$ and vectors from $\{0,1\}^n$ with 1's in exactly those positions corresponding to $S$ as minterms. Note that for a zero–one threshold function, the norm of a minterm is exactly the threshold.

## 3   Split Graphs and Hypergraphs

An undirected graph $G = (V, E)$ is a *split graph* if $V$ has an ordered partition $(V_1, V_2)$ such that $G$ induces a clique on $V_1$ and an independent set on $V_2$. We note here two useful facts about split graphs. First, there is a linear time algorithm to determine whether a graph is a split graph, and output a split if so (see [17]). Second, any split graph has at most $|V| + 1$ distinct splits.

An *r-uniform hypergraph* $H$ has the form $H = (V, E)$, where $V$ is a set and $E$ is a set of $r$-element subsets of $V$. An $r$-uniform hypergraph is a *split hypergraph* if $V$ has an ordered partition $(V_1, V_2)$ such that $E$ contains all $r$-element subsets of $V_1$, and $E$ contains no $r$-element subset of $V_2$. In this case $(V_1, V_2)$ is called a *split* of $H$.

**Lemma 1.** *For every fixed $r$, there is a polynomial-time algorithm that decides if an $r$-uniform hypergraph is a split hypergraph, and finds a split if it is.*

**Proof** Let $H$ be a split hypergraph and let $(V_1, V_2)$ be a split. Then for every other split $(U_1, U_2)$ it must hold that $|V_1 \cap U_2| < r$ and $|V_2 \cap U_1| < r$. Thus $U_1$ can be obtained by deleting fewer than $r$ elements from $V_1$ and adding fewer than $r$ elements to $V_1$. Hence the number of splits is $O(n^{2r-2})$, where $|V| = n$.

Thus *all* splits of a hypergraph can be found in polynomial time by divide and conquer. After finding all splits in the hypergraphs induced by $H$ on two arbitrarily chosen halves of $V$, we combine the splits in all possible ways. This gives $O(n^{4r})$ partitions of $V$. For each partition, we check whether it forms a split of $H$. Checking whether a partition is a split requires the examination of $O(n^r)$ subsets. Thus the overhead is polynomial. As the restriction of a split to a subset is a split of the hypergraph induced on this subset, the algorithm finds all splits of $H$. $\square$

## 4   Algorithm for Boundary Radius 1

In this section we describe our learning algorithm for the case of boundary radius 1. This is extended to the general case of radius $r$ in the next section.

Notice that for boundary radius 1, monotone conjunctions are trivially learnable: The hypothesis "always false" meets the requirements of the IBQ model. Every true instance of a conjunction is within Hamming distance 1 of a false instance: Simply turn off one bit needed in the conjunction. Thus the hypothesis "always false" errs only on instances in the boundary region. Similarly, for boundary radius 1, monotone disjunctions are trivially learned by the hypothesis "always true." These observations will be used below to handle some special cases in the beginning of the proof.

**Theorem 2.** *Zero–one threshold functions are learnable from $O(n^3)$ incomplete boundary queries with boundary radius 1.*

The algorithm has three main stages. First we find a small $(O(n))$ set of candidates that is guaranteed to contain a minterm for the target function. Next, for each candidate minterm, we find a small (again $O(n)$) set of groups of variables such that, if the candidate minterm is correct, then one of those groups of variables must be the remaining relevant variables of the target function. Sometimes in this step we instead discover that our candidate minterm is in fact not a minterm. This gives us a pool of at most $O(n^2)$ hypotheses, which must contain the target function. The third stage of our algorithm prunes this pool to a set of hypotheses that are all acceptable outputs for our algorithm.

We begin with the query $IBQ(1^n)$. If the response is 0 or $*$, then our algorithm responds "always false," and terminates. (For response 0, the target must be "always false." The "always false" function has no boundary instances, so for response $*$, the target must be a monotone conjunction.) Otherwise, the search for a minterm begins from the instance $1^n$.

## 4.1 Finding a Minterm

We now show how to find a set of candidate minterms that must contain a correct minterm.

The first step is the appropriate noisy variation of the "reduce" algorithm that is common to many algorithms using membership queries to learn some form of monotone DNF (e.g., [1]). Given that $1^n$ has IBQ 1, we set $v$ to $1^n$. Now, so long as $v$ has some child to which a membership query responds 1, we replace $v$ by that child and repeat. Thus $v$ will eventually be an instance with IBQ 1 all of whose children are classified either 0 or $*$.

For the special case $|v| \leq 1$, we output the hypothesis "always true" and terminate the entire algorithm. When $v = 0^n$, "always true" is obviously the correct hypothesis. If $|v| = 1$, then the target function must be a monotone disjunction. (Since $v$'s child, $0^n$, was classified as either 0 or $*$, the target cannot be the "always true" function. That function has no boundary instances.)

In general, when $|v| \geq 2$, there will be three cases for finding candidate minterms, depending on the children of $v$.

**Case I:** If all of $v$'s children are classified 0, then $v$ is definitely a minterm.

In general, however, the final value of $v$ from the "reduce" procedure may not be a minterm—we know only that $v$ must contain a minterm. For example, let $n = 15$, and assume that $v = 1^8 0^7$, and all of $v$'s children are classified $*$. It might be that a minterm is $x_1 \cdots x_8$, but the IBQ answers are also consistent with a minterm being $x_1 \cdots x_3$, with $x_4, \ldots, x_8$ all being irrelevant variables.

**Case II:** $v$ has at least one child classified 0. Let $k$ be the threshold of the target function. Now $v$ must contain exactly $k$ relevant 1's and an unknown number of irrelevant 1's. We determine (approximately) which 1's are relevant as follows.

We construct a complete undirected graph, $G_1$, with labeled edges. The vertices of $G_1$ are the variables that are assigned to 1 in $v$. Recall that $|v| \geq 2$. Every edge will be labeled either 0 or $*$. Each edge corresponds to a pair of variables $x_i$ and $x_j$. This pair of variables, in turn, corresponds to the grandchild of $v$ obtained by turning off $x_i$ and $x_j$. The label of this edge is the answer received from an IBQ on that grandchild. If any such grandchild has IBQ 1, then we resume the reduce process with that grandchild. Thus in what follows we assume that this does not happen.

When discussing split graphs in what follows, it is more convenient to consider complete graphs with edges having two different kinds of labels (e.g., 0 or $*$), instead of considering cliques and independent sets.

**Lemma 3.** *Graph $G_1$ is a split graph.*

*Proof sketch.* Any grandchild that had two relevant variables turned off must have classification 0, since it has distance 2 from the boundary. Also, any grandchild that had two irrelevant variables turned off must have classification $*$ (or 1 but then we would have gone back to reducing), since it is a positive instance. $\square$

We find all possible splits of $G_1$. This can be done, for example, using Lemma 1. (For the $r = 1$ case, there are more efficient algorithms.) For each split, the set of variables in the half of $G_1$ with edges labeled 0 is a candidate minterm.

**Case III:** all of $v$'s children are classified $*$. Because $v$ is a positive example, $v$ contains at least $k$ relevant 1's. It is possible that $v$ contains exactly $k$ relevant 1's, so we first do the same thing as we did in Case II. If the resulting graph is *not* a split graph, then we know that $v$ contains more than $k$ relevant 1's. If the graph is a split graph, then we obtain some candidate(s) for being a minterm.

Regardless of whether that graph was a split graph, it is possible that $v$ contains more than $k$ relevant 1's. Then $v$ must not contain any irrelevant 1's, since then at least one of its children would be classified 1 (instead of $*$). Also, $v$ cannot have more than $k+1$ relevant 1's, because in that case $v$'s children would not be in the boundary region. Thus $v$ must contain precisely $k+1$ relevant 1's, no irrelevant 1's, and all of $v$'s children are minterms. Therefore, we also add as a candidate minterm one arbitrarily selected child of $v$.

**Lemma 4.** *The procedure described above outputs a set of at most $n+2$ candidate minterms, and that set is guaranteed to contain at least one minterm of the target function.*

*Proof sketch.* The existence of the minterm was discussed in the development of the algorithm.

The number $n + 2$ is derived as follows. As noted previously, the largest possible number of splits of a graph with $|V|$ vertices is $|V| + 1$. The largest possible number of 1's in $v$ is $n$, so the split graph construction could lead to at most $n + 1$ candidates for the minterm. One other candidate can be added for a $v$ with all $*$ children. □

## 4.2 Finding the Other Relevant Variables

If our candidate minterm is $x_1 \cdots x_n$, then the only possible target function is the conjunction of all variables.

Now we assume that we have a candidate minterm $v$ with $k < n$ variables. We need to find the remaining relevant variables in our target concept. Obtain $w$ from $v$ by changing exactly one of $v$'s 1's to a 0. We then query every instance formed from $w$ by changing to 1 a pair of variables that are both assigned 0 by $v$. That is, we query all grandparents of $w$ that are not parents of $v$.

For any of those queries that returns 0, we mark both of the added variables as irrelevant, and discard them. We then form a graph $G_2^v$ on the remaining variables assigned to 0 by $v$. The definition of $G_2^v$ is analogous to that of graph $G_1$ in the previous subsection, with the queries now being of grandparents instead of grandchildren. So the edges of $G_2^v$ are all labeled either 1 or $*$. Once again, if $v$ is a minterm, then $G_2^v$ must be a split graph: Any variable setting with $k - 1$ variables from $v$ plus two additional relevant variables must be classified 1, whereas any setting with only $k - 1$ relevant variables set to 1 must be classified $*$ (or 0, but we discarded those variables).

If $G_2^v$ is not a split graph, then we know that $v$ cannot have been a minterm. Otherwise, the clique labeled 1 from each possible split gives us one possibility for the remaining relevant variables in the target function. We summarize this with a lemma.

**Lemma 5.** *The procedure described above, on input a correct minterm $v$, outputs a set of at most $n - |v| + 1$ sets of variables, and one of those sets is exactly the additional relevant variables of the target function.* □

## 4.3 Pruning the Set of Candidates

After running the algorithms of the previous two subsections, we obtain a set of of $O(n^2)$ hypotheses that contains the correct hypothesis. We must now prune this set so that it contains only acceptable hypotheses.

We call two concepts *r-indistinguishable* if their symmetric difference is in the intersection of their boundary regions of radius $r$, and *r-distinguishable* otherwise. An *r-distinguishing instance* for a pair of $r$-distinguishable concepts is an instance from their symmetric difference that is *not* in the intersection of their boundary regions of radius $r$. (We omit the $r$ when it is clear from context.)

**Lemma 6.** *Given two $r$-distinguishable concepts $f_1$ and $f_2$, and an $r$-distinguishing instance $v$, the result of $\mathrm{IBQ}(v)$ will be inconsistent with at least one of $f_1$ or $f_2$.*

*Proof sketch.* This follows immediately from the definitions, noting that a $*$ answer is inconsistent with at least one of $f_1$ or $f_2$. ☐

Lemma 6 tells us how to use an $r$-distinguishing instance to prune the set of candidate hypotheses; the following lemma tells us how to find such an $r$-distinguishing instance.

**Lemma 7.** *If two zero–one threshold functions $f_1$ and $f_2$, with thresholds $k_1$ and $k_2$, respectively, are $r$-distinguishable, then at least one of the following instances is an $r$-distinguishing instance.*

1. *Setting $k_1$ of $f_1$'s variables to 1, using as few of $f_2$'s relevant variables as possible.*
2. *Setting $k_1 + r$ of $f_1$'s variables to 1, using as few of $f_2$'s relevant variables as possible.*
3. *One of the two symmetric possibilities for $f_2$.*

*Proof sketch.* Since $f_1$ and $f_2$ are distinguishable, there must be an instance $q$ in their symmetric difference that is not in the boundary region of at least one of $f_1$ or $f_2$. We consider the case where $q$ is positive for $f_1$ and negative for $f_2$. The opposite case is symmetric.

We begin with an instance $q_1$ formed according to the rules given in Case 1 of the statement of the theorem. Since there are instances that are positive for $f_1$ and negative for $f_2$, and $q_1$ is a positive instance of $f_1$ with a minimum number of $f_2$'s relevant variables set to 1, we know that $f_2(q_1) = 0$. If $q_1$ is not in $f_2$'s boundary region, then $q = q_1$ and we are done.

Otherwise, no positive boundary instance for instance for $f_1$ is a distinguishing instance. Therefore, the distinguishing instance $q$ must be positive nonboundary for $f_1$ and negative for $f_2$. It suffices to construct $q$ to have the minimum number of $f_2$'s relevant variables set to 1 among all positive nonboundary instances of $f_1$. Case 2 of the statement of the theorem does precisely that. (An example for $r = 1$ when Case 2 is necessary is given by $f_1 = Th_2(w, x, y, z)$, $f_2 = Th_1(w)$, $q_1 = 0110$, and $q = 0111$.) ☐

*Conclusion of the proof of Theorem 2.* Lemmas 6 and 7 give us an algorithm to prune the set of hypotheses so that every remaining pair of hypotheses is 1-indistinguishable. We simply query distinguishing instances for pairs of distinguishable hypotheses, discarding those hypotheses that are inconsistent with the answer. (Note that we can compute whether a pair of hypotheses is distinguishable without making any queries.) The pruning will not delete the target function from our set of candidates. Therefore every hypothesis in the final pruned set will be 1-indistinguishable from the target concept, and so is an acceptable output for the learning algorithm.

We note that Theorem 8, which follows, tells us that there can be at most $n + 1$ hypotheses in the pool when the algorithm terminates.

A crude analysis gives a total query complexity of $O(n^3)$. Notice that all the computation is polynomial. ☐

Lemma 7 can also be used to tell precisely when two zero–one threshold functions are $r$-indistinguishable. We give this description for the case $r = 1$.

**Theorem 8.** *Two threshold functions are 1-indistinguishable if and only if they fall into one of the following categories.*

1. *They have the same set of relevant variables, and their thresholds differ by 1.*
2. *One function has one extra relevant variable, and the two functions have either the same threshold or the function with an extra relevant variable has a threshold 1 greater than the other function.*
3. *Each function contains one relevant variable that the other does not, and the two functions have the same threshold.*
4. *One function has two extra relevant variables, and that function has a threshold 1 greater than the other function.*

*Proof sketch.* It is straightforward to verify that in each of those four cases the two functions meet the definition of indistinguishability. Arguing that those are the only possibilities requires a somewhat lengthy case-by-case discussion, which we omit from this extended abstract. □

## 5  Arbitrary Constant Radius

Now we generalize Theorem 2 to the case of larger boundary radii.

**Theorem 9.** *Zero–one threshold functions are learnable from polynomially many incomplete boundary queries for any constant boundary radius $r$.*

*Proof sketch.* We will just briefly give some of the key differences between the $r = 1$ case of the previous section and the arbitrary constant $r$ case. Throughout, let $k$ be the threshold of the target function $f$.

The search for a minterm proceeds as before to some instance $v$ with IBQ 1 none of whose children have IBQ 1. There are the same three cases as before: all of $v$'s children have IBQ 0, some of $v$'s children have IBQ 0 and some have IBQ $*$, and all of $v$'s children have IBQ $*$. Again, in the first case, we know $v$ is a minterm.

In the second case, we again know that $v$ has exactly $k$ relevant 1's. If $v$ has exactly $k$ relevant 1's, then the $(r + 1)$-uniform hypergraph whose vertices are the variables that are 1 in $v$ formed by considering all $(r + 1)$-level descendants of $v$ will be a split hypergraph: If we turn off $r + 1$ of $v$'s relevant 1's, then we obtain a nonboundary negative instance, and if we turn off $r + 1$ irrelevant 1's, then we obtain a positive instance.

If none of $v$'s children has IBQ 0 (i.e., all have IBQ $*$), then we must do more. In this case, $v$ could contain as many as $k + r$ relevant 1's. Thus we run the preceding construction from every descendant of $v$ that has IBQ $*$ and is between 1 and $r$ levels below $v$. This ensures that the construction is run from some instance with exactly $k$ relevant 1's. Since $r$ is constant, we run the construction only polynomial in $n$ many times.

Now we assume that we have a candidate minterm $v$ that has $k$ relevant 1's. We turn off exactly one of $v$'s 1's, and build the hypergraph with labeled edges formed by IBQs to assignments completed by turning on all $(r + 1)$-tuples of variables assigned to 0 by $v$. As with the $r = 1$ case, an answer of 0 means that all $r + 1$ variables are irrelevant, and we can therefore discard all those variables. Among the remaining variables, the relevant variables form a clique labeled 1, and the irrelevant variables form a clique labeled $*$.

Pruning the set of candidate hypotheses is very similar to the $r = 1$ case, because Lemmas 6 and 7 are not restricted to the case $r = 1$.                □

## 6  Some Open Problems

It would be interesting to give efficient incomplete boundary query algorithms for other concept classes, which would probably require adding equivalence queries to the model. Can the results of this paper be extended to read-once disjunctions of zero–one threshold functions, or, more generally, to the class of zero–one threshold formulas [8], and to the nonmonotone versions of these classes?

Another problem is to extend the result of this paper to unreliable boundary queries, that is, to the case of lies instead of "don't know"s.

It would also be of interest to look at the relationship between the incomplete boundary query model and the incomplete membership query model [22], and to prove lower bounds for the number of incomplete boundary queries. Can zero–one threshold functions be learned with less than $\Omega(n^3)$ incomplete boundary queries?

There are some combinatorial questions related to split hypergraphs. Split graphs have a forbidden induced subgraph characterization: Split graphs are exactly those graphs which do not contain cycles of length 4 or 5, or two independent edges as induced subgraphs [9]. Peled [18] asked if split hypergraphs have a forbidden induced subgraph characterization. Another question concerns the complexity of finding a split in a split hypergraph. The algorithm described in Section 3 is far from optimal for $r = 1$. Is there a more efficient algorithm for $r > 1$?

In the discussion of split hypergraphs it was assumed that the hypergraphs are given, as usual, by a list of their edges. If the radius $r$ is constant, this representation is polynomial in $n$. On the other hand, in our setting the hypergraphs are given *implicitly* in the form of the oracle answering the queries. Thus it would be interesting to know if a split can be found using this oracle model, even when $r$ grows with $n$. This would give an efficient incomplete boundary query algorithm for learning zero–one threshold functions even when the radius of the boundary region grows with $n$.

# Acknowledgments

We would like to thank Uri Peled for helpful conversations about split graphs, and Tibor Hegedűs for valuable comments on a draft of this paper.

# References

1. D. Angluin. Queries and concept learning. *Machine Learning*, 2(4):319–342, Apr. 1988.
2. D. Angluin and M. Kriķis. Learning with malicious membership queries and exceptions. In *Proc. 7th Annu. ACM Workshop on Comput. Learning Theory*, pages 57–66. ACM Press, New York, NY, 1994.
3. D. Angluin, M. Kriķis, R. H. Sloan, and G. Turán. Malicious omissions and errors in answers to membership queries. *Machine Learning*. To appear.
4. D. Angluin and P. Laird. Learning from noisy examples. *Machine Learning*, 2(4):343–370, 1988.
5. D. Angluin and D. K. Slonim. Randomly fallible teachers: learning monotone DNF with an incomplete membership oracle. *Machine Learning*, 14(1):7–26, 1994.
6. M. Anthony, G. Brightwell, D. Cohen, and J. Shawe-Taylor. On exact specification by examples. In *Proc. 5th Annu. Workshop on Comput. Learning Theory*, pages 311–318. ACM Press, New York, NY, 1992.
7. A. Blum, P. Chalasani, S. A. Goldman, and D. K. Slonim. Learning with unreliable boundary queries. In *Proc. 8th Annu. Conf. on Comput. Learning Theory*, pages 98–107. ACM Press, New York, NY, 1995.
8. N. Bshouty, T. Hancock, L. Hellerstein, and M. Karpinski. An algorithm to learn read-once threshold formulas, and transformations between learning models. *Computational Complexity*, 4:37–61, 1994.
9. S. Földes and P. L. Hammer. Split graphs. *Congressus Numerantium*, 19:311–315, 1977.
10. S. A. Goldman and H. D. Mathias. Learning k-term DNF formulas with an incomplete membership oracle. In *Proc. 5th Annu. Workshop on Comput. Learning Theory*, pages 77–84. ACM Press, New York, NY, 1992.
11. S. A. Goldman and R. H. Sloan. Can PAC learning algorithms tolerate random attribute noise? *Algorithmica*, 14:70–84, 1995.
12. M. C. Golumbic. *Algorithmic Graph Theory and Perfect Graphs*. Computer Science and Applied Mathematics. Academic Press, New York, 1980.
13. Q. P. Gu and A. Maruoka. Learning monotone boolean functions by uniformly distributed examples. *SIAM J. Comput.*, 21:587–599, 1992.
14. T. Hegedűs. On training simple neural networks and small-weight neurons. In *Computational Learning Theory: Eurocolt '93*, volume New Series Number 53 of *The Institute of Mathematics and its Applications Conference Series*, pages 69–82, Oxford, 1994. Oxford University Press.
15. K. J. Lang and E. B. Baum. Query learning can work poorly when a human oracle is used. In *International Joint Conference on Neural Networks*, Beijing, 1992.
16. N. Littlestone. Learning quickly when irrelevant attributes abound: A new linear-threshold algorithm. *Machine Learning*, 2:285–318, 1988.
17. N. V. R. Mahadev and U. N. Peled. *Threshold Graphs and Related Topics*, volume 56 of *Annals of Discrete Mathematics*. Elsevier Science B.V., Amsterdam, The Netherlands, 1995.

18. U. Peled. Personal Communication.
19. L. Pitt and L. Valiant. Computational limitations on learning from examples. *J. ACM*, 35:965–984, 1988.
20. Y. Sakakibara. On learning from queries and counterexamples in the presence of noise. *Inform. Proc. Lett.*, 37:279–284, 1991.
21. R. H. Sloan. Four types of noise in data for PAC learning. *Inform. Proc. Lett.*, 54:157–162, 1995.
22. R. H. Sloan and G. Turán. Learning with queries but incomplete information. In *Proc. 7th Annu. ACM Workshop on Comput. Learning Theory*, pages 237–245. ACM Press, New York, NY, 1994.
23. L. G. Valiant. Learning disjunctions of conjunctions. In *Proceedings of the 9th International Joint Conference on Artificial Intelligence, vol. 1*, pages 560–566, Los Angeles, California, 1985. International Joint Committee for Artificial Intelligence.

# Generalization of the PAC-model for Learning with Partial Information (Extended Abstract)

Joel Ratsaby[1] and Vitaly Maiorov[2]

[1] Department of Electrical Engineering, Technion, Haifa 32000, Israel
[2] Department of Mathematics, Technion, Haifa 32000, Israel

**Abstract.** The PAC model of learning and its extension to real valued function classes provides a well accepted theoretical framework for representing the problem of machine learning using randomly drawn examples. Quite often in practice some form of *a priori* partial information about the target is available in addition to randomly drawn examples. In this paper we extend the PAC model to a scenario of learning with partial information in addition to randomly drawn examples. According to this model partial information effectively reduces the complexity of the hypothesis class used to learn the target thereby reducing the sample complexity of the learning problem. This leads to a clear quantitative tradeoff between the amount of partial information and the sample complexity of the problem. The underlying framework is based on a combination of information-based complexity theory (cf. Traub et. al. [18]) and Vapnik-Chervonenkis theory. A new quantity $I_{n,d}(\mathcal{F})$ which plays an important role in determining the worth of partial information is introduced. It measures the minimal approximation error of a target in a class $\mathcal{F}$ by the family of all function classes of pseudo-dimension $d$ under a given partial information which consists of any $n$ measurements which may be expressed as linear operators. As an application, we consider the problem of learning a Sobolev target class. The tradeoff between the amount of partial information and the sample complexity is calculated and by obtaining fairly tight upper and lower bounds on $I_{n,d}$ we identify an almost optimal way of providing partial information.

# 1 Introduction

The problem of machine learning using randomly drawn examples has received in recent years a significant amount of attention while serving as the basis of research in what is known as the computational learning theory field. Valiant [19] introduced the Probably Approximately Correct (PAC) learning model which in its basic form has an abstract teacher which provides the learner with a finite number $m$ of i.i.d. examples $\{(x_i, g(x_i)\}_{i=1}^m$ randomly drawn according to an unknown underlying distribution $P$ over $X$ where $g$ is the target function to be learnt to some pre-specified arbitrary accuracy $\epsilon > 0$ (with respect to the $L_1(P)$-norm) and confidence $1 - \delta$. We will refer to this as $(\epsilon, \delta)$-learning. The learner has at his discretion a hypothesis class $\mathcal{H}$ from which he is to determine a function $h_m$, sample-dependent, that approximates the unknown target $g$ to within the pre-specified accuracy and confidence levels.

In this formalization there are two primary complexity quantities which are associated with the learning problem. First, the sample complexity $m(\epsilon, \delta)$ which is defined as the sufficient sample size which guarantees $(\epsilon, \delta)$-learnability. Second, the time complexity which measures the worst-case time needed for an algorithm to produce an $(\epsilon, \delta)$-good hypothesis.

Based on the PAC model the complexity of learning has been estimated for a wide array of problems (cf. proceedings of ACM conferences on computational learning theory 1988-1996). The bulk of the work treats the scenario in which the learner has access *only* to randomly drawn samples. It is often the case in practice that some additional knowledge about the target is available. For instance, in statistical pattern classification, having some knowledge about the underlying probability distributions may crucially influence the complexity of the learning problem. If the distributions are known to be of a certain parametric form an exponentially large savings in sample size may be obtained (cf. Ratsaby & Venkatesh [12, 13]). There have been several works where the learner plays a more active role in obtaining information. Such learning scenarios may be viewed as having some form of oracle which provides partial information about the target. For instance, selecting unlabeled examples in the feature space and querying for their correct classification labels (cf. Angluin [4], Rivest and Eisenberg [15]), allowing the learner to ask arbitrary yes/no questions about the target function (Kulkarni, Mitter & Tsitsiklis [9]), or explanation-based learning where prior knowledge is used to get valid generalizations from only a few training examples (Mitchell, Keller & Kedar-Cabelli [10]). Roscheisen, Hofmann and Tresp [16] look at ways of incorporating partial knowledge into a system that learns by examples by resorting to a Bayesian model. A prior probability density over the target class is defined and a portion of the training sample is artificially generated using this prior knowledge. In Abu-Mustafa [1, 2, 3] fairly general partial information (called hints) is available for learning and is successfully used in financial prediction problems. Towell and Shavlik [17] show how rule-based prior knowledge can be incorporated into neural networks consisting of sigmoidal units.

In the above examples, experimental results demonstrate that learning methods which incorporate some form of partial information in addition to passively drawn i.i.d samples, can improve the performance of a learning system.

Our motive in this paper is to provide a quantitative view of the worth of partial information for learning. To the best of our knowledge there does not exist a theoretical framework which unites the PAC model of learning with alternative information sources. We report here what seems to be a promising avenue in this direction. Before we proceed we need to briefly introduce a branch of the field of computational complexity known as *information-based complexity* cf. Traub, Wasilkowski & Wozniakowski [18] which deals with the intrinsic difficulty of providing approximate solution to problems for which the information is partial, noisy or costly. A classical example of a problem in this field is calculating the value of a definite integral $S(f) = \int_X f(x)dx$ of a function $f$ in some infinite dimensional target class $\mathcal{F}$. Any realistic algorithm must use a finite amount of information. For instance, the Monte Carlo algorithm calculates an approximation $U(f) = \frac{1}{n}\sum_{i=1}^{n} f(x_i)$ based on uniformly distributed points $x_1, \ldots, x_n$. Thus here partial information of the functional values of $f$ at $n$ points is used to compute an $\epsilon$-approximation of $S(f)$.

Suppose that $\mathcal{F}$ consists of smooth periodic real-valued functions whose $(r-1)^{st}$ derivative is absolutely continuous, and $r^{th}$ derivative belongs to the space $L_p(0, 2\pi)$, $r \geq 1$ for some fixed $p \in [1, \infty]$. To approximate $S(f) = \int_0^{2\pi} f(t)dt$, in addition to function values, derivatives up to order $r-1$ can be computed. Hence information consists now of $n$ values $L_i(f) = f^{(j_i)}(x_i)$, $j_i \in [0, r-1]$, $x_i \in [0, 2\pi]$, $1 \leq i \leq n$. Denote by $N_n(f) = [L_1(f), \ldots, L_n(f)]$, which for this specific form of linear functionals $L_i$, $1 \leq i \leq n$, is known as the Birkhoff information for $f$. As an approximation of $S(f)$ consider any $U(f) \in \mathbb{R}$ obtained by mappings of the form $\phi : N_n(\mathcal{F}) \to \mathbb{R}$ where $N_n(\mathcal{F}) = \{N_n(f) : f \in \mathcal{F}\}$ denotes the information space. A mapping $\phi$ may be viewed as an algorithm which is given partial information $N_n(f)$ about $f$ and produces an approximation $U(f)$ to $S(f)$. The information complexity of this integration problem arises in finding the optimal set of information operators $L_i$, $1 \leq i \leq n$, or equivalently, the optimal set $\{j_i, x_i\}_{i=1}^{n}$ which minimizes the worst case approximation error $\sup_{f \in \mathcal{F}} |S(f) - U(f)|$. In other words the aim is to find a *fixed* information operator $N_n$ of the above form based upon which the approximation error of $S(f)$, in the worst-case over $\mathcal{F}$, will be minimal. The formulation of partial information for the general approximation problem is described next and is taken straight from Traub et. al. [18]. While we will limit here to the case of approximating functions $f \in \mathcal{F}$ we note that the theory is suitable for problems of approximating general functionals $S(f)$.

Let $N_n : \mathcal{F} \to N_n(\mathcal{F}) \subseteq \mathbb{R}^n$ denote a general information operator. The information $N_n(g)$ consists of $n$ measurements taken on the target function $g$, or in general, any function $f \in \mathcal{F}$, i.e.,

$$N_n(f) = [L_1(f), \ldots, L_n(f)]$$

where $L_i$, $1 \leq i \leq n$, denote any functionals. We call $n$ the *cardinality* of information and we sometimes omit $n$ and write $N(f)$. The variable $y$ denotes an ods which incorporate some form of partial information in addition to passively drawn i.i.d samples, can improve the performance of a learning system.

Our motive in this paper is to provide a quantitative view of the worth of partial information for learning. To the best of our knowledge there does not exist a theoretical framework which unites the PAC model of learning with alternative information sources. We report here what seems to be a promising avenue in this direction. Before we proceed we need to briefly introduce a branch of the field of computational complexity known as *information-based complexity* cf. Traub, Wasilkowski & Wozniakowski [18] which deals with the intrinsic difficulty of providing approximate solution to problems for which the information is partial, noisy or costly. A classical example of a problem in this field is calculating the value of a definite integral $S(f) = \int_X f(x)dx$ of a function $f$ in some infinite dimensional target class $\mathcal{F}$. Any realistic algorithm must use a finite amount of information. For instance, the Monte Carlo algorithm calculates an approximation $U(f) = \frac{1}{n}\sum_{i=1}^n f(x_i)$ based on uniformly distributed points $x_1, \ldots, x_n$. Thus here partial information of the functional values of $f$ at $n$ points is used to compute an $\epsilon$-approximation of $S(f)$.

Suppose that $\mathcal{F}$ consists of smooth periodic real-valued functions whose $(r-1)^{st}$ derivative is absolutely continuous, and $r^{th}$ derivative belongs to the space $L_p(0, 2\pi), r \geq 1$ for some fixed $p \in [1, \infty]$. To approximate $S(f) = \int_0^{2\pi} f(t)dt$, in addition to function values, derivatives up to order $r-1$ can be computed. Hence information consists now of $n$ values $L_i(f) = f^{(j_i)}(x_i), j_i \in [0, r-1], x_i \in [0, 2\pi], 1 \leq i \leq n$. Denote by $N_n(f) = [L_1(f), \ldots, L_n(f)]$, which for this specific form of linear functionals $L_i, 1 \leq i \leq n$, is known as the Birkhoff information for $f$. As an approximation of $S(f)$ consider any $U(f) \in \mathbb{R}$ obtained by mappings of the form $\phi : N_n(\mathcal{F}) \to \mathbb{R}$ where $N_n(\mathcal{F}) = \{N_n(f) : f \in \mathcal{F}\}$ denotes the information space. A mapping $\phi$ may be viewed as an algorithm which is given partial information $N_n(f)$ about $f$ and produces an approximation $U(f)$ to $S(f)$. The information complexity of this integration problem arises in finding the optimal set of information operators $L_i, 1 \leq i \leq n$, or equivalently, the optimal set $\{j_i, x_i\}_{i=1}^n$ which minimizes the worst case approximation error $\sup_{f \in \mathcal{F}} |S(f) - U(f)|$. In other words the aim is to find a *fixed* information operator $N_n$ of the above form based upon which the approximation error of $S(f)$, in the worst-case over $\mathcal{F}$, will be minimal. The formulation of partial information for the general approximation problem is described next and is taken straight from Traub et. al. [18]. While we will limit here to the case of approximating functions $f \in \mathcal{F}$ we note that the theory is suitable for problems of approximating general functionals $S(f)$.

Let $N_n : \mathcal{F} \to N_n(\mathcal{F}) \subseteq \mathbb{R}^n$ denote a general information operator. The information $N_n(g)$ consists of $n$ measurements taken on the target function $g$, or in general, any function $f \in \mathcal{F}$, i.e.,

$$N_n(f) = [L_1(f), \ldots, L_n(f)]$$

where $L_i, 1 \leq i \leq n$, denote any functionals. We call $n$ the *cardinality* of information and we sometimes omit $n$ and write $N(f)$. The variable $y$ denotes an element in $N_n(\mathcal{F})$. The subset $N_n^{-1}(y) \subset \mathcal{F}$ denotes all functions $f \in \mathcal{F}$ which share the same information vector $y$, i.e.,

$$N_n^{-1}(y) = \{f \in \mathcal{F} : N_n(f) = y\}.$$

We denote by $N_n^{-1}(N_n(g))$ the *solution set* which may also be written as $\{f \in \mathcal{F} : N_n(f) = N_n(g)\}$, which consists of all indistinguishable functions $f \in \mathcal{F}$ having the same information vector as the target $g$. Given $y \in \mathbb{R}^n$, an algorithm $\phi$ generates a single element denoted as $g_y \in N_n^{-1}(y)$. In this model partial information effectively partitions the target class $\mathcal{F}$ into infinitely many subsets $N_n^{-1}(y)$, $y \in \mathbb{R}^n$, each having a *single* representative $g_y$ which forms the approximation for any $f \in N^{-1}(y)$. Denote the radius of $N^{-1}(y)$ by

$$r(N, y) = \inf_{f' \in \mathcal{F}} \sup_{f \in N^{-1}(y)} \|f - f'\|$$

where $\|\cdot\|$ denotes some functional norm and call it the *local radius of information* $N$ at $y$. The *global radius of information* $N$ at $y$ is defined as the local radius for a worst $y$, i.e.,

$$r(N) = \sup_{y \in N(\mathcal{F})} r(N, y).$$

This quantity measures the intrinsic uncertainty or error which is associated with a fixed information operator $N$. Note that in both of these definitions the dependence on $\mathcal{F}$ is implicit.

Let $\Lambda$ be a family of functionals and consider the family $\Lambda_n$ which consists of all information $N = [L_1, \ldots, L_k]$ of cardinality $k \leq n$ with $L_i \in \Lambda$, $1 \leq i \leq n$. Then

$$r(n, \Lambda) = \inf_{N \in \Lambda_n} r(N)$$

is called the $n^{th}$ *minimal radius of information* in the family $\Lambda$ and $N_n^* = [L_1^*, \ldots, L_n^*]$ is called the $n^{th}$ *optimal information* in the class $\Lambda$ iff $L_i^* \in \Lambda$ and $r(N_n^*) = r(n, \Lambda)$.

When $\Lambda$ is the family of all *linear* functionals then $r(n, \Lambda)$ becomes a slight generality of the well known Gelfand-width of the class $\mathcal{F}$ whose classical definition is $d^n(\mathcal{F}) = \inf_{A^n} \sup_{f \in \mathcal{F} \cap A^n} \|f\|$, where $A^n$ is any linear subspace of codimension $n$. There is a wide body of literature in the field of approximation theory pertaining to estimation of this linear width as well as the related Kolmogorov $n$-width. Consequently the complexity of linear information for function approximation problems is effectively established for various target classes $\mathcal{F}$ (cf. [18]).

The PAC theory of learning is similar in many respects to approximation theory since the target is a function to be learnt to a certain degree of approximation $\epsilon > 0$ in the $L_1(P)$-norm (for 0/1-concepts) or w.r.t. other norms in the case of learning real-valued functions (cf. Haussler [8]). Thus the mathematical framework of information-based complexity, as pertaining to approximation of functions, is appropriate albeit missing the important learning-from-examples element.

In the definition of $r(N, y)$ there is a single element $g_y \in \mathcal{F}$ not necessarily in $N^{-1}(y)$ which is selected as an approximator for all functions $f$ in the subset $N^{-1}(y)$. This follows from the fact that the $\inf_{f' \in \mathcal{F}}$ precedes the $\sup_{f \in N^{-1}(y)}$. Such a definition is useful for the problem of information-based complexity since all that one is concerned with is to produce an $\epsilon$-approximation based on partial information alone. In the PAC framework there is strong significance in wanting to provide an approximator which is an element not of a subspace of $\mathcal{F}$ but of some hypothesis class which can be $(\epsilon, \delta)$-learned. In order to formulate a theory for learning based on both partial information and randomly drawn examples we will replace the single-representative of a subset $N^{-1}(y)$ by a whole approximation class of functions $\mathcal{H}_y^d$ of pseudo-dimension $d$ (for the definition of pseudo-dimension cf. Haussler [8]). Note that now partial information alone does not 'point' to a single $\epsilon$-approximation element but rather to a manifold $\mathcal{H}_y^d$, possibly non-linear, which for $any$ $f \in N^{-1}(y)$, in particular the target $g$, contains an element $h^*(g)$, dependent on $g$, such that the distance $\|g - h^*(g)\| \leq \epsilon$. Having a pseudo-dimension $d$ implies that with a finite random sample $\{(x_i, g(x_i))\}_{i=1}^m$, a learning algorithm (after being shown the partial information and hence the class $\mathcal{H}_y^d$) can determine a function $h_m \in \mathcal{H}_y^d$ which is no farther than $\epsilon$ from the optimal $h^*(g)$ with confidence greater than $1 - \delta$. Thus based on $n$ information operations on the target $g$ and $m$ labeled examples $\{(x_i, g(x_i))\}_{i=1}^m$, an element $h_m$ can be found which satisfies $\|g - h_m\| \leq 2\epsilon$ with confidence greater than $1 - \delta$.

The sample complexity $m$ does not depend on the type of hypothesis class, only on its pseudo-dimension $d$. Thus the above construction is true for any hypothesis class (or manifold) of pseudo-dimension $d$. This suggests that if the aim is to determine the tradeoff between $m$ and $n$ as a function of $d$ then we might as well permit $any$ hypothesis class of pseudo-dimension $d$ to play the role of the approximation manifold $\mathcal{H}_y^d$ of the subset $N^{-1}(y)$. Formally this amounts to replacing the outter infimum in the definition of $r(N, y)$ by $\inf_{\mathcal{H}^d}$. We then obtain the definition of a new quantity $I_{n,d}$, a variant of $r(N, \Lambda)$, which measures the minimal approximation error of a target in $\mathcal{F}$ given partial information of cardinality $n$ and using any manifold of pseudo-dimension $d$. In the next section we will present formal definitions which follow along this idea.

In this paper we restrict to the family $\Lambda$ of linear functionals. The study of the worth of linear information $N$ to problems of PAC learning is interesting albeit the obvious restriction of linear operators. One interesting example of linear information can be described in terms of having an expert or group of experts provide the partial information. Consider an expert, say a neural network, which gives the learner partial information about $g$ in the form of a projection of $g$ onto a finite $n$-dimensional subspace spanned by some fixed basis $\{\phi_1(x), \ldots, \phi_n(x)\}$. The expert provides the learner information $N_n(g) = [c_1(g), \ldots, c_n(g)]$ or equivalently a function $\hat{g} = \sum_{i=1}^n c_i(g)\phi_i(x)$ which is most similar to $g$ among all other functions in the subspace. In case of a neural network this amounts to having fixed weights in all hidden layers and variable weights $[c_1, \ldots, c_n]$ in the output layer so that given an arbitrary target $g \in \mathcal{F}$ the neural network expert adapts only the output-layer weights to fit the target. The learner is given the basis, i.e., the architecture of the network and the weights of all hidden layers, in addition to the target dependent information $[c_1(g), \ldots, c_n(g)]$. Thus here linear information is equivalent to giving the learner a linear approximation of $g$ which amounts to pointing to a subset $N_n^{-1}(N_n(g))$ of all functions which the expert takes as being identical to the target up to order $n$ of information. The learner may then proceed to PAC-learn this subset using a randomly drawn sample of side $m$ and a hypothesis class $\mathcal{H}^d$ of pseudo-dimension $d$. Suppose we consider finding the best expert or fixed basis $\{\phi_1(x), \ldots, \phi_n(x)\}$ which provides optimal information $N^*$ such that when PAC-learning over any hypothesis class of pseudo-dimension $d$, it yields the lowest approximation error in the worst-case sense over all functions $f \in \mathcal{F}$. The error of this optimal expert is related to the quantity $I_{n,d}$ mentioned earlier, the difference being that in this example we limit to linear projection functionals $L_i$ while $I_{n,d}$ is defined for *any* linear functionals $L_i$, $1 \leq i \leq n$. With the learning model to be introduced in the next section it is possible to quantitatively measure the worth of such optimal expert to the problem of PAC learning.

## 2 The Learning Framework

The information part of the learning model is based on the framework of information based complexity theory, the relevant definitions of which where introduced in Section 1. The learning-by-examples part of the model is based on the uniform SLLN work of Vapnik and Chervonenkis [22] and Haussler [8]. The target class is henceforth denoted as $\mathcal{F}$ and the hypothesis class $\mathcal{H}^d$, which we also refer to as the approximating class, is taken as any real-valued function class of pseudo-dimension $d$. The discrepancy of a hypothesis $h$ is measured by its *loss*

$$L(h) = \mathrm{E}\, |h(x) - g(x)|,$$

the expectation taken w.r.t. the probability distribution $P$ and where we choose the $L_1(P)$-norm here although any other norm $L_q$, $q \geq 1$, fits into our framework as well. The *empirical loss* which depends on the random data is defined as

$$L_m(h) = \frac{1}{m} \sum_{i=1}^{m} |h(x_i) - g(x_i)|.$$

We take the liberty in using similar notation for the $L_p$-norm, $p \geq 1$, for linear functionals $L_i$, $1 \leq i \leq n$, for a subspace $L_n$ of dimension $n$, and for the loss $L(h)$, the meaning of which should be clear from the context.

The PAC framework and its generalization to learning real-valued functions (cf. Haussler [8]) rely on algorithms which minimize the empirical expectation (based on an i.i.d. sample) of some loss functional over the hypothesis class and then output a hypothesis which minimizes this functional. Such algorithms are usually called Empirical Risk Minimization (ERM). If one wishes to consider not only empirical minimization learning algorithms but any other algorithm then the complexity of learning may become a triviality. For instance, Bartlett et. al. [5] showed that there are function classes for which for every function there exists a single example $(x, g(x))$ that can identify it exactly. In such a case it is necessary to introduce noise into the learning process which corrupts the real value of the target function at the sample points. In this paper we will only consider learning by empirical minimization algorithms.

Our primary motivation is to study the tradeoff between the sample complexity and partial information cardinality from an information theoretic standpoint, i.e., having no limitations such as algorithmic complexity, time complexity, or other (perhaps more practical) constraints. We consider the ideal scenario where the teacher has access to all possible linear information operators $N_n$ and to all hypothesis classes of pseudo-dimension $d \geq 1$. We need to define three optimal quantities, $N_n^*$, $\mathcal{H}_{N_n^*}^d$ and $h^*$, all of which implicitly depend on the unknown target $g$ and distribution $P$.

**Definition 1.** Let $g \in \mathcal{F}$ be a fixed target function. Let the optimal linear information operator $N_n^*$ of cardinality $n$ be one which minimizes the worst-case approximation error of the solution set $N_n^{-1}(g)$ using any manifold of pseudo-dimension $d$ over all linear operators $N_n$ of cardinality $n$. Formally, it is defined as one which satisfies

$$\inf_{\mathcal{H}^d} \sup_{\{f \in \mathcal{F}: N_n^*(f) = N_n^*(g)\}} \inf_{h \in \mathcal{H}^d} \|f - h\|_{L_1(P)}$$
$$= \inf_{N_n} \inf_{\mathcal{H}^d} \sup_{\{f \in \mathcal{F}: N_n(f) = N_n(g)\}} \inf_{h \in \mathcal{H}^d} \|f - h\|_{L_1(P)}.$$

The outermost infimum on the left hand side is taken over all function classes with pseudo-dimension $d$ while the outermost infimum on the right hand side is taken w.r.t. all linear information operators of cardinality $n$.

**Definition 2.** For a fixed target $g \in \mathcal{F}$ and optimal linear information operator $N_n^*$ of cardinality $n$ define the optimal hypothesis class $\mathcal{H}_{N_n^*}^d$ with pseudo-dimension $d$ as one which minimizes the worst-case approximation error of the specific solution set $N_n^{*-1}(g)$ using any manifold of pseudo-dimension $d$. Formally, it is defined as one which satisfies

$$\sup_{\{f \in \mathcal{F}: N_n^*(f) = N_n^*(g)\}} \inf_{h \in \mathcal{H}_{N_n^*}^d} \|f - h\|_{L_1(P)} = \inf_{\mathcal{H}^d} \sup_{\{f \in \mathcal{F}: N_n^*(f) = N_n^*(g)\}} \inf_{h \in \mathcal{H}^d} \|f - h\|_{L_1(P)}.$$

**Definition 3.** For a fixed target $g \in \mathcal{F}$, optimal linear information operator $N_n^*$ and optimal hypothesis class $\mathcal{H}_{N_n^*}^d$ define the optimal hypothesis $h^* \in \mathcal{H}_{N_n^*}^d$ to be any function which minimizes the loss over $\mathcal{H}_{N_n^*}^d$, namely,

$$L(h^*) = \inf_{h \in \mathcal{H}_{N_n^*}^d} L(h). \tag{1}$$

Based on these optimal quantities we define the learning model as follows: in the first stage of learning, the teacher provides partial information $N_n^*(g)$ to the learner. This effectively means first pointing to a subset $N_n^{*-1}(g) \cap \mathcal{F}$ and then to a hypothesis class $\mathcal{H}_{N_n^*}^d$ which best approximates this subset. In the second stage the learner uses the available sample $\{(x_i, g(x_i))\}_{i=1}^m$, of size $m$ to do empirical loss minimization over $\mathcal{H}_{N_n^*(g)}^d$ and obtains a hypothesis $h_m$ which satisfies

$$L_m(h_m) = \inf_{h \in \mathcal{H}_{N_n^*(g)}^d} L_m(h). \tag{2}$$

To evaluate the performance of the hypothesis $h_m$ outputted by the learner we utilize the theory of uniform SLLN pioneered by Vapnik and Chervonenkis [20, 21, 22]. We state an auxiliary theorem which is a variant of Theorem 7.3 in [22] and is based on the pseudo-dimension instead of Vapnik's capacity for real-valued functions, the former being more useful in our application.

**Theorem 4.** *Let $g \in \mathcal{F}$ be a fixed target function, $\mathcal{H}^d$ a class of functions from $X$ to $\mathbb{R}$ which has a pseudo-dimension $d \geq 7$ and assume there exists a constant $M > 0$ such that $\sup_{x \in X} |h(X) - g(X)| \leq M$ for all $h \in \mathcal{H}^d$, $g \in \mathcal{F}$. Let $\{(x_i, g(x_i))\}_{i=1}^m$, $x_i \in X$ be an i.i.d. sample of size $m > 8(d+1)\log^2(d+1)$ drawn according to any distribution $P$ on $X$. Then for arbitrary $0 < \delta < 1$, simultaneously for every function $h \in \mathcal{H}^d$ the inequality*

$$|L(h) - L_m(h)| \leq 4M \sqrt{\frac{8(d+1)\log^2(d+1)(\ln(2m)+1) + \ln\frac{9}{\delta}}{m}} \tag{3}$$

*holds with probability greater than $1 - \delta$.*

*Proof Sketch.* We follow Vapnik's proof of Theorem 7.3 in [22] but where the complexity measure of $\mathcal{H}^d$ is the pseudo-dimension instead of his capacity measure defined on p.189. Let $y \in \mathbb{R}$ and $x \in X$. It is first shown that for the indicator function class $A = \{1_{\{(x,y):|h(x)-y|>\beta\}} : h \in \mathcal{H}^d, \beta \in \mathbb{R}_+\}$ the $VC(A) \leq 8(d+1)\log^2(d+1)$. Vapnik's proof can be directly used except the set $A$ replaces a class of indicator functions of the form $\{1_{\{(x,y):(h(x)-y)^2>\beta\}} : h \in \mathcal{H}^d, \beta \in \mathbb{R}_+\}$. $\square$

We henceforth take the right hand side of (3) to be bounded from above by $c_1 \left( \sqrt{\frac{d \log^2 d \ln m + \ln \frac{1}{\delta}}{m}} \right)$ for some absolute constant $c_1 > 0$ and we refer to this quantity as $\epsilon(m, d, \delta)$. By definition of $h_m$ and $h^*$ in (1) and (2) we have

$$L(h_m) \leq L_m(h_m) + \epsilon(m, d, \delta) \leq L_m(h^*) + \epsilon(m, d, \delta) \leq L(h^*) + 2\epsilon(m, d, \delta). \tag{4}$$

Since we are really interested in assessing the absolute performance of $h_m$ as opposed to just its relative performance w.r.t. $h^*$ we need to obtain an upper bound on $L(h^*)$. We therefore have

$$L(h^*) = \inf_{h \in \mathcal{H}_{N_n^*}^d} L(h) = \inf_{h \in \mathcal{H}_{N_n^*}^d} \|g - h\|_{L_1(P)} \tag{5}$$

$$\leq \sup_{\{f \in \mathcal{F}: N_n^*(f) = N_n^*(g)\}} \inf_{h \in \mathcal{H}_{N_n^*}^d} \|f - h\|_{L_1(P)}. \tag{6}$$

From Definition 2 this is simply

$$\inf_{\mathcal{H}^d} \sup_{\{f \in \mathcal{F} : N_n^*(f) = N_n^*(g)\}} \inf_{h \in \mathcal{H}^d} \|f - h\|_{L_1(P)} \tag{7}$$

and from Definition 3 this becomes

$$\inf_{N_n} \inf_{\mathcal{H}^d} \sup_{\{f \in \mathcal{F} : N_n(f) = N_n(g)\}} \inf_{h \in \mathcal{H}^d} \|f - h\|_{L_1(P)} \tag{8}$$

which is clearly bounded from above by

$$\inf_{N_n} \sup_{y \in N_n(\mathcal{F})} \inf_{\mathcal{H}^d} \sup_{\{f \in \mathcal{F} \cap N_n^{-1}(y)\}} \inf_{h \in \mathcal{H}^d} \|f - h\|_{L_\infty}. \tag{9}$$

The quantity

$$\inf_{\mathcal{H}^d} \sup_{\{f \in \mathcal{F} \cap N_n^{-1}(y)\}} \inf_{h \in \mathcal{H}^d} \|f - h\|_{L_\infty}$$

is interesting in its own right. It represents an *n-width* as is usually referred to in the field of approximation theory (cf. Pinkus [11]). This particular width is newly introduced in this work and in its general form we denote it by

$$\rho_d(\mathcal{F}, L_p) \equiv \inf_{\mathcal{H}^d} \sup_{f \in \mathcal{F}} \inf_{h \in \mathcal{H}^d} \|f - h\|_{L_p} \tag{10}$$

for $1 \le p \le \infty$ where the outermost infimum is taken over all hypothesis classes of pseudo-dimension $d$. In the full paper we discuss some of the advantages of this non-linear width as compared to other existing non-linear $n$-widths. Here we take the $L_\infty$-norm in (10) and write $\rho_d(\mathcal{F})$. Continuing we therefore have

$$L(h^*) \le \inf_{N_n} \sup_{y \in N_n(\mathcal{F})} \rho_d\left(\mathcal{F} \cap N_n^{-1}(y)\right). \tag{11}$$

The next definition introduces a quantity of primary importance in this work.

**Definition 5.** For any target class $\mathcal{F}$ and any integers $n$, $d \ge 1$ let

$$I_{n,d}(\mathcal{F}) \equiv \inf_{N_n} \sup_{y \in N_n(\mathcal{F})} \rho_d\left(\mathcal{F} \cap N_n^{-1}(y)\right)$$

where $N_n$ runs over all linear information operators.

$I_{n,d}(\mathcal{F})$ measures the distribution-free best approximation error of the worst case element in the target class given optimal partial information about it expressed as $n$ linear operations and given that the approximating class is of pseudo-dimension $d$.

We may now break up the loss $L(h_m)$ of the algorithm-selected hypothesis $h_m$ into a *learning error* and an *information error* component,

"learning error"    "information error"

$$L(h_m) = (L(h_m) - L(h^*)) + L(h^*) = \overbrace{\Delta(m, d, \delta)} + \overbrace{L(h^*)}$$

where the learning error is defined as $\Delta(m, d, \delta) = L(h_m) - L(h^*)$. The learning error measures the extra loss suffered by outputting the algorithm's hypothesis $h_m$ as opposed to the optimal hypothesis $h^*$. The information-error which depends on the target $g$ measures the minimal error of approximating the target $g$ by a function $h^*$ given optimal partial-information $N_n^*(g)$ about $g$ and using the optimal approximating hypothesis class $\mathcal{H}_{N^*}^d$ of pseudo-dimension $d$.

We asses the goodness of $h_m$ by evaluating an upper bound on $L(h_m)$ which from (4) and (11) is

$$L(h_m) \leq 2\epsilon(m, d, \delta) + I_{n,d}(\mathcal{F}).$$

Being that $I_{n,d}$ is a useful quantity in the general learning scenario where both the probability distribution $P$ and target $g$ are unknowns we henceforth refer to $I_{n,d}(\mathcal{F})$, instead of $L(h^*)$ which does depend on $P$ and $g$, as the *information error*.

## 3 Main Results

We apply the framework introduced in the previous section to the problem of learning a Sobolev-type target class $\mathcal{F} = W_\infty^{r,s}(M)$, for some fixed $r, s \in \mathbb{Z}_+$, $M > 0$, which is defined as all functions with domain $X = [0,1]^s$ which have all partial derivatives up to order $r$ bounded in the sup-norm by $M$ (the letter $s$ is used for dimensionality of the domain as the letters $d, N, n$ are reserved for more important quantites in the sequel). Formally, let $k = [k_1, \ldots, k_s] \in \mathbb{Z}_+^s$, $\|k\| = \sum_{i=1}^{s} k_i$,

$$W_\infty^{r,s}(M) = \{f : \sup_{x \in [0,1]^s} |D^k f(x)| \leq M, \|k\| \leq r\}$$

which will henceforth be referred to as $W_\infty^{r,s}$ or $\mathcal{F}$. We now state the main results with proof sketches. The full proofs are provided in the main paper [14].

We first note the following facts. There exists a $q$-dimensional linear subspace $S_{q,r}$ of piecewise polynomials of degree $r-1$ which is spanned by the set $\{\phi_i\}_{i=1}^{q}$ and a linear operator $T_{q,r} : W_\infty^{r,s} \to S_{q,r}$ which maps any function $f \in W_\infty^{r,s}$ to an element of $S_{q,r}$.

**Lemma 6.** *Given integers $n$ and $d \geq 1$, choose $q$ such that the dimensionality of $S_{q,r}$ is $n + d$. Consider the target class $\mathcal{F} = W_\infty^{r,s}$ and the target function $g \in \mathcal{F}$. For any $f \in W_\infty^{r,s}$, let $T_{q,r}(f) = \sum_{i=1}^{n+d} L_i(f)\phi_i(x)$ for some linear functionals $L_i$, $1 \leq i \leq n + d$. Define the information operator $\hat{N}_n(f) = [L_1(f), \ldots, L_{n+d}(f)]$. Let $y = \hat{N}_n(g)$. Define the approximating class to be a linear subspace*

$$H_y^d \equiv \mathcal{H}_{\hat{N}_n(g)}^d = \left\{\sum_{i=1}^{n} y_i\phi_i(x) + \sum_{i=n+1}^{n+d} c_i\phi_i(x) : c_i \in \mathbb{R}\right\}.$$

*Then the distribution-free worst-case information error of the particular information operator $\hat{N}_n$ and class $H_y^d$ is bounded as*

$$\sup_{y \in \hat{N}_n(\mathcal{F})} \sup_{f \in \mathcal{F} \cap \hat{N}_n^{-1}(y)} \inf_{h \in H_y^d} \|f - h\|_{L_\infty} \leq \frac{c_2}{(n+d)^{r/s}}$$

*for some constant $c_2 > 0$ independent of $n$ and $d$.*

*Proof Sketch.* The upper bound follows from a result of Birman and Solomjak [6] lemma 3.1 on linear spline approximation. □

**Theorem 7.** *Let $\mathcal{F} = W_\infty^{r,s}$, $n \geq 1$, $d \geq 1$, be given integers and $c_2 > 0$ a constant independent of $n$ and $d$. Then*

$$I_{n,d}(\mathcal{F}) \leq \frac{c_2}{(n+d)^{r/s}}.$$

*Proof Sketch.* To establish an upper bound on $I_{n,d}(\mathcal{F})$ it suffices to choose a particular information operator $\hat{N}_n$ and a particular manifold $\hat{\mathcal{H}}^d$. Thus the upper bound of Lemma 6 applies. □

**Corollary 8.** *Let $\mathcal{F} = W_\infty^{r,s}$ and $g \in \mathcal{F}$ be the unknown target function. Given an i.i.d. random sample $\{(x_i, g(x_i))\}_{i=1}^m$ of size $m$ drawn according to any unknown distribution $P$ on $X$. Given an optimal partial information vector $N_n^*(g)$ consisting of $n$ linear operations on $g$. Fix any $d \geq 7$. Let $\mathcal{H}_{N_n^*}^d$ be the optimal hypothesis class of pseudo-dimension $d$. Let $h_m$ be the output hypothesis obtained from running empirical loss minimization over $\mathcal{H}_{N_n^*}^d$. Then for an arbitrary $0 < \delta < 1$, the loss of $h_m$ is bounded as*

$$L(h_m) \leq c_3 \sqrt{\frac{d \log^2 d \ln m + \ln \frac{1}{\delta}}{m}} + \frac{c_4}{(n+d)^{r/s}} \tag{12}$$

*where $c_3, c_4 > 0$ are constants independent of $m, n$ and $d$.*

The proof of Corollary 8 directly follows from Theorems 4 and 7.

In the next result we state a lower bound on the information error $I_{n,d}(\mathcal{F})$.

**Theorem 9.** *Let $\mathcal{F} = W_\infty^{r,s}$ and $n \geq 20$, $d \geq 1$ be given integers. Then*

$$I_{n,d}(\mathcal{F}) \geq \frac{1}{(1280n \ln n + 128d \ln d)^{r/s}}.$$

*Proof Sketch.* We consider a transformation which maps a function $f \in \mathcal{F}$ to a vector of its functional values at $m$ points in the domain $X$. The error of approximating the infinite dimensional subset $\mathcal{F} \cap N_n^{-1}(y)$ by a manifold $\mathcal{H}^d$ upper bounds the error of approximation of a finite $m$-dimensional set consisting of the intersection of the cube $[-1,1]^m$ with an $(m-n)$-dimensional subspace $L_{m-n}$ using a finite dimensional manifold $H^d$ of pseudo-dimension $d$. Using a classical geometric argument we show that there are exponentially-many (in $m$) vertices of the cube $[-1,1]^m$ which are close to $L_{m-n}$ while there are only a polynomial number of vertices close to $H^d$. It follows that there exist a point in $[-1,1]^m \cap L_{m-n}$ whose distance from $H^d$ is at least as large as the lower bound stated in the Theorem. □

# 4 Conclusions

Several important dependences and tradeoffs between the main parameters $m, n, d$ are apparent following the previous results. We emphasize that these dependences are specific to the particular target class $\mathcal{F} = W_\infty^{r,s}$ while extensions to other classes, in particular other Sobolev classes, are fairly straightforward.

For a fixed sample size $m$ and fixed information cardinality $n$ there is an optimal complexity

$$d^* \leq c_5 \left( \left\{ \frac{rm}{s\sqrt{\ln m}} \right\}^{2s/(s+2r)} - n \right), \tag{13}$$

which minimizes the upper bound on the loss where $c_5 > 0$ is an absolute constant. The complexity $d$ is a free parameter in this learning model and it is proportional to the amount that the estimator $h_m$ overfits the data when estimating the optimal hypothesis $h^*$. The result suggests that for a given sample size $m$ and partial information cardinality $n$, there is an optimal estimator (or model) complexity $d^*$ which minimizes the loss rate. Thus if a structure of hypothesis classes $\{\mathcal{H}^d\}_{d=1}^\infty$ is available to the learner then the best choice of a hypothesis class on which the learner should run empirical loss minimization is $\mathcal{H}^{d^*}$ with $d^*$ as in (13).

To see how $n$ and $m$ trade off we take $d$ to be the above optimal value $d^*$ and fix the total available information and sample size at some constant value $m + n = c_6$. When $s < 2r$ we find that $m$ grows polynomially in $n$ at a rate no larger than $n^{1+\frac{r}{s}}$, i.e., roughly speaking, partial information about the target $g$ is worth a polynomial number of examples. For $s > 2r$, $n$ grows polynomially in $m$ at a rate no larger than $\frac{m^2}{\ln m}$, i.e., information obtained from examples is worth a polynomial amount of partial information.

Finally, from Theorem 9 and 6 it follows that $\hat{N}_n$ and $\mathcal{H}^d_{\hat{N}_n(g)}$ incur an error which is no more than a logarithmic factor in $n$ and $d$ away from the information error $I_{n,d}(\mathcal{F})$. Thus they come close to being the optimal combination $N_n^*$ and $\mathcal{H}^d_{N_n^*}$. Hence when learning a target $g \in \mathcal{F}$ using examples and partial information, the operator $\hat{N}_n$ and the linear hypothesis class $\mathcal{H}^d_{\hat{N}_n(g)}$ guarantee a close-to optimal performance, i.e., the upper bound on $L(h_m)$, where $h_m$ is the empirical loss minimizer over $\mathcal{H}^d_{\hat{N}_n(g)}$, is almost minimal.

An additional comment is due. The fact that the linear manifold $\mathcal{H}^d_{\hat{N}_n(g)}$ achieves an almost optimal upper bound among all possible manifolds of pseudo-dimension $d$ is a consequence of the choice of the target class $W_\infty^{r,s}$ and the norm $L_\infty$ used for approximation. Suppose we consider instead another classical Sobolev class defined for fixed $1 \leq p \leq 2$ by $W_p^{r,s} = \{f : \|D^k f\|_{L_p} \leq M, \|k\| \leq r\}$, for a multi-integer $k = [k_1, \ldots, k_s] \in \mathbb{Z}_+^s$, where $\|k\| = \sum_{i=1}^s k_i$, and $D^k$ denotes the partial derivative operator. From classical results on the estimation of the Kolmogorov width of $W_p^{r,s}$, denoted here as $K_d(W_p^{r,s}, L_\infty)$, it can be shown that when using the $L_\infty$-norm for approximation, the optimal $d$-dimensional linear manifold has a worst-case approximation error which is lower bounded by $\frac{c_7}{d^{r/s-1/p}}$ for some constant $c_7 > 0$ independent of $d$. Whereas doing approximation by linear combinations of $d$ piecewise polynomial-splines of degree $r$ (but allowing the spline basis to depend on the target function which implies non-linear approximation) leads to the non-linear width introduced earlier satisfying $\rho(W_p^{r,s}, L_\infty) \leq c_8 (\frac{\ln d}{d})^{r/s}$. Thus $\rho(W_p^{r,s}, L_\infty) << K_d(W_p^{r,s}, L_\infty)$, where $a_d << b_d$ means $\frac{a_d}{b_d} \to 0$ as $d \to \infty$. The width $\rho_d()$ is hence a genuine *non-linear* width as there are target classes for which it is less than the Kolmogorov width in a strong sense.

# References

1. Abu-Mostafa Y. S. (1990), Learning from Hints in Neural Networks, *Journal of Complexity*, 6, p.192-198.
2. Abu-Mostafa Y. S. (1993), Hints and the VC Dimension, *Neural Computation*, Vol. 5, p.278-288.
3. Abu-Mostafa Y. S. (1995), Machines that Learn from Hints, *Scientific American*, Vol. 272, No. 4.
4. Angluin D., (1988), Queries and Concept Learning, *Machine Learning*, Vol 2, p. 319-342.
5. Bartlett P. L., Long P. M., Williamson R. C., (1994), Fat-Shattering and the Learnability of Real-Valued Functions, *Proceedings of the $7^{th}$ Annual Conference on Computational Learning Theory*, p. 299, 1994, ACM, New York, N.Y..
6. Birman M. S., Solomjak M. Z., (1967), Piecewise-polynomial Approximations of Functions of the Classes $W_p^\alpha$, *Math. USSR-Sbornik*, Vol. 2, No. 3, p.295-317.
7. Castelli, V., Cover T. M., (1995), On the exponential value of labeled samples, *Pattern Recognition Letters*, Vol. 16, No. 1, p.105.
8. Haussler D., (1992), Decision theoretic generalizations of the PAC model for neural net and other learning applications, *Inform. Comput.*, vol. 100 no. 1, pp. 78-150.
9. Kulkarni S. R., Mitter S. K., Tsitsiklis J. N., (1993). Active Learning Using Arbitrary Valued Queries. *Machine Learning*, Vol 11, p.23-35
10. Mitchell T. M., Keller R., Kedar-Cabelli S. (1986) Explanation-based generalization: A unifying view. *Machine Learning*, Vol. 1, pp. 47-80.
11. Pinkus A., (1985), "$n$-widths in Approximation Theory", New York: Springer-Verlag.
12. Ratsaby J., Venkatesh S.S., Learning from a mixture of labeled and unlabeled examples with parametric side information. (1995). *Proc. Eighth Annual Conference on Computational Learning Theory*, p.412, Morgan Kaufmann, San Maeto, CA.
13. Ratsaby J., Venkatesh S. S. The complexity of Learning from a Mixture of Labeled and Unlabeled Examples. (1995). *Proc. 33rd Allerton Conference on Communication, Control, and Computing*, (p. 1002-1009).
14. Ratsaby J., Maiorov V., (1996), Learning from Examples and Partial Information, Submitted to *Journal of Complexity*.
15. Rivest R. L., Eisenberg B. (1990), On the sample complexity of pac-learning using random and chosen examples. *Proceedings of the 1990 Workshop on Computational Learning Theory*, p. 154-162, Morgan Kaufmann, San Maeto, CA.
16. Roscheisen M., Hofmann R., Trespt V. (1994). Incorporating Prior Knowledge into Networks of Locally-Tuned Units, in " Computational Learning Theory and

Natural Learning Systems", Hanson S., Petsche T., Kearns M., Rivest R., Editors, MIT Pre ss, Cambridge, MA.

17. Towell G. G., Shavlik J. W. (1991). Interpretation of artificial neural networks: Mapping knowledge-based neural networks into rules. In *Advances in Neural Information Processing Systems 4*, pp. 977-984., Denver, CO. Morgan Kaufmann.

18. Traub J. F., Wasilkowski G. W. , Wozniakowski H., (1988), "Information-Based Complexity", Academic Press Inc.

19. Valiant L. G., A Theory of the learnable, (1984), *Comm. ACM* 27:11, p. 1134-1142.

20. Vapnik V. N and Chervonenkis A. Ya., (1971), On the uniform convergence of relative frequencies of events to their probabilities", *Theoret. Probl. and Its Appl.* Vol. 16 , 2, p.264-280.

21. Vapnik V. N and Chervonenkis A. Ya., (1981), Necessary and sufficient conditions for the uniform convergence of means to their expectations, *Theoret. Probl. and Its Appl.* Vol. 26, 3, p.532-553.

22. Vapnik V.N., (1982), "Estimation of Dependences Based on Empirical Data", Springer-Verlag, Berlin.

**Acknowledgments:**

J. Ratsaby thanks Dr. Santosh S. Venkatesh of the Electrical Engineering, University of Pennsylvania, for comments on an early version of the paper and to Dr. Allan Pinkus from the Faculty of Mathematics, Technion, for some comments and reference to the book of Traub [18] et. al. He also acknowledges the support of a VATAT Post-Doctorate fellowship and the Ollendorff center of the Faculty of Electrical Engineering at the Technion.

# Monotonic and Dual-Monotonic Probabilistic Language Learning of Indexed Families with High Probability

Léa Meyer

Institut für Informatik und Gesellschaft
Albert-Ludwigs-Universität Freiburg
79098 Freiburg, Germany

**Abstract.** The present paper deals with monotonic and dual-monotonic probabilistic identification of indexed families of uniformly recursive languages from positive data. In particular, we consider the special case where the probability is equal to 1.

Earlier results in the field of probabilistic identification established that - considering function identification - each collection of recursive functions identifiable with probability $p > 1/2$ is deterministically identifiable (cf. [23]). In the case of language learning from text, each collection of recursive languages identifiable from text with probability $p > 2/3$ is deterministically identifiable (cf. [20]). In particular, we have no gain of learning power when the collections of functions or languages are claimed to be inferred with probability $p = 1$.

As shown in [18], we receive high structured probabilistic hierarchies when dealing with probabilistic learning under monotonicity constraints. In this paper, we consider monotonic and dual monotonic probabilistic learning of indexed families with respect to proper, class preserving and class comprising hypothesis spaces. In particular, we can prove for proper monotonic as well as for proper dual monotonic learning that probabilistic learning is more powerful than deterministic learning *even if the probability is claimed to be 1*. To establish this result, we need a sophisticated version of the proof technique developed in [17].

## 1   Introduction

The study of probabilistic learning can be motivated by the fact that people enlarge their learning power by accepting that their learning processes may fail with a certain probability. In general, the learning power increases even if the probability has to be *close or equal to* 1. Moreover, the learning power is strictly increasing when the probability decreases. Hence, the question arises if there exist "natural" formal learning models that reflect this human abilities.

In Learning Theory, there are two important formalizations of probabilistic learning, namely *PAC-Learning*, introduced by Valiant [21], and *probabilistic inductive inference*. In this paper, we deal with several variations of probabilistic inductive inference. Probabilistic inference of recursive functions was introduced by Freivalds [6], and further investigated for example by Ambainis [1], Daley *et al.* [4], Pitt [20], and Wiehagen *et al.* [23], [24]. Considering function identification, Pitt showed that each collection of recursive functions identifiable with probability $p > 1/2$ is deterministically identifiable (cf. [20], [23]), i.e., the probabilistic hierarchy has a "gap" beginning with $1/2$. For language learning from text, Pitt showed that each collection of recursive languages identifiable from text with probability $p > \frac{2}{3}$ is deterministically identifiable (cf. [20]). In the cases of *finite probabilistic learning* and *popperian finite probabilistic learning*, Freivalds [6] and Daley *et al.* showed that the probabilistic hierarchies in these cases have a "gap" beginning with 2/3. When dealing with *identification with bounded mind changes* (cf. [23]), the situation is different. In this case, Wiehagen *et al.* showed that, for all $n \geq 2$, there is a collection of recursive functions that can be identified with arbitrary high probability making at most $n$ mind changes but every deterministic learner strictly exceeds the bound of $n$ mind changes. Furthermore. Wiehagen *et al.* [24] constructed a nonstandard hypothesis space $\mathcal{G}$ such that each infinite set of recursive functions, which is *EX*-identifiable with respect to some acceptable Gödel-numbering, is *EX*-identifiable with arbitrary high probability with respect to $\mathcal{G}$, but not deterministically *EX*-identifiable with respect to $\mathcal{G}$. The same result holds for finite identification and *BC*-identification of recursive functions with respect to nonstandard hypothesis spaces (cf. [24]). However, these nonstandard hypothesis spaces do not induce "natural" deterministic learning classes.

In particular, we notice that in all but one of these learning models. namely *BC*-identification with respect to nonstandard hypothesis spaces (cf. [24]), *the learning power is not increased when the machines are claimed to learn with probability $p = 1$.*

In the following, we give a brief introduction to the setting of *probabilistic language learning*, described for example in [20]. A *probabilistic inference machine* (abbr. PIM) is an algorithmic device that is able to flip a *t-sided coin* from time to time. The probabilistic inference machine is fed more and more information about a language to be inferred. The information the PIM is fed can consist of positive and negative examples or only positive ones. In this paper. we consider the case, where the learner is fed all strings belonging to the language to be inferred but no other strings, i.e., *learning from text*. When fed a text for a language to be learned, the PIM has to produce hypotheses about this language. Thereby, the hypotheses the probabilistic machine outputs. depend not only on the information the machine is fed, but also on the output of the coin flips. In this paper, we claim the machines to produce *grammars* for the languages to be learned. The hypotheses the learner outputs have to be members of an admissible set of hypotheses; every such admissible set is called *hypothesis space*.

Finally, we have to describe what is meant by "successful learning". A PIM $P$ is said to *identify a text $\tau$ for a language $L$ with probability $p$,* if the probability of *all infinite coin sequences $c_0, c_1, \ldots$ such that the sequence of hypotheses $P$ outputs, when fed $\tau$ and flipping $c_0, c_1, \ldots$, is converging to a hypothesis correctly describing $L$,* is greater or equal to $p$. If $P$ identifies every text for a language to be learned with probability $p$, then it is said to *identify the language from text with probability $p$.* $P$ *identifies a collection of languages from text with probability $p$* if and only if it identifies each member of this collection from text with probability $p$. In the case $t = 1$, i.e., the case where the PIM $P$ is equipped with a 1-*sided coin,* the situation described above is essentially the paradigm of *language identification in the limit* introduced by Gold [7]. For more information about identification in the limit, we refer the reader to [19] for an overview.

With respect to potential applications, we do not consider arbitrary collections of recursive languages but restrict ourselves to enumerable families of recursive languages with uniformly decidable membership, i.e., *indexed families of uniformly recursive languages* (cf. [2], [13], [14], [15], [16], [25], and the references therein).

As mentioned above, we require the learners to produce grammars for the languages to be learned. However, we do not allow every set of grammars as hypothesis space but only *enumerable families of grammars with uniformly decidable membership* (cf. for example [13], or [25]). Let $\mathcal{L} = L_0, L_1, \ldots$ be an enumerable family of target languages. Obviously, a hypothesis space for $\mathcal{L}$ has to contain at least one description for each target language. Hence, the family $\mathcal{L}$ itself may be used as hypothesis space. This leads to the notion of *proper learning*, i.e., a learner identifies $\mathcal{L}$ properly if it learns $\mathcal{L}$ with respect to $\mathcal{L}$ itself. Since the requirement to learn properly in general leads to a decrease of the learning power, we additionally consider *class preserving probabilistic learning*, i.e., $\mathcal{L}$ has to be inferred with respect to some hypothesis space having the same range as $\mathcal{L}$, and *class comprising probabilistic learning*, i.e., $\mathcal{L}$ has to be learnt with respect to some hypothesis space that has a range comprising $range(\mathcal{L})$. For more information about the impact of the hypothesis space on the learning power of inductive or probabilistic inference machines, we refer the reader for example to [15], [18] or [25].

When observing human inference processes, we notice that people in general try to "improve" the quality of their hypotheses during their learning processes. For example, people generalize from a given hypothesis when gathering new information contradicting the previous hypothesis. *Monotonicity constraints* can be viewed as an attempt to formalize *generalization strategies* and *specialization strategies*.

In this paper, we deal with monotonic and dual-monotonic learning. In the case of *monotonic learning*, the learner, fed a text for a language $L$ to be inferred, has to produce a chain of hypotheses such that $L_i \cap L \subseteq L_j \cap L$ for any two hypotheses $i$, $j$ in case $j$ is conjectured later as $i$ (cf. [22]). In the dual counterpart to monotonicity, i.e., *dual-monotonicity* (cf. [12]), we claim that the learner is never allowed to guess a grammar that generates a string that is already correctly excluded by a previously generated hypothesis. More details about monotonicity and dual-monotonicity can be found in [14], [16], [22], and [25].

In [17] and [18], we already showed that probabilistic learning under *monotonicity constraints* is able to reflect the human ability to learn with probability less than 1 without loosing to much certainty. In the sequel, we show that dual-monotonic learning, too, has this desirable property. Moreover, we are able to close a gap arising in [18] concerning *probabilistic learning with probability $p = 1$*, and show that proper monotonic and proper dual monotonic probabilistic learning with probability $p = 1$, respectively, is strictly more powerful than proper monotonic and dual-monotonic deterministic learning, respectively.

## 2 Preliminaries

We denote the natural numbers by $\mathbb{N} = \{0, 1, 2, \ldots\}$. Let $M_0$, $M_1, \ldots$ be a standard list of all Turing machines, and let $\varphi_0$, $\varphi_1, \ldots$ be the resulting acceptable programming system, i.e., $\varphi_i$ denotes the partial recursive function computed by $M_i$. Let

$\Phi_0$, $\Phi_1$, ... be any associated complexity measure (cf. [3]). Without loss of generality we may assume that $\Phi_k(x) \geq 1$ for all $k, x \in \mathbb{N}$. Furthermore, let $k, x \in \mathbb{N}$. If $\varphi_k(x)$ is defined, we say that $\varphi_k(x)$ converges and write $\varphi_k(x) \downarrow$; otherwise $\varphi_k(x)$ diverges and we write $\varphi_k(x) \uparrow$. In the sequel, we assume familiarity with formal language theory (cf. [8]). Let $\Sigma$ be any fixed finite alphabet of symbols and let $\Sigma^*$ be the free monoid over $\Sigma$. Any subset $L \subseteq \Sigma^*$ is called a language. Let $L$ be a language, and let $s = s_0, s_1, \ldots$ be a finite or infinite sequence of strings from $\Sigma^*$. Define $rng(s) := \{s_k | k \in \mathbb{N}\}$. An infinite sequence $\tau = s_0, s_1, \ldots$ of strings from $\Sigma^*$ with $rng(\tau) = L$ is called a *text* for $L$. For a text $\tau$ and a number $x$, let $\tau_x$ be the initial segment of $\tau$ of length $x + 1$. Following Angluin [2], and Lange, Zeugmann and others (cf., e.g., [25] or [16]), we exclusively deal with the learnability of indexed families of uniformly recursive languages defined as follows. A sequence $\mathcal{L} = (L_j)_{j \in \mathbb{N}}$ is said to be an *indexed family* of uniformly recursive languages provided $L_j \neq \emptyset$ for all $j \in \mathbb{N}$ and there is a recursive function $F$ such that for all $j \in \mathbb{N}$ and $s \in \Sigma^*$:

$$F(j, s) := \begin{cases} 1, & \text{if } s \in L_j, \\ 0, & \text{otherwise.} \end{cases}$$

In the following, we refer to indexed families of uniformly recursive languages as *indexed families* for short.

Now we will precise the learning models considered in this paper. Let $\mathcal{L}$ be an indexed family. An *inductive inference machine* (abbr. IIM) is an algorithmic device that takes as its input a text for a language $L \in \mathcal{L}$. When fed a text for $L$, it outputs a sequence of grammars. If, for any text for L, $M$ outputs a sequence of grammars that converges to a grammar correctly describing $L$, then $M$ is said to *identify the language in the limit from text*. This learning paradigm is called *identification in the limit* and was introduced by Gold [7]. For more information about inductive inference, we refer the reader to [19] for an overview. In this paper, we consider a nondeterministic variant of this concept, namely *probabilistic inductive inference* (cf., e.g., [6], [20], [23]). A *probabilistic inductive inference machine* (abbr. PIM) is an *algorithmic device equipped with a t-sided coin oracle*. A PIM $P$ takes as its input larger and larger initial segments of a text $\tau$ and it either takes the next input string, or it first outputs a hypothesis, i.e., a number encoding a certain computer program, and then requests the next input string. Each time, $P$ requests a new input string, it flips the $t$-sided coin. The hypotheses produced by $P$, when fed a text $\tau$, depend on the text seen so far <u>and</u> on the outcome of the coin flips.

The hypotheses the PIM outputs have to be members of an admissible set of hypotheses; every such set is called *hypothesis space*. In this paper, we do not allow arbitrary sets of hypothesis as a hypothesis space but only enumerable families of grammars $G_0, G_1, G_2, \ldots$ over the terminal alphabet $\Sigma$ such that $rng(\mathcal{L}) \subseteq \{L(G_j) | j \in \mathbb{N}\}$, and membership in $L(G_j)$ is uniformly decidable for all $j \in \mathbb{N}$, and all strings $s \in \Sigma^*$. If a PIM $P$ outputs a number $j$, then we are interpreting this number to be the index of the grammar $G_j$, i.e., $P$ guesses the language $L(G_j)$. For a hypothesis space $\mathcal{G} = (L(G_j))_{j \in \mathbb{N}}$, we use $rng(\mathcal{G})$ to denote $\{L(G_j) | j \in \mathbb{N}\}$.

Let $P$ be a PIM equipped with a $t$-sided coin. An oracle $c$ is an infinite sequence $c_0, c_1, \ldots$ where $c_i \in \{0, \ldots, t-1\}$. By $c^n$, we denote the initial segment $c_0, \ldots, c_n$ of $c$ for all $n \in \mathcal{N}$. Let $c$ be an oracle. We denote the deterministic algorithmic device defined by running $P$ with oracle $c$ by $P^c$. By $P^{c^x}(\tau_x)$, we denote the last hypothesis $P$ outputs, when fed $\tau_x$, under the condition that the first $x+1$ flips of the t-sided coin were $c^x$. If there is no such hypothesis, then $P^{c^x}(\tau_x)$ is said to be $\perp$. For the sake of readability, we now define the notion of an *infinite computation tree* (cf. [20]). Let $L \in \mathcal{L}$, and let $\tau$ be a text for $L$. Then we define $T_{P,\tau}$ to be the t-ary tree representing all possible outputs of $P$ when fed $\tau$. Each node of $T_{P,\tau}$ can be identified with a finite sequence $s \in \cup_{n\in\mathbb{N}}\{0,\ldots,t-1\}^n$ and corresponds to a hypothesis P outputs when fed $\tau$ under the assumption that the first flips of the coin were $s$.

Next we define the notion of a *converging path* in an infinite computation tree. Let $c$ be an oracle. Then the sequence $(P^{c^x}(\tau_x))_{x\in\mathbb{N}}$ is said to be a *path*. We say that $(P^{c^x}(\tau_x))_{x\in\mathbb{N}}$ *converges in the limit* to the number $j$ iff either there exists some $n \in \mathbb{N}$ with $P^{c^x}(\tau_x) = j$ for all $x \geq n$, or $(P^{c^x}(\tau_x))_{x\in\mathbb{N}}$ is finite and its last member is $j$. Let $\mathcal{G}$ be a hypothesis space. $(P^{c^x}(\tau_x))_{x\in\mathbb{N}}$ is said to *converge correctly with respect to $\mathcal{G}$* iff $(P^{c^x}(\tau_x))_{x\in\mathbb{N}}$ converges in the limit to a number $j$ and $L(G_j) = L$.

Now let $Pr$ denote the canonical Borel-measure on the Borel-$\sigma$-algebra on $\{0,\ldots, t-1\}^{\infty}$. For more details about probabilistic IIMs, measurability and infinite computation trees we refer the reader to Pitt (cf. [20]).

In the following, we define *monotonic and dual-monotonic probabilistic inference*. In general, this notions are defined for inductive inference machines (cf. [11], [12], [22]). In this paper, we directly give the definitions for probabilistic inductive inference machines and refer the reader to [11], [13], [14], [16], [22], [25] for more information about deterministic monotonic and dual-monotonic learning.

Let $c$ be an oracle, let $\tau$ be a text for a recursive language $L$, and let $P$ be a PIM. Then the path $(P^{c^x}(\tau_x))_{x\in\mathbb{N}}$ is said to be *monotonically* if and only if

$$L(G_{P^{c^x}(\tau_x)}) \cap L \subseteq L(G_{P^{c^{x+k}}(\tau_{x+k})}) \cap L$$

for all $k \in \mathbb{N}$. $(P^{c^x}(\tau_x))_{x\in\mathbb{N}}$ is said to be *dual-monotonically* if and only if

$$L(G_{P^{c^x}(\tau_x)})^c \cap L^c \subseteq L(G_{P^{c^{x+k}}(\tau_{x+k})})^c \cap L^c$$

for all $k \in \mathbb{N}$. Now we are ready to define monotonic and dual-monotonic probabilistic learning.

**Definition 1.** Let $\mathcal{L}$ be an indexed family, let $L$ be a language, let $\mathcal{G}$ be a hypothesis space, let $n \in \mathbb{N}$, and let $p \in [0,1]$. Let $\mu \in \{MON, DMON\}$ be a monotonicity constraint. Let $P$ be a PIM equipped with a t-sided coin. Set

$$S_{\tau} := \{\, c \mid (P^{c^x}(\tau_x))_{x\in\mathbb{N}} \text{ conv. correctly w.r.t. } \mathcal{G} \text{ and fulfills the condition } \mu\,\}.$$

$P\, C\mu_{prob}(p)$-*identifies* $L$ from text with respect to $\mathcal{G}$ iff $Pr(S_{\tau}) \geq p$ for every text $\tau$ for $L$. $P\, C\mu_{prob}(p)$-identifies $\mathcal{L}$ with respect to $\mathcal{G}$ iff $P\, C\mu_{prob}(p)$-identifies each $L \in rng(\mathcal{L})$ with probability $p$.

The prefix $C$ in $C\mu_{prob}(p)$ is used to denote *class comprising* learning, i.e., $\mathcal{L}$ can be $C\mu_{prob}(p)$-identified with respect to some hypothesis space $\mathcal{G}$ with $rng(\mathcal{L}) \subseteq rng(\mathcal{G})$. By $\mu_{prob}(p)$, we denote the collection of all indexed families $\mathcal{L}$ that can be $C\mu_{prob}(p)$-identified with respect to a *class preserving* hypothesis space $\mathcal{G}$, i.e., $rng(\mathcal{L}) = rng(\mathcal{G})$. The empty prefix for $LIM$ is denoted by $\varepsilon$. Furthermore, $E\mu_{prob}(p)$ denotes the collection of all indexed families that can be learned properly with probability $p$. More exactly, $\mathcal{L} \in E\mu_{prob}(p)$ iff $\mathcal{L}$ is $C\mu_{prob}(p)$-identifiable with respect to $\mathcal{L}$ itself. The corresponding *deterministic learning classes* are denoted by $C\mu$, $\mu$ and $E\mu$ for $\mu \in \{MON, DMON\}$.

In the following sections we often need a special set of recursive languages which encodes the halting problem (cf., e.g., [13]). Let $k \in \mathbb{N}$ and define

- $L_k := \{a^k b^m | m \in \mathbb{N}\}$,
- $L'_k := \begin{cases} L_k, & \text{if } \varphi_k(k) \uparrow, \\ \{a^k b^m | m \leq \Phi_k(k)\}, & \text{if } \varphi_k(k) \downarrow. \end{cases}$

## 3   Dual-monotonic probabilistic learning

In [18], we showed that the probabilistic hierarchy in the case of proper monotonic probabilistic learning is dense in $[2/3, 1]$. For class preserving probabilistic monotonic learning, we showed the probabilistic hierarchy to be strictly decreasing at points $4n/(4n+1)$, $n \in \mathbb{N}$, whereas the hierarchy in the class comprising case has a "gap" beginning with $2/3$. In this section, we show that dual monotonic probabilistic learning has similar properties.

**Theorem 2.** *Let $c, d \in \mathbb{N}$ with $gcd(c, d) = 1$, $1 > \frac{c}{d} > \frac{2}{3}$. Let $p = \frac{c}{d}$. Then there exists an indexed family $\mathcal{L}_p$ such that $\mathcal{L}_p \in EDMON_{prob}(p)$, and $\mathcal{L}_p \notin EDMON_{prob}(q)$ for all $q > p$.*

*Proof.* The key idea of the proof can be described as follows. Let $c, d \in \mathbb{N}$ with $gcd(c, d) = 1$, $c/d > 2/3$. We define an indexed family $\mathcal{L}_{c/d} = (L_{\langle k,j \rangle})_{k,j \in \mathbb{N}, j \leq 2c-d}$ as follows. For all $k \in \mathbb{N}$ set $L_{\langle k, 2c-d \rangle} = \{a^k b^0\}$. If $\varphi_k(k) \uparrow$, then all the languages $L_{\langle k,j \rangle}$ for $j \in \{0, \ldots, 2c-d-1\}$ are infinite and equal to $L_k$. If $\varphi_k(k) \downarrow$, then exactly $3c - 2d$ of the languages are finite and equal to $L'_k$. The other $d - c$ languages are infinite and equal to $L_k$. The indices $\{\langle k, j_1 \rangle, \ldots, \langle k, j_{3c-2d} \rangle\} \subset \{\langle k, 0 \rangle, \ldots, \langle k, c-1 \rangle\}$ of the finite languages depend only on the value of $\varphi_k(k)$.

Then $\mathcal{L}_{c/d}$ is dual-monotonically identifiable with probability $c/d$ but not identifiable with a probability $q > c/d$. The technical details of this proof are similar to the proof in [18] and therefore omitted.  □

**Theorem 3.** *Let $n \in \mathbb{N}$, $n \geq 3$, and let $p_n = \frac{2n-1}{2n}$. Then there exists an indexed family $\mathcal{L}_{p_n}$ such that $\mathcal{L}_{p_n} \in DMON_{prob}(p_n)$, and $\mathcal{L}_{p_n} \notin DMON_{prob}(q)$ for all $q > p_n$.*

*Proof.* Let $n \in \mathbb{N}$, $n \geq 3$, and let $p_n = (2n - 1)/2n$. For the sake of readability, we restrict ourselves to the case $n = 3$. We define an indexed family $\mathcal{L}_{5/6}$ as follows. Let $\langle . , . \rangle : \mathbb{N} \times \{1, \ldots, 6\} \to \mathbb{N}$ be an effective encoding of $\mathbb{N} \times \{1, \ldots, 6\}$. Let $k \in \mathbb{N}$. Define for $j \in \{1, 2, 3, 4\}$

$$L_{\langle k,j \rangle} := \begin{cases} L_k, & \text{if } \varphi_k(k) \uparrow, \\ \{a^k b^m | m \in \mathbb{N}, \ m \leq \Phi_k(k) + 4\} \setminus \{a^k b^{\Phi_k(k)+j}\}, & \text{if } \varphi_k(k) \downarrow. \end{cases}$$

Furthermore set

$$L_{\langle k,5\rangle} := \begin{cases} \{a^k b^0\}, & \text{if } \varphi_k(k) \uparrow, \\ \{a^k b^0\} \cup \{a^k b^m \mid m = \Phi_k(k) + 1, \Phi_k(k) + 2\}, & \text{if } \varphi_k(k) \downarrow. \end{cases}$$

and

$$L_{\langle k,6\rangle} := \begin{cases} \{a^k b^0\}, & \text{if } \varphi_k(k) \uparrow, \\ \{a^k b^0\} \cup \{a^k b^m \mid m = \Phi_k(k) + 3, \Phi_k(k) + 4\}, & \text{if } \varphi_k(k) \downarrow. \end{cases}$$

Set $\mathcal{L}_{5/6} = (L_{\langle k,j\rangle})_{k \in \mathbb{N}, j \in \{1,\dots,6\}}$. Then $\mathcal{L}_{5/6}$ witnesses the desired separation. $\quad\square$

**Theorem 4.** *There exists an indexed family $\mathcal{L}_{\frac{2}{3}} \in CDMON_{prob}(\frac{2}{3})$ such that $\mathcal{L}_{\frac{2}{3}} \notin CDMON_{prob}(q)$ for all $\frac{2}{3} < q \le 1$. If $p > \frac{2}{3}$, then $CDMON_{prob}(p) = CDMON$.*

*Proof.* Let $\mathcal{L}$ be an indexed family such that $\mathcal{L} \in \bigcup_{2/3 < p \le 1} CDMON_{prob}(p)$, let $\mathcal{G}$ be a hypothesis space, and let $P$ be a PIM such that $P$ $CDMON_{prob}(p)$-identifies $\mathcal{L}$ with a probability $p > 2/3$ with respect to $\mathcal{G}$. Let $\mathcal{H}$ be a hypothesis space extending $\mathcal{G}$ defined as follows.

Let $(s_j)_{j \in \mathbb{N}}$ be an effective enumeration of *all finite sequences of strings $s$ with range$(s) \subset L$ for some $L \in range(\mathcal{L})$.* Let $k \in \mathbb{N}$, let $\mathcal{T}_{P,s_k}$ be the finite computation tree induced by $P$ and $s_k$, and let $l_k$ be the highest level in $\mathcal{T}_{P,s_k}$. Let $x \in \mathcal{N}$, $x \le l_k$. Let $\mathcal{O} \subseteq \text{level } x$ be a set of nodes with $ind(o) \ne \bot$ for all $o \in \mathcal{O}$ and $w(\mathcal{O}) > 2/3$. Define

$$succ_{s_k}(\mathcal{O}) := \{o \in \text{level } l_k \mid \exists \text{ a node } o' \in \mathcal{O}, o' \text{ predecessor of } o\}.$$

Then define the following languages.

$$L_{s_k}^{\mathcal{O}} := \begin{cases} \cup\{L(G_{ind(o)}) \mid o \in \mathcal{O}\}, & \text{if } x = l_k, \\ \displaystyle\bigcup_{\mathcal{O}' \subset succ_{s_k}(\mathcal{O}),\, w(\mathcal{O}') > \frac{1}{3}} \bigcap_{o \in \mathcal{O}'} (L(G_{ind(o)}) \cup L^{\mathcal{O}}), & \text{if } x < l_k. \end{cases}$$

Finally, set $\mathcal{N}_x = \{\mathcal{O} \subseteq \text{level } x \mid ind(o) \ne \bot \text{ for all } o \in \mathcal{O} \text{ and } w(\mathcal{O}) > 2/3\}$ and define

$$L_{s_k} := \bigcap_{x=1}^{l_k} \left( \bigcap_{\mathcal{O} \in \mathcal{N}_x} L_{s_k}^{\mathcal{O}} \right).$$

Now let $\mathcal{H}$ be an uniformly decidable hypothesis space which contains an index for each language $L_{s_k}$, $k \in \mathbb{N}$. Denote the index for $L_{s_k}$ by $\alpha_{s_k}$ for all $k \in \mathcal{N}$. Then we can easily define an IIM $M$ which chooses its hypotheses from the infinite sequence $(\alpha_{\tau_\nu})_{\nu \in \mathbb{N}}$ by respecting the order of the sequence such that $M$ identifies $\mathcal{L}$ dual-monotonically with respect to $\mathcal{H}$.

For the separation, we define the following indexed family. Let $\langle\, ,\, \rangle : \mathbb{N} \times \mathbb{N} \to \mathbb{N}$ be an effective encoding of $\mathbb{N} \times \mathbb{N}$, and let $k \in \mathbb{N}$. Set $L_{\langle k,0\rangle} := \{a^k b^0\}$, and $L_{\langle k,1\rangle} := L_k$. Let $j \in \mathbb{N}$, $j \ge 2$, and define

$$L_{\langle k,j\rangle} := \begin{cases} L_k, & \text{if } \Phi_k(k) \ne j - 1, \\ \{a^k b^m \mid m \le \varphi_k(k) + 1\}, & \text{if } \Phi_k(k) = j - 1. \end{cases}$$

Then $\mathcal{L}_{2/3} = \{L_{\langle k,j\rangle}\}_{k,j \in \mathbb{N}}$ witnesses the desired separation.

## 4   Monotonic and dual-monotonic probabilistic learning with probability $p = 1$

When observing previous results in the field of probabilistic function or language identification, we notice that in general, the learning power is not increased when the probability is claimed to be 1. However, it seems to be a reasonable property of a learning model that there exist learning problems that strictly separate deterministic learning from probabilistic learning, since such problems could give us a deeper insight into the behaviour of the probabilistic learning model we investigate. In the sequel, we will show that $EMON_{prob}(1) \neq EMON$ and $EDMON_{prob}(1) \neq EDMON$.

Separation results in the field of learning of indexed families are usually proved by constructing indexed families encoding the halting problem in an appropriate way (cf. [13], and [25] for an overview). For probabilistic learning under monotonicity constraints, we showed in [18] that we need indexed families encoding problems that are "weaker" than the halting problem for the separation of the probabilistic learning classes in the interval $(1/2, 1]$. In the case of monotonic and dual-monotonic learning, we use a sophisticated version of this technique. However, further work will show that the problem encoded in the indexed family which separates $EMON_{prob}(1)$ from $EMON$ is "more complicated" than the problems separating the probabilistic learning classes investigated in [18].

**Theorem 5.** $EMON_{prob}(1) \neq EMON$

*Proof.* Let $\Sigma := \{a, b, d\}$. Let $\langle \ , \ \rangle$ be an effective encoding of $\mathbb{N} \times \mathbb{N} \times \{0, 1\}$, and let $st_m$ be variables for $m \in \mathbb{N}$. Set $st_m = 0$ for all $m \in \mathbb{N}$. Define the indexed family $(L_{\langle k,j,v \rangle})_{k,j,v \in \mathbb{N}, v \in \{0,1\}}$ as follows. Let $k, j, v, n, m \in \mathbb{N}$, $v \in \{0, 1\}$. If $\Phi_k(0) > n$, then $a^k b^n \in L_{\langle k,j,v \rangle}$ for all $j, v \in \mathbb{N}$, $v \in \{0, 1\}$. Furthermore, $d^{\langle j,v,t \rangle} \notin L_{\langle k,j,v \rangle}$ for all $j, t, v \in \mathbb{N}$, $t \leq n$, and $v \in \{0, 1\}$. Otherwise, i.e., if $\Phi_k(0) \leq n$, test if $\Phi_k(0) + 2 + \Phi_k(1) > n$.

We first consider the case where $\Phi_k(0) + 2 + \Phi_k(1) > n$. If $n > \Phi_k(0) + 2$, then $a^k b^n \in L_{\langle k,j,0 \rangle}$ and $a^k b^n \in L_{\langle k,j,1 \rangle}$. If $n = \Phi_k(0) + 2$, then distinguish the following two cases.

- If $\varphi_k(0) \equiv 0 \bmod 2$, then $a^k b^n \notin L_{\langle k,0,0 \rangle}$, $a^k b^n \in L_{\langle k,0,1 \rangle}$, and $d^m \in L_{\langle k,0,0 \rangle}$ for $m = \langle 0, 0, \Phi_k(0) + 2 \rangle$.
- If $\varphi_k(0) \equiv 1 \bmod 2$, then $a^k b^n \notin L_{\langle k,0,1 \rangle}$, $a^k b^n \in L_{\langle k,0,0 \rangle}$, and $d^m \in L_{\langle k,0,1 \rangle}$ for $m = \langle 0, 1, \Phi_k(0) + 2 \rangle$.

If $\Phi_k(0) + 2 + \Phi_k(1) \leq n$, then compute the least $s \in \mathbb{N}$, $s \geq 1$, such that

$$\sum_{i=0}^{s-1} (\Phi_k(i) + 2) + \Phi_k(s) \leq n \quad and \quad \sum_{i=0}^{s} (\Phi_k(i) + 2) + \Phi_k(s+1) > n.$$

Remark that in this case $\varphi_k(i) \downarrow$ for all $i \in \{0, \ldots, s\}$. If $j > s$, then $a^k b^n \in L_{\langle k,j,v \rangle}$ for $v \in \{0, 1\}$. If $j \leq s$, then the membership of $a^k b^n$ and $d^m \in L_{\langle k,j,v \rangle}$ not only depends on $j, v, n, m$, but also on the values of $\varphi_k(0), \ldots, \varphi_k(s)$.

1. $\varphi_k(s) > s$ or $\varphi_k(s) = 0$.

   If $st_j = 1$, then $a^k b^n \notin L_{\langle k,j,0\rangle}$, and $a^k b^n \notin L_{\langle k,j,1\rangle}$. Assume $st_j = 0$. If $n > \sum_{i=0}^{s-1}(\Phi_k(i) + 2) + \Phi_k(s)$, then $a^k b^n \in L_{\langle k,j,0\rangle}$ and $a^k b^n \in L_{\langle k,j,1\rangle}$. If $n = \sum_{i=0}^{s-1}(\Phi_k(i) + 2) + \Phi_k(s)$, then distinguish the following two cases.
   - If $\varphi_k(j) \equiv 0 \bmod 2$, then $a^k b^n \notin L_{\langle k,j,0\rangle}$, $a^k b^n \in L_{\langle k,j,1\rangle}$, and $d^m \in L_{\langle k,j,0\rangle}$ for $m = \langle j, 0, \sum_{i=0}^{s-1}(\Phi_k(i) + 2) + \Phi_k(s)\rangle$.
   - If $\varphi_k(j) \equiv 1 \bmod 2$, then $a^k b^n \notin L_{\langle k,j,1\rangle}$, $a^k b^n \in L_{\langle k,j,0\rangle}$, and $d^m \in L_{\langle k,j,1\rangle}$ for $m = \langle j, 1, \sum_{i=0}^{s-1}(\Phi_k(i) + 2) + \Phi_k(s)\rangle$.

2. $\varphi_k(s) \in \{1, \ldots s\}$.
   - If $st_j = 1$, then $a^k b^n \notin L_{\langle k,j,0\rangle}$, and $a^k b^n \notin L_{\langle k,j,1\rangle}$.
   - Assume $st_j = 0$. If $n = \sum_{i=0}^{s-1}(\Phi_k(i) + 2) + \Phi_k(s)$ or $n > \sum_{i=0}^{s-1}(\Phi_k(i) + 2) + (\Phi_k(s) + 2)$, then $a^k b^n \notin L_{\langle k,j,0\rangle}$, and $a^k b^n \notin L_{\langle k,j,1\rangle}$. If $n = \sum_{i=0}^{s-1}(\Phi_k(i) + 2) + (\Phi_k(s) + 1)$ or $n = \sum_{i=0}^{s-1}(\Phi_k(i) + 2) + (\Phi_k(s) + 2)$, then the membership of $a^k b^n$ to $L_{\langle k,j,0\rangle}$ and $L_{\langle k,j,1\rangle}$, respectively, depends only on the value of $j$ and $s - \varphi_k(s)$. Distinguish the following cases.
     - Let $j < s - \varphi_k(s)$. Then $a^k b^n \notin L_{\langle k,j,0\rangle}$, and $a^k b^n \notin L_{\langle k,j,1\rangle}$.
     - Let $j = s - \varphi_k(s)$. If $n = \sum_{i=0}^{s-1}(\Phi_k(i) + 2) + (\Phi_k(s) + 1)$, then $a^k b^n \in L_{\langle k,j,0\rangle}$, and $a^k b^n \notin L_{\langle k,j,1\rangle}$, and if $n = \sum_{i=0}^{s-1}(\Phi_k(i) + 2) + (\Phi_k(s) + 2)$, then $a^k b^n \notin L_{\langle k,j,0\rangle}$, and $a^k b^n \in L_{\langle k,j,1\rangle}$.
     - Let $j > s - \varphi_k(s)$. Then $a^k b^n \in L_{\langle k,j,0\rangle}$, and $a^k b^n \in L_{\langle k,j,1\rangle}$.
     Moreover, $d^m \in L_{\langle k,j,0\rangle}$ for $m = \langle j, 0, \sum_{i=0}^{s-1}(\Phi_k(i) + 2) + \Phi_k(s)\rangle$, and $d^m \in L_{\langle k,j,1\rangle}$ for $m = \langle j, 1, \sum_{i=0}^{s-1}(\Phi_k(i) + 2) + \Phi_k(s)\rangle$.
     Finally, set $st_j = 1$ for all $j \le s$.

Set $\mathcal{L} = (L_{\langle k,j,v\rangle})_{k,j,v \in \mathbb{N}, v \in \{0,1\}}$. Now we can prove the following two claims.

Claim 1: $\mathcal{L}$ is properly monotonically identifiable with probability $p = 1$.

First, we show that $\mathcal{L}$ is monotonically identifiable with probability $p = 1$. Let $L \in rng(\mathcal{L})$, let $\tau$ be a text for $L$, and let $x \in \mathbb{N}$. Let $c \in \{0,1\}^\infty$ be an oracle.

PIM P: On input $\tau_x$, $P^{c^x}$ works as follows.

1. Let $\tau_x = (\tau_{x-1}, d^{\langle j,v,z\rangle})$ for some $j, v, z \in \mathbb{N}$, $v \in \{0,1\}$. If $P^{c^{x-1}}(\tau_{x-1})$ is consistent with $\tau_x$, then output $P^{c^{x-1}}(\tau_{x-1})$. Otherwise output $L_{\langle k,j,v\rangle}$. Request the next input.

2. Let $\tau_x = (\tau_{x-1}, a^k b^z)$ for a $z \in \mathbb{N}$ and let $c^x = (c^{x-1}, c_x)$. Let $j_{x-1} \in \mathbb{N}$ with $P^{c^{x-1}}(\tau_{x-1}) \in \{\langle k, j_{x-1}, 0\rangle, \langle k, j_{x-1}, 1\rangle\}$. If $P^{c^{x-1}}(\tau_{x-1})$ is consistent with $a^k b^z$, then output $P^{c^{x-1}}(\tau_{x-1})$ and request the next input. Otherwise distinguish the following cases.
   - If $a^k b^{z+1} \in L_{P^{c^{x-1}}(\tau_{x-1})}$ and $a^k b^{z+2} \in L_{P^{c^{x-1}}(\tau_{x-1})}$, then search the least $j > j_{x-1}$ such that $\tau_x \subset L_{\langle k,j,0\rangle} \cap L_{\langle k,j,1\rangle}$. Output $\langle k, j, 0\rangle$ if $c_x = 0$, and output $\langle k, j, 1\rangle$ if $c_x = 1$. Request the next input.
   - Otherwise, $a^k b^{z+1} \notin L_{P^{c^{x-1}}(\tau_{x-1})}$ or $a^k b^{z+2} \notin L_{P^{c^{x-1}}(\tau_{x-1})}$. Thus, there must be an $s \in \mathbb{N}$, $s > j_{x-1}$, such that $\varphi_k(s) \downarrow$ and $\varphi_k(s) \in \{1, \ldots s\}$. Compute the languages $L_{\langle k,j,v\rangle}$ simultaneously for all $j, v \in \mathbb{N}$, $j > j_{x-1}$,

$v \leq 1$, in order to find this $s \in \mathbb{N}$. Now $P$ requests new inputs until the actual text either contains an element $d^m$ or the set $\{a^k b^m | m \leq \sum_{i < s}(\Phi_k(i) + 2)\}$. In the first case output the language corresponding to $d^m$; in the second case search the least $j > s$ such that $\tau_x \subset L_{\langle k,j,0 \rangle} \cap L_{\langle k,j,1 \rangle}$, output $\langle k, j, 0 \rangle$ if $c_x = 0$, and output $\langle k, j, 1 \rangle$ if $c_x = 1$. Request the next input.

<u>end</u>

Let $L \in \mathbb{N}$, let $\tau$ be a text for $L$, let $c$ be an oracle, and let $k \in \mathbb{N}$ with $L \cap L_k \neq \emptyset$.

- If $L = L_k$, then every path is monotonic, since $P$ always chooses the new hypothesis among the indices which contain more elements of $L_k$.
- If $L \neq L_k$, then $P$ eventually chooses a hypothesis $\langle k, j_2, v_2 \rangle$ after a hypothesis $\langle k, j_1, v_1 \rangle$ such that $j_2 \leq j_1$. This happens if and only if the last element of the text seen so far is an element $d^m$, and it is easy to see, that this choice does not disturb monotonicity provided $P$ never changes the hypothesis on this path again. But since the elements of the form $d^m$ are not ambiguous, $P$ identifies as soon as a such an element appears in the text.

Consequently, $P$ works monotonically on every text. To prove that $P$ identifies $\mathcal{L}$ with probability $p = 1$, we only have to consider the languages $L_k$ for $k \in \mathbb{N}$, since every other language is marked by a $d^m$ for an $m \in \mathbb{N}$, and we already argued that in this case every path converges. Considering $L_k$ for $k \in \mathbb{N}$, we have to distinguish three cases. First, let $k \in \mathbb{N}$ with $\varphi_k(i) \uparrow$ for an $i \in \mathbb{N}$. Then every path in the corresponding computation tree converges, since there is an $j_0 \in \mathbb{N}$ such that $L_{\langle k,j,v \rangle} = L_k$ for all $j \geq j_0$, $v \in \{0,1\}$. If $\varphi_k(i) \downarrow$ for all $i \in \mathbb{N}$, then either $i - \varphi_k(i) \in \{0, \ldots, i-1\}$ infinitely often or not. In the first case, $L_k \notin rng(\mathcal{L})$. The second case turns out to be more complicated, since only in this case, monotonic identification for $L_k$ may fail. Since $\varphi_k(i)$ is defined for all $i \in \mathbb{N}$ but $i - \varphi_k(i) \notin \{0, \ldots, i-1\}$ for almost all $i \in \mathbb{N}$, the language $L_k$ appears in $\{L_{\langle k,j,0 \rangle}, L_{\langle k,j,1 \rangle}\}$ for almost all $j \in \mathbb{N}$. More exactly, there exists a natural number $j_0 \in \mathbb{N}$ such that $L_{\langle k,j,v \rangle}$ is finite for every $j \leq j_0$, and $v \in \{0,1\}$, and $L_k \in \{L_{\langle k,j,0 \rangle}, L_{\langle k,j,1 \rangle}\}$ for all $j \in \mathbb{N}$, $j > j_0$. Consequently, for every $L \in \mathcal{L}$ and every text $\tau$ for $L$, there is a level $n_{\tau,0}$ of $T_{P,\tau}$ such that the weight of all paths containing an index for $L_k$ up to level $n_{\tau,0}$ is at least $1/2$. For the remaining paths, we can conclude that there is a level $n_{\tau,1} \geq n_{\tau,0}$ such the weight of all paths containing an index for $L_k$ up to level $n_{\tau,1}$ is at least $3/4$ and so on. Consequently, $P$ identifies $L_k$ with probability $p = 1$.

It remains to show that $\mathcal{L}$ is not properly monotonically identifiable. Let $M$ be an IIM which identifies $\mathcal{L}$ monotonically. We can prove the following claim.

<u>Claim 2</u>: There exists a $k_0 \in \mathbb{N}$ such that $L_{k_0} \in \mathcal{L}$ and $M$ diverges on the text $(a^{k_0} b^m)_{m \in \mathbb{N}}$ for $L_{k_0}$.

Intuitively, this claim follows from the fact, that every deterministic machine $M$ has to choose its hypotheses "probabilistically" among hypotheses in tuples of the form $(\langle k, j, 0 \rangle, \langle k, j, 1 \rangle)$, but $M$ is not allowed to change from a hypothesis $\langle k, j, 0 \rangle$ to a hypothesis $\langle k, j, 1 \rangle$ or vice versa if no element $d^m$ occurs, because if it would change like this, the path possibly would not be monotonically for $L_k$. More exactly, we define a recursive function $F : \mathbb{N} \times \mathbb{N} \to \mathbb{N}$ as follows. Let $k \in \mathbb{N}$, and let $\tau^k$ be the text

$(a^k b^m)_{n \in \mathbb{N}}$ for $L_k$. When fed $\tau^k$, $M$ outputs a sequence of hypotheses $\perp, \perp, \ldots, \perp$, $\langle k, j_0, v_0 \rangle, \langle k, j_1, v_1 \rangle, \ldots$. Without loss of generality, we may assume that this sequence is infinite.

1. Let $j \in \{0, \ldots, j_0\}$. If $v_0 = 0$, then set $F(k, j) := 2^{j_0 + 1}$. If $v_0 = 1$, then set $F(k, j) := 3^{j_0 + 1}$.
2. Assume that $F$ is defined for all $j \in \{0, \ldots, j_x\}$ for an $x \geq 0$. If $j_{x+1} = j_x$ and $v_{x+1} = v_x$, then do nothing. If $j_{x+1} > j_x$, then define $F$ for $j \in \{0, \ldots, j_{x+1}\}$ like follows.
   - If $v_{x+1} = 0$, then $F(k, j) := 2^{j_{(x+1)} + 1}$.
   - If $v_{x+1} = 1$, then $F(k, j) := 3^{j_{(x+1)} + 1}$.

   If $j_{x+1} < j_x$ or $j_{x+1} = j_x$ and $v_{x+1} \neq v_x$, then define $F$ for $j \in \mathbb{N}$, $j \geq j_x + 1\}$. like follows.

   $$F(k, j_x + 1) := (j_x + 1) - j_{x+1}, \quad \text{and} \quad F(k, j) = 0 \quad \text{for all } j > j_x + 1.$$

It is easy to see that $F$ is recursive, since $M$ is recursive. By applying the Recursion Theorem, we obtain a $k_0 \in \mathbb{N}$ with $\varphi_{k_0}(i) = F(k_0, i)$ for all $i \in \mathbb{N}$. Distinguish the following cases.

1. There is an $i \in \mathbb{N}$ with $i - \varphi_{k_0}(i) \in \{0, \ldots, i-1\}$. By construction, this happens if only if there exists an $x \in \mathbb{N}$ such that $M$ outputs a hypothesis $\langle k, j_{x+1}, v_{x+1} \rangle$ after a hypothesis $\langle k, j_x, v_x \rangle$ with $j_{x+1} < j_x$ or $j_{x+1} = j_x$ and $v_{x+1} \neq v_x$. In both cases, $L_{k_0} \in \mathcal{L}$ by construction. In the first case, $M$ works not monotonically on $(a^{k_0} b^m)_{n \in \mathbb{N}}$, since it outputs the hypothesis $\langle k_0, j_{x+1}, v_{x+1} \rangle$ for a finite language after $\langle k_0, j_x, v_x \rangle$ without the appearance of an element of the form $d^m$ in the text. Since $\langle k_0, j_{x+1}, v_{x+1} \rangle$ describes a language that is "smaller" than the language described by $\langle k_0, j_x, v_x \rangle$ with respect to $L_{k_0}$, $M$ does not work monotonically on $(a^{k_0} b^m)_{m \in \mathbb{N}}$. In the second case, $M$ does not work monotonically on $(a^{k_0} b^m)_{m \in \mathbb{N}}$, since it changes between two hypotheses in a pair $(\langle k_0, j_x, 0 \rangle, \langle k_0, j_x, 1 \rangle)$.
2. $i - \varphi_{k_0}(i) \notin \{0, \ldots, i-1\}$ for all $i \in \mathbb{N}$. Then we have to consider the case where $\varphi_{k_0}(i)$ is not defined for all $i \in \mathbb{N}$, and the case where $\varphi_{k_0}$ is total recursive. In both cases, $L_{k_0} \in \mathcal{L}$. In the first case, by construction, $M$, when fed $(a^{k_0} b^m)_{m \in \mathbb{N}}$, stabilizes on a hypothesis describing a language $L \neq L_{k_0}$. In the second case, $M$ outputs a sequence of hypotheses $(\langle k_0, j_i, v_i \rangle)_{i \in \mathbb{N}}$ with $L_{k_0} \neq L_{\langle k_0, j_i, v_i \rangle}$ for all $i \in \mathbb{N}$.

Thus, $M$ does not $EMON$-identify $\tau$. This contradiction completes the proof of Theorem 5. □

With a similar proof we can show that the same result holds for proper dual-monotonic learning.

**Theorem 6.** $EDMON_{prob}(1) \neq EDMON$

*Proof.* The proof is similar to the proof in the case of proper monotonic learning. Instead of adding identifying elements of the form $d_m$ to the languages, we define descending sets of additional elements, so that the probabilistic machine works dual-monotonic as long as it does not change its hypothesis in a pair $(\langle k, j, 0 \rangle, \langle k, j, 1 \rangle)$.

□

In the case of class preserving and class comprising monotonic probabilistic learning, there is no difference between learning with probability $p = 1$ and deterministic learning.

**Theorem 7.** $MON_{prob}(1) = MON$ and $DMON_{prob}(1) = DMON$.

*Proof.* We only give a sketch of the proof for the case of monotonic probabilistic learning. Let $\mathcal{L} \in MON_{prob}(1)$. Let $P$ be a PIM identifying $\mathcal{L}$ with respect to an appropriate class preserving hypothesis space $\mathcal{G}$. Without loss of generality, we may assume that $P$ is equipped with a two-sided coin (cf. [20]). It is easy to see that we can construct a deterministic machine $M$ that identifies $L$ and never outputs proper supersets of the language to be learned. This follows from the fact that no infinite computation tree may contain proper supersets of the language to be learned.

Now we sketch the definition of a hypothesis space $\mathcal{G}'$ such that $\mathcal{L}$ is monotonically identifiable with respect to $\mathcal{G}'$. Let $s \in \Sigma^*$ be a finite sequence of strings such that $rng(s) \subseteq L$. Let $lenght(s) = x + 1$, and let $h_{x+1}$ be the hypothesis $M$ outputs when fed $s$. Run $P$ with $s$, and set $i_{(x+1,0)} = P^{0^{x+1}}(s)$, and $i_{(x+1,1)} = P^{0^x 1}(s)$. We construct a pair of languages $(L_{(s,0)}, L_{(s,1)})$ like follows. Compare the language $L(G_{h_{x+1}})$ simulteanously with $L(G_{i_{(x+1,0)}})$ and $L(G_{i_{(x+1,1)}})$. Suppose $L(G_{h_{x+1}})$ contradicts $L(G_{i_{(x+1,r)}})$ for an $r \in \{0, 1\}$, and this contradiction is the first contradiction detected while comparing $L(G_{h_{x+1}})$ with the two languages. Then set $L_{(s,0)} = L(G_{i_{(x+1,1-r)}})$ and $L_{(s,1)} = L(G_{i_{(x+1,r)}})$. If no contradiction appears, then $L_{(s,0)} = L(G_{i_{(x+1,0)}})$ and $L_{(s,1)} = L(G_{i_{(x+1,1)}})$. This construction can be performed uniformly recursive, since $\mathcal{G}$ is uniformly recursive. However, it is not decidable whether $L_{(s,r)} = L(G_{i_{(x+1,0)}})$ or $L_{(s,r)} = L(G_{i_{(x+1,1)}})$ for $r \in \{0, 1\}$. Let $L \in rng(\mathcal{L})$, and let $\tau$ be a text for $L$. Since $M$ converges on $\tau$ to a hypothesis correctly describing $\mathcal{L}$, and since there is an $x_0 \in \mathbb{N}$ such that, for all $x \geq x_0$, at least one of the hypotheses in $\{i_{(x,0)}, i_{(x,1)}\}$ is a correct description for $L$, we can conclude that $L_{(\tau_x, 0)} = L$ for almost all $x \in \mathbb{N}$. Moreover, the sequence $(L_{(\tau_x, 0)})_{x \in \mathbb{N}}$, is monotonic. Now we can easily define a hypothesis space with the desired properties.

□

# References

1. A. Ambainis, Probabilistic and Team PFIN-type Learning: General Properties, in *Proc. 9th ACM Conf. on Comp. Learning Theory* (ACM Press, Desenzano del Garda, 1996) 157 – 168.
2. D. Angluin, Inductive Inference of formal languages from positive data, *Information and Control* **45** (1980) 117 – 135.
3. M. Blum, Machine independent theory of complexity of recursive functions, *Journal of the ACM* **14** (1967) 322 – 336.
4. R. Daley, B. Kalyanasundaram, Use of reduction arguments in determining Popperian FIN-type learning capabilities, in: *Proc of the 3th Int. Workshop on Algorithmic Learning Theory*, Lecture Notes in Computer Science **744** (Springer, Berlin, 1993) 173 – 186.

5. R. Daley, B. Kalyanasundaram, M. Velauthapillai, The power of probabilism in Popperian FINite learning, *Proc. of AII*, Lecture Notes in Computer Science **642** (Springer, Berlin, 1992) 151 – 169.

6. R. Freivalds, Finite identification of general recursive functions by probabilistic strategies, in: *Proc. of the Conf. on Fundamentals of Computation Theory* (Akademie-Verlag, Berlin, 1979) 138 – 145.

7. E.M. Gold, Language identification in the limit, *Information and Control* **10** (1967) 447 – 474.

8. J. Hopcroft, J. Ullman, *Introduction to Automata Theory Languages and Computation* (Addison-Wesley Publ. Company, 1979).

9. S. Jain, A. Sharma, Probability is more powerful than team for language identification, in: *Proc. 6th ACM Conf. on Comp. Learning Theory* (ACM Press, Santa Cruz, July 1993) 192 – 198.

10. S. Jain, A. Sharma, On monotonic strategies for learning r.e. languages, *Annals of Mathematics and Artificial Intelligence* (1994, to appear).

11. K.P. Jantke, Monotonic and non-monotonic inductive inference, *New Generation Computing* **8**, 349 – 360.

12. S. Kapur, Monotonic Language Learning, in: S. Doshita, K. Furukawa, K.P. Jantke, eds., *Proc. on ALT'92*, Lecture Notes in AI **743** (Springer, Berlin, 1992) 147 – 158.

13. S. Lange, T. Zeugmann, Types of monotonic language learning an their characterisation, in: *Proc. 5th ACM Conf. on Comp. Learning Theory*, (ACM Press, Pittsburgh, 1992) 377 – 390.

14. S. Lange, T. Zeugmann, Monotonic versus non-monotonic language learning, in: G. Brewka, K.P. Jantke, P.H. Schmitt, eds., *Proc. 2nd Int. Workshop on Nonmonotonic and Inductive Logics*, Lecture Notes in AI **659** (Springer, Berlin, 1993) 254 – 269.

15. S. Lange, T. Zeugmann, Language learning in the dependence on the space of hypotheses, in: *Proc. of the 6th ACM Conf. on Comp. Learning Theory* (ACM Press, Santa Cruz, July 1993),, 127 – 136.

16. S. Lange, T. Zeugmann, S. Kapur, Monotonic and Dual Monotonic Language Learning. *Theoretical Computer Science* **155** (1996) 365 – 410.

17. L. Meyer, Probabilistic language learning under monotonicity constraints, in: K.P. Jantke, T. Shinohara, T. Zeugmann, eds., *Proc. of ALT'95*, Lect. notes in AI **997** (Springer, Berlin, 1995), 169 – 185.

18. L. Meyer, Probabilistic learning of indexed families under monotonicity constraints, *Theoretical Computer Science, Special Issue Alt'95*, to appear.

19. D. Osherson, M. Stob, S. Weinstein, *Systems that Learn, An Introduction to Learning Theory for Cognitive and Computer Scientists* (MIT Press, Cambridge MA, 1986).

20. L. Pitt, Probabilistic Inductive Inference, *J. of the ACM* **36**, 2 (1989) 383 – 433.

21. L. Valiant, A Theory of the Learnable, *Comm. of the ACM* **27**, 11 (1984) 1134 – 1142.

22. R. Wiehagen, A Thesis in Inductive Inference, in: J. Dix, K.P. Jantke, P.H. Schmitt, eds., *Proc. First International Workshop on Nonmonotonic and Inductive Logic*, Lecture Notes in Artificial Intelligence **534** (Springer, Berlin, 1990) 184 – 207.

23. R. Wiehagen, R. Freivalds, E.B. Kinber, On the Power of Probabilistic Strategies in Inductive Inference, *Theoretical Computer Science* **28** (1984), 111 – 133.

24. R. Wiehagen, R. Freivalds, E.B. Kinber, Probabilistic versus Deterministic Inductive Inference in Nonstandard Numberings, *Zeitschr. f. math. Logik und Grundlagen d. Math.* **34** (1988) 531 – 539.

25. T. Zeugmann, S. Lange, A Guided Tour Across the Boundaries of Learning Recursive Languages, in: K.P. Jantke and S. Lange, eds., *Algorithmic Learning for Knowledge-Based Systems*, Lecture Notes in Artificial Intelligence **961** (Springer, Berlin, 1995) 193 – 262.

# Closedness Properties in Team Learning of Recursive Functions [*]

Juris Smotrovs

Institute of Mathematics and Computer Science, University of Latvia, Raiņa bulv.
29, Rīga, LV-1459, Latvia, e-mail: smotrovs@cclu.lv

**Abstract.** This paper investigates closedness properties in relation with
team learning of total recursive functions. One of the first problems
solved for any new identification types is the following: "Does the identifiability of classes $U_1$ and $U_2$ imply the identifiability of $U_1 \cup U_2$?" In
this paper we are interested in a more general question: "Does the identifiability of every union of $n-1$ classes out of $U_1, \ldots, U_n$ imply the
identifiability of $U_1 \cup \ldots \cup U_n$?" If the answer is positive, we call such
identification type $n$-closed. We show that $n$-closedness can be equivalently formulated in terms of team learning. After that we find for which
$n$ team identification in the limit and team finite identification types are
$n$-closed. In the case of team finite identification only teams in which at
least half of the strategies must be successful are considered. It turns out
that all these identification types, though not closed in the usual sense,
are $n$-closed for some $n > 2$.

## 1 Introduction

Gold in [10] introduced the learning paradigm of identification in the limit. He
also proved that in language learning this identification type is not closed under
the set union, i. e. there are such identifiable language families $\mathcal{L}_1$ and $\mathcal{L}_2$ that
$\mathcal{L}_1 \cup \mathcal{L}_2$ is not identifiable. A similar result for the learning of total recursive
functions was obtained independently by Bārzdiņš [5] and the Blums [6]. Since
then many modifications of this identification type were invented, and always
the closedness was among the first properties investigated.

Since it turned out that most of the identification types are not closed, the
idea of team learning was suggested by Case and investigated by Smith [15]:
only one of the given $n$ identification strategies must succeed on each function.
The general case where $m$ out of $n$ strategies must succeed was introduced by
Osherson, Stob and Weinstein [12].

Apsītis, Freivalds et al. showed in [3] that some identification types (for instance, identification in the limit with a bound on mindchanges) that are not
closed nevertheless have a property that much resembles closedness: there exists
such $n$ that, if every union of $n-1$ out of classes $U_1, \ldots, U_n$ is identifiable, then
the union of all $n$ classes is identifiable, too. We shall say that such identification

---

[*] This research was supported by Latvian Science Council Grant No. 93.599.

type is $n$-closed. It was shown in [3] that $n$-closedness determines which sets of requirements put on the identifiability of class unions are satisfiable and which are not. The $n$-closedness problem for identification in the limit with bounds on mindchanges and anomalies was further investigated in [16]; the paper [4] deals with a similar problem in language learning. As we shall see further in this paper, $n$-closedness can be equivalently formulated in terms of learning by a team $n - 1$ out of $n$.

The main intention of this paper is to uncover the $n$-closedness properties of team identification in the limit and team finite identification of total recursive functions. In the case of team finite identification results are presented only for teams '$m$ out of $n$' with $m/n \geq 1/2$ (the complete hierarchy of different learning powers among team finite identification types is still unknown).

The structure of this paper is as follows. Section 2 contains preliminaries. Section 3 introduces $n$-closedness and shows its relation with team learning. Section 4 contains results on $n$-closedness of team identification in the limit, while Section 5 investigates $n$-closedness of team finite identification types. In Section 6 directions for further research are presented.

## 2 Preliminaries

Any recursion theoretic notation not explained below is from [14]. $\mathbb{N}$ denotes the set of natural numbers, $\{0, 1, 2, \ldots\}$. $\langle \cdot, \ldots, \cdot \rangle$ denotes a computable one-to-one numbering of all the tuples of natural numbers. Let $\mathcal{R}$ denote the set of total recursive functions of one argument. For $f \in \mathcal{R}$, $f^{[n]}$ denotes $\langle f(0), f(1), \ldots, f(n) \rangle$.

An identification strategy $F$ is an algorithm that receives in input $f^{[n]}$, an initial segment of the total recursive function to be identified, and outputs either $\bot$ or some natural number — a hypothesis. Informally, $\bot$ means that the strategy has no hypothesis to issue. If $F(f^{[n]}) \neq \bot$, then $F(f^{[m]}) \neq \bot$ for all $m \geq n$. A team of strategies is some finite set of strategies performing identification on one and the same function $f$.

We define an identification type by the following scheme.

1. $\mathcal{I}$-identification is defined as a mapping $\mathcal{M} \to P(\mathcal{R})$, where $\mathcal{M}$ is the set of the subjects performing identification (for instance, the set of strategies or the set of teams of strategies), and $P(\mathcal{R})$ is the set of all the subsets of $\mathcal{R}$; $\mathcal{I}(M)$ is the set of all the functions identified by $M \in \mathcal{M}$;
2. a class of functions $U \subseteq \mathcal{R}$ is considered $\mathcal{I}$-identifiable iff $(\exists M \in \mathcal{M})[U \subseteq \mathcal{I}(M)]$;
3. the identification type is characterized by the set $\mathcal{I} = \{U \subseteq \mathcal{R} \mid U \text{ is } \mathcal{I}\text{-}$ identifiable$\}$.

We will concentrate on two identification types, EX and FIN, and the corresponding team learning identification types. We fix a Gödel numbering of partial recursive functions (cf. [14]) and denote it by $\varphi$.

**Definition 1.** [10] A strategy $F$ EX-*identifies* a function $f \in \mathcal{R}$ ($f \in \text{EX}(F)$) iff $(\exists h, N \in \mathbb{N})[(\forall n \geq N)[F(f^{[n]}) = h] \wedge \varphi_h = f]$.

**Definition 2.** [9] A strategy $F$ FIN-*identifies* a function $f \in \mathcal{R}$ ($f \in \text{FIN}(F)$) iff $(\exists h, N \in \mathbb{N})[(\forall n < N)[F(f^{[n]}) = \bot] \wedge (\forall n \geq N)[F(f^{[n]}) = h] \wedge \varphi_h = f]$.

Team identification was introduced in [15, 12].

**Definition 3.** Let $\mathcal{I}$ be an identification type, $k, l \in \mathbb{N}$, $k \leq l$. A class $U \subseteq \mathcal{R}$ is $\mathcal{I}$-*identifiable by a team* "$k$ out of $l$" (we denote $U \in [k, l]\mathcal{I}$) iff $(\exists M_1, \ldots, M_l \in \mathcal{M})(\forall f \in U)[\text{card}(\{i \mid f \in \mathcal{I}(M_i)\}) \geq k]$.

## 3 $n$-closedness

Here we define $n$-closedness and list some of its properties.

**Definition 4.** [4, 16] An identification type $\mathcal{I}$ is $n$-*closed* ($n \geq 1$) iff

$$(\forall U_1, \ldots, U_n \in \mathcal{I})[(\forall i \mid 1 \leq i \leq n)[ \bigcup_{j=1, j \neq i}^{n} U_j \in \mathcal{I}] \Rightarrow \bigcup_{j=1}^{n} U_j \in \mathcal{I}].$$

So "2-closed" is the same as "closed."

**Proposition 5.** *Let an identification type $\mathcal{I}$ be $n$-closed. Then $\mathcal{I}$ is $m$-closed for all $m \geq n$.*

*Proof.* Suppose $\mathcal{I}$ is $n$-closed, $m \geq n$, and sets $U_1, \ldots, U_m \in \mathcal{I}$ satisfy the property $(\forall i \mid 1 \leq i \leq m)[\bigcup_{j=1, j \neq i}^{m} U_j \in \mathcal{I}]$. Define $V_1 = U_1, \ldots, V_{n-1} = U_{n-1}, V_n = \bigcup_{j=n}^{m} U_j$. We have $\bigcup_{j=1}^{n-1} V_j \in \mathcal{I}$ because $\bigcup_{j=1}^{n-1} V_j \subseteq \bigcup_{j=1}^{m-1} U_j \in \mathcal{I}$. Since $\mathcal{I}$ is $n$-closed, $\bigcup_{j=1}^{n} V_j = \bigcup_{j=1}^{m} U_j \in \mathcal{I}$. □

The last proposition suggests that the $n$-closedness properties can be characterized by the minimal $n$ for which the identification type is $n$-closed.

**Definition 6.** [4, 16] We say that $n$ is *the closedness degree* of an identification type $\mathcal{I}$ ($n = \text{cdeg}(\mathcal{I})$) iff $n$ is the minimal number such that $\mathcal{I}$ is $n$-closed. If such $n$ does not exist, we define $\text{cdeg}(\mathcal{I}) = \infty$.

The next proposition establishes link between $n$-closedness and team learning.

**Proposition 7.** *An identification type $\mathcal{I}$ is $n$-closed iff $[n-1, n]\mathcal{I} = \mathcal{I}$.*

*Proof.* Suppose $\mathcal{I}$ is $n$-closed. Let $U \in [n-1, n]\mathcal{I}$, and let $M_1, \ldots, M_n$ be the team that $[n-1, n]\mathcal{I}$-identifies $U$. We define $U_i = \{f \in U \mid (\forall j \neq i)[f \in \mathcal{I}(M_j)]\}$. Clearly, $(\forall j \mid 1 \leq j \leq n)[\bigcup_{i=1, i \neq j}^{n} U_i \subseteq \mathcal{I}(M_j)]$. Since $\mathcal{I}$ is $n$-closed, $\bigcup_{i=1}^{n} U_i = U \in \mathcal{I}$. So $[n-1, n]\mathcal{I} \subseteq \mathcal{I}$. Obviously, $\mathcal{I} \subseteq [n-1, n]\mathcal{I}$.

Now, suppose $[n-1, n]\mathcal{I} = \mathcal{I}$. Let $U_1, \ldots, U_n$ be such classes that $(\forall j \mid 1 \leq j \leq n)[\bigcup_{i=1, i \neq j}^{n} U_i \in \mathcal{I}]$. Let $M_j$ identify $\bigcup_{i=1, i \neq j}^{n} U_i$. Then the team $M_1, \ldots, M_n$ $[n-1, n]\mathcal{I}$-identifies $\bigcup_{i=1}^{n} U_i$. So $\bigcup_{i=1}^{n} U_i \in \mathcal{I}$. Therefore, $\mathcal{I}$ is $n$-closed. □

**Corollary 8.** *Let $\mathcal{I}$ be an identification type. Then $\text{cdeg}(\mathcal{I}) = n$ iff $n$ is the minimal number for which $[n-1, n]\mathcal{I} = \mathcal{I}$. $\text{cdeg}(\mathcal{I}) = \infty$ iff for all $n \in \mathbb{N}$: $\mathcal{I} \subset [n-1, n]\mathcal{I}$.*

# 4 EX-Identification

In this section we are interested in the $\mathrm{cdeg}([m, n]\mathrm{EX})$ values. The following two theorems show which of the identification types among $[m, n]\mathrm{EX}$ have equivalent learning power and which have not.

**Theorem 9.** [15] $(\forall l \geq 1)[[1, l]\mathrm{EX} \subset [1, l + 1]\mathrm{EX}]$.

**Theorem 10.** [13] $(\forall k, l \mid 1 \leq k \leq l)[[k, l]\mathrm{EX} = [1, \lfloor l/k \rfloor]\mathrm{EX}]$.

The $\mathrm{cdeg}([1, n]\mathrm{EX})$ value follows from the next two theorems. Note that by applying Proposition 7 we use the notion "team of teams."

**Theorem 11.** [2] $(\forall n \geq 1)[\mathrm{cdeg}([1, n]\mathrm{EX}) \leq n + 2]$.

*Proof.* $[n + 1, n + 2][1, n]\mathrm{EX} \subseteq [n + 1, n \cdot (n + 2)]\mathrm{EX} = [1, n]\mathrm{EX}$, so according to Proposition 7 $[1, n]\mathrm{EX}$ is $(n + 2)$-closed. □

**Theorem 12.** $(\forall k, l \mid 1 \leq k \leq l)(\forall n \geq 1)[[k, l][1, n]\mathrm{EX} = [k, ln]\mathrm{EX}]$.

*Proof.* Clearly, $[k, l][1, n]\mathrm{EX} \subseteq [k, ln]\mathrm{EX}$.

Let $m = \lfloor ln/k \rfloor$. Then $[k, ln]\mathrm{EX} = [1, m]\mathrm{EX}$, so for each $[k, ln]\mathrm{EX}$-identifiable class $U$ there are $m$ strategies $F_1, \ldots, F_m$ such that each function from $U$ is identified by at least one of them. We now compose $l$ teams $T_0, \ldots, T_{l-1}$ with $n$ strategies in each. We put $F_i$ for each $i$, $1 \leq i \leq m$, in $k$ teams $T_{ki \bmod l}, T_{ki+1 \bmod l}, \ldots, T_{ki+k-1 \bmod l}$, where $x \bmod y$ for $y > 0$ is the smallest non-negative residue of $x$ modulo $y$. Since $mk \leq ln$, $ln - mk$ vacancies are left; we fill them with $F_1$. Suppose $f \in U$, then $f \in \mathrm{EX}(F_j)$ for some $j$. Therefore at least $k$ teams containing $F_j$ $[1, n]\mathrm{EX}$-identify $f$. Hence $U \in [k, l][1, n]\mathrm{EX}$. We have proved that $[k, ln]\mathrm{EX} \subseteq [k, l][1, n]\mathrm{EX}$. □

**Corollary 13.** $(\forall n \geq 1)[\mathrm{cdeg}([1, n]\mathrm{EX}) = n + 2]$.

*Proof.* According to Theorem 12 $[n, n + 1][1, n]\mathrm{EX} = [1, n + 1]\mathrm{EX} \supset [1, n]\mathrm{EX}$, so $\mathrm{cdeg}([1, n]\mathrm{EX}) > n + 1$. □

Theorem 12 also implies a formula for the learning power of teams of teams.

**Corollary 14.** *Let* $k_1 \leq l_1, \ldots, k_n \leq l_n$ *be positive natural numbers. Then*
$$[k_1, l_1][k_2, l_2] \ldots [k_n, l_n]\mathrm{EX} = [1, \left\lfloor \frac{l_1}{k_1} \cdot \left\lfloor \frac{l_2}{k_2} \cdot \ldots \cdot \left\lfloor \frac{l_n}{k_n} \right\rfloor \ldots \right\rfloor \right\rfloor]\mathrm{EX}.$$

# 5 FIN-Identification

The hierarchy of different learning powers among $[m, n]\mathrm{FIN}$ is still unknown. The results obtained in [1] show that this hierarchy is very complex. We shall concentrate on the more investigated case of $[m, n]\mathrm{FIN}$-identification with $m/n \geq 1/2$.

**Theorem 15.** [8, 7]

1. $(\forall n \geq 1)\left(\forall k, l \mid \frac{n+1}{2n+1} < \frac{k}{l} \leq \frac{n}{2n-1}\right)$ $[[k, l]\text{FIN} = [n, 2n - 1]\text{FIN}]$,
2. $(\forall n \geq 1)[[n, 2n - 1]\text{FIN} \subset [n + 1, 2n + 1]\text{FIN}]$.

**Theorem 16.** [18] $[1, 2]\text{FIN} \subset [2, 4]\text{FIN}$.

**Theorem 17.** [11] $(\forall k \geq 1)[[2k - 1, 4k - 2]\text{FIN} = [1, 2]\text{FIN} \wedge [2k, 4k]\text{FIN} = [2, 4]\text{FIN}]$.

So $[2, 4]\text{FIN}$, $[1, 2]\text{FIN}$ and $[n, 2n-1]\text{FIN}$ with $n \geq 1$ represent all the different learning powers among $[m, n]\text{FIN}$ with $m/n \geq 1/2$. The next theorems establish the cdeg values of these identification types. The first of them is a bit surprising because it shows that for $n$ large enough by taking team '$n - 1$ out of $n$' of $[1, 2]\text{FIN}$-teams instead of usual $[1, 2]\text{FIN}$-team we do not increase the learning power even to $[2, 4]\text{FIN}$.

**Theorem 18.** $\text{cdeg}([1, 2]\text{FIN}) \leq 9$.

*Proof.* It is enough to show that $[1, 2]\text{FIN}$ is 9-closed. Suppose all the unions of 8 out of classes $U_1, \ldots, U_9$ are in $[1, 2]\text{FIN}$. Let $T_1, \ldots, T_9$ be the teams that identify these unions. Each of these teams consists of two strategies. We are going to construct an algorithm $F$ that models strategies $F_1$ and $F_2$ $[1, 2]\text{FIN}$-identifying $\bigcup_{i=1}^{9} U_i$ using these 18 strategies as subroutines.

We shall denote by $h_{j,1}$ the first hypothesis output by any strategy of $T_j$, and by $h_{j,2}$ the hypothesis output by the other strategy from $T_j$, if any.

The algorithm for $F$ is as follows. Receiving $f^{[x]}$ in input $F$ performs $x$ steps in computing the outputs of the strategies on $f^{[0]}, \ldots, f^{[x]}$ and for any hypothesis $h_{j,\alpha}$ computed $F$ performs $x$ steps in computing $\varphi_{h_{j,\alpha}}(0), \ldots, \varphi_{h_{j,\alpha}}(x)$. $F$ switches from stage to stage according to the following scheme.

1. If in eight teams the first hypothesis is produced, $F_1$ outputs $h_1$ based on these eight hypotheses and the 16 strategies of these teams; $F$ does not consider the ninth team anymore; go to stage 2.
2. If $\varphi_{h_1}$ outputs an incorrect value (see the algorithm below) at its stage 1, go to stage 4.
   If the second hypothesis is output in four teams, let $f^{[x_0]}$ be the input segment at which the last of them was discovered; go to stage 3.
3. If $\varphi_{h_1}$ outputs an incorrect value at $x \leq x_0$ in its stage 1, go to stage 4.
   Let $k(x)$ be the amount of the teams in which $F$ has computed both hypotheses at the input $f^{[x]}$. If for some $x_1 > x_0$ the hypotheses of $8 - k(x_1) - 1$ teams among those, in which only one hypothesis has been computed by $F$, output correct values at all points in the interval $[0, x_0]$, then $F_2$ outputs $h_2$ based on the $2k(x_1)$ hypotheses of the teams that produced two hypotheses.
4. The error by $\varphi_{h_1}$ is based on the first hypotheses of four teams. Wait until in three of them the second hypothesis is produced; then $F_2$ outputs $h'_2$ based on the three new hypotheses in the following way: a value is output by $\varphi_{h'_2}$ iff at least two of the three hypotheses output this value.

The algorithm for $\varphi_{h_1}$ follows. $\varphi_{h_1}$ outputs values consequently at points $0, 1, 2, \ldots$, and switches from stage to stage if the events described below happen. After producing output at $x$, $\varphi_{h_1}$ performs $x$ steps in computing the outputs of the 16 strategies on $\varphi_{h_1}^{[0]}, \ldots, \varphi_{h_1}^{[x]}$ and for any hypothesis $h_{j,\alpha}$ computed performs $x$ steps in computing $\varphi_{h_{j,\alpha}}(0), \ldots, \varphi_{h_{j,\alpha}}(x)$. In this way $\varphi_{h_1}$ learns about new hypotheses output by strategies and can simulate the algorithm $F$ (all this in case it has correctly output the values up to $x$). After that $\varphi_{h_1}$ continues computations of $\varphi_{h_{j,\alpha}}$ until it can produce value at $x + 1$.

1. $\varphi_{h_1}$ outputs a value when four of the 8 hypotheses it was based on output one and the same value.
   If both hypotheses have been output in four teams, let us assume they are $T_1, T_2, T_3, T_4$, then go to stage 2.
2. Output a value when three hypotheses from different teams among $T_1, T_2, T_3, T_4$ produce one and the same value.
   If $F$ outputs the second hypothesis $h_2$, go to stage 3.
3. Let us assume that $h_2$ was based on both hypotheses of teams $T_1, \ldots, T_k$, $k \geq 4$.
   If $2 \cdot (k - 1)$ hypotheses from these teams produce one and the same value $y$ and the same values as $\varphi_{h_1}$ at all the previous points, then output $y$.
   If $k - 1$ hypotheses from different teams among $T_1, \ldots, T_k$ produce one and the same value $y_1$ and the same values as $\varphi_{h_1}$ at all the previous points ($y_1$ is output by $\varphi_{h_2}$, see the algorithm below), and after that $k - 1$ other hypotheses from different teams produce other value $y_2$ and the same values as $\varphi_{h_1}$ at all the previous points, then output $y_2$ and go to stage 4.
4. Output a value if $k - 1$ hypotheses from different teams among $T_1, \ldots, T_k$ produce this value and the same values as $\varphi_{h_1}$ at all the previous points.

Now, the algorithm for $\varphi_{h_2}$. Assume that $\varphi_{h_2}$ was based on both hypotheses of teams $T_1, \ldots, T_k$, $k \geq 4$, and that $h_{1,2}, \ldots, h_{4,2}$ were the first hypotheses output among $h_{j,2}$. Let $x_0$ and $x_1$ be as defined in the algorithm for $F$.

1. Output the known values of $f$ for $x \in [0, x_1]$. Simulate $\varphi_{h_{j,\alpha}}(x)$ for $1 \leq j \leq 4$, $\alpha \in \{1, 2\}$, $x_0 < x \leq x_1$ until it is clear if the first value output by three hypothesis functions from different teams is the correct value at each of these points. In other words, we check if $\varphi_{h_1}$ outputs correct values at these points in case it outputs correct values for $x \leq x_0$.
   If some incorrect value appears first at some point, go to stage 3. Otherwise go to stage 2.
2. For each $x > x_1$, wait until at least $k - 1$ hypotheses among $h_{1,1}, \ldots, h_{k,1}$, $h_{1,2}, \ldots, h_{k,2}, k \geq 4$, coming from different teams produce one and the same value $y$ at $x$ and the same values as $\varphi_{h_2}$ at all the previous points. Then output $y$.
3. Three hypotheses among $\varphi_{h_{j,\alpha}}$, $1 \leq j \leq 4$, $\alpha \in \{1, 2\}$, coming from different teams have proved to be incorrect. So by taking the other hypotheses from these teams, we obtain three hypotheses, at most one of which is incorrect.

Thus by outputting the value produced by at least two of these hypotheses $\varphi_{h_2}$ always outputs the correct value.

Let us analyse some cases to prove that the team composed by $F_1$ and $F_2$ identify any $f \in \bigcup_{i=1}^{9} U_i$.

1. *Hypothesis $h_2$ is never output.* There are two alternatives. First, no more than 3 of the 8 teams on whose hypotheses $h_1$ was based output another hypothesis. Hence at least $8 - 3 - 1 = 4$ of these first hypotheses are correct, and $\varphi_{h_1}$ either is defined at all points and equal to $f$ according to stage 1 of its algorithm, or outputs some incorrect value. In the latter case a correct hypothesis $h_2'$ is output.

   The second alternative is that no more than $8 - k - 2$ of the $8 - k$ teams that produce only one hypothesis output correct values at points between 0 and $x_0$. Then at least two teams do not identify $f$, so we have a contradiction.

2. $\varphi_{h_2}$'s *first error is an undefined value.* Suppose we have both hypotheses of $k$ teams. Since at least $k - 1$ teams correctly identify $f$, at least $k - 1$ hypotheses belonging to different teams are total recursive functions equal to $f$. Thus $\varphi_{h_2}$ always has a value to output if its previous values are correct.

3. $\varphi_{h_2}$'s *first error is an incorrect output value at some point $x$.* This incorrect value could be output only at stage 2; it was produced by $k - 1$ hypotheses that output correct values at all the previous points. The $k - 1$ correct hypotheses among the $2k$ considered output correct values at all the previous points *and* at $x$. So there are $k - 2$ teams in which both hypotheses output correct values at the previous points. Hence among the 8 hypotheses on which $h_1$ was based there are at least $(k - 2) + (8 - k - 1) = 5$ hypotheses that produce correct outputs in interval $[0, x_0]$ ($8 - k - 1$ hypotheses being checked by $F$ before producing $h_2$). So $\varphi_{h_1}$ reaches stage 2 of its algorithm. Also, since $\varphi_{h_2}$ reached stage 2, $\varphi_{h_1}$ outputs correct values in the interval $[x_0 + 1, x_1]$ and reaches stage 3. Since $k \geq 4$, we have $3 \cdot (k - 1) > 2k$, so $\varphi_{h_1}$ has at most one alternative to choose from in stages 3 and 4. We have $2k - 2$ hypotheses that output correct values in the interval $[x_1 + 1, x - 1]$, so $\varphi_{h_1}$ outputs correct values in this interval, then produces the correct value at $x$, switches to stage 4, and produces correct values thereafter.

We see that at least one of the hypotheses is correct for $f$. $\qquad\qquad\square$

**Theorem 19.** $\mathrm{cdeg}([1,2]\mathrm{FIN}) > 8$.

*Proof.* It is enough to prove that $[1,2]\mathrm{FIN}$ is not 8-closed. Let the class $V_i$ consist of functions $f \in \mathcal{R}$ that contain among their values exactly one value of kind $\langle i, 1, \cdot \rangle$ and at most one value of kind $\langle i, 2, \cdot \rangle$ such that the third component of at least one of them is a correct Gödel number for $f$. It is easy to see that $V_i \in [1,2]\mathrm{FIN}$. Let $U_i = \bigcap_{j=1, j \neq i}^{8} V_j$, $1 \leq i \leq 8$. Then $\bigcup_{i=1, i \neq j}^{8} U_i \subseteq V_j \in [1,2]\mathrm{FIN}$ for $1 \leq j \leq 8$.

Let $T$ be a team consisting of strategies $F_1$ and $F_2$. Applying multiple recursion theorem (cf. [17]) we can construct functions $\varphi_{n_1}, \ldots, \varphi_{n_{41}}$ that can be described by the following algorithm.

1. Output values as in the next table.

| | 0 | ... | 6 | ... |
|---|---|---|---|---|
| $\varphi_{n_1}, \ldots, \varphi_{n_7}$ | $\langle 1, 1, n_1 \rangle$ | ... | $\langle 7, 1, n_7 \rangle$ | $\langle \rangle$ |

The last column in the table denotes the fact that the corresponding value (in this case $\langle \rangle$) is output one by one for increasing values of argument while the algorithm is in this stage. Let $y_s$ denote the maximal point at which values have been output at the end of stage $s$. Simulate both strategies on $\varphi_{n_1}$. If a hypothesis $h_1$ is produced by one of them, let it be $F_1$, on $\varphi_{n_1}^{[x]}$, then let $x_1 \leftarrow \max(x, y_1) + 1$, and go to stage 2.

2. Output values as in the next table.

| | $x_1$ | $x_1 + 1$ | $x_1 + 2$ | $x_1 + 3$ | ... |
|---|---|---|---|---|---|
| $\varphi_{n_1}, \varphi_{n_2}, \varphi_{n_3},$ $\varphi_{n_8}, \ldots, \varphi_{n_{11}}$ | $\langle 8, 1, n_8 \rangle$ | $\langle 4, 2, n_9 \rangle$ | $\langle 5, 2, n_{10} \rangle$ | $\langle 6, 2, n_{11} \rangle$ | $\langle \rangle$ |
| $\varphi_{n_4}, \ldots, \varphi_{n_7}$ | ? | ? | ? | ? | ? |

Question marks mean that values are not output at these points in this stage. Simulate $\varphi_{h_1}(x_1 + 4)$ and $F_2$ on $\varphi_{n_1}$.
If $\varphi_{h_1}(x_1 + 4) = \langle \rangle$, go to stage 3.
If a hypothesis $h_2$ is produced by $F_2$ on $\varphi_{n_1}^{[x']}$, output the values $\varphi_{n_4}(x), \ldots,$ $\varphi_{n_7}(x)$ so that they are equal to the values $\varphi_{n_1}(x)$ as far as $\varphi_{n_1}$ is defined at the moment, let $x_2 \leftarrow \max(x', y_2) + 1$, and go to stage 5.

3. Output values as in the next table.

| | $x_1$ | $x_1 + 1$ | $x_1 + 2$ | ... |
|---|---|---|---|---|
| $\varphi_{n_4}, \ldots, \varphi_{n_7},$ $\varphi_{n_{12}}, \varphi_{n_{13}}, \varphi_{n_{14}}$ | $\langle 8, 1, n_{12} \rangle$ | $\langle 1, 2, n_{13} \rangle$ | $\langle 2, 2, n_{14} \rangle$ | $\langle 0 \rangle$ |

Simulate $F_2$ on $\varphi_{n_4}$. If a hypothesis $h_2$ is produced by $F_2$ on $\varphi_{n_4}^{[x]}$, let $x_3 \leftarrow \max(x, y_3) + 1$ and go to stage 4.

4. Output values as in the next table.

| | $x_3$ | $x_3 + 1$ | ... | $x_3 + 5$ | ... |
|---|---|---|---|---|---|
| $\varphi_{n_{13}},$ $\varphi_{n_{15}}, \ldots, \varphi_{n_{20}}$ | $\langle 3, 2, n_{15} \rangle$ | $\langle 4, 2, n_{16} \rangle$ | ... | $\langle 8, 2, n_{20} \rangle$ | $\langle \rangle$ |
| $\varphi_{n_{14}},$ $\varphi_{n_{21}}, \ldots, \varphi_{n_{26}}$ | $\langle 3, 2, n_{21} \rangle$ | $\langle 4, 2, n_{22} \rangle$ | ... | $\langle 8, 2, n_{26} \rangle$ | $\langle 0 \rangle$ |

5. Output values as in the next table.

| | $x_2$ | $x_2 + 1$ | $x_2 + 2$ | $x_2 + 3$ | $x_2 + 4$ | ... |
|---|---|---|---|---|---|---|
| $\varphi_{n_4}, \varphi_{n_5},$ $\varphi_{n_{27}}, \ldots, \varphi_{n_{31}}$ | $\langle 1, 2, n_{27} \rangle$ | $\langle 2, 2, n_{28} \rangle$ | $\langle 3, 2, n_{29} \rangle$ | $\langle 7, 2, n_{30} \rangle$ | $\langle 8, 2, n_{31} \rangle$ | $\langle \rangle$ |
| $\varphi_{n_6}, \varphi_{n_9},$ $\varphi_{n_{32}}, \ldots, \varphi_{n_{36}}$ | $\langle 1, 2, n_{32} \rangle$ | $\langle 2, 2, n_{33} \rangle$ | $\langle 3, 2, n_{34} \rangle$ | $\langle 7, 2, n_{35} \rangle$ | $\langle 8, 2, n_{36} \rangle$ | $\langle 0 \rangle$ |
| $\varphi_{n_{10}}, \varphi_{n_{11}},$ $\varphi_{n_{37}}, \ldots, \varphi_{n_{41}}$ | $\langle 1, 2, n_{37} \rangle$ | $\langle 2, 2, n_{38} \rangle$ | $\langle 3, 2, n_{39} \rangle$ | $\langle 7, 2, n_{40} \rangle$ | $\langle 8, 2, n_{41} \rangle$ | $\langle 1 \rangle$ |

*End of the algorithm.*

Let $m$ be the stage in which the algorithm remains forever. If $m = 1$, none of the strategies $F_1$ and $F_2$ produced any hypothesis on $\varphi_{n_1}$. If $m = 2$, $\varphi_{h_1}$ was undefined at $x_1 + 4$, and $F_2$ did not output any hypothesis on $\varphi_{n_1}$. If $m = 3$, $\varphi_{h_1}(x_1 + 4) \neq \varphi_{n_4}(x_1 + 4)$, and $F_2$ did not output any hypothesis on $\varphi_{n_4}$. If $m = 4$, $\varphi_{h_1}$ differs from both $\varphi_{n_{13}}$ and $\varphi_{n_{14}}$ at $x_1 + 4$; and $\varphi_{h_2}$ cannot be equal to both $\varphi_{n_{13}}$ and $\varphi_{n_{14}}$. If $m = 5$, for at least one of the functions $\varphi_{n_4}$, $\varphi_{n_6}$, $\varphi_{n_{10}}$ both hypotheses $h_1$ and $h_2$ are incorrect.

So in each case both $F_1$ and $F_2$ do not identify some function from $\bigcup_{i=1}^{8} U_i$.

$\square$

**Corollary 20.** $\mathrm{cdeg}([1,2]\mathrm{FIN}) = 9$.

The proof of the next theorem is long and use similar methods, so we omit it here.

**Theorem 21.** $\mathrm{cdeg}([2,4]\mathrm{FIN}) = 16$.

The next theorem shows the high level of cooperation needed between the hypotheses and the strategies issuing them usual in such simulation proofs.

**Theorem 22.** $(\forall n \geq 1)[\mathrm{cdeg}([n, 2n-1]\mathrm{EX}_0) \leq 2n + 2]$.

*Sketch of proof.* Suppose all the unions of $2n + 1$ out of classes $U_1, \ldots, U_{2n+2}$ are in $[n, 2n - 1]\mathrm{EX}_0$. Let $T_1, \ldots, T_{2n+2}$ be the teams that identify these unions. Each of these teams consists of $2n - 1$ strategies. We are going to construct an algorithm $F$ that models strategies $F_1, \ldots, F_{2n-1}$ $[n, 2n - 1]\mathrm{EX}_0$-identifying $\bigcup_{i=1}^{2n+2} U_i$ using the $(2n + 2)(2n - 1)$ strategies as subroutines.

We shall denote by $h_{j,i}$ the $i$-th hypothesis output in the team $T_j$, $1 \leq i \leq 2n - 1$. The algorithm $F$ outputs hypotheses as described below.

1. Receiving $f^{[x]}$ in input perform $x$ steps in computing the outputs of the strategies on $f^{[0]}, \ldots, f^{[x]}$ and for any hypothesis $h_{j,i}$ computed perform $x$ steps in computing $\varphi_{h_{j,i}}(0), \ldots, \varphi_{h_{j,i}}(x)$. This is done throughout all stages. Wait until in $2n + 1$ teams $n$ hypotheses are produced. We can assume that they are $h_{j,i}$ for $1 \leq j \leq 2n + 1$ and $1 \leq i \leq n$. Output $h_1$ by $F_1$, $h_2$ by $F_2$, ..., $h_n$ by $F_n$ based on these $(2n+1) \cdot n$ hypotheses. and the $(2n+1)(2n-1)$ strategies of the corresponding teams, discard the $(2n + 2)$-th team (do not consider it anymore), and go to stage 2.

2. Let $k_i(x)$, $1 \leq i \leq n - 1$, be the amount of the teams in which the $(n + i)$-th hypothesis has been output when $F$ has performed all the computations corresponding to the input $f^{[x]}$. Clearly, $k_i(x) \geq k_{i+1}(x)$ for $1 \leq i \leq n - 2$. Let $m$, $n \leq m \leq 2n - 2$, be the number of hypotheses $h_j$ already output. $h_{m+1}$ is output by $F_{m+1}$ at input $f^{[x]}$ if $k_i(x') \geq 2n + 1 - 2i$ for some $i > m - n$ and $x' \leq x$, and in all teams but one it is computed that at least $n$ hypotheses (among those known to $F$ at $f^{[x]}$) output correct values in the interval $[0, x']$.

Now we describe the scheme according to which the hypotheses $h_j$ cooperate. We assign priorities to the hypotheses $h_j$. The hypotheses that are output later have higher priority than those that were output sooner. If the hypotheses were output at the same time, then the lower index, the higher priority. The values are output one by one, at points $0, 1, 2, \ldots$. When $\varphi_{h_j}$ outputs value at some point $x$, it simulates all the $(2n+1) \cdot (2n-1)$ strategies on $\varphi_{h_j}(x)$ and their hypotheses with the same procedure as in $F$. Thus $\varphi_{h_j}$ can keep track of the new hypotheses (unknown when $h_i$ was output), of what hypotheses are output by $F$, and of what values are output by other hypotheses $h_{j'}$.

Let $H$ be one of the sets of hypotheses $h_j$ that have output the same values in the interval $[0, x-1]$. Let $t_i$, $n \le t_i \le 2n-1$ be the amount of hypotheses in the team $T_i$ known to the hypotheses from $H$ when they are computing what to output at $x$. Each value considered for output must satisfy the following condition: for each $i$, $1 \le i \le 2n+1$, except one, this value is output by at least $t_i - n + 1$ hypotheses in $T_i$, and these hypotheses output the same values in $[0, x-1]$ as $\varphi_{h_j}$, $h_j \in H$.

Suppose this condition is obeyed for $l \ge 1$ different values $y_1, \ldots, y_l$. When this fact becomes known for $y_j$, the hypothesis with the highest priority from $H$ that has not output any value at $x$ yet outputs $y_j$. Suppose $m \ge 1$ hypotheses from $H$ have already output $y_j$. If for some $i \ge 0$: in $2n - 2m - 2i$ teams there are $m + i + 1$ hypotheses that output $y_j$ at $x$ and the same values as $\varphi_{h_j}$, $h_j \in H$, in the interval $[0, x-1]$, then the next hypothesis from the priority queue formed in $H$ outputs $y_j$. Note that the first hypothesis that outputs $y_j$ also satisfies this condition with $m = i = 0$.

Naturally, if $h_j$ was output at $f^{[x]}$ for some $x$, then $\varphi_{h_j}$ outputs the known values of $f$ in the interval $[0, x]$ and begins to cooperate with the other hypotheses starting with point $x + 1$.

Now, let us prove that at least $n$ hypotheses among $h_j$ are correct in case $f \in \bigcup_{i=1}^{2n+2} U_i$. Since in this case all teams among $T_1, \ldots, T_{2n+2}$ but one finally output at least $n$ correct hypotheses and since, in the notation of stage 2 of the algorithm for $F$, $k_i(x)$ is a non-decreasing function, we have: if $k_i(x_0) \ge 2n + 1 - 2i$ for some $x_0$, then the needed $x'$ will be found sooner or later. Also, if the hypotheses from $H$ have output the correct values in the interval $[0, x-1]$, then there are at least $t_i - n + 1$ correct hypotheses in the team $T_i$ known to the hypotheses from $H$, for each $i$ from $[1, 2n+1]$ except one.

Let $n + m$ be the total amount of hypotheses $h_j$ output on $f$, $0 \le m \le n-1$, and let $l = n - 1 - m$. Then there are at most $2 \cdot (l - (i - n - m) + 1)$ teams in which at least $i$ hypotheses are produced, $n + m + 1 \le i \le 2n - 1$, and there are at least $2n + 1 - 2l$ teams in which at most $n + m$ hypotheses are produced. Let us denote the set of the latter teams by $S$. At least $2n - 2l$ of the teams from $S$ have at least $n - m$ correct hypotheses among their first $n$ hypotheses. Therefore, according to the conditions on which values are output by $\varphi_{h_j}$, hypotheses $h_j$, $1 \le j \le n$, at each input see sufficient information for $n - m$ hypotheses from the priority queue to output the correct values. When $h_j$, $j > n$, is output, in at least $2n + 1 - 2i$ teams there are at least $n + i$ hypotheses for some $i \geq j - n$. Then at least $2n + 1 - 2l - 2i$ of these teams are in $S$, and among their $n + i$ hypotheses known at the moment there are at least $n + i - m$ correct ones. Therefore, when $j > n$ hypotheses have been output, there is sufficient information for $j - m$ hypotheses from the priority queue to output the correct values. For $j = n + m$ that gives us $n$ correct hypotheses. The only problem is that, when a correct value is to be output, the queue may turn out to be empty. There are two possible reasons for that: some hypotheses might output incorrect values, and some hypotheses might infinitely wait at some previous argument — where less hypotheses are known, and therefore the information is insufficient for another hypothesis to output the correct value.

To show that these possibilities do not occur, let us count how many of $h_j$ can be incorrect due to producing some incorrect value. Since the values at the previous points are checked, one incorrect hypothesis cannot "cheat" the hypotheses $h_j$ twice. Let $p$ be the amount of incorrect values output (for each hypothesis $h_j$ we choose only its first error, if any), and let $s_i$ be the amount of hypotheses among $h_j$ that output the $i$-th incorrect value, $1 \leq i \leq p$. Then, according to the algorithm for $\varphi_{h_j}$, there are at least $2n + 1 - 2(s_i - 1) - 1$ teams in which at least $s_i$ hypotheses output the $i$-th incorrect value. So, there are at least $2n + 1 - \sum_{i=1}^{p}(2s_i - 1)$ teams with $\sum_{i=1}^{p} s_i$ incorrect hypotheses. If $p \geq 1$, that gives us at least $2n + 2 - 2\sum_{i=1}^{p} s_i$ such teams. If $\sum_{i=1}^{p} s_i$ reaches the value $m + 1$, we have at least $2n - 2m$ such teams. In at least $2n - 2m - 1$ of them there are at least $n$ correct hypotheses, so the total amount of hypotheses in each of them is at least $n + m + 1$. But, according to our definitions of $m$ and $l$, the amount of such teams does not exceed $2l = 2n - 2m - 2$. Contradiction. So no more than $m$ of the hypotheses $h_j$ output incorrect values.

We are going to prove that, when $u \geq n$ hypotheses $h_j$ are output, there are at least $u - m$ hypotheses in the priority queue.. Initially $u = n$, there are no more than $m$ of $h_j$ that output incorrect values, and there is sufficient information for $n - m$ hypotheses to output the correct values, so this is true for $u = n$. This can become untrue only if for some $u > n$ there are $u - m$ hypotheses in the priority queue, and one of them outputs an incorrect value at some point $x$. Let it be the $i$-th time when one of $h_j$ outputs an incorrect value. Then, for some $i' \geq 0$, there are $2n + 2 - 2(i + i')$ teams in which $i + i'$ hypotheses output this incorrect value, while at the previous points they output the correct values. $2n + 2 - 2(i + i' + l)$ of these teams are in $S$ (note that $i + i' \leq m$). Then among the first $n$ hypotheses of $2n + 2 - 2(i + i' + l)$ teams from $S$ there are at least $n - m + i + i'$ such that output correct values at least in the interval $[0, x - 1]$. Thus there is sufficient information for at least $n - m + i + i'$ hypotheses $h_j$ to output the correct values up to $x$. Let $i'' \leq i - 1$ be the amount of hypotheses $h_j$ producing incorrect outputs in the interval $[0, x - 1]$. Then at least $n - m + i + i' - i''$ hypotheses among $h_1, \ldots, h_n$ output the correct values until $h_{n+1}$ is produced. As we showed above, that implies there is sufficient information for one more strategy to output correct values, so we have at least $n + 1 - m + i + i' - i''$ hypotheses among $h_1, \ldots, h_{n+1}$ that output correct values until $h_{n+2}$ is produced, etc., we have at least $u - m + i + i' - i''$ hypotheses among $h_1, \ldots, h_u$ that output correct values up to the point $x - 1$ including. At most $i - 1 - i''$ hypotheses have an error at $x$ before the considered error, so at the moment of this error there are at least $u - m + i + i' - i'' - (i - 1 - i'') = u - m + i' + 1 > u - m$ hypotheses in the priority queue. Contradiction.

So, after $h_{n+m}$ is output, at each point there are always at least $n$ hypotheses in the priority queue, and there is sufficient information for at least $n$ hypotheses to output the correct value. Therefore, at least $n$ of $h_j$ are correct hypotheses.

$\square$

**Theorem 23.** $(\forall n \geq 1)[\mathrm{cdeg}([n, 2n - 1]\mathrm{FIN}) > 2n + 1]$.

*Proof.* $n = 1$ yields the class $[1, 1]\mathrm{EX}_0 = \mathrm{EX}_0$ that was considered in [3]. So, we suppose that $n > 1$. It is enough to show that there are such classes $U_1, \ldots, U_{2n+1}$ that the unions of $2n$ classes out of them are identifiable, while $\bigcup_{j=1}^{2n+1} U_j$ is not.

Let the class $V_i$ consist of functions $f \in \mathcal{R}$ that produce the values of kind $\langle i, l, \cdot \rangle$, where $1 \leq l \leq n$, exactly one time, and similar values with $n + 1 \leq l \leq 2n - 1$ at most one time, and the third component is correct in at least $n$ of these values. Then we have $V_i \in [n, 2n - 1]\mathrm{FIN}$. We define $U_i = \bigcap_{j=1, j \neq i}^{2n+1} V_j$, $1 \leq i \leq 2n + 1$. Then $\bigcup_{i=1, i \neq j}^{2n+1} U_i \subseteq V_j \in [n, 2n - 1]\mathrm{FIN}$, $1 \leq j \leq 2n + 1$.

We have to prove that $\bigcup_{i=1}^{2n+1} U_i \notin [n, 2n - 1]\mathrm{FIN}$. By applying the multiple recursion theorem we construct functions $\varphi_{n_i}$ that use each other's Gödel numbers. Let $T$ be an arbitrary team of $2n - 1$ strategies, $F_1, \ldots, F_{2n-1}$.

In the following algorithm for $\varphi_{n_i}$ the procedure $\mathrm{new}(x)$ assigns $x \leftarrow n_c$, and then $c \leftarrow c + 1$, where $c$ is a counter. The algorithm is constructed so that the key functions (on which the team $T$ is simulated) are from $\bigcup_{i=1}^{2n+1} U_i$.

- *Stage 0.*
  Let $c \leftarrow 1$. Execute $\mathrm{new}(s_j^i)$ for $1 \leq i \leq 2n$, $1 \leq j \leq n$. Informally, $s_j^i$ will be used as the $j$-th hypothesis for the $i$-th team. Let $y_i$ indicate the maximal value of argument at which the values have been output at the end of stage $i$. All the functions $\varphi_{s_j^i}$ output $\langle k, l, s_l^k \rangle$ at point $(k - 1) \cdot n + l - 1$ for $1 \leq k \leq 2n$, $1 \leq l \leq n$, and $\langle \rangle$ at further points, until $n$ hypotheses $h_1, \ldots, h_n$ are produced in $T$ on $\varphi_{s_1^i}^{[x]}$. Then let $x_0 \leftarrow \max(x, y_0) + 1$, output $\langle \rangle$ up to $x_0 - 1$, and go to stage 1.
- *Stage 1.*
  Execute $\mathrm{new}(s_{n+1}^i)$ for $1 \leq i \leq 2n - 2$ and $\mathrm{new}(s_j^{2n+1})$ for $1 \leq j \leq n$. The functions $\varphi_{s_j^i}$ with $i \in \{1, \ldots, 2n + 1\} - \{2n - 1\}$, $1 \leq j \leq n - 1$, $\varphi_{s_{n+1}^i}$ with $1 \leq i \leq 2n - 2$, $\varphi_{s^{2n}}$ and $\varphi_{s^{2n+1}}$ output the value $\langle i, n + 1, s_{n+1}^i \rangle$ at point $x_0 + i - 1$ for $1 \leq i \leq 2n - 2$, the value $\langle 2n + 1, j, s_j^{2n+1} \rangle$ at point $x_0 + 2n - 3 + j$ for $1 \leq j \leq n$, and $\langle \rangle$ at further points while in this stage. Suppose hypothesis $h_{n+1}$ is output in $T$ on $\varphi_{s_1^i}^{[x]}$ for some $x$. Then the functions $\varphi_{s_n^i}$ with $1 \leq i \leq 2n - 1$ and $\varphi_{s_j^{2n-1}}$ with $1 \leq j \leq n - 1$ output the values listed above in this stage, let $x_1 \leftarrow \max(x, y_1) + 1$, all the introduced functions output $\langle \rangle$ up to $x_1 - 1$, and go to stage 2.

Suppose all the functions $\varphi_{h_1}, \ldots, \varphi_{h_n}$ output $\langle\rangle$ at $x_0+3n-2$. Then execute new($s_j^i$) for $1 \leq i \leq 2n-2$, $n+1 \leq j \leq 2n-1$, new($s_j^{2n+1}$) for $1 \leq j \leq n$. The functions $\varphi_{s_j^i}$ with $1 \leq i \leq 2n-2$, $n \leq j \leq 2n-1$, $\varphi_{s_j^{2n-1}}$ and $\varphi_{s_j^{2n+1}}$ with $1 \leq j \leq n$ output the value $\langle i, j, s_j^i\rangle$ at point $x_0 + (i-1) \cdot (n-1) + j - n - 1$ for $1 \leq i \leq 2n-2$, $n+1 \leq j \leq 2n-1$, and the value $\langle 2n+1, j, s_j^{2n+1}\rangle$ at point $x_0 + (2n-2)(n-1) + j - 1$ for $1 \leq j \leq n$, and $\langle 0 \rangle$ at all the further points.

- *Stage $m$ $(2 \leq m \leq n-1)$.*
Execute new($s_{n+m}^i$) for $1 \leq i \leq 2n-2m$ and new($s_{n+m-1}^i$) for $2n-2m+3 \leq i \leq 2n+1$. The functions $\varphi_{s_j^i}$ with $i \in \{1, \ldots, 2n+1\} - \{2n-2m+1\}$, $1 \leq j \leq n-1$, $\varphi_{s_j^{2n-2m+2}}$, $\varphi_{s_{n+m}^i}$ with $1 \leq i \leq 2n-2m$, and $\varphi_{s_{n+m-1}^i}$ with $2n-2m+3 \leq i \leq 2n+1$ output the value $\langle i, n+m, s_{n+m}^i\rangle$ at point $x_{m-1}+i-1$ for $1 \leq i \leq 2n-2m$, the value $\langle i, n+m-1, s_{n+m-1}^i\rangle$ at point $x_{m-1}+i-3$ for $2n-2m+3 \leq i \leq 2n+1$, and $\langle\rangle$ at further points while in this stage.

Suppose hypothesis $h_{n+m}$ is output in $T$ on $\varphi_{s_1^1}^{[x]}$ for some $x$. Then the functions $\varphi_{s_n^i}$ with $1 \leq i \leq 2n+1$, $i \neq 2n-2m+2$, $\varphi_{s_j^i}$ with $1 \leq i \leq 2n+1$, $n+1 \leq j \leq n+m-2$, $\varphi_{s_{n+m-1}^i}$ with $1 \leq i \leq 2n-2m+2$, and $\varphi_{s_j^{2n-2m+1}}$ with $1 \leq j \leq n-1$ output the values listed above in this stage, let $x_m \leftarrow \max(x, y_m)+1$, all the introduced functions output $\langle\rangle$ up to $x_m - 1$, and go to stage $m+1$.

Suppose $n$ of the functions $\varphi_{h_1}, \ldots, \varphi_{h_{n+m-1}}$ output $\langle\rangle$ at $x_{m-1}+2n-1$. Then execute new($s_j^i$) for $1 \leq i \leq 2n-2m$, $n+m \leq j \leq 2n-1$, new($s_j^i$) for $2n-2m+3 \leq i \leq 2n+1$, $n+m-1 \leq j \leq 2n-1$. The functions $\varphi_{s_j^i}$ with $i \in \{1, \ldots, 2n+1\} - \{2n-2m+1, 2n-2m+2\}$, $n \leq j \leq 2n-1$, and $\varphi_{s_j^{2n-2m+1}}$ with $1 \leq j \leq n$ output the value $\langle i, j, s_j^i\rangle$ at point $x_{m-1}+(i-1)(n-m)+j-n-m$ for $1 \leq i \leq 2n-2m$, $n+m \leq j \leq 2n-1$, and the value $\langle i, j, s_j^i\rangle$ at point $x_{m-1} + (2n-2m)(n-m) + (i-1)(n-m+1) + j - n - m + 1$ for $2n-2m+3 \leq i \leq 2n+1$, $n+m-1 \leq j \leq 2n-1$, and $\langle 0 \rangle$ at all the further points.

- *Stage $n$.*
Execute new($s_{2n-1}^i$) for $3 \leq i \leq 2n+1$ and new($t_{2n-1}^i$) for $3 \leq i \leq 2n+1$. The functions $\varphi_{s_j^i}$ with $1 \leq i \leq 2n+1$, $1 \leq j \leq n-1$, $\varphi_{s_{2n-1}^1}$, and $\varphi_{s_{2n-1}^i}$ with $3 \leq i \leq 2n+1$ output the value $\langle i, 2n-1, s_{2n-1}^i\rangle$ at point $x_{n-1}+i-3$ for $3 \leq i \leq 2n+1$, and $\langle\rangle$ at all the further points.
The functions $\varphi_{s_j^i}$ with $1 \leq i \leq 2n+1$, $n \leq j \leq 2n-2$, $\varphi_{s_{2n-1}^2}$, and $\varphi_{t_{2n-1}^i}$ with $3 \leq i \leq 2n+1$ output the value $\langle i, 2n-1, t_{2n-1}^i\rangle$ at point $x_{n-1}+i-3$ for $3 \leq i \leq 2n+1$, and $\langle 0 \rangle$ at all the further points.

At stage $m$, $1 \leq m \leq n-1$, if at least $n$ of the hypotheses $h_i$ output the supposedly correct value $\langle\rangle$ at some fixed point, we ensure that they have an anomaly at this point. If no more than $n-1$ of these hypotheses output $\langle\rangle$ at this point, then no more than $n-1$ of them are correct hypotheses, and the team $T$ must issue another hypothesis. In stage $n$ $T$ has already issued the $2n - 1$ allowed hypotheses, and at least $n$ of them are incorrect for one of the alternatives represented by the functions $\varphi_{s_1^1}$ and $\varphi_{s_n^1}$. So in all cases at least $n$ hypotheses issued by $T$ are incorrect.

**Corollary 24.** $(\forall n \geq 1)[\mathrm{cdeg}([n, 2n - 1]\mathrm{FIN}) = 2n + 2]$.

# 6 Conclusion

There are at least two directions for further research. First, the $\mathrm{cdeg}([m, n]\mathrm{FIN})$ values with $m/n < 1/2$ can be found for the known equivalence classes (in the sense of learning power) among these identification types, since $n$-closedness seems to be a natural, set theoretical property characterizing them. Similar research can be done in team language learning, team identification in the limit with a bound on mindchanges, etc. Second, the notion "teams of teams" appeared in some of the proofs in this paper. In the case of EX-identification the situation could be easily characterized by Corollary 14. The case of FIN-identification most probably is not so simple. Maybe teams of teams give some new equivalence classes lying between those of team FIN-identification?

# Acknowledgement

The author thanks the anonymous referees for valuable comments.

# References

1. A. Ambainis. Probabilistic and team PFIN-type learning: general properties. *Proceedings of the Ninth Conference on Computational Learning Theory*, pp. 157–168, ACM, 1996.
2. K. Apsītis. Topological considerations in composing teams of learning machines. In K. Jantke, S. Lange, editors, *Algorithmic Learning for Knowledge Based Systems. LNAI*, vol. 961, pp. 146–154. Springer-Verlag, 1992.
3. K. Apsītis, R. Freivalds, M. Kriķis, R. Simanovskis, and J. Smotrovs. Unions of identifiable classes of total recursive functions. In K. Jantke, editor, *Analogical and Inductive Inference. LNAI*, vol. 642, pp. 99–107. Springer-Verlag, 1992.
4. K. Apsītis, R. Freivalds, R. Simanovskis, and J. Smotrovs. Unions of identifiable families of languages. In L. Miclet, C. de la Higuera, editors, *Grammatical Inference: Learning Syntax from Sentences. LNAI*, vol. 1147, pp. 48–58. Springer-Verlag, 1996.
5. J. Bārzdiņš. Two theorems on the limiting synthesis of functions. In J. Bārzdiņš, editor, *Theory of Algorithms and Programs*, vol.. 1, pp. 82–88. Latvian State University, Rīga, 1974. (In Russian.)
6. L. Blum and M. Blum. Toward a mathematical theory of inductive inference. *Information and Control*, vol. 28, pp. 125–155, 1975.

7. R. Daley, L. Pitt, M. Velauthapillai, and T. Will. Relations between probabilistic and team one-shot learners. In M. Warmuth and L. Valiant, editors, *Proceedings of the 1991 Workshop on Computational Learning Theory,* pp. 228–239, Morgan Kaufmann Publishers, 1991.

8. R. Freivalds. Functions computable in the limit by probabilistic machines. *Lecture Notes in Computer Science,* vol. 28, pp. 77–87, 1975.

9. R. Freivalds and R. Wiehagen. Inductive inference with additional information. *Elektronische Informationsverabeitung und Kybernetik,* vol. 15 (4), pp. 179–184, 1979.

10. E. M. Gold. Language identification in the limit. *Information and Control,* vol. 10, pp. 447–474, 1967.

11. S. Jain and A. Sharma. Finite learning by a team. In M. Fulk and J. Case, editors, *Proceedings of the Third Annual Workshop on Computational Learning Theory,* pp. 163–177, Morgan Kaufmann Publishers, 1990.

12. D. Osherson, M. Stob, and S. Weinstein. Aggregating inductive expertise. *Information and Control,* vol. 70, pp. 69–95, 1986.

13. L. Pitt and C. Smith. Probability and plurality for aggregations of learning machines. *Information and Computation,* vol. 77, pp. 77–92, 1988.

14. H. Rogers, Jr. *Theory of Recursive Functions and Effective Computability.* McGraw-Hill, New York, 1967.

15. C. Smith. The power of pluralism for automatic program synthesis. *Journal of the ACM,* vol. 29, pp. 1144–1165, 1982.

16. J. Smotrovs. Closedness properties in EX-identification of recursive functions. Submitted to the ECML-97 conference, Prague.

17. R. Smullyan. *Theory of Formal Systems. Annals of Mathematical Studies,* vol. 47, Princeton, 1961.

18. M. Velauthapillai. Inductive inference with a bounded number of mind changes. In R. Rivest, D. Haussler, and M. Warmuth, editors, *Proceedings of the 1989 Workshop on Computational Learning Theory,* pp. 200–213, Morgan Kaufmann, 1989.

# Structural Measures for Games and Process Control in the Branch Learning Model
## (Extended Abstract)

Matthias Ott[1] and Frank Stephan[2]

[1]  Institut für Logik, Komplexität und Deduktionssysteme, Universität Karlsruhe,
D-76128 Karlsruhe, Germany, Email: m_ott@ira.uka.de *
[2]  Mathematisches Institut, Universität Heidelberg, D-69120 Heidelberg, Germany,
Email: fstephan@math.uni-heidelberg.de **

**Abstract.** Process control problems can be modeled as closed recursive games. Learning strategies for such games is equivalent to the concept of learning infinite recursive branches for recursive trees. We use this branch learning model to measure the difficulty of learning and synthesizing process controllers. We also measure the difference between several process learning criteria, and their difference to controller synthesis. As measure we use the information content (i.e. the Turing degree) of the oracle which a machine need to get the desired power.

The investigated learning criteria are finite, *EX*-, *BC*-, Weak *BC*- and online learning. Finite, *EX*- and *BC*-style learning are well known from inductive inference, while weak *BC*- and online learning came up with the new notion of branch (i.e. process) learning. For all considered criteria — including synthesis — we also solve the questions of their trivial degrees, their omniscient degrees and with some restrictions their inference degrees. While most of the results about finite, *EX*- and *BC*-style branch learning can be derived from inductive inference, new techniques had to be developed for online learning, weak *BC*-style learning and synthesis, and for the comparisons of all process learning criteria with the power of controller synthesis.

## 1   Introduction

Kummer and Ott [12] have developed a theoretical model of learning winning strategies for closed recursive games [6]. Closed recursive games are games of infinite duration and a special kind of Gale-Stewart games (see e.g. [28]). These kind of games are especially interesting since process control problems can be interpreted as such games [17, 27, 29]. Closed games correspond to control problems with safety conditions, which say that the process may never reach a "bad" state [30]. An example of such a control problem is a temperature controller which has to hold the temperature in a room between $t_{\min}$ and $t_{\max}$.

---

* Supported by the Deutsche Forschungsgemeinschaft (DFG) Graduiertenkolleg "Beherrschbarkeit komplexer Systeme" (GRK 209/2-96).

** Supported by the Deutsche Forschungsgemeinschaft (DFG) grant Am 60/9-1.

Luzeaux, Martin and Zavidovique[16, 18, 19] have developed a different theoretical model of learning to control processes. An advantage of the game approach is that the setting can be shown to be equivalent to branch learning [12]. Here the learner has to find an infinite recursive branch of an infinite recursive tree. This yields a very easy model which allows a clearer theory. A further difference between the two models is that Kummer and Ott use the standard model of data input and the well known learning criteria from inductive inference while Luzeaux et al. introduce new settings for this.

The classical approach to process control is *synthesis* [7]: First, develop a complete mathematical model of the process. From this model compute the corresponding controller. The efforts to write chess programs, for example, can be classified as a synthesis problem, since the rules of the game (i.e. a program for the game tree) are completely known in advance. The synthesis problem has also been investigated theoretically for infinite games, e.g. in [4, 11, 14, 20, 29]. This classical approach fails for the control problems appearing in modern applications from, for example, robotics and manufacturing [2, 15, 22, 31]: E.g. very often the tasks to be controlled are too complex or just not completely known (e.g. robots in unknown environment, a chemical plant where not everything is accessible to measurement or completely modeled, ...) so that a complete mathematical model cannot be developed. Additionally, the synthesis of controllers only works well for more easy control problems. This has led to the application of machine learning techniques in process control [2, 21, 26, 31], taking into account that one can get more and more data over time about the processes to control.

Our concern is the theoretical foundation of these phenomena, i.e. the power of learning in process control, and the comparison of learning and controller synthesis. Here, the game model — or even better the more easy and equivalent branch learning model — allows a rigorous mathematical study of these phenomena. In recursion theoretic terminology controller synthesis is called *uniform computation* (*Uni*). In [12] it was shown that to uniformly compute and to (*EX-*)learn controllers are incomparable tasks. Moreover, there are processes for which one can learn controllers, but it is not possible to learn a complete model of the process, and vice versa. But how big is the gap between learning and uniform computation? Is there a possibility to measure the difference between these two constructive approaches?

In this paper we answer these questions in terms of oracle measures [8, 13]. Oracles improve the power of machines. Which information content do oracles need such the oracle learning machines capture uniform computation, and vice versa? The information content of a oracle is its Turing degree. We study this question for different learning criteria: finite (*FIN-*), *EX-*, *BC-* and Weak *BC-* (*WBC-*) style learning. The above are *offline* versions of learning, i.e. the learner outputs programs intended to control a process. We also study an *online* version of process learning — introduced in [12] — in which the learning machine directly outputs control actions.

Besides the comparison of different criteria — like uniform computation versus learning, or offline versus online learning — we also investigate the classical question of oracle learning: which oracles are trivial, i.e., which oracles do not help; which oracles are omniscient, i.e., which allow to find an infinite recursive branch on every tree which has one; how do the inference degrees look like, i.e., for which $A$ and $B$ does $Crit[A] \subseteq Crit[B]$ hold. (For the meaning of $Crit[A]$ see the definitions below in this paper).

Many learning criteria have direct counterparts in branch learning. The inference degrees of the counterparts of $FIN$ and $EX$ are very similar to the original ones. But this is already different at $BC$: $BC$ has two counterparts ($BranchBC$ and $BranchWBC$) and furthermore the inference-degrees of both are a very different from that of $BC$: Other than $BC$ none of them has a low omniscient oracle and $BranchWBC$ has even only recursive trivial oracles. The new criteria $BranchOnl$ behaves similar as finite learning. For $Uni$ and $BranchWBC$ new techniques had to be developed to answer the above questions.

It is fundamental that uniform computation is not captured by learning, since the identity function is trivially computable, while it is one of the most fundamental problems in function learning (namely, the $REC \in Crit$? problem). This is confirmed by our results providing exact oracle measures: We show for all learning criteria that if it is possible to capture uniform computation by using an oracle, then this oracle has to be very powerful: It is impossible for finite and online branch learning at all. For $EX$- and $BC$-style branch learning we need oracles which are omniscient for this branch learning criteria. And in the case of Weak $BC$-branch learning the oracles have to be omniscient for the class BC in the classical setting of learning functions.

On the other side $EX$-, $BC$- and $WBC$-learning are not included in uniform computation for more involved reasons. We will see that an $\emptyset'$-oracle, which is a whole Turing jump below the omniscient $Uni$-degree, suffice to capture $EX$ and $BC$-style learning. Nevertheless, this also shows that the advantage of learning over computation can be measured to correspond to a whole Turing jump. And weak BC-learning is in fact so powerful that the distance corresponds to two Turing jumps, which means that only omniscient oracles give synthesizing machines as much power.

Many of our results imply the separation of different learning criteria, e.g. $BranchBC$ versus $BranchWBC$. Because, if $Crit_1 \subseteq Crit_2[A]$ only holds for noncomputable oracles $A$, then clearly $Crit_1 \not\subseteq Crit_2$. Thus, by using oracles one gets alternative proofs for several of the separation results in [12]. Interestingly, these proofs are often easier than the direct proofs which do not use oracles. Moreover, the required degree of oracles $A$ with $Crit_1 \subseteq Crit_2[A]$ measures "the clearness" of the noninclusion.

We have already mentioned the technical advantage of the branch learning model [12]. Therefore the body of this paper is written in the terminology of branch learning. The relation between branch, game and process learning is the following: game learning is just a mathematical model of process learning, and branch learning is equivalent to strategy learning for closed recursive games. The following figure shows the correspondence between the different notions:

| Problem: | Process | Game | Tree |
|---|---|---|---|
| **Solution:** | Controller | Strategy | Branch |

The problem of finding infinite recursive branches of recursive trees is of independent interest in recursion theory [6, 23]. In [10] it is studied to which extend (in the sense of so called $k$-selectors) infinite recursive branches of trees can be computed uniformly. This approach was combined with inductive inference in [5]. Here the learner receives input/output examples of $f$ and as additional information an index of a tree $T$ such that $f$ is a branch of $T$.

Due to size constraints we can not include all proofs in this paper. The full paper is available as a technical report [25].

## 2  Notation and Definitions

The natural numbers are denoted by $\omega$. We identify sets $A \subseteq \omega$ with their characteristic function. $\#A$ denotes the cardinality of $A \subseteq \omega$.

We are using an acceptable programming system $\varphi_0, \varphi_1, \ldots$; the function computed by the $e$-th program within $s$ steps is denoted by $\varphi_{e,s}$. $W_e := dom(\varphi_e)$ is the $e$-th recursively enumerable set. We write $W_{e,s}$ for $dom(\varphi_{e,s}) \cap \{0, \ldots, s\}$. $REC$ is the set of all total recursive functions. Turing reducibility is denoted by $\leq_T$. If $A$ is a set, then $A'$ is the halting problem relative to $A$, that is $\{e : \varphi_e^A(e) \downarrow\}$. The halting problem $\emptyset'$ is denoted by $K$. $A$ is *high* iff $K' \leq_T A'$. $A$ is *low* if $A' \leq_T K$. $A$ is called *PA-complete* relative to $B$ if every partial $B$-recursive 0, 1-valued function has a total $A$-recursive extension. For $B \equiv_T \emptyset$ this is equivalent to the original definition which states that $A$ is in the Turing degree of a complete extension of Peano Arithmetic (see [23]).

For strings $\sigma, \tau \in \omega^*$, $\sigma \preceq \tau$ means that $\sigma$ is an initial segment of $\tau$. $|a_1 \ldots a_n| = n$ denotes the length of a string $a_1 \ldots a_n \in \omega^*$. Strings $\sigma \in \omega^*$ are identified with their "code numbers" according to some fixed coding $\langle \cdot \rangle$ of $\omega^*$, which satisfies $(\forall \sigma, \tau)[\sigma \preceq \tau \implies \langle \sigma \rangle \leq \langle \tau \rangle]$. Total Functions $f : \omega \to \omega$ are identified with the infinite string $f(0)f(1)\ldots$. We write $f \lceil n$ for the string $f(0) \ldots f(n-1)$.

$T \subseteq \omega^*$ is a *tree* if $T$ is closed under initial segments. If $T \subseteq \{0, 1\}^*$ then T is called a *binary* tree. Elements of a tree are called *nodes*. If $M \subseteq \omega^* \cup \omega^\omega$ is a set of finite and infinite strings, then the prefix closure $Pref(M) := \{\sigma \preceq \alpha : \alpha \in M\}$ is a tree. We often will define trees by only specifying such a set $M$. $\alpha \in \omega^\omega$ is an infinite branch of $T$, if $\{\sigma : \sigma \preceq \alpha\} \subseteq T$.

In this paper we are only interested in the class $TREE$ of all recursive trees which have an infinite recursive branch. Note that according to our conventions an infinite recursive branch of $T$ is just an recursive function $f$ with $\{f \lceil n : n \in \omega\} \subseteq T$.

The branch learning model in [12] uses binary trees. One can show that the theory remains the same if it is based on recursive trees over $\omega$:

**Theorem 1.** *For all criteria $Crit_1, Crit_2$ which we consider in this paper and all oracles $A, B$, if $Crit_1[A] \not\subseteq Crit_2[B]$, then there is a class of recursive binary trees witnessing this fact.*

Since we have discovered that it makes the proofs in this paper more simple, we base the definitions on arbitrary trees.

*EX*, *FIN*, and *BC* denote the classes of sets $S \subseteq REC$ which are identifiable by explanation, finitely identifiable by explanation and behaviorally correctly identifiable, respectively. The exact definitions for the different learning criteria are the direct counterparts to those given shortly in the context of branch learning. For background from inductive inference see e.g. [3, 8, 9, 24]. Remaining recursion theoretic notation is from [23].

## 3   Finite and Online Branch Learning

At first we define the notion of branch learning machines [12]. In the world of process control you may think of a learner which has two copies of the process to control. The first one is for experimentation ($P_E$) the second for application of the guessed controllers. We are considering machines without time and space bounds. Therefore we can assume that the machine may in the limit try all possible action sequences infinitely often on $P_E$. A sensor signals the respond of $P_e$ to the learner. $P_E$ may respond in different ways on the same action sequence due to indeterminism or disturbance by the environment. As a kind of fairness condition we assume that as long as there are possible respond sequences these will eventually appear. As a consequence we can assume that the learner gets an enumeration of all action/respond-sequences as input.

This assumption may seem a little bit strong, since the learner gets in the limit the whole information about the process. But note that the main content of our theorems is that something is *not* learnable. Thus, the significance of these results even grow if we base them on this strong input model.

While games such as chess and Go have finite game trees, these game trees are too large for exhaustive search. Thus, one has to come up with a strategy by only inspecting some part of the game tree. Similarly, the following definitions fix the question whether one can find a controller by only inspecting a finite amount of the process' behaviour (i.e. the corresponding infinite game tree).

We emphasize again that by the equivalence theorems in [12] in the following definitions the infinite recursive trees correspond to control problems (or infinite games), and the infinite recursive branches to the correct controllers (or winning strategies).

**Definition 2.** As learner we consider Turing machines $M^A$ which have access to an oracle $A$ and converge for every oracle and every input. These machines are intended to learn an infinite recursive branch of a tree $T \in TREE$. As input we feed the characteristic function of $T$ into $M^A$ such that $M^A$ outputs a sequence of guesses $h_0 h_1 \ldots$, where each $h_n$ is computed from $T{\upharpoonright}n$, i.e., $h_n = M^A(T{\upharpoonright}n)$. The guesses $h_n$ should describe some infinite recursive branch of $T$ according to the given learning criterion. The machine may also output a special symbol "?" to indicate that it has yet not seen enough data to make up its mind.

In the offline versions of branch learning (e.g. *BranchFin* below) the output of the learner is interpreted as a program for an infinite recursive branch of $T$, while in the online version the output is directly interpreted as nodes of an infinite recursive branch of $T$:

**Definition 3.** $M^A$ *finitely A-branch learns* a tree $T$ if on input $T$ the machine $M^A$ produces a sequence of guesses $?\ldots?eee\ldots$ such that $\varphi_e$ is an infinite recursive branch of $T$.

A class of trees $C$ is *finitely A-branch learnable* ($C \in BranchFin[A]$) if there is a machine $M^A$ which finitely branch learns every $T \in C$.

We write *BranchFin* for *BranchFin*$[\emptyset]$. Analogously, for the other criteria considered in this paper we write *Crit* instead of *Crit*$[\emptyset]$.

**Definition 4.** $M^A$ *online A-branch learns* a tree $T$ if on input $T$ the machine $M^A$ produces a sequence of guesses $?\ldots?b_0?\ldots?b_1?\ldots$ such that $b_0 b_1 \ldots$ is an infinite recursive branch of $T$. We will say that the machine *enumerates* the branch $b_0 b_1 \ldots$.

A class of trees $C$ is *finitely A-online learnable* ($C \in BranchOnl[A]$) if there is a machine $M^A$ which online branch learns every $T \in C$.

The following observation holds for all criteria which we consider in this paper, since queries to an oracle $A$ can be simulated by any oracle $B \geq_T A$. But we only state it explicitly for *BranchOnl*:

**Fact 5.** $A \leq_T B \implies BranchOnl[A] \subseteq BranchOnl[B]$.

From [12] we know that *BranchFin* $\subset$ *BranchOnl*. The following theorems show that this relation relativizes. This also indicates that online learning behaves in some sense similar as finite learning.

**Theorem 6.** $BranchFin[A] \subseteq BranchOnl[B] \iff A \leq_T B$.

*Proof.* Assume $A \leq_T B$ and $C \in BranchFin[A]$ via $M^A$. Then the following procedure online $A$-branch learns every $T \in C$ which implies $C \in BranchFin[B]$ by Fact 5: On input $T\restriction 0, T\restriction 1, \ldots$ wait until $M^A$ outputs it's first real guess $e$. Then enumerate the branch $\varphi_e$.

For the other direction consider the class of trees

$$C := \{xT \colon T \in TREE \land A(x)^\omega \text{ is an infinite branch of } T\}.$$

Clearly, $C \in BranchFin[A]$: Having seen $x$ output a program for $xA(x)^\omega$. Now assume that $C$ is in $BranchOnl[B]$ via $M^B$. We claim that the following procedure decides $A$ in $B$: On input $x$ apply the tree $T := x(0^\omega + 1^\omega)$ to $M^B$. Wait until $M^B$ enumerates the second node $b_1$. Output $b_1$.

Since $T \in C$ the machine $M^B$ will eventually enumerate a second node $b_1$. Then the output $b_1$ is correct, i.e. $b_1 = A(x)$: Otherwise $M^B$ would fail on some tree $x((1 - A(x))^n + A(x)^\omega)$ which is in $C$. $\square$

From Theorem 6 it follows that *BranchOnl* has no omniscient degree. Moreover, the *BranchFin* and *BranchOnl* inference degrees coincide with the Turing degrees:

**Corollary 7.** $A \leq_T B \iff BranchFin[A] \subseteq BranchFin[B] \iff$
$BranchOnl[A] \subseteq BranchOnl[B]$.

Thus, like online learning, *BranchFin* has also no omniscient degree, and the trivial degree of *BranchFin* and *BranchOnl* is the degree of $\emptyset$.

In contrast to Theorem 6 there is no oracle $A$ such that *BranchFin*[A] captures *BranchOnl*. This demonstrates that besides some similarities online learning is still a much more powerful concept than finite learning:

**Definition 8.** For $f \in REC$ let $T_f := \{f(0)f(1)\ldots\}$ be the tree which consists exactly of the infinite branch $f$.

**Theorem 9.** *BranchOnl* $\not\subseteq$ *BranchFin*[A] *for all* $A \subseteq \omega$.

*Proof.* The theorem follows from inductive inference since $\{T_f : f \in REC\}$ is in *BranchOnl*: Given $T{\upharpoonright}(n+1)$ such that $n$ codes the string $b_0 \ldots b_k$, enumerate $b_k$ if $T(n) = 1$, otherwise enumerate "?". But from $\{T_f : f \in REC\} \in BranchFin[A]$ it follows that $REC \in FIN[A]$ which is known to be impossible. □

## 4  Uniform Computation

In this section we study the synthesis of controllers from complete models of the processes:

**Definition 10.** Infinite recursive branches can be *computed uniformly in* $A$ for a class $\mathcal{C} \subseteq TREE$ ($\mathcal{C} \in Uni[A]$), if there is a partial $A$-recursive function $g$ such that
$$(\forall e)(\forall T \in \mathcal{C})[T = \varphi_e \implies g(e) \downarrow \wedge \varphi_{g(e)} \text{ is an infinite branch of } T].$$

In [12] it was shown that *BranchOnl* is strictly included in *Uni*. We now prove that it is impossible to overcome this gap by any oracle $A$. For the proof we introduce certain families of trees which will also be used later in this paper:

**Definition 11.** For $f \in REC$ we define the tree
$$R_f := \{ef(e)a_0a_1 \ldots a_n : (\forall m \leq n)[a_m = \mu s[\varphi_{e,s}(m) \downarrow = f(m)]]\}.$$

For $S \subseteq REC$ we set $\mathcal{B}(S) := \{R_f : f \in S\}$. Note, that $eb$ is in $R_f$ iff $b = f(e)$.

**Lemma 12.** *For every* $f$ *the tree* $R_f$ *is recursive and has infinite recursive branches extending* $e$ *iff* $\varphi_e = f$. *Indices for* $f$, $R_f$ *and infinite recursive branches of* $R_f$ *can be computed uniformly from each other. Moreover, enumerations of* $f$ *and* $R_f$ *can be translated effectively into each other, i.e., there are computable functions* $g_1, \ldots, g_4$ *such that* $f(n) = g_1(R_f{\upharpoonright}g_2(n))$ *and* $R_f(n) = g_3(f{\upharpoonright}g_4(n))$.

**Theorem 13.** *Uni $\not\subseteq$ BranchOnl[A] for all $A \subseteq \omega$.*

*Proof.* From Lemma 12 it follows that $\mathcal{B}(REC)$ is in *Uni*. If $\mathcal{B}(REC)$ were in *BranchOnl[A]* via $M^A$ then *REC* would be in *FIN[A]* by the following algorithm, which yields a contradiction: From the input $f(0)f(1)\ldots$ compute an enumeration of $R_f$ and feed it into $M^A$. Wait until $M^A$ enumerates the first node $b_0$ of an infinite recursive branch of $R_f$. Output $b_0$. By Lemma 12 the output $b_0$ is an index of $f$. $\qquad\square$

Compared to *BranchFin[A]*, uniform computation behaves similar as online learning, at least for $A \leq_T K$:

**Theorem 14.** *For all $A \leq_T K$: BranchFin[A] $\subseteq$ Uni[B] $\iff$ $A \leq_T B$.*

*Proof.* The proof of *BranchFin $\subseteq$ Uni* in [12] relativizes for $A \leq_T B$.

So, it remains to show the *only if* part. Since $A \leq_T K$, by the Limit Lemma there exists a computable $u : \omega^2 \to \omega$ such that $A = \lambda x.\lim_{s\to\infty} u(x,s)$. Consider the class $\mathcal{C}$ of all trees $T_x$ where

$$T_x := \{xia_0a_1\ldots a_n : i \in \{0,1\} \wedge a_0 < a_1 < \ldots < a_n \wedge$$
$$(\forall m \leq n)[u(x, a_m) = i]\}.$$

Obviously, $\mathcal{C}$ is in *BranchFin[A]*. Now assume $\mathcal{C} \in Uni[B]$ via some partial $B$-recursive function $g$. We choose an $h \in REC$ with $T_x = \varphi_{h(x)}$ for all $x$. Then $\lambda x.\varphi_{g(h(x))}(1)$ decides $A$ relative in $B$. $\qquad\square$

The omniscient degree of *Uni* has already been solved in [12]:

**Fact 15.** *TREE $\in$ Uni[A] $\iff$ $A \geq_T K'$.*

The more difficult part ($\Rightarrow$) follows also from Theorem 33 below.

A corollary of Theorem 14 is that the degree-structure of *Uni* below $K$ co-incides with the Turing degrees:

**Corollary 16.** *For all $A \leq_T K$: Uni[A] $\subseteq$ Uni[B] $\iff$ $A \leq_T B$.*

This result can even be strengthened to the following Theorem:

**Theorem 17.** *1. Uni[A] = Uni $\iff$ A recursive.*
*2. If $B \not\geq_T K$ then: Uni[A] $\subseteq$ Uni[B] $\iff$ $A \leq_T B$.*
*3. For all $A, B \geq_T K$: Uni[A] $\subseteq$ Uni[B] $\iff$ $A \leq_T B$ or $B \geq_T K'$.*

In summary, except the case $A|_T K \wedge B \geq_T K$, we were able to prove that *Uni[A] $\subseteq$ Uni[B]* iff $A \leq_T B$ or $B \geq_T K'$. The following theorem shows that this proposition indeed does not hold for arbitrary $A, B$:

**Theorem 18.** *There are oracles $A$ and $B$ not above $K'$ such that Uni[A] $\subseteq$ Uni[B] but $A \not\leq_T B$. In fact, even $A \not\leq_T B'$ can be achieved.*

From Theorems 6 and 14 we get:

**Corollary 19.** *For all $A \leq_T K$: $BranchOnl[A] \subseteq Uni[B] \implies A \leq_T B$.*

We will now show that the other direction in Corollary 19 does not hold in general, i.e. that the inclusion $BranchOnl \subseteq Uni$ from [12] does not relativize. The intuitive reason is that the $Uni$-machine can only ask finitely many queries to its oracle while the $BranchOnl$-machine may ask infinitely many queries during the enumeration of a branch.

**Theorem 20.** *For all PA-complete $A$: $BranchOnl[A] \subseteq Uni[B] \iff K' \leq_T B$, i.e. $TREE \in Uni[B]$.*

*Proof.* Kummer and Stephan [13] have constructed a family of $0, 1$-valued functions $\{\varphi_{g(i)}\}_{i \in \omega}$ $(g \in REC)$ such that

- $1^i 0 \preceq \varphi_{g(i)}$,
- $\varphi_{g(i)}(x)$ is undefined for at most one $x$,
- if $W_i$ is finite and $\varphi_e$ is a total extension of $\varphi_{g(i)}$ then $e \geq \#W_i$.

For every $i$ we define a recursive *binary* tree $T_i$ according to

$$T_i := \{a_0 \ldots a_n : 1^i 0 \preceq a_0 \ldots a_n \land (\forall m \leq n)[\neg(\varphi_{g(i),n}(m) \downarrow \neq a_m)]\}.$$

Note that the only infinite recursive branches of $T_i$ are the total recursive $0, 1$-valued extensions of $\varphi_{g(i)}$.

Since $A$ is PA-complete there is a $0, 1$-valued total $A$-recursive $h$ such that with $\{\tau \in T_i : \sigma \preceq \tau\}$ the set $\{\tau \in T_i : \sigma h(i, \sigma) \preceq \tau\}$ is also infinite, for all $\sigma$. $\mathcal{C} := \{T_i : i \in \omega\}$ is in $BranchOnl[A]$ via the machine $M^A$ which simply follows the $A$-recursive function $h$ after it has decoded $i$ from the beginning of the input tree.

Assume now that $\mathcal{C}$ is in $Uni[B]$ via some partial $B$-recursive function $\psi$. Then the index set $Inf := \{i \in \omega : W_i \text{ infinite}\}$ is r.e. in $B$, since $Inf = \{i : (\exists s)[\#W_{i,s} > \psi(u(i))]\}$ where $u \in REC$ with $(\forall i)[T_i = \varphi_{u(i)}]$. Note, that $range(u) \subseteq dom(\psi)$. If $W_i$ is infinite then clearly there is an $s$ with $\#W_{i,s} > \psi(u(i))$. And if there exists an $s$ with $\#W_{i,s} > \psi(u(i))$ then $W_i$ must be infinite since $\varphi_{\psi(u(i))}$ is a total extension of $\varphi_{g(i)}$.

$Inf$ is $\Pi_2$-complete and thus the halting problem $K$ and its complement are both $m$-reducible to $Inf$. So $K$ and its complement are enumerable relative to $B$ and thus $K \leq_T B$. So the set $Fin = \{i : W_i \text{ finite}\}$ is not only enumerable relative to $K$ but also relative to $B$. Since $Fin$ is the complement of $Inf$, it follows that $Inf$ is computable relative to $B$, i.e. $K' \equiv_T Inf \leq_T B$. □

## 5    EX-style Branch Learning

Of course, finite learning is a very restricted kind of learning. The learner gets more power if he only has to (syntactically) learn a controller *in the limit* [9]:

**Definition 21.** $M^A$ $EX[A]$-*branch learns* a tree $T$ if on input $T$ the machine $M^A$ produces a sequence of guesses $h_0 h_1 \ldots h_n eee \ldots$ such that $\varphi_e$ is an infinite recursive branch of $T$.

A class of trees $\mathcal{C}$ is $EX[A]$-*branch learnable* ($\mathcal{C} \in BranchEx[A]$) if there is a machine $M^A$ which $EX[A]$-branch learns every $T \in \mathcal{C}$.

The following results can be obtained by modifying the proofs from the corresponding results in inductive inference [1, 8, 13]. As in [8] we write $\mathcal{G}(A)$ if $A \leq_T G \leq_T K$ for some 1-generic set $G$, i.e. if $A$ is either recursive or has the same degree as a 1-generic Turing degree below $K$.

**Fact 22.** *1.* $A \leq_T K \implies BranchFin[A] \subset BranchEx$.
*2. For all $A$: $BranchEx_1 \not\subseteq BranchFin[A]$, where $BranchEx_1$ means $EX$-branch learnable with at most one mind change.*
*3. $BranchEx[A] = BranchEx \iff \mathcal{G}(A)$.*
*4. $TREE \in BranchEx[A] \iff A$ is high.*
*5. For all r.e. $A$: $BranchEx[A] \subseteq BranchEx[B] \iff A \leq_T B$ or $B$ is high.*

From [12] we know that $BranchEx$ is incomparable with $BranchOnl$ and $Uni$. In analogy to the case of $Uni$ (Theorem 13) it is also impossible to capture $BranchEx_1$ by $BranchOnl[A]$ for any oracle $A$:

**Theorem 23.** *For all $A$: $BranchEx_1 \not\subseteq BranchOnl[A]$.*

*Proof.* Consider the class $\mathcal{C} := \{T \in TREE : 0^\omega$ or $1^\omega$ is a branch of $T\}$. $\mathcal{C}$ is in $BranchEx_1$: output a program for $0^\omega$ until you find an $m$ with $0^m \notin T$. Then output a program for $1^\omega$.

But a $BranchOnl[A]$-learner $M^A$ for $\mathcal{C}$ will eventually output a first node on input $0^n + 1^n$ because $0^\omega + 1^\omega \in \mathcal{C}$. This node will be the same for $0^n + 1^\omega$ and $0^\omega + 1^n$. Thus, on one of the two trees $M^A$ fails to enumerate an infinite recursive branch. $\square$

It is fundamental that $Uni$ and $BranchOnl$ are not included in $BranchEx$: The class $\{T_f : f \in REC\}$ (see Definition 8) is in $Uni \cap BranchOnl$ but not in $BranchEx$ since $REC$ is not in $EX$. This fundamental difference between learning in the limit on the one side and online learning and uniform computation on the other side is emphasized by the following result, which shows that only omniscient oracles enable $BranchEx$ to overcome this difference.

**Theorem 24.** $Uni \subseteq BranchEx[A] \iff BranchOnl \subseteq BranchEx[A] \iff$ $A$ *is high.*

*Proof.* If $A$ is high then $Uni \subseteq BranchEx[A] = TREE$ by Fact 22.4 and if $Uni \subseteq BranchEx[A]$ then $BranchOnl \subseteq BranchEx[A]$ since $BranchOnl \subset Uni$ [12]. Finally, if $BranchOnl$ is included in $BranchEx[A]$ then $\{T_f : f \in REC\}$ is in $BranchEx[A]$. This implies $REC \in EX[A]$ and thus $A$ high [8]. $\square$

On the other side there are $EX$-branch learnable classes of trees for which infinite recursive branches cannot be computed uniformly. But in contrast to Theorem 24 $Uni$ does not need an omniscient oracle to capture $BranchEx$:

**Corollary 25.** *BranchEx* $\subseteq$ *Uni*$[A]$ $\iff$ $K \leq_T A$.

*Proof.* If *BranchEx* $\subseteq$ *Uni*$[A]$ then *BranchFin*$[K]$ $\subseteq$ *Uni*$[A]$ (Fact 22.1) which implies $K \leq_T A$ by Theorem 14. The other direction follows from [12, Proposition 19]. $\qquad\square$

## 6 BC- and Weak BC-style Branch Learning

In contrast to $EX$-style learning in $BC$-style learning the learner has only to converge *semantically* to a correct controller. Note, that there may be many correct controllers. This is the reason why there are two notions of $BC$-style branch learning, while there exists only one notion of $BC$-style function learning.

**Definition 26.** $M^A$ $BC[A]$-*branch learns* a tree $T$ if on input $T$ the machine $M^A$ produces a sequence of guesses $h_0 h_1 \ldots$ such that there is an infinite recursive branch $f$ of $T$ with $\varphi_{h_n} = f$ for almost all $n$.

$M^A$ *weakly* $BC[A]$- or $WBC[A]$-*branch learns* $T$ if $\varphi_{h_n}$ is an infinite recursive branch of $T$ for almost all $n$.

$\mathcal{C} \in BranchBC[A]$ and $\mathcal{C} \in BranchWBC[A]$ for classes $\mathcal{C} \subseteq TREE$ are defined similar to the previous definitions (e.g. $\mathcal{C} \in BranchEx[A]$ in Definition 21).

As in the case of finite versus $EX$-style branch learning it follows directly from $EX \subset BC$ that *BranchEx* $\subset$ *BranchBC*. The weak version of $BC$-style learning does not appear in classical inductive inference since there is only one target object — namely the input object itself. It was proven in [12] that *BranchBC* $\subset$ *BranchWBC*.

For the omniscient $BC$ degrees there is no nice characterization known in inductive inference. And the results in [8] suggest that there exists no nice one. Therefore it is remarkable that such a characterization exists for *BranchBC* and *BranchWBC*:

**Theorem 27.** $A$ *is high* $\iff$ $TREE \in BranchBC[A]$ $\iff$ $TREE \in BranchWBC[A]$.

*Proof.* Fact 22.4 already states: If $A$ is high then $TREE \in BranchEx[A]$. Since the inclusion *BranchEx* $\subseteq$ *BranchBC* $\subseteq$ *BranchWBC* relativizes to $A$, any high oracle is omniscient for BranchBC and BranchWBC, too. The trees from [12, Proposition 21] can be used to prove the reverse directions. $\qquad\square$

We now summarize the facts which follow from results in inductive inference by modifications of the corresponding proofs [8, 13]:

**Fact 28.** *1. $A$ high $\iff$ BranchBC $\subseteq$ BranchEx$[A]$.*
*2. BranchEx$[A]$ $\subseteq$ BranchBC $\iff$ $\mathcal{G}(A)$.*
*3. BranchBC$[A]$ = BranchBC $\iff$ $\mathcal{G}(A)$.*
*4. For all r.e. $A, B$: BranchBC$[A]$ $\subseteq$ BranchBC$[B]$ $\iff$ $A \leq_T B$ or $B$ high.*

In Theorem 24 we have seen that we need omniscient oracles $A$ to capture $Uni$ and $BranchOnl$ by $BranchEx[A]$. The following result shows that oracles $A$ with $REC \in BC[A]$ suffices to capture $BranchOnl$ by $BranchBC[A]$ and both, $BranchOnl$ and $Uni$, by $BranchWBC[A]$. This demonstrates the power of $BC$ and even more the power of $BranchWBC$ (capturing both), since only high oracles are omniscient for $BranchBC$ and $BranchWBC$ (Theorem 27) — but there are low sets $A$ with $REC \in BC[A]$ ([8]).

**Theorem 29.** *The following are equivalent:*

*(1)* $REC \in BC[A]$,
*(2)* $BranchOnl \subseteq BranchBC[A]$,
*(3)* $BranchOnl \subseteq BranchWBC[A]$,
*(4)* $Uni \subseteq BranchWBC[A]$.

*Proof of (1)* $\Rightarrow$ *(4).* Assume $C \in Uni$ via a total function $g$. On input $T \in C$ we $BC[A]$-learn an index for $T$, say by the sequence of guesses $h_1 h_2 \ldots$. Then $g(h_1)g(h_2)\ldots$ is a sequence of guesses such that almost all compute an infinite recursive branch of $T$. $\square$

Note that in the proof of $(1) \Rightarrow (4)$ we can not conclude $Uni \subseteq BranchBC$ since the sequence $h_1, h_2, \ldots$ may converge to different indices for $T$, and the branch computed by $g$ may depend on the indices for $T$, which $g$ receives as input.

The following theorem shows that we actually need an omniscient oracle $A$ to capture $Uni$ by $BranchBC[A]$. This gives a measure for the advantage of $WBC$-style over $BC$-style branch learning. This advantage of $WBC$-style over $BC$-style branch learning is additionally demonstrated by the result that for capturing $BranchWBC$ by $BranchBC[A]$ also an omniscient oracle $A$ is needed. As a corollary we get the existence of classes in $Uni$ such that the uniform computation of branches depends on the index of the input tree.

**Theorem 30.** *$A$ is high* $\Longleftrightarrow$ *$Uni \subseteq BranchBC[A]$* $\Longleftrightarrow$ *$BranchWBC \subseteq BranchBC[A]$.*

*Proof.* Since high oracles are omniscient for $BranchBC$ (Theorem 27) we only have to show that $Uni \subseteq BranchBC[A]$ and $BranchWBC \subseteq BranchBC[A]$ imply $A$ high.

Assume that $A$ is not high. Then there is a family of recursive functions $S \in BC - EX[A]$ ([13]). We consider the class $\mathcal{B}(S)$ (see Definition 11). $\mathcal{B}(S)$ is in $Uni$ by Lemma 12. $\mathcal{B}(S)$ is also in $BranchWBC$:

From the input $R_f(0), R_f(1), \ldots$ extract an enumeration $f(0), f(1), \ldots$ for $f$. Apply the $BC$-learner on $f$ which yields a sequence $h_0 h_1 \ldots$ of guesses for $f$ such that almost all guesses are correct. By Lemma 12 there is a $g \in REC$ with $(\forall e)(\forall f)[\varphi_e = f \implies \varphi_{g(e)}$ is an infinite recursive branch of $R_f]$. Thus, $g(h_0)g(h_1)\ldots$ is a sequence of guesses such that almost all compute an infinite recursive branch or $R_f$.

Assume $\mathcal{B}(S) \in BranchBC[A]$ via $M^A$. We will show that this implies $S \in EX[A]$ which is a contradiction:

Translate the input sequence $f(0), f(1), \ldots$ for $f \in S$ into an enumeration $R_f(0), R_f(1), \ldots$ (Lemma 12). By Applying $M^A$ to $R_f \upharpoonright 0, R_f \upharpoonright 1, \ldots$ we get a sequence of guesses $h_0 h_1 \ldots$ which $BC[A]$-converges to an infinite recursive branch of $R_f$. Let $k(n) := \max\{m \le n : \varphi_{h_m,n}(0)\downarrow\}$. Then $(\varphi_{h_{k(n)}}(0))_{n \in \omega}$ $EX[A]$-converges to an index for $f$ by Lemma 12. $\qquad\square$

**Corollary 31.** *There exists a class $\mathcal{C} \in Uni$ such that for all $g$ with $\mathcal{C} \in Uni$ via $g$:*
$$(\exists T \in \mathcal{C})(\exists i, j)[i \ne j \wedge \varphi_i = \varphi_j = T \wedge \varphi_{g(i)} \ne \varphi_{g(j)}].$$

In Corollary 25 we have seen that $BranchEx \subseteq Uni[A]$ iff $A \ge_T K$. This result also holds for $BC$-branch learning by the analogous proof, since Proposition 19 from [12] actually states $BranchBC \subseteq Uni[K]$:

**Corollary 32.** $BranchBC \subseteq Uni[A] \iff A \ge_T K$.

What oracle do we need to capture $BranchWBC$ by $Uni[A]$? The power of $WBC$-style branch learning appears most clearly under this "$Uni$-oracle measure". The gap between capturing $BranchBC$ and $BranchWBC$ by $Uni[A]$ is a whole Turing jump. $BranchWBC$ is so powerful that only omniscient oracles give $Uni[A]$ as much power:

**Theorem 33.** $BranchWBC \subseteq Uni[A] \iff A \ge_T K'$.

*Proof.* ($\Leftarrow$) follows by Fact 15. For the direction ($\Rightarrow$) we define
$$T_e := \{eka_0 \ldots a_n : (\forall m \le n)[(\#W_{e,m} \le k \implies a_m = 0) \wedge$$
$$(\#W_{e,m} > k \implies \#W_e \ge m \wedge a_m = \mu t[\#W_{e,t} \ge m])]\}.$$

Let $U_k^e := \{\sigma : ek\sigma \in T_e\}$ be the subtree above $ek$. If $\#W_e \le k$ then $U_k = 0^\omega$. If $\#W_e > k$ then $U_k$ contains an infinite recursive branch iff $W_e$ is infinite.

The class $\mathcal{C} := \{T_e : e \in \omega\}$ is in $BranchWBC$: Wait until you can decode $e$ from the enumeration of $T_e$. Then output in stage $s$ a program for $eka_0 a_1 \ldots$ where $k = \#W_{e,s}$ and $a_m = \mu t[\#W_{e,m} \le k \vee \#W_{e,t} \ge m]$.

If $W_e$ is finite then there is an $s$ with $W_e = W_{e,s}$. Thus, for $k = \#W_{e,s}$ we have $U_k = 0^\omega$ and all guesses from stage $s$ on will compute the branch $ek0^\omega$. If $W_e$ is infinite then every $ekU_k$ contains an infinite recursive branch and every guess computes such a branch. (Note that in this case the learner produces infinitely many different branches.)

Since $BranchWBC \subseteq Uni[A]$ there is a partial $A$-recursive $g$ with $\mathcal{C} \in Uni[A]$ via $g$. We choose an $h \in REC$ with $T_e = \varphi_{h(e)}$ for all $e$. Note, that $range(h) \subseteq dom(g)$. Then $Inf = \{e : W_e \text{ infinite}\}$ is recursively enumerable in $A$, since $Inf = \{e : (\exists s)[\#W_{e,s} > \varphi_{g(h(e))}(1)]\}$. Let $k = \varphi_{g(h(e))}(1)$. If $k > \#W_{e,s}$ then $ekU_k$ contains an infinite recursive branch, since $\mathcal{C} \in Uni$ via $g$. Then $W_e$ must be infinite because of $\#W_{e,s} > k$. And if $W_e$ is infinite then there certainly exists an $s$ with $\#W_{e,s} > \varphi_{g(h(e))}(1)$.

The fact that $Inf$ is recursively enumerable in $A$ implies $Inf \le_T A$ as shown in the proof of Theorem 20. Thus, $A \ge_T Inf \equiv_T K'$. $\qquad\square$

In summary, *BranchBC* and *BranchWBC* have the same omniscient degrees and behave similar when compared to *BranchOnl*. But in the comparisons with *Uni* the two *BC*-style branch learning notions behave very different. The two notions differ also with respect to their trivial degrees:

**Theorem 34.** *1. BranchWBC[A] = BranchWBC $\iff$ A is recursive.*
*2. For all $A \leq_T K$: BranchWBC[A] $\subseteq$ BranchWBC[B] $\iff$ $A \leq_T B$ or B high.*

**Acknowledgements:** We would like to thank John Case, Martin Kummer and Martin Riedmiller for helpful discussions and comments.

# References

1. L. Adleman and M. Blum. Inductive inference and unsolvability. *Journal of Symbolic Logic*, 56(3):891–900, 1991.
2. O. Arnold and K. P. Jantke. Therapy plan generation as program synthesis. In *Proc. 5th Int. Workshop on Algorithmic Learning Theory*, pages 40–55. Springer-Verlag, 1994.
3. L. Blum and M. Blum. Towards a mathematical theory of inductive inference. *Information and Control*, 28:125–155, 1975.
4. J. R. Büchi and L. H. Landweber. Solving sequential conditions by finite-state strategies. *Transactions of the American Mathematical Society*, 138:295–311, 1969.
5. J. Case, S. Kaufmann, E. Kinber, and M. Kummer. Learning recursive functions from approximations. In *EuroCOLT'95*, volume 904 of *LNCS*, pages 140–153. Springer-Verlag, 1995.
6. D. Cenzer and J. Remmel. Recursively presented games and strategies. *Mathematical Social Sciences*, 24:117–139, 1992.
7. O. Föllinger. *Regelungstechnik*. Hüthig, Heidelberg, 8th edition, 1994.
8. L. Fortnow, W. Gasarch, S. Jain, E. Kinber, M. Kummer, S. Kurtz, M. Pleszkoch, T. Slaman, R. Solovay, and F. Stephan. Extremes in the degrees of inferability. *Annals of Pure and Applied Logic*, 66:21–276, 1994.
9. E. M. Gold. Language identification in the limit. *Information and Control*, 10:447–474, 1967.
10. S. Kaufmann and M. Kummer. On a quantitative notion of uniformity. In *Mathematical Foundations of Computer Science*, volume 969 of *LNCS*, pages 169–178. Springer-Verlag, 1995.
11. M. Kummer and M. Ott. Effective strategies for enumeration games. In H. K. Büning, editor, *Proceedings of Computer Science Logic CSL '95*, pages 368–387, Berlin, 1996. Springer.
12. M. Kummer and M. Ott. Learning branches and learning to win closed games. In *Proceedings of Ninth Annual Conference on Computational Learning Theory*, pages 280–291, New York, 1996. ACM.
13. M. Kummer and F. Stephan. On the structure of degrees of inferability. *Journal of Computer and System Sciences*, 52(2):214–238, Apr. 1996.
14. A. H. Lachlan. On some games which are relevant to the theory of recursively enumerable sets. *Annals of Mathematics*, 91(2):291–310, 1970.

15. D. Luzeaux. Machine learning applied to the control of complex systems. In *8th International Conference on Artificial Intelligence and expert systems applications*, Paris, France, 1996.

16. D. Luzeaux and E. Martin. Steps or stages for incremental control? In *Symposium on training issues in incremental learning*, Stanford University, CA, USA, 1993. AAAI-93 Spring Symposium Series.

17. O. Maler, A. Pnueli, and J. Sifakis. On the synthesis of discrete controllers for timed systems. In *STACS 95*, volume 900 of *LNCS*, pages 229–242. Springer-Verlag, 1995.

18. E. Martin. Oracles for learning programs. In *IEEE International Conference on Systems Man Cybernetics*, Le Touquet, France, 1993.

19. E. Martin, D. Luzeaux, and B. Zavidovique. Learning and control from a recursive viewpoint. In *IEEE International Symposium on Intelligent Control*, Glasgow, Ecosse, 1992.

20. R. McNaughton. Infinite games played on finite graphs. *Annals of Pure and Applied Logic*, 65:149–184, 1993.

21. W. T. Miller, R. S. Sutton, and P. J. Werbos, editors. *Neural networks for control*. MIT Press, Cambridge, Massachusetts, 1990.

22. K. S. Narendra and S. Mukhopadhyay. Intelligent control using neural networks. *IEEE Control Systems Magazine*, 12(5):11–18, April 1992.

23. P. Odifreddi. *Classical Recursion Theory*. North-Holland, Amsterdam, 1989.

24. D. Osherson, M. Stob, and S. Weinstein. *Systems that Learn*. MIT Press, Cambridge, Massachusetts, 1986.

25. M. Ott and F. Stephan. Structural measures for games and process control in the branch learning model. Technical report 39/96, Fakultät für Informatik, Universität Karsruhe, 1996.

26. M. Riedmiller. Learning to control dynamic systems. In R. Trappl, editor, *Proceedings of the 13th. European Meeting on Cybernetics and Systems Research - 1996 (EMCSR '96)*, Vienna, 1996.

27. J. G. Thistle and W. M. Wonham. Control of infinite behavior of finite automata. *SIAM Journal on Control and Optimization*, 32(4):1075–1097, 1994.

28. W. Thomas. Automata on infinite objects. In J. van Leeuwen, editor, *Handbook of Theoretical Computer Science*, pages 133–191. Elsevier Science Publishers B. V., 1990.

29. W. Thomas. On the synthesis of strategies in infinite games. In *STACS 95*, volume 900 of *LNCS*, pages 1–13. Springer-Verlag, 1995.

30. W. Thomas and H. Lescow. Logical specification of infinite computations. In J. W. de Bakker, W.-P. de Roever, and G. Rozenberg, editors, *A Decade of Concurrency: Reflections and Perspectives*, volume 803 of *LNCS*, pages 583–621. Springer-Verlag, 1993.

31. D. A. White and D. A. Sofge, editors. *Handbook of Intelligent Control*. Van Nostrand Reinhold, New York, 1992.

# Learning under Persistent Drift

Yoav Freund[1] and Yishay Mansour[2]*

[1] AT&T Laboratories, 600 Mountain Avenue Murray Hill, NJ 07974-0636 USA
yoav@research.att.com
[2] Dept. of Computer Science Tel Aviv University Tel-Aviv 69978 ISRAEL.
mansour@math.tau.ac.il

**Abstract.** In this paper we study learning algorithms for environments which are changing over time. Unlike most previous work, we are interested in the case where the changes might be rapid but their "direction" is relatively constant. We model this type of change by assuming that the target distribution is changing continuously at a constant rate from one extreme distribution to another. We show in this case how to use a simple weighting scheme to estimate the error of an hypothesis, and using this estimate, to minimize the error of the prediction.

## 1 Introduction

One of the oversimplifying assumptions made in the PAC model [Val84] is that all the examples are drawn from the same distribution, and that the target function does not change with time. The drawbacks of this assumption have been widely recognized, and a considerable amount of work was devoted to study the cases where either the distribution [Bar92, BL96] or the target function [HL94, BBDK96] changes over time.

Clearly, without constraints on the way the distribution or target function change over time, it is hopeless to achieve any meaningful learning result. The most common and natural assumption is that the changes are not drastic. A formal way to say this is that the distance between two consecutive distributions (target functions) is bounded by some parameter. This approach was the main subject of previous research [HL94, Bar92, BL96, BBDK96], and has developed interesting learning results.

Common to the results in [HL94, Bar92, BL96] is the assumption that the rate of drift is sufficiently small that the same hypothesis is good for a sufficiently long period of time. Based on this assumption, the learning method of choice is to consider only a certain number of the most recent examples, and use them as though the distribution and target function did not change at all.

The idea of this paper is to show that if we assume that the change in the target distribution is persistent over short periods of time then we can incorporate this knowledge into our algorithm and make good predictions even when

---

* This research was supported in part by The Israel Science Foundation administered by The Israel Academy of Science and Humanities.

the drift is rapid. We define a model in which the drift in the distribution that governs the generation of examples has a simple structure. We assume that at each time point, we are sampling from a different distribution, but that within a window of size $n$ the changes in the distribution can be approximate well by a linear trajectory. In other words, we denote by $\mathcal{D}_t$ the distribution that governs the generation of examples at time $t$. This distribution is over both inputs and outputs. Thus it defines both the distribution of inputs and the (probabilistic) relationship between inputs and outputs. Consider some fixed time step $t$, at which we want to make a prediction. We assume that there is some other distribution $\mathcal{G}_t$ such that the distribution at time $t - i$, for $1 \leq i \leq n$, is approximately equal to $\mathcal{D}_t + i/n(\mathcal{G}_t - \mathcal{D}_t)$. The goal of the learner is to make a good prediction with respect to the distribution $\mathcal{D}_t$, based on the examples that it got from the distributions $\mathcal{D}_{t-n}, \ldots, \mathcal{D}_{t-1}$.

It is not hard to imagine cases in which this assumption will be reasonable. Consider, for example, the problem of predicting the occurance of rain on a particular day as a function of barometric pressure and temperature on the preceding day. As the probability of rain depends on the season, it is reasonable to expect that the best prediction function drifts with time. However, as seasons change relatively slowly, it is also reasonable to assume that the dependence of the expected performance of any fixed function on time can be approximated by a linear function within the range of one month.

One way to compare this new type of assumption to the standard one is to think of them as assumptions about a power series approximation of the way in which probabilities change with time. The standard model corresponds to the assumption about the zero-order or constant term of this expansion. It assumes that the probabilities are changing very slowly. The persistent-drift assumption is an assumption about the first order in the expansion, it assumes that it is the *rate* of change that is more or less constant.

This model has a similar motivation to the model of structured change suggested by Bartlett, Ben David and Kulkarni [BBDK96]. However, we restrict ourselves to the special case in which the change (in both the concept and the input distribution) is a linear function of time. We show that in this case a simple change to the standard method of minimizing the training error yields a simple and effective algorithm.

We design a simple estimator for the error of any fixed hypothesis and give upper bounds on its accuracy. Our algorithm uses this estimator to select a hypothesis with which to make its prediction out of a given hypothesis class. We show that the expected prediction error of this algorithm is never much worse than that of the best hypothesis in the class if the class is finite or has finite pseudo-dimension. We extend this model also to the case where past distributions are only *approximated* by linear drift.

The simplicity of the algorithm and the significance of its performance can be especially appreciated when one considers the fact that it can handle drift in both the input distribution and in the relationship between the input and the output, and that it does not assume that the input-output relationship is perfectly modeled by any of the hypotheses. If the input-output relationship is perfectly modeled by some hypothesis from a known class, and if this dependency does not change with time, then the fact that the input distribution is changing is relatively easy to deal with. Predicting by using the hypothesis that suffered the smallest loss will perform rather well. Intuitively, the worse that can happen is that the old examples might become *irrelevant* because they come from parts of the space that currently have low probability. On the other hand, in our model old examples might be *misleading*, the input-output relationship that approximates them is no longer correct and thus using the hypothesis performs best according to them is a bad idea. As we shall see, our algorithm uses an error estimate that, in effect, uses the old examples as *negative* examples, which cause it to predict in a way that is accurate for the future, rather then for the past.

The paper is organized as follows. In Section 2 we give the precise definition of our model. In Section 3 we derive an unbiased estimator for the error of a hypothesis that has minimal variance. In Section 4.1 we give a bound on the performance of an algorithm that uses a finite set of hypotheses and in Section 4.2 we sketch the derivation of a bound for hypotheses classes of finite pseudo-dimension. We conclude with a summary and some open questions in Section 5.


## 2    Preliminaries

We assume that the learner is observing a sequence of *examples*. Each example consists of an *input* $x \in X$ and an *output* $y \in [0, 1]$,[3] where $X$ is an arbitrary measurable *input space*. We denote the sequence of examples by $(x_0, y_0), (x_1, y_1), \ldots, (x_t, y_t), \ldots$.

Our goal for time $t$ is to predict the output $y_t$ given the input $x_t$. The examples are assumed to be generated independently at random according to distributions over $X \times [0, 1]$. Note that each of these distributions defines both a distribution over the input space and a distribution of outputs for each input $\text{Prob}\{y|x\}$. So far, this setup follows the standard framework of agnostic learning [Vap82, Hau92]. However, the examples are *not* identically distributed, but generated independently at random according to *different* distributions over $X \times [0, 1]$. This is the model suggested by Bartlett [Bar92], however, here we make the additional assumption that the distributions are changing with time in a way that can be approximated, for short periods of of time, by a constant rate drift.

More precisely, we denote by $\mathcal{D}_t$ the distribution according to which the $t^{\text{th}}$ example, $(x_t, y_t)$ is drawn. We assume that there are parameters $n \in N$ and $1 > \gamma \geq 0$. For any time step $t > n$, there exists a distribution $\mathcal{G}_t$ such that for any $0 \leq i \leq n$:

$$\left\| \mathcal{D}_{t-i} - \left( \mathcal{D}_t + \frac{i}{n}(\mathcal{G}_t - \mathcal{D}_t) \right) \right\|_1 \leq \gamma , \tag{1}$$

---

[3] The output domain can be easily extended to any bounded range of the reals.

where $\| \cdot \|_1$ denotes the $L_1$ norm.[4] Intuitively, $n$ corresponds to the time range where linear drift is a good approximation and $\gamma$ corresponds to the quality of this approximation.

For ease of notation we find it useful to consider a more general setup. We define a function $f : \{0, 1, \ldots, n\} \to [0, 1]$, such that $f(0) = 0$. In the linear case we have $f(i) = i/n$, and rewrite Equation (1) as follows

$$\|\mathcal{D}_{t-i} - (f(i)\mathcal{G}_t + (1 - f(i))\mathcal{D}_t)\|_1 \leq \gamma . \tag{2}$$

We assume that the learner has access to a hypothesis class $\mathcal{H}$. Each hypothesis $h \in \mathcal{H}$ is a mapping from the input space $X$ to the output space $[0, 1]$. The goal of the learner is to predict the $t^{\text{th}}$ output $(t > n)$ based on the past examples and on the $t^{\text{th}}$ input. We compare the performance of the learner with that of the best hypothesis for the $t^{\text{th}}$ step.

More precisely, we denote the prediction of the algorithm at time $t$ by $\hat{y}_t$, and the (expected) error of the algorithm at time $t$ by $\epsilon_t^{\text{alg}} = \mathrm{E}\left[|y_t - \hat{y}_t|\right]$, where expectation is taken with respect to the random choice of all examples from time 1 to $t$. Similarly, for each hypothesis $h \in \mathcal{H}$ we denote by $\epsilon_t(h)$ the error of the hypothesis $h$ at time $t$. We denote the "minimal achievable error" of the class $\mathcal{H}$ by $\epsilon_t^* = \min_{h \in \mathcal{H}} \epsilon_t(h)$. We measure the performance of our algorithm by the difference $\epsilon_t^{\text{alg}} - \epsilon_t^*$. Our goal is to find algorithms with good guaranteed upper bounds on this performance measure. The performance bounds will hold for each time step $t$ for which the assumptions on the distribution drift hold.

## 3 Estimating the error of a hypothesis

In this section our goal is to find a good estimate of the error of a fixed hypothesis $h \in \mathcal{H}$ at a fixed time step $t$ when $\gamma = 0$. We shall remove the last assumption at the end of the section.

We restrict ourselves to estimators that are linear combinations of past errors. This class of estimators is simple to calculate and to analyze. As we give no lower bounds, the possibility of improved estimators that use other functions of past observations remains open.

Formally, our estimate for the error of a hypothesis $h$ at time $t$ is of the form

$$\hat{\epsilon}_t(h) = \sum_{i=1}^{n} w_i |h(x_{t-i}) - y_{t-i}| .$$

We call $w_1, \ldots, w_n$ the *weights* and denote by $\mathbf{w}$ the weight vector which consists of these $n$ weights.

---

[4] In other words

$$\|\mathcal{D}_1 - \mathcal{D}_2\|_1 = \int_{X \times [0,1]} |\mathcal{D}_1(x, y) - \mathcal{D}_2(x, y)| d(x, y) .$$

First, we find the conditions on $\mathbf{w}$ which should be satisfied in order to make our estimator *unbiased*, i.e. $\epsilon_t(h) = \mathrm{E}\left[\hat{\epsilon}_t(h)\right]$. We denote by $\tilde{\epsilon}_t(h)$ the expected error of the hypothesis $h$ with respect to the distribution $\mathcal{G}_t$. It follows from Equation (2) that

$$\epsilon_{t-i}(h) = f(i)\tilde{\epsilon}_t(h) + (1 - f(i))\epsilon_t(h) , \tag{3}$$

for $1 \le i \le n$. Thus our requirement is that

$$\epsilon_t(h) = \sum_{i=1}^{n} w_i \left(f(i)\tilde{\epsilon}_t(h) + (1 - f(i))\epsilon_t(h)\right)$$

$$= \tilde{\epsilon}_t(h) \left(\sum_{i=1}^{n} w_i f(i)\right) + \epsilon_t(h) \left(\sum_{i=1}^{n} w_i(1 - f(i))\right) .$$

As we want the choice of weights, $\mathbf{w}$, to be independent of the unknown values of $\tilde{\epsilon}_t(h)$ and $\epsilon_t(h)$ we get the condition that the factor multiplying $\tilde{\epsilon}_t(h)$ must be equal zero, while the factor multiplying $\epsilon_t(h)$ must be equal one. Using vector notation, these conditions can be given as

$$\mathbf{w} \cdot \mathbf{f} = 0 \text{ and } \mathbf{w} \cdot (\mathbf{1} - \mathbf{f}) = 1 \tag{4}$$

where $\mathbf{f} = \langle f(1), \dots, f(n) \rangle$ and $\mathbf{1} = \langle 1, 1, \dots, 1 \rangle$. The condition can also be written as

$$\mathbf{w} \cdot \mathbf{1} = 1 \text{ and } \mathbf{w} \cdot \mathbf{f} = 0 \tag{5}$$

Unless $n = 2$, these two conditions leave a lot of freedom in the choice of $\mathbf{w}$. We use this freedom so as to minimize the variance of our estimator. (Actually, we will minimize an upper bound on the variance.) As the estimator is a sum of $n$ independent random variables, its variance is simply

$$\mathrm{Var}\left[\sum_{i=1}^{n} w_i |h(x_{t-i}) - y_{t-i}|\right] = \sum_{i=1}^{n} w_i^2 \, \mathrm{Var}\left[|h(x_{t-i}) - y_{t-i}|\right] \le \frac{1}{4} \sum_{i=1}^{n} w_i^2 .$$

Thus minimizing the $L^2$ norm of $\mathbf{w}$ is equivalent to minimizing an upper bound on the variance. Minimizing the length of $\mathbf{w}$ under the constraints given in Equation (5) implies that $\mathbf{w}$ is in the span of $\mathbf{1}$ and $\mathbf{f}$,[5] i.e., is of the form

$$\mathbf{w} = a\mathbf{1} + b\mathbf{f} .$$

Solving for $a$ and $b$ to satisfy the constraints we find that the choice of $\mathbf{w}$ that gives the unbiased estimator with least variance is

$$\mathbf{w} = \frac{F_2 \mathbf{1} - F_1 \mathbf{f}}{F_2 n - F_1^2}$$

---

[5] To see why this is so, note that any solution to the conditions in Equation (5) can be written as a sum of the two orthogonal vectors, $\mathbf{w} = \mathbf{u} + \mathbf{v}$, such that $\mathbf{u} = a\mathbf{1} + b\mathbf{f}$ and $\mathbf{v} \cdot \mathbf{1} = \mathbf{v} \cdot \mathbf{f} = 0$. It follows that $\mathbf{v} \cdot \mathbf{u} = 0$ and so $\|\mathbf{w}\|_2^2 = \|\mathbf{u}\|_2^2 + \|\mathbf{v}\|_2^2$ thus the length of $\mathbf{w}$ is minimized if $\mathbf{v} = 0$.

where

$$F_1 = \sum_{i=1}^{n} f(i) \text{ and } F_2 = \sum_{i=1}^{n} f^2(i) .$$

For the values of $f(i) = i/n$ that we are interested in, for large $n$, we have that

$$F_1 = \frac{n+1}{2} \approx \frac{n}{2}$$

$$F_2 = \frac{1}{n^2} \left( \frac{(n+1)^3}{3} - \frac{(n-1)^2}{2} + \frac{n}{6} + \frac{1}{6} \right) \approx \frac{n}{3}$$

To simplify our analysis we use the slightly sub-optimal choice of weights:

$$w_i \doteq 4/n - 6i/n^2 .$$

This is not the first time in which a weighted average of past errors has been recommended as a measure of the quality of a hypothesis. Helmbold and Long [HL94] suggested using a similar weighted average to optimize the bounds on the performance of their algorithm. The main difference is in the assumption about the rate of change. While in [HL94] the rate of change is slow, and a single function is suited to fit all the recent examples, we allow rapid changes, and it may be that a function that fits well at the start of the window will fit poorly at its end. This main structural difference manifests itself in the weights. In [HL94] all the weights are positive, and this it corresponds to the assumption that the achievable prediction error is of the same order as the rate of drift. On the other hand, our estimator, which is designed to handle rapid drifts, has some of the weights *negative* (those that correspond to steps $t - n, \ldots, t - (2/3)n$). These negative weights satisfy the need to predict the rate of change of an hypothesis and to fit it well with a linear model. (In order to gain some more intuition, consider two hypothesis that have the same average error on the distributions (each one given the same weight). Since their error changes linearly from one distribution to the other, we would like to pick the hypothesis that has the *highest* error initially, since it will have the lowest error on the last distribution, the one that we are interested in.)

We conclude this section by giving a bound on the probability that our estimator suffers a large error. To do that we use Bernstein's Inequality (see e.g. [Pol84]):

**Lemma 1 Bernstein.** *Let $Y_1, \ldots, Y_n$ be independent random variables with zero means and and bounded ranges: $|Y_i| \leq M$. Write $\sigma_i^2$ for the variance of $Y_i$. Suppose $V \geq \sigma_1^2 + \cdots + \sigma_n^2$. Then for each $\eta > 0$,*

$$\text{Prob} \{|Y_1 + \cdots + Y_n| > \eta\} \leq 2 \exp \left[ -\frac{1}{2} \eta^2 / (V + \frac{1}{3} M\eta) \right] .$$

In our setting we set $Y_i = w_i|h(x_{t-i}) - y_{t-i}| - w_i\epsilon_{t-i}(h)$, $M = \max w_i$ and $V = 1/4 \sum_{i=0}^{n-1} w_i^2$. In such a case $Y_1 + \cdots + Y_n = \hat{\epsilon}_t(h) - \epsilon_t(h)$.

If $M\eta$ is much smaller than $V$ then this bound justifies minimizing $V$, i.e., the variance of the estimator. For the special case of $f(i) = i/n$, we have $V = 1/n$ and $M = 4/n$, and therefore, for $\eta < 3/4$, we have

$$\text{Prob}\left\{|\hat{\epsilon}_t(h) - \epsilon_t(h)| > \eta\right\} \leq 2e^{-\eta^2 n/4} .$$

Going back to the case that $\gamma > 0$ we derive the following theorem.

**Theorem 2.** *For the case that $f(i) = i/n$, using $w_i = 4/n - 6i/n^2$, we guarantee that, for any hypothesis $h$ and for any time step $t$ for which the assumptions of Equation (1) hold*

$$\text{Prob}\left\{|\hat{\epsilon}_t(h) - \epsilon_t(h)| > \eta + 2\gamma\right\} \leq 2e^{-\eta^2 n/4} .$$

*Proof.* First we need to modify equation 3, to state that,

$$|\epsilon_i(h) - f(t - i)\tilde{\epsilon}_t(h) + (1 - f(t - i))\epsilon_t(h)| \leq \gamma .$$

Then we have that,

$$\epsilon_t(h) \leq \tilde{\epsilon}_t(h)\left(\sum_{i=1}^{n} w_i f(i)\right) + \epsilon_t(h)\left(\sum_{i=1}^{n} w_i(1 - f(i))\right) + \gamma\|\mathbf{w}\|_1 ,$$

The theorem follows from an application of Lemma 1, to the case where $f(i) = i/n$, and from the fact that $\sum_{i=0}^{n-1} |w_i| < 2$, for the above choice of weights.

It is interesting to compare this bound to the bound on the deviation of the estimation of the error for the case of i.i.d. drawn examples. In that case, if one uses Hoeffding's bound, one gets a similar bound, but the exponent is $-2\eta^2 n$ instead of $-\eta^2 n/4$. In other words, the sample size that we require, in order to guarantee a given accuracy and reliability level under the linear drift model is only eight times larger than the one required in the analysis standard model of fixed distribution. Most importantly, this bound is independent of the rate of the drift!

## 4 The learning algorithm

Based on the previous section it is rather straightforward to derive the learning algorithm. Given a sample $(x_i, y_i)$, for $i < t$, we use the last $n$ samples for the algorithm, i.e., $(x_i, y_i)$, for $t - n \leq i \leq t - 1$. For each hypothesis $h \in \mathcal{H}$ we compute $\hat{\epsilon}_t(h)$. The algorithm selects the hypothesis $\hat{h}_t$ that minimizes $\hat{\epsilon}_t(h)$, and returns as its prediction $\hat{h}_t(x_n)$.

In the next subsection we would like to analyze how well does this learning rule does.

## 4.1 Comparing hypotheses from a finite class

If the size of the class of hypotheses is finite, then a bound on the expected error of the hypothesis generated by our algorithm can be derived by trivial means.

**Theorem 3.** *At every time step t for which the assumptions of our model hold, the expected error of the algorithm is bounded by*

$$\epsilon_t^{alg} \le \epsilon_t^* + 2\sqrt{\frac{4}{n}\ln\frac{2|\mathcal{H}|}{\delta}} + 4\gamma + \delta$$

*Or, choosing $\delta = c/n$ for some constant $c > 0$, the error is bounded by*

$$\epsilon_t^{alg} \le \epsilon_t^* + c\sqrt{\frac{\ln n|\mathcal{H}|}{n}} + 4\gamma$$

*Proof.* Assume the opposite. As the algorithm chooses the hypothesis $h'$ whose estimated error is smallest. Denoting the best hypothesis by $h^*$ this means $\hat{\epsilon}_t(h') \le \hat{\epsilon}_t(h^*)$. This, in turn, implies that either $\hat{\epsilon}_t(h')$ or $\hat{\epsilon}_t(h^*)$ are far from their expected value. From Theorem 2 we know that either of these events can occur with small probability.

## 4.2 Comparing hypotheses from a class of finite dimension

In the case that the hypothesis class is infinite, we can still bound the error of the hypothesis if we assume that the hypothesis class has finite pseudo-dimension.

In order to prove this we need to go back to the proofs on the uniform convergence of classes of functions and reprove them for this case. We cannot use the existing theorems, because they are stated for the case in which all examples are drawn from the same distribution. Luckily, the proofs given by Haussler [Hau92], which are based on techniques of Pollard [Pol84] do not use the fact that all examples are drawn from the same distribution, and very slight alteration to these proofs lead to the following theorem, which is a slight alteration of Corollary 2 in [Hau92]:

**Theorem 4.** *Let $F$ be a permissible family of functions from a set $Z$ into $[0,1]$ with pseudo-dimension $d < \infty$. Assume $m \ge 1$. Let $z_1, \ldots, z_n$ be generated independently at random from a sequence of distributions $P_1, \ldots, P_n$, define a $s(f) = \sum_{i=1}^n w_i f(z_i)$ and denote by $\mu(f)$ the expected value of $s(f)$ then for all $0 < \epsilon \le 1$*

$$\text{Prob}\{\exists f \in F : |s(f) - \mu(f)| > \epsilon\} \le 8\left(\frac{128e}{\epsilon}\ln\frac{128e}{\epsilon}\right)^d e^{\frac{-\epsilon^2 M}{2304}}$$

*where $M = \max_i w_i - \min_i w_i$.*

We should comment that no attempt has been made to optimize the constants in this theorem.

Two observations show that the proof given by Haussler [Hau92] can be used essentially verbatim. The proof uses a trick of using two samples and permuting elements among them. The first observation is that all the permutations are done pairwise between elements with the same index in the two samples, thus all the requirements for identical distributions still hold. The second observation is that Hoeffding's bound used in the proof does not require the elements to be identically distributed but only that they are independent.

We use Theorem 4 as follows. We let the set $Z$ be the set of example pairs $(x, y)$ and define the set of functions $F$ to be $|h(x) - y|$ for $h \in \mathcal{H}$. Applying the theorem to our case we get the following theorem:

**Theorem 5.** *Let $\mathcal{H}$ be a hypothesis class of pseudo-dimension $d$ and assuming that the distribution is drifting with window size $n$ and accuracy $0 \le \gamma \le 1$. Then at each time step $t$ the error of the output hypothesis $\hat{h}_t$ is at most,*

$$\epsilon_t^{alg} \le \epsilon_t^* + c\sqrt{\frac{d}{n} \ln \frac{n}{d}} + 4\gamma ,$$

*for some constant $c$.*

## 5  Summary and open problem

We present a new model of learning under changing distributions. In our model the drift is persistent and can be well approximated by a linear drift. We show that a very simple algorithm can achieve good performance even when the drift is rapid.

There are several technical open problems. First, it would be useful to derive some lower bounds on the possible best performance in this model. This would allow us to know how much improvement might be possible. There are many potential places for improving the algorithm. We have restricted our error estimate to be a linear function of past errors and required the estimator to be consistent for the case where $\gamma = 0$. In general, there is no reason to make these restrictions. Moreover, it is clear that our choice of weights is not always optimal. For example, if $\mathcal{G}_t$ is very close to $\mathcal{D}_t$ and $\gamma$ is relatively large, it is clearly better to assume that the distribution is close to constant and use the *unweighted* average error although it is not consistent.

It is clear that there are many ways in which our analysis can be extended. First, it is clear from our derivation in Section 3 that instead of linear drift one can use many other choices for $f(i)$. Also, it is clear that more general drift structures, which involve convex combinations of more than two distributions can be similarly analyzed. It would be interesting to find choices that correspond to interesting and relevant situations.

# References

[Bar92]    Bartlett. Learning with slowly changing distribution. In *Proceedings of the Workshop on Computational Learning Theory, Morgan Kaufmann Publishers*, pages 243–252, 1992.

[BBDK96]  Peter Bartlett, Shai Ben-David, and Sanjeev Kulkarni. Learning changing concepts by exploiting the structure of change. In *Proceedings of the Workshop on Computational Learning Theory, Morgan Kaufmann Publishers*, 1996.

[BL96]     Rakesh D. Barve and Philip M. Long. On the complexity of learning from drifting distributions. In *Proceedings of the Workshop on Computational Learning Theory, Morgan Kaufmann Publishers*, 1996.

[Hau92]    David Haussler. Decision theoretic generalization of the pac model for neural net and other learning applications. *Information and Computation*, 100:78–150, 1992.

[HL94]     David Helmbold and Phill Long. Tracking drifting concepts by minimizing disagreements. *Machine Learning*, 14(1):27–46, 1994. A preliminary version appeared in Proceedings of COLT 1991, 13–23.

[Pol84]    David Pollard. *Convergence of Stochastic Processes*. Springer-Verlag, 1984.

[Val84]    Leslie G. Valiant. A theory of the learnable. *Communications of the ACM*, 27(11):1134–1142, November 1984.

[Vap82]    V. N. Vapnik. *Estimation of Dependences Based on Empirical Data*. Springer-Verlag, New York, 1982.

# Randomized Hypotheses and Minimum Disagreement Hypotheses for Learning with Noise

(extended abstract)

Nicolò Cesa-Bianchi[1], Paul Fischer[2],
Eli Shamir[3], and Hans Ulrich Simon[2]

[1] DSI, Università di Milano, Via Comelico 39 I-20135 Milano, Italy
cesabian@dsi.unimi.it
[2] Lehrstuhl Informatik II, Universität Dortmund, D-44221 Dortmund, Germany
{paulf,simon}@goedel.informatik.uni-dortmund.de
[3] Hebrew University, Jerusalem, Israel
shamir@cs.huji.ac.il

**Abstract.** In this paper we prove various results about PAC learning in the presence of malicious and random classification noise. Our main theme is the use of randomized hypotheses for learning with small sample sizes and high malicious noise rates. We show an algorithm that PAC learns any target class of VC-dimension $d$ using randomized hypotheses and order of $d/\varepsilon$ training examples (up to logarithmic factors) while tolerating malicious noise rates even slightly larger than the information-theoretic bound $\varepsilon/(1 + \varepsilon)$ for deterministic hypotheses. Combined with previous results, this implies that a lower bound $d/\Delta + \varepsilon/\Delta^2$ on the sample size, where $\eta = \varepsilon/(1 + \varepsilon) - \Delta$ is the malicious noise rate, applies only when using deterministic hypotheses. We then show that the information-theoretic upper bound on the noise rate for deterministic hypotheses can be replaced by $2\varepsilon/(1 + 2\varepsilon)$ if randomized hypotheses are used. Investigating further the use of randomized hypotheses, we show a strategy for learning the powerset of $d$ elements using an optimal sample size of order $d\varepsilon/\Delta^2$ (up to logarithmic factors) and tolerating a noise rate $\eta = 2\varepsilon/(1 + 2\varepsilon) - \Delta$. We complement this result by proving that this sample size is also necessary for any class $\mathcal{C}$ of VC-dimension $d$.

We then discuss the performance of the minimum disagreement strategy under both malicious and random classification noise models. For malicious noise we show an algorithm that, using deterministic hypotheses, learns unions of $d$ intervals on the continuous domain $[0, 1)$ using a sample size significantly smaller than that needed by the minimum disagreement strategy. For classification noise we show, generalizing a result by Laird, that order of $d/(\varepsilon\Delta^2)$ training examples suffice (up to logarithmic factors) to learn by minimizing disagreements any target class of VC-dimension $d$ tolerating random classification noise rate $\eta = 1/2 - \Delta$. Using a lower bound by Simon, we also prove that this sample size bound cannot be significantly improved.

# 1 Introduction

Any realistic learning algorithm should have the ability of coping with errors in the training data. A model of learning in the presence of *malicious noise* was introduced by Valiant [9] as an extension of his basic PAC framework for learning classes of boolean functions. In this *malicious PAC model*, each training example given to the learner is independently replaced, with fixed probability $\eta$, by an adversarially chosen one (which may or may not be consistent with the boolean target function.) A comprehensive investigation of malicious PAC learning is carried out by Kearns and Li [6]. They show that a malicious noise rate $\eta \geq \varepsilon/(1+\varepsilon)$ can make statistically indistinguishable two target functions that differ on a subset of the domain whose probability measure is at least $\varepsilon$. This implies that with this noise rate no learner can generate hypotheses that are $\varepsilon$-accurate in the PAC sense, this irrespective to the sample size (number of training examples) and to the learner's computational power. In their paper, Kearns and Li also analyze the performance of the minimum disagreement strategy in presence of malicious noise. They show that, for a sample of size[4] $d/\varepsilon$ (where $d$ is the VC-dimension of the target class) and for a noise rate bounded by any constant fraction of $\varepsilon/(1+\varepsilon)$, the hypothesis in the target class having the smallest sample error is $\varepsilon$-accurate in the PAC sense. The sample size necessary and sufficient for learning with a high noise rate, i.e. with $\eta = \varepsilon/(1+\varepsilon) - \Delta$ for $\Delta = o(\varepsilon)$, has been recently studied by Cesa-Bianchi et al. [2]. They prove that the minimum disagreement strategy PAC learns in the presence of malicious noise any target class of VC-dimension $d$ with a necessary and sufficient sample size of $d\varepsilon/\Delta^2$. Furthermore, they show a strategy RMD (which outputs deterministic hypotheses that are possibly different from any hypothesis minimizing disagreements) for learning the powerset of $d$ elements using a sample size of $d/\Delta + \varepsilon/\Delta^2$. This is optimal as they also prove a lower bound of the same order. As RMD makes essential use of the fact that the learning domain is small, one might ask whether, in the presence of malicious noise, there is an algorithm that can learn infinite target classes with fewer training examples than those required by the minimum disagreement strategy. The first result of this paper gives a positive answer to this question by showing that a variant of RMD learns the class of unions of $d$ intervals on $[0,1)$ with sample size $d/\Delta + \varepsilon/\Delta^2$.

We then consider the use of randomized hypotheses for learning with small sample sizes and high malicious noise rates, which is the main topic of this paper. An easy modification of Kearns and Li's argument shows that no learner can output $\varepsilon$-accurate randomized hypotheses with a noise rate larger or equal to $2\varepsilon/(1+2\varepsilon)$. Given the gap between this bound and the corresponding bound $\varepsilon/(1+\varepsilon)$ for learners using deterministic hypotheses, we address the problem whether allowing randomized hypotheses helps in this setting. In fact, we present an algorithm that PAC learns any target class of VC-dimension $d$ using randomized hypotheses and $d/\varepsilon$ training examples while tolerating any noise rate bounded by a constant fraction of $(7/6)\varepsilon/(1+(7/6)\varepsilon)$. The algorithm works by

---

[4] All sample size orders in this section are given up to logarithmic factors.

finding up to three functions in the target class that satisfy a certain independence condition defined on the sample. The value of the final hypothesis on a domain point is then computed by taking a majority vote over these functions (or by tossing a coin in case only two functions are found). Our investigation moves on to consider the case of a noise rate close to the information-theoretic bound $2\varepsilon/(1 + 2\varepsilon)$ for randomized hypotheses. We show a strategy for learning the powerset of $d$ elements using $d\varepsilon/\Delta^2$ training examples and tolerating a malicious noise rate of $\eta = 2\varepsilon/(1 + 2\varepsilon) - \Delta$, for any $\Delta > 0$. We also show that this sample size is optimal in the sense that *any* learner using randomized hypotheses needs at least $d\varepsilon/\Delta^2$ training examples for learning any target class of VC-dimension $d$.

In the last part of the paper, we work within the random classification noise model proposed by Angluin and Laird [1]. In this setting the boolean value of the target function is independently flipped, in each example given to the learner, with fixed probability $\eta$. Learning with random classification noise is significantly easier than in the presence of malicious noise. In [1] it is shown that the minimum disagreement strategy learns any target class with noise rate arbitrarily close to $1/2$. Subsequently, Laird [7] proves an optimal sample size of $(\ln |\mathcal{C}|)/(\varepsilon\Delta^2)$ for learning by minimizing disagreements any target class $\mathcal{C}$ of finite size $|\mathcal{C}|$ with noise rate $\eta = 1/2 - \Delta$. This sample size is matched by Simon's lower bound [8]. In this paper we generalize Laird's result by showing that $d/(\varepsilon\Delta^2)$ training examples suffice to learn any target class of VC-dimension $d$. Note that Simon's lower bound can be used to show that the sample size bound $d/(\varepsilon\Delta^2)$ cannot be significantly improved.

## 2 Definitions and notation

We recall the definitions of PAC learning and malicious PAC learning of a given *target class* $\mathcal{C}$, where $\mathcal{C}$ is a set of $\{0, 1\}$-valued functions $C$ defined on some domain $X$. We call *instance* any $x \in X$ and *labeled instance* or *example* any pair $(x, y) \in X \times \{0, 1\}$. In Valiant's PAC learning model [9], the learning algorithm (or learner) gets as input a *sample*, i.e., a multiset $\{(x_1, C(x_1)), \ldots, (x_m, C(x_m))\}$ of desired size $m < \infty$. Each instance $x_t$ in the sample given to the learner must be independently drawn from a distribution $D$ on $X$ and labeled according to the target function $C \in \mathcal{C}$. Both $C$ and $D$ are fixed in advance and unknown to the learner. In the malicious PAC model, the input sample is corrupted by an adversary using noise rate $\eta$ according to the following protocol. First, a sample $\{(x_1, C(x_1)), \ldots, (x_m, C(x_m))\}$ of the desired size is generated exactly as in the noise-free PAC model. Second, before showing the sample to the learner, each example $(x_t, C(x_t))$ is independently marked with fixed probability $\eta$, where $\eta$ is the noise rate. Finally, the adversary replaces each marked example $(x_t, C(x_t))$ in the sample by a pair $(\hat{x}_t, \hat{y}_t)$ arbitrarily chosen from $X \times \{0, 1\}$ and then feeds the corrupted sample to the learner. We call the collection of marked examples the *noisy part* of the sample and the collection of unmarked examples the *clean part*. Note that learning with this definition is harder than with the definition of malicious PAC learning given by Kearns and Li [6]. There, the examples were sequentially ordered in the sample and the adversary's choice for each marked example had to be based only on the (possibly marked) examples occurring earlier in the sample sequence.[5]

To meet the PAC learning criterion the learner, on the basis of a polynomially-sized sample (which is corrupted in case of malicious PAC learning), must output an hypothesis $H$ that with high probability is a close approximation of the target $C$. Formally, an algorithm $A$ is said to *PAC learn* a target class $C$ using hypothesis class $\mathcal{H}$ if, for all distributions $D$ on $X$, for all targets $C \in C$, and for all $1 \geq \varepsilon, \delta > 0$, given as input a sample of size $m$, $A$ outputs an hypothesis $H \in \mathcal{H}$ such that its *error probability*, $D(H \neq C)$, is strictly smaller than $\varepsilon$ with probability at least $1 - \delta$ with respect to the sample random draw, where $m = m(\varepsilon, \delta)$ is some polynomial in $1/\varepsilon$ and $\ln(1/\delta)$. We call $\varepsilon$ the *accuracy* parameter and $\delta$ the *confidence* parameter. We use $H \neq C$ to denote the symmetric difference $\{x : H(x) \neq C(x)\}$ of $H$ and $C$. A hypothesis $H$ is called $\varepsilon$-*good* (w.r.t. a distribution $D$) if it satisfies the condition $D(H \neq C) < \varepsilon$, otherwise it is called $\varepsilon$-*bad*. Similarly, an algorithm $A$ is said to *learn* a target class $C$ using hypothesis class $\mathcal{H}$ in the malicious PAC model with noise rate $\eta$ if $A$ learns $C$ in the PAC model when the input sample is perturbed by any adversary using noise rate $\eta$. Motivated by the fact (shown in [6] and mentioned in the introduction) that a noise rate $\eta \geq \varepsilon/(1 + \varepsilon)$ forbids PAC learning with accuracy $\varepsilon$, we allow the sample size $m$ to depend polynomially also on $1/\Delta$, where $\Delta = \varepsilon/(1 + \varepsilon) - \eta$.

We will occasionally use *randomized* learning algorithms that have a sequence of tosses of a fair coin as additional input source. In this case the definition of PAC learning given above is modified so that $D(C \neq H) < \varepsilon$ must hold with probability at least $1 - \delta$ also with respect to $A$'s randomization. Finally, we will use *randomized hypotheses* or *coin rules*. A coin rule is any function $F : X \to [0, 1]$ where $F(x)$ is interpreted as the probability that the boolean hypothesis defined by the coin rule takes value 1 on $x$. Coin rules are formally equivalent to *p-concepts*, whose learnability has been investigated by Kearns and Schapire in [4]. In this work, however, we focus on a completely different problem, i.e., the malicious PAC learning of boolean functions using p-concepts as hypotheses. If a learner uses coin rules as hypotheses, then the PAC learning criterion $D(C \neq H) < \varepsilon$, where $C$ is the learner's hypothesis, is replaced by $\mathbf{E}_{x \sim D}|F(x) - C(x)| < \varepsilon$, where $F$ is the coin rule output by a learner and $\mathbf{E}_{x \sim D}$ denotes expectation with respect to the distribution $D$ on $X$. Note that $|F(x) - C(x)|$ is the probability of misclassifying $x$ using coin rule $F$. Thus $\mathbf{E}_{x \sim D}|F(x) - C(x)|$, which we call the *error probability* of $F$, is the probability of misclassifying a randomly drawn instance using coin rule $F$.

Furthermore, as Proposition 2 in Section 4 shows that any noise rate larger or equal to $2\varepsilon/(1 + 2\varepsilon)$ prevents PAC learning with accuracy $\varepsilon$ using randomized hypotheses, we allow the sample size to depend polynomially also on $1/\Delta$, where $\Delta = 2\varepsilon/(1 + 2\varepsilon) - \eta$.

Throughout this paper a "hat" over a parameter denotes the estimate of

---

[5] All the results from [6] we mention here hold in our harder noise model as well.

this parameter based on the sample under consideration. In addition to the usual asymptotical notations, let $\widetilde{O}(f)$ be $O(f)$ after dropping polylogarithmic factors.

# 3  Learning $k$-Intervals with Deterministic Hypotheses

In [2] a strategy has been introduced for learning the powerset of $d$ elements tolerating a malicious noise rate of $\eta = \varepsilon/(1 + \varepsilon) - \Delta$ and using an optimal sample size of $\widetilde{O}(d/\Delta + \varepsilon/\Delta^2)$. That strategy makes an essential use of the fact that there are only $d$ domain points. We now show that there is an infinite class over a continuous domain that can be learned with the same sample size. Our technique is applicable to any target class satisfying a certain relation (see remark below.)

Let $\mathcal{I}_k$ be the class of unions of at most $k$ intervals on the unit interval $[0, 1)$. It is easy to see that the Vapnik-Chervonenkis dimension of $\mathcal{I}_k$ is $2k$. We sketch a randomized algorithm for learning $\mathcal{I}_k$ with noise rate arbitrarily close to $\varepsilon/(1+\varepsilon)$. This algorithm outputs deterministic hypotheses consisting of $O(k/\Delta)$ labeled "bins", where each bin is either a subinterval $[a, b)$ of the unit interval $[0, 1)$ or a single point.

**Theorem 1.** *For any $k \geq 1$ and any $1 \geq \varepsilon, \delta, \Delta > 0$, there is an algorithm that PAC learns the class $\mathcal{I}_k$ with accuracy $\varepsilon$, confidence $\delta$, tolerating malicious noise rate $\eta = \varepsilon/(1 + \varepsilon) - \Delta$, and using a sample of size $\widetilde{O}\left(\varepsilon/\Delta^2 + k/\Delta\right)$.*

*Proof.* The proof is similar to [2, Theorem 4.1] for learning the powerset of $d$ points. We therefore only outline the argument in this abstract, emphasizing the changes. The complete presentation will be given in the full paper. Given a sample of size $m$ the algorithm divides the unit interval $[0, 1)$ into disjoint *bins* $B_s = [a_s, b_s)$, where $a_s < b_s$. Each bin contains roughly the same number $K$ of examples, where $K = \Theta(\Delta \cdot m/k)$. A binary label is assigned to each bin $B_s$ in the the following way: If the relative frequencies of the labels 0 and 1 among the examples contained in $B_s$ are "heavily unbalanced", then the most frequent label is assigned to $B_s$. Otherwise, a fair coin is flipped to decide which label is assigned to $B_s$. The value of the final hypothesis $H$ output by the algorithm on a point $x \in [0, 1)$ is then simply the label assigned to the bin $B_s$ such that $a_s \leq x < b_s$.

The analysis of this algorithm is quite similar to the one of algorithm RMD described in [2] for learning the powerset of $d$ points. There are, however, two main differences. First, there is an additional error that is not due to the adversary action but comes from those bins $B_s = [a_s, b_s)$ that contain a point $x$ on which the target switches from 0 to 1 or vice versa. These "boundary" bins therefore contain uncorrupted examples some with label 1 and some with label 0. Giving a unique label to a boundary bin then causes an error independent of the sample corruption. However, the number of boundary bins is at most $2k$ and their total probability can be upper bounded so that we incur in a small enough error even if they all receive the wrong label. A second problem arises with a point $x \in [0,1)$ occurring in the sample with very high multiplicity. To keep a bounded number of examples in each bin, we would have to distribute the occurrences of $x$ in more than one bin. If these bins received different labels, then the final hypothesis $H$ would not have a unique label for point $x$. To avoid this, the algorithm does a preliminary step in which all the examples of each point $x$ occurring in the sample with multiplicity higher than $2K$ are removed and put in a "singleton bin" $B^x$. The remaining examples are collected into regular bins and labels are assigned to both regular and singleton bins as described before. To evaluate a point $x \in [0,1)$ in this new bin structure, the final hypothesis $H$ first checks whether $B^x$ is a singleton bin. If this is the case, then $H(x)$ is set equal to the label assigned to $B^x$. Otherwise, $H(x)$ is set equal to the label of the regular bin $B_s$ such that $a_s \le x < b_s$. □

*Remark.* The above described technique of collecting sample points into bins and assigning labels to them is applicable to other target classes as well. The crucial point is to control the additional error of the boundary bins. Our analysis always works if the following relation holds: The number of boundary bins times the VC-dimension of the class of bins is at most of the same order as the VC-dimension of the target class. Details are found in the full paper.

## 4 Learning with Randomized Hypotheses

In this section, we investigate the power of randomized hypotheses for malicious PAC learning. We start by observing that an easy modification of Kearns and Li [6, Theorem 1] yields the following result. (Recall that a target class is nontrivial if it contains two functions $C$ and $C'$ and there exist two distinct points $x, x' \in X$ such that $C(x) = C'(x) = 1$ and $C(x') \ne C'(x')$).

**Proposition 2.** *For all nontrivial target classes $C$ and all $\varepsilon < 1/2$, no algorithm can learn $C$ with accuracy $\varepsilon$ and using deterministic or randomized hypotheses tolerating malicious noise rate $\eta \ge 2\varepsilon/(1 + 2\varepsilon)$.*

Let $\eta_{\text{rand}} = \eta_{\text{rand}}(\varepsilon) = 2\varepsilon/(1 + 2\varepsilon)$ (we omit the dependence on $\varepsilon$ when it is clear from the context.) As the corresponding information-theoretic bound $\eta_{\text{det}} = \varepsilon/(1+\varepsilon)$ for learners using deterministic hypotheses is strictly smaller than $\eta_{\text{rand}}$, one might ask whether this gap is real, i.e. whether randomized hypotheses really help in this setting. In Subsection 4.1 we give a positive answer to this question by showing a general strategy that, using randomized hypotheses, learns any target class $C$ tolerating any malicious noise rate $\eta$ bounded by a constant fraction of $\frac{(7/6)\varepsilon}{1+(7/6)\varepsilon}$ and using sample size $\tilde{O}(d/\varepsilon)$, where $d$ is the VC-dimension of $C$. Note that $\frac{(7/6)\varepsilon}{1+(7/6)\varepsilon} > \eta_{\text{det}}$, whereas no learner using deterministic hypotheses can tolerate a malicious noise rate $\eta \ge \eta_{\text{det}}$, even allowing an *infinite* sample. Furthermore, the sample size used by our strategy is actually *independent* of $\eta$. Finally, in Subsection 4.2 we show an algorithm for learning the powerset of $d$ points, for any $d \ge 1$, with malicious noise rates arbitrarily close to $\eta_{\text{rand}}$. The problem of finding a general strategy for learning an arbitrary concept class with randomized hypotheses with malicious noise rate arbitrarily close to $2\varepsilon/(1+2\varepsilon)$ remains open.

## 4.1 A General Upper Bound for Low Noise Rates

We show the following result.

**Theorem 3.** *For any target class $\mathcal{C}$ with VC-dimension $d$, any $0 < \varepsilon, \delta \le 1$, and any fixed constant $c < 7/6$ a sample size of order $\frac{d}{\varepsilon}$ (ignoring logarithmic factors) is necessary and sufficient for PAC learning $\mathcal{C}$ using randomized hypotheses, with accuracy $\varepsilon$, confidence $\delta$, and tolerating malicious noise rate $\eta = c\varepsilon/(1+c\varepsilon)$.*

This, combined with [2, Theorems 3.4 and 3.7] shows that, if the noise rate is about $\eta_{\text{det}}$, then a sample size of order $d/\Delta + \varepsilon/\Delta^2$ is only needed if the final hypothesis has to be deterministic.

The idea behind the proof of Theorem 3 is the following. A sample size $\tilde{O}(d/\varepsilon)$ is too small to reliably discriminate the target (or other $\varepsilon$-good concepts) from $\varepsilon$-bad concepts. (Actually, the adversary can make $\varepsilon$-bad hypotheses perform better on the sample than target $C$.) It is, however, possible to work in two phases as follows. Phase 1 removes some concepts from $\mathcal{C}$. It is guaranteed that all concept with an error rate "significantly larger" than $\varepsilon$ are removed, and that the target $C$ is not removed. Phase 2 reliably checks whether two concepts are independent in the sense that have a "small" joint error probability (the probability to produce a wrong prediction on the same randomly drawn example). Obviously, the majority vote of three pairwise independent hypotheses has error probability at most 3 times the "small" joint error probability of two independent concepts. If there is no independent set of size 3, there must be a maximal independent set $\mathcal{U}$ of size 2 (or 1). We will show that each maximal independent set contains a concept with error probability significantly smaller than $\varepsilon$. It turns out then that $G$ or the coin rule $\frac{1}{2}(G+H)$ are $\varepsilon$-good if $\mathcal{U} = \{G\}$ or $\mathcal{U} = \{G, H\}$, respectively.

*Proof of Theorem 3.* The lower bound is evident because it holds for the noise-free case, [3]. For the upper bound, we begin with the following preliminary considerations. Let $X$ be the domain of target class $\mathcal{C}$, $D$ be any distribution on $X$, and $C \in \mathcal{C}$ be the target. Given a hypothesis $H \in \mathcal{C}$, $E(H) = \{x : H(x) \ne C(x)\}$ denotes its *error set*, and $\text{err}(H) = D(E(H))$ its error probability. The *joint error probability* of two hypotheses $G, H \in \mathcal{C}$ is given by $\text{err}(G, H) = D(E(G) \cap E(H))$. Our proof will be based on the fact that (joint) error probabilities can be accurately empirically estimated. Let $S$ be the sample. We denote the relative frequency of mistakes of $H$ on the whole sample $S$ by $\widehat{\text{err}}(H)$. The partition of $S$ into a clean and a noisy part leads to the decomposition $\widehat{\text{err}}(H) = \widehat{\text{err}}^c(H) + \widehat{\text{err}}^n(H)$, where upper indices $c$ and $n$ refer to the clean and the noisy part of the sample, respectively. Note that term $\widehat{\text{err}}^c(H)$ is an empirical estimation of $\text{err}(H)$, whereas $\widehat{\text{err}}^n(H)$ is under control of the adversary. The terms $\widehat{\text{err}}(G, H)$, $\widehat{\text{err}}^c(G, H)$, and $\widehat{\text{err}}^n(G, H)$ are defined analogously.

---

**Algorithm: SEARCH-IND-HYPOS.**

**Input:** Target class $C$, sample $S$. Accuracy and confidence parameters $\varepsilon, \delta$, upper bound $\eta_b < \dfrac{(7/6)\varepsilon}{1 + (7/6)\varepsilon}$ on true malicious noise rate $\eta$.

**Initialization:** Let $\gamma = \dfrac{(7/6) - c}{(7/6) + c}$, where $c = \dfrac{\eta_b}{(1 - \eta_b)\varepsilon}$.

**Phase 1.**

1. Remove from $C$ all concepts $H$ such that $\widehat{\mathrm{err}}(H) > (1 + \gamma)\eta_b$.
   Let $K$ be the set of remaining concepts.
2. If $K$ is empty, then output a default hypothesis.

**Phase 2.**

1. If there exists an independent set $\{F, G, H\} \subseteq K$, then output the majority vote of $F$, $G$, and $H$.
2. Otherwise, pick a maximal independent set $\mathcal{U}$ of size 1 or 2.
   If $\mathcal{U} = \{H\}$, then output $H$. If $\mathcal{U} = \{G, H\}$, then output the coin rule $\frac{1}{2}(G + H)$.

---

**Fig. 1.** A description of the randomized algorithm used in the proof of Theorem 3.

Let $\gamma, \lambda > 0$ denote two fixed constants to be determined by the analysis and recall that $\hat{\eta}$ denotes the empirical noise rate. A standard application of the Chernoff-Hoeffding bound (9) and Lemma 8 shows that, for a suitable choice of $m = \tilde{O}(d/\varepsilon)$, the following conditions are simultaneously satisfied with probability $1 - \delta$:

**Condition 1** $\hat{\eta} \leq (1 + \gamma)\eta$.

**Condition 2**
   If $H \in C$ satisfies $\mathrm{err}(H) \geq \lambda\varepsilon$, then $\widehat{\mathrm{err}}^c(H) \geq (1 - \gamma)(1 - \eta)\mathrm{err}(H)$.

**Condition 3**
   If $G, H \in C$ satisfy $\mathrm{err}(G, H) \geq \lambda\varepsilon$, then $\widehat{\mathrm{err}}^c(G, H) \geq (1 - \gamma)(1 - \eta)\mathrm{err}(G, H)$.

The proof of these conditions, which are assumed in the sequel, is omitted in this short abstract. For proving Conditions 2 and 3 we use the fact that the VC-dimensions of the classes of the error sets and the joint error sets are both $O(d)$.

We now describe the learning algorithm SEARCH-IND-HYPOS illustrated in Figure 1. For simplicity we carry out the analysis with respect to the actual noise rate $\eta$, even though this should be replaced by the upper bound $\eta_b$ given to the algorithm as input parameter.

In phase 1, all concepts $H \in C$ satisfying $\widehat{\mathrm{err}}(H) > (1 + \gamma)\eta$ are removed. Let $K = \{H \in C : \widehat{\mathrm{err}}(H) \leq (1 + \gamma)\eta\}$ denote the set of remaining concepts. Note that $\widehat{\mathrm{err}}(C) \leq \hat{\eta}$. Applying Condition 1, it follows that target $C$ belongs to $K$. Applying Condition 2 with constant $\lambda \leq c(1 + \gamma)/(1 - \gamma)$, it follows that all concepts $H \in K$ satisfy:

$$\mathrm{err}(H) \leq \frac{(1 + \gamma)\eta}{(1 - \gamma)(1 - \eta)} . \tag{1}$$

We are now in position to formalize the notion of independence, which is central for phase 2 of SEARCH-IND-HYPOS. Let us introduce another parameter $\alpha$ whose value will also be determined by the analysis. We say that $G, H \in \mathcal{K}$ are *independent* if $\widehat{\text{err}}(G, H) \leq (\alpha + \gamma)\eta$. A subset $\mathcal{U} \subseteq \mathcal{K}$ is called independent if its hypotheses are pairwise independent.

**Claim.** If $\widehat{\text{err}}^c(H) \geq (1 - \alpha)\eta$ then $H$ and $C$ are independent.

To prove the claim note that, since $C$ is the target, $\widehat{\text{err}}(H, C) \leq \widehat{\text{err}}^n(H)$. The definition of $\mathcal{K}$ and the decomposition of $\widehat{\text{err}}$ into $\widehat{\text{err}}^c$ and $\widehat{\text{err}}^n$ imply that

$$\widehat{\text{err}}^n(H) = \widehat{\text{err}}(H) - \widehat{\text{err}}^c(H) \leq (1 + \gamma)\eta - (1 - \alpha)\eta = (\alpha + \gamma)\eta,$$

proving the claim.

From Claim and Condition 2 applied with $\lambda \leq \frac{c(1-\alpha)}{(1-\gamma)}$ we obtain the following facts:

**Fact 1.** If the $\text{err}(H) \geq \frac{(1-\alpha)\eta}{(1-\gamma)(1-\eta)}$, then $H$ and target $C$ are independent.

**Fact 2** Each maximal independent set $\mathcal{U} \subseteq \mathcal{K}$ contains at least one hypothesis whose error is smaller than $\frac{(1-\alpha)\eta}{(1-\gamma)(1-\eta)}$. In particular, if $\mathcal{U} = \{H\}$, then $\text{err}(H) \leq \frac{(1-\alpha)\eta}{(1-\gamma)(1-\eta)}$. If $\mathcal{U} = \{G, H\}$, then one of $\text{err}(G)$, $\text{err}(H)$ is smaller than or equal to $\frac{(1-\alpha)\eta}{(1-\gamma)(1-\eta)}$.

We now move on to the description of phase 2 (see Figure 1.) Note that phase 2 of SEARCH-IND-HYPOS either terminates with a deterministic hypothesis, or terminates with the coin rule $\frac{1}{2}(G + H)$. The following case analysis will show that the final hypothesis output by SEARCH-IND-HYPOS is $\varepsilon$-good.

Let's first consider the case that the final hypothesis is the majority vote $\text{MAJ}_{F,G,H}$ of three independent hypothesis $F$, $G$, and $H$ (step 1 in phase 2). Then an error occurs exactly on those instances $x$ that are wrongly predicted by at least two hypotheses of $F, G, H$, that is

$$\text{err}(\text{MAJ}_{F,G,H}) \leq \text{err}(F, G) + \text{err}(F, H) + \text{err}(G, H).$$

By definition of independence, we know that

$$\widehat{\text{err}}^c(X, Y) \leq \widehat{\text{err}}(X, Y) \leq (\alpha + \gamma)\eta$$

for each pair $(X, Y)$ of distinct hypothesis in $\{F, G, H\}$. Then, observing that $c\varepsilon = \eta/(1-\eta)$ and applying Condition 3 to each such pair with $\lambda \leq c(\alpha+\gamma)/(1-\gamma)$, we get that

$$\text{err}(\text{MAJ}_{F,G,H}) \leq \frac{3(\alpha + \gamma)\eta}{(1 - \gamma)(1 - \eta)}. \tag{2}$$

If the final hypothesis is the coin rule $\frac{1}{2}(G + H)$ (from step 2 in phase 2), we may apply (1) and Fact 2 to bound the error probability as follows:

$$\text{err}\left(\frac{1}{2}(G + H)\right) = \frac{1}{2}\left(\text{err}(G) + \text{err}(H)\right)$$

$$< \frac{1}{2}\left(\frac{(1 - \alpha)\eta}{(1 - \gamma)(1 - \eta)} + \frac{(1 + \gamma)\eta}{(1 - \gamma)(1 - \eta)}\right). \tag{3}$$

If the final hypothesis is $H$ (from step 2), then $err(H) < \frac{(1-\alpha)\eta}{(1-\gamma)(1-\eta)}$ by Fact 2. This error bound is smaller than the bound (3). We now have to find choices for the parameters $\alpha, \gamma, \lambda$ such that (2) and (3) are both upper bounded by $\varepsilon$ and the previously stated conditions

$$\lambda \le c(1+\gamma)/(1-\gamma) \ , \ \ \lambda \le c(1-\alpha)/(1-\gamma) \ , \ \ \lambda \le c(\alpha+\gamma)/(1-\gamma)$$

on $\lambda$ hold. Equating bounds (2) and (3) and solving for $\alpha$ gives $\alpha = \frac{2}{7} - \frac{5}{7}\gamma$. Substituting this into (2), setting the resulting formula to $\varepsilon$ and solving for $\gamma$ yields $\gamma = \frac{(7/6)-c}{(7/6)+c}$. (Observe that the choice of $\eta = \frac{c\varepsilon}{1+c\varepsilon}$ implies the equation $\frac{\eta}{1-\eta} = c\varepsilon$.) This in turn leads to the choice $\alpha = 3\frac{c-(1/2)}{c+(7/6)}$. According to these settings one can finally choose $\lambda = 1/3$. $\qquad\square$

*Remark.* The result of Theorem 3 gives rise to a challenging combinatorial problem: Given a target class, find 3 independent hypotheses, or alternatively, a maximal independent set of less than 3 hypotheses. This replaces the "consistent hypothesis" paradigm of noise-free PAC learning and the "minimizing disagreement" paradigm of agnostic learning.

## 4.2 An Almost Optimal Coin Rule for the Powerset

In this section, we introduce and analyze a simple algorithm called Square Rule (SR) for learning with coin rules the powerset $\mathcal{C}_d$ of $d$ elements in presence of a malicious noise rate arbitrarily close to $\eta_{\mathrm{rand}}$ and using almost optimal sample size. Algorithm SR works as follows. Let $H(p,q) = q^2/(p^2 + q^2)$. For a given sample $S$, let $\widehat{p}_0(x)$ and $\widehat{p}_1(x)$, respectively, denote the relative frequency of $(x,0)$ and $(x,1)$. On input $S$, SR outputs the coin rule[6] $F(x) = H(\widehat{p}_0(x), \widehat{p}_1(x)) = \widehat{p}_1(x)^2/(\widehat{p}_0(x)^2 + \widehat{p}_1(x)^2)$. We now show a derivation of the coin rule $F$. Consider a single point $x$ and let $\widehat{p}_0 = \widehat{p}_0(x)$ and $\widehat{p}_1 = \widehat{p}_1(x)$. Now, if the true label of $x$ is 0, we say that the "empirical return" of the adversary is $\widehat{p}_0$. Likewise, the adversary's "investment" for the false label 1 is $\widehat{p}_1$. Also, as $F$ uncorrectly classifies $x$ with probability $H(\widehat{p}_0, \widehat{p}_1)$, the "empirical return to investment ratio", which we denote by $\rho$, is $H(\widehat{p}_0, \widehat{p}_1) \cdot \widehat{p}_0/\widehat{p}_1$. Similarly, if the true label of $x$ is 1, then $\rho$ is $(1 - H(\widehat{p}_0, \widehat{p}_1)) \cdot \widehat{p}_1/\widehat{p}_0$. The function $F$ that minimizes $\rho$ over all choices of $\widehat{p}_0$ and $\widehat{p}_1$ is found by letting $H(\widehat{p}_0, \widehat{p}_1) \cdot \widehat{p}_0/\widehat{p}_1 = (1 - H(\widehat{p}_0, \widehat{p}_1)) \cdot \widehat{p}_1/\widehat{p}_0$ and solving for $F$ to obtain $H(\widehat{p}_0, \widehat{p}_1) = \widehat{p}_1^2/(\widehat{p}_0^2 + \widehat{p}_1^2)$. (A plot of the functions $F$ and $\rho$ is shown in Figure 2.) Note that, as our final goal is to bound the quantity $\mathbf{E}_{x \sim D}|F(x) - C(x)|$, we should actually choose $F$ so to minimize the *expected* return to investment ratio, i.e. the ratio $|H(\widehat{p}_0, \widehat{p}_1) - C(x)| \cdot D(x)/\widehat{p}_{1-C(x)}$. However, as we will show in a moment, an estimate of the unknown quantity $D(x)$ will suffice for our purposes.

**Theorem 4.** *For any $d \ge 1$ and any $0 < \varepsilon, \delta, \Delta \le 1$, algorithm SR learns the class $\mathcal{C}_d$ with accuracy $\varepsilon$, confidence $\delta$, tolerating malicious noise rate $\eta = 2\varepsilon/(1+2\varepsilon) - \Delta$, and using a sample of size $\widetilde{O}(d\varepsilon/\Delta^2)$.*

---

[6] The function $H$ was also used by Kearns, Schapire and Sellie [5] in connection with agnostic learning.

*Proof.* We start the proof with the following preliminary considerations. Let $X = \{1, \ldots, d\}$, let $D$ be any distribution on $X$, and let $C$ be the target function. Let $t(x) = (1-\eta)D(x)$ denote the probability that $x$ is presented by the adversary with the true label $C(x)$. Fix a sample $S$. The relative frequency of $(x, C(x))$ in $S$ is denoted by $\hat{t}(x)$. We assume w.l.o.g. that the adversary does never present an instance with its true label in noisy trials. (The performance of the coin rule $F$ gets better in this case.) We denote the relative frequency of $(x, 1 - C(x))$ in $S$ by $\hat{f}(x)$. The relative frequency of noisy trials in $S$ is denoted by $\hat{\eta}$. Clearly, $\hat{\eta} = \sum_{x \in X} \hat{f}(x)$. Applying Lemma 7, it is not hard to show that there exists a sample size $m = \tilde{O}(d\varepsilon/\Delta^2)$ such that with probability $1 - \delta$ the sample $S$ satisfies the following conditions:

$$\hat{\eta} \leq \eta + \frac{\Delta}{2}, \tag{4}$$

$$\forall x \in X : t(x) \geq \frac{\Delta}{24d} \Rightarrow \hat{t}(x) \geq \frac{t(x)}{2}, \tag{5}$$

$$\forall M \subseteq X : \sum_{x \in M} t(x) \leq 16\varepsilon \Rightarrow \sum_{x \in M} \hat{t}(x) \geq \sum_{x \in M} t(x) - \frac{\Delta}{8}. \tag{6}$$

To prove (4) we apply (11) with $p' = \eta$ and $\lambda = \Delta/(2\eta)$. To prove (5) we apply (9) with $p = \Delta/(24d)$ and $\lambda = 1/2$. Finally, to prove (6) we use (9) to find that

$$\Pr\left\{ S_m \leq \left( 1 - \frac{\lambda}{p} \right) mp \right\} \leq \exp\left( -\frac{\lambda^2 m}{2p} \right) \leq \exp\left( -\frac{\lambda^2 m}{2p'} \right)$$

where the last inequality holds for all $p' \geq p$ by monotonicity. Setting $\lambda = \Delta/8$ and $p' = 16\varepsilon$ concludes the proof of (6). These three conditions will be assumed to hold in the sequel.

An instance $x$ is called *light* if $t(x) < \Delta/(24d)$, and *heavy* otherwise. Note that $\eta < \eta_{\text{rand}} \leq 2/3$ (recall that $\eta_{\text{rand}} = 2\varepsilon/(1 + 2\varepsilon)$.) Thus, $D(x) < \Delta/(8d)$ for all light points. The total contribution of light points to the error probability of the coin rule $F$ is therefore less than $\Delta/8$. The following analysis focuses on heavy points; note that for these points the implication in (5) is valid. We will show that the total error probability on heavy points is bounded by $\varepsilon - \Delta/8$.

It will be instructive to consider the error probability on $x$ of our coin rule $F$ as the return of the adversary at $x$ (denoted by return$(x)$ henceforth) and the quantity $\hat{f}(x)$, defined above, as its investment at $x$. Our goal is to show that the total return of the adversary is smaller than $\varepsilon - \Delta/8$, given that its total investment is $\hat{\eta}$. The function $R(p, q) = pq/(p^2 + q^2)$ plays a central role in the analysis of the relation between return and investment. (A plot of this function is shown in Figure 2.) Function $R$ attains its maximal value $1/2$ for $p = q$. For $q \leq p/4$ or $p \leq q/4$, the maximal value is $4/17$. Before bounding the total return, we will analyze the term return$(x)$.

If $C(x) = 0$, then

$$\hat{f}(x) = \hat{p}_1(x), \quad \hat{t}(x) = \hat{p}_0(x), \quad \text{return}(x) = F(x) \cdot D(x) = \frac{\hat{p}_1(x)^2 \cdot D(x)}{\hat{p}_0(x)^2 + \hat{p}_1(x)^2}.$$

If $C(x) = 1$, then

$$\hat{f}(x) = \hat{p}_0(x), \quad \hat{t}(x) = \hat{p}_1(x), \quad \text{return}(x) = (1 - F(x)) \cdot D(x) = \frac{\hat{p}_0(x)^2 \cdot D(x)}{\hat{p}_0(x)^2 + \hat{p}_1(x)^2}.$$

Note that in both cases $\hat{f}(x) \cdot \hat{t}(x) = \hat{p}_0(x) \cdot \hat{p}_1(x)$ and $\text{return}(x) = \hat{f}(x)^2 \cdot D(x)/(\hat{p}_0(x)^2 + \hat{p}_1(x)^2)$. Setting $\hat{\alpha}(x) = t(x) - \hat{t}(x)$, we obtain $D(x) = t(x)/(1 - \eta) = (\hat{t}(x) + \hat{\alpha}(x))/(1 - \eta)$. For the sake of simplicity, we will use the abbreviations

$$\hat{p}_0 = \hat{p}_0(x), \quad \hat{p}_1 = \hat{p}_1(x), \quad \hat{f} = \hat{f}(x), \quad \hat{t} = \hat{t}(x), \quad \hat{\alpha} = \hat{\alpha}(x).$$

With these abbreviations, $\hat{t} \cdot \hat{f} = \hat{p}_0 \cdot \hat{p}_1$ is valid and the term $\text{return}(x)$ can be written as follows:

$$
\begin{aligned}
\text{return}(x) &= \frac{\hat{f}^2 \cdot (\hat{t} + \hat{\alpha})}{(\hat{p}_0^2 + \hat{p}_1^2) \cdot (1 - \eta)} = \frac{1}{1 - \eta} \left( \frac{\hat{t} \cdot \hat{f}}{\hat{p}_0^2 + \hat{p}_1^2} \hat{f} + \frac{\hat{\alpha} \cdot \hat{f}^2}{\hat{p}_0^2 + \hat{p}_1^2} \right) \\
&= \frac{1}{1 - \eta} \left( R(\hat{p}_0, \hat{p}_1) \cdot \hat{f} + \frac{\hat{\alpha} \cdot \hat{f}^2}{\hat{p}_0^2 + \hat{p}_1^2} \right) \quad (7)
\end{aligned}
$$

We now bound separately each one of the last two terms in (7). If $\hat{f} \geq \hat{t}/4$, then

$$\frac{R(\hat{p}_0, \hat{p}_1) \cdot \hat{f}}{(1 - \eta)} \leq \frac{\hat{f}}{2(1 - \eta)}.$$

Furthermore, as either $\hat{f} = \hat{p}_0$ or $\hat{f} = \hat{p}_1$,

$$\frac{\hat{\alpha} \cdot \hat{f}^2}{(\hat{p}_0^2 + \hat{p}_1^2)(1 - \eta)} \leq \frac{\hat{\alpha}}{1 - \eta}.$$

If $\hat{f} < \hat{t}/4$, we bound the last term in (7) using (5) and get

$$\frac{\hat{\alpha} \cdot \hat{f}^2}{(\hat{p}_0^2 + \hat{p}_1^2)} = \frac{(t - \hat{t}) \cdot \hat{f}^2}{(\hat{p}_0^2 + \hat{p}_1^2)} \leq \frac{\hat{t} \cdot \hat{f}^2}{(\hat{p}_0^2 + \hat{p}_1^2)} = \frac{(\hat{p}_0 \cdot \hat{p}_1) \cdot \hat{f}}{(\hat{p}_0^2 + \hat{p}_1^2)} = R(\hat{p}_0, \hat{p}_1) \cdot \hat{f}.$$

Hence, using (7) and $R(\hat{p}_0, \hat{p}_1) \leq 4/17 < 1/4$ for $\hat{f} < \hat{t}/4$, we finally get

$$\text{return}(x) \leq \frac{2R(\hat{p}_0, \hat{p}_1) \cdot \hat{f}}{1 - \eta} < \frac{\hat{f}}{2(1 - \eta)}.$$

Piecing the above together we obtain

$$\text{return}(x) \leq \frac{\hat{f}}{2(1 - \eta)} + \begin{cases} \frac{\hat{\alpha}}{(1 - \eta)} & \text{if } \hat{f} \geq \hat{t}/4, \\ 0 & \text{otherwise.} \end{cases} \quad (8)$$

We are now in the position to bound the total return on all heavy instances $x$. For the first term in the left-hand-side of (8) we obtain the bound

$$\frac{1}{2(1 - \eta)} \sum \hat{f}(x) \leq \frac{\hat{\eta}}{2(1 - \eta)}$$

where the sum is over all heavy $x$. The treatment of the second term in the left-hand-side of (8) is more subtle. Let $M$ denote the set of heavy instances $x$ where $\widehat{f}(x) \geq \widehat{t}(x)/4$. $D(M)$ is therefore bounded as follows:

$$\sum_{x \in M} t(x) \leq 2 \sum_{x \in M} \widehat{t}(x) \leq 8 \sum_{x \in M} \widehat{f}(x) \leq 8\widehat{\eta} < 16\varepsilon.$$

From (6), we conclude that:

$$\frac{1}{1-\eta} \sum_{x \in M} \widehat{\alpha}(x) \leq \frac{1}{1-\eta} \sum_{x \in M} (t(x) - \widehat{t}(x)) \leq \frac{\Delta}{8(1-\eta)}.$$

A straightforward computation shows that

$$\frac{\widehat{\eta}}{2(1-\eta)} + \frac{\Delta}{8(1-\eta)} \leq \varepsilon - \Delta/8.$$

As the probability of all light points is at most $\Delta/8$, the expected error of SR is at most $\varepsilon$. This completes the proof of Theorem 4. □

*Remark.* In the full version of the paper we show an algorithm for learning the class of unions of at most $d$ intervals using sample size $\widetilde{O}(d\varepsilon/\Delta^2)$.

The upper bound of Theorem 4 has a matching lower bound (up to logarithmic factors). The proof, which is a somewhat involved modification of a lower bound proof for the minimum disagreement strategy presented in [2], is only sketched in this abstract.

**Theorem 5.** *For any target class $C$ with VC-dimension $d \geq 3$, for any $0 < \varepsilon \leq 1/38$, $0 < \delta \leq 1/74$, and for any $0 < \Delta = o(\varepsilon)$, the sample size needed by any strategy (even using randomized hypotheses) for learning $C$ with accuracy $\varepsilon$, confidence $\delta$, and tolerating malicious noise rate $\eta = 2\varepsilon/(1 + 2\varepsilon) - \Delta$, is $\Omega\left(d\varepsilon/\Delta^2\right)$.*

*Proof.* One uses $d$ shattered points with a suitable distribution $D$ and shows that, with constant probability, there exists a constant fraction of these points which occur with a frequency much lower than expected. The measure according to $D$ of these points is $2\varepsilon$, but the adversary can balance the occurrences of both labels on these points while using noise rate less than $\eta_{\text{rand}}$. Hence, even a randomized hypothesis cannot achieve an error smaller than $\varepsilon$. □

## 5 Minimizing Disagreements with Classification Noise

In this section we consider the classification noise model. In [7], Laird has proven an optimal sample size of $\ln |C|/(\varepsilon\Delta^2)$ for learning by minimizing disagreements any target class $C$ of finite size $|C|$ with noise rate $\eta = 1/2 - \Delta$. This sample size is matched by Simon's lower bound [8]. We now generalize Laird's result by showing that $d/(\varepsilon\Delta^2)$ training examples suffice, up to logarithmic factors, to learn any target class of VC-dimension $d$. Note that Simon's lower bound can be used to show that the sample size bound $d/(\varepsilon\Delta^2)$ can not be improved in general (the results from [8] implicitly prove this lower bound also for randomized hypotheses). The proof is omitted here.

**Theorem 6.** *For any $d \geq 1$, any target class $\mathcal{C}$ of VC-dimension $d$, and any $0 < \varepsilon, \delta, \Delta \leq 1$, the strategy that outputs any hypothesis in $\mathcal{C}$ with the smallest sample error PAC learns $\mathcal{C}$ with accuracy $\varepsilon$, confidence $\delta$, tolerating classification noise rate $\eta = 1/2 - \Delta$, and using a sample of size $\tilde{O}\left(d/(\varepsilon\Delta^2)\right)$.*

## 6  Some Statistical and Combinatorial Relations

Let $S_{m,p}$ and $S'_{m,p'}$ be the sums of successes in a sequence of $m$ Bernouilli trials each succeeding with probability respectively at least $p$ and at most $p'$.

**Lemma 7.** *For all $0 < \lambda < 1$,*

$$\Pr\{S_{m,p} \leq (1-\lambda)mp\} \leq e^{-\lambda^2 mp/2} \tag{9}$$

$$\Pr\{S_{m,p} \leq m(p-\lambda)\} \leq e^{-2\lambda^2 m}, \tag{10}$$

$$\Pr\{S'_{m,p'} \geq (1+\lambda)mp'\} \leq e^{-\lambda^2 mp'/3}. \tag{11}$$

Let $\mathcal{C}$ be a target class of VC-dimension $d$ over some domain $X$. Let $D$ be a distribution over $X$. Let $S$ be an unlabeled sample of size $m$ drawn from $X$ under $D$. For $C \in \mathcal{C}$ let $D_S(C) = |\{x \in S : x \in C\}|/m$, the empirical probability of $C$.

**Lemma 8 [10].** *For any $0 < \varepsilon, \gamma \leq 1$ and any $0 < \delta < 1$, the probability that there exists a $C \in \mathcal{C}$ such that $D(C) > \varepsilon$ and $D_S(C) \leq (1-\gamma)D(C)$ is at most $8(2m)^d e^{-\gamma^2 \varepsilon m/4}$ which in turn is at most $\delta$ if $m > \max\left\{\frac{8}{\gamma^2\varepsilon}\ln\left(\frac{8}{\delta}\right), \frac{16d}{\gamma^2\varepsilon}\ln\left(\frac{16}{\gamma^2\varepsilon}\right)\right\}$.*

## References

1. D. Angluin and P.D. Laird. Learning from noisy examples. *Machine Learning*, 2:343–370, 1988.
2. N. Cesa-Bianchi, E. Dichterman, P. Fischer, and H. Simon. Noise-tolerant learning near the information-theoretic bound. In *Proceedings of the 28th ACM Symposium on the Theory of Computing*. ACM Press, 141–150, 1996.
3. A. Ehrenfeucht, D. Haussler, M. Kearns, and L. Valiant. A General Lower Bound on the Number of Examples Needed for Learning. *Information and Computation*, 82(3):247–261, 1989.
4. M. Kearns and R.E. Schapire. Efficient distribution-free learning of probabilistic concepts. *Journal of Computer and Systems Sciences*, 48(3):464–497, 1994. An extended abstract appeared in the *Proceedings of the 30th Annual Symposium on the Foundations of Computer Science*.
5. M. J. Kearns, R. E. Schapire, and L. Sellie. Toward Efficient Agnostic Learning. *Machine Learning*, 17(2):115–141, 1994.

6. M.J. Kearns and M. Li. Learning in the presence of malicious errors. *SIAM Journal on Computing*, 22(4):807–837, 1993. A preliminary version appeared in the *Proceedings of the 20th ACM Symposium on the Theory of Computation.*

7. P.D. Laird. *Learning from Good and Bad Data.* Kluwer, 1988.

8. H.U. Simon. General bounds on the number of examples needed for learning probabilistic concepts. *Journal of Computer and Systems Sciences*, 52:239–254, 1996.

9. L. Valiant. A theory of the learnable. *Communications of the ACM*, 27(11):1134–1142, 1984.

10. V.N. Vapnik. *Estimation of Dependences Based on Empirical Data.* Springer Verlag, 1982.

# 7  Figures

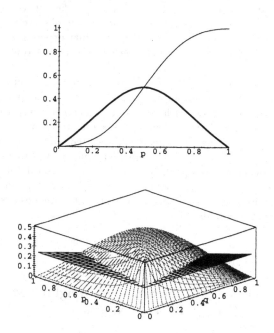

**Fig. 2. Top:** Curve of the coin rule (thin) and the return (thick); the curves are scaled to $p + q = 1$. **Bottom:** Plot of the return curve $R(p, q) = (pq)/(p^2 + q^2)$ and the constant function $c(p, q) = 4/17$, for $q \in [0, 1]$, $p \in [0, (1 - q)]$.

# Learning When to Trust Which Experts

David Helmbold[1] and Stephen Kwek[2] and Leonard Pitt[3]

[1] University of California at Santa Cruz, Department of Computer Science, Santa Cruz, CA, 95064, U.S.A., Email: dph@cse.ucsc.edu
[2] Department of Computer Science, Washington University, St. Louis, MO 63130, Email: kwek@cs.wustl.edu
[3] University of Illinois at Urbana-Champaign, Department of Computer Science, Urbana, IL 61801, U.S.A., Email: pitt@cs.uiuc.edu

**Abstract.** The standard model for prediction using a pool of experts has an underlying assumption that one of the experts performs well. In this paper, we show that this assumption does not take advantage of situations where both the outcome and the experts' predictions are based on some input which the learner gets to observe too. In particular, we exhibit a situation where each individual expert performs badly but collectively they perform well, and show that the traditional weighted majority techniques perform poorly.

To capture this notion of 'the whole is often greater than the sum of its parts', we propose an approach to measure the overall competency of a pool of experts with respect to a competency class or structure. A competency class or structure is a set of decompositions of the instance space where each expert is associated with a 'competency region' in which we assume he is competent. Our goal is to perform close to the performance of a predictor who knows the best decomposition in the competency class or structure where each expert performs reasonably well in its competency region. We present both positive and negative results in our model.

## 1 Introduction

### 1.1 The Deficiency of the Standard Weighted Majority Techniques for Prediction Using a Pool of Experts

In [LW94], Littlestone and Warmuth study the problem of making on-line prediction using a pool of experts. In their model, the learner faces a (possibly infinite) sequence of trials, with a boolean prediction to be made in each trial, and the goal of the learner is to make few mistakes. The learner is allowed to make his prediction by observing how a given pool of experts predict. The underlying assumption is that at least one of these experts will perform well but the learner does not know which one.

They propose the weighted majority algorithm which works as follows. A weight is associated with each expert. Initially, all the weights are set to one. The learner predicts 0 if the sum of the weights of all the experts that predict 0 is greater than that of the experts that predict 1, otherwise the learner predicts

1. When a mistake is made, the learner simply multiplies the weights of those experts that predict wrongly by some fixed non-negative constant $\beta$ smaller than one. The following mistake bounds are obtained for the weighted majority algorithm.

**Theorem 1.** *[LW94] Given a pool of experts $\mathcal{E}$, on any (possibly infinite) sequence of trials, the weighted majority algorithm makes at most*

a) $O(\log|\mathcal{E}| + \eta)$ *mistakes, if one of the experts makes at most $\eta$ mistakes.*

b) $O(\log(|\mathcal{E}|/k) + m/k)$ *mistakes, if there is a subset of $k$ experts making a total of $m$ mistakes.* $\qquad\square$

Observe that in this weighted majority algorithm, the weight of an expert after making $l$ mistakes is $\beta^l$ and hence, it is also known as the weighted majority algorithm using an *exponential weighting scheme*. Recently, an alternate weighting scheme, called the *binomial weighting scheme*, has been suggested by Cesa-Bianchi *et al.* [CBFHW95] and is shown to have a better mistake bound.

Suppose the experts' predictions and the actual outcome depend on some input (instance) in each trial. Notice that neither the binomial weighting scheme nor the exponential weighting scheme makes use of the instance when calculating the weights of the experts. This can be a serious disadvantage when the learner can use the instances to determine which experts are likely to predict correctly.

To illustrate this, consider the following example with a boolean instance space $\{0,1\}^n$ and two experts, $E_0$ and $E_1$ that always give opposite predictions. If $E_0$ makes at most $m_0$ mistakes if one crucial component of the instance is set to 0, and $E_1$ makes at most $m_1$ mistakes when that component is set to 1, then the weighted majority algorithm can be forced to make a mistake on almost every point in the instance space (more precisely, $2^n - |m_0 - m_1|$ mistakes), even if it uses table lookup to remember all of its previous mistakes. However, if the learner uses $E_0$'s predictions when the crucial input component was set to 0 and $E_1$'s predictions otherwise, then the learner makes at most $m_0 + m_1$ mistakes when it maintains a table of counterexamples. In other words, although neither expert is very competent, collectively they become competent if we consider restricting the use of each expert $E_i$ to the appropriate subset of the instance space.

Unfortunately, the algorithms that employ the weighted majority techniques do not take advantage of this situation. Hence, we propose two approaches that capture this notion of "the whole is often greater than the sum of its parts.":

**Competency Class:** In the first approach, each expert's area of expertise is assumed to be representable as a function chosen from some known "competency class" (of concepts).

**Competency Structure:** Alternatively, the instance space is partitioned into regions and each expert is associated with one such region as his area of expertise. Often it is assumed that the partition is representable as a $k$-valued function taken from some known class of functions, which we call *competency structure*.

With this view, the learning problem may be seen as that of determining the area of expertise of each expert. However, we illustrate later that this view is not necessarily the best.

## 1.2   The Competency Model

Suppose we have a collection of $k$ experts $\mathcal{E} = \{E_1, \cdots, E_k\}$ where each expert can be viewed as a boolean function on some finite instance space $\mathcal{X}$. Let $f$ be an arbitrary target concept (boolean function) defined over $\mathcal{X}$. The learner's goal is to use the set of experts in order to approximate the target $f$. We make no assumption on the set of experts $\mathcal{E}$ or the target $f$ other than they are functions of the instance space. As in other settings focusing on prediction with expert advice, we measure the performance of the learner relative to the "goodness" of the set of experts.

A *covering* $C = \langle c_1, \cdots, c_k \rangle$ is an ordered set of $k$ subsets of the instance space with the property that the union of the $k$ subsets is the entire instance space $\mathcal{X}$. The covering assigns the *competency region* $c_i \subseteq \mathcal{X}$ to each expert $E_i$ such that ideally, each expert should be competent (have low incompetence) in its competency region. This motivates the following definition. The *incompetence* of an expert $E_i$ with respect to the covering $C = \langle c_1, \cdots, c_k \rangle$ and target $f$, denoted by $incom(E_i, C, f)$, is defined as the number of mistakes $E_i$ makes over its competency region $c_i$. That is,

$$incom(E_i, C, f) = |\{x \in c_i : E_i(x) \neq f(x)\}|.$$

The *incompetence* of the entire collection of experts $\mathcal{E}$ with respect to the covering $C$ and target function $f$, written as $incom(\mathcal{E}, C, f)$, is defined as

$$incom(\mathcal{E}, C, f) = \sum_{i=1}^{k} incom(E_i, C, f).$$

Intuitively, if the learner makes his prediction on each input $x$ by taking a majority vote on the predictions of the set of experts whose competency regions in the covering $C$ contain $x$, then the maximum number of mistakes that the learner makes is $incom(\mathcal{E}, C, f)$ assuming that at most one mistake is made on each instance. (This can be done by storing the counterexamples in a table, provided the incompetence of each expert $E_i$ w.r.t. $C$ is not too large.) The following property follows immediately from the definition of incompetence.

**Property 2.** *If* $C = \langle c_1, \cdots, c_k \rangle$ *and* $C' = \langle c'_1, \cdots, c'_k \rangle$ *are two coverings of the instance space where* $c_i \subseteq c'_i$ *for each* $1 \leq i \leq k$ *then* $incom(\mathcal{E}, C, f) \leq incom(\mathcal{E}, C', f)$. $\quad\square$

Note that the competency regions in a covering can overlap and that the incompetence measure tends to penalize coverings with large overlaps, since the mistakes of the experts on the overlapping region are added together.

Suppose no assumptions are made about the competency regions. Consider two 'experts' (or more appropriately idiots) $E_0$ and $E_1$ where $E_0$ always predict 0 regardless of what the instance is, and $E_1$ always predict 1. Suppose we do not place any restriction on the competency regions allowed. For any boolean concept $f$, if we let $c_i$ be the part of the instance space that is classified as $i$ by $f$ then $C = \langle c_0, c_1 \rangle$ forms an optimum covering where $incom(\{E_0, E_1\}, C, f) = 0$! In other words, these two experts form a competent team in predicting any boolean concept, which means any positive result in our prediction model would imply that we can learn any boolean concept. Thus, learning arbitrary coverings is as hard as learning arbitrary functions. Therefore, we must make assumptions about the competency regions, even if the prediction strategies of the experts are simple. We use two alternative ways of restricting the possible coverings to make the learning of competency regions tractable:

**Competency Class:** We first consider restrictions on the competency regions used. Let $\mathcal{R}$ be a class of concepts. A covering $C = \langle c_1, \cdots, c_k \rangle$ is in the *competency class* induced by $\mathcal{R}$, written $\mathcal{C_R}$, if and only if each $c_i$ is a member of $\mathcal{R}$.

**Competency Structure:** When the sets of a covering are disjoint, the covering essentially maps each instance to an expert. Thus, the covering may be viewed as a classification function $C(x) = i$ where expert $E_i$ is good on instance $x$. Our second kind of restriction allows only those coverings which correspond to certain mappings. Given a mapping class $\mathcal{M}$, the *competency structure* $\mathcal{S_M}$ induced by $\mathcal{M}$ is the set of all coverings consistent with a mapping in $\mathcal{M}$.

For example, suppose DL is the class of decision lists. Then $\mathcal{C}_{\mathrm{DL}}$ is the class of coverings where the competency regions in each admissible covering can be expressed using binary decision lists and $\mathcal{S}_{\mathrm{DL}}$ is the class of coverings which partition the instance space using a $k$-valued decision list.

The *joint incompetence* of $\mathcal{E}$ with respect to a competency class or structure $\mathcal{C}$, and target $f$, $incom(\mathcal{E}, \mathcal{C}, f)$, is the minimum incompetence of the entire collection of experts $\mathcal{E}$ over all coverings of $\mathcal{X}$ in $\mathcal{C}$. That is,

$$incom(\mathcal{E}, \mathcal{C}, f) = \min_{C \in \mathcal{C}} incom(\mathcal{E}, C, f).$$

We say that $\mathcal{E}$ is *completely competent* if $incom(\mathcal{E}, \mathcal{C}, f) = 0$.

An *optimum covering* in some competency class or structure $\mathcal{C}$ is any covering $C^{opt} = \langle C_1^{opt}, \cdots, C_k^{opt} \rangle$ such that $incom(\mathcal{E}, C^{opt}, f) = incom(\mathcal{E}, \mathcal{C}, f)$. In other words, if the learner predicts using an optimal covering of $\mathcal{X}$ then its worst case number of mistakes is at most $incom(\mathcal{E}, \mathcal{C}, f)$. For instance, in the example of Section 1.1, the joint incompetence of the two experts with respect to the competency class of single literals[4] is at most $m_1 + m_2$ where the competency regions are defined by the crucial component of the input. From here on, we shall

---

[4] Actually, for this simple example we could also use the competency class of disjunctions or the competency structure of decision lists.

simply refer to the joint incompetence of $\mathcal{E}$ with respect to $\mathcal{C}$ as the incompetence of $\mathcal{E}$.

In our new model, which we call the *competency model*, the learner is given a pool of experts $\mathcal{E} = \{E_1, \cdots, E_k\}$ and we assume there exists a good covering from some known competency class or structure $\mathcal{C}$. The learning process consists of a sequence of trials as in Littlestone and Warmuth's model. On the $t$th trial, an instance $x^t \in \mathcal{X}$ is given to the learner, as well as the experts' predictions for $x^t$. The learner then predicts how the target concept $f$ classifies $x^t$ based on the experts' predictions and its past experience. After the prediction is made, the learner is told $f(x^t)$, the correct classification of $x^t$. If the prediction is incorrect, then the learner has made a *mistake*. This feedback can then be used to improve the learner's future predictions. The learner is said to be able to *learn* the competency class or structure $\mathcal{C}$ over an instance space $\mathcal{X}$ if the following criterion is met.

**Learning criterion in the competency model:** For any target concept $f$ and any set $\mathcal{E}$ of experts, if the number of mistakes the learner makes on any sequence of trials is bounded by some polynomial $poly_l(|\mathcal{E}|,\ incom(\mathcal{E},\mathcal{C},f),$ $complex(\mathcal{X}),\ complex(C^{opt}))$ for some competency class or structure $\mathcal{C}$ then we say $\mathcal{C}$ is *learnable*. Here, $complex(\mathcal{X})$ and $complex(C^{opt})$ are some appropriate complexity measures of the instance space $\mathcal{X}$ and an optimal covering $C^{opt}$ from $\mathcal{C}$. For example, if $\mathcal{C}$ is the class of disjunctions of boolean literals then $complex(\mathcal{X})$ is the number of variables and $complex(C^{opt})$ is the total number of literals that appear in $C^{opt}$. We say the learner is *efficient* if the time it consumes in each trial is bounded by some polynomial in $|\mathcal{E}|$, $incom(\mathcal{E},\mathcal{C},f)$, $complex(\mathcal{X})$ and $complex(C^{opt})$.

Furthermore, we say $\mathcal{C}$ or $C^{opt}$ is *identifiable* if we can identify each expert's competency region in the optimum covering using $\mathcal{C}$ without making more than some polynomial $poly_i(|\mathcal{E}|,\ incom(\mathcal{E},\mathcal{C},f),\ complex(\mathcal{X}),\ complex(C^{opt}))$ number of mistakes. □

It is clear that identifiability implies learnability. However, it is not clear, and probably not true, that learnability implies identifiability. There are situations where identifiability is desirable. For example, you may not have the resources to employ all the experts but are able to observe their past performance. In this case, you would like to infer their competency regions and select the subset of experts that suits your need.

Notice that the standard model used in the weighted majority algorithm is a specialization of the competency model where the competency class $\mathcal{C}$ consists of exactly two elements, the entire instance space $\mathcal{X}$ and the empty set. However, we have also relaxed the criterion for learning by not insisting that the mistake bound be polynomial in $\log k$ (as is the weighted majority's bound) but in $k$ instead. This is reasonable if the number of experts, $k$, is not extremely large.

## 1.3 Organization of This Paper

In Section 2, we present an efficient algorithm for learning the competency class (structure) of intervals in a finite linearly ordered instance space. Note that there is no distinction between competency class and structure when the competency regions are intervals, as they can be easily shown to be equivalent. The algorithm can be easily generalized to learn fixed depth $d$-ary decision trees (omitted here).

In Section 3, we begin by presenting an efficient algorithm for identifying the competency class of disjunctions of boolean literals. We do not require the instance space to be $\{0,1\}^n$ but may be a subset of $\{0,1\}^n$, as long as our optimum covering contains the subset of $\{0,1\}^n$ that may occur in our trials (a.k.a. *effective instance space*). We then continue to exhibit a simple learning algorithm for learning the same competency class with a smaller mistake bound. In doing so, we illustrate that identifying an optimum covering may not be the best way of learning a competency class. Both algorithms are based on Littlestone's [Lit88] WINNOW algorithm for learning $r$-literal disjunctions which has the ability to pick up the relevant attributes quickly even when there are (exponentially) many irrelevant attributes.

Our results also imply that the competency class of $k$-DNF formulas is identifiable and learnable when $k$ is fixed. At first glance, it may seem that our results also imply that the concept class of DNF formulas is learnable in the on-line mistake bound model by having an optimum covering consisting of one expert, which always predicts true, for each term $t$ in the target DNF formula with competency region $t$. Unfortunately, our definition of covering requires that the entire effective instance space be covered. One could cover the false instances by adding an extra expert who always predicts false and whose competency region is the entire domain. Unfortunately, this may increase the incompetence of the experts dramatically.

Knowing that we can identify the competency class of disjunctions by modifying Littlestone's WINNOW algorithm, one may ask whether we can identify the competency class of linear threshold functions over the boolean instance space, since they can be learned in the standard on-line model using WINNOW as well. Unfortunately, it is not clear how we can adapt WINNOW to do so. In fact, we show in Section 4 that identifying the competency class of conjunctions, which is a subclass of linear threshold functions, is as hard as learning decision trees in the on-line mistake bound model with a constant number of lies. The latter result, though not known to be impossible, is a difficult open problem.

In Section 5, we modify a previously known[5] on-line algorithm for learning decision lists to obtain an efficient learning algorithm for the decision list competency structures. We conclude in Section 6 with some open problems in this new frontier of prediction using experts' advice.

Throughout this paper, we assume implicitly that all the counterexamples seen are stored in a table along with their classifications. If an instance happens to be in the table, then the learner predicts with the correct classification that is stored in the table.

---

[5] This technique is due to Littlestone (private communication).

## 2  Learning the Interval Competency Class or Structure

In this section, we assume that the (finite) instance space is linearly ordered and consider the competency class $\mathcal{C}_{\mathcal{I}}$ induced by the class of intervals $\mathcal{I}$. Since the domain is linearly ordered, we can assume that the instance space is numbered $1, \ldots, d$. The class of intervals, $\mathcal{I}$, contains all subsets of the instance space of the form $i, \ldots, j$. A covering is in $\mathcal{C}_{\mathcal{I}}$ if and only if each $c_i$ is in $\mathcal{I}$.

Note that this competency class includes coverings with overlapping intervals. However, it is easy to see that there will always be an optimum covering with disjoint intervals. This follows from Property 2 and the fact that for any pair of intervals $I$ and $I'$, there are two disjoint intervals $\widehat{I} \subseteq I$ and $\widehat{I'} \subseteq I'$ such that $I \cup I' = \widehat{I} \cup \widehat{I'}$. Therefore learning the competency class of intervals is closely related to learning the competency structure which maps a (possibly empty) interval of the domain to each expert.

We now restrict our attention to coverings with disjoint intervals. When there are $k$ experts and the instance space has $d$ points then there are $\binom{d+1}{k-1}k! \leq (dk)^k$ such coverings. If the set of experts is completely competent, then the halving algorithm [LW94] can be used to learn the competency class while making at most $k \log dk$ mistakes. We refine this approach to overcome two difficulties – the halving algorithm is not generally efficient, and the experts may not be completely competent.

Assume that the $incom(\mathcal{E}, \mathcal{C}_{\mathcal{I}}, f) = \eta$, so that the optimal covering mislabels $\eta$ points. We extend the set of coverings to include one which is perfect and use dynamic programming to efficiently implement the conservative halving algorithm on this extended class of coverings. First we extend the covering by closing it to $\eta$ exceptions (at the end of the section we describe a standard doubling-trick for when $\eta$ is unknown). This ensures that one of the possible coverings is perfect. To speed up our algorithm, we also allow several of the $k$ intervals in the covering to be associated with the same expert. Thus we are actually learning a more general concept structure which can be represented as a $k$-decision list with decisions of the form "is $x \leq i$?"

We implement the conservative halving algorithm by counting the number of hypotheses that correctly label those previously seen points in the algorithm's table and also label the new point 0, and compare this with the number of hypotheses that correctly label the points in the table while labeling the new point 1. The halving algorithm predicts with the label for the new point that has the larger count, or arbitrarily if the counts are equal. Thus the halving algorithm can be implemented efficiently whenever one can efficiently count the number of hypotheses that correctly label a given sample. We show how dynamic programming can be used to do this counting.

Since there are $\binom{d}{\eta}$ ways of selecting the $\eta$ exceptions, $\binom{d+1}{k-1}$ ways of partitioning the instance space into $k$ subintervales and $k^k$ ways of assigning each subinterval to an expert, there are $\binom{d}{\eta}\binom{d+1}{k-1}k^k \leq d^\eta(dk)^k$ hypotheses in the extended class. Let $p_1, p_2, ..., p_r$ be a set $r$ labeled instances in ascending order. Define the function $\#(c, i, j, n)$ (see Figure 1) to be the number of ways that $1, ..., p_c$ can be covered with $i$ intervals such that the last interval uses expert

$E_j$ and the covering makes $n(\leq \eta)$ mistakes on points $1, ..., p_c$. The following lemma gives a recurrence relation on the function $\#(c, i, j, n)$ which allows us to compute $\#(c, i, j, n)$ for all feasible choices of $c$, $i$, $j$ and $n$, using dynamic programming[6] in $O(rk^2\eta)$ time.

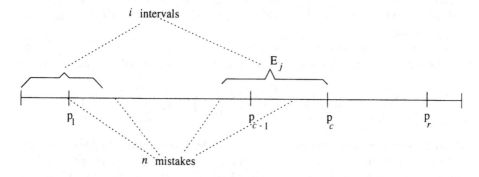

**Fig. 1.** The function $\#(c, i, j, n)$.

**Lemma 3.** *The function $\#(c, i, j, n)$ satisfies the following recurrences:*
*If expert $j$ agrees with the label of $p_c$ then*

$$\#(c, i, j, n) = \#(c - 1, i, j, n) +$$
$$\sum_{s=1}^{i-1} \binom{p_c - p_{c-1}}{s} k^{s-1} \sum_{n'=0}^{\eta} \binom{p_c - p_{c-1} - 1}{n'} \sum_{j'=1}^{k} \#(c - 1, i - s, j', \eta - n').$$
$$(1)$$

*If expert $j$ disagrees with the label of $p_c$ there will be a mistake on point $p_c$, and*

$$\#(c, i, j, n) = \#(c - 1, i, j, n - 1) +$$
$$\sum_{s=1}^{i-1} \binom{p_c - p_{c-1}}{s} k^{s-1} \sum_{n'=0}^{\eta-1} \binom{p_c - p_{c-1} - 1}{n'} \sum_{j'=1}^{k} \#(c - 1, i - s, j', \eta - 1 - n').$$
$$(2)$$

**Proof:** The first term $\#(c - 1, i, j, n)$ on the right-hand side of Equation (1) is to count those configurations where the last interval covers both $p_{c-1}$ and $p_c$. The second term counts the number of configurations where the last interval covers $p_c$ but not $p_{c-1}$.

The number of intervals, $s$, between $p_{c-1}$ and $p_c$, can range from 1 to $i - 1$. For each choice of $s$, there are $\binom{p_c - p_{c-1}}{s} k^{s-1}$ choices of $s$ intervals in the half open

---

[6] The algorithm consists of four nested loops iterating through all possible choices of $c, i, n$ and $j$ in that order.

interval $(p_{c-1}, p_c]$ and assignments of experts to these intervals. (Note that the last interval has already been assigned to expert $E_j$.) Furthermore, the number of exceptions, $n'$, in the open interval $(p_{c-1}, p_c)$ ranges from 0 to $\eta$ and for each choice of $n'$, there are $\binom{p_c - p_{c-1} - 1}{n'}$ ways of selecting $n'$ exceptions in the open interval $(p_{c-1}, p_c)$. The innermost summation is simply counting the number of ways of covering the remaining subinterval in $[1, p_c]$ after fixing both $s$ and $n'$, and the fact that there are $k$ possible experts that can be assigned to the next to last interval.

Equation (2) can be derived similarly. $\square$

The number of coverings that are consistent with the $r$ labeled sample is

$$\sum_{i=1}^{k} \sum_{j=1}^{k} \sum_{n=0}^{\eta} \left[ \#(r, i, j, k) \cdot \sum_{\alpha=1}^{k-i+1} \binom{d - p_r}{\alpha} k^{\alpha-1} \cdot \sum_{\beta=1}^{\eta-n} \binom{d - p_r}{\beta} \right] \quad (3)$$

The three outermost summations are to count the ways of specifying the portions of the coverings that cover the closed interval $[1, p_r]$ using $i$ intervals, with the last interval being assigned to expert $j$, and the $n$ exceptions on the closed interval $[1, p_r]$. The sum $\sum_{\alpha=1}^{k-i+1} \binom{d - p_r}{\alpha} k^{\alpha-1}$ counts the number of ways of covering the remaining points $p_r + 1, \cdots, d$ using at most $k - i + 1$ intervals where the leftmost interval is an extension of the last interval in the covering of the interval $[1, p_r]$, while the sum $\sum_{\beta=1}^{\eta-n} \binom{d - p_r}{\beta}$ counts the number of ways of selecting up to $\eta - n$ points, from $p_r + 1, \cdots, d$, where exceptions are made. Thus, we can count the number of coverings consistent with the sample, which allows us to implement the halving algorithm. The number of mistakes made by the halving algorithm is at most the logarithm of the number of hypotheses, or $\eta \log d + k \log(dk)$, and this quantity bounds the number of points $r$ that must be stored in the table.

The above assumed that the learner knew $\eta$, the incompetence of $\mathcal{E}$. A simple doubling trick can be used to avoid this difficulty. The learner first assumes that $\eta \leq 2$, and then when that assumption is violated, we restart and assume that $\eta = 4$, and so on. The number of mistakes made is now bounded by $2\eta \log d + k \log(dk) \log \eta$. This shows that the class of intervals is learnable in the competency model. If all the $\#(r, i, j, n)$'s for all possible choices of $i, j$ and $n$ have been computed using Lemma 3, then the sum in Equation (3) can be computed in $O(k^3 \eta^2)$ time. Thus, we have the following theorem.

**Theorem 4.** *Suppose a pool of $k$ experts has joint incompetence $\eta$ w.r.t. the competency class (structure) of intervals. We can efficiently learn the competency class or structure of $k$ intervals with mistake bound $2\eta \log d + k \log(dk) \log \eta$ and running time $O(k^3 \eta^2 + rk^2 \eta)$ per trial. Here, $r$ is the number of mistakes made so far.* $\square$

## 3 Learning and Identifying the Competency Class of Disjunctions

In this section, we show that identifying an optimum covering may not be the best way of learning a competency class of disjunctions of literals.

When the instance space is a subset of the boolean hypercube $\{0,1\}^n$, the competency class of disjunctions consists of all coverings where each expert is associated with the subset of the space satisfying a disjunction of literals. An expert can be associated with the empty set through the use of the empty disjunction. As in the previous section, we assume that the incompetence of the experts is some value $\eta$ since we can guess $\eta$ using the doubling trick described previously.

The main idea of our algorithm for learning the competency class of disjunctions of literals is to run an algorithm, which is a hybrid of Littlestone's WINNOW1 and WINNOW2 algorithms [Lit88], for each expert $E_i$ to learn its competency region $C_i^{opt}$ in an optimum covering $C^{opt}$. The learner maintains a hypothesis $h_i$ for the disjunction representing each $C_i^{opt}$ in the optimal covering. These hypotheses are linear threshold functions using one weight per variable, so that an instance $x$ is in $h_i$ if and only if $\sum_{j=1}^n w_{ij} x_j \leq kn$ (recall that $k$ is the number of experts). Initially, all the weights are set to 1, as in WINNOW. For each expert $E_i$, we also maintain a counter $\alpha_{ij}$ for each literal $x_j$ which counts the number of mistakes $E_i$ made in the previous trials when $x_j$ is set to 1.

Given an input $x$ (assuming it is not a counterexample which the learner has already seen), the learner first checks whether $x$ is *covered by* (contained in) any of the its current hypotheses $h_i$. If $x$ is covered, then for $j \in \{0,1\}$, let $\mathcal{E}_j$ be the set of experts that predict $j$ on $x$ and whose corresponding $h_i$'s contain $x$. Otherwise, the learner sets $\mathcal{E}_j, j \in \{0,1\}$, to be the set of experts that predict $j$. The learner than predicts 0 if $|\mathcal{E}_0| \geq |\mathcal{E}_1|$ and 1 otherwise. If a mistake is made, say we predicted $y$ which is wrong then we update the weights of our hypotheses according to the following rules:

$\eta$-**elimination:** Suppose $x$ is covered. For each expert $E_i$ in $\mathcal{E}_y$, if $x_j = 1$ then increment $\alpha_{ij}$ by one and check if $\alpha_{ij} > \eta$. If yes, then we can conclude that $x_j$ cannot appear in the disjunction describing the competency region of $E_i$ (since $E_i$ can make at most $\eta$ mistakes on points in its competency region) and hence, we can eliminate $x_j$ from $h_i$ by setting $w_{ij} = 0$. Otherwise, we simply do a demotion as in WINNOW1 on $w_{ij}$ by dividing it by $\alpha$.

**Promotion:** Suppose $x$ is not covered. In this case, we perform a promotion step on the weights of $h_i$ for each $i$ such that $E_i \in \mathcal{E}_{\bar{y}}$. The idea here is that at less one of the $h_i$'s is improved unless all the experts whose competency regions in the optimum covering cover $x$ predict incorrectly which happens at most $\eta$ times.

We begin by proving some simple lemmas similar to those used in proving the mistake bound of WINNOW [Lit88]. Let $u$ and $v$ be the number of promotion steps and $\eta$-elimination steps, respectively. Then the number of mistakes is simply the sum of $u$ and $v$.

**Lemma 5.**

$$v \leq \frac{\alpha}{\alpha - 1} + \alpha k u.$$

**Proof:** Consider the sum

$$S = \sum_{i=1}^{k} \sum_{j=1}^{n} w_{ij}.$$

$S$ is always non-negative. Initially, $S = kn$.

Suppose we make a mistake by predicting the classification of $x$ to be $y$. An $\eta$-elimination step occurs only if $x$ is covered and hence, only if $|\mathcal{E}_y| \geq 1$. Therefore, before the $\eta$-elimination,

$$\sum_{i:E_i \in \mathcal{E}_y} \sum_{j} w_{ij} x_j \geq |\mathcal{E}_y| kn \geq kn.$$

After an $\eta$-elimination, the above sum is reduced by a factor of $1 - \alpha^{-1}$. When a promotion step occurs, the sum $\sum_j w_{ij}$ either does not change or increases no more than $(\alpha - 1)kn$. Thus,

$$0 \leq S \leq kn + ku(\alpha - 1)kn - vkn(1 - \alpha^{-1})$$

which gives us the desired bound. □

**Lemma 6.** *For all $i, j$, $w_{ij} \leq \alpha kn$.*

**Proof:** Since a weight is promoted only if it is not greater than $kn$. □

**Lemma 7.** *After $u$ promotion steps and any number of $\eta$-elimination steps, there exists a pair $i$ and $j$ such that*

$$\log_\alpha w_{ij} \geq \frac{u - \eta L - \eta}{L}$$

*where $L$ is the sum, over all $C_i^{opt}$s, of the number of literals [7] in the disjunction describing $C_i^{opt}$.*

**Proof:** Suppose, $C_i^{opt} = x_{j_1^i} \vee \cdots \vee x_{j_{k_i}^i}$. Consider the product

$$P = \prod_{j=1}^{k} \prod_{l=1}^{k_i} w_{ij_l^i}.$$

Initially, $P = 1$. When an $\eta$-elimination occurs in the hypothesis $h_i$ for $C_i^{opt}$, the weight $w_{ij}$ is reduced only if $h_i(x) = 1$ and expert $E_i$ predicts wrongly on $x$. This can happen only at most $\eta$ times since we do a demotion on $w_{ij}$ only if $\alpha_{ij} < \eta$. Hence each $w_{il}$ can only be divided by $\alpha$ at most $\eta$ times. On the other hand, each time a promotion occurs, $P$ is increased by $\alpha$ since $x$ is covered by at least one of the $C_i^{opt}$'s, unless the expert whose competency region contains the instance $x$ predicts wrongly. The latter occurs at most $\eta$ times.

---

[7] A literal may be counted more than once in $L$ if it appears in more than one $C_i^{opt}$.

Therefore,

$$\prod_{j=1}^{k}\prod_{l=1}^{k_i} w_{ij_l} \geq \alpha^{-\eta L}\alpha^{u-\eta}.$$

This implies

$$\sum_{j=1}^{k}\sum_{l=1}^{k_i} \log_\alpha w_{ij_l} \geq u - \eta L - \eta.$$

Note that $L = \sum_{i=1}^{k} k_i$. Thus, there exists a pair $i$ and $j$ such that

$$\log_\alpha w_{ij} \geq \frac{u - \eta L - \eta}{L}.$$

$\square$

**Theorem 8.** *Suppose a pool of $k$ experts having joint incompetence $\eta$ w.r.t. the competency class of disjunctions of literals over a relevant subspace of the boolean space $\{0,1\}^n$. Then we can identify the optimum covering in $O(nk)$ time per trial and making at most*

$$\frac{\alpha}{\alpha - 1} + (1 + \alpha k)\left(L(1 + \eta + \log_\alpha(kn)) + \eta\right)$$

*mistakes. Here, $L$ is the sum, over all $C_i^{opt}$s, of the number of literals in the disjunction describing $C_i^{opt}$ and $\alpha$ is an arbitrary constant greater than 1.*

**Proof:** By Lemma 6 and Lemma 7, there exists a pair $i$ and $j$ such that

$$1 + \log_\alpha kn \geq \log_\alpha w_{ij} \geq \frac{u - \eta L - \eta}{L}.$$

Hence,

$$u \leq L(1 + \eta + \log_\alpha kn) + \eta.$$

Together with Lemma 5, we get

$$u + v \leq \frac{\alpha}{\alpha - 1} + (1 + \alpha k)\left(L(1 + \eta + \log_\alpha kn) + \eta\right).$$

$\square$

Applying Theorem 8 to the example in Section 1.1 with $\alpha$ set to 2, we can make at most $22 + 15(m_0 + m_1) + 10\log n$ mistakes instead of $2^n - |m_0 - m_1|$ mistakes. However, it turns out that if we are interested in making predictions without regard to what the optimum covering is, then we can improve the mistake bound in Theorem 8 substantially.

The idea here is to treat the prediction of each expert $E_i$ on an instance $x$ as another variable $E_i(x)$. Suppose $D_i$ is the disjunctions describing the competency region of $E_i$ w.r.t. the optimum covering $C^{opt}$. Assuming that we predict 1 when at least one expert whose competency region contains $x$ predicts 1, and

0 otherwise. Then the hypothesis $h$ (of the target concept $f$) obtained by using $C^{opt}$ for our prediction strategy on an instance $x$ corresponds to a disjunction

$$\sum_{i=1}^{k} E_i(X) \cdot D_i.$$

In other words, $h$ is a 2-DNF formula where each term is a conjunction of a literal and the variable $E_i(x)$ for some expert $E_i$.

WINNOW2 can be used to agnostically learn disjunctions of $k$ literals with a mistake bound of $O(k \log N + \mathcal{M})$ [Lit88, Lit91, AW95] where $N$ is the number of variables and $\mathcal{M}$ is the number of mistakes made in the entire sequence of trials using the best disjunction. Thus, we can apply WINNOW2 to learn $h$ agnostically and obtained a learning algorithm that has a smaller mistake bound.

**Theorem 9.** *Suppose a pool of $k$ experts having joint incompetence $\eta$ w.r.t. the competency class of disjunctions of literals over a relevant subspace of the boolean space $\{0, 1\}^n$. Then we can learn the competency class of disjunctions in $O(nk)$ time per trial and mistake bound $O(L \log(nk) + \eta)$.* □

## 4 Hardness Result for Learning Competency Class of Conjunctions

In this section, we reduce the problem of learning decision trees in the on-line mistake bound model to the problem of learning the competency class of conjunctions. In doing so, we show that if the competency class of linear threshold functions in the boolean domain, which contains the class of conjunctions, could be learned then we can learn decision trees as a concept class in the on-line mistake bound model. The latter problem, though not known to be impossible, is a difficult open problem.

Suppose we have a learner that learns the competency class of conjunctions. We illustrate below how we can make use of this learner to learn decision trees. The concept, and its complement, represented by a decision tree over the boolean domain can be expressed[8] as DNF formulas where the number of terms is bounded by the number of leaves in the decision tree. Without loss of generality, let us assume we know how many terms there are in these two formulas. We associate each term in the formulas with one expert. Those experts that are associated with the terms in the target always predict positive while the rest always predict negative. The competency region of each expert is the term that it is associated with. Clearly, the terms cover the instance space and hence form a covering. It is also easy to see that the classification of an instance by the target decision tree is the same as the classification using this covering and the corresponding experts. Thus, we have the following theorem.

---

[8] The complement of the target concept, $\overline{f}$, can be easily expressed as a DNF formula $g$ such that $g(x) = i$ if and only if $\overline{(f)}(x) = \overline{i}$.

**Theorem 10.** *If we could learn the competency class of conjunctions over $\{0,1\}^n$ then we can learn the class of decision trees in the mistake bound model.* □

## 5 Learning the Competency Structure of Decision Lists

In this section we present an algorithm that learns decision list competency structures over boolean instance spaces. More specifically, the optimum covering that we wish to learn is an ordered sequence $L$ of the form $\langle (\alpha_1, E_{i_1}), \cdots, (\alpha_{s-1}, E_{i_{s-1}}), (\alpha_s = true, E_{i_s}) \rangle$ where the $\alpha_i$'s are literals and the $E_{i_j}$'s are experts. Given an input $x \in \{0,1\}^n$ and the optimum covering $L$, the expert that we should use for predicting the classification of $x$ is $E_{i_j}$ such that $j$ is the smallest index satisfying $\alpha_j(x) = 1$. For example, consider an instance $x = \langle 10010 \rangle$ where $x_0$ and $x_3$ are set to 1, and the other variables are set to 0. If we were to use the covering $\langle (x_1, E_4), (\overline{x_3}, E_1), (\overline{x_4}, E_3), (x_0, E_2) \rangle$ as our strategy for making prediction, then we should use the advice of expert $E_3$.

We begin by assuming the incompetence of $\mathcal{E}$ is $\eta$. The idea here is to maintain a decision list $L'$ which consists of $s$ consecutive sublists $L'_1, \cdots, L'_{s+1}$ where $s$ is the length of the optimum covering (decision list). Each sublist $L'_i$ is a (possibly empty) ordered list $\langle (c_{l_i}, \mathcal{E}_{l_i}), \cdots, (c_{l_{i+1}-1}, \mathcal{E}_{l_{i+1}-1}) \rangle$ where the $\mathcal{E}_{l_j}$'s is a duplicate copy of $\mathcal{E}$ instead of a single expert and the $c_{l_j}$'s are the boolean literals. Furthermore, each boolean literal appears exactly once in $L'$. Initially, all the sublists are empty except for $L'_1$ which is set to

$$\langle (x_1, \mathcal{E}), (\overline{x_1}, \mathcal{E}), \cdots, (x_i, \mathcal{E}), (\overline{x_i}, \mathcal{E}), \cdots, (x_n, \mathcal{E}), (\overline{x_n}, \mathcal{E}), (true, \mathcal{E}) \rangle.$$

For each pair $(c_j, \mathcal{E}_j)$, we assigned an initial weight of one to each expert in $\mathcal{E}_j$. Given an instance $x$, we predict by running the weighted majority algorithm on $\mathcal{E}_j$ such that $j$ is the smallest index satisfying $c_j(x) = 1$, and we say the *rule* $(c_j, \mathcal{E}_j)$ is *fired*. If a rule $(c_j, \mathcal{E}_j)$ in sublist $L_l$ fires and causes a mistake, we simply reduce the weights of those experts in $\mathcal{E}_j$ that predict wrongly from $\mathcal{E}_j$ by half. If we predict wrongly using the rule $(c_j, \mathcal{E}_j)$ more than $a(\log k + \eta)$ time while $(c_j, \mathcal{E}_j)$ remains in the same sublist $L'_l$ then we move it to $L'_{l+1}$ and reset the weights of all the experts in $\mathcal{E}_j$ to 1. Here $a$ is the constant in the mistake bound of the weighter majority algorithm (see Theorem 1a).

Let $\alpha_i$ denotes the literal in the $i$th rule of our target optimum covering. It is clear that the rule $(\alpha_1, \mathcal{E}_\bullet)$ makes at most $a(\log k + \eta)$ mistakes while in sublist $L'_1$ and thus, does not move beyond $L'_1$. Similarly, the rule $(\alpha_2, \mathcal{E}_\bullet)$ can never move beyond $L'_2$. A simple induction allows us to argue that the rule associated with $\alpha_j$ cannot move beyond $L'_j$. Moreover, since each rule can make at most $a(\log k + \eta)$ mistakes while remaining in the same sublist, we can conclude that the total number of mistakes made is at most $ans(\log k + \eta)$.

Now, for unknown $\eta$, we can employ a standard doubling trick to guest the value of $\eta$ and run the above algorithm. Initially, our guess $\eta'$ of $\eta$ is 1 and if the number of mistakes is more than $ans(\log k + \eta)$, we double the value of $\eta'$. It is easy to show that the resulting mistake bound is $O(ns(\log k \log \eta + \eta))$.

However, this requires us to know the length $s$ of the optimum covering (so that we known our guess is wrong when we make more than $O(ns(\log k \log \eta + \eta))$ mistakes). We can overcome this difficulty by running $\log(2n + 1)$ copies of the learning algorithm, $A_1, \cdots, A_{\log(2n+1)}$ in turns where each $A_i$ assumes $s$ to be $2^i$. A simple argument shows that the mistake bound increases by at most a factor of $O(\log n)$. Thus, we have the following theorem.

**Theorem 11.** *Given a pool of $k$ experts $\mathcal{E}$ with competency $\eta$ (w.r.t. the competency structure of decision lists), we can learn the competency structure of decision lists over $n$ boolean variables with mistake bound $O(ns \log n(\log k \log \eta + \eta))$. Here, $s$ is the length of the optimum covering and $\eta$ is the incompetence of $\mathcal{E}$ w.r.t. the competency structure of decision lists. The time complexity per trial of our algorithm is $O(n + k)$.* □

## 6 Open Problems

The competency model is well motivated, there are a number of fundamental open problems yet to be explored:

*Problem 12.* What are the competency classes or structures that can be learned or cannot be learned, beside those studied in this paper?

*Problem 13.* Perhaps the model is too general. Are there other well motivated variants that warrant investigation? If a competency class or structure cannot be learned, then does augmenting the model with a membership query oracle help? Is there a PAC-like version of the competency model where the instances are drawn according to a fixed distribution?

*Problem 14.* In this paper, we only consider boolean predictions. How about real predictions with other loss function like square loss or entropic loss?

*Problem 15.* In the competency class model, an instance $x$ may fall in the competency regions of more than one expert. How will the results change if we were to predict according to the majority vote of the experts whose competency regions contain $x$?

### Acknowledgements

The authors like to thank the anonymous reviewers for their very valuable suggestions. Stephen Kwek is currently supported by NSF NYI Grant CCR-9357707 (of S. Goldman) with matching funds provided by Xerox PARC and WUTA.

## References

[AW95]    P. Auer and M. K. Warmuth. Tracking the best disjunction. In *Proc. of the 36th Symposium on the Foundations of Comp. Sci.*, pages 312–321. IEEE Computer Society Press, Los Alamitos, CA, 1995.

[CBFHW95] N. Cesa-Bianchi, Y. Freund, D. P. Helmbold, and M. K. Warmuth. On-line prediction and conversion strategies. *Machine Learning*, 1995. To appear, an extended abstract appeared in *Eurocolt '93*.

[Lit88] N. Littlestone. Learning when irrelevant attributes abound: A new linear-threshold algorithm. *Machine Learning*, 2:285–318, 1988.

[Lit91] N. Littlestone. Redundant noisy attributes, attribute errors, and linear threshold learning using Winnow. In *Proc. 4th Annu. Workshop on Comput. Learning Theory*, pages 147–156, San Mateo, CA, 1991. Morgan Kaufmann.

[LW94] N. Littlestone and M. K. Warmuth. The weighted majority algorithm. *Information and Computation*, 108(2):212–261, 1994.

# On Learning Branching Programs and Small Depth Circuits

## (Extended Abstract)

Francesco Bergadano[1] and Nader H. Bshouty[2] and Christino Tamon[*3] and
Stefano Varricchio[4]

[1] Dipartimento di Informatica, Universitá di Torino, Italy
[2] Dept. Computer Science, University of Calgary, Canada
[3] Dept. Mathematics and Computer Science, Clarkson University, U.S.A.
[4] Dipartimento di Informatica, Universitá di L'Aquila, Italy

**Abstract.** We study the learnability of branching programs and small-depth circuits with modular and threshold gates in both the exact and PAC learning models with and without membership queries. Our results extend earlier works [11, 18, 15] and exhibit further applications of *multiplicity automata* [7] in learning theory.

## 1 Introduction

Branching program is a well-studied computational model in complexity theory. The interest was in proving space and time-space tradeoff lower bounds in a non-uniform model of computation. One of the earliest famous conjectures is that majority cannot be computed by a bounded width branching program of polynomial size [8]. Barrington [4] disproved this with the surprising result that the computational power of width five permutation branching programs or $S_5$-PBPs is equivalent to $NC^1$. Recently, under the name of *binary decision diagrams*, branching programs have found numerous applications in computer-aided circuit design and verification (see [16] and the references therein).

The problem of learning branching programs has been studied in earlier works [23, 13, 15, 11]. We will review these results in the following and outline the contributions of this paper.

The learnability of bounded width branching programs was studied initially by Ergün, Ravi Kumar, and Rubinfeld [13]. In that paper they proved that restricted width two read-once branching programs with two sinks is PAC learnable under any distribution. They also showed that learning width three branching programs is as hard as learning DNF formulae. In [11] strict width two branching programs $SW_2$ (as defined by Borodin *et al.* [8]) is shown to be *properly* PAC learnable under any distribution. This is an improvement over [13] since the latter is a more general class. It was also observed that learning monotone

---

* Work done while the author was a student at the Department of Computer Science, University of Calgary.

width two branching programs (as defined by Borodin *et al.* [8]) is as hard as learning DNF formulae.

In this paper we improve the above results in two ways. First we show that any width two branching programs with a bounded number of sinks is exactly learnable using equivalence queries only. This improves upon the result of [11] showing the learnability of width two branching programs with two sinks. Second, we show that any monotone width two branching program is PAC learnable with membership queries under the uniform distribution. This extends Jackson's known result [18] on learning DNF formulae since DNF formulae form a proper subclass of monotone width two branching programs.

For branching programs with width more than two, Barrington [4] proved that width three permutation branching programs are equivalent to depth two circuits with a $mod_3$ gate at the top and parity gates at the bottom level. There is also a characterization of width four even permutation branching programs as depth three circuits with $\wedge$, $mod_2$, and $mod_3$ gates. We exploit these alternative characterizations to obtain exact learning algorithm using equivalence and membership queries for these two classes of permutation branching programs. On the other hand, by the work of Angluin and Kharitonov [2], we know that learning width five permutation branching programs with membership queries is hard under cryptographic assumptions.

The learnability of branching programs with read restrictions was studied in [23, 15]. They proved that $\mu$-branching programs (each variable appears at most once in the entire program) and ordered binary decision diagrams or Obdds (each variable appears at most once along any path) are exactly learnable using equivalence and membership queries. We prove that a constant Boolean combination of a $mod_p$ of polynomially many Obdds is exactly learnable from equivalence and membership queries, assuming that $p$ is a fixed prime.

Further in the paper, we study the problem of learning depth two circuits that consist of threshold and modular gates. We show that any depth two circuit with a $mod_p$ gate at the top, for a fixed prime $p$, and arbitrary modular gates at the bottom level (possibly with different modularities) is exactly learnable using equivalence and membership queries. Also we show that any depth two circuit with a $mod_p$ gate at the top, for a fixed prime $p$, and arbitrary threshold gates at the bottom level is exactly learnable using equivalence and membership queries. We note that by a result of Krause and Pudlák [20], DNF formulae are contained in the class of depth two circuits with a threshold gate at the top and parity gates at the bottom level. Hence learning a threshold of modular gates will imply learning DNF formulae.

Finally we prove that any Boolean combination of a constant number of concepts taken from the above classes is exactly learnable using equivalence and membership queries.

Due to space limitations we have omitted proofs from this abstract.

# 2 Preliminaries

We use $[n]$ to denote the set $\{1, 2, \ldots, n\}$ and $[a, b]$ to denote $\{a, a+1, \ldots, b\}$. The Iversonian $I[statement]$ notation means 1 if the *statement* is true and 0 otherwise. For $a \in \{0, 1\}^n$, let $a_i$ denote the $i$-th bit of $a$. The vector $e_i \in \{0, 1\}^n$ denotes the vector with all entries equal to zeros except for the $i$-th bit which is one. The all zero vector is denoted $0_n$. The Hamming weight of $a$, i.e. the number of ones in $a$, is denoted by $|a|$. The bitwise exclusive-or operation is denoted $\oplus$; sometimes we also use the $+$ sign. The inner product operation of $a \in \{0, 1\}^n$ is denoted $a^T x$ or $a \cdot x$. The ring of integers is denoted by $Z$. The finite field of $q$ elements is denoted by $GF(q)$.

## 2.1 Decision trees and parity classes

Let $A$ and $B$ be two concept classes over $\{0, 1\}^n$. An $(A, B)$-decision tree or $(A, B)$-DT is a rooted binary tree whose internal nodes are labeled with functions from $A$ and whose leaves are labeled with functions from $B$. Each internal node has precisely two outgoing edges, one labeled with 0 and the other labeled with 1. An $(A, B)$-decision tree computes a Boolean function from $\{0, 1\}^n$ to $\{0, 1\}$ in the following natural way. Given an assignment $a \in \{0, 1\}^n$, the computation starts at the root node, evaluating each function that labels the internal node according to its label, and taking the consistent edge out to the next internal node. The computation stops at a leaf node and outputs the value of the function that labels the leaf node.

An $(A, B)$-decision list or $(A, B)$-DL is a degenerate $(A, B)$-decision tree. In notation, we will write $[(f_1, g_1), (f_2, g_2), \ldots, (f_m, g_m)]$ where $f_1, f_2, \ldots, f_m \in A$ and $g_1, g_2, \ldots, g_m \in B$, to represent a $(A, B)$-DL. We implicitly assume that the last function $f_m$ is the constant one (always true) function. The class *const* consists of the constant functions always false and always true. We will shorthand $(A, const)$ to $A$, for example $(A, const)$-DT is abbreviated $A$-DT.

**Definition 1.** *(Rank of a Decision Tree)* Let $T$ be a decision tree. Then the rank of a node in $T$ is defined inductively as follows. For a non-leaf node $v$, let $v_L$ and $v_R$ be the left and right child, respectively, of $v$. Then $rank(v)$ is 0 if $v$ is a leaf, is $1 + rank(v_L)$ if $rank(v_L) = rank(v_R)$, and is $\max\{rank(v_L), rank(v_R)\}$ if $rank(v_L) \neq rank(v_R)$. The rank of the tree $T$ is the rank of its root node.

Another concept class that we consider is the class of parity functions $\oplus_k = \{a^T x + b \,|\, a \in \{0, 1\}^n, b \in \{0, 1\}, |a| \leq k\}$, where the parity may depend on at most $k$ variables. Note that $\oplus_1$ is the set of literals and $\oplus_n$ is the set of all parities. We also consider the class of parities of $k$-monomials (monomials of size at most $k$) which we denote $\oplus\cap_k$.

## 2.2 Branching programs

A branching program $M$ over $X_n = \{x_1, \ldots, x_n\}$ is an acyclic directed graph whose nodes labeled with variables from $X_n$ and whose edges are labeled with the constants $\{0,1\}$. It has a unique source (a node with no incoming edges) and at least two sinks (a node with no outgoing edges). The sinks are labeled with 0 (rejecting) and 1 (accepting), and both labels must be present. An assignment $a \in \{0,1\}^n$ to the variables induces a selection on the edges of $M$; it keeps alive all edges that are consistent with the assignment $a$. Then the branching program is said to accept $a$ if there is a directed path from the source to an accepting sink.

The *size* of a branching program is the number of nodes in the branching program. A branching program is called *leveled* if there is ordered partition $\Pi = (L_1, L_2, \dots)$ of the nodes of the branching program such that all of the edges connect nodes of one level to the next one in the partition. The *width* of a leveled branching program is the maximum number of nodes in any level in the ordered partition.

Borodin *et al.* [8] defined several variations of the width two branching programs. A width two branching program is called *strict* if it has exactly one accepting sink and one rejecting sink. A width two branching program is called *monotone* if it has exactly one rejecting sink. It was pointed out in [8] that any DNF can be converted into a width two monotone branching program. We will need the following properties of strict width two branching programs in terms of decision lists as shown in [11].

**Fact 1** *The class $\mathcal{SW}_2$ of strict width two branching programs is equivalent to $(\oplus_2, \oplus_n)$-DL. Moreover, any decision list in $(\oplus_2, \oplus_n)$-DL has length at most $n^2$.*

A width $w$ *permutation branching program* is a leveled branching program of width $w$ whose edges labeled with one form a permutation on $[w]$ and the same rule applies for edges labeled with zero. Also we require that the nodes in each level of the partition is labeled with a unique variable from $X_n$. Thus, sometimes we will say a $G$-permutation branching program or $G$-PBP, for some permutation group $G$, to denote a specific permutation used by the branching program. The notion of acceptance in a permutation branching program is slightly different. For this we need to fix some subset $S$ of $G$. Given an input assignment $a$, the entire branching program will compute a product of permutations from $G$. If this product is a permutation from $S$ then the branching program accepts otherwise it rejects.

Next we define ordered binary decision diagrams or Obdds. Let $\pi$ be an ordering or bijection of $\{1, 2, \dots, n\}$. For an assignment $x \in \{0,1\}^n$, let $\pi(x)$ be the string $x_{\pi(1)} \dots x_{\pi(n)}$. For an ordering $\pi$ and a branching program $M$, we say that $M$ is $\pi$-ordered bdd or $\pi$-Obdd if the labels of the nodes along any path in $M$ are consistent with the ordering $\pi$. An ordered branching program or decision diagram is one that is $\pi$-ordered, for some $\pi$. The notion of accepting is the same for ordinary branching programs.

## 2.3 Small depth circuits with modular and threshold gates

A $mod_p$ gate over $n$ Boolean inputs $x_1, \dots, x_n$ returns the value $x_1 + x_2 + \dots + x_n \pmod{p}$. A threshold gate or function over $n$ Boolean inputs with integer weights $a = a_1, a_2, \ldots, a_n \in Z$ and a threshold of $b \in Z$, denoted by $f_{a,b}$, returns the value

$$f_{a,b}(x) = \begin{cases} 1 & \text{if } a_1 x_1 + a_2 x_2 + \ldots + a_n x_n \geq b \\ 0 & \text{otherwise} \end{cases}$$

In another notation, $f_{a,b}(x) = [\sum_{i=1}^{n} a_i x_i \geq b]$. The class of Boolean function computable by a threshold gate with integer weights is denoted by $\widehat{LT_1}$. For a threshold function $f_{a,b}$, we define $w(f_{a,b})$ to be $|b| + \sum_{i=1}^{n} |a_i|$. The *representation size* of a threshold function $f$ is $w(f)$.

The class $mod_Z$ is the class of $mod_q$ gates, for all integers $q \in Z$. For two classes of gates $A$ and $B$, we denote $A$-$B$ circuits to be the class of functions computable by a depth two Boolean circuit with a gate from $A$ at the top and gates from $B$ at the bottom level. For example, a $mod_p$-$mod_Z$ circuit is a depth two Boolean circuit that has a $mod_p$ gate at the top and arbitrary $mod_q$ gates, $q \in Z$, at the bottom level. Note that we allow $mod_q$ gates with possibly different $q$'s at the bottom level (not just for a single value $q$).

## 2.4 Learning models

In this paper we will consider two standard learning models, namely the Probably Approximately Correct (PAC) model and the exact learning model with equivalence and membership queries.

First we define the *PAC* learning model [24]. Let $C, H$ be two classes of Boolean functions over $n$ variables, let $D$ be a probability distribution over $\{0,1\}^n$, and let $f \in C$ be a target function chosen from $C$. The learning algorithm has access to an example oracle $EX(f, D)$ which generates random labeled examples $(a, f(a))$, where $a \in \{0,1\}^n$ is drawn according the distribution $D$. We say that $C$ is *PAC learnable* using $H$ if there exists an algorithm $A$ so that: for any concept $f \in C$, for any distribution $D$ over $\{0,1\}^n$, for any $0 < \epsilon, \delta < 1$, if $A$ is given access to $EX(f, D)$ and inputs $\epsilon, \delta$, then with probability at least $1 - \delta$, $A$ outputs a hypothesis $h \in H$ satisfying $D(f \triangle h) \leq \epsilon$. The last probability is taken over the internal randomization of $A$ along with the randomization in the calls to $EX(f, D)$. We also require that the learning algorithm $A$ runs in time polynomial in $n, \frac{1}{\epsilon}, \frac{1}{\delta}$, and the size of the target function $f$.

In the *exact* learning model [1, 21] the learner asks certain oracles certain types of questions or queries about the target function $f$. In an *equivalence query*, the learning algorithm supplies any function $h \in H$ as input to $EQ_f()$ and the reply of the oracle is either *yes*, signifying that $h \equiv f$, or a *counterexample*, which is an assignment $b$ such that $h(b) \neq f(b)$. In a *membership query*, the learning algorithm supplies an assignment $b$ to $MQ_f()$ and the reply of the oracle is $f(b)$. The goal of the exact learning algorithm is to halt after time polynomial in $n$ and the *size of the representation* for $f$ in the class, and output a representation $h \in H$ that is logically equivalent to $f$.

## 2.5 Multiplicity automata

In this section we describe relevant definitions from the theory of multiplicity automata and a recent result on the learnability of multiplicity automata. We will also prove a lemma that describes a non-trivial closure operation on this class of automata.

Let $K$ be a field. A nondeterministic automaton $M$ with multiplicity is a five-tuple
$M(A, Q, E, I, F)$ where $A$ is a finite alphabet, $Q$ is the finite set of states, $I, F :
Q \to K$ are two mappings associated with the initial and final states, respectively, and $E : Q \times A \times Q \to K$ is a map that associates a multiplicity to each edge of $M$. For brevity we refer to $M$ as $K$-automaton.

Let $x = (x_1, \ldots, x_n) \in A^*$. A path $p$ for $x$ is a sequence

$$p = (p_1, x_1, p_2), (p_2, x_2, p_3), \ldots, (p_n, x_n, p_{n+1}).$$

Let $Path_M(x)$ denote the set of all paths for $x$. The *behavior* of $M$ is a mapping $S_M : A^* \to K$ defined as follows: for each $x = (x_1, \ldots, x_n) \in A^*$

$$S_M(x) = \sum_{p \in Path_M(x)} I(p_1) \left( \prod_{i=1}^n E(p_i, x_i, p_{i+1}) \right) F(p_{n+1}).$$

For a Boolean function over $f : A^* \to \{0, 1\}$, we say that a multiplicity automata $M$ computes $f$ if for all $x \in A^*$ we have $S_M(x) = f(x)$. Alternatively one may think of $f$ as a characteristic function of a language over $A^*$.

In the following we will describe several operations on multiplicity automata, namely the Hadamard product, union, and scalar multiplication.

**Definition 2.** *(Closure operations)*
Let $K$ be a field. Let $M_1(A, Q_1, E_1, I_1, F_1)$ and $M_2(A, Q_2, E_2, I_2, F_2)$ be two $K$-automata.

1. The *Hadamard product* of $M_1$ and $M_2$, denoted by $M_1 \odot M_2$, is a $K$-automaton $M(A, Q, E, I, F)$ where $Q = Q_1 \times Q_2$, and $I, F, E$ are defined as $I(q_1, q_2) = I_1(q_1) I_2(q_2)$, $F(q_1, q_2) = F_1(q_1) F_2(q_2)$, and

   $$E((q, p), a, (q', p')) = E_1(q, a, q') E_2(p, a, p').$$

   Note that $M$ has $|Q_1||Q_2|$ states. Moreover $M$ satisfies $S_M(x) = S_{M_1}(x) S_{M_2}(x)$.
2. Assume that $Q_1$ and $Q_2$ are two disjoint sets of states. The *union* of $M_1$ and $M_2$, denoted simply by $M_1 \cup M_2$, is a $K$-automaton where $M(A, Q, E, I, F)$ where $Q = Q_1 \cup Q_2$, and $I, F, E$ are defined as $I(q) = I_1(q)[q \in Q_1] + I_2(q)[q \in Q_2]$, $F(q) = F_1(q)[q \in Q_1] + F_2(q)[q \in Q_2]$, $E(q, a, p) = E_1(q, a, p)[q, p \in Q_1] + E_2(q, a, p)[q, p \in Q_2]$. Note that $M$ has $|Q_1| + |Q_2|$ states. Moreover $M$ satisfies $S_M(x) = S_{M_1}(x) + S_{M_2}(x)$.
3. For any $\lambda \in K$, the automaton $\lambda M_1$ is defined to be $M(A, Q, E, I, F)$ where $Q = Q_1$, $I = \lambda I_1$, $F = F_1$, and $E = E_1$. Note that $|Q| = |Q_1|$ and that $M$ satisfies $S_M(x) = \lambda S_{M_1}(x)$.

Next we prove a result that adds another closure operation, namely constant Boolean combinations of multiplicity automata.

**Lemma 3.** *Let $p$ be a fixed prime. Let $g_1, g_2, \ldots, g_k$ be Boolean functions that can be computed by $GF(p)$-automata of size at most $s$. Then for any Boolean function $f$ on $k$ inputs, $f(g_1, g_2, \ldots, g_k)$ can be computed by a $GF(p)$-automaton with at most $2^k s^k$ states.*

A *multiplicity oracle* $MUL_M()$ for a $K$-automaton $M$ is an oracle that receives as input a string $x \in A^*$ and returns $S_M(x)$. The following result was recently established in [12] (see also [7]).

**Theorem 4.** *[12, 7] The class of $K$-automata, for a field $K$, is exactly learnable from equivalence and multiplicity queries.*

## 3 Monotone width two branching programs

In this section we prove that monotone width two branching programs are PAC learnable with membership queries under the uniform distribution. To prove the claim we need to introduce some notation and facts for harmonic analysis of Boolean functions.

We recall the basics of the Fourier transform of Boolean functions [22]. In this setting Boolean functions will be thought of having range $\{-1, +1\}$. To avoid confusion we will denote "normal" Boolean functions, i.e., ones with the range $\{0, 1\}$, with lower-case letters, such as $f : \{0,1\}^n \to \{0,1\}$, and their *corresponding* $\{-1, +1\}$-range *counterpart* with upper-case letters, e.g., $F : \{0,1\}^n \to \{-1, +1\}$. It is easy to see that the following relations hold between $f$ and $F$: $F = 2f - 1$ and $f = \frac{1+F}{2}$. Let $F : \{0,1\}^n \to \{-1, +1\}$ be a Boolean function. The Fourier transform of Boolean functions over the uniform distribution is defined as follows. First we define the inner product over the $2^n$-dimensional vector space of all real-valued functions over $\{0,1\}^n$: $\langle F, G \rangle = 2^{-n} \sum_x F(x)G(x) = \mathbf{E}[FG]$. Next we define for each $a \in \{0,1\}^n$ the basis function $\chi_a$ as follows: $\chi_a(x) = (-1)^{\sum_{i=1}^n a_i x_i}$. These functions are *orthonormal*, i.e., $\langle \chi_a, \chi_b \rangle = [a \neq b]$, and they are *decomposable*, i.e., $\chi_{ab}(xy) = \chi_a(x)\chi_b(y)$, where $xy$ is the concatenation of strings $x$ and $y$ (possibly of different lengths). Given the orthonormality of these $\chi_a$'s we get the Fourier representation of any Boolean function $F$ as

$$F(x) = \sum_a \hat{F}(a)\chi_a(x),$$

where $\hat{F}(a) = \langle F, \chi_a \rangle = \mathbf{E}[F\chi_a]$. Also because of orthonormality we have Parseval's identity: $\sum_a \hat{F}^2(a) = 1$. Finally note that $\chi_{0_n}(x)$ is the constant function 1.

In a beautiful paper Jackson [18] proved the following theorem.

**Theorem 5.** *[18] The class of DNF formulae is PAC learnable from membership queries under the uniform distribution.*

We outline the arguments used by Jackson and illustrate how we modify it to prove the learnability of monotone width two branching programs. The first key fact about DNF formulae is that they correlate well with *some* parity function $\chi_A$, $A \in \{0,1\}^n$, under *any* distribution. In notation, if $f$ is a DNF formulae of size $s$ ($f$ has $s$ terms) and $D$ is an arbitrary distribution, then there is some $A$ such that

$$|\mathbf{E}_D[F\chi_A]| \geq \frac{1}{2s+1}.$$

We remind the reader that $F$ is the $\{-1,+1\}$-version of $f$. Using the above inequality, since $\mathbf{E}_D[F\chi_A] = \Pr_D[F = \chi_A] - \Pr_D[F \neq \chi_A]$ we derive the following. Assume without loss of generality that $\mathbf{E}_D[F\chi_A]$ is positive (the other case is symmetrically similar).

$$\mathbf{E}_D[F\chi_A] = 1 - 2\Pr_D[F \neq \chi_A] \geq \frac{1}{2s+1} \implies \Pr_D[F \neq \chi_A] \leq \frac{1}{2} - \frac{1}{2(2s+1)}.$$

This is good news since it means that the parity function $\chi_A$ is a potential hypothesis for *weak* learning $f$. The problem is that we do not know what $A$ is in relation to $F$ (other than it correlates well with $F$). The second important fact is that there is an efficient algorithm due to Kushilevitz and Mansour [19] to find parities that correlate well with certain Boolean functions assuming that the underlying distribution is uniform. So weakly learning DNF under the uniform distribution is possible by combining these two facts [9]. The third ingredient is a *boosting* algorithm, developed by Freund [14], that can turn any weak learning algorithm into a strong learning algorithm. Jackson proved that the boosting algorithm of Freund combined with a modified version of Kushilevitz and Mansour's algorithm will learn DNF formulae in the PAC model under the uniform distribution. In fact the only property that is ever needed about DNF formulae to get this learning result is the first fact. Jackson called this DNF learning algorithm the *harmonic sieve* algorithm.

To prove our PAC learning result we prove that the first fact also holds for monotone width two branching programs.

**Lemma 6.** *For any $F \in \mathcal{MW}_2$ with $s$ accepting sinks and for any distribution $D$ there is a parity $\chi_C$ that satisfies*

$$|\mathbf{E}_D[F\chi_C]| \geq \frac{1}{2sn^2+1}.$$

Using the above lemma we can then claim the following theorem.

**Theorem 7.** *The class $\mathcal{MW}_2$ of monotone width two branching programs is PAC learnable with membership queries under the uniform distribution.*

# 4 Width two branching programs with bounded number of sinks

In this section we prove width two branching programs with a constant number of sinks is exactly learnable from equivalence queries only. In notation we use $k$-sink $\mathcal{W}_2$ to denote the class of width two branching programs with at most $k$ sinks. We prove the following theorem.

**Theorem 8.** $k$-sink $\mathcal{W}_2$ is exactly learnable using equivalence queries.

In the next lemma we prove that $k$-sink width two branching program is equivalent to rank-$k$ decision trees with parity nodes.

**Lemma 9.** The class of $k$-sink, $k \geq 2$, width two branching programs is a subclass of the class rank-$k$ $\oplus_n$-DT decision trees with parity nodes.

Next, using an idea due to Blum [5], we transform further the target width two branching program into a decision list representation.

**Lemma 10.** The class of rank-$k$ decision trees with parity nodes is a subclass of decision lists whose nodes are parity of monomials, where each monomial is of size at most $k$. In notation, rank-$k$ $\oplus_n$-DT is a subclass of $\oplus \cap_k$-DL.

Finally we show in the following lemma that $\oplus \cap_k$-DL, and hence $k$-sink width two branching programs, are exactly learnable from equivalence queries. The idea is to use the closure algorithm for learning nested differences of intersection-closed concept classes due to Helmbold, Sloan, and Warmuth [17].

**Lemma 11.** The class $\oplus \cap_k$-DL of decision lists whose nodes are parity of monomials of size at most $k$ is exactly learnable using equivalence queries.

# 5 Small depth circuits and bounded width permutation branching programs

In this section we will show that some small depth circuits with modular and threshold gates and certain types of bounded width permutation branching programs are exactly learnable using equivalence and membership queries.

**Theorem 12.** For any fixed prime $p$, the class of $mod_p$-$mod_Z$ circuits is exactly learnable using equivalence and membership queries.

In the following we will exploit circuit characterizations of permutation branching programs to prove the learnability of $S_3$ and $A_4$ permutation branching programs, where $S_3$ is the symmetric group on [3] and $A_4$ is the alternating group on [4]. The following fact about $S_3$-PBPs was proved by Barrington [3].

**Fact 2** The class $S_3$-PBP is equivalent to $mod_3$-$mod_2$ circuit.

**Theorem 13.** $S_3$-*PBPs are exactly learnable using equivalence and membership queries.*

It was implicitly shown in [10] that $A_4$-PBP is equivalent to $(mod_2, mod_2)$-$mod_3$ circuit, i.e., a depth "two" circuit consisting of $mod_3$ gates at the bottom level coming into two $mod_2$ gates at the second level. The output of the two $mod_2$ gates can then be combined using *any* Boolean operation.

We will prove a more general result and as a corollary we will show that $A_4$ permutation branching programs are exactly learnable using equivalence and membership queries.

**Theorem 14.** *Let $g_1, g_2, \ldots, g_k$ be Boolean functions that can be computed by a multiplicity $GF(p)$-automata of size at most $s$. Then for any Boolean function $f$ on $k$ inputs, $f(g_1, g_2, \ldots, g_k)$ is exactly learnable using equivalence and membership queries in time $s^{O(k)}$.*

**Corollary 15.** $A_4$ *PBPs are exactly learnable using equivalence and membership queries.*

In the following we will show that Boolean functions computable by threshold gates with integer weights can be represented as a multiplicity automata.

**Lemma 16.** *The class $\widehat{LT}_1$ admits a representation as a $GF(p)$-automata, for prime $p$.*

Using the above lemma we can claim (as before) that a $mod_p$ and a constant Boolean combination of threshold functions are exactly learnable.

**Corollary 17.** *The class of $mod_p$-$\widehat{LT}_1$ is exactly learnable using equivalence and membership queries.*

**Corollary 18.** *For any Boolean function $f$ on $k$ inputs, and for $g_1, \ldots, g_k$ taken from the class $mod_p$-$\widehat{LT}_1$, the Boolean function $f(g_1, g_2, \ldots, g_k)$ is exactly learnable using equivalence and membership queries.*

We remark that proving the learnability of either $\widehat{LT}_1$-$mod_p$ or $\widehat{LT}_1$-$\widehat{LT}_1$ functions will prove the learnability of DNF formulae [20].

## 6 Ordered binary decision diagrams

In this section we provide exact learning algorithms for certain Boolean combinations of ordered binary decision diagrams (Obdds). In particular we consider any $mod_p$ and any constant Boolean combinations of Obdds. In all of our learning results we always assume that the learning algorithm is given the ordering $\pi$. As pointed out by Gavaldà and Guijarro [15] the problem of learning using the best ordering (that minimizes the size of the branching program) is hard. So from now on we will assume that the ordering is simply the identity ordering $x_1 < x_2 < \ldots < x_n$. Now we prove that a $mod_p$ of polynomially many Obdds are learnable. First we state a result that is implicit in the work of Gavaldà and Guijarro [15].

**Fact 3** *[15] For every Obbd there is an equivalent $GF(p)$-automaton, for any prime p, that accepts it. Moreover the transformation can be carried out in polynomial-time in the size of the Obdd.*

**Theorem 19.** *Let p be a fixed prime. A $mod_p$ of a polynomially many Obdds is exactly learnable using equivalence and membership queries.*

**Theorem 20.** *For any Boolean function f on k inputs, the function $f(g_1, g_2, \ldots, g_k)$, where $g_1, \ldots, g_k$ are $mod_p$ of Obdds, is exactly learnable using equivalence and membership queries.*

## Acknowledgments

We thank David A. Mix Barrington for his generosity in sending us his thesis and for his help on permutation branching programs.

## References

1. Angluin, D.: Queries and Concept Learning. Machine Learning, **2** (1988) 319–342.
2. Angluin, D., Kharitonov, M.: When Won't Membership Queries Help? Journal of Computer and System Sciences, **50** (1995) 336–355.
3. Barrington, D.A.: Bounded-Width Branching Programs. PhD thesis, Massachusetts Institute of Technology (1986).
4. Barrington, D.A.: Bounded-Width Polynomial-Size Branching Programs Recognize Exactly Those Languages in $NC^1$. Journal of Computer and System Sciences, **38** (1989) 150–164.
5. Blum, A.: Rank-$r$ Decision Trees are a Subclass of $r$-Decision Lists. Information Processing Letters, **42** (1992) 183–185.
6. Bergadano, F., Catalano, D., Varricchio, S.: Learning Sat-$k$-DNF Formulas from Membership Queries. Proc. Ann. Symp. Theory of Computing (STOC) 1996.
7. Beimel, A., Bergadano, F., Bshouty, N.H., Kushilevitz, E., Varricchio, S.: On the Applications of Multiplicity Automata in Learning. Proc. 37th IEEE Ann. Symp. on Foundations of Computer Science, (1996) 349–3 58.
8. Borodin, A., Dolev, D., Fich, F., Paul, W.: Bounds for Width Two Branching Programs. SIAM Journal on Computing, **15**:2 (1986) 549–560.
9. Blum, A., Furst, M., Jackson, J., Kearns, M., Mansour, Y., Rudich, S.: Weakly Learning DNF and Characterizing Statistical Query Learning using Fourier Analysis. Proc. 26th Ann. ACM Symp. Theory of Computing (1994) 253–262.
10. Barrington, D.A. Mix, Straubing, H., Thérien, D.: Non-uniform Automata over Groups. Information and Computation, **89** (1990) 109–132.
11. Bshouty, N.H., Tamon, C., Wilson, D.K.: On Learning Width Two Branching Programs. Proc. 9th Ann. ACM Conf. Computational Learning Theory (1996).
12. Bergadano, F., Varricchio, S.: Learning Behaviors of Automata from Multiplicity and Equivalence Queries. Proc. 2nd Italian Conference on Algorithms and Complexity (CIAC 94), Lecture Notes in Computer Science No. 778, M. Bonuccelli, P. Crescenzi, R. Petreschi (eds.), Springer-Verlag, (1994). To appear in SIAM Journal on Computing.

13. Ergün, F., Ravi Kumar, S., Rubinfeld, R.: On Learning Bounded-Width Branching Programs. Proc. 8th Ann. ACM Conf. Computational Learning Theory (1995) 361–368.

14. Freund, Y.. Boosting a Weak Learning Algorithm by Majority. Proc. 3rd Ann. Workshop on Computational Learning Theory (1990) 202–216.

15. Gavaldà, R., Guijarro, D.: Learning Ordered Binary Decision Diagrams. 6th International Workshop on Algorithmic Learning Theory, Lecture Notes in Artificial Intelligence No. 997, Jantke, Shinohara, Zeugmann (eds.), Springer-Verlag, (1995).

16. Gergov, J., Meinel, C.: MOD-2-OBDD's – A Generalization of OBDD's and EXOR-Sum-Of-Products. IFIP WG 10.5 Workshop on the Applications of Reed-Muller Expansion in Circuit Design, Hamburg, (1993).

17. Helmbold, D., Sloan, R., Warmuth, M.: Learning Nested Differences of Intersection-Closed Concept Classes. Machine Learning, **5** (1990) 165–196.

18. Jackson, J.: DNF is Efficiently Learnable under the Uniform distribution with Membership Queries. Proc. 35th Ann. Symp. on Foundations of Computer Science (1994) 42–53.

19. Kushilevitz, E., Mansour, Y.: Learning Decision Trees using the Fourier Spectrum. SIAM Journal on Computing, **22**:6 (1993) 1331–1348.

20. Krause, M., Pudlák, P.: On the Computational Power of Depth 2 Circuits with Threshold and Modulo gates. Proc. 26th Ann. ACM Symp. on the Theory of Computing (1994) 48–57.

21. Littlestone, N.: Learning Quickly When Irrelevant Attributes Abound: A New Linear-Threshold Algorithm. Machine Learning, **2** (1988) 285–318.

22. Mansour, Y.: Learning Boolean Functions via the Fourier Transform. Tutorial Notes for the Workshop on Computational Learning Theory (1994).

23. Raghavan, V., Wilkins, D.: Learning Branching Programs with Queries. Proc. 6th Ann. Workshop on Computational Learning Theory, (1993) 27–36.

24. Valiant, L.: A Theory of the Learnable. Communications of the ACM, **27**:11 (1984) 1134–1142.

# Learning Nearly Monotone $k$-term DNF[*]

Jorge Castro, David Guijarro and Víctor Lavín[**]

{castro,david,vlavin}@goliat.upc.es
Departament de Llenguatges i Sistemes Informàtics
Universitat Politècnica de Catalunya
Pau Gargallo, 5
08028 Barcelona, Spain

**Abstract.** This note studies the learnability of the class $k$-term DNF with a bounded number of negations per term. We study the case of learning with membership queries alone, and give tight upper and lower bounds on the number of negations that makes the learning task feasible. We also prove a negative result for equivalence queries. Finally, we show that a slight modification in our algorithm proves that the considered class is also learnable in the Simple PAC model, extending Li and Vitányi result for monotone $k$-term DNF.

## 1 Introduction

Among the different models of learning proposed in Computational Learning Theory , one of the most widely studied is the *exact learning via queries* model, introduced by Angluin in [Ang87b] and [Ang88].

In this model the learner's goal is to identify an unknown target function $f$, taken from some representation class $\mathcal{C}$. In order to get information about the target, the learner has available two types of queries: membership and equivalence queries. In a membership query, the learner supplies an instance $x$ from the domain and gets $f(x)$ as answer. The input to an equivalence query is a hypotesis $h$, and the answer is either "yes" if $h \equiv f$ or a counterexample in the symmetric difference of $f$ and $h$.

Many interesting results have been obtained within this framework using different combinations of queries. However, there is a great deal of problems that still remain open. In particular, one of the most challenging open problems is whether the class of DNF formulas is learnable. Although it is known that this class is not learnable using either membership or equivalence queries alone, not much can be said by now about learning using both types of queries.

Several subclasses of the class DNF have been studied from the point of view of learnability. We will focus our attention on the class $k$-term DNF, i.e., the class of DNF formulas whose number of terms is at most $k$.

---

[*] Research supported by the Esprit EC program under project 7141 (ALCOM-II), the Working Group 8556 (NeuroColt), and the Spanish DGICYT (project PB92-0709).
[**] Supported by FP93 13717942 grant from the Spanish Government.

We review now some of the results concerning this class. In [Ang87a], Angluin gives a polynomial time algorithm that learns $k$-term DNF with membership and equivalence queries. The algorithm is proper in the sense that it uses as hypotheses $k$-term DNF formulas. Improvements in the running time can be found in [BGHM93] and [Ber93].

On the other hand, it is known that the class $k$-term DNF cannot be learned with a polynomial number of membership queries. However, if we restrict that class to be monotone, then learning can be achieved in polynomial time. Thus, a natural question to ask is: What amount of non-monotonicity can we afford so that the task of learning is still feasible?

We answer this question by giving tight upper and lower bounds in the number of negations per term that make learning feasible. We prove that if the number of negations per term is bounded by a constant then we can learn in polynomial time, using membership queries. However, any bound that grows faster than a constant makes the learning task impossible in polynomial time. We also show that the number of terms is tight, i.e., if the number of terms grows faster that a constant learning becomes unfeasible. Both non-learnability proofs are information theoretic, which implies that the negative results hold even if we allow the learner to output a representation from any arbitrary class of hypotheses.

We also prove that any learning algorithm for the considered class requires a superpolynomial number of equivalence queries, if this is the only type of query allowed.

Our results, negative and positive, on membership queries apply also to $k$-term DNF formulas with a bounded number of positive literals per term, and to $k$-clause CNF formulas where the number of negative or positive literals per clause is bounded.

From [Bsh95], it can be easily obtained a learning algorithm for these classes, but it generates decision trees as hypothesis. In this work we only consider proper learning algorithms.

Finally, we consider the Simple PAC model introduced by Li and Vitányi in [LV91], and extend their result for monotone $k$-term DNF to the class considered in our paper.

The paper is organized as follows. In Section 2 we introduce notation and definitions needed along the paper. In Section 3 we describe our algorithm to learn $(k, j)$-DNF, and prove its correctness and time bounds. Section 4 is devoted to negative results. Section 5 extends our results to other classes and Section 6 deals with Simple PAC.

# 2 Definitions

As we have already mentioned, we use the model of exact learning via queries as it was proposed in [Ang88]. We refer the reader to that reference for the definitions of learnability, queries, etc.

We deal with boolean functions represented as disjunctions of conjunctions of literals (DNF). A literal is a variable, or the negation of a variable, and a term is a conjunction of literals. A $k$-term DNF formula is a disjunction of at most $k$ terms. A $(k, j)$-DNF formula is a $k$-term DNF formula with at most $j$ negated variables per term. We treat DNF formulas also as sets of terms.

Variables are considered to be indexed by natural numbers from 1 to $n$ (where $n$ is the number of variables over which the target class is defined). If $A$ and $B$ are two disjoint sets of indices of variables let $\text{Term}(A, B)$ denote the term with all its non-negated variables taken from $A$ and the negated variables taken from $B$.

For an assignment $a$, ones$(a)$ denotes the set of indices of variables where $a$ has a 1 and zeros$(a)$ denotes the set of indices of variables where $a$ has a 0. The function flip$(a, i)$ produces a new assignment equal to $a$ except in the $i$-th variable, where the value is changed.

We direct the reader to [LV91] for definitions related to Simple PAC.

## 3 A Positive Result

We present an algorithm that learns the class $(k, j)$-DNF in polynomial time, using only membership queries. This algorithm is based on [BGHM93]. In that paper Bshouty et al. give an algorithm that learns $k$-term DNF formulas with membership and equivalence queries. We show that equivalence queries are not necessary if we bound the number of negations per term. Our algorithm differs from theirs basically in the way we get counterexamples and how we produce terms from them.

Before giving a detailed description of the algorithm, we prove a simple lemma that will help us to show correctness and time bounds.

**Lemma 1** *Let $f$ and $g$ be a pair of $(k, j)$-DNF formulas such that $g$ does not imply $f$. Then there exists an assignment with at most $k + j$ zeros that satisfies $g$ but not $f$.*

*Proof.* Note that $j$ zeros are enough to satisfy a term in $g$, and since the clauses on the CNF representation of $f$ have at most $k$ literals, then $k$ zeros suffice to falsify $f$, so the lemma follows. $\square$

Let $f^*$ be the target formula. We assume that $k$ and $j$ are known. The algorithm **Learn** (Figure 1) simulates the construction of a tree of depth at most $k$, where each node contains a $(k, j)$-DNF formula that implies $f^*$. Each node branches at most $2^k j n^j$; therefore, the size of the tree is at most $O(2^{k^2} j^k n^{jk})$.

For all levels $i$ of the tree the following property holds: for each $(k, j)$-DNF representation $f$ of $f^*$ there is some node at level $i$ that contains a function $g$ of $i$ terms that coincides with a subset of $i$ terms of $f$. This property guarantees that at the end of the process some leaf of the tree will contain a $(k, j)$-DNF representation of $f^*$.

The first call to Learn is made with input parameter $g = False$. There is a global variable $S$ containing the set $\{\langle a, f^*(a)\rangle : a \in \{0,1\}^n$ and $\|\text{zeros}(a)\| \leq k+j\}$.

Whenever we need to find a counterexample to extend a current hypothesis $g$, we search for an assignment $\langle a, 1\rangle \in S$ that satisfies $g(a) = 0$. Notice that Lemma 1, together with the fact that all the hypoteses we produce imply $f^*$, guarantee that such a counterexample will be found, if some exists (otherwise, we will have $g \equiv f^*$, and consequently stop the process and output $g$).

The next step is to discover the term in the target that is satisfied by $a$. To do that we run a "minimization" process that consists on flipping ones until no more can be flipped without violating the property "$f^*(a) = 1$ and $g(a) = 0$".

Let $b$ be the minimized assignment. Two problems arise when we want to find a new term of the target formula from $b$. First, we do not know whether the target term contains negated literals (at most $j$). On the other hand, it might be that not all the ones of $b$ would correspond to positive literals in the target term, since some of them might have been kept in order to falsify the terms discovered so far, that is, in order to maintain $g(b) = 0$ along the minimization process. The number of these ones is at most $k$, for we need to falsify at most $k$ terms.

Therefore, we can consider $b$ divided in three disjoint blocks: The block $A$ of ones that keep $f^*(b) = 1$, all of which must appear as positive literals in the target term, the block $B$ of at most $k$ ones that guarantee $g(b) = 0$, some of which might be in the target term, and the block $C$ of zeros, from which at most $j$ might appear as negated literals in the target term. Note that blocks $A$ and $B$ are disjoint because $g$ implies $f^*$.

Now we create a term $\text{Term}(A \cup B', C')$ for each $B' \subseteq B$ and for each $C' \subseteq C$ of size at most $j$. Notice that the number of terms we produce after a minimized positive example is at most $2^k \sum_{i=0}^{j} \binom{n}{i}$, which is less than $2^k j n^j$.

Finally, we use Lemma 1 to eliminate from the set of terms produced those that do not imply the target function.

The function **Produce-terms** (Figure 2) gives us the terms associated to a positive assignment in the way described above.

All the previous considerations are formalized in the following lemma:

**Lemma 2** *If $g$ is a $(k,j)$-DNF formula that implies $f^*$ but not viceversa, $b$ a minimized assigment that witnesses that fact, and $T$ the result of* **Produce-terms**$(g,b)$ *then*

- *all the terms in $T$ imply $f^*$, and*
- *for any $(k,j)$-DNF representation of $f^*$ there is a term of it that is in $T$ but not in $g$.*

Once we have got the set $T$ of terms that are possible extensions of $g$, we recursively call Learn with parameter $g \vee t$ for each $t \in T$.

Lemma 2 guarantees that in the $k$-th level of the tree there will be a representation equivalent to the target, so the correctness of Learn follows.

*Query complexity.* We ask at most $(k+j)n^{k+j}$ membership queries to create $S$, and at most $n^2$, for each node of the tree, to minimize the counterexample.

procedure **Learn** $(g)$
    search $\langle a, 1 \rangle \in S$ such that $g(a) = 0$
    if none is found then halt and output $g$
    else
        if $|g| < k$ then
            let $b$ the minimization of $a$ with $g$
            $T :=$ Produce-terms$(g, b)$
            for all $t \in T$ do
                **Learn**$(g \vee t)$
            enfor
        endif
    endif

**Fig. 1.** The Learning Algorithm

This is at most $(k + j)n^{k+j} + 2^{k^2} j^k n^{jk+2}$ queries, which is polynomial in $n$. In section 6 we will show how to reduce that number to $(k + j)n^{k+j}$.

*Time complexity.* In each node we explore $S$ at most $1 + 2^k j n^j$ times to look for the counterexample and to test if the produced terms imply the target. We also spend $n^2$ steps minimizing the counterexample. This is at most $O(n^{j(k+2)+k})$.

**Theorem 3** $(k, j)$-*DNF are properly learnable with membership queries in polynomial time.*

function **Produce-terms**$(g, a)$
    $T := \emptyset$
    for each $X \subseteq \{i : i \in \text{ones}(a) \text{ and } g(\text{flip}(a, i)) = 1\}$ do
        for each $Y \subseteq \text{zeros}(a)$ such that $\|Y\| \leq j$ do
            add Term$(\text{ones}(a) - X, Y)$ to $T$
        end-for
    end-for
    delete from $T$ the terms that do not imply the target function
    return $T$

**Fig. 2.** Obtaining the terms

## 4 Lower Bounds

In this section we prove superpolynomial lower bounds on the number of queries needed to learn the class $(k, j)$-DNF when $k$ or $j$ are not constants.

In the case of membership queries we prove that our positive result is tight in two directions: we cannot afford either more than a constant number of terms or more than a constant number of negations per term.

For the first case we use a target class in [BC+95] and for the second we simply count the number of singleton sets that can be represented with a number of negations per term that is bigger than any constant.

Negative results for membership queries can be of two kinds: information theoretic and computational. Our results are of the first type, which implies that learning is unfeasible no matters what representation class is used as hypotheses class.

For equivalence queries we describe an adversary that forces a superpolynomial number of queries. The result is also information theoretic. In the case of equivalence queries this does not imply non-learnability using any hypotheses class. However, our proof of Theorem 6 implies that $(k, j)$-DNF are not learnable even if we use general $k$-term DNF as hypothesis.

## 4.1 Membership Queries

**Theorem 4** *There is no polynomial time algorithm that learns $(f(n), 0)$-DNF formulas using membership queries, if $f$ grows faster than any constant.*

*Proof.* (*sketch*) Supposse that the class is learnable with $n^c$ membership queries. We use the class $T_n$ of part (1) of Theorem 22 in [BC+95]. Let $m$ be $c+1$, $l$ be $n/m$ and $T_n$ be $\{f : f = t \vee \bigvee_{i=1}^{m} t_i\}$, where each $t_i = \bigwedge_{j=(i-1)l+1}^{il} x_j$ and $t$ is a monotone term that contains all variables except one from each $t_i$. Observe that $T_n$ is a subset of $(f(n), 0)$-DNF for $n$ such that $f(n) > c + 1$. We choose $n$ large enough such that $n^c < l^m$. Following the same argument as in [BC+95] one can show that $l^m$ queries are necessary to learn $T_n$, which proves the theorem. $\square$

We will prove that the number of negations we allow per term is also optimal.

**Theorem 5** *There is no polynomial time algorithm that learns $(1, f(n))$-DNF formulas using membership queries, if $f$ grows faster than any constant.*

*Proof.* The number of different singleton sets we can represent with $(1, f(n))$-DNF formulas is

$$\sum_{i=0}^{f(n)} \binom{n}{i} = S_f$$

We use a standard adversary argument: a teacher that answers "no" to the first $S_f - 1$ membership queries, forces any learner to ask at least $S_f - 1$ membership queries. Since $S_f$ grows faster that any polynomial the theorem follows. $\square$

## 4.2 Equivalence Queries

**Theorem 6** *For any $k > 1$ and $j \geq 0$, the class $(k,j)$-DNF is not learnable using a polynomial number of equivalence queries that are $k$-term DNF (without the $j$ restriction).*

*Proof.* Let $T_{n,k}$ be the target class of functions where each function is the disjunction of $k$ pairwise disjoint monotone terms of length $n/k$. Here, disjoint means that no pair of terms have a variable in common.

It can be shown that $|T_{n,k}| = \frac{n!}{((n/k)!)^k k!}$. We will prove that for any $k$-term $DNF$ formula $h$ there exists an assignment $a$ such that the number of functions in $T_{n,k}$ that agree with $h$ in the classification of $a$ is a "small" fraction of $|T_{n,k}|$. Therefore, providing that assignment as a counterexample to an equivalence query on input $h$ will force any learner to make a "large" number of equivalence queries, before finding out the target. To see that some $a$ satisfying these requirements exists we consider the following cases:

1. $|h| < k$. Then $h$ is falsified by some assignment containing less than $k$ 0's. Clearly, such assignment does not falsify any of the functions in $T_{n,k}$.
2. $|h| = k$ and some term $t$ of $h$ has at most $n/k$ positive literals. The assignment that satisfies those positive literals and has 0's in the remaining positions is a positive example for $h$. However, the fraction of formulas in $T_n$ satisfied by such assignment is at most

$$\frac{|T_{n-n/k,k-1}|}{|T_{n,k}|} = \frac{(n-n/k)!(n/k)!k}{n!}$$

which is smaller than $1/n^c$ for any constant $c$, and $n$ large enough.
3. Otherwise, since all the terms in $h$ have more than $n/k$ positive literals, at least two of them must share one positive literal. Therefore $h$ can be falsified by some assignment with less than $k$ 0's as in case 1.

$\square$

## 5  Applications to Other Classes

The algorithm in Figure 1 can be used to learn $k$-term DNF formulas with at most $j$ positive literals per term; it is enough to exchange the roles of ones and zeros. Furthermore, lower bounds also hold for this class.

In the case of $k$-clause CNF formulas with a bounded number of negative (positive) literals per clause, the algorithm is also appliable; it suffices to consider the complementary concept which is a $k$-term DNF formula with a bounded number of positive (negative) literals per term.

This later observation implies that negative results also hold for the considered subclasses of $k$-clause CNF.

Furthermore, we can combine the positive results to learn a subclass of $k$-term DNF (CNF) where each term (clause) has either at most $j$ negative variables or at most $j$ positive variables. Note that for boolean functions $f$ and $g$, both belonging to that class, it holds the following property similar to Lemma 1: if $g$ does not imply $f$ then there exists an assignment $x$ such that it has either at most $k + j$ zeros or at most $k + j$ ones, and $x$ satisfies $g$ but not $f$.

## 6  Simple PAC

This section is devoted to the proof of learnability of $(k, j)$-DNF in the Simple PAC setting. In [LV91], Li and Vitányi prove that the class of monotone $k$-term DNF is Simple Pac learnable. In fact, they prove a stronger result, since their algorithm outputs, with high probability, an exact representation of the target function, instead of producing a "good" approximation. The key observation in their proof is that sampling according to the universal distribution, all the assignments with at most $k$ zeros are in a polynomial-sized sample, with high probability.

We will proceed in the same manner for the class $(k, j)$-DNF. We ask for a polynomial-sized sample and get, with high probability, all the assignments with at most $k + j$ zeros. If the sample contains all those assignments we run Learn, otherwise we do nothing. Whenever Learn asks a membership query for an assignment not in the sample (as it might occur in the minimization process), we answer it correctly by ourselves using Lemmas 1 and 7.

**Lemma 7** *Let $f$ be a DNF with at most $j$ negations per term. For any assignment $a$, $f(a) = 1$ if and only if there exists a term $t$ with at most $j$ negations such that $t(a) = 1$, $t$ implies $f$, and the set of positive variables in $t$ is $ones(a)$.*

*Proof.* The if part is trivial. For the only if part, let $t'$ be a term in $f$ that accepts $a$. Clearly the positive variables of $t'$ are a subset of $ones(a)$. We define $t$ as a term with the negated variables taken from the negated variables of $t'$ and with positive variables all $ones(a)$. It is trivial to see that $t(a) = 1$. It is also easy to show that $t$ implies $f$, since $t$ implies $t'$ and $t'$ implies $f$. Moreover, $ones(a)$ are the positive variables of $t$ by construction. □

Let $b$ be the input assignment to a membership query in the minimization process. Now, we construct all the terms that have as positive literals the variables in $ones(b)$ and at most $j$ negations. Then, we use lemma 1 to test if any of those terms implies the target function. If none of them implies the target we answer NO, otherwise we answer YES.

So we have proven the following theorem

**Theorem 8** $(k, j)$-*DNF are Simple PAC learnable.*

Note that this procedure of simulating membership queries could be used to improve the query complexity stated in section 3, since the initial $(k + j)n^{k+j}$ membership queries would suffice, although at the price of increasing the time complexity.

# 7 Acknowledgments

We thank José L. Balcázar, Ricard Gavaldà and some anonymous referees for helpful comments.

# References

[Ang87a] D. Angluin. "Learning $k$-term DNF formulas using queries and counterexamples". Technical Report YALEU/DCS/RR-559, Yale University, August 1987.

[Ang87b] D. Angluin. "Learning regular sets from queries and counterexamples". Information and Computation, 75:87-106, November 1987.

[Ang88] D. Angluin. "Queries and concept learning". Machine Learning, 2(4):319-342, 1988.

[Ber93] Ulf Berggren. "Linear Time Deterministic Learning of $k$-term DNF" In Proc. 6th Annu. Workshop on Comput. Learning Theory, pages 37-40. ACM Press, New York, NY, 1993.

[Bsh95] N. Bshouty. "Simple Learning Algorithms Using Divide and Conquer". In Proc. of 8th Annu. ACM Workshop on Comput. Learning Theory, pages 447-453, 1995.

[BC+95] N. Bshouty, R. Cleve, R. Gavaldà, S. Kannan, and C. Tamon. "Oracles and queries that are sufficient for exact learning". Journal of Computer and System Sciences, 52, pp. 421-433, 1996.

[BGHM93] N. Bshouty, S. Goldman, T. Hancock, and S. Matar. "Asking queries to minimize errors". In Proc. 6th Annu. Workshop on Comput. Learning Theory, pages 41-50. ACM Press, New York, NY, 1993.

[LV91] M. Li and P. Vitányi. "Learning simple concepts under simple distributions". SIAM Journal of Computing 20, pages 911-935, 1991.

# Optimal Attribute-Efficient Learning of Disjunction, Parity, and Threshold Functions

Ryuhei Uehara[1], Kensei Tsuchida[2], and Ingo Wegener[3]

[1] Center of Information Science, Tokyo Woman's Christian University, 2-6-1 Zempukuji, Suginami-ku, Tokyo 167, Japan, email: uehara@twcu.ac.jp
[2] Faculty of Engineering, Toyo University, Kujirai, Kawagoe-shi, Saitama 350, Japan, email: kensei@krc.eng.toyo.ac.jp
[3] FB Informatik, LS II, Univ. Dortmund, 44221 Dortmund, Germany, email: wegener@ls2.informatik.uni-dortmund.de

**Abstract.** Decision trees are a very general computation model. Here the problem is to identify a Boolean function $f$ out of a given set of Boolean functions $F$ by asking for the value of $f$ at adaptively chosen inputs. For classes $F$ consisting of functions which may be obtained from one function $g$ on $n$ inputs by replacing arbitrary $n - k$ inputs by given constants this problem is known as attribute-efficient learning with $k$ essential attributes. Results on general classes of functions are known. More precise and often optimal results are presented for the cases where $g$ is one of the functions disjunction, parity or threshold.

## 1   INTRODUCTION

Decision trees are the adequate computation model, if one likes to identify an unknown object from a given universe by asking queries with a finite number of possible answers. The queries may be asked adaptively, i.e., which question is asked can depend on previous answers. The aim is to minimize the worst case number of queries which is the depth of the decision tree.

The problem in this general setting has already been discussed by Picard (1965). A lot of different problems may be treated in this general framework (see Ahlswede and Wegener (1987)). Boolean decision trees are the most important subclass of decision trees. A known Boolean function $f$ has to be evaluated at an unknown input $a$. We may query for the bits $a_i$ of $a$. The complexity measure is the number of queries. All queries have the same cost. We only remark that the minimal depth of Boolean decision trees equals the minimal depth of branching programs or binary decision diagrams (see Wegener (1987)).

Here another class of problems is considered. A class $F$ of Boolean functions on $n$ variables is given and we want to find out which function $f \in F$ is chosen by an adversary. For this purpose we may choose adaptively inputs $a \in \{0,1\}^n$ and the adversary has to answer the query $a$ with the correct value of $f(a)$. The information theoretic lower bound is $\lceil \log |F| \rceil$, since we ask binary queries. This is optimal, e.g., for the class of all $2^{2^n}$ Boolean functions. Then we have to query all $2^n$ inputs. In the following we consider much smaller classes $F$. The class of functions representable by read-once formulas has been investigated by Angluin, Hellerstein, and Karpinski (1993).

The following situation is of particular interest. The class $F$ is based on one Boolean function $g$. For some sets $S \subseteq \{1, \ldots, n\}$ (typically all sets or all sets of cardinality $k$) there exists one function $g_S \in F$ which is a subfunction of $g$ where each $x_i$, $i \notin S$, is replaced by some given constant $a_i$. The identification of the unknown function $f \in F$ is equivalent to the identification of the set of essential attributes $S$. Angluin (1988) gives an overview on query learning. The situation described above is known as attribute-efficient learning. Already Littlestone (1988) and recently Bshouty and Hellerstein (1996) have designed quite efficient algorithms for attribute-efficient learning. Their algorithms work for quite general classes of functions and are efficient in particular for small $k$. Because of their generality they do not meet the lower bound for special classes of functions.

We like to obtain more precise results for special classes of functions. The classes OR and OR($k$) are based on the disjunction of $n$ variables. The not essential variables are replaced by the constant 0. The class OR contains all OR$_S$, $S \subseteq \{1, \ldots, n\}$, i.e., the disjunction of all $x_i$, $i \in S$, and OR($k$) all OR$_S$ where $|S| = k$. In the same way we obtain the classes PAR and PAR($k$) for the parity function which decides whether the number of ones in the input is odd or even. The threshold function is the basis of discrete neural nets. The threshold function on $n$ variables and threshold $t$ decides whether the input contains at least $t$ ones. Again we replace the not essential variables by 0. Then we consider the classes THR, THR($k$), and THR$_t$($k$), i.e., we distinguish whether we consider all $S \subseteq \{1, \ldots, n\}$ or all $S \subseteq \{1, \ldots, n\}$ of cardinality $k$ and we distinguish whether the threshold $t$ is unknown or known.

Our choice of classes of functions is motivated in the following way. Our results fit into the theory of attribute-efficient learning. The functions disjunction, parity, and threshold are the most important basic gates in circuit theory and, therefore, the most fundamental functions. If we know that some wires into a gate are destroyed and we like to learn which wires are destroyed by testing the gates on chosen inputs, we obtain the considered problem. This application motivates also the investigation of large $k$, e.g., $k = n - O(1)$. This situation leads to the attribute-efficient learning with respect to the *not* essential attributes.

In the Sections 3, 4, and 5 we consider the three different classes of functions. In Section 2 we collect the information theoretical lower bounds.

## 2  SIMPLE LOWER BOUNDS

Since the queries have two possible answers, $\lceil \log |F| \rceil$ queries are necessary for the class $F$.

**Theorem 1.** *The following lower bounds hold:*

*i) $n$ for OR and PAR.*

*ii)* $\lceil \log \binom{n}{k} \rceil$ *for OR(k), PAR(k), and THR$_t$(k), if $k \geq t > 0$. This bound is larger than $k \log(n/k)$ and $(n - k) \log (n/(n - k))$.*

*iii)* $\lceil \log \left( \binom{n}{k} \cdot k + 2 \right) \rceil$ *for THR(k).*

*iv)* $n - 1 + \lceil \log(n + 1) \rceil$ *for THR.*

*Proof.* The classes OR and PAR contain $2^n$ functions and the classes OR(k), PAR(k) and THR$_t$(k) contain $\binom{n}{k}$ functions. The estimations of $\log \binom{n}{k}$ are standard calculations. For THR(k) we have the possible threshold values $t \in \{1, \ldots, k\}$ each leading to $\binom{n}{k}$ functions. For different $t$ we obtain different functions. Moreover, we obtain for $t = 0$ the constant 1 and for $t > k$ the constant 0. For the class THR we have

$$\sum_{1 \leq k \leq n} k \binom{n}{k} + 2$$

different functions, since we cannot distinguish whether a constant function "depends" on $k$ or $k'$ variables. The number of different functions equals $n2^{n-1} + 2$ and $\lceil \log(n2^{n-1} + 2) \rceil = \lceil \log 2^{n-1} \left( n + 2^{-(n-2)} \right) \rceil \geq n - 1 + \lceil \log(n + 1) \rceil$.

Later we derive for some cases better lower bounds by adversary arguments.

## 3   DISJUNCTIONS

By de Morgan's rules it easily follows that all results for disjunctions also hold for conjunctions, if the non essential variables for conjunctions are replaced by ones.

A query is an input $a \in \{0, 1\}^n$. In the following we identify queries $a$ with the query set $A = \{i \mid a_i = 1\}$.

The class of functions OR causes no problem. We meet the lower bound $n$ with the simple nonadaptive strategy asking all query sets of size 1 also called singletons.

**Proposition 2.** *The class OR(k) can be learned with at most $2k \left( \lceil \log(n/2k) \rceil + 1 \right)$ queries.*

*Proof.* We start with $2k$ query sets which build a partition of $\{1, \ldots, n\}$ and whose size is bounded by $\lceil n/(2k) \rceil$. A query set leading to the answer 1 is called a winner. By definition of the problem there are at most $k$ winners which again are split into two query sets of almost the same size. Hence, $\lceil \log(n/2k) \rceil + 1$ phases with at most $2k$ queries each are sufficient. The $k$ winners of the last phase are the essential elements (variables).

This result leads to two new problems. The upper bound is asymptotically optimal, if $k$ is not too large. But it is by the factor 2 larger than the lower bound of Theorem 1. Can we get rid of this factor? For large $k$ the lower bound is much smaller than the upper bound. What is the right value?

We answer these questions with the following two theorems.

**Theorem 3.** *The class OR(k) can be learned with at most $k\lceil \log(n/k)\rceil + 2k - 2$ queries.*

*Proof.* We partition the set of elements to $k$ sets of size at most $\lceil n/k \rceil$. We ask these $k$ sets as queries. If a set $S$ is a winner, we can find by binary search with at most $\lceil \log\lceil n/k \rceil \rceil = \lceil \log(n/k) \rceil$ queries an essential element $x$. Then we test whether $S - \{x\}$ is still a winner and continue in this way. For each of the $k$ essential elements the binary search can be done with at most $\lceil \log(n/k) \rceil$ queries. Moreover, we ask $k$ queries in the beginning. For each essential element $x$ we have found we ask an additional question (the question $S - \{x\}$ above). We can save this question for the last two essential elements. After having found the last essential element we are done. If we have found the last but one essential element, we know whether there is another set which is a winner. If and only if not, the corresponding set $S - \{x\}$ is a winner.

If $k = o(n)$, the leading term in Theorem 3 has the same constant factor as the lower bound of Theorem 1, namely 1.

**Theorem 4.** *If $n/2 \le k \le n - 1$, $n - 1$ queries are necessary and sufficient for OR(k).*

*Proof.* The claim is proved with an adversary argument. First we consider the class $OR(n - 1)$. Query sets of size larger than 1 are useless, since the answer 1 is known in advance. Hence, only singletons are tested and the adversary may answer the first $n - 1$ queries by 1.

We restrict ourselves w.l.o.g. to strategies which do not include identified elements (elements which are known to be essential or not essential) into further query sets. The adversary strategy is the following. If $k = n - 1$, we follow the strategy described above. Otherwise the adversary does the following. As long as the query sets are disjoint the adversary answers 0 for the query sets of size 1 and answers 1 for larger query sets. The answers 1 are allowed, since $k \ge n/2$. If the adversary has declared $n - k - 1$ elements as not essential, we may erase these queries and are left with the problem $OR(k)$ on $k + 1$ elements for which we can use the adversary strategy described at the beginning of this proof. If for the first time an element is contained for the second time in a query set, the adversary declares this element as essential. By the assumption that already identified elements are not contained in later query sets, the first query $A$ containing $i$ contains also another element $j$. This element is declared as not essential. In this way we may eliminate 2 queries and are left with the adversary strategy for the problem $OR(k-1)$ on $n - 2$ elements. For this problem we prove with the same strategy that $n - 3$ queries are necessary.

## 4  PARITY FUNCTIONS

The class PAR can be learned as the class OR with $n$ queries of the singletons.

Parity (or mod 2) is like disjunction a binary, associative and commutative operation with 0 as neutral element. But $(\{0,1\}, \oplus)$ is an additive group while the equation $1 \vee x = 0$ has no solution. Therefore, we obtain here results different from the previous section. The class $OR(k)$ is efficiently learnable for small $k$ and needs the maximum of $n-1$ queries if $k \geq n/2$. The group properties of the parity operation imply that for given $n$ it is the same whether we like to learn $PAR(k)$ or $PAR(n-k)$.

**Proposition 5.** *For given $n$, the complexity of learning PAR(k) is equal to the complexity of learning PAR(n − k).*

*Proof.* Let $g_1$ be the parity function on $k$ of the $n$ variables and $g_2$ be the parity function on the $n-k$ other variables. This defines a one-to-one mapping between the classes $PAR(k)$ and $PAR(n-k)$. For a query set $S$ let $a_1(S)$ and $a_2(S)$ be the answers given for $g_1$ and $g_2$ resp. Then $a_1(S) \oplus a_2(S) \equiv |S| \bmod 2$. Hence, we can compute $a_1(S)$ from $a_2(S)$ and vice versa. A strategy for $PAR(k)$ which identifies $g_1$ identifies with the corresponding answers $g_2$, if it is used for $PAR(n-k)$.

Because of Proposition 5 we assume w.l.o.g. that $k \leq n/2$. For the OR-classes, one essential variable can be identified with binary search using $\lceil \log n \rceil$ queries. For the PAR-classes the same holds, if the number of essential elements is odd. If we partition the set of elements into two parts, one has an odd number of essential elements and the other one an even number. With one query we can find out which is the "odd part" and can continue with this set. After having found one essential element, we have an even number of unknown essential elements and are in the difficult situation. We cannot make use of the already found essential element. Otherwise we may find the same essential element for a second time. If we find in the situation of an even number of unknown essential elements a set $S$ with an odd number of unknown essential elements, then the complement of $S$ with respect to the unidentified elements also contains an odd number of essential elements. We can apply the binary search technique to both sets. We get good upper bounds (see Theorem 1) for $k \in \{1, 2, 3\}$.

**Proposition 6.** *i) PAR(1) can be learned with $\lceil \log n \rceil$ queries.*
*ii) PAR(2) can be learned with $3\lceil \log n \rceil - 2$ queries.*
*iii) PAR(3) can be learned with $4\lceil \log n \rceil - 3$ queries.*

*Proof.* The first result follows from the binary search technique. For the second claim we use a so-called separating system $S_0, \ldots, S_{\lceil \log n \rceil - 1}$. That means, for $i \neq j$ there is a set $S_m$ where $i \in A_m$ and $j \notin A_m$ or vice versa. For this purpose let $A_m$ consist of the numbers $j$ whose $m$-th bit in the binary representation equals 1. First we query the sets of the separating system. If $i$ and $j$ are the essential elements, the corresponding set $A_m$ leads to the answer 1. Then we may start binary searches on $A_m$ and its complement, sets of at most $\lceil n/2 \rceil$ elements. The third result is obvious, since we may find the first essential element with binary search. Then we can apply the second result (even for a set of $n-1$ elements). We save one query, since the first query can be chosen on a set belonging to the separating system in the second round.

How can we find for larger $k$ a set with an odd number of essential objects? This question is different from the more general approach of Bshouty and Hellerstein (1996). They considered p. e. c.-classes of functions which are closed under projections and embeddings. OR($k$) and PAR($k$) are p. e. c.-classes but many other classes of functions have the property p. e. c. In the more general situation one looks for so-called $(n, k, r, \alpha)$-splitters. Actually, Bshouty and Hellerstein (1996) do not use the notion splitter.

**Definition 7.** An $(n, k, r, \alpha)$-splitter of size $s$ is a sequence $P_1, \ldots, P_s$ of partitions of $\{1, \ldots, n\}$ into $r$ sets such that for each set $S$ of cardinality $k$ at least a fraction of $\alpha > 0$ partitions put the elements of $S$ into $r$ different sets.

**Lemma 8.** *An $(n, k, r, \alpha)$-splitter of size $s$ implies that PAR(k) can be learned with $rs + k\lceil \log n \rceil$ queries.*

*Proof.* With $rs$ queries of the sets in $P_1, \ldots, P_s$ we find one partition where $k$ subsets give the answer 1. With binary search on these sets we find the $k$ essential elements.

Since the notion of splitters is quite new, the results on splitters are scattered through the literature. Moreover, it has to be distinguished whether splitters only exist or can be constructed efficiently. Friedman (1984) constructs splitters for constant $k$ leading to $O(\log n)$ learning algorithms for PAR($k$) and constant $k$. This construction was used for the construction of Boolean formulas. Ragde and Widgerson (1991) (based on Mehlhorn (1982)) and Håstad, Wegener, Wurm, and Yi (1994) also used splitters for the construction of Boolean circuits. Naor, Schulman, and Srinivasan (1995) explicitly investigate splitters under this name. The deterministic construction of splitters in Bshouty and Hellerstein (1996) is a rediscovery of the construction used by Håstad, Wegener, Wurm, and Yi (1994).

These splitters lead by Lemma 8 to the existence of learning algorithms for PAR($k$) with $O(k^3 \log n)$ queries and the efficient construction of learning algorithms with $O(k^4 \log n)$ queries (Hofmeister (1996)). Using special properties of the parity function we improve the upper bound. Since decision trees are a nonuniform computation model we concentrate our discussion on the minimal number of necessary queries and not on the efficient construction of the learning algorithms.

For the class of parity functions we may find the essential elements sequentially. We do not have to partition the essential elements in classes of size 1. For the identification of one essential element it is sufficient to find a set with an odd number of essential elements.

First we consider randomized learning algorithms with zero-error. Either we can guarantee that the algorithm always gives the right answer and that the expected number of queries is small or we guarantee an upper bound on the number of queries and a small upper bound on the probability that the algorithm answers "don't know". (For an introduction to randomized algorithms see Motwani and Raghavan (1995)). We are not the first to investigate randomized decision trees, see e. g. Saks and Widgerson (1986) and Heiman and Widgerson (1991).

Obviously, one half of the queries leads to the answer 1. Asking randomized queries we get in expected time 2 a query set with answer 1. Then, we find two essential elements with binary search. This leads to an error-free randomized algorithm with an expected number of $k(\lceil \log n \rceil + 1)$ queries. In order to meet the lower bound we should decrease the size of the query sets.

**Theorem 9.** *For PAR(k) there is a randomized error-free learning algorithm with an expected number of $k \log(n/k) + O(k)$ queries. If the number of queries is bounded by $O(k \log(n/k))$, the probability of not having identified the unknown function can be bounded by a function tending with respect to $k \log(n/k)$ exponentially fast to 0.*

*Proof.* The algorithm works as follows. If we have already found $l$ essential elements (in the beginning $l = 0$), we work on the other $n - l$ elements and query random sets of size $(n - l)/(k - l)$ (more precisely $\lceil (n - l)/(k - l) \rceil$). The probability that such a set contains an odd number of essential elements can be bounded in the following way. If $k - l$ is small, this probability tends to $1/2$ which can be proved by elementary calculations. Otherwise, the probability distribution of the number of essential elements in the random query set tends to the Poisson distribution with parameter $\lambda = 1$. Hence, the probability that the query set contains exactly one essential element tends to $e^{-1} \geq 0.36$ ($e$ the Eulerian constant $2.718\ldots$). Hence, the probability of success is for large $n$ bounded below by $1/3$. For a successful query we perform the binary search only on the small query set and not on the large complement. For the binary searches we are done in any case with

$$\sum_{1 \leq m \leq k} \lceil \log \frac{n - k + m}{m} \rceil \leq \sum_{1 \leq m \leq k} \log \frac{n}{m} + O(k) = k \log n - \log(k!) + O(k)$$

$$= k \log n - (k \log k - O(k)) + O(k) = k \log(n/k) + O(k)$$

queries. The expected number of queries to find the next set with an odd number of essential elements is bounded by 3 leading to an additional expected number of $3k$ queries.

For the second claim we get smaller upper bounds than for general error-free randomized algorithms. Only a small part of our algorithm is randomized. Furthermore, we have independent trials each with a probability of success at least $1/3$. We need $k$ successes and may perform $O(k \log(n/k))$ trials. Now the probability of less then $k$ successes can be estimated with Chernoff's bounds.

Now we look for deterministic learning algorithms. The main idea is to "recycle" query sets, i.e. to try to use them more than once. A random query set $S$ contains approximately half of the essential elements. The set is good, if it contains an odd number of essential elements. If the number of essential elements in $S$ is even, we try other sets. If we find the first essential element $i$ contained in $S$, we know without any further query that $S - \{i\}$ contains an odd number of essential elements. These ideas are made precise in the next proposition which will be improved later. Moreover, we derandomize the algorithm.

**Proposition 10.** *The class PAR(k) can be learned with* $\lceil \log \binom{n}{k} \rceil + k \lceil \log n \rceil + 2$ *queries.*

*Proof.* If $k = \Omega(n)$, the result is obvious, since $n - 1$ queries of singletons suffice. If $k \leq n/3$,

$$\binom{n}{k-1} \leq \frac{1}{2}\binom{n}{k}$$

and

$$\binom{n}{k} + \binom{n}{k-1} + \binom{n}{k-2} + \cdots + \binom{n}{1} \leq 2\binom{n}{k}.$$

We choose $m = \lceil \log \binom{n}{k} \rceil + 2$ random sets $R_1, \ldots, R_m$. Let $S \subseteq \{1, \ldots, n\}$ be one set where $|S| \in \{1, \ldots, k\}$. The probability that $S \cap R_j$ has odd cardinality equals $1/2$.

The probability that all random sets are bad for $S$, i.e. $S \cap R_1, \ldots, S \cap R_m$ all have even cardinality, equals $\frac{1}{4}\binom{n}{k}^{-1}$. Therefore, the probability that for at least one of the less than $2\binom{n}{k}$ sets $S$ all random sets are bad is bounded above by $1/2$. Hence, there exist $m$ query sets $T_1, \ldots, T_m$ such that for each $S \subseteq \{1, \ldots, n\}$ with $1 \leq |S| \leq k$ there exists a set $T_j$ such that $|S \cap T_j|$ is odd.

The sets $T_1, \ldots, T_m$ are used as query sets. Let $S$ be the unknown set of essential elements. Then $|S \cap T_{i(1)}|$ is odd for some $i(1)$ and we find an essential element $j(1)$ with binary search on $T_{i(1)}$. Let $S_1 := S - \{j(1)\}$. Then $|S_1 \cap T_{i(2)}|$ is odd for some $i(2)$ and we find an essential element $j(2)$ with binary search on $T_{i(2)} - \{j(1)\}$ and so on. Here we have used the fact that we have implicitly knowledge about the query set $T_i - \{j(1)\}$ if have asked the query $T_i$ and know that $j(1)$ is essential.

Altogether we have asked $m$ queries $T_1, \ldots, T_m$ and need $k \lceil \log n \rceil$ further queries for the binary searches.

The term $\lceil \log \binom{n}{k} \rceil$ is equal to the information theoretic lower bound. In order to obtain an asymptotically optimal algorithm the term $k \log n$ should be replaced by $O(k \log(n/k))$. If $k = O(n^{1-\varepsilon})$, nothing has to be done. Hence, we have to consider functions like $k = n/\log^2 n$ or $k = n/\log\log n$.

**Theorem 11.** *The class PAR(k) can be learned with* $O(k \log(n/k))$ *queries.*

*Proof.* Because of Proposition 5 and the simple strategy using $n - 1$ queries we can assume that $k = n/h(n)$ for some function $h(n)$ tending to $\infty$. The first idea is to replace the random sets in the proof of Proposition 10 by random sets of size $n/k = h(n)$. For sets $S$ with $k' = o(k)$ elements the intersection of $S$ and such a random set is with large probability empty. Therefore, we work with random sets of size $(n/k)^2 = h(n)^2$. The cost for each binary search is increased by a factor 2 only. For sets $S$ where $|S| \geq n/h(n)^2$ the probability of success for a random set is at least $1/3$. Hence, with $O(\log \binom{n}{k})$ sets we can identify all but $n/h(n)^2$ essential elements.

In the second phase we work with sets of size $h(n)^4$ and can identify all but $n/h(n)^4$ essential elements. This process is continued until all essential elements can be identified.

The number of query sets besides the queries in the binary searches is bounded by

$$O \left( \log \binom{n}{n/h(n)} + \log \binom{n}{n/h(n)^2} + \log \binom{n}{n/h(n)^4} + \cdots \right)$$

$$= O \left( \frac{n}{h(n)} \log h(n) + \frac{n}{h(n)^2} 2 \log h(n) + \frac{n}{h(n)^4} 4 \log h(n) + \cdots \right)$$

$$= O \left( k \log(n/k) \right).$$

We still have to estimate the number of queries during the binary searches. In the first phase we find not more than $n/h(n)$ essential elements each with a cost of $2 \log h(n)$. In the second phase we find not more than $n/h(n)^2$ essential elements each with a cost of $4 \log h(n)$ and so on. Hence, the same estimation as before shows that $O(k \log(n/k))$ queries suffice.

Again we have found asymptotically optimal algorithms. These algorithms cannot be constructed efficiently. In applications one may use the randomized algorithms.

## 5  THRESHOLD FUNCTIONS

The simple strategy of testing all singletons is optimal for the classes OR and PAR. For the class THR we obtain an optimal algorithm, if $n + 1$ is not a power of 2. Otherwise we miss the lower bound by 1.

**Theorem 12.** *The class THR can be learned with $n - 1 + \lceil \log(n + 2) \rceil$ queries.*

*Proof.* In the first phase we only use query sets of type $\{1, \ldots, m\}$. Since threshold functions are monotone, we can find with binary search and $\lceil \log(n + 2) \rceil$ queries the minimal $s \in \{0, \ldots, n\}$ such that the answer to the query $\{1, \ldots, s\}$ is 1 or we find out that such an $s$ does not exist. In the last case we are done, since the function we look for is the constant 0. If $s = 0$, the function is the constant 1. If $s \in \{1, \ldots, n\}$, we know that $s$ is an essential element. The query $\{1, \ldots, s\} - \{j\}$ decides for $j \in \{1, \ldots, s-1\}$ whether $j$ is essential and the query $\{1, \ldots, s-1, j\}$ does the same for $j \in \{s+1, \ldots, n\}$. These are $n - 1$ additional queries.

**Theorem 13.** *Let $0 \leq t \leq k \leq n$. The class $THR_t(k)$ can be learned with at most $(k - 1) \log \frac{n-1}{k-1} + 3k - 3 + \lceil \log(n + 2) \rceil$ queries.*

*Proof.* The first phase is the same as in the proof of Theorem 12. Afterwards we know the parameters $n$, $k$, and $t$. Moreover, if we are not done, we know an essential element $s$ such that the query $\{1, \ldots, s\}$ leads to the answer 1 and the query $\{1, \ldots, s - 1\}$ leads to the answer 0. Hence, we know that $\{1, \ldots, s - 1\}$

contains exactly $t-1$ essential elements and $\{s+1,\ldots,n\}$ contains the remaining $k-t$ essential elements.

We use an algorithm for $OR(k-t)$ on the set $\{s+1,\ldots,n\}$ and add to each query the set $\{1,\ldots,s-1\}$. This algorithm identifies the $k-t$ essential elements in $\{s+1,\ldots,n\}$. Then we use an algorithm for $AND(t-1)$ on the set $\{1,\ldots,s-1\}$ and add to each query the essential element $s$. This algorithm identifies the $t-1$ essential elements in $\{1,\ldots,s-1\}$.

In Section 3 we have seen that the complexity of learning AND-classes is the same as for the corresponding OR-classes. By Theorem 3 the number of queries of the second and third phase is bounded by

$$(k-t)\left\lceil \log \frac{n-s}{k-t}\right\rceil + 2(k-t) + (t-1)\left\lceil \log \frac{s-1}{t-1}\right\rceil + 2(t-1)$$

$$\leq (k-t)\log \frac{n-s}{k-t} + (t-1)\log \frac{s-1}{t-1} + 3k-3$$

$$\leq (k-1)\log \frac{n-1}{k-1} + 3k-3.$$

The last inequality is for $a = \frac{s-1}{n-1}$ and $b = \frac{t-1}{k-1}$ equivalent to

$$-b\log b - (1-b)\log(1-b) \leq -b\log a - (1-b)\log(1-a).$$

This inequality holds, since $0 \leq a, b \leq 1$, see e.g. Ahlswede and Wegener (1987), Lemma 5.3, p.20. Such inequalities are used, e.g., for the proof of the noiseless coding theorem, the left hand side is the entropy for the distribution $(b, 1-b)$.

**Theorem 14.** *The class $THR(k)$ can be learned with at most $2(k-1)\log \frac{n-1}{k-1} + 6k-6 + \lceil \log(n+2)\rceil$ queries.*

*Proof.* The first phase of the algorithms in the proofs of Theorem 12 and Theorem 13 does not need the knowledge of $t$. Hence, we can use this phase also here.

Afterwards we can solve the problem by the application of algorithms for OR (and equivalently AND). But now the number of essential elements is not known, since it depends on the unknown parameter $t$. The algorithms in the proofs of Proposition 2 and Theorem 3 rely on the fact that the number of essential elements is known. But with at most $4k$ additional queries we can make the algorithm in the proof of Proposition 2 independent of the knowledge of $k$. We start with the query $\{1,\ldots,n\}$. During the whole algorithm all winners (queries with answer 1) are split into two sets of almost the same size and these sets are used as query sets. Without knowing $k$ the algorithm does not produce more than $k$ winners in each phase. The additional queries are those during the phases $0,\ldots,\lceil \log k\rceil$ where the query sets have approximately the size $n/2^0,\ldots,n/2^{\lceil \log k\rceil}$. The number of these queries is bounded by $2^{\lceil \log k\rceil+1} \leq 4k$. Hence, the number of queries for $THR(k)$ is bounded by

$$\lceil \log(n+2)\rceil + 2(k-t)\lceil \log \frac{n-s}{2(k-t)}\rceil + 6(k-t) + 2(t-1)\lceil \log \frac{s-1}{2(t-1)}\rceil + 6(t-1).$$

Now we can use the same estimations as in the proof of Theorem 13.

We know from the Sections 2 and 3 that these upper bounds are asymptotically optimal for $k \leq n/2$. The optimal number of queries does not rely essentially on the threshold value $t$ or even on the knowledge of $t$. Does this hold also for $k > n/2$?

First we see that we get OR, if $t = 1$. We know that for this case we need $n - 1$ queries, if $k \geq n/2$. Moreover, the cases $t = 1$ and $t = k$ are equivalent. This can be generalized.

**Proposition 15.** *For given $n$, the complexity of learning $THR_t(k)$ is equal to the complexity of learning $THR_{k-t+1}(k)$.*

*Proof.* Let $S$ be the set of essential elements for the problem $THR_t(k)$. A query $Q$ leads to the answer 1 if and only if $|Q \cap S| \geq t$. If $S$ is the set of essential elements for the problem $THR_{k-t+1}(k)$, the query $Q' := \{1, \ldots, n\} - Q$ leads to the answer 1 if and only if $|Q' \cap S| \geq k - t + 1$ which is equivalent to $|Q \cap S| \leq t - 1$. Hence, we can simulate the query $Q$ for $THR_t(k)$ by the query $Q'$ for $THR_{k-t+1}(k)$ and vice versa.

We are still left with a variety of parameter choices. The case $k = n - 1$ leads to an interesting result. Afterwards we investigate the majority function, namely the case $k = n/2$.

**Theorem 16.** *Let $t \leq n/2$. To learn the class $THR_t(n - 1)$*

- *$\max\{\lceil \log n \rceil, \lceil (n - 1)/t \rceil\}$ queries are necessary and*
- *$\lceil n/t \rceil + \lceil \log t \rceil - 1$ queries are sufficient.*

By Proposition 15 we obtain similar results for the case $t > n/2$.

*Proof.* The lower bound $\lceil \log n \rceil$ is the simple information theoretical lower bound. For the lower bound $\lceil (n - 1)/t \rceil$ a simple adversary argument works. A query set of size $t + 1$ or larger is useless, since we know in advance that the answer is 1. A query set of size $t - 1$ or smaller is useless, since we know in advance that the answer is 0. Hence, all query sets have size $t$. An adversary may answer 1 for the first $\lceil (n - 1)/t \rceil - 1$ questions. Then there are still at least 2 candidates for the not essential element and another query is necessary.

For the upper bound we construct $\lceil n/t \rceil$ query sets of size $t$ such that each element is contained in at least one set. We look for a query set leading to the answer 0, since this set contains the only not essential element. At least one of the queries is good for our purposes. Hence, it is sufficient to ask $\lceil n/t \rceil - 1$ queries. Since $t \leq n/2$, we now can use binary search on this set, if we add always as many already identified elements such that the query size becomes $t$.

This result is interesting, since we now know of an example where large and small threshold values, in particular the cases AND and OR, are difficult while $t = n/2$ is easy. For $THR_{n/2}(n - 1)$ we have shown that $\lceil \log n \rceil$ queries are sufficient.

Moreover, we can prove that the threshold value $n/2$ admits efficient learning algorithms for all numbers of essential elements. We leave it to the reader to generalize this result to other threshold values.

**Theorem 17.** *The class* $THR_{n/2}(n-k)$ *can be learned with* $O(k \log(n/k))$ *queries.*

*Proof.* If $k > n/2$, nothing has to be learned and 0 queries are sufficient. If $k \leq n/2$ and $k = \Theta(n)$, the upper bound follows from Theorem 12. Hence, we may assume that $k \leq n/8$. Moreover, we assume that $k$ divides $n$. Otherwise, we may add less than $k$ elements known to be not essential. Additional not essential elements have no influence on the answer to queries and can therefore be added. This does not hold for additional essential elements.

We partition $\{1, \ldots, n\}$ into blocks $B_i, 1 \leq i \leq k$, where $B_i = \{(i-1)n/k + 1, \ldots, in/k\}$. We like to search for the $k$ not essential elements using one of the strategies for $OR(k)$ from Proposition 2 or Theorem 3. Each query set $S$ will be a subset of some $B_i$. If $S$ has size $j$, we need a set $S_j$ which is disjoint from $S$ (or even $B_i$) and which contains exactly $n/2 - j$ essential elements. The query $S \cup S_j$ then decides whether $S$ contains at least one not essential element. Hence, we may use the OR-strategies, if the so-called dummy sets $S_j$ are available. Since $|S| \leq n/k$, we only need dummy sets with $n/2 - j$ essential elements where $1 \leq j \leq n/k$.

As in the proof of Theorem 12 we determine the minimal $s$ such that $S^* = \{1, \ldots, s\}$ contains $n/2$ essential elements. We know in advance that $n/2 \leq s \leq n/2 + k$. Hence, $\lceil \log(k+1) \rceil$ queries are sufficient. By asking the queries $S^* - \{1\}, \ldots, S^* - \{k + n/k\}$ we find at least $n/k$ essential elements $e_1, \ldots, e_{n/k}$. The set $S^* - \{e_1, \ldots, e_j\}$ contains exactly $n/2 - j$ essential elements, $1 \leq j \leq n/k$. With $\lceil \log(k+1) \rceil + k + n/k$ queries we have found dummy sets which are, since $k \leq n/8$, for large $n$ disjoint from the last third of the blocks $B_i$. We may repeat the whole process twice where we shift the elements by $n/3$ and $2n/3$ resp. positions in order to find dummy sets for all blocks.

The number of queries for the computation of dummy sets is bounded by $3(\lceil \log(k+1) \rceil + k + n/k)$ and afterwards we may use the $OR(k)$-strategy from Proposition 2 or Theorem 3.

This bound is good enough if and only if $n/k = O(k \log(n/k))$. This condition is equivalent to $k = \Omega(n^{1/2}/\log^{1/2} n)$. For smaller values of $k$ we need a new strategy for the computation of dummy sets.

As usual we first determine the smallest set $S^* = \{1, \ldots, s\}$ with exactly $n/2$ essential elements. For some $l$ with $s < l \leq 2n/3$ we partition the elements $l, \ldots, n$ to $k+1$ subsets $R_1, \ldots, R_{k+1}$ of equal size $r \leq n/k$. We try to find the not essential elements in $R_1, \ldots, R_{k+1}$ by using an OR-strategy for at most $k$ essential elements. This can be done efficiently by testing only subsets of the $R$-sets. For the queries $R_1, \ldots, R_{k+1}$ we need a dummy set $D$ with exactly $n/2 - r$ essential elements. We consider the following candidates $D_0 = S^* - \{1, \ldots, r\}, \ldots, D_k = S^* - \{1, \ldots, r + k\}$. The set $D_0$ contains at least $n/2 - r$ essential elements and the set $D_k$ at most $n/2 - r$ essential elements.

What happens if we query the sets $R_1 \cup D_j, \ldots, R_{k+1} \cup D_j$? If the answers are all 0, $D_j$ is too small. Since the number of not essential elements is $k$, at least one set $R_i$ consists of $r$ essential elements only. Since also $R_i \cup D_j$ leads to the answer 0, $D_j$ is too small. Otherwise, $D_j$ may be too large. Hence, for our purposes it is sufficient to find the largest $j$ and, therefore , the smallest $D_j$ such that at least one of the queries $R_1 \cup D_j, \ldots, R_{k+1} \cup D_j$ leads to the answer 1. This can be done with binary search with $(k + 1)\lceil \log(k + 1)\rceil$ queries. Then $D_j$ contains exactly $n/2 - r$ essential elements. Moreover, the set $R_i$, such that $R_i \cup D_j$ leads to the answer 1, consists of $r$ essential elements only. Hence, larger dummy sets can be obtained easily by taking $D_j$ and the appropriate number of elements out of $R_i$. Again this procedure has to be repeated at most three times.

Altogether we need besides the queries for the corresponding $OR(k)$-strategies only $O(k \log k)$ additional queries. This is small enough if $\log k = O(\log(n/k))$ and, therefore, if $k = O(n^{1-\varepsilon})$ for some $\varepsilon > 0$.

We have proved the theorem, since at least one of the conditions $k = \Omega(n^{1/2}/\log^{1/2} n)$ and $k = O(n^{1-\varepsilon})$ is always fulfilled.

# References

Ahlswede, R. and Wegener, I. (1987). *Search Problems*. Wiley.

Angluin, D. (1988). *Queries and concept learning*. Machine Learning 2, 319–342.

Angluin, D., Hellerstein, L., and Karpinski, M. (1993). *Learning read-once formulas with queries*. Journal of the ACM 40, 185–210.

Bshouty, N. H. and Hellerstein, L. (1996). *Attribute-efficient learning in query and mistake-bound models*. Proc. of the 9th Conf. on Computational Learning Theory COLT '96, 235–243.

Friedman, J. (1984). *Constructing $O(n \log n)$ size monotone formulae for the k-th elementary symmetric polynomial of n Boolean variables*. Proc. 25th Symp. on Foundations of Computer Science, 506–515.

Håstad, J., Wegener, I., Wurm, N., and Yi, S. (1994). *Optimal depth, very small size circuits for symmetric functions in $AC^0$*. Information and Computation 108, 200–211.

Heiman, R. and Wigderson, A. (1991). *Randomized vs. deterministic decision tree complexity*. Computational Complexity 1, 311-329.

Hofmeister, T. (1996). *Personal communication*.

Littlestone, N. (1988). *Learning quickly when irrelevant attributes abound: a new linear-threshold algorithm*. Machine Learning 2, 285–318.

Mehlhorn, K. (1982). *On the program size of perfect and universal hash functions*. Proc. 23rd Symp. on Foundations of Computer Science, 170–175.

Motwani, R. and Raghavan, P. (1995). *Randomized Algorithms*. Cambridge University Press.

Naor, M., Schulman, L., and Srinivasan, A. (1995). *Splitters and near-optimal decomposition*. Proc. 36th Symp. on Foundations of Computer Science, 182–191.

Picard, C. (1965). *Théorie des Questionnaires*. Gauthier-Villars, Paris.

Ragde, P. and Widgerson, A. (1991). *Linear-size constant-depth polylog-threshold circuits.* Information Processing Letters 39, 143–146.

Saks, M. and Widgerson, A. (1986). *Probabilistic Boolean decision trees and the complexity of evaluating game trees.* Proc. of 27th Symp. on Foundations of Computer Science, 29–38.

Wegener, I. (1987). *The Complexity of Boolean Functions.* Wiley-Teubner.

# Learning Pattern Languages Using Queries

Satoshi Matsumoto* and Ayumi Shinohara

Department of Informatics,
Kyushu University 33, Fukuoka 812-81, JAPAN
e-mails:{matumoto, ayumi}@i.kyushu-u.ac.jp

**Abstract.** A pattern is a finite string of constant and variable symbols. For $k \geq 1$, we denote by $k\mu\Pi$ the set of all patterns in which each variable symbol occurs at most $k$ times. In particular, we abbreviate $\mu\Pi$ for $k = 1$. The language $L(\pi)$ of a pattern $\pi$ is the set of all strings obtained by substituting any non-null constant string for each variable symbol in $\pi$. In this paper, we show that any pattern $\pi \in k\mu\Pi$ is exactly identifiable in $O(|w|^{k+2})$ time from one positive example $w \in L(\pi)$ using $|w|^{k+1} + |\pi|^k$ membership queries. Moreover, we introduce the notion of critical pattern, and show that the number of membership queries can be reduced to $|w| + |\pi|$ if the target pattern $\pi \in \mu\Pi$ is not critical. For instance, any pattern $\pi \in \mu\Pi$ whose constant parts are of length at most 3 is not critical. Finally, we show a nontrivial subclass of $\mu\Pi$ that is identified using membership queries only, without any initial positive example.

## 1 Introduction

We investigate the feasibility of learning *pattern languages*, in the setting of exact identification using queries [4]. A pattern is a finite string of constant and variable symbols. A pattern language, which was introduced by Angluin [1], is the set of all strings obtained by substituting any non-null constant string for each variable symbol in the pattern. Because of its intuitive clearness of the expression and some desirable properties as formal languages, the learnability of pattern languages from examples has been studied in various settings. For example, pattern language learning algorithms have been proposed within the inductive inference model [1, 11, 20], the query learning setting [4, 11, 12], the PAC-learning model [9, 14]. Additionally, the average-case behavior of pattern language learners has been investigated [25], and applications in Genome Informatics have been proposed [5, 7, 21, 22].

Learning a concept from *good* examples has attracted considerable attention in recent studies [10, 11, 15, 17, 24], since it provides the best case analysis as well as the limits of learnability. Possibly, the *goodness* of the examples given heavily dependents on the properties of the languages to be identified. Informally, an

---

* This author is a Research Fellow of the Japan Society for the Promotion of Science (JSPS). The author's research is partly supported by Grants-in-Aid for JSPS research fellows from the Ministry of Education, Science and Culture, Japan.

example is regarded to be *good* if it provides a *significant* information for learning the concept.

Concerning the pattern languages, a positive example gives a learner crucial information to identify the target pattern, since the hypothesis space can be immediately restricted to a finite set [1, 2]. This is a key property for showing the class of pattern languages to be identifiable from positive examples in the framework of inductive inference [1, 2, 20]. Without any positive example, it is hard to learn a target pattern efficiently. Angluin [1] showed that the class of pattern languages is not identifiable in polynomial time using both membership and equivalence queries. The trick behind the adversary teacher is to answer equivalence queries without returning any positive example to the learner. These results provide evidence that good examples should be positive ones.

Marron [12] refined this line of research by studying pattern language learner that initially receives one positive example. Any other information concerning the target must be obtained by asking membership queries. Thus, the goodness of the initial example can be measured by the number of membership queries additionally needed until successful learning. The result suggests that *all but small fraction* of positive examples are *good* to learn a $k$-variable pattern.

Our goal is a bit more ambitious in that we would like to measure the information content provided by a positive example in dependence on its length. Intuitively, *the shorter the given positive example is, the more informative to the learner it is*, since the hypothesis space can be restricted to be a small set of patterns if the positive example is short. Especially, if the positive example is known to be a *shortest* one, the learner has only to find the positions where variable symbols occur in the target pattern. Based on the above observation, we propose a simple learning algorithm which consists of the following two phases: at the first phase, keep trying to *shrink* the given positive example by asking membership queries, until confirmation that the resulting example is a shortest one. In the second phase, identify the positions at which variable symbols occur in the target pattern. The second phase is a relatively easy task for the classes we will deal with, as we shall briefly state in Section 3. Therefore, the main part of this paper is devoted to the first phase: *how to get a shortest positive example efficiently using membership queries*, from any given (possibly very long) positive example. The process is regarded as refining the hypothesis space by shrinking the given positive example.

While our algorithm works in general, it is not necessarily efficient (measured by the number of membership queries needed). Thus, we introduce a syntactical measure, namely the maximum number of occurrences of each variable symbol in the pattern, in order to isolate the polynomially learnable subclass of pattern languages. Let $k\mu\Pi$ be the set of all patterns where each variable symbol occurs at most $k$ times, and let $k\mu\mathcal{PAT}$ be the corresponding class of pattern languages. In particular, we abbreviate $\mu\Pi$ and $\mu\mathcal{PAT}$ for $k = 1$. In Section 3, we show that any pattern $\pi_* \in k\mu\Pi$ can be identified from *any* initial positive example $w \in L(\pi_*)$ using at most $|w|^{k+1} + |\pi_*|^k$ membership queries. Provided each membership query is answered in unit time and assuming the usual RAM-model [1], the resulting learning time is $O(|w|^{k+2})$. This result nicely contrasts the fact that without membership queries, $k\mu PAT$ is not polynomial-time PAC-learnable even for the case $k = 1$ unless RP=NP [14]. Note that *without any initial positive example*, all the classes $k\mu PAT$, $k \geq 1$, are not polynomial-time query-identifiable using both membership and equivalence queries, since we can construct a malicious teacher as in [4].

Moreover, we pay special attention to subclasses of $\mu PAT$: First, reduction of the number of membership queries. Second, we ask whether the initial positive example can be dropped. A pattern in $\mu\Pi$ is called *regular*, since the generated language is regular [18, 19]. The class $\mu\Pi$ is useful for practical applications [5, 14, 16], since membership queries can be answered in linear time, while for general patterns the membership problem is NP-complete [1].

In Section 4, we reduce the number of membership queries by restricting the length of the constant parts in the pattern $\pi \in \mu\Pi$. We show that any pattern in $\mu\Pi$ whose constant parts are of length at most 3 can be exactly identified in time $O(|w|^2)$ using exactly $|w|+|\pi_*|$ membership queries. This is a natural extension of learning *subsequence languages* using membership queries as investigated in [13].

Section 5 shows a nontrivial subclass of patterns in $\mu\Pi$ with fixed length of constant parts, where a learner can enumerate effectively the candidates for positive examples: That means, any pattern in this class can be identified using membership queries only *without any initial positive example*. This is also a natural extension of the good property for subsequence languages [13].

## 2   Preliminaries

Let $\Sigma$ be a finite alphabet, i.e., a nonempty finite set of *constant symbols*, and $X = \{x, y, \ldots\}$ be a set of *variables symbols*. We assume that $\Sigma \cap X = \phi$ and $\Sigma$ contains at least two constant symbols. For an alphabet $\Delta$, let $\Delta^+$ denote the set of all nonempty strings and $\Delta^{[n]}$ the set of all strings of the length at most $n$ for $n \geq 0$. We denote by $w[i]$ the $i$-th symbol in a string $w$, and by $w[\tilde{i_1}, \cdots, \tilde{i_l}]$ the string which is obtained by eliminating $w[i_1], \cdots, w[i_l]$ from $w$. By $w[i : j]$, we denote the substring $w[i] \cdots w[j]$ of $w$. For convenience, a prefix $w[1 : i]$ is abbreviated as $w[: i]$, and a suffix $w[i : |w|]$ as $w[i :]$.

A *pattern* is a string in $(\Sigma \cup X)^+$. The set of all patterns is denoted by $\Pi$. For a pattern $\pi$, the length of $\pi$ is the number of symbols composing it, and is denoted by $|\pi|$. We denote by $k\mu\Pi$ the set of all patterns in which each variable symbol occurs at most $k$ times. Note that the class $k\mu\Pi$ is different from the set of $k$-*variable patterns*, in which at most $k$ kinds of variable symbols appear.

A *substitution* $\theta$ is a homomorphism from patterns to patterns such that $\theta(a) = a$ for each $a \in \Sigma$ and each variable symbol is replaced with any pattern. For a pattern $\pi$ and a substitution $\theta$, we denote by $\theta(\pi)$ the image of $\pi$ by $\theta$. The *pattern language of* $\pi$, denoted by $L(\pi)$, is the set $\{w \in \Sigma^+ \mid w = \theta(\pi) \text{ for some substitution } \theta\}$. We denote by $PAT$ the class of all pattern languages, and by $k\mu PAT$ the class of all pattern languages $L(\pi)$ such that $\pi \in k\mu PAT$. In particular, we write $\mu\Pi$ and $\mu PAT$ for $k = 1$. A pattern $\pi$

in $\mu\Pi$ has been called a *regular pattern* in the literature [14, 19], because the language $L(\pi)$ is regular.

In the sequel, let $\pi_*$ be a *target pattern* to be identified. A string $w$ is said to be a *positive example* if $w \in L(\pi_*)$ and a *negative example* if $w \notin L(\pi_*)$.

The problem to find a consistent pattern $\pi \in \mu\Pi$ from given positive and negative examples is shown to be NP-complete [14]. Thus the class $\mu\mathcal{PAT}$ is not polynomial-time learnable in the PAC-learning model [23], under the assumption of NP $\neq$ RP.

To overcome this computational hardness, we allow learning algorithms to use *membership queries* [3, 4, 6, 8]. A membership query is to propose a string $w$. The answer is "*yes*" if $w \in L(\pi_*)$, and "*no*" otherwise. We denote by $Mem_{L(\pi_*)}$ the *membership oracle* which answers membership queries about the language $L(\pi_*)$. We assume that it takes $|w|$ steps to use a membership query for $w \in \Sigma^*$. It is known that the class $\mathcal{PAT}$ is *not* learnable using *membership queries only* [4]. We can show that for any $k \geq 1$, the class $k\mu\mathcal{PAT}$ is *not* learnable using *membership queries only* in the same way.

A *learning algorithm* $\mathcal{A}$ may collect information about $\pi_*$ using one positive example $w \in L(\pi_*)$ and asking to the membership oracle $Mem_{L(\pi_*)}$. The goal of $\mathcal{A}$ is *exact identification* in polynomial time, that is, $\mathcal{A}$ must halt and output $\pi \in k\mu\Pi$ such that $L(\pi) = L(\pi_*)$, within the time polynomial with respect to $|\pi_*|$ and $|w|$.

## 3 Learning a pattern in $k\mu\Pi$ from one positive example using membership queries

When trying to learn an unknown target pattern $\pi_*$ from examples, a positive example $w \in L(\pi_*)$ provides crucial information to a learner, since the hypothesis space can be restricted to a finite set $\{L(\pi) \subseteq \Sigma^+ \mid \theta(\pi) = w \text{ for some } \theta\}$. This is a key property to show that the class of pattern languages is identifiable from positive examples in the framework of inductive inference [1, 20]. The shorter the positive example $w$ is, the smaller the hypothesis space is. Especially, if the positive example $w$ is a shortest one, the learner has only to find the positions where variable symbols occur in the target pattern $\pi_*$, since $|\pi_*| = |w|$. For example, if the target pattern $\pi_*$ is in $\mu\Pi$ and the given positive example $w$ is known to be a shortest one, the learner can exactly identify $\pi_*$ using $|w|$ membership queries: This is because the learner can decide whether the $i$-th symbol of the target pattern $\pi_*$ is a variable symbol or the constant symbol by asking whether $w[!i] \in L(\pi_*)$ or not, where $w[!i]$ is a string obtained from $w$ by replacing $w[i]$ with another constant symbol. In the same way, if the target pattern $\pi_*$ is in $k\mu\Pi$ and $w \in L(\pi_*)$ is a shortest positive example, $|w|^k$ membership queries are enough to identify $\pi_*$. Therefore, in the sequel, we concentrate our attention on how to get a shortest positive example by using membership queries. We denote by $SPS(L(\pi))$ the set of all shortest strings in $L(\pi)$, i.e., $SPS(L(\pi)) = \{w \in L(\pi) \mid \forall v \in L(\pi), |v| \geq |w|\}$. An element in $SPS(L(\pi))$ is called a *shortest positive string* of $L(\pi)$. Remark that $SPS(L(\pi)) = L(\pi) \cap \Sigma^{[|\pi|]}$ for any $\pi \in \Pi$.

First we consider how to find a shortest positive string of $L(\pi_*)$ when one positive example $w \in L(\pi_*)$ is given. The basic idea is quite simple: Just ask to the membership oracle whether a subsequence $w'$ of $w$ is in $L(\pi_*)$ or not. If the reply is "yes", we have the shorter positive example $w'$. Repeat this procedure until we have confirmed that $w'$ is a shortest one. Fig. 1 illustrates this scheme for the case $\pi_* \in \mu\Pi$.

---

while ( $w[\tilde{i}] \in L(\pi_*)$ for *some i* ) do
    /* Since $w[i]$ is redundant, delete it */
    $w := w[\tilde{i}]$;
return $w$

---

**Fig. 1.** The basic idea to find a shortest positive string of $L(\pi_*)$ from one positive example $w \in L(\pi_*)$ for $\pi_* \in \mu\Pi$.

The following lemma supports the correctness of the scheme in Fig. 1.

**Lemma 1.** *For a pattern $\pi_* \in \mu\Pi$ and $w \in L(\pi_*)$, $w \in SPS(L(\pi_*))$ if and only if $w[\tilde{i}] \notin L(\pi_*)$ for any i.*

*Proof.* Suppose that $w[\tilde{i}] \notin L(\pi_*)$ for any $i$, and $w \notin SPS(L(\pi_*))$. Since $w \in L(\pi_*)$, there exists a substitution $\theta$ such that $\theta(\pi_*) = w$ and $|\theta(x)| \geq 2$ for some variable symbol $x$ in $\pi_*$. By modifying $\theta$, we can construct a substitution $\theta'$ such that $\theta'(\pi_*) = w[\tilde{i}]$ for some $i$. Thus $w[\tilde{i}] \in L(\pi_*)$, which is a contradiction. The converse is trivial. $\square$

We now analyze the complexity of the procedure which implements the scheme in Fig. 1. At the first glance, the procedure *Shrink* in Fig. 2, which checks whether each $w[\tilde{i}]$ is redundant or not *only once*, may work correctly. The running time of *Shrink* is obviously $O(|w|^2)$ since it uses exactly $|w|$ membership queries.

However, unfortunately, the procedure *Shrink* does not always output a shortest positive string of $L(\pi_*)$. We present an instance where *Shrink* fails to find a shortest example.

*Example 1.* For a pattern $\pi_* = xabacy \in \mu\Pi$ and a positive example $w = $ aabacbaca $\in L(\pi_*)$, the procedure *Shrink*$(w)$ returns the string aababaca, which is not a shortest.

Procedure *Shrink(w)* /\* *shrink a positive example from left to right* \*/
Input: a string $w$ in $L(\pi_*)$.
Given: $Mem_{L(\pi_*)}$ for $\pi_* \in \mu\Pi$ .
$i := 1$;
while $(i \leq |w|)$ do
  begin
    while $(Mem_{L(\pi_*)}(w[\tilde{i}]) = \text{"}yes\text{"})$ do
      $w := w[\tilde{i}]$;
    $i := i + 1$;
  end
return $w$;

**Fig. 2.** Procedure *Shrink*

In Section 4, we will give a sufficient condition which guarantees that the output of *Shrink* is always a shortest one. In general, for $\mu\Pi$, we need the procedure *FindShortest* in Fig. 3 which calls *Shrink* as a subroutine.

Procedure *FindShortest(w)*
Input: a string $w$ in $L(\pi_*)$.
Given: $Mem_{L(\pi_*)}$ for $\pi_* \in \mu\Pi$.
Output: a string $s$ in $\mathcal{SPS}(L(\pi_*))$.
$s := w$;
do
    $s := Shrink\ (s)$
while $(\ s$ is modified $)$
output $s$;

**Fig. 3.** Procedure *FindShortest*

**Theorem 2.** *For a pattern* $\pi_* \in \mu\Pi$ *and a string* $w \in L(\pi_*)$, *the procedure FindShortest returns a string* $s \in \mathcal{SPS}(L(\pi_*))$ *in* $O(|w|^3)$ *time using at most* $|w|^2$ *membership queries.*

By these results, we can conclude that any pattern $\pi \in \mu\Pi$ can be exactly identified in polynomial time using one positive example and membership queries.

**Theorem 3.** *There exists a learning algorithm which exactly identifies every pattern $\pi_* \in \mu\Pi$ in $O(|w|^3)$ time using one positive example $w \in L(\pi_*)$ and at most $|w|^2 + |\pi_*|$ membership queries.*

We can extend the procedure *FindShortest* to treat patterns in $k\mu\Pi$ for any fixed $k \geq 1$, and we have the following theorem.

**Theorem 4.** *For a fixed $k \geq 1$, there exists a learning algorithm which exactly identifies every pattern $\pi_* \in k\mu\Pi$ in $O(|w|^{k+2})$ time using one positive example $w \in L(\pi_*)$ and at most $|w|^{k+1} + |\pi_*|^k$ membership queries.*

*Proof.* We construct a procedure *FindShortest*$^k$ to obtain a shortest positive string of $L(\pi_*)$, where the set $D_n^l$ is defined as follows:

$$D_n^l = \left\{ (i_1, i_2, \cdots, i_l) \in \{1, 2, \cdots, n\}^l \mid 1 \leq i_1 < i_2 < \cdots < i_l \leq n \right\}.$$

It is clear that $|D_n^l| = \binom{n}{l}$.

---

```
Procedure FindShortest^k(w)
Input:    a string w in L(π*).
Given:    Mem_{L(π*)} for π* ∈ kμΠ.
Output: a string s in SPS(L(π*)).
begin
   let s := w;
   Label: check_s;
      for l = 1 to k do
         foreach (i_1, ···, i_l) ∈ D^l_{|s|} do
            if Mem_{L(π*)}(s[ĩ_1, ···, ĩ_l]) = "yes" then
               begin
                  s := s[ĩ_1, ···, ĩ_l];
                  goto check_s;
               end
      output s;
end
```

---

**Fig. 4.** Procedure *FindShortest*$^k$

Since $|w| \geq |s|$, for $l \geq 1$, the foreach loop uses at most $\binom{|w|}{l}$ membership queries. We can show that $\sum_{l=1}^{k} \binom{|w|}{l} \leq |w|^k$ by induction. We see that the for loop uses at most $|w|^k$ membership queries. If $s$ is not a shortest string, the for loop deletes at least one symbol from $s$. The for loop is repeated at most $|w|$ times. Thus, the procedure $FindShortest^k$ outputs a shortest positive string of $L(\pi_*)$ and uses at most $|w|^{k+1}$ membership queries. $\qquad \square$

## 4 Reducing the number of membership queries

In the previous section, we have shown that for any target pattern $\pi_* \in \mu\Pi$, we can find a shortest positive string of $L(\pi_*)$ from one positive example $w \in L(\pi_*)$ with using $|w|^2$ membership queries. In this section, we reduce the number of membership queries into $|w|$ for some subclass of $\mu\Pi$, by showing a sufficient condition that the procedure $Shrink$ always outputs a shortest positive string of $L(\pi_*)$.

At first, we introduce the notion of components of a pattern. The *components* of a pattern $\pi$ are the constant parts of $\pi$. The component size of $\pi$ is the maximum length of components in $\pi$. For example, the components of a pattern $\mathsf{aa}\,x_1\mathsf{b}\,x_2x_3\mathsf{aba}\,x_4\mathsf{ab}\,x_5$ are $\mathsf{aa}$, $\mathsf{b}$, $\mathsf{aba}$, and $\mathsf{ab}$. Thus the component size of the pattern is 3.

Next we introduce the notion of *critical pattern*, by carefully analyzing the patterns for which the procedure $Shrink$ fails to produce a shortest one.

**Definition 5.** We say that a string $p \in \Sigma^+$ is *critical* if there exists a string $w \in \Sigma^+$ which satisfies the following conditions:

(1) $p$ is a prefix of $w$,
(2) $p$ does not appear in $w[2:]$,
(3) $p$ appears in $w[2:i-1]w[i+j_{w,p,i}:]$ for some $i \in \{1, 2, \cdots, |p|\}$, where

$$j_{w,p,i} = \max\left\{j \geq 0 \mid p \text{ appears in } w[:i-1]w[i+k:] \text{ for any } k \in \{0, \cdots, j\}\right\}.$$

We say that a pattern $\pi \in \mu\Pi$ is *critical* if some component of $\pi$ is critical.

*Example 2.* The string $p = \mathsf{abac}$ is critical, since for $w = \mathsf{abacbac}$ and $i = 4$, these conditions hold, where $j_{w,p,i} = 1$. Thus the pattern $\pi_* = x\mathsf{abac}y$ in Example 1 is critical.

Let $\pi = xpy$ be a pattern such that $p$ is not critical, and let $w$ be a string which satisfies the following conditions:

$$w \in L(\pi), \tag{a}$$
$$w[l:] \notin L(\pi) \quad \text{for any } l \geq 2. \tag{b}$$

For $i \in \{2, 3, \cdots, |p| + 1\}$, we consider the following string: $w(i) = w[: i - 1]w[i + j_i :]$ such that $w[: i - 1]w[i + k :] \in L(\pi)$ for any $k \in \{0, \cdots, j_i\}$ and $w[: i - 1]w[i + j_i + 1 :] \notin L(\pi)$. Remark that each string $w(i)$ satisfies (a) and (b) by the definition of critical patterns. The above features of critical strings is used in Lemma 6.

We now show that *Shrink* outputs a shortest positive string of $L(\pi_*)$ from a positive example $w \in L(\pi_*)$ when the target pattern $\pi_* \in \mu\Pi$ is not critical. We denote by $s_k$ the string which is obtained when the oracle $Mem_{L(\pi_*)}$ outputs "no" $k$ times in the inner while loop in *Shrink*.

**Lemma 6.** *Let* $\pi_* \in \mu\Pi$. *If* $\pi_*$ *is not critical, there exists a substitution* $\theta$ *such that* $\theta(\pi_*[: k]) = s_k[: k]$ *for any* $k \in \{1, 2, \cdots, |\pi_*|\}$.

*Proof.* Remark that the following conditions hold for any $k$, by the definition of *Shrink*,

*Condition 1:* $s_k[\tilde{k}] \notin L(\pi_*)$,
*Condition 2:* $s_k \in L(\pi_*)$.

We prove the lemma by induction on $k$. At the beginning, we consider that $k = 1$. For the case $\pi_*[1]$ is a variable symbol, we can verify it easily. For the case that $\pi_*[1]$ is a constant symbol, it is trivial by the *Condition 2*.

Assume inductively that the result holds less than $k + 1$. When $\pi_*[k + 1]$ is a variable symbol, it is easy to verify. Thus we have only to consider the case that $\pi_*[k + 1]$ is a constant symbol. If $\pi_*[: k]$ contains no variable symbol, it is clear that $\pi_*[: k + 1] = s_{k+1}[: k + 1]$. Therefore we can assume that there exist variable symbols in $\pi_*[: k]$. We consider the following two cases according to $\pi_*[k]$:

(1) In case that $\pi_*[k]$ is a variable symbol. Suppose that $s_{k+1}[k + 1] \neq \pi_*[k + 1]$. By the *Condition 2*, there exists a substitution $\theta$ such that $\theta(\pi_*[k + 1 :]) = s_{k+1}[k + 1 + j :]$ for some $j \geq 1$. Since $s_{k+1}[k + 1 + j :] = s_k[l :]$ for some $l \geq k + 2$, we have $\theta(\pi_*[k + 1 :]) = s_k[l :]$. By inductive hypothesis, $\theta'(\pi_*[: k]) = s_k[: k]$ for some $\theta'$. Since $\pi_*[k]$ is a variable symbol, using $\theta$ and $\theta'$, we can construct a substitution $\theta''$ such that $\theta''(\pi_*) = s_k[\tilde{k}]$. Thus, $s_k[\tilde{k}] \in L(\pi_*)$, which contradicts with the *Condition 1*. Thus, $\pi_*[k + 1] = s_{k+1}[k + 1]$.
(2) In case that $\pi_*[k]$ is a constant symbol. Let $l \ (< k)$ be the position of the rightmost variable symbol in $\pi_*[: k]$, and $p$ be the component of $\pi$ which contains $\pi_*[k + 1]$. Since $p$ is not critical, we can prove inductively that there exists a substitution $\theta$ such that $\theta(\pi_*[l :]) = s_{k+1}[l :]$ by the definition of critical string. Thus, $\pi_*[k + 1] = s_{k+1}[k + 1]$.

Therefore there exists a substitution $\theta$ such that $\theta(\pi_*[: k+1]) = s_{k+1}[: k + 1]$. $\square$

**Theorem 7.** *Let* $\pi_* \in \mu\Pi$ *and* $w \in L(\pi_*)$. *If* $\pi_*$ *is not critical, then Shrink$(w) \in SPS(L(\pi_*))$.*

*Proof.* Let $l = |\pi_*|$. Since $s_l$ is in $L(\pi_*)$, $l \leq |s_l|$. We show that $|s_l| \leq l$. If $\pi_*$ contains no variable, it is trivial. Thus we assume that $\pi_*$ contains variable symbols. We first consider the case that $\pi_*[l]$ is a constant symbol. Let $j < l$ be the position at which the rightmost variable symbol occurs in $\pi_*$. Thus, $\pi_*[j+1:]$ is a constant string with length $l - j$, and $\pi_*[j + 1:] = s_{j-1}[|s_{j-1}| - l + j]$. By Lemma 6, there exists a substitution $\theta$ such that $\theta(\pi_*[:j-1]) = s_{j-1}[:j-1]$. Since $\pi_*[j]$ is a variable symbol, $s_j = s_{j-1}[:j-1]s_{j-1}[|s_{j-1}| - (l-j+1):]$, which implies, $|s_l| \leq |s_j| = |s_{j-1}[:j-1]s_{j-1}[|s_{j-1}| - (l-j+1):]| = (j-1) + (l-j+1) = l$. Thus, we have $|s_l| = l$. For the case that $\pi_*[l]$ is a variable symbol, we can verify it in the same way. Since $Shrink(w) \in L(\pi_*)$ and $|s_l| \geq |Shrink(w)|$, we have $Shrink(w) \in SPS(L(\pi_*))$. $\qquad\square$

**Corollary 8.** *Let $\pi_* \in \mu\Pi$ and $w \in L(\pi_*)$. If $\pi_*$ is not critical, Shrink outputs a string in $SPS(L(\pi_*))$ in $O(|w|^2)$ time from a positive example $w \in L(\pi_*)$ using $|w|$ membership queries.*

We can show that the following theorem holds by exhaustively checking each string $w$ with $|w| \leq 3$.

**Theorem 9.** *There is no critical string $w$ with $|w| \leq 3$.*

We denoted by $\mu\Pi[l]$ the set of all patterns $\pi \in \mu\Pi$ of which component size are at most $l$. Then, by Corollary 8 and Theorem 9, the following theorem holds.

**Theorem 10.** *There exists a learning algorithm which exactly identifies every pattern $\pi_* \in \mu\Pi[3]$ in $O(|w|^2)$ time using one positive example $w \in L(\pi_*)$ and exactly $|w| + |\pi_*|$ membership queries.*

## 5 Generating a positive example using membership queries

In this section, we show a nontrivial subclass of $\mu\Pi$ where a learner can effectively enumerate a series of candidates for a positive example. As a consequent, any pattern in the class will be identifiable using membership queries only, *without any initial positive example*. The constraint which enables the effective enumeration consists of two conditions: One is that component size is fixed. The other is that the both ends of the pattern are variable symbols. These conditions are trivially hold for *subsequence languages*, for which we have developed a learning using membership queries only [13].

**Definition 11.** For an integer $l \geq 0$, let $\mu\Pi[l]^e$ be the set of all patterns $\pi \in \mu\Pi$, such that the component size of $\pi$ is at most $l$ and both the first and last symbols of $\pi$ are variable symbols.

The idea to guess a positive example using membership queries is based on the following simple observation.

*Remark.* For an alphabet $\Sigma$ and a nonnegative integer $l$, let $p_{\Sigma,l}$ be a string which contains any string in $\Sigma^{[l]}$ as a substring. For instance, the string aaabbbaabab contains any strings of length at most 3 over $\Sigma = \{a, b\}$. Let $p_{\Sigma,l}^k$ be the string $a\,p_{\Sigma,l}\,a\,p_{\Sigma,l}\,a\ldots a\,p_{\Sigma,l}\,a$, the $k$-times repetitions of $p_{\Sigma,l}$ with using $a \in \Sigma$ as a delimiter symbol. Then for any pattern $\pi \in \mu\Pi[l]^e$, there is an integer $k \leq |\pi|$ such that $p_{\Sigma,l}^k \in L(\pi)$.

**Theorem 12.** *For any fixed $l \geq 0$, any pattern $\pi_* \in \mu\Pi[l]^e$ can be exactly identified in $O(m^3 n^3)$ time using at most $m^2 n^2 + 2n$ membership queries only, where $m = l(|\Sigma| + 1)^l + 2$ and $n = |\pi_*|$.*

*Proof.* For each $k = 1, 2, \cdots$, repeat generating the string $p_{\Sigma,l}^k$ and asking to the membership oracle whether $p_{\Sigma,l}^k$ is in the target language $L(\pi_*)$, until the oracle replies "yes". Note that $k$ does not exceed the length of the target pattern $\pi_*$. In this way, we can get the positive example using at most $|\pi_*|$ membership queries. Then the target pattern can be identified by using $|p_{\Sigma,l}^k|^2 + |\pi_*|$ membership queries, as shown in Theorem 3. □

## 6 Conclusion

In this paper, we investigated exact identification of a pattern in $k\mu\Pi$ using queries for a fixed $k \geq 1$. We have shown that there exists a learning algorithm which exactly identifies every pattern $\pi_* \in k\mu\Pi$ in $O(|w|^{k+2})$ time using one positive example $w \in L(\pi_*)$ and at most $|w|^{k+1} + |\pi_*|^k$ membership queries.

In Section 4, we introduced the notion of critical patterns. Then we have shown that if a pattern $\pi_*$ is not critical, a shortest positive string of $L(\pi_*)$ is found from one positive example $w \in L(\pi_*)$ and exactly $|w|$ membership queries. In particular, since any pattern $\pi \in \mu\Pi[3]$ is not critical, we have shown that there exists a learning algorithm which exactly identifies every pattern $\pi_* \in \mu\Pi[3]$ in $O(|w|^2)$ time using one positive example $w \in L(\pi_*)$ and exactly $|w| + |\pi_*|$ membership queries. We summarize these results in Table 1.

In Section 5, for a fixed $l \geq 0$, we show that any pattern in the class $\mu\Pi[l]^e$ is exactly identifiable using membership queries only.

As future works, we will study a necessary condition of a pattern for which *Shrink* outputs a shortest positive string of $L(\pi_*)$. It may be interesting to study the learnability of a class of unions of pattern languages in our setting.

## 7 Acknowledgments

The authors wish to acknowledge Takeshi Shinohara, Thomas Zeugmann, Hiroki Ishizaka and Hiroki Arimura for their helpful suggestions and encouragement.

| $k\mu\Pi$ | | component size | |
|---|---|---|---|
| | | at most 3 | General |
| | $k = 1$ | $m + n$ queries $O(m^2)$ time | $m^2 + n$ queries $O(m^3)$ time |
| | fixed $k \geq 1$ | $m^{k+1} + n^k$ queries $O(m^{k+2})$ time | |

**Table 1.** Summary of the results in Section 3 and 4. In the table, $m$ is the length of the positive example and $n$ is the length of a pattern to be identified.

# References

1. D. Angluin. Finding patterns common to a set of strings. *Journal of Computer and System Science*, 21:46–62, 1980.
2. D. Angluin. Inductive inference of formal languages from positive data. *Information and Control*, 45:117–135, 1980.
3. D. Angluin. Learning regular sets from queries and counterexamples. *Information and Computation*, 75:87–106, 1987.
4. D. Angluin. Queries and concept learning. *Machine Learning*, 2:319–342, 1988.
5. S. Arikawa, S. Kuhara, S. Miyano, A. Shinohara and T. Shinohara. A learning algorithm for elementary formal systems and its experiments on identification of transmembrane domains. In *Proceedings 25th Hawaii International Conference on System Sciences, Vol. I*, pages 675–684, 1992.
6. H. Arimura, H. Ishizaka and T. Shinohara. Learning unions of tree patterns using queries. In *Proceedings of 6th Workshop on Algorithmic Learning Theory, Lecture Notes in Artificial Intelligence 997*, pages 66–79, 1995.
7. A. Bairoch. PROSITE: A dictionary of sites and patterns in proteins. *Nucleic Acids Research*, 19:2241–2245, 1991.
8. H. Ishizaka, H. Arimura and T. Shinohara. Finding tree patterns consistent with positive and negative examples using queries. In *Proceedings of 5th Workshop on Algorithmic Learning Theory, Lecture Notes in Artificial Intelligence 872*, pages 317–332, 1994.
9. M. Kearns and L. Pitt. A polynomial-time algorithm for learning $k$-variable pattern languages from examples. In *Proceedings of the 2nd Annual Conference on Computational Learning Theory*, pages 57–71, 1989.
10. S. Lange, J. Nessel and R. Wiehagen. Language learning from good examples. In *Proceedings of 5th International Workshop on Algorithmic Learning Theory, Lecture Notes in Artificial Intelligence 872*, pages 423–437, 1994.
11. S. Lange and R. Wiehagen. Polynomial-time inference of arbitrary pattern languages. *New Generation Computing*, 8(4):361–370, 1991.
12. A. Marron. Learning pattern languages from a single initial example and from queries. In *Proceedings of the first Annual Conference on Computational Learning Theory*, pages 311–325, 1988.
13. S. Matsumoto and A. Shinohara. Learning subsequence languages. In *6th European-Japanese Seminar on Information Modelling and Knowledge Bases*, 1996.

14. S. Miyano, A. Shinohara and T. Shinohara. Which classes of elementary formal systems are polynomial-time learnable? In *Proceedings of 2nd Workshop on Algorithmic Learning Theory*, pages 139–150, 1991.

15. H. Sakamoto. Language learning from membership queries and characteristic examples. In *Proceedings of 6th International Workshop on Algorithmic Learning Theory, Lecture Notes in Artificial Intelligence 997*, pages 55–65. Springer-Verlag, 1995.

16. S. Shimozono, A. Shinohara, T. Shinohara, S. Miyano, S. Kuhara and S. Arikawa. Knowledge acquisition from amino acid sequences by machine learning system BONSAI. *Transactions of Information Processing Society of Japan*, 35(10):2009–2018, 1994.

17. A. Shinohara. Teachability in computational learning. *New Generation Computing*, 8(4):337–347, 1990.

18. T. Shinohara. Polynomial time inference of extended regular pattern languages. In *RIMS Symposia on Software Science and Engineering(Lecture Notes in Computer Science 147)*, pages 115–127, 1982.

19. T. Shinohara. Polynomial time inference of pattern languages and its applications. In *Proceedings 7th IBM Symp. Math. Found. Comp. Sci.*, pages 191–209, 1982.

20. T. Shinohara. Inductive inference from positive data is powerful. In *Proceedings of the 3rd Annual Conference on Computational Learning Theory*, pages 97–110, 1990.

21. E. Tateishi, O. Maruyama and S. Miyano. Extracting motifs from positive and negative sequence data. In *Proceeding 13th Symposium on Theoretical Aspects of Computer Science, Lecture Notes in Computer Science 1046*, pages 219–230, 1996.

22. E. Tateishi and S. Miyano. A greedy strategy for finding motifs from positive and negative examples. In *Proceeding First Pacific Symposium on Biocomputing*, pages 599–613. World Scientific Press, 1996.

23. L. G. Valiant. A theory of the learnable. *Communications of the ACM*, 27:1134–1142, 1984.

24. T. Zeugmann. Average case analysis of pattern language learning algorithm. In *Proceedings of 5th Workshop on Algorithmic Learning Theory, Lecture Notes in Artificial Intelligence 872*, pages 8–9, 1994.

25. T. Zeugmann. Lange and Wiehagen's pattern language learning algorithm: an average-case analysis with respect to its total learing time. Technical Report RIFIS-TR-CS-111, Aplil 20, Kyushu University, 1995. (to appear in Annals of Mathematics and Artificial Intelligence).

# On Fast and Simple Algorithms for Finding Maximal Subarrays and Applications in Learning Theory

Andreas Birkendorf

Lehrstuhl Informatik II, Universität Dortmund, D-44221 Dortmund, Germany
birkendo@Ls2.informatik.uni-dortmund.de

**Abstract.** Consider the following problem $\mathrm{SUB}(k, n)$.
Given an array $A = (a_1, \ldots, a_n)$ of real elements $a_i$ and a natural number $k$, find (at most) $k$ disjoint subarrays $A_1, \ldots, A_k$ in $A$ such that the sum of the elements contained in the subarrays is maximum.

In this paper, we present a simple algorithm, based on Dynamic Programming, solving $\mathrm{SUB}(k, n)$ in time $O(kn)$. Extracting the main idea of the dynamic programming scheme, we are able to extend the algorithm such that it is applicable for a wider class of related optimization problems.

We show efficient applications of this algorithm in the area of agnostic learning by means of minimum disagreement, such as learning $k$ intervals or identifying objects in a pixel matrix. In particular, the algorithm enables us to generate optimal functions inside a special class of piecewise constant functions. In restricted settings, our algorithm is better by a factor of sample-size-order compared to solutions induced by the dynamic scheme presented in [5].

Furthermore, we develop a generalization of a tree data structure introduced in [1]. Using this tree structure, we can solve corresponding online learning tasks efficiently.

## 1 Introduction

Consider the following problem.

Given an array $A = (a_1, \ldots, a_n)$ of real elements $a_i$ and a natural number $k$, find (at most) $k$ disjoint subarrays $A_1, \ldots, A_k$ in $A$ such that the sum of the elements contained in the subarrays is maximum.

More precisely, this problem, which we denote by $\mathrm{SUB}(k, n)$, is given as follows. For a subarray $A' = (a_i, \ldots, a_j)$ of $A$, let $\|A'\|$ denote the sum $a_i + \ldots + a_j$. Hence, we are searching for $k' \leq k$ subarrays $A_i = (a_{l(i)}, \ldots, a_{r(i)})$, $1 \leq i \leq k'$, $l(i) \leq r(i) \leq l(i+1) - 2$, such that $\|A_1\| + \ldots + \|A_{k'}\|$ is maximum.

Beside the fact that this optimization problem is interesting for its own sake, applications of this problem arise in computational geometry, share analysis, pattern recognition, and learning theory.

For instance, assume that $A$ reflects the development of a special share during a period of $n$ days, i.e., $a_i$ denotes the difference between the share price on day $i$ and day $i - 1$. Now, a solution for SUB$(k, n)$ corresponds to the $k$ periods of time with maximum absolute profit.

This paper deals with efficient algorithms for SUB$(k, n)$ and related problems in the area of *agnostic learning*. In this learning model, no assumptions concerning the target, that should be learned, is made. Thus, the learner attempts to approximate the unknown target by seeking elements inside a limited hypothesis space, which describe the target in an optimal manner.

A sufficient condition to ensure agnostic learning formally is, e.g., a finite Vapnik-Chervonenkis-dimension or a finite pseudo-dimension of the underlying hypothesis space (see, e.g., [2]). This condition will be guaranteed in the sequel.

The paper is organized as follows.

In Section 2, we present a simple algorithm, named DYN$_{\text{SUB}}$, solving SUB$(k, n)$ in time $O(kn)$. The algorithm is based on Dynamic Programming. [1] A slight modification of the algorithm enables us to solve the exact variant of this problem where $k' = k$.

In Section 3, we extract the main idea of the dynamic scheme and formulate a generalized algorithm DYN, which is applicable for a wider class of related optimization problems.

In Section 4, we examine concrete applications of DYN$_{\text{SUB}}$ and DYN in the area of agnostic learning by means of *minimum disagreement*. We consider simple structured learning tasks in the fields of computational geometry, mathematics, and pattern recognition.

- First, we review the problem of learning $k$ intervals with minimum error, given a sorted sample of size $n$. Algorithms, presented in [6] and announced in [4], solve this problem in time $O(k^2 n)$ and $O(n \log n)$, respectively. A simple reduction to SUB$(k, n)$ shows a time bound of $O(kn)$ for this problem using DYN$_{\text{SUB}}$. Hence, for $k = o(\log n)$ (e.g., $k$ constant), DYN$_{\text{SUB}}$ beats these algorithms.
- After that, we point out an application in the area of *function learning*. Here, DYN enables us to generate optimal piecewise constant functions with a discrete range according to a given sample. If we measure optimality by the linear loss function, our algorithm is better by a factor of sample-size-order compared to solutions induced by the dynamic programming scheme presented in [5] for this kind of problems.

---

[1] We learnt from a referee that the same time bound can be obtained from [3] (Theorem 3) by carrying over and generalizing the formalism introduced there. However, we think that our algorithm completes and improves the algorithm presented in [3] in the following ways. Our algorithm is simpler (no preprocessing step has to be performed). Its proof of correctness is more or less evident. Our dynamic scheme can be generalized easily (see Section 3).

– At last, we briefly point out how DYN can be used as a tool to identify two dimensional objects in a pixel matrix.

In Section 5 finally, we design a special data structure, called DYN-tree. A DYN-tree is a generalization of a data structure, introduced in [1], with efficient update facilities. If we consider online variants of the problems, introduced in Section 4, we can solve them efficiently using DYN-trees.

## 2 The Algorithm DYN$_{\mathrm{SUB}}$

The general idea of the algorithm DYN$_{\mathrm{SUB}}$ is to use Dynamic Programming in the following way.

Instead of solving $SUB(k, n)$ in a direct manner, we first divide it into two disjoint subproblems which are easy to solve using Dynamic Programming. In a final step, an optimal solution for $SUB(k, n)$ is obtained simply by choosing the optimal subsolution.

Let $SUB_0(k, n)$ denote the same problem as $SUB(k, n)$, but with the additional restriction that $a_n$ must *not* be contained in any subarray $A_j$ of the solution. Analogously, let $SUB_1(k, n)$ denote the problem $SUB(k, n)$ with the additional demand that $a_n$ must be contained in a subarray $A_j$ of the solution.
Hence, if we define $G_t(k, n)$, $t \in \{0, 1\}$, to be the value (*"gain"*) of an optimal solution for $SUB_t(k, n)$, the maximum gain $G(k, n)$ of $SUB(k, n)$ is given by $G(k, n) = \max\{G_0(k, n), G_1(k, n)\}$.

The following lemma provides a dynamic programming scheme for the computation of these gains.

**Lemma 1.** *1.* $\forall t \in \{0, 1\}, \forall i \in \{0, \ldots, k\}, \forall j \in \{0, \ldots, n\}$ :
$$G_t(i, 0) = G_t(0, j) = 0.$$

*2.* $\forall i \in \{1, \ldots, k\}, \forall j \in \{1, \ldots, n\}$ :
$$G_1(i, j) = a_j + \max\{G_0(i - 1, j - 1), G_1(i, j - 1)\}.$$
$$G_0(i, j) = \max\{G_0(i, j - 1), G_1(i, j - 1)\}.$$

**Proof:** Part 1. of the lemma follows by definition of $G_t(\cdot, \cdot)$.

Let $S_t$, $t \in \{0, 1\}$, denote the set of array elements contained in *any* optimal solution for $SUB_t(i, j)$. Let $G_t$ denote its corresponding gain.
If $a_{j-1} \in S_1$ then $G_1 - a_j$ is the maximum gain of $SUB_1(i, j - 1)$.
If $a_{j-1} \notin S_1$ then $G_1 - a_j$ is the maximum gain of $SUB_0(i - 1, j - 1)$.
If $a_{j-1} \in S_0$ then $G_0 - a_j$ is the maximum gain of $SUB_1(i, j - 1)$.
If $a_{j-1} \notin S_0$ then $G_0 - a_j$ is the maximum gain of $SUB_0(i, j - 1)$.
It follows from these four implications that the matrices $G_0(i, j)$, $G_1(i, j)$ can be row-wise (or column-wise) completed as stated in the lemma. ∎

```
(* PHASE 1: Computation of Maximum Gains *)
for t = 0 to 1 do
    for i = 1 to k do G(t, i, 0) ← 0;  od;
    for j = 0 to n do G(t, 0, j) ← 0;  od;
od
for i = 1 to k do
    for j = 1 to n do
        G(0, i, j) ← max{G(0, i, j − 1), G(1, i, j − 1)};
        G(1, i, j) ← a_j + max{G(0, i − 1, j − 1), G(1, i, j − 1)};
    od;
od;
(* PHASE 2: Computation of an Optimal Solution via Backtracking *)
i ← k;  if G(0, k, n) < G(1, k, n) then S ← {a_n};  else S ← ∅;  fi;
for j = n − 1 downto 1 do
    if a_{j+1} ∉ S then  (* solve SUB_0(i, j + 1) *)
                    if G(0, i, j) < G(1, i, j) then S ← S ∪ {a_j};  fi;
                else  (* solve SUB_1(i, j + 1) *)
                    if G(0, i − 1, j) < G(1, i, j) then S ← S ∪ {a_j};
                                            else i ← i − 1;  fi;
    fi;
od;
output S.
```

**Fig. 1.** The algorithm DYN$_{\mathrm{SUB}}$ solving SUB$(k, n)$ in $O(kn)$ steps.

Equipped with Lemma 1, we can develop the algorithm DYN$_{\mathrm{SUB}}$ shown in Fig. 1 which solves SUB$(k, n)$ in $O(kn)$ steps.

In order to achieve an efficient implementation, we first compute the gains $G_t(i, j)$ in a three dimensional table $G$.

The correctness of PHASE 1 follows immediately from Lemma 1.

In PHASE 2, we create a set $S$ of array elements representing an optimal solution for SUB$(k, n)$. According to the statements of Lemma 1, a maximum gain of SUB$_0(i, j)$ is given by $\max\{G_0(i, j−1), G_1(i, j−1)\}$ and a maximum gain $G_1(i, j)$ of SUB$_1(i, j)$ is given by $a_j + \max\{G_0(i − 1, j − 1), G_1(i, j − 1)\}$.
Hence, starting with $\max\{G_0(k, n), G_1(k, n)\}$, we can construct $S$ by comparing $G_0(\cdot, j)$ and $G_1(\cdot, j)$ for the actual subproblem SUB$_0(i, j + 1)$ or SUB$_1(i, j + 1)$, respectively. Whenever $G_0(\cdot, j) < G_1(\cdot, j)$, we add $a_j$ to our actual solution set $S$ and proceed with the corresponding subproblem SUB$_t(\cdot, j)$.

Since table $G$ has size $2(k + 1)(n + 1)$ and each entry is obtained in constant time, PHASE 1 needs $O(kn)$ steps. The second phase has running time $O(n)$ which is evident from Fig. 1. We obtain

**Theorem 2.** *The problem SUB$(k, n)$ can be solved in $O(kn)$ steps.*

It is possible to sharpen the achieved time bound since w.l.o.g the input of our algorithm is an array $A^* = (a_1^*, \ldots, a_N^*)$, $N$ odd, where $a_1^* > 0$, $a_2^* < 0$, $a_3^* > 0, \ldots, a_{N-1}^* < 0$, $a_N^* > 0$. Otherwise, this *normal form* can be easily obtained from $A = (a_1, \ldots, a_n)$ in a linear time preprocessing step.[2]

**Corollary 3.** *Given an array $A$ of size $n$, the problem $SUB(k, n)$ can be solved in time $O(n + kN)$, where $N$ denotes the size of the normal form for $A$.*

Consider the problem $SUB^*(k, n)$, which is the same as $SUB(k, n)$, but with the additional demand that *exactly* $k$ subarrays are required. The following slight modification of $DYN_{SUB}$ leads to the algorithm $DYN_{SUB^*}$ solving the exact problem in $O(kn)$ steps. We only have to take care of the fact that now, by definition, there exists no solution for the problems $SUB_t(i, j)$ where $2i > j + t$.

Therefore, we introduce a symbolic value '$-\infty$', s.t. $-\infty < r$ for all $r \in \mathbf{R}$, and associate it with unsolvable problem instances, i.e., $G_t(i, j) = -\infty$ iff $SUB_t(i, j)$ is unsolvable.

For the algorithm it is sufficient to change the initialization in PHASE 1 as shown in Fig. 2. Other unsolvable instances are detected automatically by the dynamic programming scheme. We obtain

**Corollary 4.** *The problem $SUB^*(k, n)$ can be solved $O(kn)$ steps.*

> (\* *PHASE 1* \*)
> **for** $t = 0$ **to** 1 **do**
>     **for** $i = 1$ **to** $k$ **do** $G(t, i, 0) \leftarrow -\infty$; **od**;
>     **for** $j = 0$ **to** $n$ **do** ...(\* *proceed as in Fig. 1* \*)

**Fig. 2.** The algorithm $DYN_{SUB^*}$ solving $SUB^*(k, n)$ in $O(kn)$ steps.

# 3 Generalizing the Dynamic Programming Scheme

In this section, we will generalize $DYN_{SUB}$ and develop an algorithm DYN that solves a wider class of related optimization problems efficiently. Therefore, let us review the strategy of the dynamic programming scheme induced by Lemma 1 in a more abstract way.

---

[2] Find longest subsequences $(a_i, \ldots, a_j)$ where all entries are positive (or negative, respectively) and replace these sequences by a single elements $a_i^* = a_i + \ldots + a_j$. Now, drop the first (last) element in $A^*$ if negative. Note that $A^*$ may be the empty set.

Given the input array $A = (a_1, \ldots, a_n)$, DYN$_{\text{SUB}}$ generates a *decomposition* of $A$ into consecutive blocks $B_i$, i.e., a set of blocks, such that each $a_j$ of $A$ is contained in *exactly* one block $B_i$. [3] There are two types $t$ of blocks. Either $B_i$ represents a subarray $A_j$ of SUB$(k, n)$ (case $t = 1$), or $B_i$ represents a block with elements not involved in a solution of SUB$(k, n)$ (case $t = 0$).

If we associate with each element $a_j$, contained in a block of type $t(a_j)$, the gain $g(t(a_j), a_j) \overset{\Delta}{=} t(a_j) \cdot a_j$ then DYN$_{\text{SUB}}$ outputs a decomposition of $A$ into at most $k$ blocks of type 1 with maximum overall gain.

Increasing the number of possible block types and replacing the special gain function by arbitrary loss functions, we obtain the following general optimization problem OAD *(Optimal Array Decomposition)*.

Input of OAD$(k, n)$ is again an array $A = (a_1, \ldots, a_n)$ containing elements of an arbitrary set $S$. Furthermore, we have $m$ possible types $T = \{0, \ldots, m - 1\}$ of blocks and a loss function $\ell : T \times S \to \mathbf{R}$. For all inputs, $\ell$ is evaluable in constant time, e.g., given by a two dimensional table.

The goal is to find a decomposition of $A$ into at most $k$ blocks such that the overall loss $\sum_{1 \leq i \leq n} \ell(t(a_i), a_i)$ is minimum.

Note that the problem structure of OAD is slightly different from SUB. For OAD we are seeking at most $k$ blocks; for SUB we are seeking at most $k$ blocks *of type 1*. But, of course, we can reduce the OAD problem to the SUB problem easily.

Let $L(t, k, n)$ denote the minimum loss of the restricted problem OAD$_t(k, n)$ where we additionally demand $t(a_n) = t$. Then, analogously to the previous section, $\min_{t \in T} \{L(t, k, n)\}$ defines the minimum loss of OAD$(k, n)$.

Analogous reasonings as in the proof of Lemma 1 show that the following lemma is valid.

**Lemma 5.** *1.* $\forall t \in T, \forall i \in \{0, \ldots, k\}, \forall j \in \{0, \ldots, n\} :$
$$L(t, i, 0) = L(t, 0, j) = 0.$$
*2.* $\forall t \in T, \forall i \in \{1, \ldots, k\}, \forall j \in \{1, \ldots, n\} :$
$$L(t, i, j) = \ell(t, a_j) + \min\{L(t, i, j - 1), \min_{t' \in T \setminus \{t\}} \{L(t', i - 1, j - 1)\}\}.$$

Equipped with Lemma 5, the implemention of DYN is more or less straightforward (see Fig. 3). Output of DYN is the array $(t(a_1), \ldots, t(a_n))$. Note that the running time of DYN is dominated by the computation of the $m(k + 1)(n + 1)$ values $L(\cdot, \cdot, \cdot)$. The computation of each value needs time $O(m)$.

The main result of this section reads as follows.

**Theorem 6.** *For $m$ types of blocks, the problem OAD$(k, n)$ can be solved in $O(m^2 k n)$ steps.*

---

[3] Do not confuse block $B_i$ with a subarray $A_j$ of SUB$(k, n)$.

```
(* PHASE 1: Computation of Minimum Losses *)
foreach t ∈ T do
    for i = 0 to k do L(t, i, 0) ← 0;  od;
    for j = 0 to n do L(t, 0, j) ← 0;  od;
od
for i = 1 to k do
    for j = 1 to n do
        foreach t ∈ T do
            L(t, i, j) ← ℓ(t, aⱼ) + min{L(t, i, j − 1),   min   {L(t', i − 1, j − 1)}};
                                                        t'∈T\{t}
        od;
    od;
od;
(* PHASE 2: Computation of an Optimal Solution via Backtracking *)
t(aₙ) ← argminₜ{L(t, k, n)};  i ← k;
for j = n − 1 downto 1 do
    t ← t(aⱼ₊₁);
    goal ← L(t, i, j + 1) − ℓ(t, aⱼ₊₁);
    if L(t, i, j) = goal then t(aⱼ) ← t;
                      else begin
                            search t' ∈ T \ {t} such that L(t', i − 1, j) = goal;
                            t(aⱼ) ← t';
                            i ← i − 1;
                      end;
    fi;
od;
output (t(a₁), . . . , t(aₙ)).
```

**Fig. 3.** The algorithm DYN solving $OAD(k, n)$ in $O(|T^2| \, kn)$ steps.

## 4  Applications in Agnostic Learning

Since $DYN_{SUB}$ and DYN provide us with optimal solutions inside a limited (hypothesis) space, we are now prepared to give some applications of these algorithms in the area of agnostic learning by means of minimum disagreement (or minimum loss, respectively).

The first application arises in computational geometry.

We define the problem $INT(k, n)$ as follows.

> For a sequence $S = ((x_1, l_1), (x_2, l_2), \ldots, (x_n, l_n))$ of *positive* points (label $l_i = +1$) and *negative* points (label $l_i = -1$) on the real axis at position $x_i$, find (at most) $k$ disjoint intervals $I_1, \ldots, I_k$ such that the sum $\sum_{i=1}^{n} l_i \cdot \chi_i$ is maximum, where
> $$\chi_i \overset{\Delta}{=} \begin{cases} +1, & \text{if } x_i \in I_1 \cup \cdots \cup I_k, \\ -1, & \text{otherwise.} \end{cases}$$

Hence, we try to find a set of intervals that include positive and exclude negative points as far as possible.

If we assume that the sequence $S$ is sorted, i.e., $x_i < x_{i+1}$, this problem is equivalent to $\text{SUB}(k, n)$ with input array $A = (l_1, \ldots, l_n)$. We get the following corollary.

**Corollary 7.** *For a sorted sequence, the problem $INT(k, n)$ can be solved in time $O(n + kN)$, where $N$ denotes the number of changes of labels in the input sequence, i.e., $N$ is the cardinality of the set $\{1 \leq i \leq n - 1 \mid l_i \neq l_{i+1}\}$.*

The second example demonstrates a mathematical application.

For a set $T = \{y_0^*, \ldots, y_{m-1}^*\}$ of $m$ real values, let $PCF_T^k$ denote the class of piecewise constant functions $f : \mathbf{R} \to T$ where the number of constant pieces is bounded by $k$.

Given a sequence $S = ((x_1, y_1), (x_2, y_2), \ldots, (x_n, y_n))$ of real points $x_i$ and real labels $y_i$, we define the *loss* $L_\ell(f, S)$ of a function $f$ with respect to $S$ by

$$L_\ell(f, S) \overset{\Delta}{=} \sum_{i=1}^n \ell(f(x_i), y_i).$$

Examples for $\ell(\cdot, \cdot)$ may be the linear loss $\ell_1(y, y') = |y - y'|$ or the quadratic loss $\ell_2(y, y') = (y - y')^2$.

For a fixed choice of $\ell$, the problem $\text{PCF}(k, n)$ is to find a function $f \in PCF_T^k$, where $L_\ell(f, S)$ is minimum.

Obviously, we can solve PCF using DYN in a direct manner. We just feed DYN with the input array $A = (y_1, \ldots, y_n)$ (after sorting the sequence $S$ such that $x_i < x_{i+1}$) and associate with the output array $(t(a_1), \ldots, t(a_n))$ the function

$$f(x) \overset{\Delta}{=} \begin{cases} y_{t(a_1)}^*, & \text{if } x \leq x_1, \\ y_{t(a_i)}^*, & \text{if } x_{i-1} < x \leq x_i, \\ y_{t(a_n)}^*, & \text{if } x_n \leq x. \end{cases}$$

We obtain

**Corollary 8.** *For the function class $PCF_T^k$, the problem $PCF(k, n)$ can be solved in $(|T|^2 kn)$ steps.*

If we restrict ourself to the linear loss $\ell_1$ and labels $y_i \in T$, an optimal function $f \in PCF_T^k$ is even an optimal function in the class $PCF_\mathbf{R}^k$, where we allow arbitrary real values for the $k$ pieces.

The linear loss function $\ell_1$ guarantees that extending the output range $T$ from discrete values to $\mathbf{R}$ does not yield an improved solution, i.e., for every function $f^* \in PCF_\mathbf{R}^k$ there exists a function $f \in PCF_T^k$ with $L_{\ell_1}(f^*, S) = L_{\ell_1}(f, S).$[4]

---

[4] The proof of this statement is based on the well known fact that for any sequence $S = (y_1, \ldots, y_n)$ of real numbers the sum $\sum_{i=1}^n |y^* - y_i|$ is minimized if we choose $y^*$ as the *median* of $S$.

In [5], a very general scheme for constructing optimal piecewise functions is presented. This scheme would only achieve a running time of $O(|T|^2 kn^2)$ for the PCF problem in this restricted setting.

At last, we briefly mention a closely related application of the DYN algorithm in the area of pattern recognition. Consider a pixel matrix $M$ where each pixel is of a certain color. ($M$ represents a digitalized picture, for instance.) Let us take the distinct rows $r$ as input of the DYN algorithm. According to different choices of loss functions and different block types, we obtain optimal block structures in $r$. The block types $T$ may correspond to a (small) set of colors. Hence, we are able to extract a bounded number of "similar colored" blocks in $r$. Putting these block structures together for all rows $r$ in $M$, we may identify ("learn") two dimensional objects in $M$.

## 5   An On-Line Scenario

Let us review the *Optimal Array Decomposition* problem (OAD), introduced in Section 3, again. This time, we want to examine OAD in an online environment where the input array grows dynamically.

The *online* OAD$(k, n)$ problem is defined by the following process.

**Step 0:** Start with the empty array $A^{(0)} = ()$.
**Step $1 \le s \le n$:** Given $A^{(s)} = (a_1, \ldots, a_s)$, a new element $a^*$ and an array
   position $p$, $1 \le p \le s+1$, is presented. Solve the problem OAD$(k, s+1)$ with
   input array $A^{(s+1)} \triangleq (a_1, \ldots, a_{p-1}, a^*, a_p, \ldots, a_s)$.

Hence, the task is to generate $n$ solutions $S^{(1)}, \ldots, S^{(n)}$ of the OAD problem according a growing input array. Because each new element $a^*$ is inserted arbitrarily into $A^{(s)}$, we have no chance to compute $S^{(1)}, \ldots, S^{(n)}$ within a single run of the DYN algorithm, even if we may store further useful information.

Note that we need several subsolutions for the subarrays $(a_1, \ldots, a_{p-1})$ and $(a_p, \ldots, a_s)$ in order to obtain an optimum for the whole array $A^{(s)}$. But the standard DYN programming scheme provides us only with subsolutions for subarrays $(a_1, \ldots, a_j)$, $1 \le j \le s$. Of course, we can run the DYN algorithm $n$ times yielding an overall running time of $O(m^2 kn^2)$. (Remember that $m$ denotes the number of possible block types $t \in T$.)

In the remainder of this section, we design a data structure, called DYN-tree, solving the online OAD$(k, n)$ problem more efficiently for large $n$. Given $S^{(s)}$, we can generate $S^{(s+1)}$ in time $O(m^3 k^2 \log s)$. Hence, applications using DYN-trees beat "$n$-times offline algorithms" iff $mk = o(n/\log n)$.

A DYN-tree is a labeled binary tree with efficient update facilities.

In the case $m = 2$, a DYN-tree decreases to a tree data structure described in [1]. However, these trees are constructed in a single run after scanning a fixed sample. Update operations are not considered.

Given $A^{(s)} = (a_1, \ldots, a_s)$, each node $v$ of the DYN-tree $T(A^{(s)})$ corresponds to a subarray $A(v) = (a_{l(v)}, \ldots, a_{r(v)})$ of $A^{(s)}$.

Leaves correspond to the $n$ singletons $a_i$. Inner nodes $v$ with left child $u$ and right child $w$ are associated with the joint subarray $A(v) = (A(u), A(w))$, where $r(u) = l(w) - 1$. Hence, $A(u)$ and $A(w)$ refer to consecutive subarrays in $A^{(s)}$, and the root $r$ of $T(A^{(s)})$ corresponds to $A^{(s)}$.

Beside the array size $s_v = r(v) - l(v) + 1$, each node $v$ contains for all $t_l, t_r \in T$ and for all $k' \in \{1, \ldots k\}$ the following $1 + mk + m^2k$ losses according to $A(v)$.

- $L^{A(v)}(k)$, the minimum loss of a solution for the problem $OAD(k, s_v)$ with input array $A(v)$.
- $L_L^{A(v)}(t_l, k')$, which is defined as $L^{A(v)}(k')$ but with the additional restriction that the block type of the *first* element is $t_l$, i.e., $t(a_{l(v)}) = t_l$.
- $L_R^{A(v)}(k', t_r)$, which is defined as $L^{A(v)}(k')$ but with the additional restriction that the block type of the *last* element is $t_r$, i.e., $t(a_{r(v)}) = t_r$.
- $L_{LR}^{A(v)}(t_l, k', t_r)$, which is defined as $L^{A(v)}(k)$ but with restrictions $t(a_{l(v)}) = t_l$ and $t(a_{r(v)}) = t_r$.

Hence, the root $r$ of $T(A^{(s)})$ contains the minimum loss of the online $OAD(k, s)$ problem, namely $L^{A(r)}(k)$. If we want to construct an explicit solution $S^{(s)}$ we may perform a backtracking phase, similar the one in Fig. 3.

The key result is the following lemma which is, loosely speaking, the canonical "two-sided" generalization of Lemma 5. ("Two-sided" in the sense that losses of subarrays are considered where the types of *both* border elements are restricted.)

**Lemma 9.** $\forall t_l, t_r \in T, \forall k' \in \{1, \ldots k\}, \forall$ *singletons* $a, \forall$ *nodes* $u, v, w$:

1. $L_{LR}^{(a)}(t_l, k', t_r) = \begin{cases} L(t_l(a), a), & \text{if } t_l = t_r, \\ \infty, & \text{otherwise.} \end{cases}$

2. $L_{LR}^{(A(u), A(w))}(t_l, k', t_r) =$

$$\min \left\{ \begin{array}{l} \min\limits_{t \in T, 1 \le i \le k'} \{L_{LR}^{A(u)}(t_l, i, t) + L_{LR}^{A(w)}(t, k'+1-i, t_r)\}, \\ \min\limits_{1 \le i \le k'} \{L_L^{A(u)}(t_l, i) + L_R^{A(w)}(k'-i, t_r)\} \end{array} \right\}$$

3. $L_L^{A(v)}(t_l, k') = \min\limits_{t \in T}\{L_{LR}^{A(v)}(t_l, k', t)\}$

4. $L_R^{A(v)}(k', t_r) = \min\limits_{t \in T}\{L_{LR}^{A(v)}(t, k', t_r)\}$

5. $L^{A(v)}(k) = \min\limits_{t \in T}\{L_L^{A(v)}(t, k)\} = \min\limits_{t \in T}\{L_R^{A(v)}(k, t)\}$

(Statements 3., 4., and 5. follow by definition whereas statements 1. and 2. are a straightforward generalization of Lemma 5.)

Lemma 9 implies, that, given two consecutive subarrays $A(u)$ and $A(w)$, we can compute all $O(m^2k)$ losses of the joint array $A(v) = (A(u), A(w))$ in time $O((m^2k) \cdot (mk)) = O(m^3k^2)$.

Let $d$ denote the depth of $T(A^{(s)})$. For each new element $a^*$ and array position $p$, we update $T(A^{(s)})$ in time $O(m^3k^2d)$ as follows.

First, we search the leaf $u$ in $T(A^{(s)})$ containing the singleton $a_{p-1}$. (If $p = 1$, the following procedure has to be modified in a straightforward way.) Note that the path $P$ from the root of $T(A^{(s)})$ to $u$ can be found easily due to the structure of the DYN-tree.

After that, we replace the leaf $u$ by a new inner node $v$ with left child $u$ and right child $w$ where $w$ is a new leaf associated with the singleton $a^*$. Finally, we update the data of $w, u$ and all nodes on $P$ with respect to $a^*$ in a bottom-up pass. The resulting tree is a DYN-tree for $A^{(s+1)} = (a_1, \ldots, a_{p-1}, a^*, a_p, \ldots, a_s)$.

In order to keep the DYN-tree structure balanced ($d = O(\log s)$), we can organize a DYN-tree, for instance, as an AVL-tree. Now, in each phase of rebalancing $T(A^{(s)})$ at most $O(\log s)$ nodes are rearranged and their data has to be updated. Hence, one update step of a DYN-tree needs time $O(m^3k^2 \log s)$ and we obtain the following

**Theorem 10.** *Using a DYN-tree, we can solve the online $OAD(k, n)$ problem in $O(m^3k^2n \log n)$ steps.*

Online variants of the applications, introduced in Section 4, achieve corresponding running times.

Furthermore, one can think of an online scenario where the input array *shrinks* sequentially by elements $a_p$. Analogous reasonings as above yield the same time bound for this kind of problem.

# Acknowledgements

The author would like to thank Hans Ulrich Simon, Paul Fischer, Norbert Klasner, and some unknown referees for many valuable hints and discussions.

The author gratefully acknowledges the support of Deutsche Forschungsgemeinschaft grant Si 498/3-1 and the support of Deutscher Akademischer Austauschdienst grant 322-vigoni-dr.

# References

1. Peter Auer, Robert C. Holte, Wolfgang Maass. *Theory and Applications of Agnostic PAC-Learning with Small Decision Trees.* Proceedings of the 12th International Conference on Machine Learning, 1995.
2. Anselm Blumer, Andrej Ehrenfeucht, David Haussler, Manfred K. Warmuth. *Learnability and the Vapnik-Chervonenkis Dimension.* Journal of the Association for Computing Machinery, 36, 1989, p. 929–965.
3. Truxton Fulton, Simon Kasif, Steven Salzberg. *Efficient Algorithms for Finding Multi-way Splits for Decision Trees.* Proceedings of the 12th International Conference on Machine Learning, 1995, p. 244–251.
4. Michael Kearns, Yishay Mansour, Andrew Y. Ng, Dana Ron. *An Experimental and Theoretical Comparison of Model Selection Methods.* Proceedings of the 8th Annual Conference on Computation Learning Theory, 1995. p. 21–30.
5. Michael Kearns, Robert E. Schapire, Linda M. Sellie. *Towards Efficient Agnostic Learning.* Machine Learning, 17, 1994, p. 115–141.
6. Wolfgang Maass. *Efficient Agnostic PAC-Learning with Simple Hypotheses.* Proceedings of the 7th Annual Conference on Computation Learning Theory, 1994.

# A Minimax Lower Bound for Empirical Quantizer Design

Peter Bartlett[1] and Tamás Linder[2] and Gábor Lugosi[3]

[1] Department of Systems Engineering, Research School of Information Sciences and Engineering, Australian National University, Canberra 0200, Australia. (email: Peter.Bartlett@anu.edu.au)
[2] Department of Electrical and Computer Engineering, University of California, San Diego, California. (email: linder@code.ucsd.edu)
[3] Department of Economics, Pompeu Fabra University, Ramon Trias Fargas 25-27, 08005 Barcelona, Spain. (email: lugosi@upf.es)

**Abstract.** We obtain a minimax lower bound for the expected distortion of empirically designed vector quantizers. We show that the mean squared distortion of any empirically designed vector quantizer is at least $\Omega\left(n^{-1/2}\right)$ away from the optimal distortion for some distribution on a bounded subset of $\mathcal{R}^d$, where $n$ is the number of i.i.d. data points that are used to train the empirical quantizer.

## 1 Introduction

One of the basic problems of data compression is the design of vector quantizers from training data. In statistical data analysis the same problem is known as clustering. In this paper we investigate the minimax behavior of the expected mean squared distortion of a vector quantizer designed from independent identically distributed data points. The main result of the paper is a minimax lower bound which almost matches the best known upper bounds.

A $d$-dimensional $k$-point quantizer $Q$ is a mapping

$$Q(x) = y_i \quad \text{if} \quad x \in B_i,$$

where $B_1, \ldots, B_k$ form a measurable partition of $\mathcal{R}^d$, and $y_i \in \mathcal{R}^d$, $1 \leq i \leq k$. The $y_i$'s are called codepoints. The collection of codepoints $\{y_1, \ldots, y_k\}$ is the codebook. If $\mu$ is a probability measure on $\mathcal{R}^d$, the distortion of $Q$ with respect to $\mu$ is

$$D(Q) = \int_{\mathcal{R}^d} \|x - Q(x)\|^2 \mu(dx),$$

where $\|x - Q(x)\|$ is the euclidean distance between $x$ and $Q(x)$.

An empirically designed $k$-point quantizer is a measurable function $Q_n : \left(\mathcal{R}^d\right)^{n+1} \to \mathcal{R}^d$ such that for each fixed $x_1, \ldots, x_n \in \mathcal{R}^d$, $Q_n(\cdot, x_1, \ldots, x_n)$ is a $k$-point quantizer.

---

\* The work of the last two authors was supported by OTKA Grant F 014174.

In our investigation, $X, X_1, \ldots, X_n$ are i.i.d. random variables in $\mathcal{R}^d$ distributed according to some probability measure $\mu$ with $\mu(S(0, \sqrt{d})) = 1$, where $S(x, r) \subset \mathcal{R}^d$ denotes the closed ball of radius $r \geq 0$ centered at $x \in \mathcal{R}^d$. In other words, we assume that the normalized squared norm $(1/d)\|X\|^2$ of $X$ is bounded by one with probability one. (By straightforward scaling one can generalize our results to cases with $\mu(S(0, \sqrt{d}B)) = 1$ for some fixed $B < \infty$.) The distortion of $Q_n$ is the random variable

$$
\begin{aligned}
D(Q_n) &= \int_{\mathcal{R}^d} \|x - Q_n(x, X_1, \ldots, X_n)\|^2 \mu(dx) \\
&= \mathbf{E}\left[\|X - Q_n(X, X_1, \ldots, X_n)\|^2 | X_1, \ldots, X_n\right] \\
&= \mathbf{E}_\mu\left[\|X - Q_n(X, X_1, \ldots, X_n)\|^2\right].
\end{aligned}
$$

Let $D^*(k, \mu)$ be the minimum distortion achievable by the best $k$-point quantizer under the source distribution $\mu$. That is,

$$
D^*(k, \mu) = \min_Q \mathbf{E}_\mu \|X - Q(X)\|^2,
$$

where the minimum is taken over all $d$-dimensional, $k$-point quantizers. The following quantity is in the focus of our attention:

$$
J(Q_n, \mu) = ED(Q_n) - D^*(k, \mu),
$$

that is, the expected excess distortion of $Q_n$ over the optimal quantizer for $\mu$. In particular, we are interested in the *minimax expected distortion redundancy*, defined by

$$
\inf_{Q_n} \sup_\mu J(Q_n, \mu),
$$

where the infimum is taken over all empirical quantizers, and the supremum is taken over all distributions over the ball $S(0, \sqrt{d})$ in $\mathcal{R}^d$. The minimax expected distortion redundancy expresses the minimal worst-case excess distortion of any empirical quantizer.

A quantizer $Q$ is a *nearest neighbor quantizer* if for all $x$, $\|x - Q(x)\| \leq \|x - y_i\|$ for all codepoints $y_i$ of $Q$. It is easy to see that for each distribution the optimal quantizer is a nearest neighbor quantizer, and therefore, when designing a quantizer empirically, it suffices to search among such quantizers.

Let $Q_n^*$ be a quantizer that minimizes the empirical error

$$
D_n(Q) = \frac{1}{n} \sum_{i=1}^n \|X_i - Q(X_i)\|^2
$$

over all $k$-point nearest neighbor quantizers $Q$. One can prove by using standard uniform large-deviation inequalities that

$$
J(Q_n^*, \mu) \leq cd^{3/2} \sqrt{\frac{k \log n}{n}} \tag{1}
$$

for all $\mu$, where $c$ is a universal constant (see Linder, Lugosi, and Zeger [6], [7]).

The main message of the above inequality is that there exists a sequence of empirical quantizers such that for all distributions supported on a given $d$-dimensional sphere the expected distortion redundancy decreases as $O(\sqrt{\log n/n})$. With analysis based on an inequality of Alexander [1] it is possible to get rid of the $\sqrt{\log n}$ factor. More precisely, one can prove that

$$J(Q_n^*, \mu) \leq c'd^{3/2}\sqrt{\frac{k\log(kd)}{n}} \tag{2}$$

for all $\mu$, where $c'$ is another universal constant (see the discussion in [6] and Problem 12.10 in [4]). It has been an open question how tight these upper bounds are. Some have conjectured that $J(Q_n^*, \mu)$, in fact, decreases at a faster, $O(1/n)$, rate. For example, for one-codepoint quantizers (i.e., when $k = 1$), it is easy to see that $J(Q_n, \mu) = O(1/n)$ if the single codepoint of $Q_n$ is $y_1 = (1/n)\sum_{i=1}^n X_i$, the average of the $n$ data points. (For $k = 1$ it is also easy to prove a $c/n$-type lower bound for the minimax expected distortion redundancy.) Another indication that an $O(1/n)$ rate might hold was that Pollard [10] proved a central limit theorem for the codepoints of $Q_n^*$, which—as pointed out by Chou [2]—implies that the distortion redundancy decreases as $O(1/n)$ in probability. However, this result is not distribution free, it only holds for a special class of source distributions, and the conditions characterizing this class are rather complicated and very hard to check. The theorem below—the main result of this note—shows that a distribution-free $c/n$-type upper bound cannot hold, and in fact, for any empirical quantizer $Q_n$, the excess distortion is as large as a constant times $d\sqrt{\frac{k^{1-4/d}}{n}}$ for some distribution. Let $\Phi$ denote the distribution function of a standard normal random variable.

**Theorem 1.** *For any dimension $d$, number of codepoints $k \geq 3$, and sample size $n \geq 16k/(3\Phi(-2)^2)$, and for any empirically designed $k$-point quantizer $Q_n$, there exists a distribution $\mu$ on $S(0, \sqrt{d})$ such that*

$$J(Q_n, \mu) \geq c_0 d\sqrt{\frac{k^{1-4/d}}{n}},$$

*where $c_0$ is a universal constant which may be taken to be $c_0 = \Phi(-2)^4 2^{-12}/\sqrt{6}$.*

**Remark.** The constant $c_0$ of the theorem may be improved by more careful analysis.

The above theorem, together with (1) and (2), essentially describes the minimax behavior of the expected distortion in terms of the sample size $n$. However, there is still a gap if the bounds are viewed in terms of the number of codepoints $k$. For large $d$ the difference is negligible. In fact, if, according to the usual asymptotic view of information theory, $k = \lceil 2^{Rd} \rceil$ for some constant "rate" $R > 0$ (so that the output of the quantizer can be encoded using appriximately $R$ bits per vector dimension $d$), then the difference between the upper and lower bounds is merely a constant factor. The difference is more essential for very small $d$. For $d = 1, 2, 3$ the lower bound *decreases* as $k$ is increased. Elsewhere we will show that the upper bound (1) can be improved in a similar fashion, that is, this interesting behavior of the lower bound does not only occur because of the weakness of our proof, but because the minimax expected distortion indeed behaves this way (though the exact behavior is still to be characterized).

A recent work by Merhav and Ziv [9] takes the above mentioned information theoretic point of view. Their result deals with a more general setup where instead of independent training samples, the quantizer is trained by $N$ arbitrary information bits describing the source distribution. They obtain that the minimum number of training or "side information" bits necessary and sufficient for near optimal quantizer performance is approximately $N = 2^{dR}$. When specialized to the problem we investigate, it essentially implies that there exists $\epsilon > 0$ such that $J(Q_n, \mu) \geq C(\log n/n)^\epsilon$. This is a weaker statement than our Theorem 1. On the other hand, the result by Merhav and Ziv is more general in that it does not assume that the quantizer is trained from i.i.d. samples. Also, the worst-case distributions they use in proving their lower bound are in fact the $d$-dimensional marginals of certain stationary and ergodic sources.

## 2   Proof of Theorem 1.

**Step 1.** First observe that we can restrict our attention to nearest-neighbor quantizers, that is, to $Q_n$'s with the property that for all $x_1, \ldots, x_n$, the corresponding quantizer is a nearest neighbor quantizer. This follows from the fact that for any $Q_n$ not satisfying this property, we can find a nearest-neighbor quantizer $Q_n'$ such that for *all* $\mu$, $J(Q_n', \mu) \leq J(Q_n, \mu)$.

**Step 2.** Clearly,

$$\sup_\mu J(Q_n, \mu) \geq \sup_{\mu \in \mathcal{D}} J(Q_n, \mu),$$

where $\mathcal{D}$ is any restricted class of distributions on $S(0, \sqrt{d})$. We define $\mathcal{D}$ as follows: each member of $\mathcal{D}$ is concentrated on the set of $2m = 4k/3$ fixed points $\{z_i, z_i + w : i = 1 \ldots, m\}$, where $w = (\Delta, 0, 0, \ldots, 0)$ is a fixed $d$-vector, and $\Delta$ is a small positive number to be determined later. The positions of $z_1, \ldots, z_m \in S(0, \sqrt{d})$ satisfy the property that the distance between any two of them is greater than $A\Delta$, where the value of $A$ is determined in Step 5 below. For the sake of simplicity, we assume that $k$ is divisible by 3. (This assumption is clearly insignificant.) Let $\delta \leq 1/2$ be a positive number. For each $1 \leq i \leq m$, set

$$\mu(\{z_i\}) = \mu(\{z_i + w\}) = \begin{cases} \text{either} & \frac{1-\delta}{2m} \\ \text{or} & \frac{1+\delta}{2m} \end{cases}$$

such that exactly half of the pairs $(z_i, z_i + w)$ have mass $(1-\delta)/m$, and the other half of the pairs have mass $(1+\delta)/m$, so that the total mass adds up to one. Let $\mathcal{D}$ contain all such distributions. The cardinality of $\mathcal{D}$ is $M = \binom{m}{m/2}$. Denote the members of $\mathcal{D}$ by $\mu_1, \mu_2, \ldots, \mu_M$.

**Step 3.** Let $\mathcal{Q}$ denote the collection of $k$-point quantizers $Q \in \mathcal{Q}$ such that for $m/2$ values of $i \in \{1, \ldots, m\}$, $Q$ has codepoints at both $z_i$ and $z_i + w$, and for the remaining $m/2$ values of $i$ $Q$ has a single codepoint at $z_i + w/2$. If $A \geq \sqrt{2/(1-\delta)}+1$, then for any $k$-point quantizer $Q$ there exists a $\tilde{Q}$ in $\mathcal{Q}$ such that, for all $\mu$ in $\mathcal{D}$, $D(\tilde{Q}) \leq D(Q)$.

PROOF. Let $C = \{y_1, \ldots, y_k\}$ be the codebook of $Q$. Consider the Voronoi partition of $\mathcal{R}^d$ induced by the set of points $\{z_i, z_i + w; 1 \leq i \leq m\}$ and for each $i$ define $V_i$ as the union of the two Voronoi cells belonging to $z_i$ and $z_i + w$. Furthermore, let $m_i$ be the cardinality of $C \cap V_i$. A new nearest neighbor quantizer $\hat{Q}$ with codebook $\hat{C}$ is constructed as follows. Start with $\hat{C}$ empty. For all $i$

- if $m_i \geq 2$, put $z_i$ and $z_i + w$ into $\hat{C}$ ,
- if $m_i = 1$ or $m_i = 0$, put $z_i + w/2$ into $\hat{C}$.

Note that $\hat{C}$ may contain more than $k$ codepoints, but this will be fixed later. Define

$$D_i(Q) = \|z_i - Q(z_i)\|^2 \mu(\{z_i\}) + \|z_i + w - Q(z_i + w)\|^2 \mu(\{z_i + w\}).$$

Then we have the following

- if $m_i \geq 2$, then $D_i(\hat{Q}) = 0$ so that $D_i(Q) \geq D_i(\hat{Q})$,
- if $m_i = 1$, then there are two cases:
  1. $Q(z_i) = Q(z_i + w) \in V_i$. Then $D_i(Q) \geq D_i(\hat{Q})$ since $\hat{Q}(z_i) = \hat{Q}(z_i + w) = z_i + w/2$ is the optimal choice with the condition that both $z_i$ and $z_i + w$ are mapped into the same codepoint.
  2. either $z_i$ or $z_i + w$ is mapped by $Q$ to a codepoint outside $V_i$. Say $Q(z_i) \notin V_i$. Then

$$D_i(Q) \geq \frac{1 \pm \delta}{2m} \|Q(z_i) - z_i\|^2 \geq \frac{1 \pm \delta}{2m} \left( \frac{(A-1)\Delta}{2} \right)^2 ,$$

  where the second inequality follows by the triangle inequality. (Here $\pm$ means $+$ if $\mu$ puts mass $(1 + \delta)/m$ on $\{z_i, z_i + w\}$, and $-$ otherwise.) On the other hand, $D_i(\hat{Q}) = (1 \pm \delta)\Delta^2/(4m)$ so that $D_i(Q) \geq D_i(\hat{Q})$ if $A \geq \sqrt{2} + 1$.
- if $m_i = 0$, then both $Q(z_i)$ and $Q(z_i + w)$ are outside $V_i$. Thus

$$D_i(Q) \geq \frac{1 \pm \delta}{m} \left( \frac{(A-1)\Delta}{2} \right)^2 ,$$

which implies

$$D_i(Q) \geq D_i(\hat{Q}) + \frac{1 \pm \delta}{m} \left( \frac{(A-1)\Delta}{2} \right)^2 - \frac{1 \pm \delta}{m} \frac{\Delta^2}{4}, \tag{3}$$

so that $D_i(Q) \geq D_i(\hat{Q})$ if $A \geq 2$.

Thus we conclude that $D(Q) \geq D(\hat{Q})$, and we are done if $\hat{C}$ has no more than $k$ codepoints. If $\hat{C}$ contains $\hat{k} > k$ codepoints, pick $\hat{k} - k$ arbitrary pairs $\{z_i, z_i + w\} \in \hat{C}$ and replace them with the corresponding codepoint $z_i + w/2$. We thus obtain a nearest neighbor quantizer $\tilde{Q}$. Each such replacement increases the distortion by no more than $(1 + \delta)\Delta^2/(4m)$, so that

$$D(\tilde{Q}) \leq D(\hat{Q}) + (\hat{k} - k)\frac{(1 + \delta)\Delta^2}{4m}$$

On the other hand, there must be $\hat{k} - k$ indices $i$ for which $m_i = 0$. For each of these (3) holds, so that

$$D(\hat{Q}) \leq D(Q) - (\hat{k} - k)\frac{1 - \delta}{m}\frac{\Delta^2}{4}((A - 1)^2 - 1).$$

Therefore,

$$D(\tilde{Q}) \leq D(Q) + (\hat{k} - k)\frac{\Delta^2}{4m}\left((1 + \delta) - (1 - \delta)((A - 1)^2 - 1)\right),$$

and this is no more than $D(Q)$ if $A \geq \sqrt{2/(1 - \delta)} + 1$. $\qquad\square$

**Step 4.** Consider a distribution $\mu_j \in \mathcal{D}$ and the corresponding optimal quantizer $Q^{(j)}$. Clearly, from Step 3, if $A \geq \sqrt{2/(1 - \delta)} + 1$, then for the $m/2$ values of $i$ in $\{1, \ldots, m\}$ that have $\mu_j(\{z_i, z_i + w\}) = (1 + \delta)/m$, $Q^{(j)}$ has codepoints at both $z_i$ and $z_i + w$. For the remaining $m/2$ values of $i$ there is a single codepoint at $z_i + w/2$.

For any distribution in $\mathcal{D}$ and any quantizer in $\mathcal{Q}$, it is easy to see that the distortion of the quantizer is between $(1 - \delta)\Delta^2/8$ and $(1 + \delta)\Delta^2/8$.

**Step 5.** Let $\mathcal{Q}_n$ denote the family of empirically designed quantizers such that for every fixed $x_1, \ldots, x_n$, we have $Q(\cdot, x_1, \ldots, x_n) \in \mathcal{Q}$. Since $\delta \leq 1/2$, the property of the optimal quantizer described in Step 4 is always satisfied if we take $A = 3$. In particular, if $A = 3$, we have

$$\inf_{Q_n}\max_{\mu \in \mathcal{D}} J(Q_n, \mu) = \min_{Q_n \in \mathcal{Q}_n}\max_{\mu \in \mathcal{D}} J(Q_n, \mu),$$

and it suffices to lower bound the quantity on the right-hand side.

**Step 6.** Let $Z$ be a random variable which is uniformly distributed on the set of integers $\{1, 2, \ldots, M\}$. Then, for any $Q_n$, we obviously have,

$$\max_{\mu \in \mathcal{D}} J(Q_n, \mu) \geq \mathbf{E}J(Q_n, \mu_Z) = \frac{1}{M}\sum_{i=1}^{M} J(Q_n, \mu_i).$$

**Step 7.**

$$\min_{Q_n \in \mathcal{Q}_n} \mathbf{E}J(Q_n, \mu_Z) = \mathbf{E}J(Q_n^*, \mu_Z), \qquad (4)$$

where $Q_n^*$ is the "empirically optimal" (or "maximum-likelihood") quantizer from $Q$, that is, if $N_i$ denotes the number of $X_i$'s falling in $\{z_i, z_i + w\}$, then $Q_n^*$ has a codepoint at both $z_i$ and $z_i + w$ if the corresponding $N_i$ is one of the $m/2$ largest values. For the other $i$'s (i.e., those with the $m/2$ smallest $N_i$'s) $Q_n^*$ has a codepoint at $z_i + w/2$.

The proof is given in the appendix.

**Step 8.** By symmetry, we have

$$\mathbf{E}J(Q_n^*, \mu_Z) = J(Q_n^*, \mu_1).$$

The rest of the proof involves bounding $J(Q_n^*, \mu_1)$ from below, where $Q_n^*$ is the empirically optimal quantizer.

**Step 9.** Recall that the vector of random integers $(N_1, \ldots, N_m)$ is multinomially distributed with parameters $(n, q_1, \ldots, q_m)$, where $q_1 = q_2 = \cdots = q_{m/2} = (1 - \delta)/m$, and $q_{m/2+1} = \cdots = q_m = (1 + \delta)/m$. Let $N_{\sigma(1)}, \ldots, N_{\sigma(m)}$ be a reordering of the $N_i$'s such that $N_{\sigma(1)} \leq N_{\sigma(2)} \leq \cdots \leq N_{\sigma(m)}$. (In case of equal values, break ties according to indices.) Let $p_j$ $(j = 1, \ldots, m/2)$ be the probability of the event that among $N_{\sigma(1)}, \ldots, N_{\sigma(m/2)}$, there are exactly $j$ of the $N_i$'s with $i > m/2$ (i.e., the "maximum likelihood" estimate makes $j$ mistakes). Then it is easy to see that

$$J(Q_n^*, \mu_1) = \frac{\Delta^2 \delta}{2m} \sum_{j=1}^{m/2} jp_j,$$

since one "mistake" increases the distortion by $\Delta^2 \delta/(2m)$.

**Step 10.** From now on, we investigate the quantity $\sum_{j=1}^{m/2} jp_j$, that is, the expected number of mistakes. First we use the trivial bound

$$\sum_{j=1}^{m/2} jp_j \geq j_0 \sum_{j=j_0}^{m/2} p_j,$$

with $j_0$ to be chosen later. $\sum_{j=j_0}^{m/2} p_j$ is the probability that the maximum likelihood decision makes at least $j_0$ mistakes. The key observation is that this probability may be bounded below by the probability that at least $2j_0$ of the events $A_1, \ldots, A_{m/2}$ hold, where

$$A_i = \{N_i > N_{m/2+i}\}.$$

In other words,

$$\sum_{j=j_0}^{m/2} p_j \geq \mathbf{P}\left\{\sum_{j=1}^{m/2} I_{A_i} \geq 2j_0\right\}.$$

PROOF. Define the following sets of indices:

$$S_1 = \{i : \sigma(i) \leq m/2, i \geq m/2 + 1\}, \quad S_2 = \{i : \sigma(i) \leq m/2, i \leq m/2\}$$

Then the maximum likelihood decision makes $|S_1|$ mistakes. If $i \in S_2$ and $N_i > N_{m/2+i}$, then $m/2+i \in S_1$. Thus, the number of indices $i$ for which $N_i > N_{m/2+i}$ is bounded from above by $|S_1| + m/2 - |S_2| = 2|S_1|$, since $|S_2| = m/2 - |S_1|$. □

**Step 11.** Thus, we need a lower bound on the tail of the distribution of the random variable $\sum_{j=1}^{m/2} I_{A_i}$. First we obtain a suitable lower bound for its expected value.

$$\mathbf{E} \left[ \sum_{j=1}^{m/2} I_{A_i} \right] = \frac{m}{2} \mathbf{P}\{A_1\}. \tag{5}$$

Now, bounding $\mathbf{P}\{A_1\}$ conservatively, we have

$$\begin{aligned}
\mathbf{P}\{A_1\} &= \mathbf{P}\{N_1 > N_{m/2+1}\} \\
&\geq \mathbf{P}\{N_1 > n/m \text{ and } N_{m/2+1} \leq n/m\} \\
&= \mathbf{P}\{N_1 > n/m\} - \mathbf{P}\{N_1 > n/m \text{ and } N_{m/2+1} > n/m\} \\
&\geq \mathbf{P}\{N_1 > n/m\} - \mathbf{P}\{N_1 > n/m\}\mathbf{P}\{N_{m/2+1} > n/m\} \\
&= \mathbf{P}\{N_1 > n/m\}\mathbf{P}\{N_{m/2+1} \leq n/m\}.
\end{aligned}$$

The last inequality follows by Mallows' inequality (see Mallows [8]) which states that if $(N_1, \ldots, N_m)$ are multinomially distributed, then

$$\mathbf{P}\{N_1 > t_1, N_2 > t_2, \ldots, N_m > t_m\} \leq \prod_{i=1}^{m} \mathbf{P}\{N_i > t_i\}.$$

Finally, we approximate the last two binomial probabilities by normals. To this end, we use the Berry-Esséen inequality (see, e.g., Chow and Teicher [3]), which states that if $Z_1, \ldots, Z_n$ are i.i.d. random variables with $\mathbf{E}Z_1 = 0$, $\mathbf{E}[Z_1^2] = \sigma^2$, and $\mathbf{E}\left[|Z_1|^3\right] = \gamma$, then

$$\left| \mathbf{P}\left\{ \sum_{i=1}^{n} Z_i < x\sigma\sqrt{n} \right\} - \Phi(x) \right| \leq \frac{\gamma}{\sigma^3\sqrt{n}},$$

where $\Phi$ is the distribution function of a standard normal random variable. Choose $\delta = \sqrt{m/n}$. Observe that $N_1$ is the sum of $n$ i.i.d. Bernoulli$((1-\delta)/m)$ random variables. Then the Berry-Esséen inequality implies that if $n \geq 8m/\Phi(-2)^2$, then $\mathbf{P}\{N_1 > n/m\} \geq \Phi(-2)/2$, and similarly $\mathbf{P}\{N_{m/2+1} \leq n/m\} \geq \Phi(-2)/2$.

Therefore, by (5) we get

$$\mathbf{E} \left[ \sum_{j=1}^{m/2} I_{A_i} \right] \geq \frac{m\Phi(-2)^2}{8}. \tag{6}$$

**Step 12.** To obtain the desired lower bound for

$$\mathbf{P}\left\{ \sum_{j=1}^{m/2} I_{A_i} \geq 2j_0 \right\},$$

we use the following elementary inequality: if the random variable $Z$ satisfies $P\{Z \in [0, B]\} = 1$, then

$$P\left\{Z \geq \frac{EZ}{2}\right\} \geq \frac{EZ}{2B}. \tag{7}$$

To see this, notice that for $\alpha$ in $[0, B]$, $EZ \leq \alpha + B P\{Z \geq \alpha\}$, and substitute $\alpha = EZ/2$.

**Step 13.** To apply this inequality, choose $j_0 = m\Phi(-2)^2/32$. Then (6) implies that $2j_0 \leq (1/2)E\left[\sum_{j=1}^{m/2} I_{A_i}\right]$, and therefore

$$P\left\{\sum_{j=1}^{m/2} I_{A_i} \geq 2j_0\right\} \geq P\left\{\sum_{j=1}^{m/2} I_{A_i} \geq \frac{1}{2}E\left[\sum_{j=1}^{m/2} I_{A_i}\right]\right\}$$

$$\geq \frac{1}{m}E\left[\sum_{j=1}^{m/2} I_{A_i}\right]$$

$$\geq \frac{\Phi(-2)^2}{8},$$

where the second inequality follows from (7) and the last inequality follows from (6).

**Step 14.** Collecting everything, we have that

$$\inf_{Q_n} \sup_{\mu} J(Q_n, \mu) \geq \frac{\Delta^2 \Phi(-2)^4}{512}\sqrt{\frac{m}{n}},$$

where $\Delta$ is any positive number with the property that $m$ pairs of points $\{z_i, z_i + w\}$ can be placed in $S(0, \sqrt{d})$ such that the distance between any two of the $z_i$'s is at least $3\Delta$. In other words, to make $\Delta$ large, we need find a (desirably large) $\Delta$ such that $m$ points $z_1, \ldots, z_m$ can be packed into the ball $S(0, \sqrt{d} - \Delta)$. (We decrease the radius of the ball by $\Delta$ to make sure that the $(z_i + w)$'s also fall in the ball $S(0, \sqrt{d})$.) Thus, we need a good lower bound for the cardinality of the maximal $3\Delta$-packing of $S(0, \sqrt{d} - \Delta)$. It is well known (see Kolmogorov and Tikhomirov [5]) that the cardinality of the maximal packing is lower bounded by the cardinality of the minimal covering, that is, by the minimal number of balls of radius $3\Delta$ whose union covers $S(0, \sqrt{d} - \Delta)$. But this number is clearly bounded from below by the ratio of the volume of $S(0, \sqrt{d} - \Delta)$, and that of $S(0, 3\Delta)$. Therefore, $m$ points can certainly be packed in $S(0, \sqrt{d} - \Delta)$ as long as

$$m \leq \left(\frac{\sqrt{d} - \Delta}{3\Delta}\right)^d.$$

If $\Delta \leq \sqrt{d}/4$ (which is satisfied by our choice of $\Delta$ below), the above inequality holds if

$$m \leq \left(\frac{\sqrt{d}}{4\Delta}\right)^d.$$

Thus, the choice

$$\Delta = \frac{\sqrt{d}}{4m^{1/d}}$$

satisfies the required property. Resubstitution of this value proves the theorem.

□

# References

1. K. Alexander. Probability inequalities for empirical processes and a law of the iterated logarithm. *Annals of Probability*, 4:1041–1067, 1984.
2. P. A. Chou. The distortion of vector quantizers trained on $n$ vectors decreases to the optimum as $O_p(1/n)$. Proceedings of *IEEE Int. Symp. Inform. Theory*, Trondheim, Norway, 1994.
3. Y.S. Chow and H. Teicher. *Probability Theory, Independence, Interchangeability, Martingales.* Springer-Verlag, New York, 1978.
4. L. Devroye, L. Györfi, and G. Lugosi. *A Probabilistic Theory of Pattern Recognition.* Springer-Verlag, New York, 1996.
5. A.N. Kolmogorov and V.M. Tikhomirov. $\epsilon$-entropy and $\epsilon$-capacity of sets in function spaces. *Translations of the American Mathematical Society*, 17:277–364, 1961.
6. T. Linder, G. Lugosi, and K. Zeger. Rates of convergence in the source coding theorem, empirical quantizer design, and universal lossy source coding. *IEEE Transactions on Information Theory*, 40:1728–1740, 1994.
7. T. Linder, G. Lugosi, and K. Zeger. Empirical quantizer design in the presence of source noise or channel noise. *IEEE Transactions on Information Theory*, 1996. to appear.
8. C.L. Mallows. An inequality involving multinomial probabilities. *Biometrika*, 55:422–424, 1968.
9. N. Merhav and J. Ziv. On the amount of side information required for lossy data compression. submitted to IEEE Transactions on Information Theory, 1995.
10. D. Pollard. A central limit theorem for $k$-means clustering. *Annals of Probability*, 10:919–926, 1982.

# Appendix: Proof that the Maximum Likelihood Quantizer Minimizes Expected Distortion (Step 7)

PROOF. Let $(Y, Y_1, \ldots, Y_n)$ be jointly distributed as the mixture $(1/M) \sum_{i=1}^{M} \mu_i^{n+1}$, where $\mu_i^{n+1}$ is the $(n+1)$-fold product of $\mu_i$. Then for any $Q_n$,

$$EJ(Q_n, \mu_Z) = \mathbf{E}\left(\|Y - Q_n(Y, Y_1, \ldots, Y_n)\|^2\right) - \frac{(1-\delta)\Delta^2}{8}.$$

Since $Y, Y_1, \ldots, Y_n$ are exchangable random variables, the distribution of $Y$ given $(Y_1, \ldots, Y_n)$ depends only on the empirical counts $(N_1, \ldots, N_k)$. It follows that the empirical quantizer $Q_n$ achieving the minimum in (4) choses its codebook as a function of the vector $(N_1, \ldots, N_m)$. Thus, it suffices to restrict our attention to empirical quantizers that choose their codebook only as a function of

$(N_1, \ldots, N_m)$. Recall that each quantizer in $\mathcal{Q}$ is such that for each $i$ it either has one codepoint at $z_i + w/2$ or has codepoints at both $z_i$ and $z_i + w$. Since $k = 3m/2$, there must be $m/2$ codepoints of the first kind, and $m$ of the second.

We will represent the distribution $\mu_Z$ as an $m$-vector, $\gamma = (\gamma_1, \ldots, \gamma_m) \in \Gamma_m \subset \{-1, 1\}^m$, with

$$\mu_Z(\{z_i, z_i + w\}) = (1 + \gamma_i \delta)/m,$$

where

$$\Gamma_m = \left\{ \gamma \in \{-1, 1\}^m : \sum_{i=1}^m \gamma_i = 0 \right\}.$$

We write $P_{\gamma, n}(E)$ to denote the probability of the event $E$ under the multinomial distribution with parameters $(n, q_1, \ldots, q_m)$ where

$$q_i = \frac{1 + \gamma_i \delta}{\sum_{j=1}^m (1 + \gamma_j \delta)}.$$

We will represent a quantizer's choice of the codebook as a vector $\alpha = (\alpha_1, \ldots, \alpha_m) \in \Gamma_m$, with $\alpha_i = -1$ indicating one codepoint at $(i + \Delta/2)/m$ and $\alpha_i = 1$ indicating codepoints at both $i/m$ and $(i + \Delta)/m$.

Represent the quantizer $Q_n^*(\cdot, X_1, \ldots, X_n)$ by $\alpha^*(N_1, \ldots, N_m) \in \Gamma_m$ for the corresponding values of $N_i$. Define $\alpha$ similarly in terms of $Q_n$. Then it suffices to show that (with suitable abuse of notation)

$$\sum_{\gamma \in \Gamma_m} (D(\alpha(n_1, \ldots, n_m)) - D(\alpha^*(n_1, \ldots, n_m))) \, P_{\gamma, n}(\forall i, \, N_i = n_i) \geq 0$$

for all $m$-tuples of nonnegative integers $(n_1, \ldots, n_m)$ that sum to $n$ and for all functions $\alpha$.

For the numbers $n_1, \ldots, n_m$, let $\alpha = \alpha(n_1, \ldots, n_m)$ and $\alpha^* = \alpha^*(n_1, \ldots, n_m)$. Define $\beta \in \{-1, 0, 1\}^m$ by $\beta_i = (\alpha_i^* - \alpha_i)/2$. Note that $\sum_i \beta_i = 0$. It is easy to see that

$$D(\alpha) = \left( m - \delta \sum_{j=1}^m \gamma_j \alpha_j \right) \Delta^2/(8m),$$

hence the difference $D(\alpha) - D(\alpha^*)$ is some positive constant times $\sum_j \beta_j \gamma_j$, and so it suffices to show that

$$\sum_{\gamma \in \Gamma_m} P_{\gamma, n}(\forall i, \, N_i = n_i) \sum_{j=1}^m \beta_j \gamma_j \geq 0.$$

To prove this inequality, we shall split the outer sum into several parts, and show that each part is nonnegative. Each part corresponds to a set of distributions that satisfy a convenient symmetry property. First, divide the components of $\beta$ into $m/2$ pairs $(i, j)$, with $\beta_i = -\beta_j$. Without loss of generality, suppose

$$\left. \begin{array}{l} \beta_{2i-1} = -\beta_{2i}, \\ \beta_{2i-1} \leq 0, \text{ and} \\ \beta_{2i} \geq 0 \end{array} \right\} \text{ for all } 1 \leq i \leq m/2. \tag{8}$$

Then for $\tilde{\gamma} \in \{-1, 1\}^m$, let $S(\tilde{\gamma})$ denote the set of all permuted versions of $\tilde{\gamma}$ obtained by swapping the components $\tilde{\gamma}_{2i-1}$ and $\tilde{\gamma}_{2i}$, for all $i$ in some subset of $\{1, \ldots, m/2\}$. Clearly, it suffices to show that for all $\tilde{\gamma} \in \Gamma_m$,

$$\sum_{\gamma \in S(\tilde{\gamma})} \mathbf{P}_{\gamma, n}(\forall i, \, N_i = n_i) \sum_{j=1}^{m} \beta_j \gamma_j \geq 0.$$

But we have

$$\sum_{\gamma \in S(\tilde{\gamma})} \mathbf{P}_{\gamma, n}(\forall i, \, N_i = n_i) \sum_{j=1}^{m} \beta_j \gamma_j$$

$$= \sum_{\gamma \in S(\tilde{\gamma})} \mathbf{P}_{\gamma, n}(\forall i, \, N_i = n_i \, | \, \forall i, \, N_{2i-1} + N_{2i} = n_{2i-1} + n_{2i})$$

$$\times \mathbf{P}_{\gamma, n}(\forall i, \, N_{2i-1} + N_{2i} = n_{2i-1} + n_{2i}) \sum_{j=1}^{m} \beta_j \gamma_j$$

$$= \mathbf{P}_{\tilde{\gamma}, n}(\forall i, \, N_{2i-1} + N_{2i} = n_{2i-1} + n_{2i})$$

$$\times \sum_{\gamma \in S(\tilde{\gamma})} \mathbf{P}_{\gamma, n}(\forall i, \, N_i = n_i \, | \, \forall i, \, N_{2i-1} + N_{2i} = n_{2i-1} + n_{2i}) \sum_{j=1}^{m} \beta_j \gamma_j.$$

We can ignore the nonnegative constant factor, and the other probabilities are of independent events, so we can write

$$\sum_{\gamma \in S(\tilde{\gamma})} \mathbf{P}_{\gamma, n}(\forall i, \, N_i = n_i \, | \, \forall i, \, N_{2i-1} + N_{2i} = n_{2i-1} + n_{2i}) \sum_{j=1}^{m} \beta_j \gamma_j$$

$$= \sum_{\gamma \in S(\tilde{\gamma})} \prod_{i=1}^{m/2} \mathbf{P}_{(\gamma_{2i-1}, \gamma_{2i}), n_{2i-1} + n_{2i}}(N_{2i-1} = n_{2i-1}, N_{2i} = n_{2i}) \sum_{j=1}^{m} \beta_j \gamma_j.$$

So it suffices to show that for all $\tilde{\gamma} \in \{-1, 1\}^m$, all $n_1, \ldots, n_m$ summing to $n$, and all $\beta \in \{-1, 0, 1\}^m$ satisfying (8), we have

$$\sum_{\gamma \in S(\tilde{\gamma})} \prod_{i=1}^{m/2} \mathbf{P}_{(\gamma_{2i-1}, \gamma_{2i}), n_{2i-1} + n_{2i}}(N_{2i-1} = n_{2i-1}, N_{2i} = n_{2i}) \sum_{j=1}^{m} \beta_j \gamma_j \geq 0. \quad (9)$$

Without loss of generality, we can assume that $\beta_j \neq 0$ for all $j$. Indeed, suppose that $\beta_{2i-1} = \beta_{2i} = 0$ for some $i$. Then we can split the sum over $\gamma$ in (9) into a sum over the pair $(\gamma_{2i-1}, \gamma_{2i})$ and a sum over the other components of $\gamma$, and the corresponding factors in the product can be taken outside the outermost sum, since $\sum_{j=1}^{m} \beta_j \gamma_j$ is identical for both values of the pair $(\gamma_{2i-1}, \gamma_{2i})$.

Now, $\beta_{2i-1} = -1$ and $\beta_{2i} = 1$ imply that $n_{2i-1} \leq n_{2i}$. So to show that (9) holds for the cases of interest, it suffices to show that for all even $m$, for all

$n_1, \ldots, n_m$ satisfying $n_{2i-1} \leq n_{2i}$, and all $\tilde{b} \in \{-1, 1\}^m$, we have

$$\sum_{b \in S(\tilde{b})} \sum_{j=1}^{m} (-1)^j b_j \prod_{i=1}^{m/2} P_i \geq 0,$$

where

$$P_i = \mathbf{P}_{(b_{2i-1}, b_{2i}), n_{2i-1} + n_{2i}}(N_{2i-1} = n_{2i-1}, N_{2i} = n_{2i}).$$

First suppose $m = 2$. If $\tilde{b}_1 = \tilde{b}_2$, the expression is clearly zero. Otherwise, it is equal to

$$2 \left( \mathbf{P}_{(-1,1), n_1+n_2}(N_1 = n_1, N_2 = n_2) - \mathbf{P}_{(1,-1), n_1+n_2}(N_1 = n_1, N_2 = n_2) \right)$$
$$= 2 \left( \mathbf{P}_{(-1,1), n_1+n_2}(N_1 = n_1, N_2 = n_2) - \mathbf{P}_{(-1,1), n_1+n_2}(N_1 = n_2, N_2 = n_1) \right),$$

which is clearly nonnegative, since $n_2 \geq n_1$. Next, suppose the expression is nonnegative up to some even number $m$. Let $\tilde{b} \in \{-1, 1\}^{m+2}$. Then

$$\sum_{b \in S(\tilde{b})} \sum_{j=1}^{m+2} (-1)^j b_j \prod_{i=1}^{m/2+1} P_i$$

$$= \sum_{b_1, \ldots, b_m} \sum_{b_{m+1}, b_{m+2}} \left( \sum_{j=1}^{m} (-1)^j b_j + \sum_{j=m+1}^{m+2} (-1)^j b_j \right) \prod_{i=1}^{m/2} P_i P_{m/2+1}$$

$$= \sum_{b_{m+1}, b_{m+2}} P_{m/2+1} \left( \sum_{b_1, \ldots, b_m} \sum_{j=1}^{m} (-1)^j b_j \prod_{i=1}^{m/2} P_i \right)$$

$$+ \sum_{b_1, \ldots, b_m} \prod_{i=1}^{m/2} P_i \left( \sum_{b_{m+1}, b_{m+2}} \sum_{j=m+1}^{m+2} (-1)^j b_j P_{m/2+1} \right),$$

and both of these terms are nonnegative, since the expressions in parentheses are nonnegative by the inductive hypothesis. □

# Vapnik-Chervonenkis Dimension of Recurrent Neural Networks

Pascal Koiran[1]* and Eduardo D. Sontag[2]**

[1] Laboratoire de l'Informatique du Parallélisme
Ecole Normale Supérieure de Lyon – CNRS
46 allée d'Italie, 69364 Lyon Cedex 07
France
koiran@lip.ens-lyon.fr
[2] Department of Mathematics
Rutgers University
New Brunswick, NJ 08903
USA
sontag@hilbert.rutgers.edu

**Abstract.** Most of the work on the Vapnik-Chervonenkis dimension of neural networks has been focused on feedforward networks. However, recurrent networks are also widely used in learning applications, in particular when time is a relevant parameter. This paper provides lower and upper bounds for the VC dimension of such networks. Several types of activation functions are discussed, including threshold, polynomial, piecewise-polynomial and sigmoidal functions. The bounds depend on two independent parameters: the number $w$ of weights in the network, and the length $k$ of the input sequence. In contrast, for feedforward networks, VC dimension bounds can be expressed as a function of $w$ only. An important difference between recurrent and feedforward nets is that a fixed recurrent net can receive inputs of arbitrary length. Therefore we are particularly interested in the case $k \gg w$. Ignoring multiplicative constants, the main results say roughly the following:

- For architectures with activation $\sigma =$ any fixed nonlinear polynomial, the VC dimension is $\approx wk$.
- For architectures with activation $\sigma =$ any fixed *piecewise* polynomial, the VC dimension is between $wk$ and $w^2 k$.
- For architectures with activation $\sigma = \mathcal{H}$ (threshold nets), the VC dimension is between $w \log(k/w)$ and $\min\{wk \log wk, w^2 + w \log wk\}$.
- For the standard sigmoid $\sigma(x) = 1/(1 + e^{-x})$, the VC dimension is between $wk$ and $w^4 k^2$.

# 1 Introduction

In this paper we deal with questions that arise when training and testing data have a time series structure. This is a fairly common situation in many appli-

---

* This research was carried out in part while visiting DIMACS and the Rutgers Center for Systems and Control (SYCON) at Rutgers University.
** This research was supported in part by US Air Force Grant AFOSR-94-0293.

cations. It arises in control problems, when the inputs to a regulator are time-dependent measurements of plant states, or in speech processing, where inputs are windowed Fourier coefficients and signal levels at each instant.

In PAC-theoretic terms, it is natural to take into account this additional structure through the use of hypotheses classes $\mathcal{F}$ which consist of dynamical systems. We will take the inputs (for training and testing) to be functions of time, and the hypotheses classes will be defined by means of dynamical recognizers, which allow one to exploit the information inherent in the correlations and dependencies that exist among the terms of the input sequence. (As a close analogy, Kalman filtering, which relies on linear dynamical systems for extracting information — filtering of noise — from a stream of data, is perhaps the most successful known example of an application of the idea of using dynamical systems as data processors.) Through a limitation of the memory and power (dynamic order, number of adjustable parameters) of the elements of $\mathcal{F}$, and analyzing behavior for longer and longer input sequences, one is able to focus on the properties that truly reflect the dependence of $f(u)$ on long-term time correlations in the input sequence $u$. This paradigm is inspired by the use of finite automata for the recognition of languages, and the use of recursive least squares techniques in statistical problems, but the interest here is in nonlinear, continuous-state, dynamical systems. In particular, we use recurrent (sometimes "feedback" or "dynamic") neural networks. In contrast to feedforward nets, which only contain static units, recurrent nets incorporate dynamic elements (delay lines), and their behavior is described by means of systems of difference equations. (It is also possible to study *continuous-time* nets, which are defined in terms of differential equations, but we restrict attention in this paper to the discrete time case. Similar results can be obtained in the continuous-time framework, however.)

Recurrent networks are among the models considered by Grossberg and his school during the last twenty or more years, and include the networks proposed by Hopfield for associative memory and optimization. They have been employed in the design of control laws for robotic manipulators (Jordan), as well as in speech recognition (Fallside, Kuhn), speaker identification (Anderson), formal language inference (Giles), and sequence extrapolation for time series prediction (Farmer). See for instance the book [2], which emphasizes digital signal processing, or the work on language learning in [5], and the many references given in both citations. In both the areas of signal processing ([9]) and control ([10]), recurrent nets have been proposed as generic identification models or as prototype dynamic controllers. In addition, theoretical results about neural networks established their universality as models for systems approximation ([14]) as well as analog computing devices ([11, 12]).

## 2 Precise Definitions

In order to be able to formally state our main results, we now provide precise definitions of recurrent nets. Just as one does with Turing machines – or similar models of computation – in the analysis of algorithms, however, in proofs we revert to a more informal approach, leaving implicit the precise specification of networks in the formalism introduced here.

By an $n$-dimensional, $m$-input, $p$-output *initialized recurrent net* we mean a 5-tuple

$$\Sigma = (A, B, C, x^0, \sigma) \tag{1}$$

consisting of three matrices $A \in \mathbb{R}^{n \times n}$, $B \in \mathbb{R}^{n \times m}$, $C \in \mathbb{R}^{p \times n}$, a vector $x^0 \in \mathbb{R}^n$, and a diagonal mapping

$$\sigma : \mathbb{R}^n \to \mathbb{R}^n : \begin{pmatrix} x_1 \\ \vdots \\ x_n \end{pmatrix} \mapsto \begin{pmatrix} \sigma_1(x_1) \\ \vdots \\ \sigma_n(x_n) \end{pmatrix}, \tag{2}$$

where $\sigma_1, \ldots, \sigma_n$ are maps $\mathbb{R} \to \mathbb{R}$. The (discrete time) *system induced by the net* (1) is the set of $n$ coupled difference equations, plus measurement function:

$$x(t+1) = \sigma\left(Ax(t) + Bu(t)\right), \quad x(0) = x^0, \quad y(t) = Cx(t). \tag{3}$$

One also writes (3) simply as $x^+ = \sigma(Ax + Bu)$, $x(0) = x^0$, $y = Cx$. The component maps $\sigma_1, \ldots, \sigma_n$ of $\sigma$ are the *activations of the net*. If it is the case that all the $\sigma_i$ are equal to a fixed function $\sigma$, we say that the net is *homogeneous* with activation $\sigma$ and write also $\vec{\sigma}^{(n)}$ instead of $\sigma$. The spaces $\mathbb{R}^m$, $\mathbb{R}^n$, and $\mathbb{R}^p$ are called respectively the input, state, and output spaces of the net.

In the present context, one interprets the vector equations for $x$ in (3) as representing the evolution of an ensemble of $n$ "neurons" (also called sometimes "units", or "gates") where each coordinate $x_i$ of $x$ is a real-valued variable which represents the internal state of the $i$th neuron, and each coordinate $u_i, i = 1, \ldots, m$ of $u$ is an external input signal. The vector $x^0$ lists the initial values of these states. The coefficients $A_{ij}, B_{ij}$ denote the weights, intensities, or "synaptic strengths," of the various connections. The coordinates of $y(t)$ represent the output of $p$ probes, or measurement devices, each of which averages the activation values of many neurons. Often $C$ is just a projection on some coordinates, that is, the components of $y$ are simply a subset of the components of $x$.

The linear systems customarily studied in control theory (see e.g. the textbook [13]) are precisely the homogeneous initialized recurrent nets with identity activation and $x^0 = 0$.

To each initialized recurrent net $(A, B, C, x^0, \sigma)$ we associate a discrete time input/output behavior. Assume given a sequence $u = u(0), \ldots, u(k-1)$ of elements of the input space $\mathbb{R}^m$. One may iteratively solve the difference equation (3) starting with $x(0) = x^0$, thereby obtaining a sequence of state vectors $x(1), \ldots, x(k)$. In this manner, each initialized recurrent net induces a mapping, on inputs of fixed length $k$,

$$\lambda_\Sigma^k : (\mathbb{R}^m)^k \to \mathbb{R}^p : u \mapsto y(k) = Cx(k) \tag{4}$$

which assigns to the input $u$ the last output produced in response.

*Remark.* One may broaden the notion of initialized recurrent net by allowing "biases" or "offsets", i.e. nonzero vectors $d \in \mathbb{R}^n$ and $e \in \mathbb{R}^p$ in the update and the measurement equations respectively. These equations would then take the more general form $x^+ = \sigma(Ax + Bu + d)$, $y = Cx + e$. Despite the fact that biases are useful, and we employ them in proofs, we do not need to include such an extension in the formal definition. This is because the input/output behavior of any such net also arises as the input/output behavior of a net in the sense defined earlier (zero biases), with state space $\mathbb{R}^{n+1}$ and same activations. The simulation is achieved by means of the introduction of an additional variable $z$ whose value is constantly equal to a nonzero number $z_0$ in the range of one of the activations, say $\sigma$, in such a manner that the equations become $x^+ = \sigma(Ax + zd' + Bu)$, $z^+ = \sigma(a_0 z)$, $y = Cx + ze'$, where $a_0$ is chosen so that $\sigma(a_0 z_0) = z_0$ and $d', e'$ are so that $z_0 d' = d$ and $z_0 e' = e$ (if the only activation is $\sigma \equiv 0$, there would be nothing to prove).

## 2.1 Architectures

Roughly, by an "architecture" one means a choice of interconnection structure and of the activation functions $\sigma$ for each neuron, leaving weights and initial states unspecified, as parameters. One may also stipulate that the initial state, or just certain specific coordinates of it, should be zero (as with linear systems in control theory). Feedback networks with a fixed architecture provide parametric classes of dynamical systems. We formalize the notion of architecture by means of incidence matrices, employing binary matrices in order to specify the allowed interconnection patterns and initial states.

By an $n$-dimensional, $m$-input, $p$-output *recurrent architecture* we mean a 5-tuple

$$\mathcal{A} = (\alpha, \beta, \gamma, \xi, \sigma) \tag{5}$$

consisting of three matrices $\alpha \in \{0,1\}^{n \times n}$, $\beta \in \{0,1\}^{n \times m}$, and $\gamma \in \{0,1\}^{p \times n}$, a vector $\xi \in \{0,1\}^n$, and a diagonal mapping $\sigma$ as in Equation (2). An *initialized recurrent net with architecture* $\mathcal{A}$ is an instantiation obtained by choosing values for the nonzero entries, that is, any initialized recurrent net $(A, B, C, x^0, \sigma')$ such that $\sigma = \sigma'$ and the entries of the matrices and vector satisfy $A_{ij} = 0$ whenever $\alpha_{ij} = 0$, $B_{ij} = 0$ whenever $\beta_{ij} = 0$, $C_{ij} = 0$ whenever $\gamma_{ij} = 0$, and $x_i^0 = 0$ whenever $\xi_i = 0$.

We say also here that the component maps $\sigma_1, \ldots, \sigma_n$ of $\sigma$ are the activations of the net, which is homogeneous with activation $\sigma$ if all $\sigma_i$ are equal to a fixed function $\sigma$. The spaces $\mathbb{R}^m$, $\mathbb{R}^n$, and $\mathbb{R}^p$ are respectively the input, state, and output spaces of the architecture. Suppose that the binary matrices $\alpha$, $\beta$, and $\gamma$ and the vector $\xi$ have exactly $\kappa$, $\lambda$, $\mu$, and $\nu$ nonzero entries respectively; then we call the number $w := \kappa + \lambda + \mu + \nu$ the number of *parameters* or *weights* of $\mathcal{A}$, and call $\mathbb{R}^w$ the parameter or weight space. Arrange the indices of the nonzero entries in any fixed manner, for instance by listing their nonzero entries row by row, for $\alpha$, $\beta$, $\gamma$, and $\xi$ in that order. These indices are in one-to-one correspondence with the coordinates of vectors in $\mathbb{R}^w$. In this manner, one may view the architecture

$\mathcal{A}$ as representing a parameterized system $x^+ = \sigma(\alpha x + \beta u)$, $x(0) = \xi$, $y = \gamma x$ where, by substituting the parameters $\rho \in \mathbb{R}^w$ into the nonzero entries of $(\alpha, \beta, \gamma, \xi)$, every possible initialized recurrent net $\Sigma = \mathcal{A}(\rho)$ with architecture $\mathcal{A}$ results.

Recalling the notations in Equation (4), for each recurrent architecture $\mathcal{A}$ and each $k > 0$, we may introduce the set

$$\mathcal{F}_{\mathcal{A},k} := \{\lambda_\Sigma^k, \ \Sigma = \mathcal{A}(\rho), \ \rho \in \mathbb{R}^w\} \tag{6}$$

of mappings $(\mathbb{R}^m)^k \to \mathbb{R}^p$. Elements of this set are the input/output mappings induced on inputs of length $k$ by each possible initialized recurrent net with architecture $\mathcal{A}$.

## 2.2  VC Dimension

*In all our results, we will take the number of input components (m) and of output components (p) to be one, and, except in Theorem 7, we consider only homogeneous* (all activations equal) *architectures.* By $\sigma$-architecture, we mean an architecture where all activations are the same function $\sigma : \mathbb{R} \to \mathbb{R}$. The choice of $m = 1$ makes our lower bounds more interesting. It is fairly easy, though notationally somewhat more cumbersome, to extend the upper bounds to vector inputs. The same can be said about the homogeneity assumption, although it is the case that some *proofs* use nonhomogeneous nets in intermediate steps. The choice $p = 1$ is made in order to be able to see the input/output behaviors of networks as classifiers.

Given any $\mathcal{A}$ with $m = p = 1$, and any $k > 0$, we denote

$$\mathcal{B}_{\mathcal{A},k} := \{H \circ \lambda_\Sigma^k, \ \Sigma = \mathcal{A}(\rho), \ \rho \in \mathbb{R}^w, \ \xi \in \mathbb{R}^n\} \tag{7}$$

where $H$ is the threshold function: $H(x) = 0$ if $x \le 0$ and $H(x) = 1$ if $x > 0$. This is a class of mappings $\mathbb{R}^k \to \{0, 1\}$, and we write $\mathrm{VC}(\mathcal{A}, k)$ to denote its VC dimension. We refer to this quantity also as the "VC dimension of $\mathcal{A}$ when receiving inputs of length $k$".

We are particularly interested in understanding the behavior of $\mathrm{VC}(\mathcal{A}, k)$ as $k \to \infty$, for various recurrent architectures, as well as the dependence of this quantity on the number of weights and the particular type of activation being used. In particular, we continue the work described in [4] (see also [16] for related work), which had obtained estimates of these quantities for architectures with identity activations.

By a *threshold* recurrent architecture we mean a homogeneous one with $\sigma = H$. As in [15], we say that $\sigma : \mathbb{R} \to \mathbb{R}$ is *sigmoidal*, or *a sigmoid*, if:

1. $\sigma$ is differentiable at some point $x_0$ where $\sigma'(x_0) \neq 0$.
2. $\lim_{x \to -\infty} \sigma(x) = 0$ and $\lim_{x \to +\infty} \sigma(x) = 1$. (the limits 0 and 1 can be replaced by any distinct numbers).

In particular, the *standard sigmoid* is $\sigma(x) = 1/(1 + e^{-x})$. By $\sigma$-gate, or $\sigma$-unit, we mean a gate with activation $\sigma$. These two special cases are worth recording: by linear (respectively, threshold) unit we mean a unit with activation a linear or threshold function.

## 2.3 Statements of Main Results

For each $\mathcal{A}$ and $k$, by "unfolding" the iterations, one may also see the class $\mathcal{B}_{\mathcal{A},k}$ as a class of classifiers representable by feedforward neural nets (with $k$ "hidden layers"). This trivial fact allows one to easily obtain estimates, based on those bounds which were developed (cf. [3, 1], [6], [7]) for the feedforward case.

**Theorem 1.** *For recurrent architectures, with $w$ weights receiving inputs of length $k$:*

1. *The VC dimension of threshold recurrent architectures is $O(kw \log kw)$.*
2. *If $\sigma : \mathbb{R} \to \mathbb{R}$ is a fixed piecewise-polynomial function, The VC dimension of recurrent architectures with activation $\sigma$ is $O(kw^2)$.*
3. *The VC dimension of recurrent architectures with activation the standard sigmoid $O(k^2 w^4)$.*

The bounds would seem to be too conservative, since they completely disregard the fact that the weights in the different layers of the "unfolded" net are actually the same. The surprising aspect of the results to be stated next (and of the results in [4]) is that we obtain lower bounds which do not look much different. We first state two more upper bounds. The first one is interesting because for fixed $w$, it shows a $\log k$ dependence, rather than the $k \log k$ obtained by unfolding.

**Theorem 2.** *The VC dimension of an $n$-dimensional threshold recurrent architecture, with $w$ weights and receiving inputs of length $k$, is $O(wn + w \log kw)$.*

**Theorem 3.** *Let $\sigma : \mathbb{R} \to \mathbb{R}$ be a fixed polynomial function. The VC dimension of recurrent architectures with activation $\sigma$, with $w$ weights and receiving inputs of length $k$, is $O(kw)$. Moreover, if $\sigma$ is linear this bound can be improved to $O(w \log k)$.*

For a corresponding lower bound in the linear case, see [4]. We now turn to other lower bounds.

**Theorem 4.** *The VC dimension of threshold recurrent architectures, with $w$ weights and receiving inputs of length $k = \Omega(w)$, is $\Omega(w \log(k/w))$.*

Here and throughout the paper, the $\Omega$ symbol is to be interpreted as follows: "there exist universal constants $c_1, c_2, c_3 > 0$ such that for every $w \geq c_1$ and every $k \geq c_2 w$, there exists a threshold recurrent architecture with $w$ weights which has VC dimension at least $c_3 w \log(k/w)$ for inputs of length $k$."

**Theorem 5.** *Let $\sigma$ be an arbitrary sigmoid. The VC dimension of recurrent architectures with activation $\sigma$, with $w$ weights and receiving inputs of length $k$, is $\Omega(wk)$.*

It is possible to generalize Theorem 5 to even more arbitrary gate functions:

**Theorem 6.** *Let $\sigma$ be a function which is twice continuously differentiable function in an open interval containing some point $x_0$ where $\sigma''(x_0) \neq 0$. The VC dimension of recurrent architectures with activation $\sigma$, with $w$ weights and receiving inputs of length $k$, is $\Omega(wk)$.*

This is an intermediate technical result, but it seems of interest in its own right:

**Theorem 7.** *The VC dimension of recurrent architectures with threshold and linear activations, with $w$ weights and receiving inputs of length $k$, is $\Omega(wk)$.*

It is interesting to contrast the situation with the one that holds for feed-forward nets. For the latter, it holds, in general terms, that linear activations provide VC dimension proportional to $w$, threshold activations give VC dimension proportional to $w \log(w)$, and piecewise polynomial activations result in VC dimension proportional to $w^2$.

Proofs and a few additional results can be found in sections 3 and 4.

## 3  Threshold Networks

### 3.1  Lower Bounds

**Lemma 8.** *Given two integers $m, L > 0$ such that $L$ is a power of $2$, let $k = mL$ and consider the following family $\mathcal{F}$ of boolean functions on $\{0,1\}^k$: the functions in $\mathcal{F}$ are indexed by $m$ parameters $t_0, \ldots, t_{m-1} \in \{0, \ldots, L-1\}$. The corresponding function maps an input $u = (u(k-1), \ldots, u(0)) \in \{0,1\}^k$ to*

$$f_{t_0,\ldots,t_{m-1}}(u) = \bigvee_{j=0}^{m-1} u(jL + t_j),$$

*i.e., we select one input in each interval of the form $[jL, (j+1)L - 1]$ and take the logical OR of these boolean values.*

*The VC dimension of $\mathcal{F}$ is exactly $m \log L$.*

*Proof.* Since each parameter $t_j$ can take $L$ distinct values, there are at most $L^m = 2^{m \log L}$ functions in $\mathcal{F}$. Hence the VC dimension of $\mathcal{F}$ is at most $m \log L$. In order to show that this upper bound is tight, we will construct a set $S$ of $s = m \log L$ inputs $u_0, \ldots, u_{s-1}$ such that each labeling $(\epsilon_0, \ldots, \epsilon_{s-1}) \in \{0,1\}^s$ of $S$ can be obtained in the following way: let $t_j$ be the integer with binary digits (from the low-order bit to the high-order bit) $\epsilon_{j \log L}, \epsilon_{j \log L+1}, \ldots, \epsilon_{(j+1) \log L-1}$. Then $f_{t_0,\ldots,t_{m-1}}(u_i) = \epsilon_i$.

Input $u_i$ is defined as follows: write $i = q \log L + r$, with $q \in \{0, \ldots, m-1\}$ and $r \in \{0, \ldots, \log L - 1\}$. Then $u_i(t) = 0$ for every $t \notin [qL, (q+1)L - 1]$. For $t \in [qL, (q+1)L - 1]$, one can write $t = qL + r'$ where $r' \in \{0, \ldots, L-1\}$. We set $u_i(t) = 1$ if the bit of weight $2^r$ of $r'$ is equal to 1; otherwise, $u_i(t) = 0$.

To see that for any labeling $\epsilon_0, \ldots, \epsilon_{s-1}$ one has $f_{t_0,\ldots,t_{m-1}}(u_i) = \epsilon_i$ (with $t_0, \ldots, t_{m-1}$ as defined above), note that by construction of $u_i$, $u_i(jL + t_j) = 0$

for all $j \neq q$. Hence $f_{t_0,...,t_{m-1}}(u_i) = u_i(qL + t_q)$. Again by construction of $u_i$, this is just the bit of weight $2^r$ of $t_q$. However, by construction of the $t_j$'s, this bit is nothing but $\epsilon_{q \log L + r} = \epsilon_i$. Hence we get the correct output.

**Remark.** An explicit description of the inputs constructed in the above proof is as follows. Consider the $L$ by $\log L$ matrix

$$V = \begin{pmatrix} 1 & 0 & \cdots & 0 \\ 0 & 1 & \cdots & 0 \\ 1 & 1 & \cdots & 0 \\ \vdots & \vdots & \vdots & \vdots \\ 1 & 1 & \cdots & 1 \end{pmatrix}$$

which is obtained by listing all binary row vectors of size $\log L$ in the reverse of their natural order (i.e., the leftmost bit is the least significant bit). Let $U$ be the direct sum matrix $V \oplus V \oplus \cdots \oplus V$ (this is the block-diagonal matrix with $m$ copies of $V$ on the diagonal). The input set $S$ is the same as the set of columns of this matrix. We may also describe the set functions in $\mathcal{F}$ in this manner. Let $e_i$, $i = 0, \ldots, L - 1$ be the unit row vector $(0, \ldots, 0, 1, 0, \ldots, 0)$ (with a "1" in the $(i+1)$st position) and consider the row vector $E_{t_0,...,t_{m-1}} = (e_{t_0}, \ldots, e_{t_{m-1}})$. Then, $f_{t_0,...,t_{m-1}}(u_i)$ is the product of $E_{t_0,...,t_{m-1}}$ and the $i$th column of $U$.

*Proof of Theorem 4.* We first assume that $w$ is of the form $8m + 2$, for some $m \geq 1$. We also assume that $L = \kappa/m$ is a power of 2, where $\kappa = k - 2$, and that $L \geq 2$. The (straightforward) generalization to arbitrary values of $w$ and $k$ is explained at the end of the proof.

We shall construct an architecture $\mathcal{N}$ of $w$ weights which implements the family $\mathcal{F}$ of Lemma 8 for inputs of length $\kappa$. It will become clear that in the initialized recurrent network implementation, we need two additional inputs at time $\kappa$ and $\kappa + 1$. This explains why $k = \kappa + 2$. According to Lemma 8, our shattered set $S'$ will be of size $m \log L = [(w-2)/8] \cdot \log[8(k-2)/(w-2)]$. This is indeed $\Omega(w \log(k/w))$.

$S'$ is defined as follows. For each input $u$ in the shattered set $S$ of Lemma 8 there is an input $u' \in S'$ satisfying $u'(t) = 2t + u(t_i)$ for $t = 0, \ldots, \kappa - 1$. There are two additional "dummy" inputs $u'(\kappa) = 0$ and $u'(\kappa + 1) = 0$ (the values $(0, 0)$ can be replaced by an arbitrary pair of real numbers).

Let us now describe network $\mathcal{N}$. We need $m$ subnetworks to perform the tests "$u(jL + t_j) = 1$ ?" for $j = 0, \ldots, m - 1$. By construction of $S'$, this question has a positive answer if and only if there exists $t \in \{0, \ldots, \kappa - 1\}$ such that $u'(t) = 2(jL + t_j) + 1$. The outcome $e_j$ of this test can be computed by a simple network of 3 threshold units and 7 weights:

$$e_j = H[H(u' - \theta_j + 0.5) + H(\theta_j + 0.5 - u') - 1.5]$$

where $\theta_j = 2(jL + t_j) + 1$. The network has one additional threshold gate $o$ which serves as output unit. It keeps computing the OR of the $e_j$'s and of the previous output (to make sure that is some $e_j$ is equal to 1 at some time, the output remains 1 ever after). This can be implemented with $m + 2$ weights as follows: $o^+ = H(o + \sum_{j=1}^{m} e_j - 0.5)$. Therefore $\mathcal{N}$ has $7m + (m+2) = w$ weights.

Note that the last two inputs $u'(\kappa)$ and $u'(\kappa + 1)$ are "wasted", i.e., they do not influence the final output $o(k)$. All gates are initialized to 0. This guarantees that the outputs at $t = 1$ and $t = 2$ are both 0. These outputs are "bogus" in the sense that they occur before even the first input $u'(0)$ is processed. If one of these bogus outputs was equal to 1 then the final output would be 1, no matter what the input sequence is (and we certainly don't want that to happen).

The generalization to arbitrary values of $w$ and $k$ is as follows: let $m = \lfloor (w - 2)/8 \rfloor$ and $L$ the largest power of 2 which is not larger than $(k - 2)/m$ (we can assume that $L \geq 2$). The construction above yields a network of $w' = 8m + 2$ weights with VC dimension $m \log L$. This is still $\Omega(w \log(k/w))$, albeit with a slightly smaller constant. One can obtain a network of exactly $w$ weights by adding to the present construction $w' - w$ "dummy" units which are completely disconnected from the rest of the network (for instance, each dummy unit might be of the form $x^+ = H(x)$).

## 3.2 Upper Bounds

*Proof of Theorem 1 (threshold case).* By unfolding, the recurrent network can be simulated by a (depth $k$) feedforward threshold network with $kw$ weights (note that the only effect of having the initial $x(0) \in \mathbb{R}^n$ as a programmable parameter is to change the threshold values in the first layer of that feedforward net). The result then follows from the Baum-Haussler bound [1].

*Proof of Theorem 2.* Let $S = \{u_1, \ldots, u_s\}$ be a set of $s$ inputs. We will bound the number of distinct transition functions of the architecture for inputs in $S$. The transition function is of the form

$$\phi : (x, u) \mapsto \vec{H}^{(n)}(Ax + Bu),$$

where the network state $x$ is in $\{0, 1\}^n$ and the input $u$ in $\mathbb{R}$. Since we are considering only inputs from $S$, $u$ can take any of the (at most) $ks$ values $u_i(t)$ ($i = 1, \ldots, s; t = 0, \ldots, k-1$). Hence the domain $D$ of $\phi$ has at most $|\{0, 1\}^n|ks = 2^n ks$ elements. Let $T_i$ be the threshold function computed by gate number $i$. If this gate has $w_i$ incoming weights, then $T_i$ can induce at most $2|D|^{w_i}$ distinct functions on $D$ by, e.g., Sauer's lemma. Hence there are at most $\prod_{i=1}^{n} 2|D|^{w_i} = 2^n |D|^{w-\nu}$ distinct transition functions, where $\nu$ is the number of entries equal to 1 in $\xi$ (in other words, $\nu$ is the number of "unspecified" coordinates of initial states; by definition, the total number of parameters is $w = \sum_{i=1}^{n} w_i + \nu$). If two settings of the architecture's parameters give rise to the same transition function and the initial states are the same, the functions induced on $S$ will be identical. Therefore if $S$ is to be shattered, $2^s \leq 2^n(2^n ks)^{w-\nu} \times 2^\nu \leq 2^n(2^n ks)^w$. This implies that $s \leq n(w + 1) + w \log k + w \log s$, hence $s/2 \leq n(w + 1) + w \log k$ or $s/2 \leq w \log s$. In both cases, $s = O(wn + w \log kw)$.

We don't know if a $O(w \log kw)$ bound applies for all values of $k, w \geq 2$. It is clear from the proof of this theorem that the "extra" term $wn$ comes from the $2^n$ bound on the number of network states. One may be able to give better bounds for networks with a smaller number of "accessible" states.

**Theorem 9.** *The VC dimension of a recurrent architecture of $n$ threshold units and $w$ weights receiving* boolean *inputs of length $k$ is $O(wn + w \log w)$. (Note that this bound is independent of $k$.)*

*Proof.* This follows from the proof of Theorem 2. The domain of the transition function $\phi$ has only $2^{n+1}$ elements since $u \in \{0, 1\}$. Hence one can set $|D| = 2^{n+1}$ in the proof of that theorem.

The same result applies to architectures taking their inputs in any fixed finite set. This is in sharp contrast with the case of feedforward architectures, where maximum VC dimension $\Omega(w \log w)$ can be achieved with boolean inputs.

# 4 Sigmoidal Networks

## 4.1 Upper Bounds

*Proof of Theorem 1 (piecewise-polynomial case).* It takes $O(w)$ arithmetic operations to update the network's state after a new input component is received. Hence the whole computation requires $O(kw)$ operations for inputs of length $k$. The architecture has $w + n \leq 2w$ programmable parameters, where $n$ is the number of units in the network. Hence by [6] (Theorem 2.3) its VC dimension is $O(w \times kw)$.

Interestingly, one can give a better upper bound for polynomial activation functions than for piecewise-polynomial activation functions. The linear case is included in [4].

*Proof of Theorem 3.* We denote by $W$ the vector listing all weights in the three systems matrices $\alpha, \beta, \gamma$, so that the parameter vector $\rho$ can be partitioned as $(W, \rho_0)$, where $\rho_0$ lists the weights in $\xi$. Let $P : \mathbb{R}^{w - \nu + 1 + n} \rightarrow \mathbb{R}^n$ be the function mapping $W$, the input $u \in \mathbb{R}$, and the network's current state $x \in \mathbb{R}^n$ to the next state $x^+ \in \mathbb{R}^n$. For instance, the network's state after reading $u(0)$ and $u(1)$ is $P(W, u(1), P(W, u(0), x(0)))$. If $\sigma$ is a degree-$d$ polynomial then each component of $P$ is a polynomial of degree $2d$. (this twofold increase is due to multiplications between weight and input or state variables; the degree in the weight variables is only $d$.) After the whole input $u \in \mathbb{R}^k$ has been read, the state of any unit in the network (and in particular the state of the output unit) can be expressed as a polynomial $P_k$ in $u \in \mathbb{R}^k$, $W \in \mathbb{R}^{w - \nu}$ and the parameters $\rho_0$ for the nonzero coordinates of $x(0) \in \mathbb{R}^n$. The degree of $P_k$ in the programmable parameters is at most $D = 2d^k + \sum_{j=1}^{k-1} d^j$. By [6] (Theorem 2.2) the VC dimension is bounded by $2w \log(8eD)$. (note that the degree in the input variables does not appear in this bound.) The theorem follows from the obvious observations: $D = k + 1$ for $d = 1$ and $D < 2d^{k+1}$ for $d \geq 2$.

*Proof of Theorem 1 (standard-sigmoidal case).* By unfolding, the recurrent architecture can be simulated by a feedforward net with $kn$ nodes, where $n$ be the number of nodes in the original architecture, and the same number $w$ of programmable parameters. By [7] there is a $O((kn)^2 w^2)$ upper bound on the VC dimension of that architecture. This is $O(k^2 w^4)$ as claimed.

Note: one can argue that the feedforward net has $kw$ weights, but many of those weights are "shared" and there are only $w + n \leq 2w$ programmable parameters. The result in [7] explicitly allows such weight-sharing arrangements (see condition $e$ in section 4.1 of their paper).

## 4.2 Lower Bounds

Theorem 6 shows that the $O(kw)$ upper bound of Theorem 3 is tight (for nonlinear polynomials). In fact, the matching $\Omega(kw)$ lower bound applies to a much wider class of functions than just polynomials. Let us consider first the simpler case of sigmoidal functions.

*Proof of Theorem 5.* This follows from Theorem 7 and the fact on any finite set of inputs, linear and threshold gates can be simulated by gates with activation $\sigma$.

*Proof of Theorem 7.* We can assume that $\kappa = k - 2 \geq 1$. We also assume that $w$ is of the form $14\nu + 2$. As in Theorem 4, the generalization to other values of $w$ is straightforward. We first define the shattered set $S$: a sequence $u \in \mathbb{R}^\kappa$ is in $S$ if it has exactly one non-zero component, and that component is in $\{1, \dots, \nu\}$ (obviously, $|S| = \kappa\nu$). Next we define a family $\mathcal{F}$ of functions which shatters $S$. The functions in this family are indexed by $\nu$ parameters $w_1, \dots, w_\nu \in [0, 1]$. Each parameter is assumed to have a finite $\kappa$-bit binary expansion $0.w_{i1} \dots w_{i\kappa}$. Given an input $u \in S$ with $i = u(j)$ as non-zero component, the corresponding output simply is $f_{w_1, \dots, w_\nu}(u) := w_{ij}$ (i.e., we select bit number $j$ of $w_i$). It is clear that $\mathcal{F}$ shatters $S$: any function $f : S \to \{0, 1\}$ can be implemented by setting $w_{ij} = f(ie_j)$ ($e_j$ denotes the element of $S$ with a 1 in the $j$-th position).

In a recurrent network implementation of this, the set $S'$ of shattered sequences is obtained by adding two "dummy" inputs $u(\kappa) = u(k - 2) = 0$ and $u(\kappa + 1) = u(k - 1) = 0$ at the end of a sequence $(u(0), \dots, u(\kappa - 1)) \in S$, as in the proof of Theorem 4.

The parameters $w_1, \dots, w_\nu$ are stored in the initial states of units $x_1, \dots, x_\nu$. As the computation proceeds, these units will store shifted versions of the parameters. The leading bits of $x_1, \dots, x_\nu$ are stored in $\nu$ other units $y_1, \dots, y_\nu$. The initial state of $x_i$ is $w_i/2$; all other units are initialized to 0. (note that this implies in particular that at $t = 0$, $y_i$ indeed stores the leading bit of $x_i$.) New values of $x_i$ and $y_i$ can be computed at each time step by the following 5-weight system:

$$x_i^+ = 2x_i - y_i$$
$$y_i^+ = H(4x_i - 2y_i - 1)$$

The network should output 1 if the current input $u$ is equal to $i \neq 0$, and $y_i = 1$. This can be checked by computing $e_i = H[H(u - i + 0.5) + H(i + 0.5 - u) + y_i - 2.5]$ (this requires $3\nu$ threshold gates and $8\nu$ weights). There is one additional threshold gate $o$ which serves as output unit. It keeps computing the OR of the $e_i$'s and of the previous output This can be implemented with $\nu + 2$ weights as in the proof of Theorem 4: $o^+ = H(o + \sum_{i=1}^{\nu} e_i - 0.5)$.

The architecture described above has $5\nu + 8\nu + (\nu + 2) = 14\nu + 2 = w$ weights. The output $f_{w_1,\ldots,w_\nu}(u(0),\ldots,u(\kappa - 1))$ is carried by the output unit at time $(\kappa - 1) + 3 = k$. Note that the last two inputs $u(\kappa)$ and $u(\kappa + 1)$ are "wasted", i.e., they do not influence the final output $o(k)$. Note also that the outputs at $t = 1$ and $t = 2$ are both 0 as needed.

Theorem 6 generalizes Theorem 5 to even more arbitrary activations. For this we need some of the machinery of [8]. In particular, we need to allow networks with multiplication and division gates. These gates have fan-in two and number of weights also two (even though there is no natural numerical parameter associated to the gate; we need to assign weights to multiplication and division gates to account for the numerical parameters that will occur when simulating these gates by $\sigma$-gates). The output of a multiplication gate is defined as the product of its two inputs. The output of a division gate is defined as the quotient of its two inputs, assuming that the second input is nonzero. An input to a circuit is said to be *valid* if it does not cause a division by zero at any division gate. We will only work with sets of valid inputs (so the domain of the function computed by such a generalized network is a subset of $\mathbb{R}^m$ and shattering is only defined for subsets of this domain).

We will use *feedforward architectures* as building blocks in our recurrent architectures. The necessary background is standard and can be found for instance in [8]. To be self-contained, we recall that the units of feedforward architecture are grouped into *layers*. We use the same type of units as in recurrent architectures (in particular, multiplication and division gates are allowed, as mentioned earlier in this section). The inputs to the architecture are fed to units in the first layer. For $i > 1$, units in layer $i$ receive their inputs from layer $i - 1$. The last layer is made of a single gate: the output gate. The function computed by a gate is defined by a straightforward induction on its depth in the architecture. The function computed by the architecture is the function computed by the output gate.

Readers familiar with feedforward nets will notice that we do not allow connections between non-adjacent layers. For synchronization reasons, such connections are to be avoided in recurrent nets. One can always convert a non-layered feedforward architecture into a layered one by introducing delays (identity gates).

The following two lemmas from [8] are needed (the first one is well-known and easy to prove).

**Lemma 10.** Let $\phi : [0,1] \to [0,1]$ be the logistic map $\phi(x) = 4x(1 - x)$. For every $n \geq 1$ and every $\epsilon \in \{0,1\}^n$ there exists $x_1 \in [0,1]$ such that the sequence $(x_k)_{1 \leq k \leq n}$ defined by $x_{k+1} = \phi(x_k)$ for $k = 1,\ldots,n-1$ satisfies the following property: $0 \leq x_k < 1/2$ if $\epsilon_k = 0$ and and $1/2 < x_k \leq 1$ if $\epsilon_k = 1$.

The next result is essentially Lemma 1 from [8].

**Lemma 11.** *For every $n \geq 0$, there is a feedforward architecture $\mathcal{A}$ with inputs $(x, W_0, \ldots, W_n)$ in $\mathbb{R}^{n+2}$ such that the following property holds: for every $\epsilon > 0$ there exists a choice of the weights of $\mathcal{A}$ such that the function $f_\epsilon$ implemented by the network satisfies $\lim_{\epsilon \to 0} f_\epsilon(i, W_0, \ldots, W_n) = W_i$ for $i = 0, \ldots, n$.*

*This architecture is made of linear, multiplication and division gates. It has $\Theta(n)$ weights and depth $\Theta(\log n)$.*

**Lemma 12.** *The VC dimension of recurrent architectures of linear, multiplication and division gates with $w$ weights receiving inputs of length $k = \Omega(\log w)$ is $\Omega(wk)$.*

*Proof.* It is similar to that of Theorem 7. In particular, the shattered set $S \subseteq \mathbb{R}^\kappa$ is the same and the class $\mathcal{F}$ of functions shattering $S$ is indexed in the same way. Hence we will just sketch the main differences with the linear-threshold case in the implementation of $\mathcal{F}$ on a recurrent network. The bit-extracting device in Theorem 7 can be replaced by the following system:

$$x_i^+ = 4x_i(1 - x_i). \tag{8}$$

A value of $x_i$ smaller than $1/2$ should be understood as encoding the binary digit 0 ("reject") and a value larger than $1/2$ the digit 1 ("accept"). By Lemma 10, any (finite) binary sequence can be produced by (8) with a suitable choice of $x_i(0)$. This system can be implemented by a subnetwork of two linear gates (computing $1 - x_i$ and $4x_i$) and one product gate. It produces an output at every other time step. Therefore we can only feed an input to the network at every other time step, too (the gaps in the input sequence can be filled by arbitrary, meaningless values).

The output of (8) should be selected if the current input $u$ is equal to $i \neq 0$. By Lemma 11, this can be done (approximately) as follows:

$$e = f_\epsilon(u, 0, x_1, \ldots, x_\nu). \tag{9}$$

Note that the subnetwork implementing this function has depth $\Theta(\log w)$, whence the condition $k = \Omega(\log w)$ in the lemma's statement (we need to add $\Theta(\log w)$ dummy inputs at the end of the input sequence). Since the network has to work only on a finite set of inputs, the construction will be correct if $\epsilon$ is small enough (this can be justified as in [8]).

Finally, the output unit accumulates the values of $e$, starting from the initial state $o = 0$. Note that these accumulated values are all (approximately) zero, except at most one of them. This is because any input in the shattered set $S$ of Theorem 9 has only one non-zero component. And whenever the current input component $u$ is zero, the function $f_\epsilon$ in (9) selects the first number in the sequence $(0, x_1, \ldots, x_\nu)$, that is, 0.

In order to implement this on a recurrent network, we have to introduce a delay since meaningful values of $e$ come only at every other time step. Therefore one would like to write

$$o^+ = \text{Id}(o) + e \tag{10}$$

where the identity function Id is implemented by a linear gate. An input would be rejected if the output at time $k$ is smaller than $1/2$; it would accepted if the output is larger than $1/2$. The only problem with this construction is that the output unit might accumulate non-zero values of $e$ which occur even before the first input can be processed. In the proof of Theorem 7 we have checked "by hand" that this problem does not occur. Here we prefer to use instead a special-purpose device: we replace (10) by

$$o^+ = I(o) + s_0 e \qquad (11)$$

where $s_0$ is designed to output 0 for the first few $T = O(\log \nu)$ time steps, and 1 thereafter. This can be done with the following system of $T+1$ units: $s_i^+ = s_{i+1}$ for $i = 0, \ldots, T-1$ and $s_T^+ = s_T$. These units are initialized as follows: $s_i(0) = 0$ for $i = 0, \ldots, T-1$, and $s_T(0) = 1$.

**Theorem 13.** *The VC dimension of recurrent architectures of linear and multiplication gates with $w$ weights receiving inputs of length $k = \Omega(\log w)$ is $\Omega(wk)$.*

*Proof.* The theorem follows from Lemma 12 and the (simple) simulation of networks with linear, multiplication and division gates by networks with linear and multiplication gates only ([8]). This simulation applies to feedforward as well as to recurrent networks. Note that since the length of the longest path in the network increases by a constant factor, it is necessary to pad the input sequence with $O(\log w)$ dummy inputs. This changes only the implied constants in the $\Omega$ symbols.

As in [8], this result makes it possible to prove good VC dimension lower bounds for a wide class of transfer functions. The most important case is the following:

*Proof of Theorem 6.* Linear and multiplication gates can be simulated by $\sigma$-gates as in [8]. The input sequence must be padded by a small number of dummy inputs as in the proof of Theorem 13.

## 5   Final Remarks

We have left several questions unanswered:

1. For piecewise-polynomial functions, can one close the gap between the $O(kw^2)$ upper bound and the $\Omega(kw)$ lower bound ?
2. This gap is even bigger for the standard sigmoid: $O(k^2 w^4)$ versus $\Omega(kw)$. A tight bound is probably too much to ask for since even for feedforward architectures there is a gap: $O(w^4)$ versus $\Omega(w^2)$. A less ambitious goal would be to replace the $k^2$ factor in the upper bound by $k$.
3. For threshold architectures, we have a tight $\Theta(w \log k)$ bound for $k \gg w$. However this tight bound applies only when $k$ is exponentially larger than $w$. It would be interesting to have a tight bound when $k$ is polynomial in $w$.

# References

1. E.B. Baum and D. Haussler, "What size net gives valid generalization?", *Neural Computation*, 1(1989), pp. 151-160.
2. Y. Bengio, *Neural Networks for Speech and Sequence Recognition*, Thompson Computer Press, Boston, 1996.
3. T.M. Cover, "Capacity problems for linear machines", in: *Pattern Recognition* (L. Kanal ed.), *Thompson Book Co.*, 1968, pp. 283-289
4. B. Dasgupta and E.D. Sontag, "Sample complexity for learning recurrent perceptron mappings," *IEEE Trans. Inform. Theory*, September 1996, to appear. (Summary in *Advances in Neural Information Processing Systems 8 (NIPS95)* (D.S. Touretzky, M.C. Moser, and M.E. Hasselmo, eds.), MIT Press, Cambridge, MA, 1996, pp. 204-210.)
5. C.L. Giles, G.Z. Sun, H.H. Chen, Y.C. Lee and D. Chen, "Higher order recurrent networks and grammatical inference", in *Advances in Neural Information Processing Systems 2*, D.S. Touretzky (ed.), Morgan Kaufmann, San Mateo, CA, 1990.
6. P. Goldberg and M. Jerrum, "Bounding the Vapnik-Chervonenkis dimension of concept classes parametrized by real numbers," *Machine Learning* 18(1995), pp. 131-148.
7. M. Karpinski and A. Macintyre, "Polynomial bounds for VC dimension of sigmoidal and general Pfaffian neural networks," *J. Computer Sys. Sci.*, to appear. (Summary in "Polynomial bounds for VC dimension of sigmoidal neural networks," in *Proc. 27th ACM Symposium on Theory of Computing, 1995*, pp. 200-208.)
8. P. Koiran and E.D. Sontag, "Neural networks with quadratic VC dimension," *J. Computer Sys. Sci.*, to appear. (Summary in *Advances in Neural Information Processing Systems 8 (NIPS95)* (D.S. Touretzky, M.C. Moser, and M.E. Hasselmo, eds.), MIT Press, Cambridge, MA, 1996, pp. 197-203.)
9. M. Matthews, "A state-space approach to adaptive nonlinear filtering using recurrent neural networks," *Proc. 1990 IASTED Symp. on Artificial Intelligence Applications and Neural Networks*, Zürich, pp. 197-200, July 1990.
10. M.M. Polycarpou, and P.A. Ioannou, "Neural networks and on-line approximators for adaptive control," in *Proc. Seventh Yale Workshop on Adaptive and Learning Systems*, pp. 93-798, Yale University, 1992.
11. H. Siegelmann and E.D. Sontag, "On the computational power of neural nets," *J. Comp. Syst. Sci.* 50(1995): 132-150.
12. H. Siegelmann and E.D. Sontag, "Analog computation, neural networks, and circuits," *Theor. Comp. Sci.* 131(1994): 331-360.
13. E.D. Sontag, *Mathematical Control Theory: Deterministic Finite Dimensional Systems*, Springer, New York, 1990.
14. E.D. Sontag, "Neural nets as systems models and controllers," in *Proc. Seventh Yale Workshop on Adaptive and Learning Systems*, pp. 73-79, Yale University, 1992.
15. E.D. Sontag, "Feedforward nets for interpolation and classification," *J. Comp. Syst. Sci.* 45(1992): 20-48.
16. A.M. Zador and B.A. Pearlmutter, "VC dimension of an integrate-and-fire neuron model," *Neural Computation* 8(1996): 611-624.

# Linear Algebraic Proofs of VC-Dimension Based Inequalities

Leonid Gurvits*

NEC Research Institute

4 Independence Way

Princeton, NJ 08540

and

DIMACS, Rutgers University

New Brunswick, NJ 08903

## Abstract

We apply linear algebra(polynomial) techniques to various VC-Dimension based inequalities. We explore connections between the sample compression and this technique for so called *maximum* classes and prove that *maximum* classes are connected subgraphs of a Boolean cube. We provide a fast(linear in the cardinality of the class for the fixed VC-dimension) interpolational algorithm for *maximum* classes. A new method to bound a pseudo-dimension for a class of cell-wise constant functions is proposed.

## Introduction

Like many important results (consider, for instance, Hall's theorem about perfect matchings) Sauer's Lemma [Sa72] already has several proofs. What is a reason to invent a new proof? Perhaps, to simplify, to shorten, but what is the most important, is to discover some new relations and properties; behind, in our case, the formal definition of VC-Dimension. (One mathematician has said that a good proof is one where you learned something after you did it.)

Returning to our subject, we think that the most enlightening (simple and short) proof of Sauer's Lemma is a Linear-Algebraic proof by P. Frankl and J. Pach

*Research at Rutgers partially supported by the US Air Force Grant AFOSR-94-0293.

[FP83, BF92], We will use the idea of this proof throughout in this paper.

The main three examples we consider below are Sauer-like inequality for k-valued case (Sauer's Lemma corresponds to binary case); projections, maximum classes and Welzl's approach to sample compression; and bounds on pseudo-dimension of so called cell-wise constant (polynomial) functions. In the first example we use, similarly to the binary case, only the spanning property of "short" monomials; in the second one we use their linear independence property; and in the third example we use the "new" property of VC-Dimension discovered in Frankl-Pach proof to get an upper bound on the pseudo-dimension of some important classes of functions.

The goal of this paper is twofold: it contains (we hope) new results and approaches, but also it could be very useful in teaching. We hope that our treatment of Welzl's approach to sample compression will be helpful to attack the still open problem how to compress nonmaximum classes.

## 1.  Spanning and Independence, Francl-Pach Theorem

Let us consider a finite set $X = \{x_1, ..., x_m\}$ and a system of functions $F = \{f_1, \cdots f_k\}, f_j : X \to R, 1 \le j \le k$.

Define a matrix,

$$M_{X,F} = (M_{X,F}(i,j); 1 \le i \le m, 1 \le j \le k), \quad M_{x,F}(i,j) = f_j(x_i).$$

In other words, functions are just m-dimensional vectors. If they span the entire m-dimensional linear space we say $F$ is spanning on $X$; if they are linearly independent we say $F$ is independent on $X$.

The following proposition is immediate.

**Proposition 1.**  If $F$ is spanning on $X$ then $m \le k$; if $F$ is independent on $X$ then $m \ge k.\square$

Surprisingly, **Proposition 1** allows sometimes to prove rather sophisticated combinatorial inequalities (see, for instance, [BF92]).

Let us first introduce some notations:

1.  **Boolean vectors** are just vectors with 0,1 entries, the set of all $N$-Dimensional Boolean vector (i.e. the Boolean cube) is $B_N$. The support of a Boolean vector $b \in B_N$ is the subset $S_b \subset 1, \cdots, N$ such that $i \in S_b$ iff $b_i = 1$. VC-Dimension of a family $X \subset B_N$ of Boolean vectors is the usual VC-Dimension of the set of their supports, i.e. the maximum $d$ such that there exists a subset $S \subset \{1, \cdots, N\}$ with cardinality $d$ and the restriction of $X$ on $S$

is equal to $B_d$. In other words $S$ is shattered by supports of vectors in $X$ .

2. **Monomials.** We will use the following notation: $x_1^{d_1} \cdots x_n^{dn}$ will be written as $x_D$, $D = (d_1, \cdots d_n)$;
$x_{i_1} \cdots x_{i_k}$ is denoted as $x_w$, where $w$ is a Boolean vector with $\{i_1, \cdots i_k\}$ being its support, $|w|$ as usual is the weight (number of ones) of $w$.

The following theorem was proved by P. Francl and J. Pach in 1983 [BF92].

**Theorem 1. (Francl-Pach, 83)**
If a set of Boolean vectors $X \subset B_N$ has VC-Dimension $d$ then a set of monomials of $x_w, w \in B_N, |w| \le d$ is spanning on $X$. $\square$

Before we go to the proof, we would like to make the following simple but useful comment: if $X = (Y_1, \cdots Y_m)$ then the family of all monomials $x_w$ such that $|w| \le d$ is spanning on $X$ iff any function $f : X \to R$ can be represented as $f = \sum_{|w| \le d} \alpha_w x_w$ (i.e. as a linear combination of short monomials). (The proof below is due to Jim Reeds [personal communication], but apparently it was already known in the coding community with $log(m)$ instead of VC-dimension.)

Proof of Theorem 1. From the comment just given it suffices to show that any interpolational problem $f(Y_i) = a_i$ can be solved by a linear combination of "short" monomials $x_w$ with $|w| \le d$. Obviously, it can be solved as a linear combination of all monomials $x_w, w \in B_N$. Therefore it is enough to prove that any monomial $x_w$ is a linear combination of "short" monomials when restricted to $X$. By a simple induction argument we need to prove this only for monomials $x_w, |w| = d + 1$. Consider without loss of generality $x_w = x_1 \cdots x_{d+1}$.
Since $VC(X) = d$ there exists at least one $d + 1$-dimensional boolean vector $(V_1, \cdots V_{d+1})$ such that there is no $Y_i \in X$ given that $Y_i = (V_1, \cdots V_{d+1}, \cdots)$. Consider the following change of variables

$$z_i = \begin{cases} x_i, & \text{if } V_i = 1 \\ 1 - x_i, & \text{if } V_i = 0. \end{cases}$$

Then the product $z_1 \cdots z_{d+1}$ restricted to $\{Y_1, \cdots Y_m\}$ is identically zero. But $0 \equiv z_1 \cdots z_{d+1} = \pm x_1 \cdots x_{d+1} + \sum(\pm \text{products of length} \le d)$. So, $x_1 x_2 \cdots x_{d+1}$ is the needed linear combination of short monomials. $\square$

Remark 1.    The original result by P. Frankl and J. Pach was formulated in terms of $s^*$-independence. The original proof was based on Moebius Transform, i.e. they used the "inclusion-exclusion" argument. In a binary case practically all "inclusion-exclusion" formulas can be obtained via a polynomial (moments) approach. This is basically what happened with the proof above. Also, perhaps the "polynomial nature" of Frankl-Pach result was lost in their proof(and formulation) and this explains why it was rediscovered a few times afterwards. But the Moebius Transform allows to generalize the Theorem 1 to more general partially ordered sets (see corresponding results in [BF92]).

**Example 1.  (Improved Sauer's Lemma )**
**Theorem 2.**
Suppose that $X \subset B_N, VC(X) = d$ and all boolean vectors in $X$ have the same weight, say $L$. Then $|X| \le \binom{N}{d}$.

Proof. We will prove that the family of monomials of length $d$ is spanning on $X$,from which it follows that $|X| \le \binom{N}{d}$.

First, it is clear that $L \ge d$.
Also, if $(x_1, \cdots x_N) \in X$ then $\frac{1}{L}(x_1 + \cdots + x_N) \equiv 1$.
Consider a monomial $x_{i_1} \cdots x_{i_k}, k < d$.
Then $x_{i_1} \cdots x_{i_k} = \frac{1}{L}(x_{i_1} \cdots x_{i_k})(x_1 + \cdots + x_N) = \frac{K}{L} x_{i_1} \cdots x_{i_k} + $ (monomials of length K+1).
Since $k < L$ hence $(1 - \frac{k}{L}) \ne 0$ and $x_{i_1} \cdots x_{i_k}$ is a linear combination of monomials of length $k + 1$. From this by simple induction it follows that any monomial of length less than $d$ is a linear combination of monomials of length $d$. The last observation and Theorem 1 proves the needed spanning property. $\square$

**Example 2.  k-valued Sauer's Lemma and Pollard's Pseudo-dimension.**

**Definition 1**
Let us consider a subset $Y \subset X_1 \times \cdots \times X_N, |X_i| = m_i + 1$. Assume WLOG that $X_i \subset R$.
Also, let us consider a cartesian product of families of maps $M = G_1 \times \cdots \times G_N$ where $G_i \subset \{0,1\}^{X_i}$. In other words, if $f = (f_1, \cdots, f_N) \in M$ and $x = (x_1, \cdots, x_N) \in Y$, then $f(x) = (f(x_1), \cdots, f(x_N)) \in \{0,1\}^N$. We define $f(Y) = \{f(x), x \in Y\}$. So, $f(Y)$ is a subset of a Boolean cube $B_N$.
Define M-VC dimension of $Y$ (will be denoted as $VC_M(Y)$) as a maximum $VC(f(Y))$ over $f \in M$. $\square$

Let us consider some popular examples:

Order each set $X_i = \{\alpha_1^i < \alpha_2^i \cdots < \alpha_{m(i)+1}^i\}$. Let us define $G_i = (f_i^1, \cdots f_i^{m(i)+1})$, where

$$f_i^k(\alpha_l^i) = \begin{cases} 1, & l \le k \\ 0, & l > k. \end{cases}$$

In a matrix form the family $G_i$ corresponds to $m(i) + 1$ by $m(i) + 1$ lower triangular matrix with the lower part including diagonal having all ones and upper part having all zeroes. This family gives the subgraph or Pollard's dimension. If the corresponding matrix is an identity matrix $I$ then the corresponding M-VC dimension is known as a graph dimension.

**Theorem 3.**

If $G_i$ is a spanning family of functions on $X_i (1 \le i \le N)$ then the set of monomials

$$\{x_{n_1}^{d_{n_1}} \cdots x_{n_i}^{d_{n_i}} \cdots x_{n_k}^{d_{n_k}} : 1 \le i \le k, 0 \le d_{n_i} \le m_{n_i}, 0 \le k \le d\}$$

is spanning on $Y$, where $d = VC_M(Y)$.

**Corollary 3.** Under assumptions of the Theorem 3

$$|Y| \le S_a(m_1, \cdots, m_N, d) = 1 + \sum_{i=1}^{N} m_i + \sum_{i<j} m_i m_j + \cdots + \sum_{1 \le i_1 < i_2 \cdots \le i_d \le N} m_{i_1} m_{i_2} \cdots m_{i_d}.$$

Note that if $m_i = R$, then $|Y| \le 1 + R \binom{N}{1} + \cdots + \binom{N}{d} R^d$.

Our proof will use the following claim.

**Claim 1.** Suppose that family of function $G_i$ is spanning on $X_i$. Then the family of functions $\prod_M =: \{f_1(x_1) \cdot f_2(x_2) \cdots f_N(x_N) : f_i \in G_i, 1 \le i \le N\}$ is spanning on $X_1 \times X_2 \cdots \times X_N$.

Proof of Claim 1. Let us associate with $G_i$, the matrix $M_{X_i, G_i}$ as defined in the beginning of the paper.
Then $M_{X_1 \times X_2 \cdots \times X_N, G_1 \times G_2 \cdots \times G_N} = M_{X_1, G_1} \otimes M_{X_2, G_2} \cdots \otimes M_{X_N, G_N}$, where $\otimes$ stands for the usual tensor product of matrices. It is well known and easy to prove that Rank $(A \otimes B) =$ Rank $(A) \cdot$ Rank $(B)$.
The spanning property means that Rank $(M_{X_i, G_i}) = |X_i|$.
So Rank $(M_{X_1 \times X_2 \cdots \times X_N, G_1 \times G_2 \cdots \times G_N}) = |X_1| \cdot |X_2| \cdots |X_N|$, which proves the claim. $\square$

(This claim above is a standard statement in Linear Algebra. It is included in order to make the paper self contained.)

**Proof of Theorem 3**
Since $G_i$ is spanning on $X_i$ hence it follows from the Claim 1 that any function on $Y$ can be represented as a linear combination of products $f_1(x_1) \cdots f_N(x_N)$, $f_i \in G_i$. Now we can use the "Boolean" result about usual VC-Dimension, i.e. Theorem 1:

$f_1(x_1) \cdots f_N(x_N)$ is a linear combination of short products, i.e.

$$f_{n_1}(x_{n_1}) \cdots f_{n_k}(x_{n_k}), k \leq d = VC_M(Y).$$

Also, any function $f_i(x_i)$ can be represented as a polynomial: $f_i(x_i) = a_{m_i} x_i^{m_i} + \cdots + a_0$, which is a standard Lagrange interpolating polynomial.
Putting all this together we get that the set of monomials $\{x_{n_1}^{d_{n_1}} \cdots x_{n_k}^{d_{n_k}} : 0 \leq d_{n_i} \leq m_{n_i}, 0 \leq k \leq d\}$ is spanning on $Y$. To prove the corollary we just count the number of corresponding monomials and apply Proposition 1. $\square$

**Remark 2.** It may seem that we "cooked" Definition 1 "for the sake" of the proof of Theorem 3. But this is not the case since the corresponding inequality for Pollard's and Graph Dimensions was proved rather recently in [HL].
In our opinion, the proof from [HL] followed the combinatorial proof of Sauer's Lemma. Our proof, which is also more general, instead to follow previous proof used an extra property (spanning) discovered in Frankl-Pach Theorem. The same can be said about our next example.

**Example 3. (Projections, Welzl's Approach to Sample Compression, Connectivity of Maximum Classes.).**

In all examples above we used only spanning property. Below we will take advantage of an independence.

**Definition 2.** Consider $Y \subset X_1 \times X_2 \times \cdots \times X_N$, $S \subset \{1, \cdots, N\}$. Then the S-projection of $Y$ denoted as $P_S(Y)$ is the set of all restriction of $Y$ on $X_{i_1} \times X_{i_2} \times \cdots \times X_{i_l}$, where $S = \{i_1, \cdots, i_l\}$.

**Proposition 2.** Let us consider $Y \subset X_1 \times X_2 \times \cdots \times X_N$.
If the set of monomials $\{x_{n_1}^{d_{n_1}} \cdots x_{n_k}^{d_{n_k}} : 0 \leq d_{n_i} \leq m_{n_i}, 0 \leq k \leq d\}$ is independent on $Y$, then the S-projected set of monomials $\{x_{n_1}^{d_{n_1}} \cdots x_{n_k}^{d_{n_k}} : 0 \leq d_{n_i} \leq m_{n_i}, n_i \in S, 0 \leq k \leq d\}$ is independent on $P_S(Y)$ for all $S \subset \{1, \cdots, N\}$. $\square$

This proposition is also obvious, it just uses the fact that any subset of an independent set is also independent. Now we have the theorem.

**Theorem 4.**

Consider, as in Theorem 3, $Y \subset X_1 \times X_2 \cdots \times X_N, VC_M(Y) = d$ and $|Y| = S_a(m_1, m_2, \cdots, m_N, d)$. Then for any $S = \{i_1, \cdots i_k\} \subset \{1, 2, \cdots N\}$ a cardinality of S-projection $|P_S(Y)| = S_a(m_{i_1}, \cdots m_{i_k}, d)$.

Proof. If $|Y| = S_a(m_1, m_2, \cdots, m_N, d)$ then the set of monomials $\{x_{n_1}^{d_{n_1}} \cdots x_{n_k}^{d_{n_k}} : 0 \le d_{n_i} \le m_{n_i}, 0 \le k \le d\}$ is independent on $Y$ by the Theorem 3.

From Proposition 2 the $S$-projected set of monomials is also independent on $P_S(Y)$, so $|P_S(Y)| \ge S_a(m_{i_i}, \cdots, m_{i_k}, d)$ by the Proposition 1. But $VC_M(P_S(Y)) \le VC_M(Y) = d$. So, $|P_S(Y)| \le S_a(m_{i_1}, \cdots, m_{i_k}, d)$, which gives that $|P_S(Y)| = S_a(m_{i_1}, \cdots, m_{i_k}, d)$. $\square$

It is clear that the above theorem works in 2-valued and k-valued cases as well. The Boolean case was proved by E.Welzl (see [We], [FW95]) by a purely combinatorial inductive counting argument.

Let us go now to the Boolean case. We consider $Y \subset B_N$, $VC(Y) = d$ and
$$|Y| = 1 + \binom{N}{1} + \cdots + \binom{N}{d} = \Phi(N, d),$$
such $Y$ is called *maximum* class.

It follows from Theorem 1 that the family of all $d$-short monomials $\{x_w, w \subset \{1, \cdots N\}, |w| \le d\}$ is spanning and independent on $Y$.

Let us fix a first bit, i.e.

$$Y = \begin{pmatrix} 1 & A \\ 0 & A \\ 1 & B \\ 0 & C \end{pmatrix};$$

$A, B, C$ are pairwise disjoint subsets of $B_{N-1}$.
We group above all elements in $Y$ which are adjacent in $B_N$ through first bit (corresponds to $A$) and all others correspond to $B$ and $C$.

Let us define

$$\hat{Y} = \begin{pmatrix} 1 & A \\ 0 & A \\ 0 & B \\ 0 & C \end{pmatrix}.$$

It is clear that $\hat{Y}$ also has $\Phi(N, d)$ distinct elements and $VC(\hat{Y}) \le VC(Y)$. ( This elegant transformation is known as shifting and was already used for another proof of Sauer's Lemma).

**Claim 1 ([We],[FW95].** A subset $A \subset B_{N-1}$ is not empty, $VC(A) = d - 1$ and $|A| = \Phi(N - 1, d - 1)$.

Proof. Indeed,the $\{2, \cdots, N\}$-projection of $Y$ is $\{A, B, C\}$.It follows from Theorem 4 that the cardinality $|\{A, B, C\}| = \Phi(N - 1, d)$. But $\Phi(N, d) = |Y| = |A| + |\{A, B, C\}|$. So,$|A| = \Phi(N, d) - \Phi(N - 1, d) = \Phi(N - 1, d - 1)$.From this it follows that $VC(A) = d - 1$ since ,obviously, $VC(A) \leq d - 1$. $\square$

Combining Claim 1 and the shifting technique it is not difficult to prove the following result connecting VC-dimension and geometry in a rather surprising way.

**Theorem 5.** If $Y \subset B_N$ is a maximum class then it is a connected subgraph of $B_N$. $\square$

Proof of Theorem 6. It follows from the Theorem 5 that the number of edges in a maximum class with VC-dimension $d$ is equal to number of edges in the "canonical" class of all boolean vectors with the weight less or equal than $d$. It is known(follows by a standart reasoning) that in this maximum case the shifting will end up at the "canonical" class and each step in the shifting can only add extra edges.So,the number of edges in
$G1 =: \{(1A), (0A), (1B), (0C)\}$ is the same as in $G2 =: \{(1A), (0A), (0B), (0C)\}$.
From this it follows that there are no edges between $(0B)$ and $(0C)$. It is enough now to prove that the connectivity of $G2$ implies the connectivity of $G1$. We claim that any path in $G2$ can be transformed into a path in $G1$.
Indeed,sinse we don't have edges between $(0B)$ and $(0C)$ the only problem is with edges from $(0B)$ to $(0A)$ (these edges don't present in $G1$). But any such edge $(0b) \rightarrow (0a)$ in $G2$ can be replaced by the path of length 2 in $G1 : (1b) \rightarrow (1a) \rightarrow (0a)$.This ends the proof. $\square$

We conjecture that in Theorem 6 the maximum class $Y$ is at least $d$-connected, i.e. removing any $d - 1$ vertices won't destroy its connectivity.

**Example 4. Cell-Wise Constant Functions.**

Let us consider a set $X$ with $\sigma$-algebra $F$ and a measure $\mu$. Suppose that $X_1, \cdots, X_m \in F$ and define cells generated by the family $\{X_1, \cdots X_m\}$ as the following subset of $B_m$ :$C_e = \{(I_{X_1}(x), I_{X_2}(x), \cdots I_{X_m}(x)) : x \in X\}$, where $I_{X_i}$ is an indicator function of a subset $X_i$. So, each cell $b \in C_e$ corresponds to some measurable subset of $X$. Function $f : X \rightarrow R$ is called cell-wise constant if it is constant on each cell.

**Proposition 3.** If $VC(C_e) = d$ then $\int_X f(x)\mu(dx) = C_0 + \sum C_{i_1, \cdots, i_k}\mu(X_{i_1} \cap \cdots \cap X_{i_k})$, where $1 \leq i_1 < \cdots < i_k \leq m, k \leq d; C_0, C_{i_1, \cdots, i_k}$ depend on $f$. $\square$

Obviously, this result is a direct corollary of the Theorem 1 since the function

$f$ can be represented as a linear combination of "short" product of indicator functions. One of the possible important applications of the Proposition 3 is an exact shortening of the inclusion-exclusion formula.

Let us consider $m$ perceptrons in $R^d$; i.e. $h_i = sgn(< a_i, x > +b_i)$, where $a_i \in R^d$ and $b_i \in R(1 \leq i \leq m)$. The corresponding hyperplanes partitioned $R^d$ into cells, it is easy to see that VC-Dimension of cells is equal to $d$ in this case. So any cell-wise constant function $f = f(h_1(x), \cdots, h_m(x)) = C_o + \sum C_{i_1, \cdots, i_k} h_{i_1} \cdots h_{i_m}$,
where $1 \leq i_1 < \cdots < i_k \leq m, k \leq d; C_0, C_{i_1, \cdots, i_k}$ depend on $f$. $\square$

This representation allows us to estimate a pseudo-dimension $D$ of the class of these cell-wise constant functions using Theorem 2.3 in [GJ93], it is at most quadratic in the number of weights, i.e. $D \leq O(m^{2d})$.

We think that this bound could be improved but the most important conclusion is that in this way one can estimate a pseudo-dimension for a rather wide class of cell-wise constant functions. Instead of $sgn$ one could have more complicated $k$-valued logical transformer (in this case one has to apply Theorem 3) and instead of affine functions one could have, for instance, polynomials. Also, in the very same way one can deal with functions which are cell-wise polynomial.

Let us discuss some computational aspects of cell-wise constant functions. Natural questions to ask are:

1. How difficult is it to compute coefficients $C_{i_1, \cdots, i_k}$?

2. What is a bound on $l_1$ norm of coefficients $\sum |C_{i_1, \cdots, i_k}|$ in terms of $max_x |f(h_l(x), \cdots, h_m(x))|$.

We will answer the above questions in the case when the class of cells is maximum.
Suppose that $Y \subset B_N$ is a maximum class and $VC(Y) = d; F$ is a set of all $d$-short monomial $\{x_\omega, |\omega| \leq d, \omega \in B_N\}$.
Then the matrix $M_{X,F}$(see the beginning of the Chapter 1) is square and invertible by Theorem 1.Moreover its determinant $det(M_{X,F}) = \pm 1$ since Theorem 1 clearly holds for any commutative field(even ring).The complexity question is about the complexity of a solution of the system of linear equations $M_{X,F}x = y$; the second question is about an upper worst case bound for the norm $\| M_{X,F}^{-1} \|_{l_\infty \to l_1}$, where we consider $M_{X,F}^{-1} : l_\infty \to l_1$. We will use below the notation $C(N, d)$ for the worst case complexity and the notation $L(N, d)$ for the largest $\| M_{X,F}^{-1} \|_{l_\infty \to l_1}$ over all maximum classes $Y \subset B_N$ with $VC(Y) = d$.

We again fix the first bit and consider

$$Y = \begin{pmatrix} 1 & A \\ 0 & A \\ 0 & B \\ 1 & C \end{pmatrix}$$

and $Y \subset B_N$ is a maximum class with VC-Dimension equal to $d$.

We know that $A$ is not empty, $A$ is a maximum class with VC equal to d-1 and $A \cup B \cup C$ is a maximum class with VC equal to $d$.

Let us consider an interpolational problem:

$$Y = \left. \begin{array}{ccc} 0A & \rightarrow & f_1 \\ 1A & \rightarrow & f_2 \\ 0B & \rightarrow & f_3 \\ 1C & \rightarrow & f_4 \end{array} \right\} = f.$$

The function $f$ has unique representation $f = \sum_{|w| \leq d} C_w x_w = x_1 P_1(x_2, \cdots x_n) + Q_1(x_2, \cdots, x_N)$, where $deg(P_1) \leq d - 1$, $\deg(Q_1) \leq d$ .

Let us define $\tilde{P}_1(x_2, \cdots x_n)$ as a unique solution to the following interpolational problem:
$A \rightarrow f_2 - f_1$ (remember $A$ is also maximum class with VC dimension equal to d-1).
So, $deg(\tilde{P}) \leq d - 1$, and $\tilde{P}$ is unique.

Then

$$f - x_1 \tilde{P}_1 = \left. \begin{array}{ccc} 0A & \rightarrow & f_1 \\ 1A & \rightarrow & f_1 \\ 0B & \rightarrow & f_3 \\ 1C & \rightarrow & f_4 - \tilde{P}_1(C) \end{array} \right\} \rightarrow q$$

We can interpolate $q$ by solving the following interpolational problem in $(x_2, \cdots x_n)$:

$$\begin{array}{ccc} A & \rightarrow & f_1 \\ B & \rightarrow & f_3 \\ C & \rightarrow & f_4 - \tilde{P}(C) \end{array}$$

Again, $A \cup B \cup C$ is a maximum class with VC dimension equal to $d$, so $q = \tilde{Q}_1(x_2, \cdots x_N), deg(\tilde{Q}_1) \leq d$. Using uniqueness we get that $P_1 = \tilde{P}_1$ and $Q_1 = \tilde{Q}_1$, which gives a recursive way to solve the above interpolational problem for maximum classes excluding bit by bit.

But this "depth" recursion is not the best way unless the class $C$ is always empty. The problem is in evaluating $\tilde{P}_1(C)$.Fortunatelly,the polynomial nature of our problem suggests that we do not need to compute $\tilde{Q}_1$ at all. Indeed,we can do the same procedure using any bit(Theorems 4 and 5),which will produce $N$ unique decompositions:

$$f = \sum_{|w| \leq d} C_w x_w = x_i P_i + Q_i, \text{ where } deg(P_i) \leq d-1, \deg(Q_i) \leq d; 1 \leq i \leq N$$

.The polynomials $P_i = \tilde{P}_i$ and $Q_i = \tilde{Q}_i$ depend on all variables but $x_i$.

Again using uniqueness,we notice that the part $x_i P_i$ contains all monomials which contain the variable $x_i$ and this is it.Of course,we should find out a constant term but this is easy.Moreover,let us assume, to make life a bit simpler, that the vector of all zeroes is in $Y$. Putting all this together, we get the following inequalities:

$C(N,d) \leq N(C(N-1,d-1) + \Phi(N-1,d-1))$ and $L(N,d) \leq 2N(L(N-1,d-1)) + 1$.

Notice that the term $\Phi(N-1,d-1)$ in the first inequality and the factor 2 in the second one are there because of the $\Phi(N-1,d-1)$ substraction in the definition of polynomials $\tilde{P}_i$.

Since $\Phi(N,d) = O(N^d)$ for a fixed $d$ hence we have the following theorem.

**Theorem 6.** Both $C(N,d)$ and $L(N,d)$ are $O(\Phi(N,d))$ for the fixed $d$. $\square$

(It is not difficult to prove using tensor products that $L(d,d) = 3^d$.)

The next theorem also follows directly from the above considerations.

**Theorem 7.**Suppose that $Y$ is a maximum class and $f : Y \to R$.Then the function $f$ can be represented as a polynomial of degree less or equal than $k$ iff $deg(\tilde{P}_i) \leq k-1$ for all $1 \leq i \leq N$. (For $k = 1$ this result holds for all connected subgraphs of $B_N$.)$\square$

**Remark 3.** The "depth" recursion above also has its merits.It can be applied to any(nonmaximum) class $Y$ with $VC$-dimension equal to $d$ to find out an interpolational(nonunique) polynomial $P$ with $deg(P) \leq d$.Moreover,this recursion gives an alternative, recursive in $N$ and $d$, proof of Theorem 1. Indeed,we used only two clear facts to consruct $P$: $VC(A) \leq d-1$ and $VC(\{A,B,C\}) \leq d$.Notice how it really close to the inductive proof of Sauer's Lemma:

$$|Y| = |A| + |\{A, B, C\}| \leq \Phi(N - 1, d - 1) + \Phi(N - 1, d) = \Phi(N, d). \quad \square$$

## Conclusions and future work.

The linear(in number of cells) interpolational algorithm for maximum classes presented above seems to be very related to the corresponding compession algorithm (Theorem 10 in [FW]). We think that a linear algorithm(if any) for general classes with VC-dimension equal to $d$ will provide good clues to the general compression case.Another natural future work is an extension of Theorems 5,6,7 to the $k$-valued case.We think this should not be that difficult.We anticipate several "compexity" applications of Theorem 6 based on Proposition 3: volume computation,estimation of means of maximums of random variables,covering times for Markov Chains and so on.Perhaps, graphs studied in Theorem 5 deserve much deeper treatment. It is easy to see that Theorem 1 holds not just for monomials but for any product-basis, say for parities $\{-1^{<x,w>}, w \in B_N, |w| \leq d\}$. This simple observation can also lead to some new complexity results.There are many combinatorial inequalities with the same right side and "polynomial background" as in Sauer's. One of them is famous Frankl-Wilson inequality [FrWi81].By the way,it is our guess that this inequality suggested the Frankl-Pach result about the VC-dimension.Are there analogs of Theorems 5,6,7 for the corresponding maximum classes?

### Acknowledgments

This work benefited from discussions with S. Ben-David, P. Bartlett, R. Williamson, P. Coiran, E. Sontag, and M. Warmuth. The paper (and the author) owes a lot to comments of anonymous referees. It is my pleasure to acknowledge a great influence on this paper of a great book [ BF92] .

## References

[BF92] L.Babai and P.Frankl. Linear algebra methods in combinatorics with applications to geometry and computer science. (Preliminary Version 2),1992, Dept. of Computer Science,The University of Chicago.

[FrWi81] P.Frankl and R.M.Wilson. Intersection theorems with geometric consequences. Combinatorica 1(1981),357-368.

[FW95] S.Floyd and M.Warmuth. Sample compression,learnability,and the Vapnik-Chervonenkis dimension, Machine Learning,,1-36,1995.

[We] E. Welzl.(1987). Complete range spaces.Unpublished notes.


[HL] D.Haussler and Phil Long.(1991) A generalization of Sauer's lemma, UCSC-CRL-90-15.


[GJ93] P.Goldberg and M.Jerrum (1993). Bounding the Vapnik-Chervonenkis dimension of concepts classes parameterized by real numbers. In proc. 6th Annual ACM Conference on Computational Learning Theory.


[Sa72] N.Sauer (1972). On the density of families of sets. J.Comb. Theory,Series A 13(1972), 145-147.

# A Result Relating Convex n-widths to Covering Numbers with Some Applications to Neural Networks

Jonathan Baxter and Peter Bartlett

Department of Systems Engineering
Research School of Information Sciences and Engineering
Australian National University
Canberra 0200, Australia

**Abstract.** In general, approximating classes of functions defined over high-dimensional input spaces by linear combinations of a fixed set of basis functions or "features" is known to be hard. Typically, the worst-case error of the best basis set decays only as fast as $\Theta\left(n^{-1/d}\right)$, where $n$ is the number of basis functions and $d$ is the input dimension. However, there are many examples of high-dimensional pattern recognition problems (such as face recognition) where linear combinations of small sets of features do solve the problem well. Hence these function classes do not suffer from the "curse of dimensionality" associated with more general classes. It is natural then, to look for characterizations of high-dimensional function classes that nevertheless are approximated well by linear combinations of small sets of features. In this paper we give a general result relating the error of approximation of a function class to the covering number of its "convex core". For one-hidden-layer neural networks, covering numbers of the class of functions computed by a single hidden node upper bound the covering numbers of the convex core. Hence, using standard results we obtain upper bounds on the approximation rate of neural network classes.

## 1    Introduction

A common approach to solving high-dimensional pattern recognition problems is to choose a small set of relevant features, linear combinations of which approximate well the functions in the target class. Another way of viewing the small set of features is as a low-dimensional representation of the input space. Recently there have been a number of papers showing how such feature sets can be *learnt* (*e.g.* [1, 8, 2]) using neural network and related techniques.

The assumption that a class of functions can be approximated well by linear combinations of a small set of features is a very strong one, for it is known that approximating the class of functions with domain $[0, 1]^d$ and bounded first derivative to within error $\varepsilon$ requires at least $1/\varepsilon^d$ basis functions. The purpose of this paper is to gain a better understanding of the factors governing whether a function class possesses a low-dimensional representation or not. A theorem is presented showing that the dimension of the representation required to achieve an approximation error of less than $\varepsilon$ is closely related to the size of the smallest $\varepsilon$-covering number of the "convex core" of the function class. We show that the covering numbers of the convex core of a single-hidden-layer neural network are upper-bounded by covering numbers of the class of functions computed by a single hidden node, which enables an easy calculation of upper bounds on the approximation error in this case. We give upper bounds for several hidden node classes, including general VC classes, linear threshold classes and classes smoothly parameterized by several real variables.

The remainder of the paper is organized as follows. Introductory definitions are presented in Section 2 along with some simple results. The main theorem is given in Section 3, along with examples showing that it is tight. Applications of the theorem to neural networks are given in Section 4.

## 2 Preliminary Definitions

Let $(X, \|\cdot\|)$ be a Banach space. For any $S \subset X$ and any $f \in X$, define

$$\|f - S\| := \inf_{s \in S} \|f - s\|.$$

We say that $S$ is *convex* if $s_1, \ldots, s_n \in S$ implies $\sum_{i=1}^n \lambda_i s_i \in S$ for any real $\lambda_1, \ldots, \lambda_n$ such that $\sum_{i=1}^n |\lambda_i| \le 1$. For any $S \subseteq X$, define

$$\mathrm{con}(S) := \left\{ \sum_{i=1}^n \lambda_i s_i : \sum_{i=1}^n |\lambda_i| \le 1, s_i \in S, i = 1, \ldots, n \right\},$$

*i.e.* $\mathrm{con}(S)$ is the set of all convex combinations of $n$ elements from $S$. Let $\overline{\mathrm{co}}(S)$ denote the set of all $f \in X$ such that $\lim_{n \to \infty} \|f - \mathrm{con}(S)\| = 0$. Similarly, define

$$\mathrm{lin}_n(S) := \left\{ \sum_{i=1}^n \lambda_i s_i : s_i \in S, i = 1, \ldots, n \right\},$$

and let $\overline{\mathrm{lin}}(S)$ denote the set of all $f \in X$ such that $\lim_{n \to \infty} \|f - \mathrm{lin}_n(S)\| = 0$.

**Definition 1** *For any $K \subseteq X$, define the* convex n-width *of $K$ by*

$$c_n(K) := \inf_{\phi_1, \ldots, \phi_n \in X} \sup_{f \in K} \|f - \mathrm{con}(\{\phi_1, \ldots, \phi_n\})\|.$$

Note that $c_n(K)$ is similar to the *Kolmogorov n-width* $d_n(K)$ [7], except that instead of arbitrary linear combinations of the $\phi_1, \ldots, \phi_n$, the approximation has to be achieved with convex combinations.

**Definition 2** *The* Kolmogorov n-width *of $K \subseteq X$ is*

$$d_n(K) := \inf_{\phi_1, \ldots, \phi_n \in X} \sup_{f \in K} \|f - \mathrm{lin}_n(\{\phi_1, \ldots, \phi_n\})\|.$$

For $K \subseteq X$, let $\mathcal{N}(\varepsilon, K)$ denote the size of the smallest $\varepsilon$-cover of $K$, i.e. the size of the smallest set $\{\phi_1, \ldots, \phi_N\} \subset X$ such that for all $f \in K$ there exists $\phi_i$ such that $\|f - \phi_i\| \leq \varepsilon$. If there is no such set then set $\mathcal{N}(\varepsilon, K) := \infty$.

**Definition 3** *For any $K \subseteq X$, define*

$$\mathcal{N}_{\text{co}}(\varepsilon, K) := \min_{S \subseteq X : \overline{\text{co}}(S) \supseteq K} \mathcal{N}(\varepsilon, S). \tag{1}$$

*If $S \subseteq X$ is such that $\overline{\text{co}}(S) \supseteq K$ and $\mathcal{N}(\varepsilon, S) = \mathcal{N}_{\text{co}}(\varepsilon, K)$, then we say $S$ is a convex $\varepsilon$-core of $K$.*

Note that there always exists at least one convex $\varepsilon$-core of $K$ (if $\mathcal{N}_{\text{co}}(\varepsilon, K) = \infty$ then we can set $S = K$, otherwise the fact that $\mathcal{N}(\varepsilon, S)$ is integer valued means that the min in (1) must be attained for some $S$).

**Definition 4** *A space $X$ is centred if, for every $\varepsilon > 0$ and every subset $S \subseteq X$ with diameter $\sup_{a,b \in S} \|a - b\| = 2\varepsilon$, there is a point $c$ in $X$ from which every point in $S$ is no further than $\varepsilon$.*

## 3  Results

**Theorem 1** *For any set $K \subseteq X$ and for all $\varepsilon > 0$,*

1. *if $n < \mathcal{N}_{\text{co}}(\varepsilon, K) - 1$ then $c_n(K) \geq \varepsilon$, and if in addition $X$ is centred then $c_n(K) > \varepsilon$,*
2. *if $n \geq \mathcal{N}_{\text{co}}(\varepsilon, K)$ then $c_n(K) \leq \varepsilon$.*

**Proof**
*Part 1:* Suppose first that $X$ is centred. We show that $c_n(K) \leq \varepsilon$ implies $n + 1 \geq \mathcal{N}_{\text{co}}(\varepsilon, K)$. Fix $\delta > 0$. If $c_n(K) \leq \varepsilon$ then there exists $\phi_1, \ldots, \phi_n$ such that for all $f \in K$ there exists $\lambda_1, \ldots, \lambda_n$ with $\sum_{i=1}^{n} |\lambda_i| \leq 1$ and

$$\left\| f - \sum_{i=1}^{n} \lambda_i \phi_i \right\| \leq \varepsilon + \delta.$$

Set $\phi_0 := 0$, $\alpha := \varepsilon + \delta$ and let

$$S := \bigcup_{i=0}^{n} B_\alpha(\phi_i),$$

where $B_\alpha(\phi_i) := \{f \in X : \|f - \phi_i\| \leq \alpha\}$. Note that $\mathcal{N}(\alpha, S) \leq n + 1$. We show that $\overline{\text{co}}(S) \supseteq K$ and so $\mathcal{N}_{\text{co}}(\alpha, K) \leq \mathcal{N}(\alpha, S) \leq n + 1$. Letting $\delta \to 0$ (*i.e.* $\alpha \to \varepsilon^+$) gives the result because in a centred space the covering numbers are continuous from the right (see Theorems III and V in [5]).

So fix $f \in K$ and choose a convex combination $\sum_{i=1}^{n} \lambda_i \phi_i$ so that $\|f - \sum_{i=1}^{n} \lambda_i \phi_i\| \le \alpha$ as above. Set $\lambda_0 := 1 - \sum_{j=1}^{n} |\lambda_j|$ and for each $i = 0, \dots, n$,

$$\phi_i' := \phi_i + \text{sign}(\lambda_i) \left( f - \sum_{j=1}^{n} \lambda_j \phi_j \right)$$

Note that $\sum_{j=0}^{n} |\lambda_j| = 1$ and for each $i = 0, \dots, n$,

$$\|\phi_i - \phi_i'\| = \left\| f - \sum_{j=1}^{n} \lambda_j \phi_j \right\| \le \alpha,$$

hence $\phi_i' \in S$ for each $i = 0, \dots, n$. Now,

$$\left\| f - \sum_{i=0}^{n} \lambda_i \phi_i' \right\| = \left\| f - \lambda_0 \left( f - \sum_{j=1}^{n} \lambda_j \phi_j \right) - \right.$$
$$\left. \sum_{i=1}^{n} \lambda_i \left[ \phi_i + \text{sign}(\lambda_i) \left( f - \sum_{j=1}^{n} \lambda_j \phi_j \right) \right] \right\|$$
$$= \left\| \left( 1 - \lambda_0 - \sum_{i=1}^{n} |\lambda_i| \right) f + \sum_{i=1}^{n} \lambda_i \phi_i \left( \lambda_0 - 1 + \sum_{j=1}^{n} |\lambda_j| \right) \right\|$$
$$= 0,$$

and so $f \in \overline{\text{co}(S)}$, as required. (We have actually proved the stronger result that $f \in \text{co}_n(S)$.)

The argument when $X$ is not centred is almost identical. In this case, we show that $c_n(K) < \epsilon$ implies the existence of $\phi_1, \dots, \phi_n$ satisfying similar conditions, but with $\alpha$ replaced by a quantity smaller than $\epsilon$. In this case, we do not need continuity of the covering numbers.

*Part 2:* We show that if $n = \mathcal{N}_{\text{co}}(\epsilon, K)$ then $c_n(K) \le \epsilon$. Part 2 then follows because if $n' > n$ then $c_{n'}(K) \le c_n(K)$. So let $n = \mathcal{N}_{\text{co}}(\epsilon, K)$ and let $S$ be a convex $\epsilon$-core of $K$ (recall by the remarks following Definition 3 that such an $S$ always exists). By definition, there exists $\hat{S} := \{\phi_1, \dots, \phi_n\} \subset X$ such that for all $s \in S$ there exists $\phi_i \in \hat{S}$ such that $\|s - \phi_i\| \le \epsilon$. As $\overline{\text{co}(S)} \supseteq K$, for all $f \in K$ and $\delta > 0$ we can find $f_1, \dots, f_N \in S$ and $\lambda_1, \dots, \lambda_N$ such that $\sum_{i=1}^{N} |\lambda_i| \le 1$ and $\|f - \sum_{i=1}^{N} \lambda_i f_i\| \le \delta$. For each $i = 1, \dots, N$, choose $\hat{f}_i \in \hat{S}$ such that $\|f_i - \hat{f}_i\| \le \epsilon$. Note that each $\hat{f}_j$ is one of the $\phi_i$'s, so for each $i = 1, \dots, n$ define $\lambda_i' := \sum_{j: \hat{f}_j = \phi_i} \lambda_j$. Note that $\sum_{i=1}^{n} |\lambda_i'| \le \sum_{i=1}^{N} |\lambda_i| \le 1$, hence $\sum_{i=1}^{n} \lambda_i' \phi_i$ is a convex combination of the $\phi_i$'s. Now,

$$\left\| f - \sum_{i=1}^{n} \lambda_i' \phi_i \right\| = \left\| f - \sum_{i=1}^{N} \lambda_i \hat{f}_i \right\|$$

$$\leq \left\| f - \sum_{i=1}^{N} \lambda_i f_i \right\| + \left\| \sum_{i=1}^{N} \lambda_i f_i - \sum_{i=1}^{N} \lambda_i \hat{f}_i \right\|$$

$$\leq \delta + \sum_{i=1}^{N} |\lambda_i| \left\| f_i - \hat{f}_i \right\|$$

$$\leq \delta + \varepsilon.$$

Letting $\delta \to 0$ shows that $c_n(K) \leq \varepsilon$, as required. $\square$

### 3.1 Theorem 1 is as tight as possible

There is a gap of "1" in Theorem 1, in the sense that when $n = \mathcal{N}_{co}(\varepsilon, K) - 1$ we don't know whether $c_n(K) \leq \varepsilon$ or $c_n(K) \geq \varepsilon$. In this section we show the gap is necessary: there exist classes for which $c_{\mathcal{N}_{co}(\varepsilon, K)-1}(K) > \varepsilon$ and also classes for which $c_{\mathcal{N}_{co}(\varepsilon, K)-1}(K) \leq \varepsilon$. The first case is trivial; just consider the class consisting of a single non-zero element $K = \{\phi \neq 0\}$. Clearly $\mathcal{N}_{co}(\varepsilon, K) = 1$ for all $\varepsilon \geq 0$, but $c_0(K) = \|\phi\| > 0$.

To demonstrate the second case we need a lemma.

**Lemma 2** *If $c_n(K) < \infty$ then $c_n(K) = d_n(K)$.*

**Proof**
For any $S \subseteq X$, define

$$\text{lin}_n^{\Lambda}(S) := \left\{ \sum_{i=1}^{n} \lambda_i s_i : \sum_{i=1}^{n} |\lambda_i| \leq \Lambda, s_i \in S, i = 1, \ldots, n \right\}.$$

Let $\varepsilon = d_n(K) \leq c_n(K) < \infty$ and suppose that for all $\delta > 0$ there exists $\phi_1, \ldots, \phi_n \in X$ and $\Lambda < \infty$ such that

$$\sup_{f \in K} \left\| f - \text{lin}_n^{\Lambda}(\{\phi_1, \ldots, \phi_n\}) \right\| < \varepsilon + \delta.$$

Then $c_n(K) = \varepsilon$ also because $\text{co}_n(\Lambda S) = \text{lin}_n^{\Lambda}(S)$. So we need only consider the case in which there exists $\delta > 0$ such that for all $\phi_1, \ldots, \phi_n$ and $\Lambda < \infty$,

$$\sup_{f \in K} \left\| f - \text{lin}_n^{\Lambda}(\{\phi_1, \ldots, \phi_n\}) \right\| \geq \varepsilon + \delta.$$

Equivalently, we assume that for all $S = \{\phi_1, \ldots, \phi_n\}$ for which $\sup_{f \in K} \|f - \text{lin}_n(S)\| < \varepsilon + \delta$, there exists a sequence $(f_N)_{N=1}^{\infty}$ in $K$ such that if $\lambda_{N1}, \ldots, \lambda_{Nn}$ satisfy

$$\left\| f_N - \sum_{i=1}^{n} \lambda_{Ni} \phi_i \right\| < \varepsilon + \delta \tag{2}$$

then $\sum_{i=1}^{n} |\lambda_{Ni}| > N$. Fix such an $S = \{\phi_1, \ldots, \phi_n\}$, a sequence $(f_N)_{N=1}^{\infty}$, and for each $f_N$ a set of coefficients $\lambda_{N1}, \ldots, \lambda_{Nn}$ satisfying (2). We show that if

$c_n(K) < \infty$ this leads to a contradiction. Note that without loss of generality we can assume $\phi_1, \ldots, \phi_n$ are linearly independent.

As $c_n(K) < \infty$, there exists $\psi_1, \ldots, \psi_n$ such that

$$\sup_{f \in K} \|f - \mathrm{co}_n(\{\psi_1, \ldots, \psi_n\})\| = \beta,$$

for some $\beta < \infty$. So for each $f_N$, choose $\lambda'_{N1}, \ldots, \lambda'_{Nn}$ such that $\sum_{i=1}^n |\lambda'_{Ni}| \leq 1$ and

$$\left\| f_N - \sum_{i=1}^n \lambda'_{Ni} \psi_i \right\| \leq \beta. \tag{3}$$

Equations (2) and (3) imply that

$$\left\| \sum_{i=1}^n \lambda_{Ni} \phi_i - \sum_{i=1}^n \lambda'_{Ni} \psi_i \right\| < \beta + \varepsilon + \delta. \tag{4}$$

In addition,

$$\left\| \sum_{i=1}^n \lambda_{Ni} \phi_i - \sum_{i=1}^n \lambda'_{Ni} \psi_i \right\| \geq \left\| \sum_{i=1}^n \lambda_{Ni} \phi_i \right\| - \left\| \sum_{i=1}^n \lambda'_{Ni} \psi_i \right\|$$

$$\geq \left\| \sum_{i=1}^n \lambda_{Ni} \phi_i \right\| - \|\psi \mathrm{max}\|,$$

where $\|\psi\mathrm{max}\| := \max_i \|\psi_i\|$. However, $\|\sum_{i=1}^n \lambda_{Ni} \phi_i\| \to \infty$ as $N \to \infty$[1], which contradicts (4). $\square$

Now we can exhibit a class for which $c_{\mathcal{N}_{\mathrm{co}}(\varepsilon,K)-1}(K) = c_{\mathcal{N}_{\mathrm{co}}(\varepsilon,K)}(K) = \varepsilon$. Let $\mathbf{T}$ denote the unit circle. The *Sobolev space* $W_2^r(\mathbf{T})$ is the set of all functions $f$ on $\mathbf{T}$ for which $f^{(r-1)}$ (the $r-1$th derivative of $f$) is absolutely continuous and $\|f^{(r)}\|_2 := (\int_{\mathbf{T}} [f^{(r)}(t)]^2 \, dt)^{1/2} < \infty$. Define

$$B_2^r(\mathbf{T}, C) := \left\{ f \in W_2^r(\mathbf{T}) : \|f^{(r)}\|_2 \leq 1, \left| \int_{\mathbf{T}} f(t) \, dt \right| \leq C \right\}.$$

Consider approximation within the Banach space of all measurable functions on $\mathbf{T}$ with norm $\|\cdot\|_2$. The following theorem follows easily from a similar result of Kolmogorov [4, 6].

**Theorem 3** *For $n, r = 1, 2, \ldots$ and $C > 2\pi$,*

$$d_{2n-1}(B_2^r(\mathbf{T}, C)) = d_{2n}(B_2^r(\mathbf{T}, C)) = n^{-r}. \tag{5}$$

*The subspace $\{1, \sin t, \cos t, \ldots, \sin(n-1)t, \cos(n-1)t\}$ is an optimal $2n-1$ dimensional subspace.*

---

[1] To see this set

$$a := \inf_{\alpha_1, \ldots, \alpha_n : \sum |\alpha_i| = 1} \left\| \sum_{i=1}^n \alpha_i \phi_i \right\|.$$

$a > 0$ because the $\phi_1, \ldots, \phi_n$ are linearly independent. As $\sum_{i=1}^n |\lambda_{Ni}| > N$ (by assumption), $\|\sum_{i=1}^n \lambda_{Ni} \phi_i\| > Na$.

**Lemma 4** *For all* $n, r = 1, 2, \ldots$ *and* $C > 2\pi$,

$$c_n \left( B_2^r(\mathbf{T}, C) \right) = d_n \left( B_2^r(\mathbf{T}, C) \right).$$

**Proof.** If $f \in B_2^r(\mathbf{T}, C)$ it has a representation

$$f(t) = a_0 + \sum_{k=1}^{\infty} (a_k \cos kt + b_k \sin kt)$$

with $|a_0| \leq C/(2\pi)$ and

$$\|f^{(r)}\|_2^2 = \pi \sum_{k=1}^{\infty} k^{2r} (a_k^2 + b_k^2) \leq 1. \tag{6}$$

$\sum_{k=1}^{\infty} |a_k| + |b_k|$ will be maximized subject to the constraint (6) if $r = 1$. In that case, a variational argument shows that if

$$a_k = b_k = \frac{\sqrt{3}}{\pi k^2}$$

then $\sum_{k=1}^{\infty} |a_k| + |b_k|$ is maximal, and has value $\pi/\sqrt{3}$. Hence each optimal linear approximation will have the sum of the absolute values of its coefficients less than $C/(2\pi) + \pi/\sqrt{3}$, which implies that $c_n(B_2^r(\mathbf{T}, C)) < \infty$. Applying Lemma 2 gives the result. $\square$

As $c_{2n-1}(B_2^r(\mathbf{T}, C)) = c_{2n}(B_2^r(\mathbf{T}, C)) = n^{-r}$, we know that the gap in Theorem 1 must be necessary, for if there was no gap the approximation error would have to decrease *every* time the number of basis functions is increased, not every second time as is the case with this example.

## 4   Neural Network Applications

In this section Theorem 1 is used to calculate upper bounds on the convex n-widths of various function classes computed by one-hidden-layer "neural networks" for which the sum of the absolute values of the output weights is bounded by 1. With this restriction on the output weights, neural network classes $K_{nn}$ are equal to co$(S)$ where $S$ is the set of all functions computed by a single hidden node. Hence $\mathcal{N}_{co}(\varepsilon, K_{nn}) \leq \mathcal{N}(\varepsilon, S)$, which via Theorem 1 gives

$$c_{\mathcal{N}(\varepsilon, S)}(K_{nn}) \leq \varepsilon.$$

It would be nice to show that the node classes are convex $\varepsilon$-cores, *i.e.* that $\mathcal{N}_{co}(\varepsilon, K_{nn}) = \mathcal{N}(\varepsilon, S)$, for then we would obtain almost tight lower bounds on the approximate rates also.

**Lemma 5** *If* $K = \overline{\text{co}}(S)$ *then* $S$ *is a convex* $\varepsilon$-*core of* $K$ *(i.e.* $\mathcal{N}(\varepsilon, S) = \mathcal{N}_{co}(\varepsilon, K)$) *if and only if* $\mathcal{N}(\varepsilon, S) = \mathcal{N}_{co}(\varepsilon, S)$.

**Proof.** Suppose $K = \overline{\text{co}\,(S)}$ and $S$ is a convex $\varepsilon$-core of $K$. Let $T$ be a convex $\varepsilon$-core of $S$, so trivially $\mathcal{N}(\varepsilon, T) \leq \mathcal{N}(\varepsilon, S)$. Now, $K = \overline{\text{co}\,(S)} \subseteq \overline{\text{co}\left(\overline{\text{co}\,(T)}\right)} = \overline{\text{co}\,(T)}$, which implies $\mathcal{N}(\varepsilon, T) \geq \mathcal{N}(\varepsilon, S)$, so $\mathcal{N}(\varepsilon, T) = \mathcal{N}(\varepsilon, S)$, as required.

Suppose $K = \overline{\text{co}\,(S)}$ and $\mathcal{N}(\varepsilon, S) = \mathcal{N}_{\text{co}}(\varepsilon, S)$. Clearly $\mathcal{N}(\varepsilon, S) \geq \mathcal{N}_{\text{co}}(\varepsilon, K)$. Let $T$ be a convex $\varepsilon$-core of $K$, which implies $\overline{\text{co}\,(T)} \supseteq S$ and so $\mathcal{N}_{\text{co}}(\varepsilon, K) = \mathcal{N}(\varepsilon, T) \geq \mathcal{N}_{\text{co}}(\varepsilon, S) = \mathcal{N}(\varepsilon, S)$. $\square$

So one way to verify that the node function class $S$ is a convex $\varepsilon$-core of $K$ is to show that $\mathcal{N}(\varepsilon, S) = \mathcal{N}_{\text{co}}(\varepsilon, S)$, however this seems difficult, so we present only the upper bounds.

## 4.1 VC classes $S$

Let $\mathcal{N}\,(\varepsilon, S, L_p(P))$ denote the smallest $\varepsilon$-cover of $S$ under the $L_p(P)$ norm for some $1 \leq p < \infty$ and some distribution $P$. Let $V(S)$ denote the VC dimension of $S$. Haussler [3] proved:

$$\mathcal{N}\,(\varepsilon, S, L_p(P)) \leq K V(S)(4e)^{V(S)} \left(\frac{1}{\varepsilon}\right)^{p(V(S)-1)}$$

(see also [9], Theorem 2.6.4). Hence,

$$c_n(K_{nn}(S)) \leq \frac{C}{n^{\frac{1}{p(V(S)-1)}}},$$

where

$$C = \left(K V(S)(4e)^{V(S)}\right)^{1/(p(V(S)-1))}.$$

So neural networks whose node classes have small VC dimension can be well approximated by convex combinations of fixed sets of basis functions.

## 4.2 Linear Threshold $S$

This is a special case of the previous section. The VC dimension of the class of linear threshold functions on $\mathbb{R}^d$ is $d+1$ and so for the $L_p(P)$ norm

$$c_n(K) \leq \frac{C}{n^{\frac{1}{p(d+1)}}}.$$

## 4.3 Smoothly parameterized classes

Suppose $S$ is indexed by $k$ real parameters, that is there exists a "mother function" $f: \mathbb{R}^d \times [0,1]^k \to [0,1]$ such that $S = \{f(\cdot, y) : y \in [0,1]^k\}$. If we assume that the parameterization satisfies $\|f(\cdot, y) - f(\cdot, y')\| \leq \|y - y'\|$ for all $y, y' \in [0,1]^k$, then $\mathcal{N}(\varepsilon, S) \leq (1/\varepsilon)^k$ which gives an approximation rate of

$$c_n(K) \leq \frac{1}{n^{\frac{1}{k}}}.$$

# Acknowledgements

The first author was supported in part by EPSRC grant numbers K70366 and K70373. Part of this work was conducted while the first author was at Royal Holloway College and The London School of Economics. Thanks to Mostefa Golea for helpful discussions.

# References

1. Jonathan Baxter. Learning Internal Representations. In *Proceedings of the Eighth International Conference on Computational Learning Theory*, Santa Cruz, California, 1995. ACM Press.
2. Shimon Edelman and Nathan Intrator. Learning low dimensional representations of visual objects with extensive use of prior knowledge. In Sebastian Thrun, editor, *Explanation-Based Neural Network Learning*. Kluwer Academic, 1996. To Appear.
3. David Haussler. Sphere packing numbers of the boolean n-cube with bounded VC-dimension. *Journal of Combinatorial Theory A*, 69:217–232, 1995.
4. A N Kolmogorov. Über die beste Annäherung von Funktionen einer gegebenen Funktionenclasse. *Ann. Math.*, 37:107–110, 1936.
5. A N Kolmogorov and V M Tihomirov. $\epsilon$-entropy and $\epsilon$-capacity of sets in functional spaces. *AMS Translations Series 2*, 17:277–364, 1961.
6. George G Lorentz, Manfred v. Golitschek, and Yuly Makovoz. *Constructive Approximation: advanced problems*. Springer Verlag, Berlin, 1996.
7. Allan Pinkus. *n-Widths in Approximation Theory*. Springer-Verlag, Berlin, 1985.
8. Sebastian Thrun and Tom M Mitchell. Learning One More Thing. Technical Report CMU-CS-94-184, CMU, 1994.
9. Aad W van der Vaart and Jon A Wellner. *Weak Convergence and Empirical Processes*. Springer-Verlag, New York, 1996.

# Confidence Estimates of Classification Accuracy on New Examples*

John Shawe-Taylor

Department of Computer Science
Royal Holloway, University of London
Egham, TW20 0EX, UK
Email: jst@dcs.rhbnc.ac.uk

**Abstract.** Following recent results [6] showing the importance of the fat shattering dimension in explaining the beneficial effect of a large margin on generalization performance, the current paper investigates how the margin on a test example can be used to give greater certainty of correct classification in the distribution independent model. The results show that even if the classifier does not classify all of the training examples correctly, the fact that a new example has a larger margin than that on the misclassified examples, can be used to give very good estimates for the generalization performance in terms of the fat shattering dimension measured at a scale proportional to the excess margin. The estimate relies on a sufficiently large number of the correctly classified training examples having a margin roughly equal to that used to estimate generalization, indicating that the corresponding output values need to be 'well sampled'. If this is not the case it may be better to use the estimate obtained from a smaller margin.

## 1 Introduction

It has been known for a long time that large margin hyperplane classification can improve the generalization performance of a classifier [8, 4]. Recently a distribution free analysis was made of this effect in which the fat shattering dimension was shown to effectively replace the pseudo-dimension as the key parameter in bounding the generalization error [6]. Bartlett [3] generalized this idea to agnostic learning where errors are allowed on the training set and also derived bounds on the fat shattering dimensions of neural like structures.

The approach suggests that the margin could perhaps be an estimate of the confidence with which a particular classification is made. In other words if a new example has an output value well clear of the margin we should be more confident of the associated classification than when the output value is closer to the margin. The current paper places this intuition on a firm footing by showing that there is indeed a relationship between the margin and the corresponding estimation of error probability, though it is not simply the margin that enters into the equation. It is important that the training set contains points which have margins similar to that measured on the test example. This appears to

---

* This work was supported by the ESPRIT Neurocolt Working Group No. 8556.

link with the idea that the space should have been sampled in the corresponding region, though paradoxically it is the output values that are required to be sampled and not the region of the input space where the new example is located.

One by-product of the analysis is a confidence of classification that would normally be associated with a perfectly matched training set being obtained for new examples on which the output value exceeds the error margins for points in the training set.

## 2 Background to the Analysis

We begin with definitions of covering numbers which will be needed in the analysis.

**Definition 1.** Let $(X, d)$ be a (pseudo-) metric space, let $A$ be a subset of $X$ and $\epsilon > 0$. A set $B \subseteq X$ is an $\epsilon$-*cover* for $A$ if, for every $a \in A$, there exists $b \in B$ such that $d(a, b) < \epsilon$. The $\epsilon$-*covering number* of $A$, $\mathcal{N}_d(\epsilon, A)$, is the minimal cardinality of an $\epsilon$-cover for $A$ (if there is no such finite cover then it is defined to be $\infty$).

The idea is that $B$ should be finite but approximate all of $A$ with respect to the pseudometric $d$. We will use the $l^\infty$ distance over a finite sample $\mathbf{x} = (x_1, \ldots, x_m)$ for the pseudo-metric in the space of functions,

$$d_{\mathbf{x}}(f, g) = \max_i |f(x_i) - g(x_i)|.$$

We write $\mathcal{N}(\epsilon, \mathcal{F}, \mathbf{x})$ for the $\epsilon$-covering number of $\mathcal{F}$ with respect to the pseudo-metric $d_{\mathbf{x}}$.

In general we are concerned with classifications obtained by thresholding real valued functions. Hence, typically we will consider a set $\mathcal{F}$ of functions mapping from an input space $X$ to the reals. We will then fix for a particularly learning problem a threshold $\theta$ and implicitly use the classification functions

$$H = T_\theta(\mathcal{F}) = \{T_\theta(f) : f \in \mathcal{F}\},$$

where $T_\theta(f) = T_\theta \circ f$ and

$$T_\theta(x) = \begin{cases} 1; & \text{if } x \geq \theta, \\ 0; & \text{otherwise.} \end{cases}$$

Consider a hyperplane defined by $(w, \theta)$, where $w$ is a weight vector and $\theta$ a threshold value. Let $X_0$ be a subset of the Euclidean space that does not have a limit point on the hyperplane, so that

$$\min_{x \in X_0} |\langle x, w \rangle + \theta| > 0.$$

We say that the hyperplane is in *canonical form* with respect to $X_0$ if

$$\min_{x \in X_0} |\langle x, w \rangle + \theta| = 1.$$

Let $\| \cdot \|$ denote the Euclidean norm.

The following results are needed for bounding covering numbers in the subsequent proofs.

**Lemma 2 Alon** *et al.* **[1].** *Let $\mathcal{F}$ be a class of functions $X \to [0, 1]$ and $P$ a distribution over $X$. Choose $0 < \epsilon < 1$ and let $d = \text{Fat}_{\mathcal{F}}(\epsilon/4)$. Then*

$$E\left(\mathcal{N}(\epsilon, \mathcal{F}, \mathbf{x})\right) \le 2 \left(\frac{4m}{\epsilon^2}\right)^{d \log(2em/(d\epsilon))},$$

*where the expectation $E$ is taken w.r.t. a sample $\mathbf{x} \in X^m$ drawn according to $P^m$.*

**Corollary 3.** *[6] Let $\mathcal{F}$ be a class of functions $X \to [a, b]$ and $P$ a distribution over $X$. Choose $0 < \epsilon < 1$ and let $d = \text{Fat}_{\mathcal{F}}(\epsilon/4)$. Then*

$$E\left(\mathcal{N}(\epsilon, \mathcal{F}, \mathbf{x})\right) \le 2 \left(\frac{4m(b-a)^2}{\epsilon^2}\right)^{d \log(2em(b-a)/(d\epsilon))},$$

*where the expectation $E$ is over samples $\mathbf{x} \in X^m$ drawn according to $P^m$.*

As in [6] we introduce the following transformation in order to translate a margin problem into a maximum problem. We define the mapping $\hat{\ } : \mathbb{R}^X \to \mathbb{R}^{X \times \{0,1\}}$ by

$$\hat{\ } : f \mapsto \hat{f}(x, c) = f(x)(1 - c) + (2\theta - f(x))c, \tag{1}$$

for some fixed real $\theta$. For a set of functions $\mathcal{F}$, we define $\hat{\mathcal{F}} = \hat{\mathcal{F}}_\theta = \{\hat{f} : f \in \mathcal{F}\}$. The idea behind this mapping is that for a function $f$ the corresponding $\hat{f}$ maps the input $x$ and its classification $c$ to an output value, which will be less than $\theta$ provided the classification obtained by thresholding $f(x)$ at $\theta$ is correct. In a mild abuse of notation, we will also write $\hat{f}(x)$ in place of $\hat{f}(x, t(x))$, where $t$ is the target function. We have the following Lemmas and Theorems from [6] which give the current state of knowledge in this type of analysis.

**Lemma 4.** *[6] Let $\mathcal{F}$ be a set of real valued functions from $X$ to $\mathbb{R}$. Then for all $\gamma \ge 0$,*

$$\text{Fat}_{\hat{\mathcal{F}}}(\gamma) = \text{Fat}_{\mathcal{F}}(\gamma).$$

In the following theorem quoted from [6] the use of AFat in place of Fat is simply an artifact to ensure that it can always be chosen continuous from the right. Ignoring this detailed technical point, one may read Fat in place of AFat.

**Lemma 5.** *[6] Suppose $\mathcal{F}$ is a set of functions that map from $X$ to $\mathbb{R}$ with finite fat-shattering dimension bounded by the function $\text{AFat} : \mathbb{R} \to \mathbb{N}$ which is continuous from the right. Then for any distribution $P$ on $X$, and any $k \in \mathbb{N}$ and any $\theta \in \mathbb{R}$*

$$P^{2m} \left\{ \mathbf{x}\mathbf{y} : \exists f \in \mathcal{F}, r = \max_j \{f(x_j)\}, 2\gamma = \theta - r, k = \text{AFat}(\gamma/4), \right.$$

$$\left. \frac{1}{m} |\{i : f(y_i) \ge r + 2\gamma\}| > \epsilon(m, k, \delta) \right\} < \delta,$$

*where $\epsilon(m, k, \delta) \ge \frac{1}{m}(k \log \frac{8em}{k} \log(32m) + \log \frac{2}{\delta})$.*

**Theorem 6.** *[6] Consider a real valued function class $\mathcal{F}$ having fat shattering function bounded above by the function* AFat $: \mathbb{R} \to \mathbb{N}$ *which is continuous from the right. Fix $\theta \in \mathbb{R}$. If a learner correctly classifies $m$ independently generated examples $\mathbf{z}$ with $h = T_\theta(f) \in T_\theta(\mathcal{F})$ such that $er_{\mathbf{z}}(h) = 0$ and $\gamma = \min |f(x_i) - \theta|$, then with confidence $1 - \delta$ the expected error of $h$ is bounded from above by*

$$\epsilon(m, k, \delta) = \frac{2}{m} \left( k \log \left( \frac{8em}{k} \right) \log(32m) + \log \left( \frac{8m}{\delta} \right) \right),$$

*where $k = $ AFat$(\gamma/8)$.*

**Lemma 7.** *[6] Let $\mathcal{F}$ be the set of linear functions with unit weight vectors,*

$$\mathcal{F} = \{x \mapsto \langle w, x \rangle + \theta : \|w\| = 1\}. \tag{2}$$

*restricted to points in a ball of $n$ dimensions of radius $R$ about the origin and with thresholds $|\theta| \le R$. The fat shattering function of $\mathcal{F}$ can be bounded by*

$$\text{Fat}_{\mathcal{F}}(\gamma) \le \min\{9R^2/\gamma^2, n + 1\} + 1.$$

Combining the previous two results gives the following bound on the generalisation.

**Theorem 8.** *[6] Suppose inputs are drawn independently according to a distribution whose support is contained in a ball in $\mathbb{R}^n$ centered at the origin, of radius $R$. If we succeed in correctly classifying $m$ such inputs by a canonical hyperplane with $\|w\| = 1/\gamma$ and with $|\theta| \le R$, then with confidence $1 - \delta$ the generalization error will be bounded from above by*

$$\epsilon(m, \gamma) = \frac{2}{m} \left( k \log \left( \frac{8em}{k} \right) \log(32m) + \log \frac{8m}{\delta} \right),$$

*where $k = \lfloor 577R^2/\gamma^2 \rfloor$.*

The aim of the current paper is to apply similar proof techniques to bound the generalisation error on particular novel examples based on the margin of the output of the real valued function prior to classification. The intuition is that for examples where the margin is large we should be more confident about the accuracy of the associated classification. The results in the following sections define in a precise sense situations where this intuition holds true.

## 3 Further Analysis

We quote a technical lemma, which will be useful in the proposition that follows. The group $\Sigma$ consists of all $2^m$ permutations which exchange corresponding points in the first and second halves of the sample, i.e. $x_j \leftrightarrow y_j$ for $j \in \{1, \ldots, m\}$.

**Lemma 9.** *[6] Let $\Sigma$ be the swapping group of permutations on a $2m$ sample of points* **xy**. *Consider any fixed set $z_1, \ldots, z_d$ of the points. For $3k < d$ the probability $P_{d,k}$ under the uniform distribution over permutations that exactly $k$ of the points $z_1, \ldots, z_d$ are in the first half of the sample is bounded by*

$$P_{d,k} \leq \binom{d}{k} 0.5^d.$$

We will need a further result in order to carry through the analysis of conditional probabilities. The result aims to show that the relative frequency of certain events does not vary by a very large amount with respect to the fat shattering dimension.

Let n-th$\{A\}$ denote the $n$-th smallest value in the set $A$. Hence, 1-th$\{A\}$ is the smallest and $|A|$-th$\{A\}$ the largest value in $A$.

**Lemma 10.** *Suppose $\mathcal{F}$ is a set of functions that map from $X$ to $[a, b]$ with finite fat-shattering dimension bounded by the function* $\mathrm{AFat} : \mathbb{R} \to \mathbb{N}$. *Then for any distribution $P$ on $X$, and any $\gamma \in \mathbb{R}$, the probability*

$$P^{2m} \{\mathbf{xy} \colon \exists f \in \mathcal{F}, r_n = n\text{-}th\{f(x_j)|1 \leq j \leq m\}, |\{i : f(y_i) \leq r_n + 2\gamma\}| < n/2\}$$

*is less than $\delta$, provided $n \geq \frac{4}{\log 1.2}(k \log \frac{2em(b-a)}{k\gamma} \log \frac{4m(b-a)^2}{\gamma^2} + \log \frac{2}{\delta})$,*
*where $k = \mathrm{AFat}(\gamma/4)$.*

*Proof.* We use the symmetrisation technique with the group $\Sigma$. Let $B_{\mathbf{xy}}$ be a minimal $\gamma$-cover of $\mathcal{F}$ in the pseudo-metric $d_{\mathbf{xy}}$. Let $f \in \mathcal{F}$ satisfy the conditions given and let $\tilde{f} \in B_{\mathbf{xy}}$ be within $\gamma$ of $f$. Hence, at least $n$ of the points $x$ in **x** satisfy $\tilde{f}(x) < r_n + \gamma$, while less than $n/2$ of the points in **y** satisfy this condition. Let the number of points that satisfy the condition on the left be $d_L \geq n$ and the number on the right is $d_R < n/2$. Hence, $3d_L < d_L + d_R$ and we can apply Lemma 9 to bound the probability of this occurring for fixed $\tilde{f}$ by

$$\binom{d_L + d_R}{d_L} 0.5^{d_L + d_R} \leq \binom{d_L + n}{d_L} 0.5^{d_L + n} \leq \binom{3n/2 - 1}{n/2 - 1} 0.5^{3n/2 - 1} \leq \left(\frac{5}{6}\right)^{n/4}.$$

Hence, the probability of it occurring for some $\tilde{f}$ can be bounded by

$$E(|B_{\mathbf{xy}}|) \left(\frac{5}{6}\right)^{n/4} \leq 2 \left(\frac{4m(b-a)^2}{\gamma^2}\right)^{k \log(2em(b-a)/k\gamma)} \left(\frac{5}{6}\right)^{n/4}.$$

This will be less than $\delta$ provided

$$n \geq \frac{4}{\log 1.2}(k \log \frac{2em(b-a)}{k\gamma} \log \frac{4m(b-a)^2}{\gamma^2} + \log \frac{2}{\delta}).$$

$\square$

**Proposition 11.** *Suppose $\mathcal{F}$ is a set of functions that map from $X$ to $[a, b]$ with finite fat shattering dimension bounded by the function* AFat : $\mathbb{R} \to \mathbb{N}$. *Fix $\gamma \in \mathbb{R}$ and $n \in \mathbb{N}$. Then for sufficiently large $n$*

$$P^m \Big\{ \mathbf{x} : \exists f \in \mathcal{F}, r_n = n\text{-}th\{\hat{f}(x_j) | 1 \leq j \leq m\},$$

$$P\{y | \hat{f}(y) < r_n + 2\gamma\} < n/4m \Big\} < \delta$$

*provided*

$$n \geq \tfrac{4}{\log 1.2}(k \log \tfrac{2em(b-a)}{k\gamma} \log \tfrac{4m(b-a)^2}{\gamma^2} + \log \tfrac{4}{\delta}).$$

*where $k = $ AFat$(\gamma/4)$.*

*Proof.* We first apply a similar technique to Vapnik [7, page 168].

$$P^{2m} \Big\{ \mathbf{xy} : \exists f \in \mathcal{F}, r_n = n\text{-}th\{\hat{f}(x_j)|1 \leq j \leq m\}, |\{i : f(y_i) \leq r_n + 2\gamma\}| < n/2 \Big\}$$

$$\geq P^{2m} \Big\{ \mathbf{xy} : \exists f \in \mathcal{F}, r_n = n\text{-}th\{f(x_j)|1 \leq j \leq m\},$$

$$P\{y | \hat{f}(y) < r_n + 2\gamma\} < n/4m, |\{i : f(y_i) \leq r_n + 2\gamma\}| < n/2 \Big\}$$

$$\geq 0.5 P^m \Big\{ \mathbf{x} : \exists f \in \mathcal{F}, r_n = n\text{-}th\{\hat{f}(x_j)|1 \leq j \leq m\},$$

$$P\{y | \hat{f}(y) < r_n + 2\gamma\} < n/4m \Big\},$$

for sufficiently large $n$. The last inequality follows by considering for a fixed $\mathbf{x}$ and $f$ which satisfy the first two conditions, the probability over $\mathbf{y}$ that the final condition is satisfied. This will be greater than 0.5 for sufficiently large $n$. Using Chernoff bounds the value of $n$ required is 9. □

## 4 Margin on Test Examples

The motivation for the following theorem is a situation in the folded space where the margin on a new example from the threshold plus the margin on the training examples is greater than $2\gamma$. Hence, this margin is potentially much bigger than that observed on the examples. Indeed, the result applies even in cases where the training examples are misclassified. The value $\eta$ is the margin of the new example to the threshold. Figure 1 illustrates the relationship between the different parameters.

The $y$ axis of the diagram represents the output of $\hat{f}$ for $f \in \mathcal{F}$, the set of real valued functions considered. Hence, misclassification corresponds to being above the threshold value. The left side of the diagram details the situation on the left hand side $\mathbf{x}$ of the double sample, while the right hand side illustrates the second half $\mathbf{y}$. Hence, on the left hand side all output values are below $\theta + \eta - 2\gamma$ though some of them may be between $\theta$ and $\theta + \eta - 2\gamma$ and so be misclassified (if $\eta > 2\gamma$). However, at least $n$ points have output values below $r = \theta - \eta - 2\gamma$, and so are very safely correctly classified. Note that the theorems do not require $2\gamma < \eta$. In fact if the training examples are all correctly classified then we can take $2\gamma > \eta$.

Corollary 14 reformulates these parameters in a way that is more appropriate for application of the results.

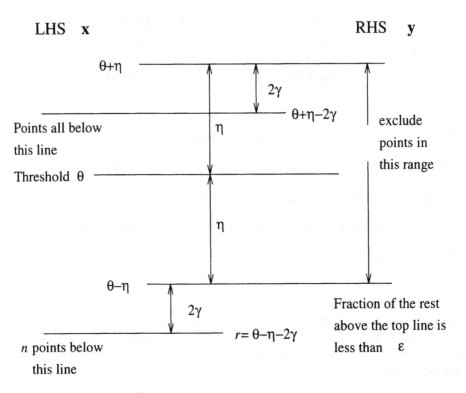

**Fig. 1.** Relationship of various parameters

**Theorem 12.** *Suppose $\mathcal{F}$ is a set of functions that map from $X$ to $[a, b]$ with finite fat-shattering dimension bounded by the function* $\mathrm{AFat} : \mathbb{R} \to \mathbb{N}$. *Then for any distribution $P$ on $X$, and any $n \in \mathbb{N}$ and any $\theta, \gamma, r \in \mathbb{R}, \eta = \theta - (r + 2\gamma)$*

$$P^{2m} \left\{ \mathbf{xy} : \exists f \in \mathcal{F}, n \geq |\{j : f(x_j) \leq r\}|, f(x_i) < \theta + \eta - 2\gamma \right.$$

$$\left. \text{for all } i, |\{i : f(y_i) \geq \theta + \eta\}| > \epsilon(m, n, k, \delta) |\{i : |f(y_i) - \theta| \geq \eta\}| \right\} < \delta,$$

*where* $\epsilon(m, n, k, \delta) = \frac{2}{n}(k \log \frac{8em(b-a)}{k\gamma} \log \frac{32m(b-a)^2}{\gamma^2} + \log \frac{2}{\delta})$ *and* $k = \mathrm{AFat}(\gamma/4)$.

*Proof.* Using the standard permutation argument (as in [2]), we may fix a sequence **xy** and bound the probability under the uniform distribution on swapping permutations $\Sigma$ that the permuted sequence satisfies the condition stated. Let $A_f(\gamma, r)$ denote the event, that the function $f$ satisfies the 'bad' conditions on the sample **xy**

$$n \geq |\{j : f(x_j) \leq r\}|, \; f(x_i) < \theta + \eta - 2\gamma, \text{ for all } i,$$
$$|\{i : f(y_i) \geq \theta + \eta\}| > \epsilon(m, n, k, \delta) \, |\{i : |f(y_i) - \theta| \geq \eta\}|$$

Consider a minimal $\gamma$-cover $B_{\mathbf{xy}}$ of $\mathcal{F}$ in the pseudo-metric $d_{\mathbf{xy}}$. We have that for any $g \in \mathcal{F}$, there exists $\tilde{g} \in B_{\mathbf{xy}}$, with $|g(x) - \tilde{g}(x)| < \gamma$ for all $x \in \mathbf{xy}$. Thus since for $n$ of the $x \in \mathbf{x}$, $f(x) \leq r$, and so $\tilde{f}(x) < r + \gamma$. Furthermore for $x \in \mathbf{x}$, $f(x) < \theta + \eta - 2\gamma$ and so $\tilde{f}(x) < \theta + \eta - \gamma$. Let the size of the following two sets be given by

$$l^+ = |Y^+|, \text{ where } Y^+ = \{i : f(y_i) \geq \theta + \eta\}$$
$$l^- = |Y^-|, \text{ where } Y^- = \{i : f(y_i) \leq \theta - \eta\}$$

It will be sufficient if we bound the probability that $l^+ > \epsilon(l^+ + l^-)$ since this is equivalent to

$$|\{i : f(y_i) \geq \theta + \eta\}| > \epsilon(m, n, k, \delta) \, |\{i : |f(y_i) - \theta| \geq \eta\}|.$$

Note that for $i \in Y^+$, $f(y_i) \geq \theta + \eta$ and so $\tilde{f}(y_i) > \theta + \eta - \gamma$. On the other hand for $y_i \in \mathbf{y}$ for which $\tilde{f}(y_i) < r + \gamma = \theta - \eta - \gamma$, $f(y_i) < \theta - \eta$ and so $i \in Y^-$. In contrast on the left hand half of the double sample, all points $x$ satisfy the condition $\tilde{f}(x) < \theta + \eta - \gamma$, while at least $n$ points $x$ satisfy the condition $\tilde{f}(x) < r + \gamma$. We will exploit these discrepancies to place an upper bound on the probability of this situation occurring under the swapping permutations $\Sigma$. In bounding the probabilities, the worst case will occur if for all $i \in Y^-$, $\tilde{f}(y_i) < r + \gamma$ and

$$l^+ = \left\lceil \frac{\epsilon}{1 - \epsilon} l^- \right\rceil.$$

Hence, we assume that this holds. We consider two cases. First consider $l^- \geq n/2$. In this case $l^+ \geq \epsilon n/(2(1 - \epsilon))$ and so the probability is bounded by

$$2^{-\epsilon n/2}.$$

If on the other hand $l^- < n/2$ we can apply Lemma 9 to obtain the bound

$$2^{-l^+} \binom{n + l^-}{l^-} 2^{-(n + l^-)} = 2^{-l^-/(1 - \epsilon) - n} \binom{n + l^-}{l^-}$$

This will attain a maximum when $l^- = n/2 - 1$. Hence, in both cases the value is bounded by $2^{-\epsilon n/2}$. Thus by the union bound

$$P^{2m} \left\{ \mathbf{xy} : \exists f \in \mathcal{F}, A_f(\gamma, r) \right\} \leq E(|B_{\mathbf{xy}}|) 2^{-\epsilon(m, n, k, \delta)n/2},$$

where the expectation is over **xy** drawn according to $P^{2m}$. Hence, by Corollary 3 (setting $\epsilon$ to $\gamma$, and $m$ to $2m$),

$$E(|B_{\mathbf{xy}}|) = E(\mathcal{N}(\gamma, \pi(\mathcal{F}), \mathbf{xy})) \leq 2 \left( \frac{8m(b-a)^2}{\gamma^2} \right)^{d \log(4em(b-a)/(d\gamma))},$$

where $d = \mathrm{Fat}_{\mathcal{F}}(\gamma/4) \leq k$. Thus

$$E(|B_{\mathbf{xy}}|) \leq 2 \left( \frac{32m(b-a)^2}{\gamma^2} \right)^{k \log(8em(b-a)/(k\gamma))},$$

and so $E(|B_{\mathbf{xy}}|)2^{-\epsilon(m,n,k,\delta)n/2} < \delta$, provided

$$\epsilon(m, n, k, \delta) \geq \frac{2}{n} \left( k \log \frac{8em(b-a)}{k\gamma} \log \frac{32m(b-a)^2}{\gamma^2} + \log \frac{2}{\delta} \right),$$

as required. $\qquad\qquad\qquad\qquad\qquad\qquad\qquad\qquad\qquad\qquad\qquad\qquad\square$

We will use the following notation in the proof of the main theorem. Let the expected error of a hypothesis $h = T_\theta(f)$ on examples $x$ for which $|f(x) - \theta| \geq \gamma$ be er$(h|\gamma)$. The result is uniform over all choices of $n$ and $k$, so that in applying the result the optimal choice of $n$ and $k$ can be used for a particular classification margin. Note that the result does not require correct classification on the training set. If there are misclassifications, it is sufficient that the margin on the new example is $2\gamma_k$ larger than the size of the largest margin among the misclassified examples.

**Theorem 13.** *Consider a real valued function class $\mathcal{F}$ with range $[a, b]$ having fat shattering function bounded above by the function* AFat $: \mathbb{R} \to \mathbb{N}$ *which is continuous from the right. Fix $\theta \in \mathbb{R}$. Suppose a learner classifies $m$ independently generated examples $\mathbf{z}$ with $h = T_\theta(f) \in T_\theta(\mathcal{F})$ and let $r_n = n\text{-th}\{\hat{f}(x_j)|1 \leq j \leq m\}$, $\gamma_k = \min\{\gamma'|\mathrm{AFat}(\gamma'/4) = k\}$. Then for all $n, k$, such that $r_m < \theta + \eta_{nk} - 2\gamma_k$, where $\eta_{nk} = \theta - (r_n + 2\gamma_k)$, with confidence $1 - \delta$ the expected error* er$(h|\eta_{nk})$ *is bounded from above by*

$$\epsilon(m, n, k, \delta) = \frac{4}{n}(k \log \frac{8em(b-a)}{k\gamma_k} \log \frac{32m(b-a)^2}{\gamma_k^2} + \log \frac{2(2m)^2}{\delta}),$$

*provided $n/4 - 2\epsilon m > 8/\epsilon$ and $n \geq \frac{4}{\log 1.2}(k \log \frac{2em(b-a)}{k\gamma} \log \frac{4m(b-a)^2}{\gamma^2} + \log \frac{4(2m)^2}{\delta})$.*

.

*Proof.* For each $n$ and $k$, we will divide the probability into two parts. We use the trick of moving to estimating the maximum of a function using the mapping (1). Note that $r_i = r_i(f)$ always refers to the function $f$ being considered in the particular expression.

$$P^m\Big\{\mathbf{x} \colon \exists f \in \mathcal{F},\, r_m < \theta + \eta_{nk} - 2\gamma_k,\, \mathrm{er}(T_\theta(f)|\eta_{nk}) > \epsilon(m, n, k, \delta)\Big\}$$

$$\leq P^m\Big\{\mathbf{x} \colon \exists f \in \mathcal{F}, r_m < \theta + \eta_{nk} - 2\gamma_k,\, P\{y|f(y) < r_n + 2\gamma_k\} < n/(4m)\Big\}$$

$$+ P^m\Big\{\mathbf{x} \colon \exists f \in \mathcal{F}, r_m < \theta + \eta_{nk} - 2\gamma_k,$$

$$P\{y|\hat{f}(y) < r_n + 2\gamma_k\} \geq n/(4m),\quad \mathrm{er}(T_\theta(f)|\eta_{nk}) > \epsilon(m, n, k, \delta)\Big\}$$

The first probability is bounded by Proposition 11 to be less than $\delta/2$ provided

$$n \geq \tfrac{4}{\log 1.2}(k \log \tfrac{2em(b-a)}{k\gamma} \log \tfrac{4m(b-a)^2}{\gamma^2} + \log \tfrac{4(2m)^2}{\delta}),$$

allowing for the $2m^2$ possible values for $n$ and $k$. For the second we apply a trick similar to that used by Vapnik [7, page 168] to bound the probability of deviation from true probability by the deviation of relative frequencies on two samples. In this case there is a slight complication as we are considering conditional probabilities.

$$P^{2m}\left\{ \mathbf{xy} \colon \exists f \in \mathcal{F}, r_m < \theta + \eta_{nk} - 2\gamma_k, \right.$$

$$\left. \left|\left\{i : \hat{f}(y_i) \geq \theta + \eta_{nk}\right\}\right| > 0.5\epsilon(m,n,k,\delta)\left|\left\{i : |\hat{f}(y_i) - \theta| \geq \eta_{nk}\right\}\right| \right\}$$

$$\geq P^{2m}\left\{ \mathbf{xy} \colon \exists f \in \mathcal{F}, r_m < \theta + \eta_{nk} - 2\gamma_k, \right.$$

$$P\{y|\hat{f}(y) < r_n + 2\gamma_k\} \geq n/(4m), \quad \mathrm{er}(T_\theta(f)|\eta_{nk}) > \epsilon(m,n,k,\delta),$$

$$\left. \left|\left\{i : \hat{f}(y_i) \geq \theta + \eta_{nk}\right\}\right| > 0.5\epsilon(m,n,k,\delta)\left|\left\{i : |\hat{f}(y_i) - \theta| \geq \eta_{nk}\right\}\right| \right\}$$

The first three conditions are those we wish to bound and relate only to the first half of the sample. Consider a fixed $\mathbf{x}$ and $f$ for which these hold. We will now show that with probability at least one half (for sufficiently large $n$ and $m$) the second half of the sample will satisfy the final condition. Hence, the probability over the double sample will be greater than half the desired probability over $m$-tuples.

First consider the case where there are fewer than $n/4 - 2m\epsilon$ points in the second half of the sample for which $\hat{f}(y_j) < r_n + 2\gamma_k$. The probability of this occurring can be bounded by 0.5 provided $m > 8/\epsilon$ by Chebyshev's inequality. If on the other hand at least $n/4 - 2m\epsilon$ points satisfy the condition, then the probability that among these points the relative frequency of those for which $\hat{f}(y_i) \geq \theta + \eta_{nk}$ being greater than $\epsilon/2$ is less than 0.5, again by Chebyshev's inequality provided $n/4 - 2m\epsilon > 8/\epsilon$. Hence, we have

$$2P^{2m}\left\{ \mathbf{xy} \colon \exists f \in \mathcal{F}, r_m < \theta + \eta_{nk} - 2\gamma_k, \right.$$

$$\left. \left|\left\{i : \hat{f}(y_i) \geq \theta + \eta_{nk}\right\}\right| > 0.5\epsilon(m,n,k,\delta)\left|\left\{i : |\hat{f}(y_i) - \theta| \geq \eta_{nk}\right\}\right| \right\}$$

$$\geq P^m\left\{ \mathbf{x} \colon \exists f \in \mathcal{F}, r_m < \theta + \eta_{nk} - 2\gamma_k, \right.$$

$$\left. P\{y|\hat{f}(y) < r_n + 2\gamma_k\} \geq n/(4m), \quad \mathrm{er}(T_\theta(f)|\eta_{nk}) > \epsilon(m,n,k,\delta) \right\}$$

We can now apply Theorem 12 to bound this expression, substituting $\epsilon/2$ in place of $\epsilon$ and $\delta/(2m)^2$ in place of $\delta$ to ensure uniformity over all choices of $k$ and $n$. This shows that for

$$\epsilon(m, n, k, \delta) = \tfrac{4}{n}(k \log \tfrac{8em(b-a)}{k\gamma_k} \log \tfrac{32m(b-a)^2}{\gamma_k^2} + \log \tfrac{2(2m)^2}{\delta}),$$

$$P^m\Big\{\mathbf{x}: \exists f \in \mathcal{F}, r_m < \theta + \eta_{mk} - 2\gamma_k, P\{y|\hat{f}(y) < r_n + 2\gamma_k\} \geq n/m - \epsilon,$$

$$\mathrm{er}(T_\theta(f)|\eta_{mk}) > \epsilon(m, n, k, \delta)\Big\} \leq \delta/(2m)^2.$$

Combining this with the result of Proposition 11 gives the result, since there are only $2m^2$ possible values for $k$ and $n$. □

It is worth noting that if the second condition on $n$ is not satisfied the bound is not significant in any case and so this condition can effectively be ignored.

The following Corollary summarises the results for a particular observed margin. Since the bound is uniform over the different values of $n$ and $k$, the user can choose the values to minimise the estimate provided the associated conditions are satisfied.

**Corollary 14.** *Consider a real valued function class $\mathcal{F}$ with range $[a, b]$ having fat shattering function bounded above by the function* AFat $: \mathbb{R} \to \mathbb{N}$ *which is continuous from the right. Fix $\theta \in \mathbb{R}$. Suppose a learner classifies $m$ independently generated examples $\mathbf{z}$ with $h = T_\theta(f) \in T_\theta(\mathcal{F})$ and let $r_n = n\text{-}th\{\hat{f}(x_j)|1 \leq j \leq m\}$, $\gamma_k = \min\{\gamma'|\mathrm{AFat}(\gamma'/4) = k\}$. Suppose further that a new example is observed with margin $\eta$, then the classification given by $h$ is with probability greater than $1 - \delta$ less than*

$$\epsilon(m, n, k, \delta) = \tfrac{4}{n}(k \log \tfrac{8em(b-a)}{k\gamma_k} \log \tfrac{32m(b-a)^2}{\gamma_k^2} + \log \tfrac{2(2m)^2}{\delta}),$$

*for all $n, k$, such that $\eta > \max\{r_m - \theta + 2\gamma_k, \theta - (r_n + 2\gamma_k)\}$, provided $n/4 - 2\epsilon m > 8/\epsilon$ and*

$$n \geq \tfrac{4}{\log 1.2}(k \log \tfrac{2em(b-a)}{k\gamma_k} \log \tfrac{4m(b-a)^2}{\gamma_k^2} + \log \tfrac{4(2m)^2}{\delta}),$$

*Proof.* The result just lists the bounds of the theorem that apply for observed margin of $\eta$. □

The implication of the result is that we can measure the fat shattering dimension up to scales given by the distance between the margin of the new example plus that of the worst training example (counted as negative if the example is misclassified). The reason for considering smaller scales will be the possibility that taking $\gamma$ large may result in too small a value for $n$. Hence, a trade-off may need to be made between the different choices of $\gamma_k$ and $n$.

# 5 Conclusions

We have shown how the margin on a novel example can be used to give improved confidence estimates for the accuracy of the classification given by a classifier which is based on thresholding a real valued function from a class with small fat shattering dimensions. The estimate involves the number of examples that give outputs with a similar margin to that measured on the new example, suggesting that this region of the *output* space has been well sampled!

The results are analogous to those obtained using a Bayesian analysis [5], though we should emphasise that strong assumptions are made in that case both about the nature of the distributions and the quality of certain approximations. The results presented here do not depend on any such assumptions, apart from the usual 'benign' measurability conditions necessary for uniform convergence.

The paper suggests that the results obtained by Bayesian analysis may be amenable to a more general analysis, perhaps also considering situations in which the assumptions used in this paper concerning the fat shattering function of the underlying space of functions do not apply.

# References

1. Noga Alon, Shai Ben-David, Nicolò Cesa-Bianchi, David Haussler, "Scale-sensitive Dimensions, Uniform Convergence, and Learnability," in *Proceedings of the Conference on Foundations of Computer Science (FOCS)*, 1993. Also to appear in *Journal of the ACM*.
2. Martin Anthony and John Shawe-Taylor, "A Result of Vapnik with Applications," *Discrete Applied Mathematics*, **47**, 207–217, (1993).
3. Peter Bartlett, "The Sample Complexity of Pattern Classification with Neural Networks: the Size of the Weights is More Important than the Size of the Network," Technical Report, Department of Systems Engineering, Australian National University, May 1996.
4. Bernhard E. Boser, Isabelle M. Guyon, and Vladimir N. Vapnik, "A Training Algorithm for Optimal Margin Classifiers," pages 144–152 in *Proceedings of the Fifth Annual Workshop on Computational Learning Theory*, Pittsburgh ACM, (1992)
5. D.J.C. MacKay, Bayesian Methods for Adaptive Models, Ph.D. Thesis, Caltech, 1991.
6. John Shawe-Taylor, Peter Bartlett, Robert Williamson and Martin Anthony, Structural Risk Minimization over Data-Dependent Hierarchies, NeuroCOLT Technical Report, NC-TR-96-51.
7. Vladimir N. Vapnik, *Estimation of Dependences Based on Empirical Data*, Springer-Verlag, New York, 1982.
8. Vladimir N. Vapnik, *The Nature of Statistical Learning Theory*, Springer-Verlag, New York, 1995.

# Learning Formulae from Elementary Facts [*]

Jānis Bārzdiņš [**1], Rūsiņš Freivalds [***1] and Carl H. Smith [†2]

[1] Institute of Math and Computer Science, University of Latvia, Raiņa bulvāris 29, LV-1459, Rīga, Latvia
[2] Institute for Logic, Language and Computation University of Amsterdam, lantage Muidergracht 24, NL-1018 TV Amsterdam, The Netherlands

**Abstract.** Since the seminal paper by E.M. Gold [Gol67] the computational learning theory community has been presuming that the main problem in the learning theory on the recursion-theoretical level is to restore a grammar from samples of language or a program from its sample computations. However scientists in physics and biology have become accustomed to looking for interesting assertions rather than for a universal theory explaining everything.

The language for the formulation of the interesting statements is, of course, most important. We use first order predicate logic. Three types of the formulae learning machines are considered. Machines of the first type produce each result in a finite number of steps. This learning type is very restricted. Machines of the second type produce the output in the limit. The third type machine supplies the result with what we call *assurance levels*. For success, we require that the assurance level grows indefinitley.

We have proved that there is the best finite formulae learner and there is the best nondeterministic assurance formulae learner while for the other types of learning there is no best learner. No $\forall x(P(x))$ type formula is learnable in a finite mode. All $\exists x \forall y(P(x,y))$ type formulae are assurance learnable but not vice versa. Formulae involving only monadic predicates are both learnable in the limit and assurance learnable. Nondeterministic assurance learners can learn all the predicate formulae while probabilistic assurance learners can learn only $\exists x \forall y \exists z(P(x,y,z))$ type formulae. Nondeterministic and probabilistic limit learners can be simulated by deterministic ones.

## 1 Introduction

In the standard paradigm of inductive inference, the sample data is taken to encode some phenomenon or concept. The goal of the learning is to find a program

[*] This project was supported by an International Agreement under NSF Grant 9421640.
[**] The first author was supported by Latvian Science Council Grant No. 93.593.
[***] The second author was supported by Latvian Science Council Grant No. 93.599.
[†] On leave from the Department of Computer Science, University of Maryland, College Park, MD 20742 USA, The third author was supported in part by NSF Grant 9301339 and a grant from the Netherlands Organization for Scientific Research.

that computes the function that generates the input. Since the function can be used to predict the outcome of any experiment, it is regarded as a complete explanation of phenomenon that is encoded by the data. The first use of such models was by philosphers of science who pretended the model captured the fundamental aspects of the scientific method. While most scientific disciplines have overarching goals, such as discovering the nature of the universe, most science is directed to achieving much more modest goals.

In order to bring the models of inductive inference closer to practical matters, we revisit the orginal philosphical motivations and propose the investigation of learning algorithms that do not attempt to discover explantations of phenomena, but rather try to reveal certain truths about the data that describe the phenomenon. The hope is to arrive at practical techniques for synthesising facts from data. The need for such techniques is tremendous. The new automated data gathering techniques have enabled empirical scientist to collect more data than can possibly be assimilated by a human. For example, "Mission to Planet Earth" is expected to generate terabytes of data. Radio Astronomy data sets, from 40,000 different viewing angles, run to 3 terabytes in aggregate. The Scripps Institute has a project to analyze the temperature of the world's oceans by analyzing the propogation of low-frequency sound waves. The data collection will take a year, and result in a 600 gigabyte data set that must be inverted. NASA is sponsoring a project to assimilate remote sensing data into a global weather model, generating a terabyte of data per year. Their goal is to analyze a decades worth of data. These are only a few of many such examples.

Clearly, automated techniques are needed to analyze such large data sets. The goal of our work is to develope such techniques. We start with the more modest goal of adapting the standard model from inductive inference to discuss sythesising facts, instead of explanations, from the data. Much of this work is a meticulous developement of the first principles and proving preliminary results which give boundary conditions. We start with revierwing the notions from logic that we employ in our investigation.

A *model* will be a triple $\langle \Sigma, N, I \rangle$ where $\Sigma$ is a finite set of predicate symbols, called a *signature*, with designated arities, $N$ is the domain of the variables used in the predicates and $I$ is the interpretation of the predicates. Unless otherwise noted, the domain will be the natural numbers, $\mathbb{N}$. For example consider the model $M_0 = \langle \Sigma_0, \mathbb{N}, I_0 \rangle$ where $\Sigma_0$ contains three binary predicates, $P_1, P_2$ and $P_3$. The interpretation $I_0$ is given by three formulas: $\hat{P}_1(x, y) : x \leq y$, $\hat{P}_2(x, y) : y = 5x$ and $\hat{P}_3(x, y) : y = x^2$. The *elementary facts* of a model are all of the instantiated predicate symbols of the model with associated truth values. The elementary facts of our example model $M_0$ include $P_1(2, 5) = T$, $P_1(6, 2) = F$, $P_1(4, 5) = T$, $P_2(2, 10) = T$, $P_3(3, 10) = F$. In some of the proofs that follow it will be more convenient to list these elementary facts as $P_1(2, 5)$, $\neg P_1(6, 2)$, $P_1(4, 5)$, $P_2(2, 10)$, $\neg P_3(3, 10)$. A *term* is either a notation for a member of the domain or a variable. The *elementary formulae* of a model $M = \langle \Sigma, N, I \rangle$ are formulae of the form $P(n_1, \cdots, n_k)$ where $P$ is a $k$-ary predicate symbol in $\Sigma$ and $n_i, i = 1, \ldots, k$, is a term. *Formulae* are first order predicate formulae constructed from the elementary formulae in the traditional way. Notions of *validity*, and any other logical notions not defined explicitly here are standard notions and can be found in some text such as [Kle52]. The set of all elementary facts of a model $M$ will be denoted by $E_M$ and the set of all enumerations of elements of $E_M$ will be denoted by $D_M$. A similar study was done previously [OSW91] obtaining a result similar to our Theorem 6. Our results concern only effective algorithms for discovery.

## 2 Learning Formulae from Elementary Facts

In this section we will discuss algorithms that input the elementary facts of some model and output true formulae fom the model. For example, from the elementary facts of $M_0$ in the previous section, we would like to be able to produce true formulae like $\exists x \exists y (P_2(x, y) \& P_1(x, y))$ without producing false formulae like $\exists x \forall y (P_2(x, y) \& P_1(25, y))$.

We proceed to define *finite formulae learning* algorithms. The word "finite" comes from the analogy with FIN type inference (see, e.g., [Wie76]), sometimes called "one shot" learning. This is because any output by such a machine is never later reconsidered.

**Definition 1.** A *finite formulae learning machine* (abbreviated: FFL) $L$ is a deterministic algorithmic device that takes input from an enumeration $D$ of elementary facts of some model $M$ and produces first order predicate logic formulae, each one in a finite number of steps. The set of formae so produced is denoted by $L(D)$.

**Definition 2.** A FFL $L$ is *correct* iff for arbitrary model $M$, and for arbitrary enumeration of the elementary facts, all the formulae produced by $L$ are true for $M$. (In symbols: $\forall M \forall D \in D_M \forall f \in L(D)$ ($f$ is true for $M$)).

For example, consider the machine $L_1$ that outputs only one formula

$$\forall x \forall y (P_2(x, y) \supset P_1(x, y))$$

whatever the input. This formula is true for some models, for instance for the model $M_0$ considered above. However the formula is false for some other models. Hence the machine $L_1$ is not correct.

**Definition 3.** A formula $f$ is learnable by FFL if there is a correct FFL $L$ outputting $f$ on elementary facts of every model $M$ such that $f$ is true in $M$.

**Definition 4.** A formula $f$ is decidable by FFL if there is a correct FFL $L$ learning both $f$ and $\neg f$.

Hence a correct $L$ decides for arbitrary model $M$ whether $f$ is true or false. The power of FFL's is inherently limited as no correct FFL can output a formula such as: $\forall x (P(x))$. To see this, assume from the contrary, that a correct FFL $L$

outputs $\forall x(P(x))$. This output is produced after $L$ has seen only finitely many of the elementary facts. Let $D'$ denote the set of all the elementary facts observed by $L$ up to the time it produced $\forall x(P(x))$ as output. Suppose the subset of $D'$ relevant to the predicate $P$ is $\{P(a_1), P(a_2), \cdots, P(a_n)\}$. Let $a$ denote an element different from $\{a_1, \cdots, a_n\}$. It is possible to construct a model that is consistent with $D'$ that has $\neg P(a)$ as an elementary fact. This shows that $L$ is not correct.

On the other hand, any formula $\exists x(P(x))$ is learnable by FFL. There is a correct FFL outputting this formula whenever $P(c)$ is observed in the elementary facts for some number $c$.

One should not think that the learnable formulas are all that simple. Arbitrary tautology, e.g. $\forall x \forall u \exists y \exists v(\neg P(x, y) \vee P(v, u))$ is decidable by FFL, not merely learnable. Some complicated formulae not being tautologies are decidable as well. For instance, $\forall x \forall u \exists y \exists v(\neg P(x, y) \vee P(v, u)) \wedge P_2(13)$ is decidable.

**Definition 5.** A correct FFL $L$ is called *best* if $L'(D) \subseteq L(D)$ holds for arbitrary correct FFL $L'$, for arbitrary model $M$ and arbitrary enumeration of elementary facts $D \in D_M$.

**Theorem 6.** *There is a best FFL.*

Proof: In proceeding towards this goal, we must introduce some new terminology. Let $K = \{e_1, \ldots, e_s\}$ be a finite set of elementary facts about some model. A formula $f$ is *semantically implied* by $K$ (written $K \| \models f$) iff for all models where $K$ is true, $f$ is true. Let $F_K = \{f \mid K \| \models f\}$, the set of formulae semantically implied by $K$. Let some model $M = \langle \Sigma, \mathbb{N}, I \rangle$ be given. Select $D \in D_M$ and let $D = \{e_1, e_2, \cdots\}$. Form initial segments of $D$ by defining, for each $i > 0$, $D_i = (e_1, \cdots, e_i)$. Notice that the set of models for which $D_{i+1}$ is true is a subset of the set of models for which $D_i$ is true, for any $i$. It is easy to see that if $i < j$ then $F_{D_i} \subseteq F_{D_j}$. Define then

$$F_D = \lim_{i \to \infty} F_{D_i}.$$

Since for any $D, D' \in D_M$, $F_D = F_{D'}$, we will write $F_M$ for $F_D$ as the set of formulae that are semantically implied by the elementary facts is dependent on the model, and not the particular enumeration of the elementary facts. For arbitrary FFL $L$, if $L$ is correct then for arbitrary model $M$ and arbitrary $D \in D_M$, $L(D) \subseteq F_M$. Obviously, the Theorem will be proved if we prove existence of a FFL $L_0$ such that $L_0(D) = F_M$.

Chose as an appropriate axiom system, $A$, any of the standard ones for the first order predicate logics, see for example [Men87]. If it is possible to derive a formula $f$ from the elementary facts about some model $M$ via the axiom system, we write $E_M \overset{A}{\vdash} f$. Notice that if $E_M$ is, for example, $\{\neg P(0), P(1), \cdots\}$ then $E_M \overset{A}{\vdash} \exists x(P(x))$. This follows from the observation that "$P(1) \Rightarrow \exists x(P(x))$" is in $A$. The axiom system and the elementary facts about a model produce a set of formulae. We call this set $A_M$ and formally define it as $A_M = \{f \mid E_M \overset{A}{\vdash} f\}$.

The desired FFL $L_0$ uses the axiom system to derive all possible formulae from the elementary facts provided as input. The validity of our Theorem follows from

**Lemma 7.** $A_M = F_M$.

Sketch of Proof: Our proof follows the proof of Gödel's first theorem (as presented in [Men87]), strengthening some of the key lemmas. Fix some model $M$, and use the notation $D_i$, $F_{D_i}$ introduced earlier. Define $A_{D_i} = \{f \mid D_i \overset{A}{\vdash} f\}$. We show that $A_{D_i} = F_{D_i}$, for any $i$. This result does not follow directly from Gödel's first theorem as we are restricting the use of constants and we are using a fixed domain.

Fix an $i \in \mathbb{N}$. By the soundness of the first order theory $A$, $A_{D_i} \subseteq F_{D_i}$. The remainder of the proof is devoted to showing that $F_{D_i} \subseteq A_{D_i}$. Assume from the contrary that there is a formula $f$ such that $D_i \models f$, but it is not the case that $D_i \overset{A}{\vdash} f$. Equivalently, it is not the case that $\overset{U}{\vdash} f$, where $U = A \cup D_i$. We may suppose without loss of generality that $f$ is closed. Let $C$ be the set of constant symbols appearing in either $D_i$ or $f$. It is easy to see that $C$ is finite. By Lemma 2.9 [Men87], if a closed formula is not provable in some theory, then it's negation can be consistently added as an axiom. Hence, we can add $\neg f$ to $A \cup D_i$ and get a consistent axiom system. Proposition 2.12 of [Men87] says that the for any consistent theory there is a countable model. In fact, the proof of Proposition 2.12 given in [Men87] actually proves a slightly stronger result, which we need, that says not only such a model exists but additionally it can be arranged that different constants have different interpretations. Let $M'$ be such a model in case of $\{\neg f\} \cup A \cup D_i$.

Recall that our constants are notations for natural numbers. If $c$ is a constant, then we denote by $\bar{c}$ the natural number described by $c$. We enumerate the elements of the model $M'$ so that arbitrary constant $c \in C$ gets the number $\bar{c}$. This is possible since $C$ is finite. Simultaneously we re-define the predicates in the model $M'$ as predicates not over the elements of the model but rather as predicates over their numbers. In the result we obtain a new model $M''$ with domain set $\mathbb{N}$ such that the set $D_i$ of the elementary facts and the formula $\neg f$ are true in $M''$ This contradicts to $D_i \models f$ thus concluding the proof. ⊠

**Theorem 8.** *If a formula $f$ is decidable by FFL then $f$ is equivalent to a quantifierless formula $g$ not containing variables.*

Proof: Assume there is a correct FFL $L$ deciding $f$. The machine $L$ outputs $f$ on all the models where $f$ is true and outputs $\neg f$ on all the models where $f$ is false. Consider a standard order of input for the elementary facts (for example, the elementary facts are input in the order $P_1(0,0)$, $P_2(0)$, $P_1(0,1)$, $P_2(1)$, $P_1(1,0)$, $P_3(1)$, $P_1(1,1), \ldots$). Consider a binary tree of possible values of these predicates. Each model corresponds to an infinite path in this tree. For each model we cut the path at the position where $L$ outputs its final TRUE or FALSE. Notice that if two models have the same values of the observed elementary facts, then $L$ stops at the same moment and produces the same result. Since the tree is binary, it follows from König's lemma [Kön26] that there is a constant $c$ such that all the paths are cut at depth not exceeding $c$. Hence the formula $f$ is equivalent to a quantifierless formula $g$ depending only of the first $c$ values of the predicates (in our standard order of presenting them). ⊠

## 3 Learning Formulae in the Limit

In Section 2 we introduced finite formulae learners and found them to be limited. Now we consider formulae learning process in the limit which is a counterpart to E. M. Gold's notion of computation in the limit.

**Definition 9.** A *limit formulae learning machine* (abbreviated LFL) is a deterministic algorithmic device that takes as the input an enumeration of the elementary facts of some model and produces as the output a sequence of the first order predicate logics formulae paired with values TRUE and FALSE.

A LFL can output the same formula several times, some instances with TRUE, some instances with FALSE. If $L$ is LFL and $D$ is its input data and $f$ is a predicate logic formula, then $A(L, D, f) = (a_1, a_2, \ldots)$ is the sequence of statements TRUE and FALSE associated with $f$.

**Definition 10.** We say that LFL $L$ learns a formula $f$ from the input data $D$ if and only if $A(L, D, f)$ is a finite sequence with the last element TRUE.

**Definition 11.** A LFL $L$ is correct iff for all models $M$, all $D \in D_M$ and all formulae $f$, the LFL $L$ learns $f$ from $D$ only when $f$ is true in $M$.

As in Section 2, we distinguish formulae learnable by LFL (a correct LFL can learn the formula) from formulae decidable by LFL (a correct LFL can learn both the formula and its negation). It is easy to see that LFL machines are more powerful than FFL machines. For instance, formula $\forall x(P(x))$ (which cannot be learned by any correct FFL machine) is decidable by LFL. Indeed, if no false $P(c)$ is found, the output concerning $\forall x(P(x))$ is TRUE, otherwise FALSE.

**Theorem 12.** *Let $A$ be arbitrary Boolean formula with predicate symbols $P_1$, ..., $P_n$ from signature $\Sigma$, and $x_1, \ldots, x_u, y_1, \ldots, y_v$ be variables of the involved predicates. Then the formula*

$$\exists x_1 \cdots x_u \forall y_1 \cdots \forall y_v (A(P_1, \ldots, P_n, x_1, \ldots, x_u, y_1, \ldots, y_v))$$

*is learnable by a correct LFL.*

Proof: Let $\alpha_0, \alpha_1, \alpha_2, \ldots$ be an enumeration of all possible $u$- tuples of nonnegative integers and $\beta_0, \beta_1, \beta_2, \ldots$ be an enumeration of all possible $v$- tuples of nonnegative integers. LFL systematically takes $u$- tuples $\alpha_0, \alpha_1, \alpha_2, \ldots$ and for the current $\alpha_i$ outputs FALSE immediately followed by TRUE, goes on in systematic consideration of all $v$- tuples until the formula $A$ turns out to be false. Then LFL goes to another $u$- tuple $\alpha_{i+1}$. If the formula is true, only finite number of outputs related to this formula is output, and the last one is TRUE. If the formula is false, the sequence of outputs is infinite. Hence the LFL is correct. ⊠

**Theorem 13.** *There is no correct LFL which learns formula "$\forall x \exists y (P(x,y))$".*

Proof: Assume from the contrary that this formula (called $f$ for the sequel) is learnable by a correct LFL $L$. We construct a specific $P(x,y)$. If a value of this predicate is defined, it is never changed later. We put $P(x,y)$ true until $L$ outputs first TRUE for $f$. Since only finite number of values $P(x,y)$ are observed till this moment, we define $P(x,y)$ true for all these pairs $(x,y)$. After that we put new values $P(x,y)$ FALSE. If this goes on infinity, $P$ becomes a predicate for which $f$ is false. Since $L$ is a correct LFL, $L$ is to change its output to FALSE at some moment. After that we put new values $P(x,y)$ TRUE. If this goes on infinity, $P$ becomes a predicate for which $f$ is true. Since $L$ learns $f$, $L$ is to change its output to TRUE. This way, changing TRUE and FALSE alternately, we get in the limit a predicate $P$ for which the formula $f$ is true but $L$ does not learn it. Contradiction. ☒

**Corollary 14.** *The formula "$\exists x \forall y (P(x,y))$" is learnable but not decidable by LFL.*

**Theorem 15.** *There is no best LFL.*

Proof: Consider the formula "$\forall x \exists y (P(x,y))$". It is not learnable by a correct LFL. On the other hand, there are correct LFL machines $L_1, L_2, \ldots$ learning only this formula only on very limited models $M_1, M_2, \ldots$ where $M_n$ is a model where $P(x,0)$ is true for all $x \geq n$. For $L_n$ it remains to find out from the elementary facts whether $\exists x (P(0,y)) \& \exists x (P(1,y)) \& \cdots \& \exists x (P(n-1,y))$ and whether $\forall x \geq n (P(x,0))$.

Assume from the contrary that there is the best LFL $L$. Then $L$ is to learn this formula for all $M_1, M_2, \ldots$. However an argument similar to the proof of Theorem 13 shows that this is impossible. ☒

**Theorem 16.** *If $f$ is a first order predicate logics formula involving only monadic predicates, then $f$ is decidable by LFL.*

Proof: Without loss of generality, we assume that the target formula $f$ is in prenex form. We prove our Theorem by induction. For quantifierless formulae the Theorem is obvious. Assume that the Theorem is true for $n-1$ quantifiers and the target formula $f$ contains $n$ quantifiers.

Let $Qx$ be the outermost quantifier of the formula $f$. Suppose that $P_1, \ldots, P_m$ is a complete list of all monadic predicates in $f$ which contain the variable $x$. To simplify the proof, assume that $m = 2$. The generalization to larger values of $m$ is obvious. We define 4 formulae $f_1, f_2, f_3, f_4$ (in general $2^m$ formulae) derived from $f$ substituting, respectively, $P_1(x) = T, P_2(x) = T$ for $f_1$, $P_1(x) = T, P_2(x) = F$ for $f_2$, $P_1(x) = F, P_2(x) = T$ for $f_3$, $P_1(x) = F, P_2(x) = F$ for $f_4$. It is important that $f_1, f_2, f_3, f_4$ have at most $n-1$ quantifiers. The target formula is equivalent to $Qx((P_1(x) \& P_2(x) \& f_1) \vee (P_1(x) \& P_2(x) \& f_1) \vee (P_1(x) \& P_2(x) \& f_1) \vee (P_1(x) \& P_2(x) \& f_1))$.

By the induction assumption there are LFLs $L_1, l_2, L_3, L_4$ deciding $f_1, f_2, f_3,$ $f_4$ respectively. If $Qx$ is the existence quantifier $\exists x$, the machine $L$ finds out in the limit which of the 4 formulae $g_1 : \exists x(P_1(x)\&P_2(x))$, $g_2 : \exists x(P_1(x)\&\neg P_2(x))$, $g_3 : \exists x(\neg P_1(x)\&P_2(x))$, $g_4 : \exists x(\neg P_1(x)\&\neg P_2(x))$ are true in the model $M$. These formulae are decidable by LFL $K_1, K_2, K_3, K_4$. In parallel, $L$ outputs the disjunction of the outputs of all the machines $L_1, L_2, L_3, L_4$ with the corresponding indices.

If $Qx$ is the universal quantifier $\forall x$, the machine $L$ finds out in the limit which of the 4 machines $L_1, L_2, L_3, L_4$ output TRUE (this subset stabilizes in the limit), reacting to every mind change by outputting sequence TRUE, FALSE, and outputs the disjunction of the outputs of all the machines $K_1, K_2, K_3, K_4$ with the corresponding indices. ☒

**Comment.** Theorem 16 holds in a more general case. It suffices that in the target formula $\exists x \forall y \forall z \exists u \exists v \exists w \forall q (P_1(u,v)\&(P_2(y,z)\lor P_3(q))\&(P_4(x) \supset P_1(z,y)))$ the variables involved in one occurence of a predicate are all from the same group of the quantifiers of the same type in the prenex form.

# 4 Learning Formulae with Assurance Levels

Now we consider another learning process which is essentially infinite. The machine attaches to each output a level of assurance. For some formula the assurance level may grow while for some other formula the assurance level stabilizes at some intermediate level. This notion was introduced by us in an earlier paper [BFS96] where we considered only a Gold style learning of programs.

The main notion from [BFS96] that we need is that of "assurance level." A *assurance level* is a rational number between 0 and 1, inclusive. A 0 represent a vote of no assurance and 1 indicates absolute certainty.

**Definition 17.** A *assurance formulae learning machine* (abbreviated AFL) is a deterministic algorithmic device that takes as the input an enumeration of the elementary facts of some model and produces as the output an infinite sequence of first order predicate logics formulae paired with assurance levels.

A AFL will produce a sequence of outputs, like an FFL, but unlike the FFL case, the same formula may appear over and over again, with different assurance levels. If $L$ is AFL and $D$ is its input data and $f$ is a predicate logics formula, then $B(L, D, f) = (b_1, b_2, \cdots)$ is the sequence of assurance levels associated with $f$ that $L$ produces when given $D$ as input, in the order of appearance in the output stream.

**Definition 18.** We say that AFL $L$ learns a formula $f$ from the input data $D$ if and only if $B(L, D, f)$ monotonically converges to 1.

It is easy to observe that an equivalent definition of the AFL-learnability can be proposed as follows.

**Definition 19.** We say that LFL $L$ AFL-learns a formula $f$ from the input data $D$ if and only if $L$ outputs formula $f$ infinitely many times.

However, we use Definition 18 as the primary definition since it allows useful generalizations. It is easy to see that AFL machines are more powerful than FFL machines. For instance, formula $\forall x(P(x))$ (which cannot be output by any correct FFL machine) can be decided by a correct AFL. Indeed, let $\omega(n) = 2^{-n-1}$. If AFL finds out that $P(0)\&P(1)\&\cdots\&P(n)$ is true, AFL outputs the formula $\forall x(P(x))$ with assurance level $\sum_{i=0}^{n}\omega(i)$. Hence AFL decides $\forall x(P(x))$ iff it is true for the considered model.

**Theorem 20.** *Let $A$ be arbitrary Boolean formula with predicate symbols $P_1$, ..., $P_n$ from signature $\Sigma$, and $x_1,\ldots,x_u,y_1,\ldots,y_v$ be variables of the involved predicates. Then the formula*

$$\forall x_1 \cdots \forall x_u \exists y_1 \cdots \exists y_v A(P_1,\ldots,P_n,x_1,\ldots,x_u,y_1,\ldots,y_v)$$

*is learnable by a correct AFL.*

Proof: Let $\alpha_0,\alpha_1,\alpha_2,\ldots$ be an enumeration of all possible $u$- tuples of nonnegative integers and $\beta_0,\beta_1,\beta_2,\ldots$ be an enumeration of all possible $v$- tuples of nonnegative integers. Let $\omega(n) = 1 - \frac{1}{2^{n+1}}$. If AFL finds out that for $u$- tuple $(x_1,\ldots,x_u)$ from the set $\{\alpha_0,\alpha_1,\alpha_2,\ldots\}$ there is a set $\{\beta_0,\beta_1,\beta_2,\ldots\}$ such that $A(P_1,\ldots,P_n,x_1,\ldots,x_u,y_1,\ldots,y_v)$ is true, then AFL outputs the formula

$$\forall x_1 \cdots \forall x_u \exists y_1 \cdots \exists y_v A(P_1,\ldots,P_n,x_1,\ldots,x_u,y_1,\ldots,y_v)$$

with assurance level $\sum_{i=0}^{n}\omega(i)$. Hence AFL learns this formula iff the formula is true for the considered model. ☒

**Theorem 21.** *There is no correct AFL which learns formula "$\exists x \forall y(P(x,y))$."*

Proof: Assume by way of contradiction that a AFL $L$ learns this formula denoted by $f$. We construct, in effective stages of finite extension, an interpretation for the predicate $P(x,y)$ such that $L$ outputs $f$ with assurance levels converging to 1 but the formula $f$ is not true under this interpretation of the predicate. Each stage will employ an auxiliary predicate that is defined prior this stage. By way of initialization, $P_0$ is the predicate over two arguments that is always true. We define an increasing sequence of integers $\{m_s\}$ to mark boundaries of areas where $P$ is equal to $P_s$. The first integer $m_0$ is defined to be 0. Execute the following stages for $s = 0, s = 1, \ldots$.

Begin stage $s$. Use values of $P_s$ as the elementary facts for $L$ until $L$ produces an output $f/c$ for $c \geq 1 - 1/2^{s+1}$. Since $\exists x \forall y(P_s(x,y))$ is true, such an output will eventually be produced. Let $D_s$ be the set of pairs $(x,y)$ such that the value

$P_s(x, y)$ was read from the input by $L$ to produce $f/c$. Of course, $D_s$ is a finite set. Let $m_{s+1}$ be the largest value $x$ in pairs $(x, y) \in D_s$. Define $P_{s+1}$ as follows

$$P_{s+1}(x, y) = \begin{cases} T, \text{ if } (x, y) \in D_s, \\ T, \text{ if } x > m_{s+1}, \\ F, \text{ otherwise.} \end{cases}$$

End stage $s$.

Define $P(x, y) = P_s(x, y)$ for $m_{s_1} < x \leq m_s$, $s = 1, 2, \ldots$. Notice that $P$ coincides with $P_s$ on all the values used by $L$ to produce $f/c$ with some $c \geq 1 - 1/2^s$. Hence, when the values of $P$ are used as the elementary facts for $L$, $L$ will produce assurance levels for $f$ converging to 1. In other words, $L$ learns $f$. However, for arbitrary $x$, and for all sufficiently large $y$'s, $P(x, y) = F$. Hence $f$ is false for this interpretation of $P$. Contradiction. ⊠

**Theorem 22.** *If a formula is decidable by LFL, then it is decidable by AFL as well.*

Proof: Since the formula $f$ is decidable by LFL $L$, the outputs concerning $f$ stabilize on TRUE or FALSE. Hence the correct answer is the current output at infinitely many moments, while the incorrect answer is the current output at only finite number of moments. Hence AFL can raise assurance level for the current output of the LFL.

**Theorem 23.** *If $f$ is a first order predicate logics formula involving only monadic predicates, then $f$ is decidable by AFL.*

Proof: Immediate from Theorems 16 and 22.

**Theorem 24.** *There is no best AFL.*

Proof: The proof starts by the construction of a sequence of AFL's $L_0, L_1, \cdots$. The idea is to make each of the AFLs behave correctly and in particular, for any model $M$ and any enumeration of elementary facts $D \in D_M$, $B(L_i, D, \exists x \leq i \forall y (P(x, y))$ monotonically approaches 1 iff $\exists x \leq i \forall y (P(x, y))$ is true in $M$. Of course, since we have no way of expressing "$\exists x \leq i$" directly in the standard first order theory we must really use the notationally cumbersome, but logically equivalent formulation:

$$\exists x \leq i \forall y (P(x, y)) \equiv (\forall y (P(0, y)) \vee \forall y (P(1, y)) \vee \cdots \vee \forall y (P(i, y))).$$

The machine $L_i$ is really quite simple, it outputs only formulas equivalent to $\exists x \leq k \forall y (P(x, y))$, for some $k \leq i$ and keeps on increasing the assurance level towards 1 as long as for some $j \leq k$ no elementary fact has been received as input which contradicts the truth of the formula "$\forall y (P(j, y))$." Furthermore, every time some $L_i$ outputs $\exists x \leq k \forall y (P(x, y))$ with some assurance level, then it also outputs $\exists x \forall y (P(x,y))$ with the same assurance level. Clearly, each $L_i$ is correct and for all models $M$, for all $D \in D_M$, $L_i(D) \subset L_{i+1}(D)$.

Choose any model $M$ for which $\exists x \forall y (P(x,y))$ is true. Then, in $M$ $\forall y (P(m_0, y))$ is true for some $m_0$. Then for all $m \geq m_0$, for all $D \in D_M$, $B(L_m, D, \exists x \leq m \forall y (P(x,y)))$ and $B(L_m, D, \exists x \forall y (P(x,y)))$ monotonically approach 1.

Suppose by way of contradiction that $L$ is a best AFL. Choose any $D \in D_M$. We claim that $\exists x \forall y (P(x,y)) \in L(D)$, contradicting Theorem 21. For any $i \geq m_0$, $\exists x \leq i \forall y (P(x,y)) \in L_i(D)$ for any model where $\exists x \leq i \forall y (P(x,y))$ is true. Hence, since $L$ is the best learner, $\exists x \forall y (P(x,y)) \in L(D)$ for any $D \in D_M$ in all models $M$ where $\exists x \forall y (P(x,y))$ is true. Let $\mathcal{M}_i$ be set of models where $\exists x \leq i \forall y (P(x,y))$ is true. Then $\mathcal{M}_i \subseteq \mathcal{M}_{i+1}$. Let $\mathcal{M}$ be the limit of the sequence of models $\mathcal{M}_i$ as $i$ increases. Hence, $B(L, D, \exists x \forall y (P(x,y)))$ monotonically approaches 1 for all $D \in D_M$ for any model $M \in \mathcal{M}$. But $\mathcal{M}$ is precisely the set of models where $\exists x \forall y (P(x,y))$ is true. Therefore, $\exists x \forall y (P(x,y)) \in L(D)$, contradicting Theorem 21. ☒

## 5 Nondeterministic Learning

The best formulae learning machine in Section 3 was based on an axiom system. Axiom systems are adequately described by nondeterministic algorithms rather than by deterministic ones. This consideration suggests that nondeterministic formulae learning machines are to be considered as well.

A nondeterministic FFL machine (abbreviated as NFFL) differs from the FFL machines considered is Section 3 only in being nondeterministic, thus allowing differing performances of the same machine over the same input data.

**Definition 25.** We say that a NFFL $L$ learns a formula $f$ from the input data $D$ if and only if there is a performance of $L$ over $D$ such that $L$ outputs the formula $f$.

**Definition 26.** An NFFL is correct iff for arbitrary model $M$ and for arbitrary enumeration of the elementary facts about $M$, all the formulae learned by $L$ are true over $M$.

**Theorem 27.** *If a formula $f$ is learnable by a correct nondeterministic FFL, then $f$ is learnable by a correct deterministic FFL as well.*

Proof: Obvious. The deterministic FFL systematically overviews all the performances of the given nondeterministic FFL over the given input and outputs every formula produced by the NFFL in at least one performance. Correctness of the deterministic FFL is implied by the correctness of the nondeterministic FFL. ☒

**Theorem 28.** *If a formula $f$ is learnable by a correct nondeterministic LFL, then $f$ is learnable by a correct deterministic LFL as well.*

**Theorem 29.** *There is a nondeterministic AFL correctly learning all the formulae in the first order predicate logics.*

Proof: Suppose the formula $f$ is in form

$$\exists x_1 \cdots \exists x_a \forall y_1 \cdots \forall y_b \, \exists z_1 \cdots \exists z_c \forall u_1 \cdots \forall u_d \cdots \forall v_1 \cdots \forall v_q \exists w_1 \cdots \exists w_r \quad (1)$$

$$(A(P_1, \ldots, P_n, x_1, \ldots w_r)) \quad (2)$$

where $A$ is a Boolean formula made of the predicate symbols $P_1, \ldots, P_n$ with variables $x_1, \ldots, w_r$.

The needed NAFL nondeterministically guesses exactly one $a$- tuple of natural numbers $x^0 = (x_1^0, \ldots, x_a^0)$ and goes into an infinite process of enumeration of all possible $b$- tuples of natural numbers $y^0 = (y_1^0, \ldots, y_b^0)$. For each pair $(x^0, y^0)$ the nondeterministic AFL guesses exactly one $c$- tuple $z^0 = (z_1^0, \ldots, z_c^0)$ and goes into infinite process of enumeration of all possible $d$- tuples $u^0 = (u_1^0, \ldots, u_d^0)$. Going along the quantifier prefix, the NAFL finally, for each $(x^0, y^0, \ldots, v^0)$ guesses exactly one $w^0 = (w_1^0, \ldots, w_r^0)$ and checks whether $A(P_1, \ldots, P_n, x_1, \ldots w_r)$ is true.

Let $\omega(k) = 1 - \frac{1}{2^{k+1}}$. If the series of guesses described in the preceeding paragraph ends in finding the formula $A(P_1, \ldots, P_n, x_1, \ldots w_r)$ true, NAFL adds the value $\bar{\omega} = \omega(y_1) \cdot \omega(y_2) \cdots \omega(y_b) \cdot \omega(u_1) \cdot \omega(u_2) \cdots \omega(u_d) \cdots \omega(v_1) \cdot \omega(v_2) \cdots \omega(v_q)$ to the assurance level already reached.

Since $\sum_{k=0}^{\infty} \omega k = 1$ and all $\omega(k) > 0$, the total of all the $\bar{\omega}$ equals 1 if and only if the formula $f$ is true. ☒

**Corollary 30.** *There is a best NAFL.*

## 6 Probabilistic Learning

In Computational Complexity in ir often tha case that the nondeterministic complexity class is presumably larger than the corresponding deterministic complexity class. For instance, it is presumed that $P \subset NP$, $L \subset NL$ and so on. As for the probabilistic classes, unbounded probabilistic classes usually are larger than the nondeterministic classes while the bounded probabilistic classes are proper subclasses of the nondeterministic ones ($P \subset NP \subset PP$). However in the formulae learning the position of probabilistic learners and their capabilities is different. We consider probabilistic finite formula learning (PFFL) machines and probabilistic assurance formula learning (PAFL) machines.

**Definition 31.** We say that a PFFL $L$ learns a formula $f$ from the input data $D$ if and only if the probability of $f$ being output when $L$ processes $D$, strictly exceeds $1/2$.

**Definition 32.** We say that a PAFL $L$ learns a formula $f$ from the input data $D$ if and only if the probability of $f$ getting assurance level converging to 1, strictly exceeds $1/2$.

The two definitions do not bound the probability of the correct result away from the cut point $1/2$.

**Theorem 33.** *If a formula $f$ is learnable by a correct probabilistic FFL, then $f$ is learnable by a correct deterministic FFL as well.*

**Theorem 34.** *If a formula $f$ is learnable by a correct probabilistic LFL, then $f$ is learnable by a correct deterministic LFL as well.*

**Theorem 35.** *Let $A$ be arbitrary Boolean formula with predicate symbols $P_1$, $\ldots$, $P_n$ from signature $\Sigma$, and $x, \ldots, x_u, y_1, \ldots, y_v, z_1, \ldots, z_w$ be variables of the involved predicates. Then the formula*

$$\exists x_1 \cdots \exists x_u \forall y_1 \cdots \forall y_v \exists z_1 \cdots \exists z_w (A(P_1, \ldots, P_n, x_1, \ldots, x_u, y_1, \ldots, y_v, z_1, \ldots, z_w))$$

*is learnable by a correct PAFL.*

Proof: For the sake of conciseness we consider only a "typical" case when the formula $f$ is

$$\exists x \forall y \exists z (P(x, y, z)).$$

The needed PAFL outputs $f$ with assurance level $1 - \frac{1}{2^{v+1}}$ with probability $1 - \frac{1}{2^{v+1}}$ whenever the PAFL finds out that $\exists z_0(P(x, 0, z_0)) \& \exists z_1(P(x, 1, z_1)) \& \cdots \& \exists z_y(P(x, y, z_y))$. The probability of outputting $f$ with assurance converging to 1 strictly exceeds $1/2$ if and only if $f$ is true. $\boxtimes$

**Theorem 36.** *There is no correct PAFL which learns formula $\forall x \exists y \forall z (P(x, y, z))$.*

# 7 Conclusions

The notion of formulae learning and the results already obtained suggest really many open problems. We list only few of them:

1. Theorem 15 shows that there is no best LFL for the learnability. Is there a best LFL for the decidability?
2. Similarly, Theorem 24 shows that there is no best AFL for the learnability. Is there a best AFL for the decidability?
3. Theorem 22 asserts that decidability by LFL implies decidability by AFL. Is the converse true?
4. It is easy to see that if a formula $f$ is learnable by LFL, and $f$ is equivalent to $g$, then the formula $g$ is also learnable by LFL. Is the same true for AFL's?
5. Lemma 7 shows that for the finite learnability there is a complete axiom system. Is anything similar possible for limit learnability and assurance learnability?

# References

[BFS96]  J. Bārzdiņš, R. Freivalds, and C. Smith. Learning with confidence. In C. Puech and R. Reischuk, editors, *Proceedings of the 13<sup>th</sup> Symposium on the Theoretical Aspects of Computer Science*, volume LNCS1046, pages 207–218. Springer, 1996.

[Gol67]  E. M. Gold. Language identification in the limit. *Information and Control*, 10:447–474, 1967.

[Kle52]  S. Kleene. *Introduction to Metamathematics*. American Elsevier, 1952.

[Kön26]  D. König. Sur les correspondances multivoques des ensembles. *Fund. Math*, 8:114–134, 1926.

[Men87]  E. Mendelson. *Introduction to Mathematical Logic, 3ed*. Wadsworth and Brooks/Cole, 1987.

[OSW91]  D. Osherson, M. Stob, and S. Weinstein. A universal inductive inference machine. *Journal of Symbolic Logic*, 56(2):661–672, 1991.

[Wie76]  R. Wiehagen. Limes-erkennung rekursiver funktionen durch spezielle strategien. *Elektronische Informationsverarbeitung und Kybernetik*, 12:93–99, 1976.

# Control Structures in Hypothesis Spaces: The Influence on Learning

John Case[1] and Sanjay Jain[2] and Mandayam Suraj[1]

[1] Department of Computer and Information Sciences
University of Delaware
Newark, DE 19716, USA
{case,suraj}@cis.udel.edu
[2] Department of Information Systems and Computer Science
National University of Singapore
Singapore 119260
Republic of Singapore
sanjay@iscs.nus.sg

**Abstract.** In any learnability setting, hypotheses are conjectured *from some hypothesis space*. Studied herein are the effects on learnability of the *presence or absence of certain control structures* in the hypothesis space. First presented are control structure *characterizations* of some rather specific but illustrative learnability results. Then presented are the main theorems. Each of these characterizes the invariance of a learning class over hypothesis space $V$ (and a little more about $V$) as: $V$ has suitable instances of *all* denotational control structures.

## 1  Introduction

In any learnability setting, hypotheses are conjectured *from some hypothesis space*, for example, in [OSW86] from general purpose programming systems, in [ZL95, Wie78] from subrecursive systems, and in [Qui92] from very simple classes of classificatory decision trees.[3] Much is known theoretically about the restrictions on learning power resulting from restricted hypothesis spaces [ZL95].

In the present paper we begin to study the effects on learnability of the *presence or absence of certain control structures* in the hypothesis space. We consider herein general purpose systems $V$ for the entire class of r.e. languages, which systems may or may not have available particular control structures. [BS94] considered, in effect, whether a particular learnability result **P** characterized the general purpose hypothesis spaces having available all possible control structures; they discovered their particular **P** failed very badly to do so. We began our study with the idea in mind of seeing if certain control structures (in general purpose systems) were necessary and sufficient to maintain the invariance (compared with a system with all possible control structures available) of standard learning classes. We haven't quite achieved that, and our paper is an initial progress report on the endeavor.[4]

---

[3] For example, with the latter one can, nonetheless, train an autopilot from flight simulator data on real pilots [CSM92].

[4] [Wie96] quite interestingly characterizes learning criteria invariances, but as in [Wie78, FKW84], not in terms of control structures.

In Section 2.1 we present the basics of the sorts of general purpose recognizing systems we consider.

We treat (see Section 2.2) mostly the standard learning criteria of learning in the limit and learning in one-shot, recognizers (or grammars [HU79, Wei87]) for r.e. languages — from text (or positive information).

In Section 2.3 we provide sufficient background material from [Ric80, Ric81, Roy87] about control structures in general purpose programming systems.

In Section 3 we first present control structure *characterizations* of some rather specific but illustrative learnability results. In the remainder we consider, for the control structures involved, whether or not they *must* be available in any hypothesis space.

In Section 4 we present our two main characterization theorems, Theorems 35 and 36. Each, essentially, characterizes the invariance of a learning class over hypothesis space $V$ (and a little more about $V$) as: $V$ has suitable instances of *all* denotational control structures. Some parts of these theorems are the most difficult in the paper.

Lastly in Section 5 we briefly sketch some problems and future directions.

## 2 Notations and Definitions

We let $N$ denote the set of natural numbers, i.e., $\{0, 1, 2, 3, \ldots\}$. We let $i, j, k, m, n, p, q, s, v, w, x, y, z$ (with or without subscripts, superscripts, ...) range over $N$.

$\emptyset$ denotes the empty set. $\in, \notin, \subseteq, \subset$ respectively denote 'is a member of', 'is not a member of', 'is a subset of' and 'is a proper subset of'.

For sets $A$ and $B$, $A \oplus B \stackrel{\text{def}}{=} (\{2 \cdot x \mid x \in A\} \cup \{2 \cdot x + 1 \mid x \in B\})$ [Rog67]. When iterating the $\oplus$ operator, we will assume left-associativity (to avoid excessive parenthesization).

For $S$, a subset of $N$, $\text{card}(S)$ denotes the cardinality of $S$. $\max(S)$ and $\min(S)$ denote, respectively, the maximum and minimum of the set $S$, where $\max(\emptyset) = 0$ and $\min(\emptyset) = \infty$. $D_x$ denotes the finite set with canonical index $x$ [Rog67].

$\langle \cdot, \cdot \rangle$ denotes a fixed *pairing function* [Rog67], a computable, surjective and injective mapping from $N \times N$ into $N$. $\langle \cdot, \cdot \rangle$ is useful, for example, for speaking of two inputs to a one-input program.

$f, g, h$ and $t$ with or without decorations range over *total* (not necessarily computable) functions with arguments and values from $N$.

Let $\varphi_p$ be the partial computable function: $N \to N$ computed (according to some standard I/O conventions) by Turing machine number $p$ is some standard numbering of Turing machines [Rog58, Rog67, Ric80, Ric81, Roy87]. Let $W_p$ denote the domain of $\varphi_p$. Then $W_p$ is the set $\subseteq N$ *recognized* [HU79, Wei87] by Turing machine number $p$, i.e., the set of natural number inputs on which Turing machine $p$ halts. Let $\Phi$ denote a step-counting Blum complexity measure for $\varphi_p$ [Blu67, DSW94]. We let

$$\varphi_{p,s}(x) \stackrel{\text{def}}{=} \begin{cases} \varphi_p(x) & \text{if } x \leq s \text{ and } \Phi_p(x) \leq s; \\ \text{undefined} & \text{otherwise.} \end{cases}$$

We then let $W_{p,s}$ be the domain of $\varphi_{p,s}$.

The set of all recursively enumerable languages is denoted by $\mathcal{E}$. $L$ and $S$, with or without decorations, range over $\mathcal{E}$. $\mathcal{L}$, with or without decorations, ranges over subsets of $\mathcal{E}$. For a set $L$, we use $\chi_L$ to denote the characteristic function of $L$, the function which is 1 on $L$ and 0 off $L$. $\overline{L}$ denotes complement of $L$, i.e., $N - L$.

The quantifiers '$\stackrel{\infty}{\forall}$', and '$\stackrel{\infty}{\exists}$' essentially from [Blu67], mean 'for all but finitely many' and 'there exist infinitely many', respectively.

We next define a *limiting-computable function*.

First, we define

$$\lim_{t\to\infty} h(x,t) \stackrel{\text{def}}{=} \begin{cases} y & \text{if } (\stackrel{\infty}{\forall} t)[h(x,t) = y]; \\ \text{undefined} & \text{otherwise.} \end{cases}$$

We write $h(x,\infty)$ for $\lim_{t\to\infty} h(x,t)$. $g : N \to N$ is *limiting-computable* $\stackrel{\text{def}}{\Leftrightarrow}$ ($\exists$ computable $h : (N \times N) \to N)(\forall x)[g(x) = h(x,\infty)]$.

Intuitively, $h(x,t)$ is the output at discrete time $t$ of a mind changing algorithm for $g$ (acting on input $x$); hence, for $g$ limiting computable as just above, for all $x$, for all but finitely many times $t$, the output of the mind changing algorithm on input $x$ is $g(x)$.

In this paper we freely use Church's lambda notation [Chu41, Rog67, All78] to define functions: $N \to N$. For example, $\lambda x. x + 1$ denotes the function that maps each $x \in N$ to $x + 1$.

## 2.1 Computable Recognizing Systems

As we noted in Section 1, in any learnability setting, hypotheses are conjectured *from some hypothesis space*. Furthermore, we noted that in the present paper we focus our attention on hypothesis spaces for recognizing the entire class of r.e. sets. The collection of Turing machines (or their code numbers) defining the sets $W_p$, $p = 0, 1, 2, \ldots$ from Section 2.3 forms such an hypothesis space. We write $W$ as the name of this particular hypothesis space. Of course Turing machines have a universal interpreter which is also a Turing machine. We are also interested in the present paper in focusing our attention on hypothesis spaces containing a universal interpreter for the hypothesis space. Formally this can be handled as follows, where for mappings $V$ in this definition, we write $V_p$ for the value of the mapping $V$ at $p$.

**Definition 1.** $V$ is a *computable recognizing system* (abbreviated: c.r.s.) $\stackrel{\text{def}}{\Leftrightarrow}$ $V : N \stackrel{\text{onto}}{\to} \mathcal{E}$ such that for some computable $t$, for every $p$, $V_p = W_{t(p)}$

Intuitively, for a c.r.s. $V$, each r.e. set is some $V_p$, and we have some uniform computable way to map any $V$-recognizer $p$ into a corresponding Turing machine recognizer $t(p)$ which recognizes the set $V_p$.

**Definition 2.** Suppose $V$ is a c.r.s. For $L$ r.e., $\mathrm{MinGram}_V(L)$ denotes $\min(\{p \mid V_p = L\})$.

We define next some interesting senses in which one can translate from one c.r.s. into another. Part (b) of this definition is based on a definition in [Rog58]. [ZL95] notes the relevance to learning theory of the sense in part (c).

**Definition 3.** Suppose $V^1$ and $V^2$ are c.r.s.'s

(a) We say that $t$ *translates* $V^1$ *into* $V^2$ (written: $t : V^1 \le V^2$) $\overset{\text{def}}{\Leftrightarrow}$ $(\forall p)[V^2_{t(p)} = V^1_p]$.[5]

(b) $V^1$ *computably translates into* $V^2$ (written: $V^1 \le V^2$) $\overset{\text{def}}{\Leftrightarrow}$ ($\exists$ computable $t)[t : V^1 \le V^2]$.

(c) $V^1$ *limiting-computably translates into* $V^2$ (written: $V^1 \le_{\lim} V^2$) $\overset{\text{def}}{\Leftrightarrow}$ ($\exists$ limiting-computable $t)[t : V^1 \le V^2]$.

The next definition is also based on a definition in [Rog58].

**Definition 4.** (a) $V$ is an *acceptable recognizing system* (abbreviated *a.r.s.*) $\overset{\text{def}}{\Leftrightarrow}$ $V$ is a c.r.s. and $(\forall$ c.r.s. $U)[U \le V]$.

(b) $V$ is a *limiting-acceptable recognizing system* (abbreviated *lim-a.r.s.*) $\overset{\text{def}}{\Leftrightarrow}$ $V$ is a c.r.s. and $(\forall$ c.r.s. $U)[U \le_{\lim} V]$.

Clearly, $W$ is an acceptable system (intuitively, a system in which one can interpret an arbitrary c.r.s.). The acceptable systems are the ones maximal with respect to $\le$, the limiting-acceptable systems are the ones maximal with respect to $\le_{\lim}$.

**Definition 5.** $V_{p,s} \overset{\text{def}}{=} W_{t(p),s}$, where $t$ is some arbitrary but fixed computable function such that $t\colon V \le W$.

**Definition 6.** *Friedberg computable recognizing systems* are (by definition) c.r.s.'s in which there exists *exactly* one recognizer for each r.e. set.

Such systems were first shown to exist by Friedberg [Fri58], and they are useful in providing counterexamples.

$U$ and $V$, with or without superscripts, range over c.r.s.'s.

## 2.2 Learning Theory Definitions

A *sequence* $\sigma$ is a mapping from an initial segment of $N$ into $(N \cup \{\#\})$. The *content* of a sequence $\sigma$, denoted content$(\sigma)$, is the set of natural numbers in the range of $\sigma$. The *length* of $\sigma$, denoted by $|\sigma|$, is the number of elements in $\sigma$. $\Lambda$ denotes an empty sequence. SEQ denotes the set of all finite sequences. The set of all finite sequences of natural numbers and #'s, SEQ, can be coded onto $N$. This latter fact will be used implicitly in some of our proofs.

---

[5] I.e, for each $p$, $t(p)$, the translation of $V^1$-recognizer $p$, is a $V^2$-recognizer equivalent to $p$.

A *text* $T$ for a language $L$ is a mapping from $N$ into $(N \cup \{\#\})$ such that $L$ is the set of natural numbers in the range of $T$. The *content* of a text $T$, denoted content$(T)$, is the set of natural numbers in the range of $T$.

Intuitively, a text for a language is an enumeration or sequential presentation of all the objects in the language with the #'s representing pauses in the listing or presentation of such objects. For example, the only text for the empty language is just an infinite sequence of #'s

We let $T$, with or without superscripts, range over texts. $T[n]$ denotes the finite initial sequence of $T$ with length $n$. Hence, domain$(T[n]) = \{x \mid x < n\}$.

A *language learning machine* is (by definition) an algorithmic device that maps SEQ into $N \cup \{?\}$.

Intuitively, the output ?'s represent the machine not yet committing to an output *program*. The reason we allow the ?'s is so that a learning machine can wait until it has seen a long enough input before it outputs its first numerical output, if at all.

$M$ ranges over language learning machines. In this paper we assume, without loss of generality, that for all $\sigma \subseteq \tau$, $[M(\sigma) \neq ?] \Rightarrow [M(\tau) \neq ?]$.

Suppose $M$ is a learning machine and $T$ is a text. $M(T){\downarrow}$ (read: $M(T)$ *converges*) $\overset{\text{def}}{\Leftrightarrow} (\exists i)(\overset{\infty}{\forall} n) [M(T[n]) = i]$. If $M(T){\downarrow}$, then $M(T)$ is defined $=$ the unique $i$ such that $(\overset{\infty}{\forall} n)[M(T[n]) = i]$.

We now introduce a criterion for a learning machine to be considered *successful* on languages.

**Definition 7.** Suppose $V$ is a c.r.s.
  (a) $M$ **TxtEx**$_V$-*identifies* $L \overset{\text{def}}{\Leftrightarrow} (\forall$ texts $T$ for $L)(\exists i \mid V_i = L)[M(T){\downarrow} = i]$.
  (b) For all $M$, **TxtEx**$_V(M) = \{L \mid M$ **TxtEx**$_V$-identifies $L\}$.
  (c) **TxtEx**$_V = \{\mathcal{L} \mid (\exists M)[\mathcal{L} \subseteq$ **TxtEx**$_V(M)]\}$.

Gold [Gol67] introduced the criterion we call **TxtEx**$_W$.

We next introduce one-shot language identification for which the first program conjectured must be correct.

**Definition 8.** Suppose $V$ is a c.r.s.
  (a) $M$ **TxtFin**$_V$-*identifies* $L \overset{\text{def}}{\Leftrightarrow} (\forall$ texts $T$ for $L)(\exists i \mid V_i = L)(\exists n)[(\forall n' \geq n)[M(T[n']) = i] \wedge (\forall n' < n)[M(T[n']) =?]]$.
  (b) For all $M$, **TxtFin**$_V(M) = \{L \mid M$ **TxtFin**$_V$-identifies $L\}$.
  (c) **TxtFin**$_V = \{\mathcal{L} \mid (\exists M)[\mathcal{L} \subseteq$ **TxtFin**$_V(M)]\}$.

**Definition 9.** Suppose $V$ is a c.r.s.
  (a) $M$ **TxtMinEx**$_V$-*identifies* $L \overset{\text{def}}{\Leftrightarrow} (\forall$ texts $T$ for $L)[M(T){\downarrow} = \text{MinGram}_V(L)]$.
  (b) For all $M$, **TxtMinEx**$_V(M) = \{L \mid M$ **TxtMinEx**$_V$-identifies $L\}$.
  (c) **TxtMinEx**$_V = \{\mathcal{L} \mid (\exists M)[\mathcal{L} \subseteq$ **TxtMinEx**$_V(M)]\}$.

We sometimes write **TxtEx** for **TxtEx**$_W$ and similarly for the other criteria just discussed.

## 2.3 Control Structures in C.R.S.'s

[Ric80, Ric81, Roy87] show how to define control structures in the context of programming systems (effective numberings) for the partial computable functions [Rog58]. These ideas can be straightforwardly adapted to the context of c.r.s.'s. We will omit some of the details of this adaptation, but Definition 11 below will provide all that is really essential to the present paper.

Of course, **while-loop** and **if-then-else** are natural (intuitive) example control structures for systems for the partial computable functions. We exhibit in the next definition two natural example control structures in the context of c.r.s.'s.[6]

**Definition 10.**
(a) An *instance of the control structure* **union** *in* $V$ is (by definition) a function $f$ such that, for all $p$ and $q$, $V_{f(p,q)} = \{x \mid x \in V_p \lor x \in V_q\}$.

(b) An *instance of the control structure* **intersect** *in* $V$ is (by definition) a function $g$ such that, for all $p$ and $q$, $V_{g(p,q)} = \{x \mid x \in V_p \land x \in V_q\}$.

Intuitively, for example, an instance $g$ of **intersect** in $V$ applied to constituent $V$-programs $p$ and $q$, produces $g(p, q)$, a composite $V$-program for recognizing the intersection of the respective sets recognized by $p$ and $q$.

In the present paper, it will suffice for us to consider the *extensional* [Roy87] (synonym: *denotational* [Sto77]) control structures.[7] Instances of *extensional control structures* provide a means of forming a composite program from given constituent programs (and/or data), *where* the I/O behavior of that composite program depends only on the I/O behavior of the constituent programs (and on the data).[8] Clearly, in the context of c.r.s.'s, **union** and **intersect** from Definition 10 above are extensional. Also, instances of each combine *two* programs (and no data) to form a third (composite) recognizer program.

Formally, each control structure for c.r.s.'s is determined by an enumeration operator $\Theta$. [Rog67] provides an excellent discussion of enumeration operators.[9] As noted earlier, we provide below the definition of extensional (or denotational) control structures only since that is all that is really essential to the present paper. Also, as noted above, this definition is the obvious analog for c.r.s.'s of the corresponding concepts in [Roy87].

---

[6] We believe it is pedagogically useful to present these examples before we present some formal notions about control structures in general.

[7] [Ric80, Ric81, Roy87] provide an even more general type of control structure called *intensional* (synonym: *connotational*). Also, the extensional control structures, as rigorously defined in [Roy87], include ([Roy87, Theorem 2.3.3]) the *recursive* extensional control structures under minimal fixed point semantics.

[8] So, for example, when applying extensional control structures, the I/O behavior of a composite program cannot generally depend on the number of symbols in or the run-time complexity of a constituent program.

[9] Roughly, an *enumeration operator* $\Theta$ is (by definition) a mapping from all sets of natural numbers into the same such that some algorithm transforms arbitrary enumerations of any set $A$ into correspondings enumerations of $\Theta(A)$.

In [Ric80, Ric81, Roy87] we see that control structures in the context of programming systems for the partial computable functions are determined instead by *recursive operators* [Rog67].

**Definition 11.**

(a) Suppose $n > 0$. Suppose $0 \leq m \leq n$. Suppose $\Theta$ is an enumeration operator. Suppose $V$ is a c.r.s.

$f : N^n \to N$ *is an instance of the extensional control structure in $V$ determined by $(m, n, \Theta)$* $\overset{\text{def}}{\Leftrightarrow}$ $(\forall p_1, \ldots, p_m, x_1, \ldots, x_{n-m})[V_{f(p_1, \ldots, p_m, x_1, \ldots, x_{n-m})} = \Theta(V_{p_1} \oplus \ldots \oplus V_{p_m})(x_1, \ldots, x_{n-m})].$[10]

(b) Suppose $n > 0$. Suppose $0 \leq m \leq n$. Suppose $\Theta$ is an enumeration operator.

*The extensional control structure determined by $(m, n, \Theta)$* is (by definition) $\{(V, f) \mid V$ is a c.r.s. $\wedge f : N^n \to N$ is an instance of the extensional control structure in $V$ determined by $(m, n, \Theta)\}$.

(c) **s** *is an extensional control structure* $\overset{\text{def}}{\Leftrightarrow}$ $(\exists n > 0)(\exists m \mid 0 \leq m \leq n)(\exists$ enumeration operator $\Theta)[$ **s** is the extensional control structure determined by $(m, n, \Theta)]$.

If $f$ is an instance of a control structure in $V$, then $f$ may or may not be computable or even limiting-computable. In the c.r.s. $W$, one has, of course, *computable* instances of **union** and **intersect**. Similarly, in typical, practical programming languages, one has instances of **while-loop** and **if-then-else** which are not only computable, but, since they can be realized by simple substitution of the constituent programs into some fixed template, they are computable in linear-time [Roy87, Mar89].

The learning criteria we consider in Section 3 below feature converging to a correct hypothesis *in the limit*. Hence, it is not surprising that only *limiting-*computable instances of the control structures are relevant there. However, in Section 4 further below, *computable* instances are sometimes relevant.

Case showed [Ric80, Roy87] that the acceptable programming systems (for the partial computable functions) are characterized by having a computable instance of *each* control structure. This result easily carries over to a corresponding control structure characterization of acceptable c.r.s.'s. It is a straightforward lift to show the following

**Theorem 12.** A c.r.s. is limiting-acceptable $\Leftrightarrow$ it has a limiting-computable instance of each *extensional* control structure.

It is currently open whether in Theorem 12 just above, the word 'extensional' can be removed. It is straightforward to show that 'extensional' can be added (before 'control structure') with no problem in the characterization of *acceptable* c.r.s.'s. These control structure characterizations of acceptability and limiting-acceptability motivate their partly *learning-theoretic* characterizations in Section 4 below.

---

[10] Clearly, $p_1, \ldots, p_m$ are program arguments, and $x_1, \ldots, x_{n-m}$ are data arguments. $f(p_1, \ldots, p_m, x_1, \ldots, x_{n-m})$ is the resultant composite $V$-program whose I/O behavior depends on that of the program arguments and which also depends on the data arguments.

It is easy to argue that all the examples in the present paper of instances of control structures in a c.r.s. $V$ satisfy this definition for suitably chosen $(m, n, \Theta)$. In these examples we suppress explicit mention of the $(m, n, \Theta)$.

**Definition 13.** We write $V \models \mathbf{s}$ to mean there is a computable instance of the control structure $\mathbf{s}$ in $V$, and we write $V \models \text{lim-}\mathbf{s}$ to mean that there is a limiting-computable instance of $\mathbf{s}$ in $V$.

We present next, examples of (extensional) control structures of relevance to the sections which follow. In the remainder of the paper, for convenience, we will many times drop the modifier 'extensional' in discussions of extensional control structures.

The first example, **s-1-1**, is a control structure intuitively for storing a datum $x$ in a recognizing program $p$, more specifically, for replacing the first of two (coded) input parameters to $p$ by the constant $x$. In the c.r.s. $W$, Kleene's S-m-n function [Rog67] essentially provides a computable instance.

**Definition 14.** An *instance of the control structure* **s-1-1** *in* $V$ is (by definition) a function $f$ such that, for all $p$ and $x$, $V_{f(p,x)} = \{y \mid \langle x, y \rangle \in V_p\}$.

[Rog58] characterized acceptability for programming systems (numberings) of the partial recursive functions in terms of Kleene's S-m-n Theorem. His proof straightforwardly adapts to show the following

**Theorem 15.**
(a) For all c.r.s. $V$, $V$ is acceptable $\Leftrightarrow V \models \mathbf{s}\text{-}\mathbf{1}\text{-}\mathbf{1}$.
(b) For all c.r.s. $V$, $V$ is limiting-acceptable $\Leftrightarrow V \models \text{lim-}\mathbf{s}\text{-}\mathbf{1}\text{-}\mathbf{1}$.

The next example, **fin**, is a control structure which has no program arguments and one data argument $x$. Its instances, applied to $x$, return a recognizer for the canonical finite set $D_x$.

**Definition 16.** An *instance of the control structure* **fin** *in* $V$ is (by definition) a function $f$ such that, for all $x$, $V_{f(x)} = D_x$.

The next example, **coinit**, is a control structure which has no program arguments and one data argument $x$. Its instances, applied to $x$, return a recognizer for the set of all integers $\geq x$.

**Definition 17.** An *instance of the control structure* **coinit** *in* $V$ is (by definition) a function $f$ such that, for all $x$, $V_{f(x)} = \{y \mid y \geq x\}$.

The next example, **cosingle**, is a control structure which has no program arguments and one data argument $x$. Its instances, applied to $x$, return a recognizer for the set of all natural numbers $\neq x$.

**Definition 18.** An *instance of the control structure* **cosingle** *in* $V$ is (by definition) a function $f$ such that, for all $x$, $V_{f(x)} = \{y \mid y \neq x\}$.

The next example, **proj**, is a control structure which has one program argument $p$ and no data arguments. For **proj**, it is useful to think of $V_p$ as a (coded) set of ordered pairs. Then an instance of **proj**, applied to $p$, returns a recognizer for the first (or $x$-axis) projection of $V_p$.

**Definition 19.** An *instance of the control structure* **proj** *in* $V$ is (by definition) a function $f$ such that, for all $p$, $V_{f(p)} = \{x \mid (\exists y)[\langle x, y \rangle \in V_p]\}$.

# 3  Control Structure Characterizations of Learnability Results

As we noted in Section 1, in any learnability setting, hypotheses are conjectured *from some hypothesis space*. Furthermore, we noted that in the present paper we focus our attention on hypothesis spaces for recognizing the entire class of r.e. sets, and any such hypothesis space will have available some control structures but perhaps not others. The availability of certain control structures is, as we will see in this section, essential to certain learnability results. In the present section we first present control structure *characterizations* of some rather specific but illustrative learnability results. In the remainder we consider, for the control structures involved, whether or not they *must* be available in any hypothesis space (of the sort we consider herein). As we will see, some are always available and some are not.

**TxtEx**-learnability in c.r.s.'s is closely connected to the presence or absence of limiting-computable instances of control structures in them.

Here are some standard classes in **TxtEx**.

**Definition 20.**

   (a) FiniteSets $\stackrel{\text{def}}{=} \{D_i \mid i \in N\}$.

   (b) Co-Single $\stackrel{\text{def}}{=} \{L \mid (\exists j)[L = \overline{\{j\}}]\}$.

   (c) Co-Init $\stackrel{\text{def}}{=} \{L \mid (\exists j)[L = \overline{\{i \mid i \geq j\}}]\}$.

We have the following characterizations for each class from Definition 20 just above of its being in **TxtEx$_V$**. Each characterization is in terms of the availability of certain *limiting*-computable control structures in the hypothesis space $V$.

**Theorem 21.** Suppose $V$ is a c.r.s.. Then,

   (a) FiniteSets $\in$ **TxtEx$_V$** $\Leftrightarrow V \models$ lim-**fin**.

   (b) Co-Init $\in$ **TxtEx$_V$** $\Leftrightarrow V \models$ lim-**coinit**.

   (c) Co-Single $\in$ **TxtEx$_V$** $\Leftrightarrow V \models$ lim-**cosingle**.

*Proof.* We only prove part (b). Rest of the parts can be proved similarly.

Suppose $V$ is a c.r.s.

($\Rightarrow$): Suppose Co-Init $\in$ **TxtEx$_V$** as witnessed by $M$. We define $f_2(.,.)$ as follows.

Given any $i$, it is possible to compute a text $T_i$ for the language $\{n \mid n \geq i\}$ *uniformly in* $i$. For all $i, n$, let $f_2(i, n) = M(T_i[n])$. Further, let $f = \lambda i . \lim_{n \to \infty} f_2(i, n)$.

It is straightforward to show that $f$ is an instance of lim-**coinit** in $V$.

($\Leftarrow$): Suppose $V \models$ lim-**coinit** as witnessed by limiting computable $f$. Suppose $f$ is limiting-computable as witnessed by computable $f_2(.,.)$.

We define $M$ as follows.

$M(\sigma) = f_2(\min(\text{content}(\sigma) \cup \{|\sigma|\}), |\sigma|)$. It is straightforward to show that $M$ **TxtEx$_V$**-identifies Co-Init. ∎

**Definition 22.** A class $\mathcal{L}$ of languages is *uniformly decidable* $\stackrel{\text{def}}{\Leftrightarrow} \mathcal{L}$ can be written as $\{L_0, L_1, \ldots\}$, where $(\exists$ computable $f)(\forall i)[\lambda x . f(i, x) = \chi_{L_i}]$.

Uniformly decidable classes of languages are ubiquitous in computational learning theory [ZL95] and are many times also called *indexed families of recursive languages*. Important examples of such classes are the class of all context free languages [HU79] and the class of all pattern languages [Ang80b, Ang80a]. Other examples, of relevance to the present section, are FiniteSets, Co-Init, and Co-Single.

Next, we define a class of control structures useful for uniformly decidable classes. Just after that we provide Theorem 24 which generalizes Theorem 21 above.

Let $\mathcal{L} = \{L_i \mid i \in N\}$ be a uniformly decidable class of recursive languages (where $(\exists$ computable $f)(\forall i)[\lambda x . f(i, x) = \chi_{L_i}]$). We associate with $\mathcal{L}$ a control structure $\mathbf{cs}_{\mathcal{L}}$ which has no program arguments and one data argument $i$. An instance of $\mathbf{cs}_{\mathcal{L}}$, applied to $i$, returns a recognizer for the language $L_i$.[11]

**Definition 23.** For $\mathcal{L}$ as just above, an *instance of the control structure* $\mathbf{cs}_{\mathcal{L}}$ *in* $V$ is (by definition) a function $f$ such that, for all $i$, $V_{f(i)} = L_i$.

Theorem 21 generalizes as follows.

**Theorem 24.** Suppose $\mathcal{L} \in \mathbf{TxtEx}$ is a uniformly decidable class. Then, $(\forall V)[\mathcal{L} \in \mathbf{TxtEx}_V \Leftrightarrow V \models \lim\text{-}\mathbf{cs}_{\mathcal{L}}]$.

From Theorem 25 and Theorem 27 below, we will see that FiniteSets can be **TxtEx**-identified in all c.r.s.'s, but that there is a c.r.s. in which Co-Init cannot be **TxtEx**-identified. From this perspective, then, FiniteSets is *easier* than Co-Init. By contrast, with respect to an *intrinsic complexity* notion from [FKS95, JS94], FiniteSets is *harder* than Co-Init for **TxtEx**-identification.

**Theorem 25.** For all c.r.s.'s $V$, FiniteSets $\in \mathbf{TxtEx}_V$.

From Theorem 21 and 25, we have the following

**Corollary 26.** For all c.r.s. $V$, $V \models \lim\text{-}\mathbf{fin}$.

For the class Co-Init, however, we get the following result. Its proof is technically interesting since it involves a pleasing, subtle non-constructivity in the way the entire class of r.e. sets is embedded in the example c.r.s. of the Theorem.

**Theorem 27.** There exists a c.r.s. $V$, $V \not\models \lim\text{-}\mathbf{coinit}$ (and hence Co-Init $\notin \mathbf{TxtEx}_V$).

*Proof.* We use the symbol $\downarrow$ to denote that a computation halts. We define $V$ in stages below. Go to stage 0.

Begin stage $n$
    For all $i \leq n$, do the following steps. For all $i$, let $s_i = \max(\{s \mid \varphi_{i,n}(i, s)\downarrow\})$; let $p_i = \varphi_i(i, s_i)$, if $s_i \neq 0$ (recall that $\max(\emptyset) = 0$); otherwise, $p_i$ is undefined.
    1    For all $q \in \{p_i \mid i \leq n\}$, let $\mathrm{ClaimSet}_q = \{i \leq n \mid p_i = q\}$; for all other $q$, let $\mathrm{ClaimSet}_q = \emptyset$.

---

[11] N.B. The parameter $i$ here *within the system* $V$ does serve as a datum; however, within the subrecursive system $\langle L_i \mid i \in N \rangle$ it can be construed as a program (for deciding $L_i$).

2    If $\min(\{W_{i,n}\}) \notin \text{ClaimSet}_{2i}$, then enumerate $W_{i,n}$ into $V_{2i}$.
3    If $\min(\{W_{i,n}\}) \notin \text{ClaimSet}_{2i+1}$, then enumerate $W_{i,n}$ into $V_{2i+1}$.
End stage $n$.
Go to stage $n+1$.

**Claim 28.** $V \not\models$ lim-**coinit** (and hence Co-Init $\notin$ **TxtEx**$_V$).

**Claim 29.** For all $p$, there exists an $i$ such that $V_i = W_p$.

It follows from the above claims that $V$ is a c.r.s., $V \not\models$ lim-**coinit** and Co-Init $\notin$ **TxtEx**$_V$.                   ■ (Theorem 27)

The proof of Theorem 27, can be easily generalized to uniformly decidable classes of *infinite* recursive languages to give

**Theorem 30.** Suppose $\mathcal{L} \in$ **TxtEx** is a *infinite* uniformly decidable class containing only *infinite* (recursive) languages. Then, $(\exists$ a c.r.s. $V)[\mathcal{L} \notin$ **TxtEx**$_V]$.

We then have the following

**Corollary 31.** There exists a c.r.s. $V$ such that Co-Single $\notin$ **TxtEx**$_V$.

In another vein, Theorem 25 gives us the following

**Corollary 32.** $(\exists \mathcal{L} \mid \text{card}(\mathcal{L})$ infinite$)(\forall$ c.r.s. $V)[\mathcal{L} \in$ **TxtEx**$_V]$.

The immediately above corollary contrasts with [FKS94, Lemmas 25 & 26] which yield programming systems (for the partial computable functions) with respect to which one cannot learn in the limit any infinite class of (total) computable functions.[12]

As an even more contrasting result, an easy generalization of the proof of Theorem 25 gives,

**Theorem 33.** Suppose $\mathcal{L} \in$ **TxtEx** contains at most *finitely* many *infinite* sets (with no restriction on how many finite sets it contains). Then $(\forall$ c.r.s. $V)[\mathcal{L} \in$ **TxtEx**$_V]$.

# 4    Partly Learning-Theoretic Characterizations of Having "All" Control Structures

In this section we present our two main characterization theorems, Theorems 35 and 36. The first, in effect, characterizes **TxtFin**$_V$ being $=$ **TxtFin** (and a little more about $V$) as: $V$ has computable instances of all (extensional) control structures. The second, in effect, characterizes **TxtEx**$_V$ being $=$ **TxtEx** (and a little more about $V$) as: $V$ has limiting-computable instances of all extensional control structures. Of course, by remarks in Section 2.3 above, these are just characterizations of acceptability and limiting-acceptability, respectively; hence, we express them in such terms. As we will see, the hardest part of each of these theorems is the *furthermore* clause.

---

[12] An explanation for this and the next contrasting result is that in learning computable functions: there are no finite objects to be learned.

After our main theorems we consider a number of related matters and consequences.

The following Theorem is useful in proving part of our first main theorem and is of interest in its own right. Efim Kinber suggested the c.r.s. used in the proof of this

**Theorem 34.** There exists a limiting-acceptable c.r.s. $V$ that is not acceptable, such that $\mathbf{TxtEx}_V = \mathbf{TxtEx}$ and $\mathbf{TxtFin}_V = \mathbf{TxtFin}$.

*Proof.* We define a c.r.s. $V$ as follows.
$V_i = \{0\}$, if $i = 0$; $\emptyset$, if $i > 0$ and $W_i = \{0\}$; $W_i$, otherwise.
We omit verifying that this $V$ works.

■

Here is our first main

**Theorem 35.** $V$ is acceptable $\Leftrightarrow [\mathbf{TxtFin}_V = \mathbf{TxtFin} \wedge V \models \mathbf{proj}]$.
Furthermore, the clauses in the right hand side are independent of each other.

The proof of the $\Leftrightarrow$ part of Theorem 35 is a straightforward variant of the proof of the $\Leftrightarrow$ part of Theorem 36 below. For the *furthermore* part:
$(\exists V)[V \models \mathbf{proj} \not\Rightarrow \mathbf{TxtFin}_V = \mathbf{TxtFin}]$ follows from Theorem 37 below;
$(\exists V)[\mathbf{TxtFin}_V = \mathbf{TxtFin} \not\Rightarrow V \models \mathbf{proj}]$ follows from Theorem 34.
Our second main theorem follows.

**Theorem 36.** $V$ is limiting-acceptable $\Leftrightarrow [\mathbf{TxtEx}_V = \mathbf{TxtEx} \wedge V \models \text{lim-}\mathbf{proj}]$.
Furthermore, the clauses in the right hand side are independent of each other.

We mostly omit the proof of the $\Leftrightarrow$ part of this theorem.[13]. We break up the *furthermore* part into two separate theorems, Theorems 37 and 38, and sketch some of the proof of the second one only.

**Theorem 37.** $(\exists V)[V \models \text{lim-}\mathbf{proj}$ and $\mathbf{TxtFin} \not\subseteq \mathbf{TxtEx}_V$ (and hence $V$ is not limiting-acceptable) ]

**Theorem 38.** $(\exists V)[V$ is not limiting-acceptable and $\mathbf{TxtEx}_V = \mathbf{TxtEx}]$.

The sketch of the proof of this theorem proceeds employing a series of lemmas and propositions.
Let $\text{Init} \stackrel{\text{def}}{=} \{L \mid (\exists j)[L = \{i \mid i < j\}]\}$.

**Lemma 39.** Suppose $V$ is a c.r.s. such that $V_0 = N$. Then one can effectively (in algorithmic description of $V$) obtain a Friedberg c.r.s. $U$ and a limiting recursive function $f$ such that,
$(\forall i \mid V_i \notin (\{N\} \cup \text{Init}) \wedge i = \text{MinGram}_V(V_i))[U_{f(i)} = V_i]$.

*Proof.* Odifreddi's construction ( [Odi89, Theorem II.5.22, Page 230]) proves this lemma. ■ (Lemma 39)

---

[13] For the ($\Leftarrow$) direction we use the class $\mathcal{L}_{\mathbf{TxtEx}}$ from [JS94].

**Proposition 40.** Suppose $\mathcal{L}'$ is finite, $U$ is a c.r.s., $\mathcal{L} \cup \mathcal{L}' \in \mathbf{TxtEx}$, and $\mathcal{L} \in \mathbf{TxtEx}_U$. Then $\mathcal{L} \cup \mathcal{L}' \in \mathbf{TxtEx}_U$.

As a corollary to Theorem 25 we have,

**Corollary 41.** For all c.r.s. $U$, Init $\in \mathbf{TxtMinEx}_U$.

The following Lemma is proved using Lemma 39 and Proposition 40, and Corollary 41.

**Lemma 42.** Suppose $V$ is a c.r.s. Then one can effectively (in algorithmic description of $V$) construct a Friedberg c.r.s. $U$ such that $\mathbf{TxtMinEx}_V \subseteq \mathbf{TxtEx}_U = \mathbf{TxtMinEx}_U$.

**Lemma 43.** Suppose $M$ is given. Let $\mathcal{L} = \mathbf{TxtEx}(M)$. Then one can effectively construct a c.r.s. $V$ such that
(a) $M$ $\mathbf{TxtEx}_V$-identifies $\mathcal{L}$, and
(b) For infinite $L \in \mathcal{L}$, $M$ $\mathbf{TxtMinEx}_V$-identifies $L$.

**Lemma 44.** Suppose $V$ is a c.r.s. Further suppose $M$ and $\mathcal{L}$ are such that
(a) $M$ $\mathbf{TxtEx}_V$-identifies $\mathcal{L}$, and
(b) For all infinite $L \in \mathcal{L}$, $M$ $\mathbf{TxtMinEx}_V$-identifies $L$.
Then, $\mathcal{L} \in \mathbf{TxtMinEx}_V$.

We get the following proposition from Lemmas 43 and 44.

**Proposition 45.** For any inductive inference machine $M$, one can effectively (in $M$) construct a c.r.s. $V$ such that $\mathbf{TxtEx}(M) \in \mathbf{TxtMinEx}_V$.

A sequence of c.r.s.'s $V^0, V^1, \ldots$ is an *an r.e. sequence of c.r.s.'s* just in case the set $\{\langle\langle i, j\rangle, x\rangle \mid x \in V^i_j\}$ is recursively enumerable. The *direct sum* of an r.e. sequence of c.r.s.'s, $V^0, V^1, \ldots$ is defined to be the c.r.s. $V$ such that for all $i, j$, $V_{\langle i,j\rangle} = V^i_j$.
Finally, by an straightforward modification of the proof of the main theorem in [Kum89], we get the following

**Lemma 46.** The direct sum of an r.e. sequence of Friedberg c.r.s.'s is *never* limiting-acceptable.

PROOF OF THEOREM 38. Theorem follows directly from Lemmas 42 and 46 and Proposition 45. ∎ (Theorem 38)

Theorems 37 and 38 together give us the *furthermore* part of Theorem 36, and, with the $\Leftrightarrow$ part, we have ∎ (Theorem 36)

It is straightforward to show that Friedberg c.r.s.'s are *not* limiting-acceptable, yet we can show, by a straightforward modification of the proof of Theorem 4 from [FKW82], that Friedberg c.r.s.'s do not witness the truth of Theorem 38 above.
We can show that a c.r.s. $V$ is limiting-acceptable just in case one can computably (or equivalently, limiting-computably) translate $\mathbf{TxtEx}$-identifying machines to $\mathbf{TxtEx}_V$-identifying machines. We omit the formal statement and proof.

# 5 Further Directions and Problems

What we originally set out to do (for the principal learning criteria of this paper) was to

1. Find a set of control structures **S** such that $\mathbf{TxtFin}_V = \mathbf{TxtFin} \Leftrightarrow (\forall s \in \mathbf{S})[V \models s]$; and
2. Find a set of control structures **S** such that $\mathbf{TxtEx}_V = \mathbf{TxtEx} \Leftrightarrow (\forall s \in \mathbf{S})[V \models \lim\text{-}s]$.

This remains to be done.

It would be interesting to get learnability results about control structures in *sub*recursive hypothesis spaces [Roy87].

Are there pure learning-theoretic results completely characterizing each of acceptability and limiting-acceptability?

## Acknowledgements

We would like to thank Ganesh Baliga for helpful discussions, encouragement, and for suggesting some lines of research that, in part, led to the present paper. We would also like to thank each of Efim Kinber and Rolf Wiehagen for helpful discussions and examples.

## References

[All78]   J. Allen. *Anatomy of Lisp*. McGraw-Hill, New York, NY, 1978.

[Ang80a]  D. Angluin. Finding patterns common to a set of strings. *Journal of Computer and System Sciences*, 21:46–62, 1980.

[Ang80b]  D. Angluin. Inductive inference of formal languages from positive data. *Information and Control*, 45:117–135, 1980.

[Blu67]   M. Blum. A machine independent theory of the complexity of recursive functions. *Journal of the ACM*, 14:322–336, 1967.

[BS94]    G. Baliga and A. Shende. Learning-theoretic perspectives of acceptable numberings. In *Third International Symposium on Artificial Intelligence and Mathematics*, January 1994.

[Chu41]   A. Church. *The Calculi of Lambda Conversion*. Princeton Univ. Press, 1941.

[CSM92]   D. Kedzier C. Sammut, S. Hurst and D. Michie. Learning to fly. In D. Sleeman and P. Edwards, editors, *Proceedings of the Ninth International Conference on Machine Learning*. Morgan Kaufmann, 1992.

[DSW94]   M. Davis, R. Sigal, and E. Weyuker. *Computability, Complexity, and Languages*. Academic Press, second edition, 1994.

[FKS94]   R. Freivalds, M. Karpinski, and C. H. Smith. Co-learning of total recursive functions. In *Proceedings of the Seventh Annual Conference on Computational Learning Theory, New Brunswick, New Jersey*, pages 190–197. ACM-Press, July 1994.

[FKS95]   R Freivalds, E. Kinber, and C. H. Smith. On the intrinsic complexity of learning. In Paul Vitanyi, editor, *Proceedings of the Second European Conference on Computational Lear ning Theory*, pages 154–169. Springer-Verlag, March 1995. Lecture Notes in Artificial Intelligence 904.

[FKW82]   R. Freivalds, E. Kinber, and R. Wiehagen. Inductive inference and computable one-one numberings. *Zeitschrift für Mathematische Logik und Grundlagen der Mathematik*, 28:463–479, 1982.

[FKW84]  R. Freivalds, E. Kinber, and R. Wiehagen.  Connections between identifying functionals, standardizing operations, and computable numberings. *Zeitschrift für Mathematische Logik und Grundlagen der Mathematik*, 30:145–164, 1984.

[Fri58]  R. M. Friedberg. Three theorems on recursive enumeration. *Journal of Symbolic Logic*, 23(3):309–316, September 1958.

[Gol67]  E. Gold. Language identification in the limit. *Information and Control*, 10:447–474, 1967.

[HU79]  J. Hopcroft and J. Ullman. *Introduction to Automata Theory Languages and Computation*. Addison-Wesley Publishing Company, 1979.

[JS94]  S. Jain and A. Sharma. On the intrinsic complexity of language identification. In *Proceedings of the Seventh Annual Conference on Computational Learning Theory, New Brunswick, New Jersey*, pages 278–286. ACM-Press, July 1994.

[Kum89]  M. Kummer. A note on direct sums of friedbergnumberings. *Journal of Symbolic Logic*, 54(3):1009–1010, September 1989.

[Mar89]  Y. Marcoux. Composition is almost as good as s-1-1. In *Proceedings, Structure in Complexity Theory–Fourth Annual Conference*. IEEE Computer Society Press, 1989.

[Odi89]  P. Odifreddi. *Classical Recursion Theory*, volume 125 of *Studies in Logic and the Foundations of Mathematics*. North Holland, Amsterdam, 1989.

[OSW86]  D. Osherson, M. Stob, and S. Weinstein. *Systems that Learn, An Introduction to Learning Theory for Cognitive and Computer Scientists*. MIT Press, Cambridge, Mass., 1986.

[Qui92]  J. Quinlan. *C4.5: Programs for Machine Learning*. Morgan Kaufmann Publishers, San Mateo, CA, 1992.

[Ric80]  G. Riccardi. *The Independence of Control Structures in Abstract Programming Systems*. PhD thesis, SUNY Buffalo, 1980.

[Ric81]  G. Riccardi. The independence of control structures in abstract programming systems. *Journal of Computer and System Sciences*, 22:107–143, 1981.

[Rog58]  H. Rogers. Gödel numberings of partial recursive functions. *Journal of Symbolic Logic*, 23:331–341, 1958.

[Rog67]  H. Rogers. *Theory of Recursive Functions and Effective Computability*. McGraw Hill, New York, 1967. Reprinted, MIT Press, 1987.

[Roy87]  J. Royer. *A Connotational Theory of Program Structure*. Lecture Notes in Computer Science 273. Springer Verlag, 1987.

[Sto77]  J. Stoy. *Denotational Semantics: The Scott-Strachey Approach to Programming Language Theory*. MIT Press, 1977.

[Wei87]  K. Weihrauch. *Computability*. Springer-Verlag, 1987.

[Wie78]  R. Wiehagen. Characterization problems in the theory of inductive inference. *Lecture Notes in Computer Science*, 62:494–508, 1978.

[Wie96]  R. Wiehagen. Characterizations of learnability in various hypothesis spaces. Private communication, 1996.

[ZL95]  T. Zeugmann and S. Lange. A guided tour across the boundaries of learning recursive languages. In Klaus P. Jantke and Steffen Lange, editors, *Algorithmic Learning for Knowledge-Based Systems*, volume 961 of *Lecture Notes in Artificial Intelligence*, pages 190–258. Springer-Verlag, 1995.

# Ordinal Mind Change Complexity of Language Identification

Andris Ambainis[1] and Sanjay Jain[2] and Arun Sharma[3]

[1] Institute of Mathematics and Computer Science
University of Latvia
Raiņa bulv. 29, Riga, Latvia
Email: ambainis@cclu.lv
[2] Department of Information Systems and Computer Science
National University of Singapore
Singapore 119260, Republic of Singapore
Email: sanjay@iscs.nus.sg
[3] School of Computer Science and Engineering
The University of New South Wales
Sydney, NSW 2052, Australia
Email: arun@cse.unsw.edu.au

**Abstract.** The approach of ordinal mind change complexity, introduced by Freivalds and Smith, uses constructive ordinals to bound the number of mind changes made by a learning machine. This approach provides a measure of the extent to which a learning machine has to keep revising its estimate of the number of mind changes it will make before converging to a correct hypothesis for languages in the class being learned. Recently, this measure, which also suggests the difficulty of learning a class of languages, has been used to analyze the learnability of rich classes of languages. Jain and Sharma have shown that the ordinal mind change complexity for identification from positive data of languages formed by unions of up to $n$ pattern languages is $\omega^n$. They have also shown that this bound is essential. Similar results were also established for classes definable by length-bounded elementary formal systems with up to $n$ clauses. These later results translate to learnability of certain classes of logic programs.

The present paper further investigates the utility of ordinal mind change complexity. It is shown that if identification is to take place from both positive and negative data, then the ordinal mind change complexity of the class of languages formed by unions of up to $n+1$ pattern languages is only $\omega \times_o n$ (where $\times_o$ represents ordinal multiplication). This result nicely extends an observation of Lange and Zeugmann that pattern languages can be identified from both positive and negative data with 0 mind changes.

Existence of an ordinal mind change bound for a class of learnable languages can be seen as an indication of its learning "tractability." Conditions are investigated under which a class has an ordinal mind change bound for identification from positive data. It is shown that an indexed family of computable languages has an ordinal mind change bound if it has finite elasticity and can be identified by a conservative machine. It is also shown that the requirement of conservative identification can be sacrificed for the purely topological requirement of $M$-finite thickness. Interaction between identification by monotonic strategies and existence of ordinal mind change bound is also investigated.

# 1  Introduction

Natural numbers have been used as counters for bounding the number of mind changes. However, such bounds do not take into account the scenario in which a learning machine, after examining an element of the language is in a position to issue a bound on the number of mind changes it will make before the onset of convergence. For example, consider the class $COINIT = \{L \mid (\exists n)[L = \{x \mid x \geq n\}]\}$. Intuitively, $COINIT$ is the collection of languages that contain all natural numbers except a finite initial segment. Clearly, a learning machine that, at any given time, finds the minimum element $n$ in the data seen so far and emits a grammar for the language $\{x \mid x \geq n\}$ identifies $COINIT$ in the limit from positive data. It is also easy to see that the class $COINIT$ cannot be identified by any machine that is required to converge within a constant number of mind changes. However, the machine identifying $COINIT$ can, after examining an element of the language, issue an upper bound on the number of mind changes. It turns out that the class of pattern languages ($PATTERN$), first introduced by Angluin [Ang80] who also showed that this class can be identified in the limit from only positive data (texts), displays similar behavior. This is because any string in a pattern language yields a finite set of patterns that are candidate patterns for the language being learned. Such scenarios can be modeled by the use of constructive ordinals as mind change counters introduced by Freivalds and Smith [FS93]. We illustrate the idea with a few examples; the formal definition is presented later.

**TxtEx** denotes the collection of language classes that can be identified in the limit from texts. **TxtEx**$_\alpha$ denotes the collection of languages classes that can be identified in the limit from texts with an ordinal mind change bound $\alpha$. Let $\omega$ denote the first limit ordinal. For $\alpha \prec \omega$, the notion coincides with the earlier notion of bounded mind change identification. For $\alpha = \omega$, **TxtEx**$_\omega$ denotes learnable classes for which there exists a machine that, after examining some element(s) of the language, can announce an upper bound on the number of mind changes it will make before the onset of successful convergence. Both, $COINIT$ and $PATTERN$ are members of **TxtEx**$_\omega$. Proceeding on, the class **TxtEx**$_{\omega \times o2}$ contains classes for which there is a learning machine that after examining some element(s) of the language announces an upper bound on the number of mind changes, but reserves the right to revise this upper bound once. Similarly, in the case of **TxtEx**$_{\omega \times o3}$, the machine reserves the right to revise its upper bound twice, and so on. **TxtEx**$_{\omega^2}$ contains classes for which the machine announces an upper bound on the number of times it may revise its conjectured upper bound on the number of mind changes, and so on.

Shinohara [Shi86] showed that the class of pattern languages is not closed under union and many rich concepts can be represented by unions of pattern languages; these languages have been applied to knowledge acquisition from amino acid sequences (see Arikawa et al. [AMS+92]). In [JS96], the ordinal mind change complexity of the classes of languages formed by taking unions of pattern languages was derived. For $n > 1$, it was shown that the class formed by taking unions of up to $n$ pattern languages, $PATTERN^n$, is in **TxtEx**$_{\omega^n}$. It was also shown that there are cases for which the $\omega^n$ bound is essential because $PATTERN^n \not\subseteq \textbf{TxtEx}_\alpha$, for all $\alpha \prec \omega^n$.

In this paper we investigate the ordinal mind change bounds for identification in the limit of unions of pattern languages from both positive and negative data (informants). **InfEx** denotes the collection of language classes that can be identified in the limit from informants and **InfEx**$_\alpha$ denotes the collection of those classes identifiable with an ordinal mind change bound of $\alpha$. Lange and Zeugmann [LZ93] have observed that *PATTERN* can be identified from informants with 0 mind changes. So, it is to be expected that the ordinal mind change bounds for identification from informants of unions of pattern languages be lower than those for identification from texts. We show that this is indeed the case as $PATTERN^{n+1} \in \textbf{InfEx}_{\omega \times_O n}$.

It is interesting to note that although the unbounded union of pattern languages is not identifiable from texts, it is identifiable from informants. Unfortunately, there is no ordinal mind change bound for identification from informants of unbounded unions of pattern languages. This is because this class contains the class of finite languages, *FIN*, for which there is no ordinal mind change complexity bound. It may be argued that in terms of mind change complexity, *FIN*, is a very difficult problem.[4] Since the existence of ordinal mind change bound for a class is a reflection of its learning "tractability", it is therefore useful to investigate conditions under which an ordinal mind change bound can be guaranteed. We consider a number of possibilities, including identifiability by conservative strategies, topological properties like finite thickness, $M$-finite thickness, and finite elasticity, and monotonicity requirements. We preview some of our results.

We first establish a useful technical result which states that if a learning machine makes a finite number of mind changes on any text, then the class of languages that can be identified by this machine has an ordinal mind change bound. This result is used to show that if an indexed family of computable languages has finite elasticity and can be conservatively identified then there is an ordinal mind change bound for this class. We also show that the requirement of conservative identification can be sacrificed in the previous result for the purely topological requirement that the class have $M$-finite thickness in addition to finite elasticity. Since finite thickness implies finite elasticity and $M$-finite thickness, the above results imply that any indexed family of computable languages with finite thickness has an ordinal mind change bound.

The results discussed above give general sufficient conditions for identifiability with ordinal bound on mind changes. However, the mind change bound $\alpha$ may be arbitrarily large. An interesting question to ask is whether the ordinal mind change bound remains arbitrarily large if some other constraints such as monotonicity are added. We show a negative result in this direction as for every constructive ordinal bound $\alpha$, there exists an indexed family of computable languages that can be identified strong-monotonically and has finite thickness, but cannot be identified with the ordinal mind change bound of $\alpha$. A similar result also holds for dual strong-monotonicity.

We now proceed formally.

---

[4] A similar conclusion can be drawn from the study of intrinsic complexity of *FIN* [JS94], where it turns out that *FIN* is a complete class with respect to weak reduction.

## 2 Preliminaries

$N$ denotes the set of natural numbers, $\{0, 1, 2, \ldots\}$; $N^+$ denotes the set of positive integers. Any unexplained recursion theoretic notation is from [Rog67]. Cardinality of a set $S$ is denoted by card($S$). $\emptyset$ denotes the empty set. The maximum and minimum of a set are denoted by $\max(\cdot), \min(\cdot)$, $\subseteq, \supseteq, \subset, \supset, \emptyset$ respectively denote, subset, superset, proper subset, proper superset, and emptyset. A language is any subset of $N$. $L$ denotes a typical variable for a language. $\overline{L}$ denotes the complement of $L$, that is, $\overline{L} = N - L$.

### 2.1 Identification

We first define the notion of texts for languages.

**Definition 1.**

(a) A *text* for a language $L$ is a mapping $T$ from $N$ into $N \cup \{\#\}$ such that $L$ is the set of natural numbers in the range of $T$.

(b) *content*($T$) denotes the set of natural numbers in the range of $T$.

(c) The initial sequence of text $T$ of length $n$ is denoted $T[n]$.

(d) The set of all finite initial sequences of $N$ and $\#$'s is denoted SEQ.

Members of SEQ are inputs to machines that learn grammars (acceptors) for r.e. languages. We let $\sigma$ and $\tau$, with or without decorations[5], range over SEQ. $\Lambda$ denotes the empty sequence. content($\sigma$) denotes the set of natural numbers in the range of $\sigma$ and length of $\sigma$ is denoted $|\sigma|$. We say that $\sigma \subseteq \tau$ ($\sigma \subseteq T$) to denote that $\sigma$ is an initial sequence of $\tau$ ($T$).

**Definition 2.** A language learning machine is an algorithmic mapping from SEQ into $N \cup \{?\}$.

A conjecture of ? by a machine is interpreted as "no guess at this moment". This is useful to avoid biasing the number of mind changes of a machine. For this paper, we assume, without loss of generality, that $\sigma \subseteq \tau$ and $\mathbf{M}(\sigma) \neq ?$ implies $\mathbf{M}(\tau) \neq ?$.

$\mathbf{M}$ denotes a typical variable for a language learning machine. We also fix an acceptable programming system and interpret the output of a language learning machine as the index of a program in this system. Then, a program conjectured by a machine in response to a finite initial sequence may be viewed as a candidate accepting grammar for the language being learned. We say that $\mathbf{M}$ converges on text $T$ to $i$ (written: $\mathbf{M}(T)$ converges to $i$) just in case for all but finitely many $n$, $\mathbf{M}(T[n]) = i$. The following definition introduces Gold's criterion for successful identification of languages.

**Definition 3.** [Gol67]

(a) $\mathbf{M}$ **TxtEx**-*identifies* a text $T$ just in case $\mathbf{M}(T)$ converges to a grammar for content($T$).

---

[5] Decorations are subscripts, superscripts and the like.

(b) **M TxtEx-*identifies*** an r.e. language $L$ (written: $L \in$ **TxtEx(M)**) just in case **M TxtEx**-identifies each text $T$ for $L$.

(c) **TxtEx** denotes the set of all collections $\mathcal{L}$ of r.e. languages such that some machine **TxtEx**-identifies each language in $\mathcal{L}$.

The next two definitions describe the notion of informants as a model of both positive and negative data presentation and identification in the limit from informants.

**Definition 4.** An informant for $L$ is an infinite sequence (repetitions allowed) of ordered pairs such that for each $n \in N$ either $(n, 1)$ or $(n, 0)$ (but not both) appear in the sequence and $(n, 1)$ appears only if $n \in L$ and $(n, 0)$ appears only if $n \notin L$.

$I$ denotes a typical variable for informants. $I[n]$ denotes the initial sequence of informant $I$ with length $n$. content($I$) $= \{(x, y) \mid (x, y)$ appears in sequence $I\}$. content($I[n]$) is defined similarly.

PosInfo($I[n]$) $= \{x \mid (x, 1) \in$ content($I[n]$)$\}$. NegInfo($I[n]$) $= \{x \mid (x, 0) \in$ content($I[n]$)$\}$.

We now define identification from both positive and negative data.

**Definition 5.** [Gol67]

(a) **M InfEx-*identifies*** an r.e. language $L$ just in case **M**, fed any informant for $L$, converges to a grammar for $L$. In this case we say that $L \in$ **InfEx(M)**.

(b) **M InfEx-*identifies*** a collection of languages, $\mathcal{L}$, just in case **M InfEx**-identifies each language in $\mathcal{L}$.

(c) **InfEx** denotes the set of all collections $\mathcal{L}$ of r.e. languages such that some machine **InfEx**-identifies $\mathcal{L}$.

## 2.2 Ordinals as Mind Change Counters

We assume a fixed notation system, $O$, and partial ordering of constructive ordinals as used by, for example, Kleene [Kle38, Rog67, Sac90]. $\preceq, \prec, \succeq$ and $\succ$ on ordinals below refer to the partial ordering of ordinals which is provable in the notation system used. Similarly, $\times_O$ and $+_O$ refer to the addition and multiplication in the ordinal system used. We do not go into the details of the notation system used, but instead refer the reader to [Kle38, Rog67, Sac90, CJS95, FS93].

**Definition 6.** **F**, an algorithmic mapping from **SEQ** into constructive ordinals, is an *ordinal mind change counter function* just in case $(\forall \sigma \subseteq \tau)[\mathbf{F}(\sigma) \succeq \mathbf{F}(\tau)]$.

**Definition 7.** [FS93] Let $\alpha$ be a constructive ordinal.

(a) We say that **M**, with associated ordinal mind change counter function **F**, **TxtEx$_\alpha$-*identifies*** a text $T$ just in case the following three conditions hold:
  (i) $\mathbf{M}(T)$ converges to a grammar for content($T$),
  (ii) $\mathbf{F}(\Lambda) = \alpha$ and
  (iii) $(\forall n)[? \neq \mathbf{M}(T[n]) \neq \mathbf{M}(T[n+1]) \Rightarrow \mathbf{F}(T[n]) \succ \mathbf{F}(T[n+1])]$.

(b) **M**, with associated ordinal mind change counter function **F**, **TxtEx$_\alpha$-*identifies*** $L$ (written: $L \in$ **TxtEx$_\alpha$(M, F)**) just in case **M**, with associated ordinal mind change counter function **F**, **TxtEx$_\alpha$**-identifies each text for $L$.

(c) $\mathbf{TxtEx}_\alpha = \{\mathcal{L} \mid (\exists \mathbf{M}, \mathbf{F})[\mathcal{L} \subseteq \mathbf{TxtEx}_\alpha(\mathbf{M}, \mathbf{F})]\}$.

Similarly to the above definition, we can define $\mathbf{InfEx}_\alpha$ to denote classes of languages that can be identified from informants with $\alpha$ as the ordinal mind change bound.

The following Lemma is useful in proving some of our theorems.

**Lemma 8.** *Fix a constructive ordinal $\alpha$. There exists an r.e. sequence of pairs of learning machines and corresponding ordinal mind change counter functions, $(\mathbf{M}_0, \mathbf{F}_0), (\mathbf{M}_1, \mathbf{F}_1), \ldots$, such that*

*(a) for all $\mathcal{L} \in \mathbf{TxtEx}_\alpha$, there exists an $i$ such that $\mathcal{L} \subseteq \mathbf{TxtEx}_\alpha(\mathbf{M}_i, \mathbf{F}_i)$.*
*(b) for all $i$, $\mathbf{F}_i(\Lambda) = \alpha$.*
*(c) for all $i$, for all texts $T$, for all $n$, $\mathbf{M}_i(T[n]) \neq \mathbf{M}_i(T[n+1]) \Rightarrow \mathbf{F}_i(T[n]) \succ \mathbf{F}_i(T[n+1])$.*

The above lemma can be proved on the lines of the proof of Lemma 4.2.2B in [OSW86].

## 3 Ordinal Mind Change Complexity of Unions of Pattern Languages

Let $\Sigma$ and $X$ be mutually disjoint sets. $\Sigma$ is finite and its elements are referred to as *constant symbols*. Elements of $X$ are referred to as *variables*. For the present section, we let $a, b, \ldots$ range over constant symbols and $x, y, z, x_1, x_2, \ldots$ range over variables.

**Definition 9.** A *term* or a *pattern* is an element of $(\Sigma \cup X)^+$. A *ground term* (or a *word*, or a *string*) is an element of $\Sigma^+$.

A *substitution* is a homomorphism from terms to terms that maps each symbol $a \in \Sigma$ to itself. The image of a term $\pi$ under a substitution $\theta$ is denoted $\pi\theta$. We next describe the language defined by a pattern. Note that there exists a recursive bijective mapping between elements of $\Sigma^+$ and $N$. Thus we can name elements of $\Sigma^+$ with elements of $N$. We implicitly assume such a mapping when we discuss languages defined using subsets of $\Sigma^+$ below. (We do not explicitly use such a bijective mapping for ease of notation).

**Definition 10.** [Ang80] The language associated with the pattern $\pi$ is defined as $\mathbf{Lang}(\pi) = \{\pi\theta \mid \theta \text{ is a substitution and } \pi\theta \in \Sigma^+\}$. We define the class $PATTERN = \{\mathbf{Lang}(\pi) \mid \pi \text{ is a pattern}\}$.

Angluin [Ang80] showed that $PATTERN \in \mathbf{TxtEx}$. Shinohara [Shi86] showed that pattern languages are not closed under union, and hence it is useful to study identification of languages that are unions of more than one pattern language, as they can be used to represent more expressive concepts.

We next define unions of pattern languages. Let $S$ be a set of patterns. Then $\mathbf{Lang}(S)$ is defined as $\bigcup_{\pi \in S} \mathbf{Lang}(\pi)$. Intuitively, $\mathbf{Lang}(S)$ is the language formed by the union of languages associated with patterns in $S$.

**Definition 11.** [Shi86, Wri89] Let $n \in N$. $PATTERN^n = \{\mathbf{Lang}(S) \mid \mathrm{card}(S) \le n\}$.

Shinohara [Shi86] and Wright [Wri89] showed that for $n > 1$, $PATTERN^n \in \mathbf{TxtEx}$. Jain and Sharma [JS96] showed that $PATTERN^n \in \mathbf{TxtEx}_{\omega^n}$ and $PATTERN^n \notin \mathbf{TxtEx}_\alpha$ for $\alpha \prec \omega^n$.

We now consider the ordinal mind change complexity of identifying unions of pattern languages from informants. Let $PAT$ denote the set of all canonical patterns [Ang80]. Let $PAT^i = \{S \mid S \subseteq PAT \wedge \mathrm{card}(S) = i\}$.

Angluin showed that, for $p, p' \in PAT$, $\mathbf{Lang}(p) = \mathbf{Lang}(p')$ iff $p = p'$. This result does not hold for elements of $PAT^i$ where $i > 1$.

Suppose Pos and Neg are disjoint finite sets such that Pos $\neq \emptyset$. Then let

$$X_i^{\mathrm{Pos,Neg}} = \{S \in PAT^i \mid [\mathrm{Pos} \subseteq \mathbf{Lang}(S)] \wedge [\mathrm{Neg} \subseteq \overline{\mathbf{Lang}(S)}]\}$$

**Lemma 12.** *Suppose we are given finite disjoint sets* Pos, Neg, *where* Pos $\neq \emptyset$, *and a natural number* $i$, *such that* $(\forall j \le i)[X_j^{\mathrm{Pos,Neg}} = \emptyset]$. *Then, effectively in* Pos, Neg, *and* $i$, *we can determine* $X_{i+1}^{\mathrm{Pos,Neg}}$. *(Note that* $X_{i+1}$ *must be finite in this case!)*

*Proof.* Suppose Pos, Neg, and $i$ are as given in the hypothesis of the lemma. Let

$$P = \{p \in PAT \mid [\mathrm{Pos} \cap \mathbf{Lang}(p) \neq \emptyset] \wedge [\mathrm{Neg} \cap \mathbf{Lang}(p) = \emptyset]\}$$

Let

$$X = \{S \in PAT^{i+1} \mid [\mathrm{Pos} \subseteq \mathbf{Lang}(S)] \wedge [S \subseteq P]\}$$

It is easy to verify that $X = X_{i+1}^{\mathrm{Pos,Neg}}$. Also note that $X$ can be obtained effectively from Pos, Neg and $i$. $\square$

**Corollary 13.** *Suppose* Pos *and* Neg *are disjoint finite sets such that* Pos $\neq \emptyset$. *Then effectively in* Pos, Neg, *one can find* $i$, *and corresponding* $X_i^{\mathrm{Pos,Neg}}$ *(which must be finite) such that* $i = \min(\{j \mid X_j^{\mathrm{Pos,Neg}} \neq \emptyset\})$.

*Proof.* Note that $PATTERN^0$ contains only the empty language. The corollary now follows by repeated use of Lemma 12, until one finds an $i$ such that $X_i^{\mathrm{Pos,Neg}} \neq \emptyset$. $\square$

**Theorem 14.** (a) $PATTERN^1 \in \mathbf{InfEx}_0$.
 (b) $(\forall i \ge 1)[PATTERN^{i+1} \in \mathbf{InfEx}_{\omega \times_O i}]$.

*Proof.* (a) Shown by Lange and Zeugmann [LZ93]. Also follows from the proof of Part (b).
(b) Fix $i$. Let $\mathbf{M}(I[n]), \mathbf{F}(I[n])$ be defined as follows.
 Let Pos = PosInfo($I[n]$) and Neg = NegInfo($I[n]$).
 If Pos $= \emptyset$, then $\mathbf{M}(I[n]) = ?$ and $\mathbf{F}(I[n]) = \omega \times_O i$.
 If Pos $\neq \emptyset$, then let $j = \min(\{j' \mid X_{j'}^{\mathrm{Pos,Neg}} \neq \emptyset\})$. Note that $j$ (and corresponding $X_j^{\mathrm{Pos,Neg}}$) can be found effectively in $I[n]$, using Corollary 13.
 If $j = 1$ and $\mathrm{card}(X_j^{\mathrm{Pos,Neg}}) > 1$, then $\mathbf{M}(I[n]) = ?$. $\mathbf{F}(I[n]) = \omega \times_O i$.
 If $j > 1$ or $\mathrm{card}(X_j^{\mathrm{Pos,Neg}}) = 1$, then $\mathbf{M}(I[n]) = $ lexicographically least element in $X_j^{\mathrm{Pos,Neg}}$. $\mathbf{F}(I[n]) = \omega \times_O (i + 1 - j) +_O (\mathrm{card}(X_j^{\mathrm{Pos,Neg}}) - 1)$.

It is easy to verify that $\mathbf{M}, \mathbf{F}$ witness the theorem. $\qquad\qquad\qquad\qquad\qquad\square$

It is open at this stage whether we can do better than the $\omega \times_O i$ bound for $PATTERN^{i+1}$. However, if we consider unions of $i + 1$ simple pattern languages[6], then it is easy to see that the mind change bound for identification from informants is simply $i$.

## 4  Ordinal Complexity and Conservativeness

We first establish an important technical result.

**Theorem 15.** *Let $\mathbf{M}$ be a learning machine such that, for any text $T$ (irrespective of whether $\mathbf{M}$ identifies $T$ or not), $\mathbf{M}$ makes only finitely many mind changes on $T$ as input. Let $\mathcal{L}$ denote the class of all languages $\mathbf{TxtEx}$-identified by $\mathbf{M}$. Then, for some ordinal mind change counter function $\mathbf{F}$, and constructive ordinal $\alpha$, $\mathcal{L} \subseteq \mathbf{TxtEx}_\alpha(\mathbf{M}, \mathbf{F})$.*

*Proof.* We define a *conjecture tree* $\mathcal{T}_\mathbf{M}$ for machine $\mathbf{M}$. The root of $\mathcal{T}_\mathbf{M}$ corresponds to the empty sequence, $\Lambda$. Other nodes of the tree correspond to finite initial sequences of texts, $T[n + 1]$, such that $\mathbf{M}(T[n]) \neq \mathbf{M}(T[n + 1])$. Let $S = \{\Lambda\} \cup \{T[n + 1] \mid n \in N, T$ is a text and $\mathbf{M}(T[n]) \neq \mathbf{M}(T[n + 1])\}$. For $\sigma \in S$, we use $V_\sigma$ to denote the node corresponding to the sequence $\sigma$. Node $V_{\sigma_1}$ is a descendent of node $V_{\sigma_2}$ iff $\sigma_2 \subset \sigma_1$.

We will now define a constructive ordinal, $\alpha_\sigma$, corresponding to each $\sigma \in S$. For $\sigma \in S$, let $S_\sigma = \{\tau \in S \mid \sigma \subset \tau\}$. Intuitively $S_\sigma$ denotes the proper descendants of $\sigma$ in the tree $\mathcal{T}_\mathbf{M}$. Note that $S_\sigma$ is recursively enumerable (effectively in $\sigma$). Let $S_\sigma^s$ denote the finite set enumerated in $s$ steps in some, effective in $\sigma$, enumeration of $S_\sigma$.

$\alpha_\sigma$ is defined as follows. $\alpha_\sigma$ is the limit of $f_\sigma(0), f_\sigma(1), \ldots$, where $f_\sigma$ is defined as as follows.

$f_\sigma(0) = 0$. $f_\sigma(i + 1) = f_\sigma + \alpha_{\tau_1} + \ldots +_O \alpha_{\tau_k} +_O 1$, where $\tau_1, \tau_2, \ldots, \tau_k$, are the elements of $S_\sigma^i$.

We first need to show that $\alpha_\sigma$ are correct notation.

**Lemma 16.** *(a) Let $V_\sigma$ be a leaf of $\mathcal{T}_\mathbf{M}$. Then $\alpha_\sigma$ is a correct ordinal notation.*

*(b) Suppose $\sigma \in S$, and $\alpha_\tau$ is a correct ordinal notation for each $\tau \in S_\sigma$. Then $\alpha_\sigma$ is a correct ordinal notation.*

*(c) For any $\sigma \in S$, $\alpha_\sigma$ is a correct ordinal notation.*

*(d) If $\sigma \in S$ and $\tau \in S_\sigma$, then $\alpha_\tau \prec \alpha_\sigma$.*

*Proof.* (a) If $V_\sigma$ is a leaf, then $S_\sigma$ is empty. Hence,

$f_\sigma(0) = 0, f_\sigma(1) = 0 +_O 1 = 1, \ldots, f_\sigma(n) = f_\sigma(n - 1) +_O 1 = (n - 1) +_O 1 = n, \ldots.$

It follows that $\alpha_\sigma$ is a notation for $\omega$.

(b) Since, $\alpha_\sigma$ is a limit of $f_\sigma(0), f_\sigma(1), \ldots$, it suffices to show that each $f_\sigma(i)$ is a correct ordinal notation. Now, for each $\tau \in S_\sigma$, $\alpha_\tau$ is correct notation. Thus, since

---

[6] A simple pattern language is formed by substituting, for each variable, strings of length exactly one.

$f_\sigma(i+1)$ is defined using $f_\sigma(i)$, $\alpha_\tau$, 1 and $+_O$ operation only, $f_\sigma(i+1)$ is a correct ordinal notation.

(c) Suppose by way of contradiction that $\alpha_\sigma$ is not a correct notation. We then construct an infinite sequence $\sigma_0 \subset \sigma_1 \subset \ldots$ such that, for each $i$, $\sigma_i \in S$ and $\alpha_{\sigma_i}$ is not a correct notation.

Let $\sigma_0 = \sigma$. Suppose $\sigma_i$ has been defined. Let $\sigma_{i+1}$ be such that $\sigma_{i+1} \in S_{\sigma_i}$ and $\alpha_{\sigma_{i+1}}$ is not a correct notation. The existence of such a $\sigma_{i+1}$ follows from parts (a) and (b).

Consider the text $T = \bigcup_{i \in N} \sigma_i$. Now, since each $\sigma_i \in S$, we have that $\mathbf{M}$ on $T$ makes infinitely many mind changes (after reading last element of $\sigma_1$, after reading last element of $\sigma_2$, and so on). This yields a contradiction to hypothesis of the theorem.

(d) Note that $\alpha_\sigma \succ f_\sigma(i)$, for each $i$. Suppose $\tau \in S_\sigma^s$. Then it is easy to see that $f_\sigma(s+1) \succ \alpha_\tau$. Thus $\alpha_\tau \prec \alpha_\sigma$.

This proves the Lemma. $\square$

Let $\alpha = \alpha_\Lambda$. We now construct an $\mathbf{F}$ such that $\mathcal{L} \subseteq \mathbf{TxtEx}_\alpha(\mathbf{M}, \mathbf{F})$. $\mathbf{F}$ is defined as follows.

$$\mathbf{F}(T[n]) = \begin{cases} \alpha_\Lambda, & \text{if } T[n]) = \Lambda; \\ \mathbf{F}(T[n] - 1), & \text{if } n > 0, \text{ and } \mathbf{M}(T[n+1]) = \mathbf{M}(T[n]); \\ \alpha_{T[n]}, & \text{otherwise.} \end{cases}$$

From the definition of $\alpha_\sigma$ and Lemma 16, it is easy to verify that $\mathbf{TxtEx}(\mathbf{M}) \subseteq \mathbf{TxtEx}_\alpha(\mathbf{M}, \mathbf{F})$.
$\square$

Theorem 15 allows us to establish several sufficient conditions for the existence of ordinal bounds on mind changes in the context of identification of indexed families of computable languages.

A sequence of nonempty languages $L_0, L_1, \ldots$ is an indexed family just in case there exists a computable function $f$ such that for each $i \in N$ and for each $x \in N$,

$$f(i, x) = \begin{cases} 1, & \text{if } x \in L_i, \\ 0, & \text{otherwise.} \end{cases}$$

In other words, there is a uniform decision procedure for languages in the class. Here, $i$ may be thought of as a grammar for the language $L_i$. It makes sense to learn an indexed family of computable languages in terms of a hypothesis space that also describes an indexed family. In the following we only consider hypothesis spaces which describe an indexed family. We will abuse the notation slightly and use $\mathcal{L}$ to refer to both the concept class and the hypothesis space; it will be clear from context which interpretation is intended. To differentiate the concept class $\mathcal{L} = \{L_i \mid i \in N\}$ from the hypothesis space $\mathcal{L}$, we sometimes say that the class of languages $\{L_i \mid i \in N\}$ is the range of the hypothesis space $\mathcal{L}$ (written: range($\mathcal{L}$)). The next definition adapts Gold's criterion of identification in the limit to the identification of indexed families with respect to a given hypothesis space.

**Definition 17.** Let $\mathcal{L}$ be an indexed family and let $\mathcal{L}' = \{L_0', L_1', \ldots\}$ be a hypothesis space.

(a) Let $L \in \mathcal{L}$. A machine $\mathbf{M}$ **TxtEx**-*identifies* $L$ with respect to hypothesis space $\mathcal{L}'$ just in case for any text $T$ for $L$, $\mathbf{M}(T)\!\downarrow = j$ such that $L = L_j'$.

(b) A machine **M** **TxtEx**-*identifies* $\mathcal{L}$ with respect to $\mathcal{L}'$ just in case for each $L \in \mathcal{L}$, **M** **TxtEx**-identifies $L$ with respect to $\mathcal{L}'$.

There are three kinds of identification that have been studied in the literature. (a) class comprising; (b) class preserving; and (c) exact. If the indexed family $\mathcal{L}$ is identified with respect to a hypothesis space $\mathcal{L}'$ such that $\mathcal{L} \subseteq \text{range}(\mathcal{L}')$ then the identification is referred to as class comprising. However, if it is required that the indexed family be identifiable with respect to a hypothesis space $\mathcal{L}'$ such that $\mathcal{L} = \text{range}(\mathcal{L}')$ then the identification is referred to as class preserving. Finally, if the identification of the indexed family $\mathcal{L}$ is required to be with respect to $\mathcal{L}$ itself, then the identification is referred to as exact. The reader is referred to the excellent survey by Zeugmann and Lange [ZL95] for discussion of these issues.

We can similarly define **TxtEx**$_\alpha$-identification with respect to hypothesis space $\mathcal{L}'$. Note that Theorem 15 holds with respect to all hypothesis spaces.

We next describe certain topological conditions on language classes that yield sufficient conditions for identifiability of indexed families of computable languages. The following notion was introduced by Angluin [Ang80].

**Definition 18.** [Ang80] $\mathcal{L}$ has *finite thickness* just in case for each $n \in N$, $\text{card}(\{L \in \mathcal{L} \mid n \in L\})$ is finite.

*PATTERN* has finite thickness. Angluin [Ang80] showed that if $\mathcal{L}$ is an indexed family of computable languages and $\mathcal{L}$ has finite thickness then $\mathcal{L} \in$ **TxtEx**. A more interesting topological notion was introduced by Wright [Wri89] (see also Motoki, Shinohara, and Wright [MSW91]) described below.

**Definition 19.** [Wri89, MSW91] $\mathcal{L}$ has *infinite elasticity* just in case there exists an infinite sequence of pairwise distinct numbers, $\{w_i \in N \mid i \in N\}$, and an infinite sequence of pairwise distinct languages, $\{A_i \in \mathcal{L} \mid i \in N\}$, such that for each $k \in N$, $\{w_i \mid i < k\} \subseteq A_k$, but $w_k \notin A_k$. $\mathcal{L}$ is said to have *finite elasticity* just in case $\mathcal{L}$ does not have infinite elasticity.

Wright [Wri89] showed that if a class $\mathcal{L}$ has finite thickness then it has finite elasticity. He further showed that if a class $\mathcal{L}$ is an indexed family of computable languages and $\mathcal{L}$ has finite elasticity, then $\mathcal{L} \in$ **TxtEx**.

Finite elasticity is a sufficient condition for identification of indexed families of computable languages. Also, the property of finite elasticity is preserved under finite unions. As already noted, it was shown in [JS96] that for each $n > 0$, $PATTERN^n \in$ **TxtEx**$_{\omega^n}$. It would be interesting to investigate whether, for each indexed family of computable languages $\mathcal{L}$ that has finite elasticity, there is an $i$ such that $\mathcal{L} \in$ **TxtEx**$_{\omega^i}$. The following result established in [JS96] showed that the answer to this question is negative.

**Theorem 20.** [JS96] *There exists a class $\mathcal{L}$ such that the following hold: (a) $\mathcal{L}$ is an indexed family of recursive languages; (b) $\mathcal{L}$ has finite elasticity; and (c) for each $i > 0$, $\mathcal{L} \notin$ **TxtEx**$_{\omega^i}$.*

However, we are able to show that an indexed family of computable languages with finite elasticity has an ordinal mind change bound if it can be identified conservatively. The next definition describes conservative identification.

**Definition 21.** Let $\mathcal{L} = \{L_0, L_1, \ldots\}$ be a hypothesis space. $\mathbf{M}$ is said to be a *conservative learning machine with respect to hypothesis space* $\mathcal{L}$ just in case for all $\sigma$ and $\tau$ such that $\sigma \subseteq \tau$ and content$(\tau) \subseteq L_{\mathbf{M}(\sigma)}$, $\mathbf{M}(\sigma) = \mathbf{M}(\tau)$.

Intuitively, conservative machines do not change their hypothesis if the input is contained in the language conjectured.

**Theorem 22.** *Let $\mathcal{L}'$ be an indexed family of computable languages with finite elasticity. Assume that $\mathcal{L}$ is identifiable by a conservative learning machine with respect to the hypothesis space $\mathcal{L}'$. Then $\mathcal{L} \in \mathbf{TxtEx}_\alpha$ with respect to hypothesis space $\mathcal{L}'$, for some constructive ordinal $\alpha$.*

*Proof.* Let $\mathbf{M}$ be a conservative learning machine which identifies $\mathcal{L}$ with respect to hypothesis space $\mathcal{L}'$. We will describe a machine $\mathbf{M}'$ which identifies $\mathcal{L}$ with respect to $\mathcal{L}'$, and changes its mind at most finitely often on any text. Theorem 15 will then imply the theorem.

For a given text $T$, $n \in N$, let lmc$(\mathbf{M}', T[n])$ be defined as follows:

$$\text{lmc}(\mathbf{M}', T[n]) = \max(\{m + 1 \mid m < n \,\wedge\, \mathbf{M}'(T[m]) \neq \mathbf{M}'(T[m + 1])\})$$

Intuitively, lmc denotes the last point where $\mathbf{M}'$ made a mind change. Note that if $\mathbf{M}'(T[0]) = \mathbf{M}'(T[1]) = \cdots = \mathbf{M}'(T[n])$, then lmc$(\mathbf{M}', T[n]) = 0$. $\mathbf{M}'$ is now defined as follows:

$$\mathbf{M}'(T[n]) = \begin{cases} ?, & \text{if } n = 0 \text{ or } \mathbf{M}(T[n]) =?; \\ \mathbf{M}(T[n]), & \text{if content}(T[\text{lmc}(\mathbf{M}', T[n-1])]) \subseteq L'_{\mathbf{M}(T[n])}; \\ \mathbf{M}'(T[n-1]), & \text{otherwise.} \end{cases}$$

It is easy to verify that $\mathbf{M}'$ $\mathbf{TxtEx}$-identifies with respect to $\mathcal{L}'$ any language which $\mathbf{M}$ $\mathbf{TxtEx}$-identifies with respect to $\mathcal{L}'$. We prove that $\mathbf{M}'$ makes only finitely many mind changes on any text $T$. By Theorem 15, this implies that $\mathcal{L} \in \mathbf{TxtEx}_\alpha$ with respect to hypothesis space $\mathcal{L}'$, for some constructive ordinal $\alpha$.

Suppose by way of contradiction that $\mathbf{M}'$ makes infinitely many mind changes on a text $T$. Let $n_1 < n_2 < \ldots$ be such that, for each $i$, $\mathbf{M}'(T[n_i]) \neq \mathbf{M}'(T[n_i + 1])$. Then, it is verify from the construction of $\mathbf{M}'$ that, for all $i$, content$(T[n_i + 1]) \subseteq L'_{\mathbf{M}'(T[n_{i+2}])}$. Moreover, since $\mathbf{M}$ is conservative, we have content$(T[n_i + 1]) \not\subseteq L'_{\mathbf{M}'(T[n_i])}$. It follows that $\mathcal{L}'$ has infinite elasticity. A contradiction. $\square$

**Definition 23.** $L_j$ is a *minimal concept of* $L$ in $\mathcal{L}$ just in case $L \subseteq L_j$, $L_j \in \mathcal{L}$, and there is no $L_i \in \mathcal{L}$ such that $L \subseteq L_i$ and $L_i \subset L_j$.

**Definition 24.** [SM94] $\mathcal{L}$ satisfies *MEF-condition* if for any finite set $D$ and any $L_i \in \mathcal{L}$ with $D \subseteq L_i$ there is a minimal concept $L_j$ of $D$ within $\mathcal{L}$ such that $L_j \subseteq L_i$. $\mathcal{L}$ satisfies *MFF-condition* if for any nonempty finite set $D$, the cardinality of $\{L_i \in \mathcal{L} \mid L_i \text{ is a minimal concept of } D \text{ within } \mathcal{L}\}$ is finite. $\mathcal{L}$ has *M-finite thickness* if $\mathcal{L}$ satisfies both MEF-condition and MFF-condition.

**Theorem 25.** *Let $\mathcal{L}$ be an indexed family of computable languages. Assume that $\mathcal{L}$ has M-finite thickness and finite elasticity. Then $\mathcal{L} \in \mathbf{TxtEx}_\alpha$ with respect to hypothesis space $\mathcal{L}$, for some constructive ordinal $\alpha$.*

*Proof.* We consider the following learning machine M. Suppose $T$ is an arbitrary text. Define $M(T[n])$ as follows. Let $L_i^{(n)}$ denote $L_i \cap \{x \mid x < n\}$.

If $\emptyset \in \mathcal{L}$, then let $G_\emptyset$ denote a grammar for $\emptyset$ in $\mathcal{L}$; otheriwse let $G_\emptyset = 0$.

$M(T[n])$
    Let $C_n = \text{content}(T[n])$.
    If $C_n = \emptyset$ then output $G_\emptyset$.
    Let $S_n = \{i \leq n \mid C_n \subseteq L_i \wedge \neg(\exists j \leq n)[C_n \subseteq L_j \wedge L_j^{(n)} \subset L_i^{(n)}]\}$.
    If $S_n$ is not empty then output $\min(S_n)$, else output $M(T[n-1])$.
End

The above learning machine is a slight modification of the machine of Mukouchi [Muk94].

Let $T$ be an arbitrary text (for a language $L$). Assume without loss of generality that $\text{content}(T) \neq \emptyset$. We shall prove that M makes finitely many mind changes on $T$. Suppose by way of contradiction, M changes its mind infinitely often on $T$. First note that, if $M(T[n]) \neq M(T[n+1])$ then $\text{content}(T[n+1]) \subseteq L_{M(T[n+1])}$. Consider two cases:

*Case 1.* M, on $T$, outputs infinitely many distinct conjectures $i$ such that $\text{content}(T) \not\subseteq L_i$. (That is $\text{card}(\{M(T[n]) \mid n \in N \wedge \text{content}(T) \not\subseteq L_{M(T[n])}\}) = \infty$.)

    Let $n_1 < n_2, \ldots$, be such that $M(T[n_i]) \neq M(T[n_{i+1}])$, and $\text{content}(T[n_{i+1}]) \not\subseteq L_{M(T[n_i])}$. Note that there exist such $n_i$ by hypothesis of the case. Also, by construction, we have $\text{content}(T[n_i]) \subseteq L_{M(T[n_{i+1}])}$ (since, any *new* hypothesis output by M is consistent with the input).

    It follows that $\mathcal{L}$ has infinite elasticity (by considering the languages $L_{M(T[n_{2i}])}$, we see that $\text{content}(T[n_{2i+1}]) \subseteq L_{M(T[n_{2i+2}])}$ but, $\text{content}(T[n_{2i+1}]) \not\subseteq L_{M(T[n_{2i}])}$.) A contradiction.

*Case 2.* M, on $T$, issues only finitely many distinct conjectures $i$ such that $\text{content}(T) \not\subseteq L_i$.

Then, for large enough $n$, $L_{M(T[n])} \supseteq \text{content}(T) = L$ (since M changes its hypothesis infinitely often and if $M(T[n]) \neq M(T[n+1])$ then $\text{content}(T[n+1]) \subseteq L_{M(T[n+1])}$).

Mukouchi [Muk94] showed the following lemma.

**Lemma 26.** [Muk94] *Let $\mathcal{L} = \{L_i \mid i \in N\}$ be a class satisfying MEF-condition and having finite elasticity. Let $L$ be a nonempty language. If for some $n$, $L \subseteq L_n$, then there is a minimal concept $L_j$ of $L$ within $\mathcal{L}$ such that $L_j \subseteq L_n$.*

Since, we have already shown that, for large enough $n$, $L_{M(T[n])} \supseteq L$, Lemma 26 implies that there is a minimal concept $L_j$ of $L$ within $\mathcal{L}$.

Let $S = \{L_j \mid L_j$ is a minimal concept for $L$ within $\mathcal{L}\}$. Let $m$ be such that, for all $L' \in S$, there exists a $j < m$ such that $L_j = L'$ (that is, all minimal concepts of $L = \text{content}(T)$ are represented by an index $\leq m$). Let $j_m$ be the minimum number such that $L_{j_m} \in S$.

For large enough $n$ $(> m)$, the following hold

(i) $L_{\mathbf{M}(T[n])} \supseteq L$.

(ii) For all $j < m$, either content$(T[n]) \not\subseteq L_j$, or $L_j \in S$, or there exists an $L' \in S$, such that $L_j^{(n)} \supset L'^{(n)}$.

(iii) For all minimal concepts $L' \in S$, such that $L' \neq L_{j_m}$, $L'^{(n)} - L_{j_m}^{(n)} \neq \emptyset$.

Note that (i) and (ii) imply that, $\mathbf{M}(T[n])$ will only output an index for one of the minimal concepts. (iii) implies that this index must be $j_m$. Hence, $\mathbf{M}$ converges to $j_m$ on the text $T$, i.e., $\mathbf{M}$ makes only finitely many mind changes on $T$. A contradiction.

Thus, $\mathbf{M}$ must make only finitely many mind changes on any text $T$. Similarly to Case 2, we can show that on any text for a language $L_j$, $\mathbf{M}$ converges to the smallest index for $L_j$. So, $\mathbf{M}$ makes finitely many mind changes on any input and TxtEx-identifies $\mathcal{L}$ with respect to $\mathcal{C}$. Thus, Theorem 15 implies that $\mathcal{L} \in$ TxtEx$_\alpha$ with respect to $\mathcal{C}$, for some constructive ordinal $\alpha$. $\qquad\square$

**Corollary 27.** *Let $\mathcal{L}$ be an indexed family of computable languages with finite thickness. Then $\mathcal{L} \in$ TxtEx$_\alpha$ with respect to $\mathcal{L}$, for some constructive ordinal $\alpha$.*

*Proof.* If $\mathcal{L}$ has finite thickness, then $\mathcal{L}$ has finite elasticity (cf. Wright [Wri89] and Shinohara [Shi94]) and M-finite thickness (cf. Mukouchi [Muk94]). Hence, by Theorem 25, $\mathcal{L} \in$ TxtEx$_\alpha$ with respect to $\mathcal{L}$, for some constructive ordinal $\alpha$. $\qquad\square$

A special case of Theorem 25 is the learnability of length-bounded elementary formal systems with ordinal-bounded mind changes. (Shinohara [Shi94] has proved that $LBEFS^{(\leq n)}$, the class of languages defined by length-bounded elementary formal systems with at most $n$ axioms, has finite elasticity and Sato and Moriyama [SM94] have proved that $LBEFS^{(\leq n)}$ has M-finite thickness.) The learnability of $LBEFS^{(\leq n)}$ was shown by Shinohara [Shi94]. Jain and Sharma [JS96] proved that $LBEFS^{(\leq n)}$ is learnable with the number of mind changes bounded by ordinal $\omega^n$.

The results discussed in the present paper give general sufficient conditions for identifiability with ordinal bound on mind changes. However, they do not give explicit ordinals $\alpha$. In all these theorems we have "$\mathcal{L} \in$ TxtEx$_\alpha$ for some ordinal $\alpha$." It appears that ordinal $\alpha$ can be arbitrarily large. An interesting question to ask is if the ordinal bound $\alpha$ is still arbitrarily large if attention is restricted to classes that are identifiable by strategies that show monotonicity properties. The next result implies that even if we require that a class $\mathcal{L}$ has finite thickness and that it is identifiable by a strong-monotonic learning machine, the ordinal mind change bound can be arbitrarily large. The reader should however note that strong-monotonicity together with finite elasticity implies the existence of an ordinal bound because strong-monotonicity implies conservatism.

# 5 Ordinal Complexity and Monotonicity

Below we describe the notion of strong-monotonic identification.

**Definition 28.** (Jantke [Jan91])

(a) Let $\mathcal{L}' = \{L'_0, L'_1, \ldots\}$ be a hypothesis space. A learning machine **M** is said to be *strong monotonic with respect to* $\mathcal{L}'$ just in case for all $\sigma$ and $\tau$ such that $\sigma \subseteq \tau$, $L'_{\mathbf{M}(\sigma)} \subseteq L'_{\mathbf{M}(\tau)}$.

(b) A learning machine **M** is said to *strong-monotonically* **TxtEx**-*identify* $L$ *with respect to* $\mathcal{L}'$ just in case **M** **TxtEx**-identifies $L$ with respect to $\mathcal{L}'$ and **M** is strong monotonic with respect to $\mathcal{L}'$.

(c) **M** *strong-monotonically* **TxtEx**-*identifies* $\mathcal{L}$ *with respect to* $\mathcal{L}'$ just in case, for each $L \in \mathcal{L}$, **M** strong-monotonically **TxtEx**-identifies $L$ with respect to $\mathcal{L}'$.

**Theorem 29.** *Let $\alpha$ be a constructive ordinal. There exists an indexed family $\mathcal{L}$ such that $\mathcal{L}$ can be **TxtEx**-identified strong-monotonically with respect to hypothesis space $\mathcal{L}$, $\mathcal{L}$ has finite thickness, and $\mathcal{L} \notin \mathbf{TxtEx}_\alpha$ with respect to any hypothesis space.*

Due to space limitation, we omit the proof.

A similar result for class comprising dual strong monotonic identification will be presented in the full version of the paper.

# 6 Conclusion

The present paper further illustrated the utility of ordinal mind change bound as a measure of the difficulty of learning a class of languages. This technique yields a useful measure to compare the learnability of rich classes of concepts which are not very amenable to analysis by more restricted notions of learnability. This is especially true of concept classes that go beyond propositional representation, e.g., elementary formal systems and logic programming systems.

It was argued that the existence of an ordinal mind change bound can be viewed as a measure of learning "tractability." Several sufficient conditions were derived for the existence of such a bound in terms of various topological properties of language classes.

ACKNOWLEDGEMENT We thank the referees for helpful comments. Andris Ambainis was supported in part by Latvia's Science Council Grant 93.599. Arun Sharma was supported in part by a grant from the Australian Research Council.

# References

[AMS+92] S. Arikawa, S. Miyano, A. Shinohara, T. Shinohara, and A. Yamamoto. Algorithmic learning theory with elementary formal systems. *IEICE Trans. Inf. and Syst.*, E75-D No. 4:405–414, 1992.

[Ang80] D. Angluin. Finding patterns common to a set of strings. *Journal of Computer and System Sciences*, 21:46–62, 1980.

[CJS95] J. Case, S. Jain, and M. Suraj. Not-so-nearly-minimal-size program inference. In Klaus P. Jantke and Steffen Lange, editors, *Algorithmic Learning for Knowledge-Based Systems*, volume 961 of *Lecture Notes in Artificial Intelligence*, pages 77–96. Springer-Verlag, 1995.

[FS93]     R. Freivalds and C. Smith. On the role of procrastination in machine learning. *Information and Computation*, pages 237–271, 1993.

[Gol67]    E. M. Gold. Language identification in the limit. *Information and Control*, 10:447–474, 1967.

[Jan91]    K. P. Jantke. Monotonic and non-monotonic inductive inference. *New Generation Computing*, 8:349–360, 1991.

[JS94]     S. Jain and A. Sharma. On the intrinsic complexity of language identification. In *Proceedings of the Seventh Annual Conference on Computational Learning Theory, New Brunswick, New Jersey*, pages 278–286. ACM-Press, July 1994.

[JS96]     S. Jain and A. Sharma. Elementary formal systems, intrinsic complexity, and procrastination. In *Proceedings of the Ninth Annual Conference on Computational Learning Theory*, pages 181–192. ACM-Press, June 1996.

[Kle38]    S. C. Kleene. Notations for ordinal numbers. *Journal of Symbolic Logic*, 3:150–155, 1938.

[LZ93]     S. Lange and T. Zeugmann. Monotonic versus non-monotonic language learning. In *Proceedings of the Second International Workshop on Nonmonotonic and Inductive Logic*, pages 254–269. Springer-Verlag, 1993. Lecture Notes in Artificial Intelligence 659.

[MSW91]    T. Motoki, T. Shinohara, and K. Wright. The correct definition of finite elasticity: Corrigendum to identification of unions. In L. Valiant and M. Warmuth, editors, *Proceedings of the Fourth Annual Workshop on Computational Learning Theory, Santa Cruz, California*, page 375. Morgan Kaufman, 1991.

[Muk94]    Y. Mukouchi. Inductive inference of an approximate concept from positive data. In S. Arikawa and K. P. Jantke, editors, *Algorithmic Learning Theory, 4th International Workshop on Analogical and Inductive Inference, AII'94 and 5th International Workshop on Algorithm Learning Theory, ALT'94*, Lecture Notes in Artificial Intelligence, 872, pages 484–499. Springer-Verlag, 1994.

[OSW86]    D. Osherson, M. Stob, and S. Weinstein. *Systems that Learn, An Introduction to Learning Theory for Cognitive and Computer Scientists*. MIT Press, Cambridge, Mass., 1986.

[Rog67]    H. Rogers. *Theory of Recursive Functions and Effective Computability*. McGraw-Hill, New York, 1967. Reprinted, MIT Press 1987.

[Sac90]    G. E. Sacks. *Higher Recursion Theory*. Springer-Verlag, 1990.

[Shi86]    T. Shinohara. *Studies on Inductive Inference from Positive Data*. PhD thesis, Kyushu University, Kyushu, Japan, 1986.

[Shi94]    T. Shinohara. Rich classes inferable from positive data: Length–bounded elementary formal systems. *Information and Computation*, 108:175–186, 1994.

[SM94]     M. Sato and T. Moriyama. Inductive inference of length bounded EFS's from positive data. Technical Report DMSIS-RR-94-2, Department of Mathematical Sciences and Information Sciences, University of Osaka Prefecture, Japan, 1994.

[Wri89]    K. Wright. Identification of unions of languages drawn from an identifiable class. In R. Rivest, D. Haussler, and M. K. Warmuth, editors, *Proceedings of the Second Annual Workshop on Computational Learning Theory, Santa Cruz, California*, pages 328–333. Morgan Kaufmann Publishers, Inc., 1989.

[ZL95]     T. Zeugmann and S. Lange. A guided tour across the boundaries of learning recursive languages. In K.P. Jantke and S. Lange, editors, *Algorithmic Learning for Knowledge-Based Systems*, pages 190–258. Lecture Notes in Artificial Intelligence No. 961, Springer-Verlag, 1995.

# Robust Learning with Infinite Additional Information*

Susanne Kaufmann[1] and Frank Stephan[2] **

[1] Interactive Systems Laboratories, Am Fasanengarten 5, Universität Karlsruhe, 76128 Karlsruhe, Germany, kaufmann@ira.uka.de.
[2] Mathematisches Institut, Im Neuenheimer Feld 294, Universität Heidelberg, 69120 Heidelberg, Germany, fstephan@math.uni-heidelberg.de.

**Abstract** The present work investigates Gold style algorithmic learning from input-output examples whereby the learner has access to oracles as additional information. Furthermore this access has to be robust, that means that a single learning algorithm has to succeed with every oracle which meets a given specification. The first main result considers oracles of the same Turing degree: Robust learning with any oracle from a given degree does not achieve more than learning without any additional information.

The further work considers learning from function oracles which describe the whole class of functions to be learned in one of the following four ways: the oracle is a list of all functions in this class or a predictor for this class or a one-sided classifier accepting just the functions in this class or a martingale succeeding on this class.

It is shown that for learning in the limit (Ex), lists are the most powerful additional information, the powers of predictors and classifiers are incomparable and martingales are of no help at all. Similar results are obtained for the criteria of predicting the next value, finite, Popperian and finite Popperian learning. Lists are omniscient for the criterion of predicting the next value but some classes can not be Ex-learned with any of these types of additional information. The class REC of all recursive functions is Ex-learnable with the help of a list, a predictor or a classifier.

## 1 Introduction

Gold style inductive inference [7, 13] is an abstract model for learning: the learner receives the course of values $f(0), f(1), \ldots$ of a recursive function to be learned and synthesizes from this information a program for $f$. This synthesis has to meet certain convergence requirements. The special model considered in the present paper is that the learner has in addition access to nonrecursive information on the class $S$ from which the function $f$ is taken. This information is provided as a

---

* A long version of this paper is available as a technical report [18].
** Supported by the Deutsche Forschungsgemeinschaft (DFG) grant Am 60/9-1.

function oracle. But the access to this oracle has to be robust, i.e., ignorant of the actual coding of this information. So the learner has to cope with every oracle which meets a given specification. Four types of such specifications are used in this paper: (1) the oracle is a list of all functions in $S$; (2) the oracle is a predictor which predicts every $f \in S$ under the model "next value"; (3) the oracle is a one-sided classifier which converges on a function $f$ to 1 iff $f \in S$; (4) the oracle is a martingale which succeeds on every function in $S$. Learning with additional information has several roots in the literature which are presented now.

Adleman and Blum [1] as well as Gasarch and Pleszkoch [12] transferred the concept of using nonrecursive oracles to inductive inference. Such oracles can be very helpful, for example every high oracle allows to learn all recursive functions in the limit [1]. Also every nonrecursive oracle allows to learn some class finitely which can not be finitely learned without any oracle. But in these models, the machines always depend on the actual form of the oracle. Indeed Theorem 2.1 shows the following: if a class $S$ can be learned via a fixed machine succeeding with any oracle inside a given Turing degree then $S$ can be learned without any help of an oracle. So it is in this context more suitable to specify the oracles by some structural properties which allow to derive some information in a uniform way than by their Turing degree.

A second root is the notion of learning with additional information in the way as introduced by Freivalds and Wiehagen [11]. They presented a model where the additional information is just a number (and not an infinite object as an oracle) which depends on the function $f$ (and not only on the class $S$). One important result is the following: they presented in addition to the values of the function an upper bound of the size of some program of $f$. This finite information is already sufficient to learn the whole class of all recursive functions, REC, in the limit. Jain and Sharma [15] extended this work.

Baliga and Case [4] modified this setting such that the learner receives as additional information an index of a higher-order program instead of this upper bound of the program size. This concept is not so powerful as that of Freivalds and Wiehagen [11], as it does not allow the inference of REC. But it still permits inference of larger classes than without any additional information. Jain and Sharma [14] gave as additional information programs which are defined on a "sufficiently large" domain and coincide with the function $f$ to be learned on their domain.

Case, Kaufmann, Kinber and Kummer [9] considered as additional information an index of a certain tree such that among other requirements the function to be learned is an infinite branch of it. These trees had to fulfill certain requirements as having bounded width; they showed that – depending on the parameters of the tree – the class REC of all recursive functions is learnable via a team of machines using this additional information. Furthermore, Merkle and Stephan [20] showed, that there is a class $S$ which can be learned in the limit only if as additional information an index of such a tree is provided, on which the function to be learned is an isolated infinite branch.

Finally Osherson, Stob and Weinstein [24] already went in the direction of the present paper by synthesizing learner for a whole class from additional information on the class $S$ to be learned.

The third root is the work of Angluin [3] whose notion of "minimal adequate teacher" is some kind of infinite additional information. The infinity is given by the fact that the teacher has to answer each query from a given infinite query-language correctly. The answers to the queries are not always unique; e.g., there may be several ways to select counterexamples to a learner's hypothesis. So the learner has in her model to be robust in the sense that learning has to succeed with every teacher which meets the specification. Similarly robust learning in the present paper is modelled by the infinite concept of a "minimal adequate oracle".

Main recursion theoretic notions follow the books of Odifreddi [22] and Soare [27]. $\mathbb{N}$ is the set of natural numbers. $A, B, C$ denote subsets of $\mathbb{N}$ and are identified with their characteristic function: $A(x) = 1$ for $x \in A$ and $A(x) = 0$ for $x \notin A$. $f$ and $g$ denote total recursive functions from $\mathbb{N}$ to $\mathbb{N}$. REC denotes this class of all total recursive functions and $\text{REC}_{0,1} = \{f \in \text{REC} : (\forall x)\,[f(x) \leq 1]\}$. Strings $\sigma, \tau, \eta \in \mathbb{N}^*$ are finite sequences of natural numbers and binary strings $\alpha, \beta, \gamma$ range over $\{0,1\}^*$. Strings are also identified with a partial function: If $\sigma = abcc$ then $\sigma(x)$ equals $a$ for $x = 0$, $b$ for $x = 1$, $c$ for $x = 2, 3$ and is undefined for $x > 3$. A string $\sigma$ is prefix of some other string $\tau$ (or function $f$ or set $A$) iff $\sigma(x) = \tau(x)\!\downarrow$ ($f(x)$ or $A(x)$, respectively) for all $x$ in the domain of $\sigma$ (which is denoted by $dom(\sigma)$). $\preceq$ denotes the prefix-relation ($\sigma \preceq \tau$). $\varphi_e$ is the $e$-th partial recursive function w.r.t. some fixed acceptable numbering. This numbering is also always used as hypotheses space unless explicitly stated otherwise.

Now an overview on the most important definitions from learning theory [7, 13, 23] is included for the readers' convenience.

**Learning functions and classes:** A machine learns a class $S$ iff it learns every function $f \in S$ according to the given criterion. The classes $S$ contain always only recursive functions.

**Finite Learning (Fin):** $M$ learns a function $f$ finitely if $M(\sigma) \in \{?, e\}$ for all $\sigma \preceq f$, $M(\sigma) = e$ for some $\sigma \preceq f$ and $\varphi_e = f$. That means $M$ first outputs the symbol "?" to indicate that it wants to see more data on $f$ and then eventually decides to make a guess $e$ which has to be correct.

**Explanatory Learning (Ex):** $M$ learns a function $f$ explanatorily if $M(\sigma) = e$ for almost all $\sigma \preceq f$ and $e$ is a fixed program for $f$. That means that $M$ first outputs some arbitrary guesses and then converges eventually to a correct program for $f$.

**Popperian Finite Learning (PFin):** This is finite learning combined with the additional constraint that any output (also for input not belonging to any function in $S$) is either the symbol "?" or a program for a total function.

**Popperian Explanatory Learning (PEx):** This is explanatory learning combined with the additional constraint that any output is either the symbol "?" or a program for a total function.

**Predicting the Next Value (NV):** A machine $M$ predicts a function $f$ iff $M$ is defined everywhere and $M(f(0)f(1)\ldots f(x)) = f(x+1)$ for almost all $x$.

Now these five concepts (Ex, Fin, PEx, PFin, NV) are combined with different types of oracles. The definitions are stated for Ex but it is easy to see how they are adapted to the other four learning criteria. The general model is, that the learner $M$ receives the course of values of the function $f$ and in addition has access to a function oracle describing a certain information on the class $S$ (and so very indirectly also on the single function $f$). $M$ accesses the oracle $O$ via queries for $O(x)$ at certain numbers or strings $x$. $M$ has to learn every $f \in S$ with any "minimal adequate" oracle meeting the specification. Together with the definition an overview on the results is given.

**List:** A class $S$ is in Ex[List] iff there is a machine $M$ such that $M$ equipped with a function oracle $F$ Ex-learns every $f \in S$ whenever $F$ is a list of $S$, i.e., $S = \{F_0, F_1, \ldots\}$ where $F_x$ is the function given by $F_x(y) = F(x,y)$. The most common inference classes as the class REC of all recursive functions and the class $REC_{0,1}$ of all $\{0,1\}$-valued recursive functions are in Ex[List], but there is also some $S \notin$ Ex[List]. Furthermore every class is in NV[List] but PEx[List], Fin[List] and PFin[List] are weaker than PEx[List].

**Predictor:** A class $S$ is in Ex[Predictor] iff there is a machine $M$ such that $M$ equipped with a function oracle $P$ Ex-learns every $f \in S$ whenever $P$ is a device which NV-learns all $f \in S$. Predictors are strictly weaker than lists, e.g., $REC_{0,1} \in$ Ex[List] $-$ Ex[Predictor]. Interestingly this is one of the few cases in inductive inference where a criterion fails for $REC_{0,1}$ but succeeds for REC, i.e., REC $\in$ Ex[Predictor]. By definition, predictors are omniscient for the criterion NV but on the other hand they are useless for the criteria PFin, Fin and PEx, i.e., anything learned with a predictor under one of these criteria can also be learned without any additional help under the same criterion.

**Classifier:** A class $S$ is in Ex[Classifier] iff there is a machine $M$ such that $M$ equipped with a function oracle $C$ Ex-learns every $f \in S$ whenever $C$ is a one-sided classifier for $S$. A one-sided classifier $C$ converges on all $f \in S$ to 1, i.e., $(\forall^{\infty} \sigma \preceq f)\,[C(\sigma) = 1]$, and does not converge to 1 on every (also nonrecursive) $f \notin S$, i.e. $(\exists^{\infty} \sigma \preceq f)\,[C(\sigma) = 0]$. Classifiers allow to Ex-learn and NV-learn the classes REC and $REC_{0,1}$ but they are not omniscient for these criteria. For Fin, PEx and PFin they are useless.

**Martingale:** A class $S$ is in Ex[Martingale] iff there is a machine $M$ such that $M$ equipped with a function oracle $m$ Ex-learns every $f \in S$ whenever $m$ is a martingale succeeding on $S$. A martingale is a total function with positive rational values such that $m(\lambda) = 1$ and for each $\sigma$ there is a rational number $q$ with $0 \leq q < m(\sigma)$ and a prediction $a$ such that $m(\sigma a) = m(\sigma)+q$ and $m(\sigma b) = m(\sigma) - q$ for all $b \neq a$. It turns out that martingales are useless for all considered learning criteria.

**Inside Given Degrees:** The oracles in this notion are (other than the previous ones) independent of $S$. A class $S$ is robust learnable inside a given degree **a** of oracles iff there is a machine $M$ which Ex-learns every $f \in S$ with any oracle $A \in \mathbf{a}$. It is shown that for all common notions of degrees (Turing, tt, wtt, btt, m) except the notion of 1-degrees this kind of additional information allows only to learn classes which can already be learned without access to any oracle.

Now the concepts are presented in detail each in one section starting with the notion of learning inside given degrees.

## 2 Robust Learning inside given Degrees

For a given oracle $A$, the Turing degree of $A$ is the collection of all oracles $B$ which have the same computational complexity as $A$, i.e., which are Turing equivalent to $A$. There are refinements of the notion of a Turing degree such as m-degree and 1-degree: A set $A$ is m-reducible to $B$ iff there is a recursive function $f$ such that $A(x) = B(f(x))$ for all $x$. If this $f$ is furthermore one-to-one, then $A$ is 1-reducible to $B$. $A$ and $B$ are called m-equivalent, i.e., $A$ and $B$ have the same m-degree, if $A$ is m-reducible to $B$ and $B$ is m-reducible to $A$. Similarly 1-equivalence and 1-degrees are defined. Odifreddi [22, Chapter VI] gives an overview on these and other degrees. The following theorem states that robust learning from an m-degree does not help. The same result also holds for the degrees given by the reductions btt, tt, wtt and Turing as defined in [22] since each such degree is the union of several m-degrees.

**Theorem 2.1** *Assume that a single machine $M$ Ex[$B$]-learns (NV[$B$]-learns) $S$ via access to oracle $B$ for any $B$ in the m-degree of $A$. Then $S$ can be Ex-learned (NV-learned) without any oracle.*

**Proof** (for Ex-learning; the proof for NV-learning is similar). Let $S \in \text{Ex}[B]$ via $M^B$ for all oracles $B$ in the m-degree of $A$. W.l.o.g. $M$ is total also for the oracles outside the m-degree of $A$ and $M(\sigma)$ is computed with oracle access only below $|\sigma|$ – these conditions can be satisfied via delaying mind changes [10, Note 2.14]. For any function $f$ let $M^\alpha(f)$ abbreviate $M^\alpha(f(0)f(1)\ldots f(|\alpha|))$. There are two cases:

(I) There is a function $f \in S$ with $(\forall \alpha)(\exists \beta \succeq \alpha)[M^\beta(f) \neq M^\alpha(f)]$. Now it is possible to compute inductively binary strings $\alpha_0, \alpha_1, \ldots$ such that for each $n$ and $a_0, a_1, \ldots, a_n \in \{0, 1\}$ there are $\alpha, \beta$ with $a_0\alpha_0 a_1\alpha_1 \ldots a_n \preceq \alpha \preceq \beta \preceq a_0\alpha_0 a_1\alpha_1 \ldots a_n\alpha_n$ and $M^\alpha(f) \neq M^\beta(f)$. Here $\alpha_n$ is produced by concatenating strings $\gamma_k$ for $k = 0, 1, \ldots, 2^{n+1} - 1$ where the $\gamma_k$ are defined inductively: if $a_0 a_1 \ldots a_n$ is the binary representation of $k$ and if $\alpha = a_0\alpha_0 a_1\alpha_1 \ldots a_n\gamma_0\gamma_1 \ldots \gamma_{k-1}$ then $\gamma_k$ is the first string found which enforces $M^\alpha(f) \neq M^\beta(f)$ for $\beta = \alpha\gamma_k$.

It follows that $M$ does not converge for any oracle of the form $a_0\alpha_0 a_1\alpha_1 \ldots$, in particular not for $B = A(0)\alpha_0 A(1)\alpha_1 \ldots$ which is m-equivalent to $A$. So the case (I) does not hold.

(II) For each function $f \in S$ there is an $\alpha$ with $M^\beta(f) = M^\alpha(f)$ for all

$\beta \succeq \alpha$. Now the Ex-learner $N$ for $S$ works as follows: On input $f(0)f(1)\ldots f(n)$, $N$ searches for the first string $\alpha$ (according to some enumeration of all strings) such that $M^\beta(f(0)f(1)\ldots f(|\beta|)) = M^\alpha(f(0)f(1)\ldots f(|\alpha|))$ for all strings $\beta \succeq \alpha$ of length up to $n$ and outputs $M^\alpha(f(0)f(1)\ldots f(|\alpha|))$.

Some first string $\alpha$ satisfies the condition at (II) for the given function $f$ and thus $N$ converges to the value $M^\alpha(f)$. Since there is some oracle $B$ in the m-degree of $A$ with $B \succeq \alpha$, $M^B$ converges also to $M^\alpha(f)$ and $M^\alpha(f)$ is the correct value. So $N$ infers $S$ without the help of any oracle. ∎

For the criteria Fin, PEx and PFin the same result holds also with 1-degrees in place of m-degrees.

**Theorem 2.2** *Assume that a single machine $M$ PEx[$B$]-learns $S$ via access to oracle $B$ for any $B$ in the 1-degree of $A$. Then $S$ can be PEx-learned without any oracle. The same result holds also for the criteria Fin and PFin.*

**Proof** First it is necessary to note that each finite binary string can be extended to a set in the 1-degree of $A$ since $A$ is not recursive and therefore infinite and coinfinite – otherwise one could fix $A$ and replace queries to the oracle by computations. Now let $S$ be PEx-learnable via uniform access to some oracle in the 1-degree of $A$ via a machine $M$. The set

$$E = \{M^B(\sigma) : B \equiv_1 A \text{ and } \sigma \in \mathbb{N}^*\}$$
$$= \{e : (\exists \beta \in \{0,1\}^*)\,(\exists \sigma \in \mathbb{N}^*)\,[M^\beta(\sigma) = e]\}$$

is an enumerable set of indices: since $M$ uses for any output only a finite prefix of $B$, the search can go over all binary strings instead over all oracles 1-equivalent to $A$. Since any such string can be extended to an oracle 1-equivalent to $A$, each index in $E$ is an index of a total recursive function. On the other hand, $E$ contains all guesses $M^A(f(0)f(1)\ldots f(n))$ for each $f \in S$. Since $M$ learns $S$ from oracle $A$, $E$ contains for each $f \in S$ and index. Thus $E$ is an enumerable set containing only indices of total recursive functions and for each function in $S$ there is an index in $E$. It follows that $S$ is PEx-learnable.

The proofs for the criteria Fin and PFin are based on the same idea. For each $\sigma$ define – similarly to above – the sets

$$E(\sigma) = \{M^\beta(\sigma) : \beta \in \{0,1\}^*\}$$
$$G(\sigma) = \cup_{\tau \prec \sigma}\, E_{|\sigma|}(\tau)$$

where the $E_s(\tau)$ are a recursive enumeration of the $E(\tau)$ uniform in $\tau$. The algorithm outputs "?" until it reaches some $\sigma \preceq f$ such that $G(\sigma)$ is not empty. Then the algorithm outputs some $e \in G(\sigma)$ and abstains from any mind change. This first guess is computed relative some finite binary string $\beta$ and since some $B \equiv_1 A$ extends $\beta$, the output must be a correct index for $f$ provided that $f \in S$. Furthermore in the case PFin $e$ has to be a total index, also if $\sigma$ does not belong to any $f \in S$. So again it follows that uniform access to 1-degrees does not support learning for the criteria Fin and PFin. ∎

Some 1-degrees are also trivial for Ex-learning and NV-learning. For example the 1-degree of a cylinder $A$ (which satisfies $A(\langle x, y \rangle) = A(\langle x, 0 \rangle)$ for all pairs $\langle x, y \rangle$). But if $A$ is sufficiently thin then the class REC of all recursive functions can be Ex-learned and NV-learned uniformly relative to every $B \equiv_1 A$ by a single machine $M$.

**Theorem 2.3** *If the principal function $p_A$ of $A$ dominates every recursive function $f \in$ REC then there is a machine $M$ which Ex-learns REC relative to any oracle $B$ in the 1-degree of $A$. The same holds for NV.*

**Proof** Recall that the principal function $p_A$ of $A$ assigns to each $x$ the $x$-th element of $A$. It can be shown that for each $B \equiv_1 A$, the principal function $p_B$ of $B$ also dominates every recursive function: $B = \{f(x) : x \in A\}$ for some recursive bijection $f$ and if $p_B$ would not dominate the recursive function $g$ then $p_A$ would also not dominate the recursive function $n \to \max\{f(m) : m \leq g(n)\}$.

Now the following algorithm $M^B$ Ex-learns all recursive functions $g$: On input $\sigma \preceq g$ of length $n$, $M^B$ first computes $x = p_B(n)$. Then $M^B$ searches for the least $e$ such that $\varphi_e(y) \downarrow = \sigma(y)$ within $x$ computation steps for all $y \in dom(\sigma)$. If $M^B$ finds such an $e$ below $n$ then $M^B$ outputs this program $e$. Otherwise $M^B$ outputs the symbol "?" to indicate that $M^B$ could not make up its mind because of either too few data or too few computation time.

$M^B$ converges to the minimal index $e$ of $g$: Since the principal function $p_B$ dominates the computation time of $\varphi_e$, the learner $M^B$ outputs almost always either $e$ or an index below $e$. The second case only occurs finitely often because there are only finitely many indices $i < e$ and each $\varphi_i$ either diverges or computes a value different form $f$ on some $x_i$. So for all $x > x_0 + x_1 + \ldots + x_{i-1}$, $M^B$ does no longer output a value below $e$ and thus converges to $e$.

The modification from Ex-learning to NV-learning is that $M^B$ in place of outputting $e$ simulates $\varphi_e(n+1)$ for $x$ computation steps and outputs the result if it is found within $x$ steps. Otherwise it outputs 0. Since $p_B$ dominates the computation-time of $\varphi_e$ whenever $\varphi_e$ is total (and in particular equals $f$) the procedure predicts almost always every recursive function. Note that $M$ must be total only for oracles $B \equiv_1 A$ and may diverge on others, in particular on oracles represented by finite sets. ∎

This proof gives the nice (and already well-known) fact that whenever a dominating function can be computed from the oracle then REC can be learned under the criterion Ex using this dominating function. This function needs not to be the same for all permitted oracles but each permitted oracle must give a dominating function via the same algorithm. The construction will be used in several proofs below.

# 3 Lists

Angluin [2] discovered that it is very much easier to learn a class of languages if it is a uniformly recursive family of functions (in her case: sets) whose index is known to the learner. Jantke [16] introduced within this model the intensively studied notions of monotonic inference and Zeugmann [29] gives an overview on these studies.

In the present work such a uniformly recursive computation procedure is replaced by an oracle which consists of a list of all functions in $S$. It is investigated how much such an oracle supports learning.

For a given array $F$ let $F_x$ denote the function $F_x(y) = F(x, y)$. Such an array $F$ is a list for a class $S$ iff $S = \{F_x : x \in \mathbb{N}\}$, so a list for $S$ contains just all functions in $S$ (but no nonmembers of $S$). First it is shown that some famous classes can be learned using a list.

A folklore result is that every uniformly recursive class can be learned w.r.t. its enumeration as hypothesis space. Some anonymous referee of the European Conference on Computational Learning Theory 1997 pointed out to the authors that this proof transfers to the setting of learning lists: if the entries to the rows of the list are used as hypothesis space then every class $S$ can be learned in the limit with help of a list. Furthermore Case, Jain and Sharma [8] introduced learning w.r.t. limiting programs as a space of hypothesis and showed that they increase the learning power. This is still true for learning with lists as additional information. Nevertheless in the present work only the restricted version is considered where the learner still has to use the given acceptable numbering $\varphi_e$ as hypothesis space for learning from lists under the criteria Ex, PEx, Fin and PFin.

**Theorem 3.1** *The classes* REC *of all recursive functions,* $\mathrm{REC}_{0,1}$ *of all* $\{0, 1\}$-*valued recursive functions,* $S_0 = \{f : (\exists e)\,[\varphi_e = f \wedge 0^e 1 \preceq f]\}$ *of all self describing functions,* $S_1 = \{f : (\forall^\infty x)\,[f(x) = 0]\}$ *of all functions with "finite support" and* $S_0 \cup S_1$ *are in* Ex[List]*, i.e., they are learnable in the limit from a list.*

**Proof** $S_0$ and $S_1$ are in Ex, so it remains to show the other three results. The proof for REC is based on the fact that every high oracle allows to infer all recursive functions [1] and the result for $\mathrm{REC}_{0,1}$ uses a construction of Jockusch [17].

If $F$ is a list for REC then the function $h(x) = F_0(x) + F_1(x) + \ldots + F_x(x)$ dominates each $F_y$ and therefore all recursive functions. Arguing as in Theorem 2.3, REC can be Ex-learned using the dominating function $h$ obtained from the given list $F$ of REC.

Similarly it is shown that $S_0 \cup S_1 \in$ Ex[List]. As above, a function $h$ is constructed which dominates every function in $S_0 \cup S_1$. This function indeed dominates all recursive functions and thus enables to learn every subset of REC, in particular $S_0 \cup S_1$. So the domination property remains to be shown:

Note that a self describing function codes its index, i.e., there is an $e$ such that $0^e 1 \preceq f$ and $f = \varphi_e$. For any total recursive function $\varphi_e$ let $\varphi_{s(e,a)}(x) = 0$ for $x < a$, $\varphi_{s(e,a)}(a) = 1$ and $\varphi_{s(e,a)}(x) = \varphi_e(x)$ for $x > a$. The recursion-theorem states that there is an $a$ with $\varphi_{s(e,a)} = \varphi_a$, so one of these functions is self describing and in $S_0 \cup S_1$. Thus $h$ dominates this $\varphi_a$ and also the finite variant $\varphi_e$ of $\varphi_a$.

The case $\mathrm{REC}_{0,1}$ is more difficult, since no dominant function can be computed from a list of $REC_{0,1}$. But the following method from [17] can be applied: Let $\psi$ be a $\{0,1\}$-valued function which has no recursive extension. Now define via dovetailing

$$\varphi_{g(i)}(x) = \begin{cases} 0 & \text{if } \varphi_i(y) \text{ converges for all } y \leq x; \\ \psi(x) & \text{if } \psi(x) \text{ converges before the condition above is satisfied;} \\ \uparrow & \text{otherwise.} \end{cases}$$

The function $\varphi_{g(i)}$ has a recursive $\{0,1\}$-valued extension iff $\varphi_i$ is total. Now the inference-algorithm always outputs the $i$ from the least pair $\langle i,j\rangle$ such that the input $f(0)f(1)\ldots f(x)$ is compatible with $\varphi_{i,x}$ and that $\varphi_{g(i),x}$ is extended by $F_j$. Such a pair $\langle i,j\rangle$ exists, since each $\{0,1\}$-valued total recursive function has an index $i$ and then the function $\varphi_{g(i)}$ is also total and recursive and equals some $F_j$. Furthermore all false pairs $\langle i,j\rangle$ are thrown out since either $\varphi_i(x)\downarrow \neq f(x)$ for some $x$ or $\varphi_{g(i)}$ has no extension within the list of all $\{0,1\}$-valued recursive functions and in particular differs from $F_j$. ∎

**Theorem 3.2** *There are two classes $S_2, S_3 \in$ PFin[List] such that their union $S_2 \cup S_3$ and their difference $S_2 - S_3$ are not in Ex[List].*

**Proof** Let $S_3$ contain all constant functions. The class $S_2$ is defined using a construction from [19, Theorem 7.1]. This theorem shows that there is a family $\varphi_{g(i)}$ and an array $A$ of low Turing degree such that

- $range(\varphi_{g(i)}) = \{0,1\}$ and $0^i 1 \preceq \varphi_{g(i)}$;
- For all $i$ there is at most one $x$ with $\varphi_{g(i)}(x)\uparrow$;
- $A_i$ extends $\varphi_{g(i)}$ and is recursive;
- The class $S_4 = \{A_i : i \in \mathbb{N}\}$ is not Ex-learnable relative to $A$.

Now let $S_2$ contain all functions in $S_4$ plus all constant functions of the form $f(x) = \langle i,j\rangle + 2$ where $(\forall j \geq i)\,[\varphi_{g(i)}(j)\downarrow]$. The following four observations hold:

- $S_2 \in$ PFin[List]: Learning a function $f \in S_2$, the learner $M$ checks whether $f(0) > 1$. If so, the function is a constant function and $M$ outputs a total index for it. If not, $M$ outputs "?" until an $i$ is known with $0^i 1 \preceq f$ and a $j$ is found such that the function $h$ with $h(0) = \langle i,j\rangle + 2$ is in the list. Then the function $\varphi_{g(i)}$ is total beyond $j$ and $M$ outputs the index $g'(i,j)$ of

$$\varphi_{g'(i,j)}(x) = \begin{cases} f(x) & \text{if } x \leq j; \\ \varphi_{g(i)}(x) & \text{otherwise;} \end{cases}$$

where $f$ is the function on the input. Only its first $j$ values are necessary, but the $j$ can depend on the concrete form of the list. By the choice of the constant functions in $S_2$ and the fact that the list contains exactly those functions which belong to $S_2$, the algorithm always outputs exactly one total program and this one is correct if the data belongs to some $f \in S_2$.
- $S_3 \in$ PFin[List]: This follows directly from the fact, that a constant function $f$ is known after seeing the value $f(0)$.

- $S_2 - S_3 \notin$ Ex[List]: $S_4 = S_2 - S_3$ and $A$ is a list for $S_4$. By the choice of $A$ and $S_4$, the class $S_4$ can not be learned with $A$-oracle, in particular not under the criterion Ex[List] since the list presented can be exactly $A$.
- $S_2 \cup S_3 \notin$ Ex[List]: There is also an $A$-recursive array for $S_4 \cup S_3 = S_2 \cup S_3$. Since $S_4 \notin$ Ex[$A$], the same holds for the superclass $S_2 \cup S_3$ and so this class can also not be learned with the help of a list. Indeed the point is that by the union the particular information, from where on a function $\varphi_{g(i)}$ is total, is overwritten.

These observations give directly the theorem. ∎

A direct corollary is, that the class $S_2$ can be learned under the criteria PFin[List], PEx[List], Fin[List] and Ex[List], but not under the criteria PFin, PEx, Fin or Ex. So lists are really a help for several learning criteria.

## 4 Predictors

Barzdins [5] and Blum and Blum [7] introduced the learning criterion NV where the learner has to interpolate the next value from the previous ones. In this section it is investigated to which extent such a predicting device can be uniformly translated into a learner for one of the other four criteria. Formally, a total device $P$ is called a predictor for $S$ iff

$$(\forall f \in S)\,(\exists x)\,(\forall y > x)\,[P(f(0)f(1)\ldots f(y)) = f(y+1)],$$

i.e., if it predicts each function $f \in S$ at almost all places $y+1$ from the data $f(0), f(1), \ldots, f(y)$. Any list can be turned into a predictor as follows: Let $F$ be a list and define

$$P(a_0 a_1 \ldots a_y) = \begin{cases} F_x(y+1) & \text{for the first } x \le y \text{ with} \\ & F_x(0) = a_0, F_x(1) = a_1, \ldots, F_x(y) = a_y; \\ 0 & \text{if there is no such } x \le y. \end{cases}$$

This translation is not reversible: a predictor may also predict functions outside the class $S$ to be learned and so hide the information which functions belong to $S$ and which not. The translation from lists to predictors has the following immediate application.

**Theorem 4.1** $S \in$ NV[List] *for all* $S \subseteq$ REC, *i.e., lists are omniscient for NV.*

While lists help under all inference-criteria, predictors are no longer helpful for PFin, Fin and PEx. This is due to the fact, that every finite modification of a predictor is again a predictor and so the inference machine has to fulfill the requirements for these three learning criteria also under all finite modifications of the predictors. Then it follows by an easy adaption of the proof of Theorem 2.2 that the criteria are not supported by predictors as additional information.

**Theorem 4.2** PEx[Predictor]=PEx, Fin[Predictor]=Fin *and* PFin[Predictor] = PFin.

While predictors are omniscient for NV-learning (by definition) and trivial for Fin, PFin and PEx, they are intermediate for Ex-learning. In particular the natural class REC is learnable by predictor while the also natural class $REC_{0,1}$ is not.

**Theorem 4.3** $REC \in Ex[Predictor]$ *and* $REC_{0,1} \notin Ex[Predictor]$.

**Proof** The first result is due to the fact that a dominating function can be computed using a predictor. For each $\sigma$ the predictor $P$ defines inductively a total function $f_\sigma$ via extending the string $\sigma$ by $P$:

$$f_\sigma(n) = \begin{cases} \sigma(n) & \text{for } n \in dom(\sigma). \\ P(f_\sigma(0)f_\sigma(1)\ldots f_\sigma(n-1)) & \text{for } n \notin dom(\sigma). \end{cases}$$

Let $\sigma_0, \sigma_1, \ldots$ be an enumeration of all strings. Now

$$g(x) = f_{\sigma_0}(x) + f_{\sigma_1}(x) + \ldots + f_{\sigma_x}(x)$$

is uniformly recursive in the given predictor $P$ and dominates every recursive function. As in Theorem 2.3 it follows that REC can be learned in the limit using this $g$ obtained from $P$.

The construction fails in the case of $REC_{0,1}$. Indeed there is a low oracle predicting all $\{0,1\}$-valued functions. This oracle gives a predictor, but the predictor is not sufficiently powerful to learn $REC_{0,1}$ in the limit since this requires a high oracle [1, 10]. ∎

## 5  Classifiers

A one-sided classifier $C$ [28] assigns to every string $\sigma$ a binary value. $C$ classifies $S$ iff

$$(\forall f)\,[f \in S \Leftrightarrow (\forall^\infty \sigma \preceq f)\,[C(\sigma) = 1]].$$

Note that the quantifier also ranges over nonrecursive functions, i.e., $C$ must not converge to 1 on any nonrecursive function. Two-sided classification requires in addition, that $C$ converges on the functions outside $S$ to 0. So one-sided classes are the $\Sigma_2^{(s)}$-classes and two-sided classes are the $\Delta_2^{(s)}$-classes according to the notation of Rogers [21, Chapter 15.1]; they are also called $\Sigma_2^0$-classes and $\Delta_2^0$-classes. There are classes of recursive functions, which have no two-sided classifier, even not relative to any oracle, e.g., REC and $S_1$ [6, 21, 28]. On the other hand, every countable class has a (not necessarily recursive) one-sided classifier. So the concept of one-sided classification is more suitable. One-sided classifiers still do not help the criteria PEx, Fin and PFin via the same argument as in the case of 1-degrees and predictors. So the following theorem is stated without proof, since the one for Theorem 2.2 could be adapted with minor changes.

**Theorem 5.1** PEx[Classifier] = PEx, Fin[Classifier] = Fin *and* PFin[Classifier] = PFin.

Reliable inference means, that a machine converges on a function $f$ iff it learns this function. The next theorem shows, that every class $S$ learnable in the limit using a classifier can even be learned reliably using this classifier.

**Theorem 5.2** Ex[Classifier] = REx[Classifier].

**Proof** The criterion Ex is more general than REx, thus it is sufficient to show only the direction Ex[Classifier] $\rightarrow$ REx[Classifier]. Let $S \in$ Ex[Classifier] via a classifier $C$ and an inference-machine $M$. Furthermore let *pad* be an injective padding-function such that $\varphi_{pad(i,j)} = \varphi_i$ for all $i$ and $j$. The new REx-learner $N$ uses *pad* to enforce a mind change whenever $C$ takes the value 0 (let $M(\lambda) = a$ for some $\varphi_a \notin S$):

$$N(\sigma) = pad(M(\sigma), \tau) \text{ for the longest } \tau \preceq \sigma \text{ with } C(\tau) = 0 \vee M(\tau) \neq M(\sigma).$$

$N$ is a reliable inference algorithm for $S$: If $f \in S$, then $C$ converges on $f$ to 1 and $M$ converges to some index $e$ with $\varphi_e = f$. There is a smallest $\tau \preceq f$ which satisfies $C(\sigma) = 1$ and $M(\tau) = M(\sigma) = e$ for all $\sigma$ with $\tau \preceq \sigma \preceq f$. Thus the $N$ converges to $pad(e, \tau)$. If $f$ is not in $S$ then there are infinitely many $\tau \preceq f$ with $C(\tau) = 0$. For all these $\tau$, $N$ takes the value $pad(M(\tau), \tau)$ and all these values are different, i.e., $N$ does not converge. It follows that $S$ is learned via the reliable machine $N$. ∎

The next Theorem uses – as the corresponding Theorem 3.1 for lists – Jockusch's construction [17] in order to show that every class containing all $\{0,1\}$-valued self describing functions is learnable using a classifier.

**Theorem 5.3** *If* $REC_{0,1} \cap S_0 \subseteq S$ *then* $S \in$ Ex[Classifier] $\cap$ NV[Classifier].

Any list can be transferred into a one-sided classifier: The classifier determines for every $\sigma$ the smallest index $e \leq |\sigma|$ such that $\sigma \preceq F_e$. If this index for $\sigma a$ is greater than that for $\sigma$ or if $\sigma a$ does not have such an index, then the classifier outputs 0. Otherwise it outputs 1. The algorithm can be easily verified. So everything which can be learned from a classifier can also be learned from a list.

**Theorem 5.4** Ex[Classifier] $\subseteq$ Ex[List].

So both concepts Ex[Classifier] and Ex[Predictor] are weaker than Ex[List]. The next theorem shows that they are incomparable and thus both concepts are strictly weaker than Ex-learning from a list.

**Theorem 5.5** Ex[Classifier] *and* Ex[Predictor] *are incomparable.*

**Proof** Since $REC_{0,1} \in$ Ex[Classifier] $-$ Ex[Predictor], only the other noninclusion remains to be shown: Ex[Predictor] $\not\subseteq$ Ex[Classifier]. The class to witness this noninclusion is the union of the following two classes:

– The class $S_4$ from Theorem 3.2.

– The class $S_5 = \{\Phi_e : e \in \mathbb{N}\} \cap REC$ of all total step-counting functions. Thereby $\Phi_e(x)$ is defined as the time to compute $\varphi_e(x)$ if $\varphi_e(x) \downarrow$; otherwise $\Phi_e(x)$ is undefined.

The class $S_4$ has a list relative to some low oracle $A$ and therefore it also has a classifier relative to $A$. $S_5$ even has a recursive one-sided classifier $C$: The uniform graph $G = \{(x, y, e) : \Phi_e(x) \downarrow = y\}$ of all step-counting functions is decidable. There is a one-sided computable classifier $C$ such that $C(f(0)f(1) \ldots f(n)) = 0$ iff $n = 0$ or $a_n = \max\{i \leq n : (\forall j \leq i)(\exists x < n)[(x, f(x), j) \notin G]\} > a_{n-1}$ where $a_{n-1}$ is defined analogously; $C(f(0)f(1) \ldots f(n)) = 1$ otherwise. So the union of $S_4 \cup S_5$ has a classifier of degree $A$, but as already mentioned in Theorem 3.2, $S_4$ and every superclass can only be learned from oracles of high degree. Therefore $S_4 \cup S_5 \notin$ Ex[Classifier].

On the other hand, if $M$ is a predictor for $S_5$ then $M$ must predict the computation-time for each function $\varphi_e$ almost everywhere. So uniformly in $M$ some function dominating all computation-times can be calculated and using this function it is possible to infer every recursive function – in particular every function in $S_4 \cup S_5$. ∎

A direct corollary is, that whenever $M$ is a predictor for $S_5$, then a dominating and therefore nonrecursive function can be computed relative to $M$. In particular $S_5$ has no predictor which uses only the computable above constructed classifier as oracle and thus $S_5 \notin$ NV[Classifier].

**Theorem 5.6**  *The class $S_5$ of all total step-counting functions can not be learned under the criterion NV[Classifier].*


# 6   Martingales

A martingale calculates the gambling-account of someone who always tries to predict the next value of a function. In each round the gambler places an amount $q$ on some number $a$, i.e., for each string $\sigma$ there is a rational number $q$, $0 \leq q < m(\sigma)$, such that $m(\sigma a) = m(\sigma) + q$ for some $a$ and $m(\sigma b) = m(\sigma) - q$ for all $b \neq a$. The gambler wins on a function $f$ iff the martingale takes on prefixes of $f$ arbitrary large amounts of money. $m$ is a martingale for $S$ iff $m$ wins on every function $f \in S$. The interested reader finds more on martingales in Schnorr's book [25].

**Theorem 6.1**  *If $S \in$ Ex[Martingale] then $S \in$ Ex. The same holds for all other inference criteria. In short: martingales do not help.*

This result is due to two facts: (1) there are oracles which are trivial for Ex-learning and NV-learning but which enable to construct a martingale succeeding on every computable function; (2) the set of all finite functions which can be extended to a martingale succeedings on REC is enumerable.

So martingales are on the bottom of the inclusion-structure of these four types of additional information as it is summarized in the following theorem.

**Theorem 6.2** *The inclusion-structure of the four types of additional information with respect to the learning criteria* Ex *and* NV *are given by the following diagrams.*

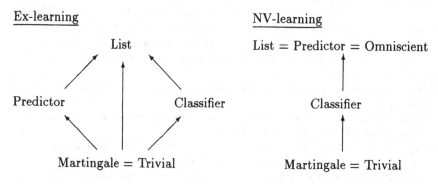

For the criteria Fin, PFin *and* PEx *only lists provide some help while the other three types of additional information are trivial, i.e., do not increase the learning-power.*

**Acknowledgment** We would like to thank Arun Sharma and the anonymous referees of the European Conference on Computational Learning Theory 1997 for useful suggestions and comments.

# References

1. Lenny Adleman and Manuel Blum (1991): Inductive Inference and Unsolvability. Journal of Symbolic Logic 56:891–900.
2. Dana Angluin (1980): Inductive Inference of Formal Languages from Positive Data. Information and Control 45:117–135.
3. Dana Angluin (1987): Learning Regular Sets From Queries and Counterexamples. Information and Computation 75:87–106.
4. Ganesh Baliga and John Case (1994): Learning with Higher Order Additional Information. Proceedings of the Fifth Workshop on Algorithmic Learning Theory (ALT) 64–75.
5. Janis Barzdins (1971): Prognostication of automata and functions. Information Processing '71 (1) 81–84. Edited by C. P. Freiman, North-Holland, Amsterdam.
6. Shai Ben-David (1992): Can Finite Samples Detect Singularities of Real-Valued Functions? Proceedings of the 24th Annual ACM Symposium on the Theory of Computer Science, Victoria, B.C., 390–399.
7. Leonard Blum and Manuel Blum (1975): Towards a Mathematical Theory of Inductive Inference. Information and Control 28:125–155.
8. John Case, Sanjay Jain and Arun Sharma (1992): On learning limiting programs. International Journal of Foundations of Computer Science 1:93–115.
9. John Case, Susanne Kaufmann, Efim Kinber and Martin Kummer (1995): Learning Recursive Functions From Approximations. Proceedings of the second European Conference on Computational Learning Theory (EuroCOLT) 140-153.

10. Lance Fortnow, William Gasarch, Sanjay Jain, Efim Kinber, Martin Kummer, Steven Kurtz, Mark Pleszkoch, Theodore Slaman, Robert Solovay and Frank Stephan (1994): Extremes in the Degrees of Inferability. Annals of Pure and Applied Logic 66:231–276.

11. Rusins Freivalds and Rolf Wiehagen (1979): Inductive inference with additional information. Elektronische Informationsverarbeitung und Kybernetik 15:179–185.

12. William Gasarch and Mark Pleszkoch (1989): Learning via queries to an oracle. Proceedings of the Second Annual Conference on Computational Learning Theory (COLT) 214–229.

13. Mark Gold (1967): Language Identification in the Limit. Information and Control 10:447–474.

14. Sanjay Jain and Arun Sharma (1991): Learning in the Presence of Partial Explanations. Information and Computation 95:162–191.

15. Sanjay Jain and Arun Sharma (1993): Learning with the Knowledge of an Upper Bound on Program Size. Information and Computation 102:118–166.

16. Klaus-Peter Jantke (1991): Monotonic and Non-Monotonic Inductive Inference. New Generation Computing 8:349–360.

17. Carl Jockusch (1972): Degrees in which recursive sets are uniformly recursive. Canadian Journal of Mathematics, 24:1092–1099.

18. Susanne Kaufmann and Frank Stephan (1996): Robust Learning with Infinite Additional Information (long version of this paper). *Forschungesberichte Mathematische Logik 26 / 1996 des Mathematischen Institut an der Universität Heidelberg*, Heidelberg, 1996.

19. Martin Kummer and Frank Stephan (1993): On the Structure of Degrees of Inferability. Proceedings of the Sixth Conference on Computational Learning Theory (COLT) 117–126.

20. Wolfgang Merkle and Frank Stephan (1996): Trees and Learning. Proceedings of the Ninth Conference on Computational Learning Theory (COLT) ACM-Press, pp. 270–279.

21. Hartley Rogers, Jr. (1967): Theory of Recursive Functions and Effective Computability. McGraw-Hill Book Company, New York.

22. Piergiorgio Odifreddi (1989): Classical Recursion Theory. North-Holland.

23. Daniel Osherson, Michael Stob and Scott Weinstein (1986): Systems that Learn. Bradford – The MIT Press, Cambridge, Massachusetts.

24. Daniel Osherson, Michael Stob and Scott Weinstein (1988): Synthesizing inductive expertise, Information and Computation 77(2):138–161.

25. Claus Peter Schnorr (1971): Zufälligkeit und Wahrscheinlichkeit. Lecture Notes in Mathematics, Springer-Verlag, Berlin, 1971.

26. Theodore Slaman and Robert Solovay (1991): When Oracles Do Not Help. Proceedings of the Fourth Conference on Computational Learning Theory (COLT) 379–383.

27. Robert Soare (1987): Recursively Enumerable Sets and Degrees. Springer-Verlag Heidelberg.

28. Frank Stephan (1996): On One-Sided Versus Two-Sided Classification. Forschungsberichte Mathematische Logik 25 / 1996, Mathematisches Institut, Universität Heidelberg.

29. Thomas Zeugmann (1993): Algorithmisches Lernen von Funktionen und Sprachen. Habilitationsschrift an der Technischen Hochschule Darmstadt.

# Author Index

# Springer
# and the
# environment

At Springer we firmly believe that an
international science publisher has a
special obligation to the environment,
and our corporate policies consistently
reflect this conviction.
We also expect our business partners –
paper mills, printers, packaging
manufacturers, etc. – to commit
themselves to using materials and
production processes that do not harm
the environment. The paper in this
book is made from low- or no-chlorine
pulp and is acid free, in conformance
with international standards for paper
permanency.

Springer

# Lecture Notes in Artificial Intelligence (LNAI)

# Lecture Notes in Computer Science